Contractual Relations

Contractual Relations

A Contribution to the Critique of the Classical Law of Contract

DAVID CAMPBELL

Lancaster University Law School

OXFORD
UNIVERSITY PRESS

OXFORD
UNIVERSITY PRESS

Great Clarendon Street, Oxford, OX2 6DP,
United Kingdom

Oxford University Press is a department of the University of Oxford.
It furthers the University's objective of excellence in research, scholarship,
and education by publishing worldwide. Oxford is a registered trade mark of
Oxford University Press in the UK and in certain other countries

First Edition published in 2022

Impression: 1

Published in the United States of America by Oxford University Press
198 Madison Avenue, New York, NY 10016, United States of America

British Library Cataloguing in Publication Data
Data available

Library of Congress Control Number: 2022940277

ISBN 978–0–19–885515–6

DOI: 10.1093/oso/9780198855156.001.0001

Printed and bound by
CPI Group (UK) Ltd, Croydon, CR0 4YY

To my wife Jill Campbell, who embodies the virtue extolled in this book; but also, thankfully for me, also possesses other virtues quite opposed to it.

Acknowledgements

I first studied the law of contract in 1976; first gave tutorials on it in 1983; first gave lectures in 1985; and first published on the subject in 1987. Between that time and the appearance of this book, I have been fortunate to receive a great deal of valuable criticism and other help, and it seemed appropriate to thank all those who provided this, especially as some ideas expressed here are traceable to the mid-1980s. The resulting list assumed what I felt were the embarrassing dimensions of the sort of acknowledgements one sees in some contemporary novels, and I have omitted it, with apologies to the many who would have been included in it.

I should, however, like to thank the members of two smaller groups. First, the arguments of this book have been directly shaped by personal conversation and correspondence with Allan Beever, John Carter, Hugh Collins, Ryan Cushley-Spendiff, Kevin Dowd, John Gava, Richard Lewis, Roger Halson, the late Don Harris, John Holmwood, Matthias Klaes, Richard Lewis, Jonathan Morgan, Sol Picciotto, David Sugarman, and Warren Swain.

The second group is of those without whom there would be no relational theory of contract of the type I have tried to develop in this book, one which calls into question the basic categories of economic action and legal contract. These are the late Ian Macneil and what may be called the core contributors to the Wisconsin tradition of contract teaching: the late John Kidwell, Stewart Macaulay, and William Whitford. Enjoying the support and friendship of these outstanding scholars has been a great privilege in my life.

It is, however, particularly with Bill and Stewart in mind that I insist that none of those mentioned bear responsibility for the arguments made here.

I should also like to thank Jill Campbell for allowing a detail of one of her paintings, Spring Blue, to be used as the cover of my book. Neil Duxbury and Carl Stychin made some otherwise unobtainable materials available to me. The staff of the Library of Lancaster University have often gone beyond what duty required in order to help me. The Lancaster University Law School supported the writing of this book with generous research leave and grants. Marie Selwood, though on this occasion with assistance from Ryan Cushley-Spendiff, has again indispensably assisted me with copy-editing tasks beyond my own competence, and has furnished this book with its, if I may say so, excellent tables and index.

Though substantial alterations to quoted passages are indicated, I have made many silent alterations to the punctuation and spelling of quotations, particularly from older works, in aid of readability.

I have stated the law on the basis of materials available to me at Christmas 2021.

David Campbell
Lynesack
County Durham
St Valentine's Day 2022

Contents

Table of Cases

UNITED KINGDOM

AUSTRALIA

SINGAPORE

UNITED STATES

Table of Legislation

STATUTES

STATUTORY INSTRUMENTS

INTERNATIONAL INSTRUMENTS

AUSTRALIA

UNITED STATES

PART 1
INTRODUCTION: ECONOMIC EXCHANGE AND LEGAL CONTRACT

1

Choice, Mutual Advantage in Exchange, and Freedom of Contract

The Argument of this Book

In a market economy, resources are allocated principally through the countless exchanges of economic goods by economic actors which together constitute that economy.[1] Ideal typically, economic actors exchange 'goods' in the economic sense,[2] which goods may take various legal forms, principally 'real' or 'personal' property, 'goods' in the legal sense, and 'service' or 'services', for money, money serving its principal function as the 'universally employed medium of exchange' for all particular goods.[3] Economic actors may be human beings which are legally recognised to have a 'natural' personality, or business organisations (possibly of only one member but also possibly employing multitudes) which are legally recognised to have a form of 'corporate' personality.[4] A business organisation may be a private firm, a public authority, or a hybrid structure, but, unless the contrary is occasionally indicated, all will here be considered only as they are subject to the general principles of the private law of contract. A contractual relationship arises when economic actors give their economic

[1] JA Schumpeter, *History of Economic Analysis* (Allen and Unwin 1954) 241:

> Actually the economic life of a non-socialist society consists of millions of relations or flows between individual firms or households . . . we can never observe all of them.

[2] C Menger, *Principles of Economics* (Libertarian Press 1994) 52 (hereafter Menger, *Principles*):

> external things . . . that can be placed in a causal connection with the satisfaction of human needs we term *useful things*. If, however, we both recognise this causal connection and have the power actually to direct the useful things to the satisfaction of our needs, we call them *goods*.

[3] L von Mises, *The Theory of Money and Credit* (Liberty Classics 1981) 45.

[4] FW Maitland, 'Moral Personality and Legal Personality' in *State, Trust and Corporation* (CUP 2003) 63–64.

Contractual Relations. David Campbell, Oxford University Press. © David Campbell 2022.
DOI: 10.1093/oso/9780198855156.003.0001

exchange the status of a legal contract, thereby giving themselves the legal status of being parties to a contract.

The answers one gives to all questions of personal and political morality ultimately rest on the concept one has formed of the nature of human being, or one's 'philosophical anthropology'. This book is written by a 'liberal socialist' who believes, firstly, that the most attractive yet plausible such philosophical anthropology is that of classical liberalism, which focuses on 'unsocial sociability'[5] as a specific characteristic of humankind,[6] and, secondly, that, considering such natural human beings as economic actors, the market economy, when institutionalised in, *inter alia*, an adequate law of contract, is the best possible general system for the production and consumption of economic goods. This seems a very strange thing for a socialist of any stripe to say. In part, of course, this is because communism has had the abolition of the market, and thus of contract, at its heart, and, certainly after Friedrich Engels and Karl Marx, socialism and communism, when not effectively identified with one another, are distinguished by the former being seen only as a stage of transition towards the latter as a final goal.[7] In this book, a 'revisionist' attempt will be made to distinguish liberal socialism from communism in a most clear manner.[8] But, even were this attempt successful, this would not reduce the initial strangeness of socialist enthusiasm for the law of contact, because, though it is avowedly non-communist, the welfare state has become intimately identified with a thoroughgoing antipathy towards the market, and thus towards contract.

In the liberal-democracies, the *laissez faire* market economy legally institutionalised in the classical law of contract has been developed into the 'maximalist'[9] welfare state,[10] the policy of which towards the law of contract is 'welfarism'. As it was put in the particularly influential 1980s formulations of the late John Adams, Roger Brownsword, and Hugh Collins,[11] in the modern law of contract the pursuit of 'ideals of social justice

[5] I Kant, 'Idea for a Universal History with a Cosmopolitan Aim' in *Anthropology, History and Education* in *The Cambridge Edition of the Works* (CUP 2007) 113:

> All the culture and art that adorn humanity, and the most beautiful social order, are the fruits of unsociability, through which [humanity] is necessitated by itself to discipline itself, and so by an art extorted from it, to develop completely the germs of nature.

[6] I Kant, *Anthropology from a Pragmatic Point of View* in *Anthropology, History and Education*, ibid 417:

> the characteristic of the human species is this: that nature has planted in it the seed of discord, and has willed that its own reason bring concord out of this, or at least the constant approximation to it.

[7] K Marx, *The Class Struggles in France 1848–50* in K Marx and F Engels, *Collected Works*, vol 10 (Lawrence and Wishart 1978) 127 (emphases omitted):

> Socialism is the declaration of the permanence of the revolution, the class dictatorship of the proletariat as the necessary transit point to the abolition of class distinctions generally, to the abolition of the relations of production on which they rest, to the abolition of all the social relations that correspond to these relations of production, to the revolutionising of all the ideas that result from these social relations.

[8] E Bernstein, *The Preconditions of Socialism* (CUP 1993) 147:

> with respect to liberalism as a historical movement, socialism is its legitimate heir, not only chronologically but intellectually.

[9] N Barry, *Welfare* (Open University Press 1990) 104–07.

[10] S Fine, *Laissez-faire and the General-welfare State* (University of Michigan Press 1964).

[11] If we leave aside the pathbreaking work of Wolfgang Friedman (D Campbell, 'Socio-Legal Analysis of Contract' in PA Thomas (ed), *Socio-legal Studies* (Dartmouth Publishing 1997)) as having (for its purpose

[embodying] the communitarian values comprising assistance to the weak and handicapped, fairness in the distribution of wealth, and altruistic concern for the interests of others which gave birth to the welfare state,'[12] is intended to effect a fundamental shift from 'market-individualism' to 'consumer-welfarism'.[13] The core moral value of *laissez faire* and the classical law is the autonomy of the parties entering into a voluntary exchange. But the maximalist welfare state, going beyond the essentially Beveridgean bounds[14] within which the welfare state is legitimate,[15] has been developed 'at the expense of the autonomous status of individual actors'.[16] Though it has sought to remedy the inadequacies of the classical law which have been particularly exposed by the huge expansion of participation in contracting,[17] welfarism has subordinated contract to

perfectly justified) only a limited engagement with the doctrinal detail of the law of contract, the most influential UK statement of welfarism has been that of PS Atiyah, and this statement will be discussed in chs 5 and 6. Acknowledgement of the success of the neo-liberal criticism of the maximalist welfare state (PS Atiyah, *An Introduction to the Law of Contract* (4th edn, Clarendon Press 1989) vi–vii) caused Atiyah to effect a remarkable *volte face*, abandoning a promised volume in continuation of PS Atiyah, *The Rise and Fall of Freedom of Contract* (pbk edn, Clarendon Press 1985) vii, and taking up positions he had done much to show were untenable: PS Atiyah, 'Freedom of Contract and the New Right' in *Essays on Contract* (rev edn, Clarendon Press 1990). As this *volte face* had to cast doubt on his earlier reasoning, it must be said that Atiyah left his magisterial work on contract in an incoherent state: D Campbell, 'The Undeath of Contract: A Study in the Degeneration of a Research Programme' (1992) 22 Hong Kong Law Journal 20, 41–47.

Always cautious about the extent of the ambition of maximalist welfarism (R Brownsword, 'The Philosophy of Welfarism and Its Emergence in the Modern Law of Contract' in R Brownsword, G Howells, and T Wilhelmsson (eds), *Welfarism in Contract Law* (Dartmouth Publishing 1994), Adams, Brownsword, and Collins have repeatedly revised the early welfarist positions cited in succeeding notes in order to accommodate their increasing acceptance of the desirability of the market economy, and these revisions are arguably the most thought-provoking things of recent vintage written on the law of contract by UK writers. Perhaps the clearest example of the extent of the rethinking is the treatment of market-individualism in the last edition of JN Adams and R Brownsword, *Understanding Contract Law* (5th edn, Sweet & Maxwell 2007) ch 8. But though certain arguments of these authors will be repeatedly discussed in this book, including in this chapter, no attempt will be made to give an overall account of their positions. An attempt to do this up to 2000 was made in D Campbell, 'Reflexivity and Welfarism in the Modern Law of Contract (Review of H Collins, *Regulating Contracts*)' (2000) 20 Oxford Journal of Legal Studies 477.

[12] H Collins, *The Law of Contract* (1st edn, Weidenfeld and Nicolson 1986) 1 (hereafter Collins, *Contract*).

[13] JN Adams and R Brownsword, 'The Ideologies of Contract' (1987) 7 Legal Studies 207.

[14] WH Beveridge, *Full Employment in a Free Society* (George Allen & Unwin 1944) 187:

> The right division between the scope of the state and of private citizens ... may well be found in the ... principle of a social minimum ... The democratic state must be guided, and can safely be guided, by social priorities up to that minimum. The scope for free action by the citizens is in spending above that minimum.

[15] Sir William Beveridge, *Social Security and Allied Services* (Cmd 6404, 1942) para 294:

> to give by compulsory insurance more than is needed for subsistence is an unnecessary interference with individual responsibilities. More can be given only by taking more in contributions or taxation. That means departing from the principle of a notional minimum, above which citizens shall spend their money freely, and adopting instead the principle of regulating the lives of individuals by law.

[16] J Habermas, 'Paradigms of Law' in M Rosenfeld and A Arato (eds), *Habermas on Law and Democracy* (University of California Press 1998) 17.

[17] W Friedmann, *Law and Social Change in Contemporary Britain* (Stevens & Sons 1951) 34:

> The social function of contract in the formative era of modern industrial and capitalist society may be summed up in four elements: freedom of movement; insurance against calculated economic risks; freedom of will; and equality between parties ... The problems of legal adjustment and interpretation ... which they have posed in a rapidly changing society [and] The difficulty of bridging the gap between the formal and substantive aspects of both freedom [of will] and

the pursuit of social goals in such a way as to, if not explicitly replace autonomy,[18] then constantly challenge it by reference to 'paternalism' as a core moral value of contract, the benignity of which cannot alter its unacceptable authoritarianism.[19]

I wish to distinguish a liberal socialist law of contract from welfarism because I believe that, of its nature, such a law will indeed remedy the inadequacies of the classical law, but will do so, not in opposition to freedom of contract, but by making that freedom actual in the Hegelian sense of gaining clear (or adequate, or rational) understanding of existing institutions and practices, which are thereby open to restatement in light of this understanding of their adequate form.[20] The actualisation of freedom of contract does not require, indeed it must reject, the imposition of exogenous moral standards. It stands, or falls, as the understanding of what is.[21] It requires that contracting parties be made fully conscious that a moral foundation of what (introduced in the next chapter) will be called a relationship of mutual recognition of each other's

> equality is evident in the pathetic contrast between the law of contract as it is taught in most textbooks, and modern contract as it functions in society.

This was written in 1951. Friedmann thoroughly revised this book, which later appeared as *Law in a Changing Society*, but this passage was preserved through to W Friedmann, *Law in A Changing Society* (2nd edn, Penguin Books 1972) 119, to which we shall return in the next chapter.

[18] F Wieacker, *A History of Private Law in Europe* (Clarendon Press 1995) 434:

> Unlike economies which are centrally planned or controlled in one way or another, the principle of freedom of contract is upheld in the market economy of the social state, but not with the same role as in a liberal economy ... the classical conception of private law as a complex of private spheres of action must defer to the solidarity of the economy as a whole.

The first edition of Wieacker's book appeared in 1952. Such is its relevance today that it must be seen as an act of private law clairvoyance comparable to the public law clairvoyance of AV Dicey, *An Introduction to the Study of the Law of the Constitution* in *The Oxford Edition of Dicey*, vol 1 (OUP 2013) 417–85 and AV Dicey, *Law and Public Opinion in England During the Nineteenth Century* (2nd edn, Liberty Fund 2008) 359–401. The current position of the English private law is described in JNE Varuhas, 'The Socialisation of the Private Law: Balancing Private Right and Public Good' (2021) 137 Law Quarterly Review 141.

[19] I Kant, 'On the Common Saying: That May be Correct in Theory But It Is Of No Use in Practice' in *Practical Philosophy* in *The Cambridge Edition of the Works* (CUP 1996) 291 (hereafter Kant, 'Theory and Practice'):

> a paternal government ... in which the subjects ... are constrained to behave only passively, so as to wait upon the judgement of the head of state as to how they should be happy ... is the greatest despotism thinkable.

[20] GWF Hegel, *Elements of the Philosophy of Right* (CUP 1991) 11, 20 (translation modified) (hereafter Hegel, *Philosophy of Right*):

> The truth concerning right, ethics, and the state is ... as old as its exposition and promulgation in public laws and public morality and religion. What more does this truth require, given that the thinking mind is not content to possess it in this manner? What it needs is to be comprehended as well, so that the content which is already rational in itself may also gain a rational form and thereby appear justified to free thinking ... since philosophy is the exploration of the rational, it is for that very reason the comprehension of the present and the actual ... not the setting up of a world beyond, which exists God knows where—or rather, of which we can very well say that we know where it exists, namely in the errors of ... empty ratiocination ... What is rational is actual, and what is actual is rational.

See further GWF Hegel, *The Encyclopaedia Logic* (Hackett 1991) s 6.

[21] Hegel, *Philosophy of Right*, ibid 21 (translation modified):

> such instruction as [philosophy] may contain cannot be aimed at instructing the state on how it ought to be, but rather at showing how the state ... should be *recognised* ... To comprehend what is is the task of philosophy, for what is is reason.

interests is, as it always has been, necessary to make a market economy based on general voluntary exchange actual.

The argument, of which Polanyi's formulation is probably now the most influential, that a 'pure' general market economy was never possible, and that a literal *laissez faire* is therefore fictitious, has been largely carried by showing that public institutions providing what I shall persist in calling 'social security' have necessarily been created throughout that economy's history.[22] An argument that private economic action could never have been based on 'purely economic' motives is not absent from Polanyi's thought,[23] but it is a minor theme obscured, and in a sense contradicted by, the way he stressed the necessity of public institutions in vehement criticism of what he called 'the liberal creed'.[24] I will return to social security in Chapter 6, but the focus of this book is on the fictitious nature of pure economic motivation, for economic action through contracting is intrinsically moral. This has been, and is, very inadequately understood, and so the classical law of contract, judged as an institutional 'vesting' of the morality of contract, is itself very inadequate.[25] But this book nevertheless rests on the belief that Orwell was right to claim that socialism's 'only possible justification' is that it is

[22] K Polanyi, *The Great Transformation* (Beacon Press 2001) ch 7 (hereafter Polanyi, *Transformation*).

[23] As Polanyi understood (K Polanyi, 'Economics and the Freedom to Shape Our Social Destiny' in *For a New West* (Polity 2014) 35), the ideology of *laissez faire* maintained that 'Economic motives' now reigned supreme in a world of their own, and the individual was made to act on them under 'penalty of extinction', whilst in fact:

> man was never as selfish as the theory demanded [and] On closer investigation he was still found to be acting on remarkably 'mixed' motives, not excluding those of duty to himself and others.

Whilst I am anxious that my merely making one adverse point here should not indicate a wish to detract from the deserved influence of Polanyi's seminal book, that much of what he says has to be interpreted as a claim that *laissez faire* actually excluded duties to others is indicative of the non-negligible extent to which Polanyi's market economy—and the importance of this is that he is very representative—is a straw man. It is very significant that the later part of *The Great Transformation*, is an explanation of the rise of fascism as the all but inevitable result of the internal 'strains and stresses' which 'destroyed' 'Nineteenth Century [ie including Anglo-Saxon as well as continental] civilisation' (ibid 257). I do not think it is just the advantage of hindsight that allows us to say that another 'great transformation' has been far more important than fascism. This transformation is the very extensive self-critical socialisation of *laissez faire* liberalism (L Seidentop, 'Two Liberal Traditions' in A Ryan (ed), *The Idea of Freedom* (OUP 1979)), of which Churchill's and Lloyd George's 'new' or 'social' liberalism was the principal British expression, which Jaques Barzun called 'the Great Switch', made under 'the pressure of socialist ideas', in the history of liberalism: J Barzun, *From Dawn to Decadence* (Harper Collins 2000) 688. One readily understands how it could have looked very different to Polanyi, an exemplar of *Mitteleuropean* civilisation effectively driven from Germany in 1933, who wrote his *magnum opus* in the early 1940s.

For reasons of economic and social theory rooted in the difference between Polanyi's identification of labour as one of three fictitious commodities and Marx's labour theory of value, I believe Polanyi's criticism of capitalism to be fundamentally far weaker than Marx's. This point cannot be discussed here, but it is with a discussion of the fetishism of commodities, the aspect of the labour theory that is crucial to our concerns, that this book concludes. Polanyi felt obliged to briefly distinguish fictious commodities from commodity fetishism in *Transformation* (n 22) 76 n, doing so in a way that took it for granted that Marx's views were wrong. He almost certainly was unaware that Marx's general criticism of fetishism involved a specific criticism of the 'enchanted, perverted, topsy-turvy world' of the nineteenth century economics of the 'trinity formula' of land, labour, and capital: K Marx, *Capital*, vol 3 in K Marx and F Engels, *Collected Works*, vol 37 (Lawrence and Wishart 1998) 817.

[24] Polanyi, *Transformation* (n 22) chs 12 and 13.

[25] S Veitch, *Moral Conflict and Legal Reasoning* (Hart 1999) 4:

> In order to hold true to its premises ... a theory of liberalism must challenge the institutional vesting it presently receives at the hands of the legal system.

necessary to 'preserve and even enlarge the atmosphere of liberalism'.[26] The core of liberal socialism is the preservation and indeed expansion of the individual's freedom to act,[27] which, in regard of the allocation of economic goods, should take the form of the economic actor's freedom to choose, legally institutionalised as freedom of contract.[28]

The starting point of this liberal justification of socialism is the criticism of the market economy most famously expressed in Anatole France's observation that: '[t]he law in its majestic egalitarianism forbids the rich as well as the poor to sleep under bridges, to beg in the streets and to steal bread'.[29] However, to the enormous attention

[26] G Orwell, 'Inside the Whale' in *A Patriot After All* in *Complete Works*, vol 12 (rev edn, Secker and Warburg 2000) 110. Orwell earlier had written: 'Socialists ... have never made it sufficiently clear that the essential aims of socialism are justice and liberty': G Orwell, *The Road to Wigan Pier* in *Complete Works*, vol 5 (Secker and Warburg 1986) 199. A further brief comment on Orwell's position will be made in the conclusion of this book.

[27] GDH Cole, 'Western Civilisation and Individual Rights' in *Essays in Social Theory* (Oldbourne 1962) 156:

> I for one am not the less individualist in my outlook for being a socialist: indeed I regard socialism, not as an end, but as a means to the enlargement of individual capacities and liberties.

An explicit claim to be developing a 'liberal socialism' was articulated by a number of British social democracy's highly influential economists: eg JE Meade, *Planning and the Price Mechanism: The Liberal-socialist Solution* (William Pickering 1994). In my opinion, however, the extent of the roles typically given to central planning and to the recognition of externalities was not reconcilable with the undoubted liberal aspiration. Meade's views on externalities were the subject of what became a reference point in the development of the Coasean critique of welfare economics on which the argument of this book relies heavily: SNS Cheung, 'The Fable of the Bees: An Economic Investigation' (1973) 16 Journal of Law and Economics 11.

[28] Liberal socialism is specifically a rejection of the political and economic beliefs that lie behind the claim exemplified by EP Thompson, 'At the Point of Decay' in EP Thompson (ed), *Out of Apathy* (Stevens & Sons 1960) 3 that:

> The socialist end has been the creation—*not* of equality of opportunity within an acquisitive society—but of a society of equals, a co-operative community. The pre-requisite for this is the replacement of production for profit by production for use.

The broad conception of the possibilities of social organisation that must lie behind this rejection of equality of opportunity and of profit is briefly set out in EP Thompson, 'An Open Letter to Leszek Kolakowski' in *The Poverty of Theory* (Merlin Press 1978) 170, and is criticised in the conclusion of this book.

[29] A France, *The Red Lily* (The Bodley Head 1908) 95. France is placing in the mouth of a fictional character views clearly traceable to Louis Blanc, *The Organisation of Labour* (HG Clarke 1848) 20:

> the poor man has the free *right* to ameliorate his position ... And pray what of that if he has not the *power*? ... This free right, considered in the abstract, is the mirage which since 1783 keeps the people in delusion. This right is the metaphysical and lifeless protection which has replaced the active protection the people are entitled to. This right, pompously and barrenly proclaimed in charters, has but served to mark all the injustice of a system of individualism, and all the barbarity of abandoning the poor to their own resources. It is because liberty has been defined by the word *right* that men have come to be called free who are in fact the slaves of ignorance and the slaves of chance. Let it be said once and for all. Liberty consists not only in the rights accorded, but in the power given to men to exercise and develop their faculties under the empire of justice and the safeguard of the law.

The most sustained statement of this basic idea in the context of acceptance of Bernstein's revisionism is C Roselli, *Liberal Socialism* (Princeton UP 1994) 86:

> Socialism is nothing more than the logical development ... of the principle of liberty. Socialism ... is liberalism in action. It means that liberty comes into the life of poor people. Socialism says, the abstract recognition of liberty of conscience and political freedoms for all, though it may represent an essential moment in the development of political theory, is a thing of very limited value when the majority of men, forced to live as a result of circumstances of birth and environment in moral and material poverty, are left without the possibility of appreciating its significance and taking any actual advantage of it. Liberty, without the accompaniment and

paid to the distribution of initial endowments and therefore, it was intended, the equalisation of opportunity to participate in the market economy, and to the also enormous attention paid to the occasions for intervention when it was believed that market exchange would not enhance welfare, I hope to add a critical understanding of the way that the general legal institutionalisation of exchange *in the operation* of the positive law of contract has both facilitated and frustrated liberal aspiration. This, I fear, would not prevent me from being counted amongst the group Friedrich Hayek identified as 'well-meaning but unthinking people who did not understand that they were undermining the foundations of impartial justice' by repeating France's 'famous phrase'.[30] However, I am perhaps unique[31] amongst that number in that I very much would wish to have had my views found acceptable by Hayek. For not only is the socialism I have in mind very significantly akin to Hayek's liberal political morality, but the account of exchange and contract in this book will draw heavily on the understanding of the co-ordination of economic information by competition to which Hayek gave perhaps the twentieth century's leading expression. If contracting is to give optimal effect to freedom to choose and therefore to welfare-enhancing competition, it must be made self-conscious of its moral basis in a relationship of mutual recognition. Consciousness of this necessity is, for reasons which will emerge over the course of this book, best called socialism.

When writing the preface to a 1976 edition of *The Road to Serfdom*, Hayek bemoaned the way that the prevalent definition of 'socialism', which when he first drafted the book in the early 1940s 'unambiguously' had meant 'nationalisation of the means of production and … central economic planning', now meant 'the extensive redistribution of incomes through taxation and the institutions of the welfare state'.[32] If it was Hayek's point that in debate one should not evasively shift the meaning of crucial terms, then, of course, his point had merit, for the principled conduct of debate does require something of the discipline of the duel from its participants. But he was also acknowledging a different point. He recognised that the shift in its meaning he described had made socialism far more acceptable, though he did not at all concede that it made it ultimately acceptable, and the last book he wrote was a restatement of his profound rejection of socialism in terms suitable to the late 1980s.[33]

support of a minimum of economic autonomy, without emancipation from the grip of pressing material necessity, does not exist for the individual; it is a mere phantasm.

[30] FA Hayek, *The Constitution of Liberty* in *Collected Works*, vol 17 (University of Chicago Press 2011) 343 (hereafter Hayek, *Constitution*). See also FA Hayek, 'The Political Ideal of the Rule of Law' in *The Market and Other Orders* in *Collected Works*, vol 15 (Routledge 2014) 181.

In 1938, a colloquium was held in Paris to mark the publication the previous year of Walter Lippmann's *The Good Society*. Hayek attended, and had both the colloquium in mind when setting up the Mont Pelerin Society and *The Good Society* in mind when writing *The Road to Serfdom*. In his opening remarks, the organiser of the colloquium, the French philosopher Louis Rougier, specifically asserted 'that a liberal socialism is a contradiction in terms': L Rougier, 'Foreword' in J Reinhoudt and S Audier (eds), *The Walter Lippmann Colloquium* (Palgrave Macmillan 2018) 98.

[31] P Boettke, 'Why Are there No Austrian Socialists?' in *Calculation and Co-ordination* (Routledge 2001).

[32] FA Hayek, *The Road to Serfdom* in *Collected Works*, vol 2 (University of Chicago Press 2007) 54–55 (hereafter Hayek, *Serfdom*).

[33] FA Hayek, *The Fatal Conceit* in *Collected Works*, vol 1 (Routledge 1988).

Socialism as Hayek understood it in the 1940s had by 1976 become theoretically indefensible, in part because central economic planning had over that period itself become generally acknowledged to impose impossible burdens of *inter alia* information gathering on planning agencies. This was, of course, to no little extent a result of Hayek's own contributions to the pre-war 'socialist calculation' debate,[34] and to the eventual political success of the 'neo-liberal revolution' in the 1970s,[35] on the basis of an acceptance of much of both, and therefore of an acceptance of the necessity of an essential restatement of socialism, this book has been written.[36]

I am about to argue for a yet different form of belief in socialism, though in doing so I by no means wish to present another literally *de novo* novelty for consideration, but to present a belief which can secure agreement only if it is able to persuade those considering it that, though rooted in the insistence upon equality that we have traced to France, it is a socialism that is immanent within, and necessary for the realisation of the aspirations of, the classical liberalism of which Hayek was so outstanding a champion. One is abashed to say so, but I intend to subject the law of contract to 'immanent critique' in the tradition of Kant,[37] Hegel,[38] and Marx in the belief that, as Marx put it, 'these petrified relations must be forced to dance by singing their own tune to them!'.[39] Marx's second period of economic studies which culminated in *Capital* involved an extremely extensive engagement with what he called classical political economy, represented principally by Adam Smith and David Ricardo, and it was through this that Marx arrived at what can properly be regarded as his own mature economic views, which he then, by tortuous effort, sought to express in a convincing way. The positions of classical political economy were initially accepted, and the argument for socialism

[34] FA Hayek, 'The Present State of the Debate' in *Socialism and War* in *Collected Works*, vol 10 (Liberty Fund 1997).

[35] FA Hayek, 'The Pretence of Knowledge' in *The Market and Other Orders* in *Collected Works*, vol 15 (Routledge 2014).

[36] R Plant, *The Neo-liberal State* (OUP 2010) 251:

> contrary to the neo-liberal's own perspective, there is, in fact, no categorical distinction to be drawn between social democracy and neo-liberalism.

[37] I Kant, *Critique of the Power of Judgement* in *The Cambridge Edition of the Works* (CUP 2000) 33 (hereafter Kant, *Critique of Judgement*):

> If in place of certain unsuccessful attempts in philosophy one would introduce a different principle and make it influential, then it is very satisfying to understand how and why the former had to go wrong.

[38] GWF Hegel, *Phenomenology of Spirit* (CUP 2018) 53–57:

> [An extant system of belief] will prove to be not real knowing. But while it … regards itself as real knowing, this path has a negative meaning for it, and … will count to it as the loss of itself, it loses its truth. The path can accordingly be regarded as the path of doubt, or more properly the path of despair [The extant belief] suffers this violence at its own hands and brings to ruin its own restricted satisfaction. With the feeling of this violence, anxiety over the truth might well withdraw and strive to hold on to what it is in danger of losing. But this anxiety can find no rest, even if it wants to remain in thoughtless indolence, thought spoils the thoughtlessness, and its unrest disturbs its indolence … thus we do not need to bring standards with us and in the investigation to apply *our* ideas and thoughts. By leaving these aside, we succeed in considering the matter at issue as it is *in and for itself* [From] This *dialectical* movement which [an extant belief] practices in its own self … *the new, true object arises.*

[39] K Marx, 'Contribution to the Critique of Hegel's Philosophy of Law: Introduction' in K Marx and F Engels, *Collected Works*, vol 3 (Lawrence & Wishart 1975) 178.

and communism were to arise from pursuit of the resolution of the severe difficulties—contradictions Marx often said—which those positions contained, and which critique exposed. Initially addressing the beliefs central to the existing dominant position, Marx's argument could succeed only by persuading those holding those beliefs to alter them in order to resolve the difficulties their critique had exposed. It was in principle an argument which had to work, and could only work, through persuasion.

It is in this tradition that this book will put forward an explanation and evaluation of the positive law of contract and, behind this, the understanding of economic action expressed in neo-classical economics. The result of this critique will be adequate consciousness of a relationship of mutual recognition. This relationship is always present in economic action and contract, for without it neither are possible, but the classical law of contract and neo-classical economics express this only very inadequately.[40] Conscious mutual recognition by economic actors and contracting parties is what I mean by socialism, actualised in the social market.[41] But it is wrong, as Marx said, 'to anticipate results which still have to be substantiated', and it was for this reason[42] that he courageously omitted from the two books he published on political economy—*A Contribution to the Critique of Political Economy* in 1859 and volume one of *Capital* in 1867—an introduction he had drafted[43] which set out the general conclusions he had reached through studies reaching back decades. I believe that Marx took this sacrifice too far. This introduction would have much assisted in the understanding of *Capital* (as indeed it has, but only after a century had elapsed after Volume 1's publication),[44] and anyway I don't have Marx's courage, so I shall, particularly in the next chapter, anticipate results. But I do basically intend to discuss the classical law and neo-classical economics in the way immanent critique requires by initially taking them at face value. Let us, then, straightaway turn to exchange and contract, specifically to their theoretical expression in the basic welfare claim of neo-classical economics—Pareto optimality—and to their doctrinal expression in freedom of contract.

[40] I believe that Polanyi's views are far less fruitful overall than Marx's, the description of the 'double movement' of capitalism in Polanyi, *Transformation* (n 22) has more vividly captured this core aspect of the critique of *laissez faire* than Marx, despite his awareness of the 'social' regulation of capitalism, was ever able to do: K Polanyi, 'The Trend Toward an Integrated Society' in *For a New West* (Polity Press 2014) 216–18:

> the apparently simple proposition that all factors of production must have free markets implies in practice that the whole society must be subordinated to the needs of the market system [But this is] a utopia bound for destruction ... The utopian character of a market economy explains why it never could really be put into practice [and why] the separation of economics and politics was never carried completely into effect. The integration of society began even before the movement for a market economy had reached its climax.

[41] Save as it will be found necessary, principally in ch 6, to ground the treatment of the law of contract, I will not discuss the redistributive features of the social market (including the welfare state), but it is my fundamental belief that consciousness of the moral foundation of exchange in mutual recognition will greatly strengthen the legitimacy of those features, and this will be argued in the conclusion of this book.

[42] K Marx, *A Contribution to the Critique of Political Economy* in K Marx and F Engels, *Collected Works*, vol 29 (Lawrence and Wishart 1987) 261 (hereafter Marx, *Contribution*).

[43] K Marx, 'Economic Manuscripts of 1857–8 [*Grundrisse*]' in K Marx and F Engels, *Collected Works*, vols 28–29 (Lawrence and Wishart 1986–7) vol 28, 17–48 (hereafter Marx, *Grundrisse*).

[44] T Carver, *Texts on Method* (Basil Blackwell 1975) pt 1.

Pareto Optimality, Autonomy, and Freedom of Contract

Kenneth Arrow, one of those most responsible for the neo-classical statement of the conditions of existence of a general competitive equilibrium, put the claim to legitimacy of the market economy thus: 'First theorem of welfare economics: every competitive equilibrium is Pareto efficient.'[45] This is a claim that a generally competitive economy will spontaneously yield an equilibrium which realises the maximum possible economic welfare. The statement of maximum welfare, due to Vilfredo Pareto, is 'Pareto efficiency' or 'optimality':

> the members of a community enjoy, in a certain situation, maximum [utility] when it is impossible to move slightly away from this position in such a way that the [utility] enjoyed by each member of the community increases or decreases. That is to say, every small displacement from the position must necessarily have the effect of increasing the [utility] enjoyed by some individuals and decreasing that enjoyed by others, ie of being agreeable to some and disagreeable to others.[46]

Pareto optimality is a completely non-substantive criterion. It identifies economic welfare entirely as the product of the voluntary choices of self-interested economic actors. At a general competitive equilibrium, goods have been exchanged whenever actors have identified what they believe to be all the beneficial possibilities of doing so. The possibilities of exchange are exhausted because any further exchange would leave at least one actor worse off, ie no further exchange can be agreed. Vitally importantly, equilibrium is established by, and could be established only by, voluntary exchange, which spontaneously identifies Pareto optimality by ceasing at equilibrium. The beautiful symmetry of the model[47] lies in its being driven by voluntary exchange motivated by subjectively defined self-interest, and working only because it is so driven. There is no possible substantive justification for a Pareto optimal equilibrium. Its justification is that it completely realises economic actors' choices made in their self-interest.

As a goal, Pareto optimality is attractive, or even intelligible, only given the classical liberal philosophical anthropology of the natural person as an economic actor.[48] The aspect of this that it is essential to emphasise at this point of a discussion of exchange

[45] KJ Arrow, 'Pareto Optimality with Costly Transfers' in *Collected Papers*, vol 2 (Belknap Press 1983) 290.

[46] V Pareto, *Manual of Political Economy* (OUP 2014) 179 (ch 6, s 33) (hereafter Pareto, *Manual*). On the use of the word 'utility' in this quotation, see the text accompanying n 77 and n 121.

[47] R Dorfman, PA Samuelson, and RM Solow, *Linear Programming and Economic Analysis* (McGraw-Hill 1958) 410:

> Every competitive equilibrium is a Pareto optimum; and every Pareto optimum is a competitive equilibrium.

[48] In a very successful criticism of the theory of general competition as involving a 'liberal paradox', Amartya Sen argued that the liberal value of 'unrestricted' choice was incompatible with Pareto optimisation. If a 'prude' chose, not merely to her or himself refrain from reading *Lady Chatterley's Lover*, but wanted to choose to prevent others reading it because their doing so diminished her or his satisfactions, and a 'lewd' wanted to choose read it her or himself and to have everyone read it because that increased her or his satisfactions, then it was impossible to establish a non-contradictory schedule of their preferences: A Sen, 'The Impossibility of a Paretian Liberal' in *Choice, Welfare and Measurement* (Harvard University Press 1982). This is indeed the case, but the conclusion we should draw is quite the opposite of the one Sen draws, for, as

and contract is that the human being is a finite, sensuous being living within its natural environment, of which its own body is part, and so is subject to the laws of physical causality; but that the human being is more than a natural being because it also possesses a 'supersensible' or 'noumenal' faculty of freedom making it capable of self-determination or 'autonomy'.[49] The exercise of autonomy in such a way as to preserve and develop that autonomy, and so the human being's more than natural character, is 'the supreme principle of morality'.[50] In exercising and seeking to develop its faculties, the finite but free human being can only look on its current overall situation as a limit which it must surpass in its deeds,[51] and, as we shall see in the conclusion of this book, this development in relation to economic goods is 'betterment'.[52] But when seeking to better itself, the human being experiences its natural environment in a way that, whatever the extent of its technological powers, has an ineluctable sense of being external and resistant to those powers.[53] Even for Marx, who in collaboration with Engels took

is pointed out in B Barry, 'Lady Chatterley's Lover and Doctor Fischer's Bomb Party' in *Democracy, Power and Justice* (OUP 1989) 360–69, Sen does not address liberalism at all.

Liberalism is not a commitment to unrestricted choice in the way Sen means. It is a commitment to each individual's autonomy, which precisely requires, not embracing, but strenuously limiting interference with others' choices. The implication of Sen's argument is, not that liberalism fails, but that, if we wish to pursue Pareto optimality, we should not attempt to give effect to the 'nosy' preferences which give rise to what Sen regards as a paradox. Such paradoxes run counter to the *de gustibus* principle, and behind this Mill's harm principle (it is hard to understand how Sen deals with Mill). Sen actually demonstrates the value of one of the pure theoretical conclusions that may be drawn from general competitive equilibrium. That an argument of this quality could have enjoyed such success is ultimately traceable to the way that, by claiming to radically undermine Pareto optimality, that argument apparently demonstrates the necessity of welfarist intervention to guide socially optimal choice.

[49] Kant, *Critique of Judgement* (n 37) 302 (translation amended):

> Now we have in the world only a single sort of being whose causality is teleological, ie aimed at ends, and yet at the same time so constituted that the law in accordance with which the being has to determine ends is represented by itself as unconditioned and independent of natural conditions, but yet as necessary in itself. The being of this sort is the human being considered as noumenon: the only being which is natural but in which we can nevertheless cognise, on the basis of its own constitution, a supersensible faculty of freedom.

[50] I Kant, *Groundwork of the Metaphysics of Morals* in *Practical Philosophy* in *The Cambridge Edition of the Works* (CUP 1996) 89 (hereafter Kant, *Groundwork*).

[51] I Kant, *The Metaphysics of Morals* in *Practical Philosophy* in *The Cambridge Edition of the Works* (CUP 1996) 518 (hereafter Kant, *Metaphysics of Morals*):

> When it is said that it is in itself a duty for the human being to make his end the perfection belonging to a human being ... this duty can ... consist only in cultivating one's faculties ... A human being has a duty to raise himself from the crude state of his nature ... more and more towards humanity, by which he alone is capable of setting himself ends.

[52] B de Mandeville, *Fable of the Bees* (Liberty Classics 1988) vol 2, 181, 128:

> [The desire of] ameliorating our condition [is] I believe ... as [much] a characteristic of our species as any [that] can be named ... This is what is not to be perceived in any creature but man ... The restless industry of man to supply his wants, and his constant endeavours to meliorate his condition upon Earth, have produced and brought to perfection many useful arts and sciences.

[53] JS Mill, *Principles of Political Economy* in *Collected Works*, vols 2–3 (University of Toronto Press 1965) 199 (hereafter Mill, *Principles*):

> The laws and conditions of the production of wealth partake of the character of physical truths. There is nothing optional or arbitrary in them. Whatever mankind produces must be produced in the modes, and under the conditions, imposed by the constitution of external things, and

as wide-ranging a view of humanity's possibilities in its relationship with nature as has ever been taken, to which we shall return in the conclusion of this book, the natural world was in this sense found,[54] and the labour process was conceived, not as one of literal creation, but of creative transformation of the, in this sense, refractory material of what is given.[55]

Though disdain for the cultural and ethical aridity of what Tawney influentially called the 'acquisitive society'[56] is, of course, a prominent strophe of social criticism of capitalism of widely varying degrees of sophistication, advocacy of an acquisitive spirit in Tawney's sense is not a characteristic feature of neo-classical economics. It is not only that action in 'the market sphere' is but a part of life, and so that sphere should be appropriately delimited;[57] it is that, beyond the gratification of 'physiological' necessity, which in affluent liberal democratic societies does not really speak to the formation of a human being's character,[58] the acquisition of economic goods should *never* itself be the goal of human beings.[59] However, the improvement of a human

> by the inherent properties of their own bodily and mental structure. Whether they like it or not, their productions will be limited by the amount of their previous accumulation, and, that being given, it will be proportional to their energy, their skill, the perfection of their machinery, and their judicious use of the advantages of combined labour ... howsoever we may succeed in making for ourselves more space within the limits set by the constitution of things, we know that there must be limits. We cannot alter the ultimate properties either of matter or mind, but can only employ those properties more or less successfully, to bring about the events in which we are interested.

[54] In K Marx, *Capital*, vol 1 in K Marx and F Engels, *Collected Works*, vol 35 (International Publishers 1996) 194 (hereafter Marx, *Capital*, vol 1) 53 n 1, Marx quotes (from an Italian edition of) P Verri, *Reflections on Political Economy* (Augustus M Kelley 1993) 10:

> Our perception of everything in this world, whether produced by the hand of man or by the universal laws of physics, is not of actual creation but only of transformation of matter. The only elements human ingenuity finds in analysing the idea of reproduction are bringing together and separating, and thus if, in the fields, soil, air and water are transformed into grain, this is reproduction of value and wealth.

[55] K Marx and F Engels, *The German Ideology* in K Marx and F Engels, *Collected Works*, vol 5 (Lawrence and Wishart 1976) 38–39:

> for the practical materialist ... it is a question of revolutionising the existing world, of practically coming to grips with and changing the things found in existence.

[56] RH Tawney, *The Acquisitive Society* (Fontana Books 1961) 33–34 (hereafter Tawney, *Acquisitive Society*):

> [In] Acquisitive Societies [the] whole tendency and interest and preoccupation is to promote the acquisition of wealth ... Under the impulse of such ideas men do not become religious or wise or artistic ... they become powerful and rich.

In addition to their discussion in this chapter, Tawney's views will be considered in the conclusion of this book.

[57] H Röpke, *A Humane Economy* (pbk edn, ISI Books 2014) 91 (hereafter Röpke, *Humane Economy*):

> the market economy is not everything. It must find its place in a higher order of things which is not ruled by supply and demand, free prices and competition.

[58] AH Maslow, *Motivation and Personality* (3rd edn, Harper and Row 1987) 37.

[59] PH Wicksteed, *The Commonsense of Political Economy* (rev edn, Routledge & Kegan Paul 1933) (hereafter Wicksteed, *Commonsense*):

> since ... no ultimate object of desire can ever be the direct subject of exchange at all ... to regard the 'economic man' (as he is often called) as actuated solely by the desire to possess wealth

being, even when what is pursued is not so much a material goal as the symbolic representation[60] of the being's cultural qualities,[61] ultimately must rest on the utilisation, and therefore acquisition, of economic goods.[62] One cannot just appreciate 'a symphony' or 'a novel'; one must listen to a live or recorded performance or play an instrument or read a book.[63] Given natural limits and human aspiration, economic goods are ultimately scarce,[64] and so a method for allocating those goods is required which can reconcile ultimately competitive, alternative demands.[65]

As a response to these conditions, Pareto optimality could not be a more powerful claim to legitimacy: it is a state of perfect freedom to choose[66] by natural persons, each of whose capacity to choose is regarded of equal worth.[67] A natural person's power to

> is to think of him as only desiring to collect tools and never desiring to do or make anything with them.

[60] TM Scanlon, *What We Owe to Each Other* (Belknap Press 1998) 251–53.

[61] A Smith, *Theory of Moral Sentiments* in *The Glasgow Edition of the Works and Correspondence*, vol 1 (Clarendon Press 1976) 50 (hereafter Smith, *Moral Sentiments*):

> what are the advantages which we propose by that great purpose of human life which we call bettering our condition? To be observed, to be all attended to, to be taken notice of with sympathy, complacency and approbation, are all the advantages which we can propose to derive from this.

[62] FA Hayek, *Law Legislation and Liberty* (corrected edn, Routledge 1982) vol 3, 113 (hereafter Hayek, *Law*):

> There are, in the last resort, no economic ends. The economic efforts of … individuals … consist in an allocation of means for … competing ultimate purposes which are always non-economic.

[63] HD Dickinson, 'The Failure of Economic Individualism' in GDH Cole (ed), *Studies in Capital and Investment* (Victor Gollancz 1935) 13:

> Even the most intellectual and spiritual needs make some call on material resources … for their satisfaction.

[64] L Walras, *Elements of Pure Economics* (Orion Editions 1984) 65:

> By social wealth I mean all things, material or immaterial … that are *scarce*, that is to say, on the one hand *useful* to us and, on the other hand, only available *in limited quantity*.

The limitation of quantity is in regard to the fulfilment of desired alternative uses: Lord Robbins, *Essay on the Nature and Significance of Economic Science* (Macmillan 1969) 16 (hereafter Robbins, *Essay*):

> Economics is the science which studies human behaviour as a relation between ends and scarce means which have alternative uses.

[65] G Simmel, *The Philosophy of Money* (3rd edn, Routledge 2004) 311:

> If one starts out from the assumption that the quantity of goods available for consumption is limited [and] that this quantity does not satisfy the given demands … then it follows that whatever is given to one person must be taken away from another.

[66] M Rothbard, *The Ethics of Liberty* (New York University Press 2002) 42:

> Each man's power, then, is always necessarily limited by the facts of the human condition, by the nature of man and the world; but it is one of the glories of man's condition that each person *can* be absolutely free, even in a world of complex interaction and exchange.

[67] Robbins, *Essay* (n 64) 140:

> In Western democracies we assume for certain purposes that men in similar circumstances are capable of equal satisfactions [as opposed to] the representative of some other civilisation [who might assure] us that we were wrong [and] that members of his caste (or his race) were capable of experiencing ten times as much satisfaction from given incomes as members of an inferior caste (or race).

As Robbins notes, this position in neo-classical economics is derived from 'the historical association of English Economics with Utilitarianism', and in particular with what Mill called 'Bentham's *dictum*' that

choose reflects that person's ability to translate her or his subjective desires into effective demand through the expenditure of money to buy goods, the prices of which conveys their scarcity as a function of demand and supply.[68] This of course, raises profound issues of inequality to which we shall turn in Chapter 6, but considering it only as the medium of exchange, money translates scarcity into the prices at which a natural person as consumer is offered economic goods. All choice is constrained ultimately because economic goods are scarce, but an equilibrium which is established only by every economic actor having the power to choose, and exercising it so as to exhaust the possibilities of voluntary exchange, reflects the self-determined choices of those actors in the light of relative scarcities expressed in prices. In this way, Pareto optimality is the expression in the economic sphere of actualised autonomy.

The law of contract is at its root the legal institutionalisation of autonomy in exchange:

> Among the basic conceptions of contract law the most pervasive and indispensable is the principle of private autonomy. This principle simply means that the law views private individuals as possessing a power to effect, within certain limits, changes in their legal relations. The man who conveys property to another is exercising this power; so is the man who enters a contract. When a court enforces a promise it is merely arming with legal sanction a rule or *lex* previously established by the party himself.[69]

This is, of course, principally expressed in the doctrine of freedom of contract. Though so very often quoted as to have become the epitome of cliché,[70] Sir George Jessel MR's 1875 affirmation of freedom of contract as the paramount, as it were, 'public policy' pursued by contract, is still the cornerstone of the law:

> [I]f there is one thing more than another that public policy requires it is that men of full age and competent understanding shall have the utmost liberty of contracting, and that their contracts when entered into freely and voluntarily shall be held sacred and shall be enforced by courts of justice. Therefore, you have this paramount

'everybody [is] to count for one and nobody for more than one': JS Mill, *Utilitarianism* in *Collected Works*, vol 10 (University of Toronto Press 1969) 257.

68 IM Kirzner, *Market Theory of the Price System* in *Collected Works* (Liberty Fund 2011) 68–69:

> The consumer decides ... what goods to buy, and in what quantities to buy them, on the basis of *three* sets of factors. *First*, the consumer consults his own scale of values, built on his personal tastes, and the requirements of his own particular situation. *Second*, the consumer ... finds himself with a limited amount of money with which to buy ... *Third*, the consumer faces a market with which each good he is interested in is available only at a definite price. The consumer finds ... that ... expenditure ... might ... provide a large number of alternative combinations of purchases, the contents of each combination being, with given expenditure, rigidly determined by the prices of the goods entering into the combination ... The essence of the problem facing the consumer thus consists in choosing one out of an immense number of alternative assortments of goods.

69 LL Fuller, 'Consideration and Form' (1941) 41 Columbia Law Review 799, 807.

70 Sir John Baker pointedly eschewed quoting this *dictum*: J Baker, 'From Sanctity of Contract to Reasonable Expectation' (1979) 32 Current Legal Problems 17, 17 n 3.

> public policy to consider—that you are not lightly to interfere with this freedom of contract.[71]

As part of an argument for resisting the temptation to, in the public interest, revise a possibly oppressive contract because of the trumping public interest in freedom of contract, Jessel MR held that the policy of freedom of contract has two aspects. The first, the core of 'negative' freedom,[72] is that contracting parties should be at liberty to form subjective intentions to contract for such goods as they wish, and to enter into such contracts as it is within their personal powers to conclude. It is by the exercise of those powers that the contracting party is able to determine its own life and character:

> It is a first principle of liberal political morality that we be secure in what is ours, so that our persons and property not be open to exploitation by others, and that from a sure foundation we may express our will and expend our powers in the world. By these powers we may create good things or low, useful articles or luxuries, things extraordinary or banal, and we will be judged accordingly—as saintly or mean, skilful or ordinary, industrious and fortunate or debased, friendly and kind or cold and inhuman. But whatever we accomplish and however that accomplishment is judged, morality requires that we respect the person and property of others, leaving them free to make their lives as we are left free to make ours. This is the liberal ideal.[73]

The second aspect of freedom of contract, which at this point of the argument can equally be regarded as negative in character though it unarguably involves an 'active' power to make actual the 'passive' first aspect,[74] is that economic actors' contracts as agreed should be legally enforced: this is the doctrine of sanctity of contract.[75] Though sanctity is derived from what we shall see, principally in Chapters 2 and 8, is contract's principal function of providing the parties with security when making an exchange, sanctity also speaks to the promotion of autonomy, for it makes the parties' responsible for the consequences of their choices, and recognition of their responsibility is essential to their autonomy:

> If we decline to take seriously the assumption of an obligation because we do not take seriously the promisor's prior conception of the good that led him to assume it, to that extent we do not take him seriously as a person. We infantilise him, as we

[71] *Printing and Numerical Registering Co v Sampson* (1875) LR 19 Eq 462 (Ch) 465.

[72] I Berlin, 'Two Concepts of Liberty' in *Four Essays on Liberty* (OUP 1969) 122–23 (hereafter Berlin, 'Two Concepts'):

> I am normally said to be free to the degree to which no man or body of men interferes with my liberty. Political liberty in this sense is simply an area within which a man can act unobstructed by others ... The wider the area of non-interference, the wider my freedom.

[73] C Fried, *Contract as Promise* (2nd edn, OUP 2015) 7 (hereafter Fried, *Contract as Promise*).

[74] Berlin, 'Two Concepts' (n 72) 165 always encompassed this:

> Perhaps the chief value for liberals of political—'positive'—rights, of participating in the government, is as a means for protecting what they hold to be an ultimate value, namely individual—'negative'—liberty.

[75] DH Parry, *The Sanctity of Contracts in English Law* (Stevens & Sons 1959).

> do quite properly when we release the very young from the consequences of their choices ... over the last two centuries citizens in liberal democracies have become increasingly free to dispose of their talents, labour and property as seems best to them. The freedom to bind oneself contractually to a future disposition is an important and striking example of this freedom.[76]

Despite, as I have said, Jessel MR's *dictum* having come to be regarded as the epitome of cliché, so that it is only with hesitation that one would now cite it even with the purpose of mounting a serious criticism of it, I nevertheless cite it because, though the freedom, as Jessel MR recognised, has always, and in principle uncontroversially, been subject to 'certain limits', in the prevailing state of our understanding of contract, the negative liberty that economic actors should be able to contract for such goods as they choose requires some discussion of its basic principle.

When earlier setting out Pareto optimality, I inserted the word 'utility' in the seminal passage quoted from Pareto. This was not the word Pareto himself used. In order to make it plain that the acknowledgement of the value accorded to a good by an economic actor does not imply morally endorsing that actor's judgement, and therefore that the existence of general equilibrium confers no such endorsement on the economy as a whole, Pareto used the term rendered in English as 'ophelimity', from the Greek *ophelos*: benefit, rather than use the term 'utility', which arguably conveys some approbation of the outcome, and used a choice to recreationally use morphine to illustrate this.[77] Neo-classical economics are wholly relativistic, absolutely avoiding evaluations of the substance of actors' preferences, in an attempt to come to terms with the fundamental problem of economic and legal policy which Pareto's morphine example emphasises.[78] Neo-classical analysis evaluates an actor's choices (viewed 'ordinally') in terms of their rational consistency in maximising the actor's self-defined satisfactions without passing a judgement on the substance (viewed 'cardinally') of those choices.[79] The severe criticism made of this limitation by those who think the value neutrality of economics is an abnegation of its role, which will be discussed in Chapter 3, does not, in my view, give nearly sufficient weight to the desirability of the negative political morality of requiring the state to take a stance of neutrality towards human beings as natural, autonomous persons who make economic choices.[80] We shall return to this requirement of neutrality.

The argument that the choice between ultimate values is not rationally determinable enjoys the support of high authority indeed. But if Hume, for example, did not,

[76] Fried, *Contract as Promise* (n 73) 20–21.

[77] Pareto, *Manual* (n 46) 78 (ch 3, sec 30):

> morphine is not useful, in the ordinary sense of the word, since it is harmful to the morphine addict; on the other hand it is economically *useful* to him since it satisfies one of his wants.

[78] JR Hicks, *Value and Capital* (2nd edn, Clarendon Press 1946) 18:

> If one is a utilitarian in philosophy, one has a perfect right to be a utilitarian in one's economics. But if one is not ... one also has the right to an economics free of utilitarian assumptions.

[79] PA Samuelson, *Foundations of Economic Analysis* (enlarged edn, Harvard University Press 1947) 90–91.

[80] R Nozick, *Anarchy, State and Utopia* (Basic Books 1974) 33 (hereafter Nozick, *Anarchy*):

> a state or government that claims ... allegiance ... scrupulously must be neutral between its citizens.

in my opinion, capture the nature of personal moral philosophy when he maintained that 'reason is, and ought to be, the slave of the passions, and can never pretend to any office other than to serve and obey them',[81] he nevertheless certainly did capture the essence of liberal political policy towards economic action. Whether or not ultimate values are open to rational debate (as I believe they are), awaiting the definitive outcome of such debate (and not short-circuiting it by the authoritarian imposition of an outcome) before determining the allocation of goods obviously would completely paralyse decision-making,[82] and contestation is the central feature of moral and political dispute even for those who think such debate must posit a theoretical end-point of perfectibility.[83] Liberalism's unique response to ineluctable disagreement is, not to seek to realise such an end-point, but, by making a political principle of 'value pluralism',[84] to give equal legal weight to each person's opinion[85] in a way which is intended to:

> enable those who espouse widely different and incompatible conceptions of the good life for human beings to live together peaceably within the same society, enjoying the same political status and engaging in the same economic relationships.[86]

The essential character of neo-classical economics is that they do not attempt to second-guess the basic values guiding economic actors' choices. *A fortiori* a liberal democratic legal system should not seek to give force to political judgements by refusing to enforce actors' choices or imposing 'choices' upon them. The liberal economy must be based on a 'want-regarding' rather than an 'ideal-regarding' principle, in that each economic actor's want must be respected, rather than politically evaluated from a claimed ideal position.[87] Of course, this does not mean that wants

[81] D Hume, *A Treatise of Human Nature* in *The Clarendon Edition of the Works* (Clarendon Press 2007) 266.

[82] When discussing 'those ends which, upon account of their peculiar importance, may be regarded, if such an expression is allowable, as the favourite ends of nature', Smith, *Moral Sentiments* (n 61) 76 tells us that:

> Mankind are endowed with a desire of those ends, and an aversion to the contrary ... But ... it has not been entrusted to the slow and uncertain determinations of our reason, to find out the proper means of bringing them about.

[83] One need not, then, accept all that Hayek sometimes means by 'our irremediable ignorance' (Hayek, *Law* (n 62) vol 1, 13) to accept the conclusion he draws in Hayek, *Serfdom* (n 32) 102 from 'the fundamental fact on which the whole philosophy of individualism is based':

> the indisputable fact that the limits of our powers of imagination make it impossible to include in our scale of values more than a sector of the needs of the whole society, and that [therefore] nothing but partial scales of values exist—scales which are inevitably different and often inconsistent with each other. From this the individualist concludes that the individuals should be allowed, within defined limits, to follow their own values rather than somebody else's; that within these spheres the individual's system of ends should be supreme and not subject to any dictation by others.

[84] B Barry, *Justice as Impartiality* (Clarendon Press 1995) ch 6 and J Raz, *The Morality of Freedom* (Clarendon Press 1986) ch 5. Of course, there must be a consensus, enforced by law, about value pluralism itself: B Barry, *Culture and Equality* (Polity 2001).

[85] BA Ackerman, *Social Justice in the Liberal State* (Yale University Press 1980) 11.

[86] A MacIntyre, *Whose Justice? Which Rationality?* (Duckworth 1988) 335–36.

[87] B Barry, *Political Argument* (reissued edn, Harvester Wheatsheaf, 1990) 38–42.

should not be subject to debate. But it absolutely does mean that an actor's choice, once made, should not normally be politically overridden.

De gustibus non est disputandum is indeed a foolish maxim for the guidance of one's personal conduct. Reflection, especially in light of the particular views of others and of general moral standards,[88] on the wisdom of one's courses of action, including choices of economic goods, is so much a personal moral duty that it very arguably is itself part of autonomy or of human action as such. What is more, the legitimacy of an economy ultimately cannot inhere in satisfying wants regardless of the moral value of those wants. An economy 'must be judged ethically ... by ... the type of character which it forms in its people, rather than by its efficiency in satisfying wants as they exist at any given time.'[89] But such a judgement must be a matter of debate over, rather than the imposition of, standards, and the 'tolerant ... economic ... attitude'[90] of *de gustibus non est disputandum* is the basis of wisdom in the evaluation of the operation of a system for the allocation of economic goods which rests on respect for autonomy.[91] The market is in this vital sense a system, as Gauthier has it, of 'freedom from morality'.[92]

This reasoning is, of course, specific to natural legal persons and cannot be directly applied to business organisations. That it does indirectly apply to them is, however, analytically essential to the legitimacy of the market economy. In Carl Menger's *Principles of Economics*, one of the three foundational statements of marginal economic analysis, economic goods that 'directly' serve the needs of natural legal persons *qua* consumers are called 'goods of the first order'.[93] The goods that are used, overwhelmingly by business organisations, to produce goods of the first order, are goods of the second order. Goods of the second order obviously overlap with various concepts

[88] Though, as discussed in ch 3, the rejection of paternalism in JS Mill, *On Liberty* in *Collected Works*, vol 18 (University of Toronto Press 1977) 223 is obviously one foundation of the views advocated in this book, to the extent that Mill applied the same reasoning to what he termed the 'moral coercion of public opinion' as to legal sanction, then the lack of an essential nuance in that reasoning leads in principle to a radical individualism inadequately respectful of tradition. In respect of our concerns at this point in the argument, it should be noted that this radical individualism is, despite the preponderance of contemporary opinion, open to Arnold's criticisms of the philosophy of 'Doing As One Likes': M Arnold, *Culture and Anarchy* (pbk edn, CUP 1960) 50:

> The aspirations of culture ... are not satisfied, unless what men say, when they may say what they like, is worth saying—has good in it, and more good than bad ... culture indefatigably tries, not to make what each raw person may like the rule by which he fashions himself; but to draw ever nearer to a sense of what is indeed beautiful, graceful and becoming, and to get the raw person to like that.

[89] FH Knight, 'The Ethics of Competition' in *The Ethics of Competition* (Transaction Publishers 1997) 43. The conclusion of FH Knight, 'Some Fallacies in the Interpretation of Social Cost' in *The Ethics of Competition*, ibid 227–28, one of the most important papers in the entire history of neo-classical economics, is a comprehensive list of the limitations of the market economy and an indication of the role of those economics in light of these.

[90] FH Knight, 'Ethics and the Economic Interpretation' in *The Ethics of Competition*, ibid 14.

[91] L Robbins, *The Economic Problem in Peace and War* (Macmillan 1947) 18 (hereafter Robbins, *Peace and War*):

> I do not agree with many of the preferences of my fellow citizens. I yield to no-one the right to describe them as silly, vulgar, self-frustrating, even wrong, if you wish to use that sort of language. But I hold that these are matters for argument and persuasion rather than coercion.

[92] D Gauthier, *Morals By Agreement* (Clarendon Press 1986) 83 (hereafter Gauthier, *Morals By Agreement*).

[93] Menger, *Principles* (n 2) 56.

of factors of production and of business capital, but the claim that underlies the way Menger identifies goods of the second order is that they 'are in indirect causal connection with the satisfaction of human needs'.[94] Bread is a good of the first order; flour, salt, and other ingredients of bread are (analysed in relationship to bread) goods of the second order, as are the labour and plant involved in bread's production. The allocation and use of goods of the second order is ultimately determined by the production for consumption of goods of the first order. Through all the swiftly accumulating complexity of linkages between goods in an economy runs the thread of the satisfaction of human needs:

> The fact that goods of the first order have a direct and goods of the second order an indirect causal relation with the satisfaction of our needs gives rise to no difference in the essence of that relationship, since [both display] some causal connection, but not necessarily one that is direct, between things and the satisfaction of human needs.[95]

Menger's identification of this common essence of consumer goods and factors of production is an important statement of the claim, traceable to Smith,[96] that the allocation of economic goods in a market economy ultimately is determined by the free, subjective choices of natural legal persons acting as the end-consumers of goods, to which business organisations as the producers of goods in pursuit of profit respond. The existence of this 'consumer sovereignty' is essential to the market economy's claim to legitimacy, and this will be examined at length in Chapter 3. But it is appropriate to deal here with two points about this claim.

First, although it is absurd to directly apply the *de gustibus* principle to business organisations, the liberal commitment to autonomy must indirectly apply to them, if their actions are to institutionalise that commitment.[97] Preventing a natural legal person from directly satisfying a desire and preventing a business organisation indirectly satisfying it is just a difference of authoritarian technique. Though influential 'corporate social responsibility' arguments for adopting this indirect technique now make up a considerable part of what passes for the study of company law[98] and strategy,[99] criticism of the structure and resultant action of in particular the public

[94] ibid 57.

[95] ibid.

[96] A Smith, *The Wealth of Nations* in *The Glasgow Edition of the Works and Correspondence*, vol 2 (Clarendon Press 1976) 660 (hereafter Smith, *Wealth of Nations*):

> Consumption is the sole end and purpose of all production; and the interest of the producer ought to be attended to, only so far as it may be necessary for promoting that of the consumer.

[97] L von Mises, *Socialism* (Liberty Classics 1979) 240 (hereafter von Mises, *Socialism*):

> In his capacity as a businessman a man is servant of consumers, bound to comply with their wishes. He cannot indulge in his own whims and fancies. But his customers whims and fancies are for him ultimate law, provided these customers are ready to pay for them ... If the consumers, without a taste for the beautiful, prefer things ugly and vulgar, he must ... supply them with such things.

[98] D Millon, 'Communitarianism in Corporate Law: Foundations and Law Reform Strategies' in LE Mitchell (ed), *Progressive Corporate Law* (Westview Press 1995).

[99] RE Freeman, *Strategic Management* (CUP 1983).

company[100] which is consistent with the values which inform the argument of this book cannot possibly take a line which in principle requires refusing to satisfy consumers' revealed preferences.[101]

Secondly, in an economy which respects consumers' preferences,[102] taking decisions about the production and utilisation of factors of production by business organisations, which turns on the entrepreneurial identification of existing and potential consumer demand[103] which a particular organisation can plan to profitably satisfy,[104] must be overwhelmingly left to those organisations because complete planned direction of those factors is an impossibility.[105] Reflection on the previous example of bread leads to some perception of the complexity of linking the factors of production in the general economy, but this is before we acknowledge that 'bread' is a collective noun which embraces very many existing and potential future goods. In an important sense, the modern conception of economics arose from the extraordinary influence of Smith's recognition that an economy with a developed division of labour is simply too complex to be directed:

> Observe the accommodation of the most common artificer or day-labourer in a civilised and thriving country and you will perceive that the number of people in whose industry a part, though but a small part, has been employed in procuring him this accommodation, exceeds all computation. The woollen coat, for example, which covers the day-labourer, as coarse and rough as it may appear, is the produce of a great multitude of workmen ... without the assistance and co-operation of many thousands, the very meanest person in a civilised country could not be provided, even according to, what we very falsely imagine, the easy and simple manner in which he is commonly accommodated.[106]

The policy which Smith believed it essential to adopt in light of this has come down to us as '*laissez faire*'. In a paper the text of which is lost, Smith is reported as saying that:

> it requires no more than to leave [Nature] alone and give her fair play in the pursuit of her own ends that she may establish her own designs ... Little else is required to

[100] Of the absolute necessity of which I would hope, on the basis of previous work, not to be thought unaware.

[101] M Friedman, 'The Social Responsibility of Business Is to Increase its Profits' (13 September 1970) *The New York Times (Sunday Magazine)* SM17:

> The executive is exercising a distinct 'social responsibility', rather than serving as an agent of the stockholders or the customers or the employees, only if he spends the money in a different way than they would have spent it.

[102] In total war, the normal absence in a liberal democracy of a social goal for output was replaced with a social goal, survival, which was given a 'peculiar overriding status' 'to which all other aims are subordinate', and this effected a 'drastic ... simplification of the allocation problem ... so great as to ... virtually ... change its nature': Robbins, *Peace and War* (n 91) 30, 47–48.

[103] FA Hayek, 'Competition as a Discovery Procedure' in *The Market and Other Orders* in *Collected Works*, vol 15 (Routledge 2014).

[104] E Penrose, *The Theory of the Growth of the Firm* (OUP 2009) 71–75.

[105] FA Hayek, 'The Economics of Planning' in *Socialism and War* in *Collected Works*, vol 10 (Liberty Fund 1997).

[106] Smith, *Wealth of Nations* (n 96) 22–23.

> carry a state to the highest degree of affluence ... brought about by the natural course of things.[107]

Though the criticism (in the sense of actualisation) of *laissez faire* is the core of this book, I should make it clear at this early stage that I accept that part of Smith's reasoning which turns on the claim that the market economy is the only possible form of welfare-enhancing general economy of consumer choice because only it can deal with the co-ordination problems of such an economy. It is essential that:

> The sovereign is completely discharged from a duty, in the attempting to perform which he must always be exposed to innumerable delusions, and for the proper performance of which no human wisdom or knowledge could ever be sufficient; the duty of superintending the industry of private people, and of directing it towards the employments most suitable to the interests of that society.[108]

But in what sense can acceptance of the *de gustibus* principle and the necessity of market ordering be thought consistent with the regulation of exchange by the law contract?

Pareto Optimality, Autonomy, and Contractual Agreement

The way I have derived freedom of contract from Pareto optimality has been intended to convey the centrality of autonomy to these fundamentals of economics and of law, but whilst I trust this derivation is accurate, the accounts of Pareto optimality and autonomy have both involved a literally tendentious misrepresentation. It has been insisted that Pareto optimality must be a matter only of self-interested, voluntary choices. The very concept of rational economic action does indeed require that an economic actor evaluate the goods potentially available to it, and to subjectively rank them in terms of their desirability set against their cost. But, the indispensability of such analysis notwithstanding, the solipsistic concept of self-interest involved[109] does not capture the actual source of Pareto optimality's claim to legitimacy, which is that it portrays a social system of *mutual* advantage. With this shift of focus to the social, the solipsistic self-interest that motivates exchange must be abandoned for a self-interest that makes exchange actually possible, which is based on a relationship of mutual recognition.

[107] D Stewart, 'Account of the Life and Writings of Adam Smith LLD' in A Smith, *Essays on Philosophical Subjects* in *The Glasgow Edition of the Works and Correspondence*, vol 3 (Clarendon Press 1980) 322.

[108] Smith, *Wealth of Nations* (n 96) 687.

[109] The solipsistic flavour of the analysis is perfectly conveyed in Heinrich Gossen, *The Laws of Human Nature* (MIT Press 1983), a work which was all but completely ignored for decades after its publication in 1854, but which is now recognised as having anticipated Menger, Jevons, and Walras in putting forward the first systematic statement of marginal analysis. Having in pt 1 on 'The Economy of the Isolated Individual' set out 'the basic principles that must guide the individual in evaluating the external world ... for his actions to obtain a maximum of life pleasure', Gossen sought confirmation of those principles from the 'experiences provided by actuality' to be found by reading *Robinson Crusoe*, but only 'up to the point when Crusoe finds Friday': ibid 54. It is in pt 2 that Gossen turns to 'The Exchange Economy'.

We have seen that a Pareto optimal equilibrium is a position from which 'every small displacement … must necessarily have the effect of increasing the ophelimity enjoyed by some individuals and decreasing that enjoyed by others, ie of being agreeable to some and disagreeable to others'. At such an equilibrium, it may well be the case that some, indeed perhaps all, economic actors can see possibilities of further improvement through exchange, but they cannot realise any of them unilaterally.[110] If an actor goes to an isolated place and reveals its preference for a good by declaiming it to the wind, this has no economic significance. An actor reveals its preferences in a significant manner, ie actually makes a choice rather than having the relevant subjective intention, by making an economic exchange.[111] And an exchange cannot take place because one economic actor believes it will benefit from the exchange.[112] It can take place only when a pair of actors both believe they will benefit, and for this reason voluntarily enter into the exchange.

Pareto optimality cannot, then, be seen as being capable of being realised in the sense of one economic actor enjoying autonomy in exchange, the one actor then being multiplied to the number of all the actors in the economy. Optimality can be realised only if two, paired actors both enjoy autonomy in every exchange, for though acting from self-interest, they enter into a relationship in which the legitimate realisation of the self-interest of one is conditional on the legitimate realisation of the self-interest of the other. The only method by which legitimate exchange may take place is by reciprocal persuasion, with the war of transfer by exercise of solipsistic self-interest by, for example, force being replaced by contractual transfer by consent:

> The workings of [self-interest] may be viewed under two aspects, according as the agents act *without*, or *with*, the consent of others … the first species of action may be called *war*; the second *contract*.[113]

[110] G Simmel, 'The Problem of Sociology' in *On Individuality and Social Forms* (University of Chicago Press 1971) 24:

> Any social form or process is composed of two elements which in reality are inseparable: on the one hand, an interest, a purpose, or a motive; on the other, a form or mode of interaction among individuals through which, or in the shape of which, that content attains social reality.

[111] I put to one side the collection of 'stated preferences' by eg opinion surveys which may be used as evidence for state intervention, the stated preference being distanced from the commitment of resource which is intrinsic to the revelation of preference by a choice to make an exchange.

[112] J von Neumann and O Morgenstern, *The Theory of Games and Economic Behaviour* (60th Anniversary edn, Princeton University Press 2004) 10–11:

> [Robinson] Crusoe faces an ordinary [maximisation] problem … a participant in a social exchange economy [faces] a problem [which] has many elements in common [with] this … But [his problem] also contains some, very essential, elements of an entirely different nature. He too tries to obtain an optimum result. But to achieve this, he must enter into relations of exchange with others. If two … persons exchange goods with each other, then the result for each one will depend in general not merely upon his own actions but on those of others as well … each participant attempts to maximise a function … of which he does not control all variables. This is … a peculiar and disconcerting mixture of several conflicting maximisation problems. Every participant is guided by another principle and neither determines all variables which affect his interest.

[113] FY Edgeworth, *Mathematical Psychics* in *Mathematical Psychics and Further Papers on Political Economy* (OUP 2003) 16–17. There are numerous social theoretical variants of this distinction, and that of von Mises will be mentioned in the text accompanying n 137.

Actual choices, rather than subjective intentions to choose, require voluntary exchange, and so should express the self-interest of both actors in relationship with each other. Contract institutionalises this by requiring exchange to be an *agreement*,[114] which has an essential, if most inadequately recognised, active aspect. This aspect may best be approached by considering the way that Smith strove to develop a concept of self-interest in exchange which had to be exercised through acknowledgement of and engagement with the self-interest of others, so that agreement is the result of what each party has *persuaded* the other to do in its own interest:

> The offering of a shilling, which to us appears to have so plain and simple a meaning, is in reality offering an argument to persuade one another to do so as it is for his interest.[115]

The legitimacy of the market economy entirely rests on this, and it is bearing the significance of persuasion in mind that we should understand the morality informing what may be the most influential passage in all of modern European social thought:

> In civilised society [man] stands at all times in need of the co-operation and assistance of great multitudes [and] has almost constant occasion for the help of his brethren, and it is in vain for him to expect it from their benevolence only. He will be more likely to prevail if he can interest their self-love in his favour ... and it is in this manner that we obtain from one another the far greater part of those good offices which we stand in need of. It is not from the benevolence of the butcher, the brewer, or the baker, that we expect our dinner, but from their regard to their own interest. We address ourselves, not to their humanity but to their self-love, and never talk to them of our own necessities but of their advantages.[116]

This passage is very commonly interpreted as a justification of self-interest, which indeed it is, but only a self-interest which is pursued through persuasion, and so is respectful of the autonomy of others. It is the aim of this entire book to develop the implications of these views of Smith's on self-interest and persuasion.

[114] Put the other way round, each actor can withhold agreement by rejecting an offer and so 'veto' a transfer desired by the offeror. This is the essence of a 'property' rule of ownership, seminally distinguished from a liability rule in G Calabresi and AD Melamed, 'Property Rules, Liability Rules and Inalienability: One View of the Cathedral' (1972) 85 Harvard Law Review 1089, 1092:

> An entitlement is protected by a property rule to the extent that someone who wishes to remove the entitlement from its holder must buy it from him in a voluntary transaction in which the value of the entitlement is agreed upon by the seller. It is the form of entitlement which gives rise to the least amount of state intervention: once the original entitlement is decided upon, the state does not try to decide its value. It lets each of the parties say how much the entitlement is worth to him, and gives the seller a veto if the buyer does not offer enough

[115] A Smith, *Lectures on Jurisprudence* in *The Glasgow Edition of the Works and Correspondence*, vol 5 (Clarendon Press 1978) 352. 'Persuasion' can, of course, carry an opposed, even sinister, connotation, and in the now forgotten but then very influential V Packard, *The Hidden Persuaders* (Ig Publishing 2007), this connotation was made an important theme of the US criticisms of mass consumerism in the 1950s and 1960s, discussed in Chapter 3.

[116] Smith, *Wealth of Nations* (n 96) 26–27.

It is, in truth, a more complicated matter than it initially seems to derive economic action and contract autonomy understood in Kantian terms. As it is a matter of the human being's relationship with its natural environment, the acquisition of economic goods is ultimately motivated by what Kant would call desire, and conduct of any sort which is motivated in an unmediated manner by desire cannot be moral.[117] To act according to unmediated desire is to surrender the noumenal faculty of freedom to natural influences, and so in a sense is not to 'act'. To act, or to act freely, the human being must decide for itself whether to act upon the impulse of desire, or not. 'Autonomy' as such in fact emerges in Kant's reasoning as a single moral principle which is distinguished from the 'heteronomy' of all the various impulses of desire experienced in interaction with the natural world.[118]

Striving not to go further than necessary into Kant's practical philosophy or its vocabulary, Kant formulates the 'Fundamental Law of Pure Practical Reason', the categorical imperative, in this way: 'So act that the maxim of your will could always hold at the same time as a principle of a giving of universal law'.[119] When addressing a specific empirical situation, a moral action is one which may be regarded as self-legislation in that, if the specific decision were universalised, it would perpetuate autonomy. The law emerges from the freedom to will, and makes the preservation of self-legislation the measure of morality. To sustain moral experience, the subject is to be committed to the freedom of self-legislation, and the adequacy of the legislation is to be assessed by considering how far it (re)produces autonomy. Autonomy, then, is both the revealed condition of morality, and the continuously renewed achievement of respect for the moral law.

The reproduction of autonomy in exchange has two aspects which we must distinguish. First, we must register that there are crucial issues at the level of what Kant called 'duties to oneself' (or 'self-regarding duties') which must be observed to reproduce one's own autonomy,[120] of which the duty to discuss one's choices that we have mentioned in connection with *de gustibus* is the one most relevant to us. The unavoidable question arises whether some exceptional, 'specialised vices' would be so harmful, with Pareto's example of the recreational use of morphine coming to mind, that a policy of coercively eliminating those vices might be wise.[121] I do not pretend to add to previous consideration of this problem,[122] but merely aim to make the basic position taken in this book clear when I say that I myself am open to the possibility of such a policy, but only if it is not defended in terms of extending autonomy, its defence perforce acknowledging it must have the opposite effect.[123]

[117] I Kant, *Critique of Practical Reason* in *Practical Philosophy* in *The Cambridge Edition of the Works* (CUP 1996) 155.

[118] ibid 166.

[119] ibid 164.

[120] I Kant, *Lectures on Ethics* in *The Cambridge Edition of the Works* (CUP 1997) 122–28 (hereafter Kant, *Lectures*).

[121] J Raz, *The Morality of Freedom* (Clarendon Press 1986) 380–81.

[122] G Dworkin, 'Paternalism' in RA Wassterstrom (ed), *Morality and the Law* (Wadsworth 1971).

[123] L Kolakowski, 'How To Be a Conservative-Liberal-Socialist: A Credo' in *Modernity on Endless Trial* (University of Chicago Press 1990) 226:

> A socialist believes [that] There are good reasons why freedom of economic activity should be limited.

Our focus here, however, is on the second level of 'duties to others',[124] for the reproduction of autonomy in the social relationship of exchange is a question of an actor's conduct towards other actors, with the law of contract turning on the recognition that a party's freedom to choose is crucially influenced by the conduct of the other parties involved in negotiations and contracts. When the question is one of legally enforceable duties to others, this is a question of 'justice'. Kant states the universal principle of justice as 'Every action is just if it can coexist with everyone's freedom in accordance with a universal law, or if on its maxim the freedom of choice of each can coexist with everyone's freedom in accordance with a universal law.'[125] The key to this is not to treat others as mere means to the realisation of one's own ends, but to recognise that others also have the status of ends-in-themselves.[126] This is the necessary condition of realising Pareto optimality as a social system of *mutual* advantage, and it will be argued throughout this book that the positive law of contract has been, and is being, formed by the development of consciousness of this necessity in a concept of good faith which expresses the duties to each other of both parties to a contract. Coherently understanding these duties has long involved and now involves rejection of a classical law that cannot free itself from a commitment to solipsistic self-interest.

Autonomy and the Regulation of Contract

Laissez faire and minimalism

Autonomy as the basis of freedom of contract is first of all a question of negative freedom from coercion allowing the formation of solipsistically self-interested subjective intentions. But as the basis of a just law of contract, autonomy has a very different character. As it must not override economic actors' own conceptions of the good, autonomy is 'a genuinely second-order conception ... there is no substantive conception of the good that it rules out, just so long as that conception has been arrived at autonomously'.[127] As we have seen, this requires the state to be neutral between economic actors' as human beings who choose, but to give practical effect to such neutrality in the law of contract requires us to see that this does not mean 'neutrality between conceptions of the good ... because [we must attribute value] only to those conceptions with the right pedigree'.[128] It is a fundamental function of the law of contract to conduct this test of pedigree, and it does so by requiring that contracts, whatever the substance of their terms, into which it seeks to make no inquiry, be voluntary agreements (of a type called bargains). Requiring agreement requires that each party's legitimate self-interest must take a form which allows the autonomy of the other party, and it is this *relationship* of mutual autonomy, rather than the solipsistically self-interested

But the limitation should be called precisely that, and should not be called a higher form of freedom.

124 Kant, *Lectures* (n 120) 177–84. I discuss what I regard as an unacceptable equivocation about this in the law of vitiating factors and consumer law in ch 6.

125 Kant, *Metaphysics of Morals* (n 51) 387 (translation amended).

126 Kant, *Groundwork* (n 50) 80.

127 B Barry, *Justice as Impartiality* (Clarendon Press 1995) 133.

128 ibid.

economic actor (or even two solipsistically self-interested economic actors making an exchange),[129] that should be the basic concept of our understanding of the law of contract.[130]

It is wrong to claim that neo-classical economics has characteristically claimed that self-interest should be allowed 'unlimited scope' and 'free play'.[131] Though those economics are based on the claim that, as AC Pigou put it one of the works that established the welfare economic critique of *laissez faire*, 'the working of self-interest is generally beneficent',[132] they have centrally acknowledged that exchange being beneficent does not entail that the exercise of self-interest will be confined to exchange. Pareto himself recognised a fundamental 'division in men's activity: some of them will endeavour to produce goods … some of them will endeavour, not to produce, but to appropriate the goods produced by others'.[133] Commenting on this, Pigou argued that Smith, in a way to which we will return in the conclusion of this book, had assumed 'the existence of laws designed, and, in the main, competent to prevent acts of *mere* appropriation, such as those perpetrated by highwaymen and card-sharpers', in order to ensure that 'exchange was not a matter of 'seizure'.[134] Self-interest, in sum, is generally beneficent only because its 'free play is … confined to certain directions by our general social institutions, especially the family, private property and the territorial state'.[135] It was on this basis that von Mises identified 'the maintenance of peace [in order] to assure economic continuity'[136] as the central role of law in creating liberal democratic society based on 'contractual bonds',[137] and that Weber made peacefulness intrinsic to the concept of economic action: 'economic action is any peaceful exercise of an actor's control over resources which is in its main impulse directed towards economic ends'.[138]

All this is, of course, ultimately based on the analysis of human motivation which has set the framework for all modern political theory: Hobbes' argument that in a

[129] Kant argued that the contractual transfer of goods requires a 'common' or 'united' will irreducible to the 'separate' wills of the parties: Kant, *Metaphysics of Morals* (n 51) 422–24. See also JG Fichte, *The Science of Rights* (Routledge & Kegan Paul 1970) 210–12 and Hegel, *Philosophy of Right* (n 20) 104–06.

[130] IR Macneil, 'Reflections on Relational Contract' (1985) 141 Journal of Institutional and Theoretical Economics 541, 542:

> What is essential to any sound theoretical approach to contracts of any kind is a *Grundnorm* recognising the embeddedness of all exchange in relations.

Macneil's views were formed prior to the appearance of what has become the reference point in the modern discussion of the 'embeddedness' of economic action in social relations: M Granovetter, 'Economic Action and Social Structure: The Problem of Embeddedness' (1985) 91 American Journal of Sociology 481. Embeddedness is discussed in ch 2.

[131] Tawney, *Acquisitive Society* (n 56) 32.

[132] AC Pigou, *The Economics of Welfare* (Transaction Publishers 2002) 128; quoting E Cannan, 'Review of NG Pierson *Principles of Economics* (1913)' 23 Economic Review 331 (hereafter Pigou, *Welfare*).

[133] Pareto, *Manual* (n 46) 235 (ch 9, s 17).

[134] Pigou, *Welfare* (n 132) 128.

[135] ibid; quoting E Cannan, *The History of the Local Rates in England* (2nd edn, PS King 1912) 176.

[136] von Mises, *Socialism* (n 97) 36.

[137] L von Mises, *Human Action* (4th rev edn, Fox and Wilkes 1996) 195–98. HC Havighurst, *The Nature of Private Contract* (Northwestern University Press 1961) 21 placed von Mises at the heart of its analysis of contractual 'peace'.

[138] M Weber, *Economy and Society* (reissued edn, University of California Press 1978) 63. Weber preceded this definition by saying that action is 'economically oriented' if it 'is concerned with the satisfaction of a desire for "utilities"'.

pre-political state of nature the unconstrained exercise of self-interest would lead to a 'warre ... of every man, against every man' in which life would be 'solitary, poor, nasty, brutish and short'.[139] Given the philosophic anthropology accepted here, some legal solution to the 'Hobbesian problem of order'[140] must be reached for exchange generally to take place.[141] In this sense regulation, defined as the establishment and maintenance of a legal framework within which legitimate economic activity may be carried out,[142] is necessary for economic action constitutive of a general market economy to be possible.[143]

What has undermined the *laissez faire* understanding of self-interest (and the welfarist response to it which shares this understanding) is, not a denial of the necessity of limits to self-interest, but the narrowness of its concept of, precisely, limitation. In the first instance, this is, as it were, a quantitative matter. Though to do so involves great oversimplification,[144] one is basically right to say that the characteristic of *laissez faire* is its tediously unrelieved (ultra-)minimalism.[145] It sees the optimum role of the state as, as Mill aptly said, the mere prevention of force or fraud.[146] But the situation this would leave, of 'anarchy plus a street constable' as Carlyle put it, is not only wholly unattractive but, as Carlyle himself saw, wholly unsustainable,[147] and so vacuous as a guide to government policy.[148] Though *laissez faire* minimalism follows from a commitment to the autonomy of the parties, that minimalism simply cannot encompass the complexity and extent of the continuous, reflexive process of active 'institutional direction',[149] *inter alia* by the principles of the law of contract, necessary even to

[139] T Hobbes, *Leviathan* (rev student edn, CUP 1996) 88, 89. The specific role of the law of contract in providing security is discussed ibid 96–97.

[140] T Parsons, *The Structure of Social Action* (pbk edn, Free Press, 1968) 89–94.

[141] Gauthier, *Morality by Agreement* (n 92) 85:

> Before Smith's invisible hand can do its beneficent work, Hobbes' war of every man against every man must first be exorcised.

[142] This definition is based on RH Coase, 'Advertising and Free Speech' (1977) 6 Journal of Legal Studies 1, 5. Noting the conventional confinement of 'regulation' to direct or indirect control by a public agency, Coase said that 'regulation is also the result of legislative and judicial actions, and it would be unwise not to take these into consideration'.

[143] OH Taylor, 'Non-economic Elements in Social Life' in *Economics and Liberalism* (Harvard University Press 1955) 126:

> It is only within a strong framework ... of socially enforced rules limiting the 'rational' pursuit of private interests to modes of action involving no coercive exploitation of others that such activity can go on in the ways and with the results which economic theory describes.

[144] AJ Taylor, *Laissez-faire and State Intervention in Nineteenth-century Britain* (Macmillan 1972).

[145] Nozick, *Anarchy* (n 80) 26–28. Though I shall continue to eschew use of the term 'minimalism', and indeed remain critical of its use, that use in J Morgan, *Contract Law Minimalism* (CUP 2013), which is discussed in ch 4, is not merely not susceptible to the argument I am trying to make here, but it is a condition of that argument's success that it should be able to accommodate the substance of Dr Morgan's views.

[146] Mill, *Principles* (n 53) 936.

[147] T Carlyle, *Latter-day Pamphlets* (Chapman and Hall 1850) 17–18.

[148] Hayek, *Constitution* (n 30) 340:

> The old formulae of laissez faire or non-intervention do not provide us with an adequate criterion for distinguishing between what is and what is not admissible in a free system.

[149] D Campbell and M Klaes, 'The Principle of Institutional Direction: Coase's Regulatory Critique of Intervention' (2005) 29 Cambridge Journal of Economics 263. Klaes and I had particularly Bastiat's formulations in mind: F Bastiat, 'The Law' in *'The Law', 'The State' and Other Political Writings 1843–50* in *Collected Works*, vol 2 (Liberty Fund 2012) 65–66:

prevent force or fraud, much less to generally regulate exchange. But it is necessary to add an, as it were, qualitative dimension to this quantitative criticism of *laissez faire*, because discussion of the merely quantitative cannot fully expose the effect of the ethical shortcomings of *laissez faire* on our understanding of the way in which the general principles of contract are followed and developed.

It would simply be an affectation to deny that problems of, as it were, technique inherent in the regulatory task give rise to an unavoidable degree of difficulty in the law of contract. It is, and always will be, difficult to hand down the correct rules. But an in fact extremely large part of the difficulty of the core doctrines of the positive law of contract can simply be eliminated if the morality which underlies those doctrines was clearly articulated in their statement. It is just this, however, that the classical law is incapable of doing because it contradictorily regards solipsistic self-interest as legitimate, and so has grave difficulty when rationalising what appear to be limitations on freedom of contract, though there is no serious argument about the necessity of limitation in principle, nor that the positive law has come to be absolutely replete with such limitations. In 1960, in the first thing he ever published, Ian Macneil both noted the paradox of the ubiquity of limitations in a system of *laissez faire* freedom, and gave a clear indication of how the paradox should be resolved. The limitations, Macneil told us:

> appear as exceptions to some general rule permitting the parties fully to define their legal status [but] if the role of the law in creating contracts were more completely presented this distortion would not occur, and these matters would be seen not as exceptions to freedom of contract but as simply part of the law's definition of contract.[150]

Welfarism and purpose

I have earlier argued that Tawney's famous criticism of the ethical and cultural barrenness of the acquisitive society misses its mark if it is intended to be a criticism of a feature that economic action necessarily displays. The inaccuracy of the criticism is, however, wider than this. Having made his criticism, Tawney goes on to acknowledge that:

> When law and force confine a man within the bounds of justice, they do not impose anything on him but a mere negation. They impose on him only the obligation to refrain from injuring others. They do not infringe on his personality or his liberty or his property. They merely safeguard the personality, the liberty, and the property of others. They stand on the defensive; they defend the equal right of all … This is so true that … to say that *the object of the law is to make justice prevail* is to use an expression that is not strictly exact. One should say: *The object of the law is to prevent injustice from prevailing.*

[150] IR Macneil, 'Review of H Shepherd and BD Sher, *Law in Society: An Introduction to Freedom of Contract*' (1960) 46 Cornell Law Quarterly 176, 177.

> The appeal of this conception must be powerful, for it has laid the whole modern world under its spell ... The secret of its triumph is obvious. It is an invitation to men to use the powers with which they have been endowed ... without enquiring whether there is any principle by which their exercise should be limited ... By fixing men's minds, not upon the discharge of social obligations, which restricts their energy, because it defines the goal to which it should be directed, but upon the exercise of the right to pursue their own self-interest, it offers unlimited scope for the acquisition of riches, and therefore gives free play to one of the most powerful of human instincts.[151]

Tawney's views turn on his inability to recognise a limit to self-interest other than would be set by the discharge of 'social' obligations.[152] But there is an ethical limit to self-interest even if one does not recognise, indeed thinks it essential to deny, social, ie collective, 'purpose' in the market sphere. The necessary implication of what I have said of *de gustibus* in regard to the choices of individuals is that, as a collective matter, market order in liberal democratic society's best claim to legitimacy rests, not on the moral value of particular social goals set by 'society', but on the extent of the freedom of actors to set their own goals. One may say that the goal of liberal democratic society should be to eschew the pursuit of social goals and be, in this sense, 'purposeless'.[153] But this does not mean that the market economy is devoid of morality, because the stability of that economy entirely rests on economic actors' recognising the legitimacy of each others' pursuit of the goals they define for themselves, and of the social institutions, including the law of contract, which make that pursuit possible. The moral practice of the law of contract is absolutely not the pursuit of a social goal, but is the reproduction of the 'conditions of [the] practice'[154] of contracting in a form of civil association consisting of:

> each pursuing his own interest or even joined with some others in seeking common satisfactions, but related to one another in the continuous acknowledgement of the authority of rules of conduct indifferent to the pursuit or the achievement of any purpose.[155]

The success of the neo-liberal revolution particularly called into question views such as Tawney's because the more extensive the identification of social goals, the smaller must be the market sphere which *should* be driven by personally chosen goals.[156] Perhaps the most telling neo-liberal criticism made of this on the grounds of

[151] Tawney, *Acquisitive Society* (n 56) 32. In the passages omitted from this quotation Tawney distinguishes, or rather fails properly to distinguish, between 'natural' and 'social' powers, but this is distinction which would run against Tawney's blanket idea of equality, in which 'economic' arguments for inequality are dismissed as 'mere superstitions, for which no shadow of convincing evidence has as yet been adduced': RH Tawney, *Equality* (4th edn, William Pickering 1994) 11. These issues are taken up in ch 6.

[152] M Oakeshott, *On Human Conduct* (Clarendon Press 1975) 109: 'Some writers ... find it impossible to imagine association except in terms of common purpose' (hereafter Oakeshott, *Human Conduct*).

[153] Hayek, *Law* (n 62) vol 2, 109–11.

[154] Oakeshott, *Human Conduct* (n 152) 60, 118–19.

[155] ibid 201.

[156] M Walzer, *Spheres of Justice* (Blackwell 1983) 112–15.

political morality was Nozick's criticism, derived from his insistence on neutrality, of 'patterning':

> no end-state principle or distributional patterned principle of justice can be continuously realised without continuous interference with people's lives ... To maintain a pattern one must either continuously interfere to stop people from transferring resources as they wish to, or continually (or periodically) interfere to take from some persons resources that for other reasons some people chose to transfer to them.[157]

The liberal socialist position taken in this book obviously entails something like the criticism of patterning, and the task is to actively give it, and therefore neutrality, effect.

The predominant response of left-wing regulatory theory, and as part of this of welfarism in contract, to this aspect of neo-liberalism has been to seek to avoid the choice which Tawney and Nozick pose. Let us recall Collins' influential statement of the 'ideals of social justice' of the modern law. The 'purpose' of that law accordingly was 'the channelling and regulation of market transactions according to [those] ideals'.[158] Collins here acutely anticipated the shift in the meaning of 'regulation' by which left-wing regulatory theory has sought to reconcile social purpose with an acknowledgement of the superior 'efficiency' of 'the market' made necessary by neo-liberalism. Expressed in an extremely varied terminology of 'hybrids', 'quasi-markets', 'networks', etc, and applied far beyond the private law of contract to embrace a general economy of 'regulatory capitalism', the essential claim is that sufficiently sophisticated design of (meta-)regulation will ensure that market transactions are, as Collins expressed it, so channelled that their outcomes will yield social justice. In what may be the most influential contribution to this argument from within the law of contract,[159] Collins told us that:

> The great strength of ... private law regulation of contracts is plainly its responsive or reflexive quality. It devolves an extensive discretionary power of self-regulation to the parties. Subject to the requirement of a negotiated consensus, the rules produced will then be routinely enforced by the legal system through the agency of the ordinary courts. By conferring autonomy on the parties to devise their own regulation, private law achieves considerable flexibility, which in turn achieves the advantage that the regulation permits experimentation with novel types of business transaction that might enhance potential business efficiency.[160]

[157] Nozick, *Anarchy* (n 80) 163.

[158] Collins, *Contract* (n 12) 1.

[159] In particular, an important collection of papers sought to generalise Collins' approach in *Regulating Contracts*, which he summarises and develops in the collection's first chapter, to, in principle, all the laws of the regulatory capitalist state: C Parker, C Scott, N Lacey, and J Braithwaite (eds), *Regulating Law* (OUP 2004).

A valuable overall statement of Brownsword's thinking may be found in the introduction he and his co-editors have provided to R Brownsword, RAJ van Gestel, and H-W Micklitz (eds), *Contract and Regulation* (Edward Elgar 2017).

[160] H Collins, *Regulating Contracts* (OUP 1999) 67.

It is, as has earlier been claimed, correct to view the private law of contract as a form of regulation, but, with respect, Collins, though he very valuably argues against 'the tasks of regulating contracts being passed to new public regulatory systems, which has been the predominant response in the twentieth century to distributive problems in contracts',[161] does not take sufficient distance from the 'public' connotations of regulation. He summarises his achievement by saying that:

> By viewing all legal intervention in markets, including private law, as types of regulation, we have been able to launch an investigation into the comparative advantages of different regulatory strategies with respect to the objectives of the legal regulation of contracts.[162]

The private law and the market are conceived as strategies for reaching the predetermined purpose, or set of purposes, of social justice. Though there will be numerous specific instances when the spontaneous intentions of the parties are endorsed because they coincide with social justice, it is the exogenous standard that dominates, and inconsistent voluntary choices will be ruled out, not by being forbidden, but by being made impossible in the first place.[163] This sophisticated refinement of the technique of positive freedom[164] is the attraction of Collins' approach. This approach, however, runs counter to the praise of the market that motivated the entire effort, for it contradicts the market's essential purposelessness. A market, indeed, that seeks to give effect to such a purpose is not a market at all.[165]

The core sense of economic action is misunderstood when such action is to be rendered amenable to social purpose. The market is seen as a 'mechanism' for the 'efficient' 'technical' production of results. But the fundamentals of the market cannot be approached in this way,[166] for that economy 'is the economic order proper to a definite social structure and to a definite spiritual and moral setting'.[167] That setting is the purposelessness of self-interested choice, for this is the only possible basis of Pareto optimality. If general exchange is to be possible; the principal legal institution for what *has* to be the voluntary transfer of what *has* to be private property *has* to be the private

[161] ibid 358.

[162] ibid.

[163] Berlin, 'Two Concepts' (n 72) 133:

> [I may] conceive of myself as coercing others for their own sake, in their, not my, interest. I am claiming that I know what they truly need better than they know it themselves ... I may declare that they are actually aiming at what in their benighted state they consciously resist, because their exists within them an occult entity ... their 'true' purpose ... and that this entity, although it is belied by all that they overtly feel and do say, is their 'real' self.

[164] I do not want to delve into the literature of regulatory capitalism but I will say that the first use of the term 'regulatory state' of which I am aware was in the telling subtitle of H Seidman and R Gilmour, *Politics, Position and Power: From the Positive to the Regulatory State* (4th edn, OUP 1986). The prosaic subtitle of earlier editions, *The Dynamics of Federal Organisation*, was restored for the 5th and last edition.

[165] D Campbell, 'The "Hybrid Contract" and the Merging of the Public and Private Law of the Allocation of Economic Goods,' in D Campbell and ND Lewis (eds), *Promoting Participation: Law or Politics?* (Cavendish 1999) in D Campbell, 'Relational Contract and the Nature of Private Ordering: A Comment on Vincent-Jones' (2007) 14 Indiana J Global Legal Studies 279.

[166] Röpke, *Humane Economy* (n 57) 93.

[167] ibid.

law of contract.[168] Efficiency cannot be a technical matter of the realisation of an exogenous purpose;[169] the 'efficiency' of Pareto optimality *has* to inhere in the actualisation of individual actors' voluntary, ie self-determined, choices.

A distinction must be drawn between 'social regulation' or 'intervention' and 'economic regulation', the distinction turning, not on the presence or absence of regulation at all, but the presence or absence of purpose.[170] The economic regulation which is necessary for the existence of a general market economy is ultimately a public matter, but the paramount public policy which must be pursued by such regulation is Jessel MR's freedom of contract, which we now see is a matter, not of passive negative freedom, but of active regulation for negative freedom. The point has never been better expressed than it was by Walter Lippmann:

> in a free society the state does not administer the affairs of men. It administers justice among men who conduct their own affairs.[171]

The seeming unacceptability of making a public commitment to purposeless regulation of this sort, which has no 'social' dimension, has been the basic impulse to welfarism. But this unacceptability is not nearly so formidable as it has appeared, because it is misconceived. Though 'social' purpose must be eschewed in the market sphere, the purposeless purpose of Pareto optimisation, far from lacking moral justification, has moral legitimacy as an essential, constitutive feature.

Constraint and Facilitation in the Law of Contract

The concept of 'constraint' has played a crucially important role in the formulation of sociology's claim to be a science with a specific subject matter of causal influences upon individuals' actions which emerge from, but are not reducible to, the wills of those individuals. After examining cases such as legal rules, social conventions, professional practices, and methods of business competition,[172] Durkheim defined a 'social fact' as 'any way of acting, whether fixed or not, capable of exerting over the individual an external constraint ... having an existence of its own independent of its individual manifestations'.[173] Though it served its main purpose of demonstrating the

[168] A striking unintended demonstration of this has recently been furnished by the proposal, ultimately derived from Henry George, to make private property always open to a compulsory auction in EA Posner and EG Weyl, *Radical Markets* (Princeton University Press 2018). I have described the resultant loss of the freedom to choose whether or not to sell what one owns as 'hideous': D Campbell, 'The Non-existence of Markets in the Economic Analysis of Law *à la Mode* (Review of EA Posner and EG Weyl, *Radical Markets: Uprooting Capitalism and Democracy for a Just Society*)' (2019) 83 Modern Law Review 951, 959.

[169] Röpke, *Humane Economy* (n 57) 94:

> [Those] who,] speaking in the name of the market economy, work out the most elaborate projects for regulating the movements of [that] economy ... seem to be unaware of the question whether such a machine is compatible with the atmosphere of the market, to which freedom is essential.

[170] D Campbell, 'The "Market" in the Theory of Regulation' (2018) 27 Social and Legal Studies 545, 549–55.

[171] W Lippmann, *The Good Society* (Transaction Publishers 2005) 267.

[172] E Durkheim, *The Rules of Sociological Method* (Macmillan 1982) 59 (hereafter Durkheim, *Rules*).

[173] ibid 51.

sui generis ontology of the social influences upon individual action,[174] the concept of the social fact obviously is, as Durkheim always perceived[175] but only gradually came to more fully appreciate, inadequate to the relationship of social institutions and individual actors in a number of ways, two of which are of great interest here.

First, 'constraint' does not capture the 'enabling' or 'facilitative'[176] aspect of social institutions. Perhaps Durkheim's most famous example of a constraint was that for a French person 'it was impossible to do otherwise' than speak French with her or his compatriots.[177] As the adoption of one of a range of alternative possibilities implies the exclusion of others—*determinatio est negatio*[178]—Durkheim's example unarguably is one of constraint, but how greatly enabled is the actor, even if its range of possibility is constrained, by the use of the French, or any one other, language.[179] In light of this, it is wrong, or only very partial, to give precedence to the constraining rather than the facilitative aspect of the market economy as it institutionalises the values of a liberal democracy.[180] (And criticism of this economy when it does not do this is in fact blunted by a general focus on constraint.) For reasons turning on the necessity of securing peacefulness which we have discussed, Weber was right, despite the indisputable counter-evidence, to affirm the long standing[181] overall identification of the national and global development of the market economy with the generally civil conduct of economic activity.[182] Of even more relevance to the argument to be made

[174] This of course involved distinguishing 'social' causality from, not only individuals' wills, but from the causal influences upon action of the natural environment: ibid 50.

[175] Leaving aside other parts of Durkheim's work, his doctoral dissertation and first major published work contains passages on contract that clearly show this, and thus to an extent anticipate the argument of this book: eg E Durkheim, *The Division of Labour in Society* (Macmillan 1984) 320:

> liberty itself is the product of regulation. Far from being a type of antagonist to social action, it is the resultant.

[176] RB Seidman, 'Contract Law, The Free Market and State Intervention: A Jurisprudential Perspective' (1973) 7 Journal of Economic Issues 553, 553–59.

[177] Durkheim, *Rules* (n 172) 51.

[178] Letter from Baruch de Spinoza to Jarig Jelles (letter 50) (2 June 1674) in *Complete Works* (Hackett Publishing 2002) 892.

[179] A Giddens, *The Constitution of Society* (Polity Press 1984) 170:

> Since any language presumes a range of rule-governed properties, the process of language learning sets certain limits to cognition and activity. But by the very same token the learning of a language greatly expands the cognitive and practical capacities of the individual.

[180] S Deakin, C Lane, and F Wilkinson, 'Contract Law, Trust Relations and Incentives for Co-operation' in S Deakin and J Michie (eds), *Contracts, Co-operation and Competition* (OUP 1997) 133:

> Institutional forces do not simply constrain individual agency, but channel contractual behaviour in the sense of opening up options for co-operative behaviour which would not otherwise be feasible.

[181] C de Montesquieu, *The Spirit of the Laws* (CUP 1989) 48:

> the spirit of commerce brings with it the spirit of frugality, economy, moderation, work, wisdom, tranquility, order and rule.

The widespread modern use of essentially this claim in the institutional explanation of the economic success of the western nations has interestingly been developed in relation to the detail of the law of contract in NB Othman, *The Dignity of Commerce* (University of Chicago Press 2016).

[182] M Weber, 'Prefatory Remarks to *Collected Essays on the Sociology of Religion*' in *The Protestant Ethic and the Spirit of Capitalism* (OUP 2011) 237:

> [The] naïve manner of conceptualising capitalism by reference to a 'pursuit of gain' must be relegated to the garden of cultural history ... and abandoned once and for all. A fully unconstrained

in this book, that economy has engendered a growth of wealth so immense[183] that it has fundamentally changed the nature of human aspiration.[184] Even in the eyes of Engels and Marx, capitalism's most profound critics, the 'bourgeoisie, historically, has played a most revolutionary part'.[185] The unprecedented material achievement of capitalism,[186] the latest of a succession of historical 'mode[s] of production', represented the closure of the 'pre-history of human society'[187] because it furnished the indispensable conditions[188] for a 'leap ... to the kingdom of freedom'[189] which could be plausibly considered only because of that achievement.

Though there is no shortage of defects in the national and global market economies which demand criticism, and no shortage of criticism which addresses or far exceeds that demand, those economies, and the positive law of contract when its role in the market economy is focused upon, are generally regarded as overall legitimate because they are on balance enormously—this word is not strong enough—facilitative. In Part 2 of this book it is argued that the basic doctrinal shape of the law of contract has emerged in order to serve this facilitative function, and that the core doctrines of the positive law of contract can be fully understood only by acknowledging the role that the legitimacy gained by performance of this function plays in the way contract's rules are followed.

For a second way in which 'constraint' fails to capture the relationship of social institutions and individual wills is that constraint may even be said to express the

compulsion to acquire goods cannot be understood as synonymous with capitalism, and even less with its 'spirit'. On the contrary, capitalism can be identical with the taming of this irrational motivation.

183 Smith, *Wealth of Nations* (n 96) 24:

> the accommodation of an European prince does not always so much exceed that of an industrious and frugal peasant as the accommodation of the latter exceeds that of many an African king, the absolute master of the lives and liberties of ten thousand naked savages.

184 Marx, *Grundrisse* (n 43) vol 29, 251:

> capital forces labour beyond the limits of natural need and thus creates the material elements for the development of the rich individuality ... as varied in its production as its consumption [in which] labour no longer appears as labour but as the full development of activity itself ... natural necessity has disappeared in its immediate form ... replaced by historically produced need.

185 K Marx and F Engels, *Manifesto of the Communist Party* in *Collected Works*, vol 6 (Lawrence and Wishart 1976) 486.

186 ibid 486–87:

> The bourgeoisie ... has been the first to show what man's activity can bring about. It has accomplished wonders far surpassing Egyptian pyramids, Roman aqueducts, and Gothic cathedrals; it has conducted expeditions that put in the shade all former exoduses of nations and crusades ... The bourgeoisie, during its rule of scarce one hundred years has created more massive and more colossal productive forces than have all previous generations together.

187 Marx, *Contribution* (n 42) 263–64.

188 Marx, *Capital*, vol 1 (n 54) 588:

> Fanatically bent on making value expand itself [the capitalist] ruthlessly forces the human race to produce for production's sake; he thus forces the development of the productive powers of society, and creates that material conditions which alone can form the real basis of a higher form of society ... in which the full and free development of every individual forms the ruling principle.

189 F Engels, *Anti-Dühring* in K Marx and F Engels, *Collected Works*, vol 25 (Lawrence and Wishart 1987) 270.

'opposite'[190] of the way that an actor may actively subscribe to the constraint because he or she has the capacity to evaluate it and agrees with it:

> while institutions bear down upon us, we nevertheless cling to them; they impose obligations on us, and yet we love them; they place constraints upon us, and yet we find satisfaction in the way they function, and in that very constraint.[191]

In our previous discussion of Kant's principle of justice, we focused on duties to others, and specifically on legally enforceable duties. Now, as legal enforcement is analytically a matter of coercion, Kant calls the principle of justice and the rules derived from it matters of 'external' legislation.[192] Obedience to such legislation can be compelled, and action under compulsion has no direct moral virtue for the actor is responding to the natural influence of fear of hurt, not making a moral choice, and indeed may be doing something with which he or she does not agree. Kant sought the justification of this in the social contract as a general, second-order solution to the Hobbesian problem of order,[193] but this, in my hesitant view,[194] left a significant gap in Kant's ability to relate the external aspect of a legal duty to the 'internal' aspect of possible moral commitment to that specific duty. It is not to deny the truth of Austin's answer to the question 'what is law?', which of course turns on ultimately coercive 'command',[195] to maintain that in a liberal democracy commands *should* be such that an actor's internal self-legislation *should* be able to map onto them, so that the actor makes a free moral choice (either as a specific decision or as a habit which can be reviewed) to follow a (latent) command.[196] In the cases in which the internal belief does map onto a command, then viewed in its moral aspect, the command thereby becomes (also) a rule.[197] Obedience to a command and the following of a rule involve very different relationships between law and action.

190 Durkheim, *Rules* (n 172) liv n 4.

191 ibid.

192 Kant, *Metaphysics of Morals* (n 51) 394–95, 526.

193 Kant, 'Theory and Practice' (n 19) 290–91.

194 D Campbell, 'Individualism, Equality and the Possibility of Rights' (1991) 6 The Connecticut Journal of International Law 507, 511–14. As it relates to our concerns, and in particular as these are discussed in the text accompanying n 199, the claim in I Kant, 'Towards Perpetual Peace' in *Practical Philosophy* in *The Cambridge Edition of the Works* (CUP 1996) 335 that 'The problem of establishing a state … is soluble even for a nation of devils' is so partial as to be wrong.

195 J Austin, *The Province of Jurisprudence Determined* (Dartmouth 1998) 18.

196 J-J Rousseau, *The Social Contract* in *The Social Contract and other Later Political Writings* (CUP 1997) 79–80:

> What makes the constitution of a state genuinely solid and lasting is when what is appropriate is so well attended to that natural relations and the laws always agree on the same points, and the latter as it were only secure, accompany and rectify the former. But if the lawgiver mistakes his subject, if he adopts a principle different from the nature of things, if one principle tends towards servitude while the other tends towards freedom … then the laws will be found imperceptibly to weaken, the constitution to deteriorate, and the state will not be free of turmoil.

197 M Oakeshott, 'The Rule of Law' in *On History* (Liberty Fund 1999) 140:

> [in contrast to commands] rules assume agents wishing to perform and performing self-chosen actions in pursuit of substantive satisfactions.

The great stress Hart's 'descriptive sociology'[198] placed on the 'internal aspect' of an actor's attitude towards a command or rule has, of course, very much furthered our understanding how the command or rule was followed, and this is essential to describing what the positive law, including the positive law of contract, is. Leaving aside the implications for the political legitimacy of the system of law of which the rule is part, addressing actors' beliefs that they 'had an obligation' and were not merely 'obliged' to follow a rule allows us to give due weight to the active and creative process of following rules that are regarded as legitimate.[199] Hart's strong inclination to justify the interventionist state led him, however, to try to integrate the internal aspect into Austin's concept of the positive law when disentangling these was Austin's precise intention. Austin was fundamentally right because even in liberal democracies the coincidence of the internal and external aspects should not be achieved by conceptual fiat but must be seen to be a continuously live political issue.[200] Law ultimately *is* coercion, and morality must be analytically separated from law. But law nevertheless should try to express morality, and the law of contract is a vast, though now much underrated in theoretical discussion, success in this respect. Understanding the positive law of contract[201] requires us to grasp the central fact of the general legitimacy of the market order which its classical principles attempt to institutionalise. Telling criticism of the classical law can be only of a failure to actualise those principles, not a rejection of them on exogenous grounds, though this is precisely what welfarism does.

Citing Sir George Jessel MR's *dictum*, the distinguished consumer lawyer JK Macleod described *laissez faire* as the holding of a 'ring between two equal parties whilst they achieved a true bargain.'[202] Consumer law, and behind this welfarism, is, of course, a response to a belief that the equality was often illusory, and we shall turn to this in Chapter 6, but the point I wish to make here is that it is the basic mistake of welfarism to believe that, once inside the ring, the contracting parties, and in particular the party enjoying superior bargaining power, continue to act as they would have done outside of it,[203] up to what then are the necessary limits which contract and consumer law therefore has to set. But this fails to recognise that the ethical nature of the parties' normal, legitimate action, allowing mutual advantage in exchange and freedom

[198] HLA Hart, *The Concept of Law* (3rd edn, Clarendon Press 2012).

[199] ibid 82. Hart's views are applied to the interpretation of contract in ch 4.

[200] Fuller, in my opinion, typically underestimated what satisfaction of the requirements of legality he identified as the 'inner morality' of law itself achieves in the interests of good government, but his estimation certainly had the virtue of keeping the limits of the moral approbation conveyed by what we say when we say something is 'the law' to the forefront of our minds: LL Fuller, *The Morality of Law* (rev edn, Yale University Press 1969) 44:

> With respect to the demands of legality . . . the most we can expect of constitutions and courts is that they save us from the abyss; they cannot be expected to lay out very many compulsory steps toward truly significant accomplishment.

[201] Within contract scholarship, by far the most valuable classification of the 'external' and 'internal' aspects of the 'contractual norms' is IR Macneil, 'Values in Contract: Internal and External' (1983) 78 Northwestern University Law Review 340.

[202] JK Macleod, *Consumer Sales Law* (2nd edn, Routledge-Cavendish 2007) para 1.02.

[203] A fundamental theme of Elias' magisterial discussion of the 'civilising process' in the widest sense is the way that 'constraints through others from a variety of angles were converted into self-restraints': N Elias, *On the Process of Civilisation* in *Collected Works*, vol 3 (University College Dublin Press 2012) 403.

of contract in agreement, is changed by being inside the ring.[204] The law of contract's rules enjoy—and can only work because they enjoy—the active support of those engaged in legitimate exchange.

Contract may indeed be seen as a constraint in a quite literal sense by parties which seek to engage in illegitimate transfers, and the rules seeking to prevent force and fraud are paradigm instances of this. But though they play a (far too) large role in our thinking about the law of contract, force and fraud (and the mandatory rules to which they give rise) are exceptional, and the overwhelming bulk of the rules of contract is not seen as a constraint in the same way. The internal aspect of these rules is a consciousness of their legitimacy, which is the product of contracting parties acknowledging that those rules make it possible for them to pursue and realise their *legitimate* self-interest.

Contracting parties can legitimately realise their self-interest only by entering into Pareto optimising exchanges which must be mutually advantageous. Solipsistic self-interest cannot generate this possibility because it is in principle inimical to respect for mutual advantage. And indeed, not only does the legitimacy of the rules of the law of contract inhere in their providing that the pursuit of solipsistic self-interest is illegitimate, but understanding what those rules are follows from respect for both contracting parties as they exhibit their self-interest in ways consistent with the power of all to voluntarily agree to exchange. The law of contract can coherently be conceived only as, not a set of limitations upon potential illegitimate action, but as the facilitative conditions of all legitimate economic action.

This is, of course, precisely what the classical law of contract and its corollary neoclassical economics are unable adequately to express, because, whilst we have seen that it would not be right to say that they regard solipsistic self-interest as entirely legitimate, as they have no alternative, more adequate concept of self-interest, they see the law's role in the minimalist terms of limiting inevitable excess. Hume counselled against basing policy on the assumption that citizens are ordinarily 'knaves',[205] but that is precisely what the concept of the contracting party in the classical law leads us to

[204] I hope not to be too literal when I say that the *Rules of Boxing* are, as might be expected, highly restrictive of how boxers may conduct themselves, and, indeed, in addition to specifying 'acts ... not permitted ... during a contest', those rules purport to give the referee an 'absolute discretion' to disqualify a boxer the referee 'feels' 'has conducted himself in an unsportsmanlike manner': British Boxing Board of Control Ltd, *Rules and Regulations 2021*, reg 2 <https://bbbofc.com/build/documents/Rules_and_Regulations_2021.pdf> accessed 14 July 2022. Of course, punches below the belt are thrown, and worse, but this is not legitimate conduct inside the ring, and it is only by internalising the rules that boxers can normally successfully fight, doing so in line with the entire point of the contest and their participation in it, which is determining who is the better opponent in ways that reflect agreed desired qualities of aggression, speed, strength, etc, and absolutely not a willingness to do anything to hurt. The rules have to deal with the persistence of illegitimate action, but this is not their main function, which is to guide legitimate action.

In B Suits, *The Grasshopper* (Scottish Academic Press 1978) 24–25, Bernard Suits has compellingly argued that 'It is impossible ... to win [a] game and at the same time break one of its rules', but has gone on to observe that, for example, 'one can ... decide to cheat in order to gain ... money'. Suits nevertheless insists that 'the alternatives of winning [a] game honestly and winning the game by cheating' are not available, 'since in the latter case [one] would not be playing the game at all and thus could not, *a fortiori*, win it'. Equivalently, it may possible to maximise one's advantage by solipsistic conduct of a process of transfer, but it is not possible to make a contract proper in this way.

[205] D Hume, 'Of the Independency of Parliament' in *Essays: Moral, Political and Literary* in *The Clarendon Edition of the Works* (Clarendon Press 2021) 57:

> Political writers have established it as a maxim that, in contriving any system of government, and fixing the several checks and controls of the constitution, every man ought to be supposed

do. We are back to Carlyle, for this is war, if war with certain weapons ruled out. But it is not in this moral atmosphere that the law of contract generally facilitates exchange and settles disputes. Accepting that the law of contract sometimes does have to deal with knaves, it nevertheless is the case that that law overwhelmingly deals with parties of good will whose action in accordance with their subjective intentions gives rise to disputes about the objectively correct position, which, when determined, the parties then accept, and to which they reorient their subjective beliefs as the basis of their subsequent action. To do this, both parties must relate their subjective intentions to what the objective standard of the law (which I will argue expresses the moral relationship of mutual recognition), and this is impossible if the parties deal with each other with an attitude of solipsistic self-interest. The development of the modern law of contract has been a process of the growing acknowledgment of this impossibility in a concept of good faith, which has involved a shift in the very meaning of contracting parties' intentions in agreement.

Conclusion: Subjectivity, Objectivity, and Mistake in Contract Law

Subjectivity and objectivity of intention

It would seem that the first way in which the issues we have just discussed were systematically understood in the law of contract was *subjectively*.[206] An agreement was taken to be a meeting of the minds, a *consensus ad idem*, with the implications both that a lack of consensus should vitiate any apparent agreement and, conversely, that when interpreting contracts the court should seek to give effect to the wills of the parties when they do reach consensus. The acceptance of the will theory was heavily influenced by the publication in 1806 of a translation by the barrister William David Evans of RJ Pothier's *Law of Obligations*. Originally published in French between 1761 and 1764 with the 'express purpose of providing … general principles',[207] Pothier's book

> a *knave*, and to have no other end in all his actions than private interest. By this interest we must govern him, and by means of it make him, notwithstanding his insatiable avarice and ambition, co-operate to public good.

B de Mandeville, *The Fable of the Bees* (Liberty Classics 1988) 17 of course begins (after its preface) by reproducing a long poem which Mandeville had earlier published to no great notice entitled 'The Grumbling Hive, or Knaves Turned Honest', and Hume, who elsewhere was explicitly critical of Mandeville, will have had Mandeville in mind. The shortcomings which modern scholarship has exposed in Hume's criticism of Mandeville does not affect the criticism of the position with which Mandeville has been all but universally associated.

[206] I must say that I find this conceptually very difficult to accept, and so find the argument in JM Perillo, 'The Origin of the Objective Theory of Contract Formation and Interpretation' (2000) 69 Fordham Law Review 427, 428 that 'objective approaches have predominated … since time immemorial' highly persuasive. Such doubts can be put to one side in comments which are really directed at the view of agreement bound up in *consensus ad idem*, which view certainly is a reality. It is telling that the *festschrift* marking the retirement of Sir Guenter Treitel, surely the foremost Commonwealth representative of the classical law in its decline, could be given this title: FD Rose (ed), *Consensus Ad Idem* (Sweet & Maxwell 1996).

[207] PS Atiyah, *The Rise and Fall of Freedom of Contract* (pbk edn, Clarendon Press 1985) 399.

has had an important role in the formation of the modern English law of contract.[208] In one of his appendices giving English amplifications of Pothier's principles, Evans put the point thus:

> As every contract derives its effect from the intention of the parties, that intention … must be the ground of every decision respecting its operation and intent, and the grand object of consideration in every question with regard to its construction.[209]

The will theory has the enormous virtue that it recognises the freedom of choice that is of the essence of Pareto optimisation. However, it does so only very imperfectly, for it is, to put the point as strongly as the case demands, worthless as a legal technique for giving expression to the parties' choices. Whatever its previous importance, the will theory should now function only as a spur to theoretical reflection, for its manifest shortcomings make it abundantly clear that any workable doctrine of agreement must be objective:

> commercial contracts cannot be arranged by what people think in their inmost minds. Commercial contracts are made according to what people say.[210]

The subjectivity of the will theory requires direct access to the minds of the parties, whereas, of course, the first point that must be made is that this is just what we do not have.[211] All we ever have is the physical behaviour (including speech and writing) of the parties, some of which signifies meaningful action, with the understanding of the act, even if initially it is performed solitarily, being possible only if the act expresses a social relationship of meaning. The implications of this for exchange and contract emerge clearly from Weber's famous use of exchange as an example of the understanding of the meaning of action from its observable signs:

> Let us suppose that two men … meet and 'exchange' two objects. We are inclined to think that a mere description of what can be observed during this exchange—muscular movements and, if some words were 'spoken', the sounds which, so to say, constitute the 'matter' or the 'material' of the behaviour—would in no sense comprehend the 'essence' of what happens. This is quite correct. The 'essence' of what happens is constituted by the 'meaning' which the two parties ascribe to their observable behaviour, a 'meaning' which 'regulates' the course of their future conduct. Without this 'meaning', we are inclined to say, an 'exchange is neither empirically possible

[208] AWB Simpson, 'Innovation in Nineteenth Century Contract Law' in *Legal Theory and Legal History* (Hambledon Press 1987) 179–80 and W Swain, *The Law of Contract 1670–1870* (CUP 2015) 176–77.

[209] RJ Pothier, *A Treatise on the Law of Obligations or Contracts* (A Strahan 1806) vol 2, app 5, 35.

[210] *Muirhead and Turnbull v Dickson* (1905) 7 F 686 (IH) 694. This case is discussed in ch 7.

[211] In *Brogden v The Metropolitan Railway* (1877) 2 App Cas 666 (HL) 692, Lord Blackburn drew on the words of Sir Thomas Brian, the Chief Justice of the Common Pleas, in a case from the reign of Edward IV (I believe 1477–78) recorded in the *Year Books* to give what has become the principal modern statement of the point: 'it is trite law that the thought of man is not triable, for even the Devil does not know what the thought of man is'. Whilst a Barrister, Mr Colin Blackburn had discussed the case at length in a book on sales, with the later editions of which he remained involved whilst on the Bench: C Blackburn, *The Contract of Sale* (William Benning and Co 1845) 190–200 (Brian CJ's *dictum* is at 193).

> nor conceptually imaginable'. Of course! The fact that 'observable' signs function as 'symbols' is one of the constitutive presuppositions of all 'social' relations.[212]

It is wrong, however, to regard objectivity of agreement as a sort of, as it were, evidentiary approach to the subjective intentions which really matter, which is bound to make it seem that 'Freedom of contract is . . . difficult to reconcile with the . . . "objective theory"', not least because, as we will see, objectivity 'can lead to the imposition of non-consensual obligations'.[213] But the issue, as Williston said in regard of 'direct evidence of intention', is 'not one of evidence but of substantive law'.[214] The law of contract sets up an objective standard of agreement with which the parties must comply. This standard was famously described by Blackburn J in *Smith v Hughes*:

> If, whatever a man's real intention may be, he so conducts himself that a reasonable man would believe that he was assenting to the terms proposed by the other party, and that the other party upon that belief enters into the contract with him, the man thus conducting himself would be equally bound as if he had intended to agree to the other party's terms.[215]

The meaning of a statement made in the course of negotiations is assessed from the objective perspective of a reasonable person in the situation of the party to whom the statement was made, and a party who acts in such a way as to signify agreement to such a reasonable person will be held to have agreed, whatever her or his subjective intention. (An example will be given shortly.) This is to say, in the passage from subjective to objective theories of agreement, the law of contract makes the determination of agreement a matter, not of delving into the subjective will, but of requiring an action to meet an objective, normative standard. An actor may have a subjective intention to exchange which leads it to place itself in a situation in which it may be said to have agreed a contract, but whether it has done so is determined, not by its subjective intention (or by the sum of this actor's intention plus another actor's subjective intention), but by both actor's intentions as immediately understood in terms of their objective relationship. A competent contracting party will consciously orient itself to this requirement of objectivity. If such a party wants its subjective intention endorsed by the law of contract, it is required to express that intention in the objective terms the law will recognise. Before turning, in Part 2 of this book, to the way this requirement is institutionalised in the values of mutual advantage in exchange and bargained-for agreement on which the core doctrines of the law of contract turn, it is, however, productive to turn to the, as it were, negative example provided by a doctrine in which the issues are, representatively, so poorly understood that that doctrine has no place in an adequate law of contract. This is the doctrine of agreement mistake.

[212] M Weber, *Critique of Stammler* (Free Press 1977) 109.
[213] J Beatson, A Burrows, and J Cartwright, *Anson's Law of Contract* (31st edn, OUP 2020) 7.
[214] S Williston, *The Law of Contracts* (Baker, Voorhis and Co 1924) vol 2, s 612; now RA Lord, *Samuel Williston, A Treatise on the Law of Contracts* (4th edn, West Group 1999) vol 11, ss 3.32–3.33 states that the claim that the entire parole evidence rule is 'not a rule of evidence [or] interpretation or construction, but is a rule of substantive law . . . may be said to be universally accepted'.
[215] (1871) LR 6 QB 597 (QB) 607.

The impossibility of operative mistake

The influential attempt by Geoffrey Cheshire to bring a basic coherence to the very wide and disparate range of legal issues evoked by the idea that when entering into a contract a defendant had made a 'mistake' that nullified its consent turned on distinguishing three categories of unilateral, mutual, and common mistake.[216] The basis of the distinction was the parties' subjective states of mind: it is believed that in a common mistake both parties make the same mistake; in a mutual mistake both parties make a different mistake; and in a unilateral mistake only one party is mistaken.[217] It would be supererogatory to add to the large case law and vast commentary in which the, with great respect, shortcomings of this classification have been demonstrated. The argument here is that these shortcomings cannot be avoided until the subjective approach is entirely eliminated, which will require the entire elimination of 'operative' mistake as an excuse for non-performance. This, however, may be easily done in one respect as, properly understood, the principal cases do not turn on mistake at all,[218] and eliminating agreement mistake from the law of contract will only help our understanding of agreement.[219] What is more difficult is changing the understanding which places a weight on the subjective that demonstrates a basic misunderstanding of the nature and function of the law of contract.[220]

Except on the basis of a most literal understanding of *consensus ad idem*, so that excuse from non-performance simply logically follows the will theoretical definition of agreement, Cheshire's classification, as he himself was well aware, does not answer the question why, as subjective mistake is not normally an excuse, *some* subjective mistakes have been thought to be operative. Citing *inter alia Tamplin v James*[221] in

[216] GC Cheshire, 'Mistake as Affecting Contractual Consent' (1944) 60 Law Quarterly Review 175 (hereafter Cheshire, 'Mistake').

[217] Cheshire, ibid 183–89, included within unilateral mistake what would now be called 'personality mistake', ie the mistake in *Cundy v Lindsay* (1877–78) LR 3 App Cas 459 (HL). Though it is the case that only one party is mistaken, personality mistake raises an issue connected with fraud which is materially different to unilateral mistake proper, and should not be treated in this way. The legal argument about personality mistake was an ingenious attempt to shift loss onto a purchaser in good faith which was completely unhelpful when formulating a policy to deal with that loss. This is one of many instances in which, not only is fraud shown to be a criminal matter to which the law of contract is unsuited, but persistence in regarding fraud as central to contract has unwelcome doctrinal consequences: C Macmillan, *Mistakes in Contract Law* (Hart 2010) ch 8.

[218] CJ Slade, 'The Myth of Mistake in the English Law of Contract' (1954) 70 Law Quarterly Review 385.

[219] See n 227.

[220] Lord Steyn, 'Contract Law: Fulfilling the Reasonable Expectations of Honest Men' (1977) Law Quarterly Review 433:

> It is a defensible position for a legal system to give predominance to the subjective intentions of the parties. Such a policy can claim to be committed to the ideal of perfect individualised justice.

Though Lord Steyn said this in order to contrast it to 'the English way . . . generally based on an objective theory of contract', he was quite unable to say why, other than in some way providing 'commercial certainty', giving any such a predominance is completely inappropriate to the law of contract.

Legal pleas which are of importance in the current law which are, as it were, at the margins of the general principles of the law of contract, such as *non est factum* and rectification, are a mixture of a small proportion of technical matters which cannot be ignored, and a preponderant proportion of scarcely credible antediluvianism about the place of subjectivity in contract which will not be specifically discussed here.

[221] (1880) LR 15 Ch D 215 (CA) (hereafter *Tamplin v James*). If I understand the procedure correctly, Bagally LJ's judgment was handed down in the Chancery Division, where he sat in place of Malins VC who

support of his observations that there is 'no general rule that ... mistake inevitably excludes agreement', and that 'it is well established by a series of cases that the existence of a ... mistake does not *per se* prevent the formation of a contract', Cheshire insisted that 'if the test of intention in the formation of contract were subjective' 'there would be no certainty in business transactions, no fidelity in apparent contracts. Chaos and injustice would ensue.'[222] The universally accepted reason for this was given by Bagally LJ in *Tamplin v James*:

> The defendant cannot be allowed to evade ... performance by the simple statement that he has made a mistake. Were such to be the law the performance of a contract could rarely be enforced upon an unwilling party who was also unscrupulous.[223]

In *Tamplin v James*, the purchaser bid at auction for a plot of land. The purchaser 'had known the property from [the time he was] a boy'[224] and made his bid without consulting the plans which the vendor had made available at the auction. The purchaser thought the plot being sold included land which it did not and, presumably for this reason offering more than other bidders, made the successful bid. When he found out that the plot did not include the land he believed, he refused to complete the purchase because, in sum, he had made a mistake. It was accepted that he had made a subjective mistake, but as that mistake, caused by his failure to consult the plans, was unreasonable, and would if allowed to be an excuse be a specific instance of the 'great temptation to perjury'[225] the subjective position offered to the unscrupulous, it was given no objective weight, and the contract was enforced.

Cheshire's first response to the question why some mistakes were excuses—when mistake normally is not—was to distinguish the mischief that lay behind the common mistake, which, as will be discussed in Chapter 10, is now recognised to turn on the impossibility of performing an obligation which had nevertheless been agreed, from the mischief that lay behind mutual and unilateral mistake, which is want of agreement. This, of course, really reduces Cheshire's categories of mistake from three to two, and the basic structure of the treatment of mistake in the fourth edition of Cheshire and Fifoot was an attempt to make this clear.[226]

This reduction does not, however, take us far, for why only some *agreement* mistakes are singled out remains wholly obscure.[227] The answer requires us to see that the

had recently suffered the riding accident that was to contribute to his death, and this judgment was appealed to a Court of Appeal consisting of James, Brett, and Cotton LJJ.

[222] Cheshire, 'Mistake' (n 216) 180, 179. These comments were addressed to mutual mistake but would apply to unilateral mistake as well.

[223] *Tamplin v James* (n 221) 217–18.

[224] ibid 216.

[225] ibid 219.

[226] GC Cheshire and CHS Fifoot, *Law of Contract* (4th edn, Butterworths 1956) 173–74.

[227] An undeniable but nevertheless, it is submitted, more apparent than real difficulty (this was the opinion of the court that decided the case) which should now just be set aside has been posed by the significance given to *Raffles v Wichelhaus and Busch* (1864) 2 H and C 906; 159 ER 375. This case cannot be explained on any of the bases on which agreement mistake is about to be explained, but this is because the parties had failed to put their intentions into a form capable of *any* interpretation which would lead to an agreement being objectively held to exist, or the facts were so unclear as to make this conclusion

mistake, though it is the reason an excuse is pleaded, is irrelevant to cases of operative unilateral and mutual mistake. The excuse turns, not on the mistake by the party pleading the excuse, but on the action of the party wishing to enforce the contract. In *Hartog v Colin and Shields*[228] the defendant seller made a clerical error when communicating an offer price that was absurdly low. The buyer realising what had happened—and so the mistake was unilateral—nevertheless purported to accept that price, but the seller was excused performance. This case *cannot* be distinguished from *Tamplin v James* on the basis of subjective mistake as the defendants in both cases were subjectively mistaken in fundamentally the same way. The distinction between the cases is that in *Hartog v Colin and Shields* the offer was so absurdly low that it would have been obvious to a reasonable third party that it was made in error, and so the claimant 'could not reasonably have supposed that that offer contained the offeror's real intention',[229] and the law will not permit 'agreement' on this basis. A case[230] in which a party had 'snapped at' an obviously mistaken offer was specifically distinguished in *Tamplin v James*,[231] leading one to surmise the offered price in *Tamplin v James*, though high, cannot have been startlingly high. The point is that it is not the purchaser's mistake that mattered; it was the seller's attempt to take advantage of an obvious want of agreement that mattered.

In *Scriven Bros and Co v Hindley and Co*,[232] a consignment of the textile tow was sold at auction. The buyer bought the tow thinking it was hemp, a more valuable textile, but on finding it was tow, sought to escape the contract, and was allowed to do so. This case also obviously needs carefully to be distinguished from *Tamplin v James*, to which it seems identical. It *is* identical on the facts of the defendant's mistake. It is distinguished in that the defendant's mistake was induced by the seller's (or rather the auctioneer's as its agent) negligent catalogue description of the goods for sale, which misled the buyer and would have misled a reasonable person. The seller and the buyer were mutually mistaken in that the buyer made a mistake, but the auctioneer, the jury found, did not know this, thinking the bid high but not demonstrating a complete misunderstanding about the goods.[233] This is to say, the seller's mistake is not to know the buyer is mistaken, whereas in a unilateral mistake the party seeking to take advantage obviously does know of the other party's mistake. Nevertheless, the excuse again stems from the seller's conduct, which is what was at issue in the case. A crucial point of dispute was whether the defendant had a duty to inspect which would have meant it could not rely on the auctioneer's description. The distinction between this situation and *Tamplin v James* is even more clear in *Denny v Hancock*,[234] a sale of land in which the purchaser made a mistake about the extent of land for sale four square with

unavoidable. This case was incomprehensible prior to the appearance of AWB Simpson, 'The Beauty of Obscurity: *Raffles* v *Wichelhaus and Busch*' (1864)' in AWB Simpson, *Leading Cases in the Common Law* (reprinted edn, OUP 2001).

228 [1939] 3 All ER 566 (KB).
229 ibid 568F.
230 *Webster v Cecil* (1861) 30 Beav 62; 54 ER 812.
231 *Tamplin v James* (n 221) 221.
232 [1913] 3 KB 564 (KB).
233 ibid 566.
234 (1870–71) LR 6 Ch App 1 (CA).

Tamplin v James, but was excused performance because the mistake was caused by an error in the information made available by the claimant vendor.

Despite its undoubted value, Bagally LJ's criticism of the subjective position as an opening to fraud is, with respect, very insufficient. One has to bar the way to the unscrupulous, but what is the point of the law of contract if parties were so scrupulous that they would not take advantage of the subjective position? The point is that even perfectly good faith parties would not acknowledge liability if the law was that subjective mistake was an excuse. But parties recognise that this cannot possibly be the law. One's subjective mistake in negotiation cannot be an excuse if one has led the other party to enter into a contract on the basis of that negotiation, and that one has a duty to absorb the liability which arises from the objective relationship thus created is the basis of exchange and contract. One has to be learned in the law not to immediately acknowledge this elementary duty of citizenship in liberal democracies based on a market economy, and the doctrine of agreement mistake in which legal scholarship has badly obfuscated this elementary duty should be abolished.[235]

The operative agreement mistakes are nothing of the sort. They are failures of the party wishing to enforce the contract to perform some of what we will see, particularly in Chapter 4, are the extensive range of duties which parties owe each other in order for objective agreement of a contract to be possible. Unilateral mistake is actually a duty not to 'snap up' what is known to be a statement which does not express the other party's intention, part of a wider duty to refrain from 'sharp dealing'; mutual mistake is part of a duty not to secure agreement by misleading the other party. The law of contract is not a law of the subjective wills of parties but of their objective duties to one another. It is a law which institutionalises a *relationship*. Prior to demonstrating in Part 2 of this book that the positive law of contract can be understood only on this basis, let us first turn to the principal theoretical attempts which have been made to insist on this relational basis of the law of contract.

[235] For different, if ultimately related, reasons to be set out in ch 10, I also believe that impossibility mistake has no place in the law of contract, and so I would abolish the doctrine of mistake *in toto*.

2
Exchange, Relational Contract, and Mutual Recognition

Introduction: Relational Contract as a Legal Concept

In his remarkable 2013 judgment in *Yam Seng Pte Ltd v International Trade Corporation Ltd*,[1] Leggatt J, as he then was, drew the concept of a relational contract out of the obscurantist disdain with which the English law had previously regarded it,[2] and, after an initially unsympathetic response,[3] the subsequent citations of this judgment allowed Fraser J to claim in 2019 that 'the concept of relational contracts is an established one in English law'.[4] Though we shall place *Yam Seng* and its influence in the proper context of its positive implications for the law of agreement in Chapter 4, it is necessary to start here by noting that something of a false step would appear to have been taken. For Fraser J was right to say that this recognition of the relational contract has been a matter of recognising the existence of a 'specie' of contract[5] distinct from what we might, at this point, call the standard contract.[6] But though this

[1] [2013] EWHC 111 (QB); [2013] 1 All ER (Comm) 1321 (hereafter *Yam Seng*).
[2] *Baird Textiles Holdings Ltd v Marks and Spencer plc* [2001] EWCA Civ 274; [2002] 1 All ER (Comm) 737 [16]. This case will be discussed at length in ch 10.
[3] *Mid Essex Hospital Services NHS Trust v Compass Group UK and Ireland Ltd (t/a Medirest)* [2013] EWCA Civ 200, [2013] BLR 265 [105] and *Globe Motors Inc v TRW Lucas Varity Electric Steering Ltd* [2016] EWCA Civ 396; (2016) 168 Con LR 59 [67]–[68]. Very shortly after his appointment to the Court of Appeal, Leggatt LJ reviewed the more positive of the 'divergent reactions' to *Yam Seng* (n 1), including one aspect of *Globe Motors*, in *(Al) Nehayan v Kent* [2018] EWHC 333 (Comm); [2018] 1 CLC 216 [168]–[171] (hereafter *Nehayan v Kent*).
[4] *Bates v The Post Office (No 3)* [2019] EWHC 606 (QB); [2019] All ER (D) 100 (Mar) [705] (hereafter *Bates v PO*).
[5] In *Nehayan v Kent* (n 3) [167], Leggatt LJ spoke of his having drawn attention to 'a category of contract' in *Yam Seng* (n 1).
[6] *Bates v PO* (n 4) [703]. In *Essex County Council v UBB Waste Disposal (Essex) Ltd (No 2)* [2020] EWHC 1581 (TCC); (2020) 191 Con LR 77 [104]–[105], Pepperall J endorsed the recognition of the relational contract, but differed from the list Fraser J had given (*Bates v PO* (n 4) [725]) of the 'helpful indicia' of the existence of one.

Contractual Relations. David Campbell, Oxford University Press.
DOI: 10.1093/oso/9780198855156.003.0002

approach does follow from the preponderant view that has been formed of 'the relational theory of contract' associated with, in particular, Stewart Macaulay[7] and the late Ian Macneil, it is not, it will be argued, the best view of that theory. It is evident that Stewart Macaulay and Ian Macneil reached that pinnacle of scholarly achievement at which the significance of one's work is demonstrated by it being intimately associated with a universally known position, but a position which misunderstands that work.[8] It will be argued in Chapter 10 that the law of contract does indeed require a legal concept of a specifically 'relational' contract. But this concept must be understood in light of a prior recognition that the most valuable contribution of the relational theory is its demonstration that contracting—negotiating contracts, performing them, adjudicating them—is possible at all only because the law of contract is embedded in the social relations of the market economy (which will later be described as based on a relation of mutual recognition).

Though we should trace the history of the relational theory[9] to the publication in 1963 of Macaulay's truly seminal paper[10] on 'Non-contractual Relations in Business: A Preliminary Study',[11] the interpretation of that theory as being based on recognising the specie of the relational contract is principally due to Grant Gilmore's 1970 lectures published as *The Death of Contract*, in which he called Macaulay 'the Lord High Executioner of the Contracts is Dead School'.[12] This resounding formulation has led to a general belief that Macaulay believed that the law of contract is tantamount to irrelevant to contractual action.[13] Especially as Macaulay was then playing a leading

[7] Macaulay would be the first to say that he was reliant on the collaboration with others working in a distinct tradition associated with the University of Wisconsin Law School (S Macaulay, 'Willard's Law School?' [1997] Wisconsin Law Review 1163), and in particular with those in the 'Wisconsin Contracts Group', the central members of which were the late John Kidwell, Macaulay, and William Whitford. Others who have been involved in the writing of what is now S Macaulay, W Whitford, K Hendley, and J Lipson, *Contracts: Law in Action*, 2 vols (Carolina Academic Press 2017) (hereafter Macaulay and others, *Contracts*) were the late Jean Braucher, Marc Galanter, Kathryn Hendley, and Jonathan Lipson. On the aims of Wisconsin contracts teaching see, in addition to the introduction to this casebook, L Friedman and S Macaulay, 'Contract Law and Contract Teaching: Past, Present and Future' [1967] Wisconsin Law Review 805, and S Macaulay and W Whitford, 'The Development of *Contracts: Law in Action*' (2015) 87 Temple Law Review 793.

[8] RW Emerson, 'Self-reliance' in *Essays: First Series* in *Essays and Lectures* (The Library of America 1983) 265: 'To be great is to be misunderstood.'

[9] Of express suggestions prior to Macaulay and Macneil that the shortcomings of the classical law should be attributed to its failure to accommodate the 'relational', perhaps the first, which was brought to my attention by Arthur Jacobson (AJ Jacobson, 'The Equitable Administration of Long-term Relations: An Appreciation of Judge Clark's Opinion in *Parev Products*' in P Petruck (ed), *Judge Charles Edward Clark* (Oceana Publications 1991) nb 58 n 27), is the opinion of Clark J in the US restraint of trade case *Parev Products Co, Inc v I Rokeach and Sons Inc* 124 F 2d 147 (US 2d Cir 1941).

[10] It is supererogatory to provide authority for this description of this paper but it might be mentioned that it was included in the authoritative D Kennedy and WW Fisher III (eds), *The Canon of American Legal Thought* (Princeton University Press 2006), which ranges not just across contract but, as its title says, across all legal thought.

[11] (1963) 28 *American Sociological Review* 55 (hereafter Macaulay, 'Non-contractual Relations'). I regard S Macaulay, 'The Use and Non-use of Contracts in the Manufacturing Industry' (1963) 9(7) Practical Lawyer 13 (hereafter Macaulay, 'Non-use') as a valuable companion paper, but, published in journal more focused on a professional rather than an academic audience, it has played, save for the term 'non-use' itself, a small role in subsequent discussion.

[12] G Gilmore, *The Death of Contract* (2nd edn, Ohio State UP 1995) 1 n 1 (hereafter Gilmore, *Death of Contract*).

[13] RW Gordon, 'Macaulay, Macneil, and the Discovery of Solidarity and Power in Contract Law' [1985] Wisconsin Law Review 565, 571, 573: 'marginality', 'relative insignificance', and 'relatively trivial status'.

role in establishing the 'law in action' (or its synonyms) approach,[14] not merely to contract, but to legal issues in general,[15] ultimately the issue was the replacement of the 'economic' orientation of action informing the standard contract with a 'sociological analysis'[16] of non-contractual relations which invited the development of a welfarist orientation.[17]

It was in this broad atmosphere that Macneil's first major statement of the relational theory, his 1974 'The Many Futures of Contract',[18] has largely been read to the effect that his intentions were similar. In a formulation which I select from amongst very many because it can be read together with Macneil's informatively highly critical response to it,[19] Gunther Teubner claimed that Macneil committed 'a fatal error' in putting forward a 'warm, human, co-operative ... relation' as the basis of:

> a wrong juxtaposition between an economic and a sociological interpretation of contract where economics stands for self-interest, rational choice and market exchange, and sociology for solidarity, co-operation and community.[20]

Macneil cited his complete rejection of this account in 2003 in the last thing he wrote on contract,[21] his general point being that:

> A widespread perception has long existed that relational contract theory is an analytical tool biased in favour of state intervention in contractual relations; of co-operation rather than conflict; of communitarian, liberal, and/or radical values; of the continuance rather than the break-up of relations; and of many other 'soft and cuddly' values, often associated with ... a naïve and dangerous humanitarianism ... This misconceived perception has been utilised, repeatedly, to discredit relational approaches to contracts ... Those who have asserted that [that relational

[14] The first formulation of the underlying idea in the terms of 'law in action' of which I am aware was R Pound, 'Law in Books and Law in Action' (1910) 44 American Law Review 12.

[15] S Macaulay, L Friedman, and E Mertz, *Law in Action: A Socio-Legal Reader* (Foundation Press 2007) (hereafter Macaulay and others, *Law in Action*).

[16] Gilmore, *Death of Contract* (n 12) 1.

[17] However, the approach of the paper that was mentioned in ch 1 has become a reference point in the discussion of these issues, M Granovetter, 'Economic Action and Social Structure: The Problem of Embeddedness' (1985) 91 American Journal of Sociology 481, is highly nuanced. The understanding of economic action does indeed require an appreciation of its 'embeddedness' in social relations, but Granovetter attempts to marry the critique of 'under-socialised' economic accounts to a critique of 'over-socialised' sociological accounts by insisting that economic actors (ibid 487):

> do not behave or decide as atoms outside a social context, nor do they adhere slavishly to a script written for them by the particular intersection of sociological categories they happen to occupy.

On this basis, adequate analysis of all economic action:

> threads its way between the over-socialised approach of general morality and the under-socialised one of impersonal ... arrangements: ibid 493.

[18] (1974) 47 Southern California Law Review 691 (hereafter Macneil, 'Many Futures').

[19] IR Macneil, 'Contracting Worlds and Essential Contract Theory' (2000) 9 Social and Legal Studies 431.

[20] G Teubner, 'Contracting Worlds: The Many Autonomies of Private Law' (2000) 9 Social and Legal Studies 398.

[21] IR Macneil, 'Reflections on Relational Contract After a Neo-classical Seminar' in D Campbell, H Collins, and J Wightman (eds), *Implicit Dimensions of Contract* (Hart 2003) 212 n 5 (hereafter Macneil, 'Reflections').

> theory] is biased in particular social directions ... have done so in disregard of my repeatedly stressing ... that [the relational theory] can lead to hard and tough conclusions just as well as to soft and cuddly, ie humanitarian, ones [That the relational theory] *appears* to [its critics] to favour humanitarian views is entirely the product of the non-neutrality of their own tools of analysis: [neo-classical economics] and classical contract law.[22]

It would be quite wrong to deny that the work of Macaulay and of Macneil clearly expresses unproductive tensions between values generally identified with the classical law and values generally identified with welfarism; all post-war writing of interest on the law of contract expresses such tensions. The principal significance of their work, however, is that the relational theory which may be derived from it can accommodate those tensions in a way which breaks down the opposition between the standard contract and the relational contract on which that work has predominantly been taken to turn, and in doing so indicates a way in which those tensions may be handled other than unproductively in a general theory of relational contract.

Macaulay and the Function of Contract

The claim of non-use

In previous work I have called Gilmore's description of Macaulay as Lord High Executioner the 'Gilmore myth'.[23] I did not do so in order to pre-empt the question of the description's accuracy, but to try to capture its undeniable importance in the development of contract theory. It is as well nevertheless to first establish that the myth is false. One is immediately struck by the difficulty of reconciling advocacy of the death of contract with the great labour behind the achievement of establishing the Wisconsin approach to the teaching of the subject, and along with the criticisms of the positive law, there are very many passages in Macaulay's writing which expressly proclaim the value, and even more the potential value, of contract.[24] Macaulay's express attempts to raise objections to the Gilmore myth go back so long ago as, to my knowledge, 1985,[25] and continued to be made throughout and beyond his retirement from the full-time faculty of the University of Wisconsin Law School.[26] On his Wisconsin Law School web page Macaulay continues to tell us, as he for decades has told us there,

22 ibid 207, 212–13, 217.

23 D Campbell, 'What Do We Mean by the Non-use of Contract?' in J Braucher, J Kidwell, and WC Whitford (eds), *Revisiting the Contracts Scholarship of Stewart Macaulay: On the Empirical and the Lyrical* (Hart 2013) (hereafter Campbell, 'Non-use').

24 The point acutely emerges from Macaulay's firm opposition to an episode of enthusiasm for the claim that 'Parties have decided that they will rely on relational norms and sanctions rather than the law': S Macaulay, 'Freedom From Contract: Solutions in Search of a Problem?' [2004] Wisconsin Law Review 777.

25 S Macaulay, 'An Empirical View of Contract' [1985] Wisconsin Law Review 465.

26 S Macaulay, 'The Death of Contract: Dodos and Unicorns or Sleeping Rattlesnakes?' in RW Gordon and MJ Horwitz (eds), *Law, Society and History: Themes in the Legal Sociology and Legal History of Lawrence M Friedman* (CUP 2011) 204.

that he 'declined the honour' of being Lord High Executioner, and believed 'only that academic contract was dead while the real institution was alive and well'.[27]

Gilmore has, of course, been subject to some pretty severe criticism of the accuracy of his own history of the 'doctrinal disintegration' of contract law,[28] and a considerable number of attempts have been made to disentangle what of Gilmore's death of contract is and is not of value in light of such criticism.[29] What I will argue here is that, however little value there is in the idea of the death of contract, it transpires that Gilmore chose his words rather carefully when he said that Macaulay was the Lord High Executioner because, as Gilmore precisely put it, Macaulay had shown 'the irrelevance of traditional contract theory'.[30] This is much more nearly accurate a description of what Macaulay has done. It is the classical law of contract that Macaulay has done so much to call into question, though, of course, to the considerable extent that the classical law still influences 'contract law in practice', then the positive law remains 'a flawed product'.[31] But this evaluation must be separated from Macaulay's overall positive attitude towards the legal institution of the law of contract, which, he hopes, is not entirely '*perdido* (lost)' and may have a better future.[32]

A myth as powerful as the Gilmore myth must, however, have a basis in fact, and, leaving other issues aside, the basic concepts of 'non-use' and 'non-contractual relations' introduced in Macaulay's two great 1963 papers only inadequately capture the relationship between economic exchange and legal contract that Macaulay has done so much to reveal to us. It is in an obvious sense foolish to criticise the coining[33] of terms which have given rise to such valuable discussion, but surely one cannot be surprised if these terms have been interpreted as a claim that the positive law *is* irrelevant. On their face, they depict the relationship between what we might call the legal, economic, and social aspects of contract in a way which does invite disregard of the law of contract as such, and, in my opinion, they should no longer be used.

I am by no means the first to question the appositeness of the terms 'non-use' and 'non-contractual relations'.[34] The earliest such questioning of which I am aware was

[27] *Stewart Macaulay, Professor Emeritus* (nd) University of Wisconsin Law School, <https://secure.law.wisc.edu/profiles/smacaula@wisc.edu> (accessed 23 December 2021).

[28] The late Professor Simpson had a very low opinion of Gilmore as a legal historian, describing him as a mere 'amateur' (AWB Simpson, 'Contract: The Twitching Corpse' (1980) 1 Oxford Journal of Legal Studies 265, 273), or even as someone 'who never felt inhibited by mere ignorance from writing legal history' whose work 'needs to be treated with extreme caution on matters historical' (AWB Simpson, 'The Beauty of Obscurity: *Raffles* v *Wichelhaus and Busch*' (1864)' in AWB Simpson, *Leading Cases in the Common Law* (reprinted edn, OUP 2001) 162). This did not prevent Simpson from insisting upon the other than historical value of *The Death of Contract.*

[29] My own contribution is D Campbell, 'The Undeath of Contract: A Study in the Degeneration of a Research Programme' (1992) 22 Hong Kong Law Journal 20.

[30] Gilmore, *Death of Contract* (n 12) 1.

[31] S Macaulay, 'Relational Contracts Floating on a Sea of Custom? Thoughts About the Ideas of Ian Macneil and Lisa Bernstein' (2000) 94 Northwestern University Law Review 775, 804 (hereafter Macaulay, 'Relational Contracts').

[32] S Macaulay, 'Contracts, New Legal Realism and Improving the Navigation of The Yellow Submarine' (2006) 80 Tulane Law Review 1161, 1194.

[33] More correctly, Macaulay accepted the title suggested for 'Non-contractual Relations in Business' by the great American sociologist RK Merton: S Macaulay, 'Crime and Custom in Business Society' (1995) 22 Journal of Law and Society 248, 251.

[34] I am restricting to a footnote a highly interesting reservation about 'non-use' entered by Macaulay himself in 2007: Macaulay and others, *Law in Action* (n 15) 90:

that of Schur in 1967, who told us that Macaulay's findings 'do not refer to the express failure of legal norms but rather to the limitations of legal control and the tendency for non-legal norms to complement legal ones'.[35] I learned of Schur by reading the first British paper attempting to reproduce Macaulay's research, by Beale and Dugdale in 1975, which had, for a paper with that intent, the provocative subtitle (the key word of which I have emphasised) of 'Planning and the *Use* of Contractual Remedies'.[36] This correctly indicated what the paper itself confirms, that the law is not unused, but that its use is matter of the way that the parties' action is influenced by the role the legal rule plays in constituting the parties' economic relationship, the influence being a complex matter which cannot be reduced to the explanation of action as a direct result of the positive law as cause.

As is known by every competent commentator on contract, the basic thrust of 'Non-contractual Relations in Business' is that, though 'legal sanctions, while not an everyday affair, are not unknown in business', 'there is little evidence that … today's businessmen would use the courts to settle disputes'.[37] Macaulay's identification of non-use led him to argue that:

> Two questions need to be answered: (a) How can businesses successfully operate exchange relationships with relatively so little attention to detailed planning or to legal sanctions, and (b) Why does business ever use contract in light of its success without it?[38]

Macaulay's answer to the first question has been the basis of the Gilmore myth. Macaulay described 'a hesitancy to speak of legal rights or to threaten to sue'[39] which arose for three reasons. First, 'In most situations contract is not needed' as most failures to perform are relatively clear cut and easily resolved 'because usually there is little room for honest misunderstandings or good faith differences of opinion [amongst] experienced professionals who will know the customs of their industry and of those industries with which they deal'.[40] Secondly, 'contract and contract law are often thought unnecessary because there are many effective non-legal sanctions', in particular, 'the most obvious' sanction of preserving an ongoing relationship between 'business units [which] want to deal with each other again', and to enjoy a good 'general business reputation'.[41] Thirdly, the use of 'contract and contract law … may have,

> 'Non-contractual Relations in Business' is a study of when business people use formal processes of law and, more importantly, when they do not. Would it be accurate, however, to say that [that paper] was a study of the "non-use" of law or would it be more to the point to say it was a study about informal rules, norms and practices – which happen not to coincide with the rules "on the books"?'

[35] EM Schur, *Law and Society* (Random House 1967) 131.

[36] H Beale and T Dugdale, 'Contracts Between Businessmen: Planning and the Use of Contractual Remedies' (1975) 2 British Journal of Law and Society 45, 46 n 4.

[37] Macaulay, 'Non-contractual Relations' (n 11) 62.

[38] ibid.

[39] ibid 61.

[40] ibid 62–63.

[41] ibid 63–64.

or may be thought to have, undesirable consequences' such as delay, loss of 'flexibility' in the handling of the exchange relationship, legal and related costs (which are unlikely to be fully recovered even in the event of successful litigation), and the generation of an unhelpful working atmosphere, 'turning a co-operative venture into an antagonistic horse trade'.[42] All this led to the identification of what was described in 'Use and Non-use of Contracts in the Manufacturing Industry' as a 'common' 'attitude toward contracts that can best be described as indifferent or even hostile to the whole idea',[43] and to the then startling conclusion that 'many, if not most, exchanges reflect no planning, or only a minimal amount of it, especially concerning legal sanctions and the effect of defective performances'.[44]

The principal conclusion that Macaulay drew from this account of the non-use of contract and of the work done by non-contractual relations was that 'To understand the functions of contract the whole system of conducting exchanges must be explored more fully.'[45] This was and is true, and in pursuing its implications Macaulay has made the principal contribution to the law in action approach to the study of the law of contract, producing some of the most interesting studies of specific contracting practices and reviews of our understanding of contracting in general that have ever been written. A now large literature has taken Macaulay's apparent demonstration of non-use as its starting point when purporting to describe the non-contractual relations that explain what really happens in law in action.[46] I should hope to be the last to deny the interest of this literature, but I do think it has largely taken a mistaken tack, in which confusion over 'trust' has played a large part.[47]

We must carefully distinguish between two senses of the now hugely overworked concept of trust.[48] In the first, 'economic' sense, trust plays an essential role in facilitating market exchange by, as will be argued in Chapter 4, providing an essential background to the interpretation of the intentions of the contracting parties. But in the second, 'sociological' sense, trust is set against the market and the parties' intentions. Now, Macaulay has been right to tell us that some notion of trust is 'necessary to make any economic system work',[49] and understanding the first sense of trust turns on this. But the width of Macaulay's notion of trust has allowed the second sense

[42] ibid 64.

[43] Macaulay, 'Non-use' (n 11) 14.

[44] Macaulay, 'Non-contractual Relations' (n 11) 60.

[45] ibid 67.

[46] In the pathbreaking R Danzig, '*Hadley and Another v Baxendale and Others*' in R Danzig and GR Watson, *The Capability Problem in Contract Law* (2nd edn, Foundation Press 2004) 87 n 134, Macaulay is cited as authority for the claim that parties are 'likely ... to resolve difficulties by negotiation which bears little if any relation to formal law doctrine'.

[47] S Wheeler, 'Contracts and Corporations', in P Cane and HM Kritser (eds), *The Oxford Handbook of Empirical Legal Research* (OUP 2010) 147.

[48] S Deakin, C Lane, and F Wilkinson, 'Contract Law, Trust Relations and Incentives for Co-operation: A Comparative Study' in S Deakin and J Michie (eds), *Contracts, Co-operation and Competition: Studies in Economics, Management and Law* (OUP 1997) 105. These contributors had made an important attempt to avoid the 'polarisation' of trust, not only in this paper but also in S Deakin and F Wilkinson, 'Contracts, Co-operation and Trust: The Role of the Institutional Framework' in D Campbell and P Vincent-Jones (eds), *Contract and Economic Organisation* (Dartmouth 1996); and S Deakin, C Lane, and F Wilkinson, 'Trust or Law? Towards an Integrated Theory of Contractual Relations Between Firms' (1994) 21 Journal of Law and Society 329.

[49] Macaulay, 'Relational Contracts' (n 31) 804.

to come to the fore in the analyses of contracting which take his work as their starting point. There can be no doubt that Macaulay himself contributed to this, and indeed himself furnished perhaps the outstanding empirical study illustrating the approach by taking an unduly positive view[50] of how SC Johnson and Son Ltd managed to complete the construction of its subsequently architecturally very famous Administration Building, despite conduct by the architect, Frank Lloyd Wright, which, leaving other issues aside, made it inevitable that the finished masterpiece was wildly over time and over budget.[51]

In the sociological analysis, the unused contract generally falls entirely out of consideration and attention entirely shifts to non-contractual relations. This analysis turns to what I have here followed the dominant usage in calling the 'embeddedness' of exchange in social relations, in which an idea of trust very largely displaces contract.[52] This second sense of trust is social, not only in that it is grounded in sociological theory, but in the sense that, though it is very amorphous, one can say of it that it is anti-economic. The role of non-contractual relations of trust is taken to be evidence, not merely of the non-use of contract, but of the non-use of economics. These non-contractual relations are regarded as social in the double sense of being, indeed, social relations, but also social relations which articulate an orientation of action opposed to the self-interest claimed to be analysed in economics, which is identified with contract. This second sense of social relations turns on the idea that a welfarist organisation of exchange should, to a lesser or greater degree falling short of a complete rejection of the market, replace self-interest.

I repeat that this argument certainly can be recognised in Macaulay's work, but disregard of economics is far from easy to identify in his 1963 papers. It will be recalled that Macaulay thought that his findings required us to answer, not only the question 'How can businesses successfully operate exchange relationships with relatively so little attention to detailed planning or to legal sanctions?', but also the question 'Why does business ever use contract in light of its success without it?'[53] A very considerable part of 'Non-contractual Relations in Business' addressed the question 'Why do relatively contractual practices ever exist?'[54] The picture that emerges from the 1963 papers is not one of literal non-use but of a complex interplay between the use of legal and non-legal sanctions which Macaulay explains by reference to 'the functions and dysfunctions of using contract to solve exchange problems'.[55] Macaulay's ability to mount an analysis of 'the functions and dysfunctions of using contract to solve exchange problems' does not turn on the general social embedding of legal issues, although this is of course a feature of his work, but his conception of contracting specifically turns on the relationship of law to economics manifested in the way contract law facilitates economic exchange.

[50] Campbell, 'Non-use' (n 23) 168–77.

[51] S Macaulay, 'Organic Transactions: Contract, Frank Lloyd Wright and the Johnson Building' [1996] Wisconsin Law Review 75.

[52] See n 17.

[53] Macaulay, 'Non-contractual Relations' (n 11) 62.

[54] ibid 65.

[55] ibid 56.

Devices for conducting exchanges

A proper understanding of 'Non-contractual relations in Business' must begin with its definition of 'contracts' as 'devices for conducting exchanges':

> Contract is not treated as synonymous with an exchange itself, which may or may not be characterised as contractual. Nor is contract used to refer to a writing recording an agreement. Contract, as ... the term [is used] here, involves two distinct elements: (a) rational planning of the transaction with careful planning for as many future contingencies as can be foreseen, and (b) the existence or use of actual or potential legal sanctions to induce performance of the exchange or to compensate for non-performance.[56]

These devices, Macaulay goes on to tell us:

> may be used or may exist in greater or lesser degree, so that transactions can be described relatively as involving a more or a less contractual manner (a) of creating an exchange relationship or (b) of solving problems arising during the course of such a relationship.[57]

The great virtue of this definition of contract is that it breaks the complete identification of economic exchange and legal contract, which in effect extinguishes the former, in the classical law's conception of contract. In the first edition of the oldest of the contract textbooks still in general use in England and Wales, that of Sir William Anson first published in 1879, contract is defined 'as a combination of the two ideas of agreement and obligation. It is that form of agreement which directly contemplates and results in an obligation.'[58] In the 25th, centenary edition, 'the law of contract' was described as 'that branch of law which determines the circumstances in which a promise shall be legally binding on the person making it'.[59] Approaching contract in this way identifies the contract with legally enforceable promises, and the economic exchange which is its proper foundation does not feature. On this basis, it is inevitable that the classical approach to the subject will be 'to analyse the concept of a promise'.[60] A complicated legal doctrine of contract and an elaborate speculative ethics of promising may be erected, but there is nothing to the classical conception of contract other than law, and this is not what is essential. Economic exchange is what is essential.[61]

[56] ibid.

[57] ibid.

[58] WR Anson, *Principles of the English Law of Contract* (Clarendon Press 1879) 1.

[59] AG Guest, *Anson's Law of Contract* (25th edn, Clarendon Press, 1979) 2.

[60] ibid.

[61] A number of valuable recent criticisms of promise theory intended to develop Fried's analysis of contract law in terms of autonomy are, it is submitted, undermined, so that their undoubted insights remain *ad hoc*, because of their failure to base their analysis on this: P Benson, *Justice in Transactions* (Belknap Press 2019) (hereafter Benson, *Justice*); H Dagan and M Heller, *The Choice Theory of Contracts* (CUP 2017); and P Saprai, *Contract Law Without Foundations* (OUP 2019).

Professor Benson's is a fascinating case. Perhaps because he generally conflates neo-classical economics with essentially Posnerian law and economics when the latter are in fact a form of welfare economic

Why parties make promises in the form of contracts cannot naturally emerge from the classical understanding of the subject, and this question has been either entirely ignored, so that the whole thing seemed a sort of abstract legal game in the way so memorably parodied by Llewellyn,[62] or, especially more recently, as some feeling of disquiet about the purely legal approach has had to be acknowledged by all but the most antediluvian, has been discussed only as an appendix to the basic concept of promise. In the most recent edition of *Anson*, a discussion of the economic 'functions of contract'[63] now follows the definition of contract, but this definition remains that given in the centenary edition,[64] and so this discussion, though welcome, is a mere 'social scientific' addition to what remains a purely legal concept of contract as promise, which the social science does not deepen, nor indeed relate to in any sustained way.

In contrast to this entirely legal conception of contract, Macaulay's definition of contract as devices for conducting exchanges has an integral economic component, with the economic exchange the object and the legal contract a means of achieving that object. Now, it is analytically essential to realise that parties do not have to intend that their promises to exchange will be legally binding. Nevertheless, exchange and contract are (with exceptions discussed in Chapter 5) congruent because in the conditions of the general market economy the law of contract is, 'as a practical matter', necessary for exchange.[65] By putting their exchange commitments into the legal form of a contract, parties obtain security, ultimately backed by the state, against

alternative to Pareto optimisation (D Campbell, 'Welfare Economics for Capitalists: The Economic Consequences of Judge Posner' (2012) 33 Cardozo Law Review 2233), Benson is at pains to insist on the radical separation of the 'juridical' from the 'economic', leading to a claim which could not more contradict the approach of the present book: 'the fact that contract law takes up economic interactions as its appropriate content does not make it dependent upon or rooted in the latter' (Benson, *Justice* 445). Leaving aside the merits of this view of juridical relations, it is my opinion that Benson's position is fundamentally inconsistent with that of Rawls.

In my view, Rawls' principal achievement, writing against a background of general if not universal commitment to egalitarianism to which he himself largely subscribed and which led him to focus on reining in inequality, has been to give inequality of outcome a legitimate basis in liberal democratic societies in which equality is a paramount value. The trade-off between 'efficiency' and 'fairness' and the difference principle itself make basic sense only if one accepts the legitimacy of a proportionality between personal effort and self-interested betterment, and this follows from an 'economic' philosophic anthropology expressed in J Rawls, *A Theory of Justice* (rev edn, OUP 1999) 87:

> the distribution of natural talents ... is neither just nor unjust ... These are simply natural facts.
>
> Perhaps Rawls' clearest brief expression of this came, however, not in *A Theory of Justice*, but in his later statement of 'realistic utopianism' in J Rawls, *The Law of Peoples* (Harvard UP 1999) 12–13.

Though at one level Benson's juridical approach does not detract from the interest of his argument, it does mean that the foundation of that argument is, one is obliged to conclude, quite opposed to the one drawing upon Rawls that Benson believes it to be.

[62] KN Llewellyn, 'Our Case Law of Contract: Offer and Acceptance II' (1939) 48 Yale Law Journal 779, 785.

[63] J Beatson, A Burrows, and J Cartwright, *Anson's Law of Contract* (31st edn, OUP 2010) 2–4. A ritual reference to 'Non-contractual Relations in Business' made in the course of this discussion completely plays down its significance.

[64] ibid 1–2.

[65] H Havighurst, *The Nature of Private Contract* (Northwestern University Press 1961) 22–23:

> Theoretically exchange is possible without the use of any promises at all ... But as a practical matter ... it will rarely be possible to achieve it without some use of the promise ... the promise plays a part in the facilitation of exchange.

non-performance. Contract then emerges as a unity of economic exchange and legal device for providing security for the exchange. As was mentioned in the previous chapter, in his pathbreaking discussion, Wolfgang Friedmann identified the provision of 'insurance against calculated economic risks' as one of four 'elements' of the social function of contract,[66] and though Friedman's other elements, including providing basic freedom of movement and of will, are of the first importance, they are the results of economic action under the law of contract and not, as is 'insurance' against breach, the functional reason parties enter into a contract.[67]

This understanding of the nature of contract lies behind the vital distinction between 'primary' and 'secondary' obligations, which will be discussed at length in Chapter 8. The former are the parties' generally express promises to exchange. The latter are the parties' generally implicit promises to provide a remedy in the event of breach. Secondary obligations arise at the time of agreement, but remain latent during the performance of primary obligations, crystallising only if a breach is committed, when the defendant must provide a remedy.

There is an immense theoretical benefit to this conception of contract as a unity of economic exchange and legal security which has, in my opinion, underpinned Macaulay's contribution to the subject. Whilst it was perhaps not entirely inevitable, the classical law's purely legal conception of contract was highly likely to lead, and has led, to the core belief that the function of contract should be the literal enforcement of legally binding promises, for if one asks how one should adequately enforce a promise, then literal enforcement is the natural answer. How else could one really enforce a promise? But all we know of the way contract remedies work, especially as understood in the light of what Macaulay has told us about this,[68] is counter-evidence to this literal belief in *pacta sunt servanda*, which is the fundamental error of the classical law. These issues will be examined at length in Chapter 8, but the main point may be anticipated here.

Parties enter into an exchange in order to maximise the satisfactions they obtain from their ownership of economic goods. They exchange goods they own prior to the exchange in order to realise a surplus satisfaction from the transferred goods they own after it. It is this surplus that is the basis of the fundamental concept in the analysis of remedies: the expectation interest. The crucial advantage which Macaulay's approach enjoys over the purely legal classical law is that it generates an integral flexibility in the relationship between economic exchange and the form of the legal security provided by the contract. For, as I have said, the legal contract is not what is essential. It is the exchange, or more precisely the surplus that is the entire point of the exchange, that is essential. The actual performance of primary obligations is incidental to obtaining that surplus, indeed, creating legal contractual obligations is a cost of obtaining that surplus. Macaulay's approach allows us to see that what really matters is not 'performance'

[66] W Friedmann, *Law in a Changing Society* (2nd edn, Penguin 1972) 119.

[67] Putting promises to exchange in the form of a contract has other functions than providing security, such as clarifying the intentions of the parties. But it is not essential that such clarification take the legal form of agreeing a contract, whereas the provision of security underwritten by the state analytically must have a legal form.

[68] S Macaulay, 'Almost Everything that I Did Want to Know About Contract Litigation: A Comment on Galanter' [2001] Wisconsin Law Review 629, 630.

but 'expectation', and to assess the way the contract device facilitates the exchange in terms of how well it protects expectation. This is the true function of contract, but it is not something that can coherently emerge from the classical law.

Taking this approach allows Macaulay to analyse 'the functions and dysfunctions of using contract to solve exchange problems', and to distinguish cases of the adoption of a 'more or less contractual manner' of solving these problems, depending on the costs and benefits imposed by those functions and dysfunctions. On the basis of the economic argument 'that economic actors will employ the litigation process to settle disputes only to the extent that (1) the present value of continuing relationships is low, and (2) the anticipated return from the litigation process is high',[69] Macaulay has given the main impetus to the relational theory by empirically showing to us many cases where the litigation process has such costs as to be entirely dysfunctional. In regard of these cases, Macaulay has been able to build on the evidence of 'indifferent or even hostile' attitude of business towards law set out in his 1963 papers to show the great and troubling distance between the 'real deal' and the 'paper deal'.[70] But these cases have typically been relational in the sense of being members of the distinct specie of relational cases, non-standard in that they are characterised by long duration, the difficulty of initially specifying the allocation of risks over that duration, etc, for such cases have an economic form to which the default law of contract, particularly the default law of remedies, is very poorly suited, and attempting to govern such contracts with this unsuitable law can be, as has been said, dysfunctional. This will be discussed at length in Chapters 9 and 10.

The point that must be made here, however, is that, to focus on remedies, the default remedies are not unsuited to standard cases, indeed they are remarkably well suited to them, but in these cases these remedies work so well that we might say that the returns to litigation would be low in the sense that litigation is quite unnecessary. The outcomes normally produced by the default law are in the interests of both parties, which therefore unproblematically regard the legal position as the basis of legitimate action in the way that is generally regarded as the epitome of regulatory success. I am very gratified to be able to say that a previous formulation of this claim, which, to repeat, will be set out length in Chapter 8, has found a certain favour with Macaulay.[71] The vital issue which Macaulay did more than anyone else to bring to proper attention is drawing a distinction between standard and non-standard cases and evaluating the very differing performances of the law in 'solving [the] problems arising' in the different classes of cases. This distinction is, however, best approached by turning to Ian Macneil.

[69] S Macaulay, 'Elegant Models, Empirical Pictures, and the Complexities of Contract' (1977) 11 Law and Society Review 507, 509.

[70] S Macaulay, 'The Real Deal and the Paper Deal: Empirical Pictures of Relationships, Complexity and the Urge for Transparent, Simple Rules' in D Campbell, H Collins, and J Wightman (eds), *Implicit Dimensions of Contract* (Hart 2003).

[71] S Macaulay, 'Renegotiations and Settlements: Dr Pangloss' Notes on the Margins of David Campbell's Papers' (2007) 29 Cardozo Law Review 261. It is clear enough from this paper that Macaulay by no means entirely agreed with my argument about remedies in particular and relational contract in general, and it was never my belief that, in light of my views on welfarism, it would be possible for him to do so.

Macneil's View of the Discrete and the Relational

I can be brief about that part of Macneil's work which is the basis of the view of the relational contract as a distinct specie of contract. In his earlier work, of which 'The Many Futures of Contract' is the centrepiece, Macneil showed that the classical law rests on a model of a standard contract which he called the 'discrete contract', but that the empirical forms of contract are by no means entirely composed of discrete contracts. Rather, discrete contracts form one pole of a 'spectrum' of contracts, at the other pole of which stands the relational contract:

> contractual ordering of economic activity takes place along a spectrum of discrete and relational behaviour. At one end are relatively discrete transactions. Discrete transactions are contracts of short duration, involving limited personal interactions, and containing precise party measurements of easily acquired objects of exchange, for example money and grain. They require a minimum of future co-operative behaviour between the parties and no sharing of benefits or burdens. They bind the parties tightly and precisely. The parties view such transactions as free of entangling strings, and they expect no altruism. The parties see everything connected with such transactions as clearly defined ... If trouble is anticipated at all, it is anticipated only if someone or something turns out unexpectedly badly ... At the other end of the contract spectrum are ongoing relations ... The relations are of significant duration ... Close whole person relations form an integral part of the relation ... The object of exchange typically includes both easily measured quantities ... and quantities not easily measured ... Future co-operative behaviour is expected ... benefits and burdens of the relation are to be shared rather than entirely divided and allocated ... The entangling strings of friendship, reputation, interdependence, morality, and altruistic desires are integral ... Trouble is expected as a matter of course ... Finally, the participants view the relation as an ongoing integration of behaviour to grow and vary with events.[72]

Exemplified by major construction works,[73] long-term natural resource exploitation contracts,[74] long-term supply contracts,[75] long-term distributorships,[76] etc, these relational contracts are, no doubt, numerically a small category by comparison to standard contracts, but they are an integral feature of the provision of goods through industrialised processes.[77] Throughout his work, Macneil added to Macaulay's

[72] IR Macneil and PJ Gudel, *Contracts: Exchange Transactions and Relations* (3rd edn, Foundation Press 2001) 14–15 (hereafter Macneil and Gudel, *Contracts*). The first two editions of this casebook, prepared by Macneil himself, were published in 1971 and 1978.

[73] TJ Stipanowich, 'Reconstructing Construction Law: Reality and Reform in a Transactional System' [1998] Wisconsin Law Review 463.

[74] JH Mulherin, 'Complexity in Long-term Contracts: An Analysis of Natural Gas Provisions' (1986) 2 Journal of Law, Economics and Organisation 105.

[75] PL Joskow, 'Contract Duration and Relationship Specific Investments: Empirical Evidence from Coal Markets' (1987) 77 American Economic Review 168.

[76] S Macaulay, 'Long-Term Continuing Relations: The American Experience Regulating Dealerships and Franchises' in Christian Joerges (ed), *Franchising and the Law: Theoretical and Comparative Approaches in Europe and the United States* (Nomos Verlagsgesellschaft, 1991).

[77] Macneil, 'Many Futures (n 18) 693–96.

demonstration that the classical law and its model of contract is markedly inadequate to the understanding of these contracts by extensively showing how attempting to force them onto the procrustean bed of the classical law led to the doctrinal incoherence,[78] and so to the practical irrelevance or active unhelpfulness,[79] of the law. Macneil's main object of criticism was not, in fact, what he understood to be the classical law, but the prevailing body of what he called the 'neo-classical law', formed by inadequate attempts to reconcile the classical law with its deficiencies, rather than restate the law of contract on a fundamentally different, relational basis.[80] The point that must be noted is that, as with Macaulay, the critique is not of the law of contract *tout court*, but of the inadequate form of the existing understanding of the law of contract.[81]

What Macneil principally added to Macaulay was a coherent explanation of why differing contracts are distributed along a spectrum, based on the concept of 'presentiation'. The proper understanding of this explanation has to build on a detailed exposure of the shortcomings of the classical law, and in particular of the doctrine of consideration, and so it will be reserved for Chapter 10, where the great value of the distinction between discrete and relational contracts will emerge. At this point, it is enough to turn to the resultant picture of the difference between the attitudes of parties to discrete and relational contracts. In the quotation above, the discrete contract 'free of entangling strings' such as 'sharing' and altruism' is contrasted to the relational contract to which such strings are 'integral'. It is this that has been seized on in the idea of a specie of relational contract as a 'warm, human, co-operative ... relation' in contrast to the discrete contract of 'self-interest, rational choice and market exchange'.

It should be said that this view does, as Macneil himself came to acknowledge at least up to a point,[82] have a basis in a confusion in the work that brought his ideas to such prominence, which it would be fruitless to deny can be legitimately interpreted as allowing the possibility of a truly discrete contract. To the extent he did allow this possibility, Macneil was mistaken, for his consistent position should have been that it is impossible that there can be any such thing. It would be very unfair to fail to acknowledge either that those passages in which Macneil allowed the possibility of a truly discrete contract are often very hedged about,[83] or that there have *always* been

[78] In early work, principally a number of entries in RB Schlesinger (ed), *Formation of Contracts: A Study of the Common Core of Legal Systems*, 2 vols (Oceana Publications 1968), Macneil exposed the doctrinal inadequacies of fundamental concepts such as offer, rejection, and acceptance in a way entirely comparable to Atiyah's criticisms of consideration.

[79] Macneil, 'Many Futures' (n 18) 693:

> A long and unsuccessful struggle to reconcile [the classical law's] pure and simple concept with what seems to me the real life of contractual behaviour has led to this essay.

[80] IR Macneil, 'Contracts: Adjustment of Long-term Economic Relations Under Classical, Neo-classical and Economic Analysis' (1978) 72 Northwestern University Law Review 854, 865–86 (hereafter Macneil, 'Adjustment').

[81] IR Macneil, 'Whither Contracts? (1969) 21 Journal of Legal Education 403.

[82] IR Macneil, 'Relational Contract Theory: Challenges and Queries' (2000) 94 Northwestern University Law Review 877, 895 (hereafter Macneil, 'Challenges and Queries').

[83] Even his famous, or notorious, gas station example, the first more than 'bare definitional' discrete contract in Macneil, 'Many Futures' (n 18) 720–21, was stated with numerous, not then fully thought-through, caveats, and these caveats were later worked up as a statement that the example was of only an 'apparently discrete transaction': Macneil, 'Adjustment', ibid 857 n 10 and IR Macneil, 'Values in Contract: Internal and External' (1983) 78 Northwestern University Law Review 340, 344 (hereafter Macneil, 'Values').

other passages that deny this possibility[84] (and, conversely, insist that '*all* contracts are relational'),[85] and we shall see that Macneil sought to emphasise this denial (and its converse) in later work.

Behind the concession of the possibility of the truly discrete contract lies a concession of the possibility of a system of welfare-enhancing exchange based on solipsistic self-interest, a grave contradiction in Macneil's work, for no other contributor conversant with the detail of the law of contract has done more to show that all contracting integrally has an other-regarding aspect. The elaborate and repeatedly revised normative schemas that became the most familiar feature of Macneil's work are normative schemas applying to *all* contracts, particularly in the identification of essential 'common contract norms'.[86] If we step away from Macneil a little, we can say that it is not only that a truly discrete contract would not enhance welfare because, as was argued in the previous chapter, it would not capture the mutual advantage of Pareto exchange; it is that it is impossible to make a truly discrete contract because, without social relations facilitative of voluntary agreement, a general market economy could not possibly be stable.

Though the problem ultimately is one about the understanding of the discrete contract, the problem that has vexed the reception of Macneil's work is the converse difficulty over the relational contract, for arguing that all contracts are relational meant that he was using 'relational' both to describe an aspect of all contracts and *also* to describe a set of contracts distinct from the discrete contract. In his later work, Macneil sought to deal with this by stressing that all contracts are relational and relabelling what formerly he had called relational contracts as 'intertwined' contracts,[87] so that the spectrum of discrete and intertwined contracts was but 'an adjunct'[88] of a general theory of relational contract which he came to call 'essential contract theory'.[89]

Macneil was himself well aware that, however determined,[90] his efforts to correct a wrong impression which was in part caused by what he acknowledged were early

[84] IR Macneil, 'Restatement (Second) of Contracts and Presentiation' (1974) 60 Virginia Law Review 589, 594:

> No one was ever so naïve as to believe that contract law could indeed achieve total presentiation, but there are some kinds of contracts where close approximations may be possible.

[85] Macneil, 'Values' (n 83) 341–42:

> the contract dimension ... I take to be the relations among people in the course of projecting exchange into the future. So viewed, *all* contracts are relational. Nevertheless, some contracts ... are far more relational than others.

A later refinement relabelled discrete contracts as 'as-if discrete': Macneil, 'Challenges and Queries' (n 82) 895–96.

[86] IR Macneil, *The New Social Contract* (Yale University Press 1980) (hereafter Macneil, *New Social Contract*) and Macneil, 'Values' (n 83). An interesting attempt to simplify Macneil's schemas to bring out the essential point is made in R Austen-Baker, 'Comprehensive Contract Theory: A Four Norm Model of Contractual Relations' (2009) 25 Journal of Contract Law 216.

[87] This was first put forward in IR Macneil, 'Relational Contract Theory as Sociology: A Reply to Professors Lindberg and de Vos' (1987) 143 Journal of Institutional and Theoretical Economics 272, 276.

[88] Macneil, 'Challenges and Queries' (n 82) 894 n 63.

[89] ibid 892–93. In Macneil, 'Reflections' (n 21) 207 n 1, Macneil said he took this step 'belatedly'.

[90] When compiling a selection from Macneil's works which was published in 2001, I very hesitantly suggested that 'The Many Futures of Contract' be completely omitted, though in minor part this was for reasons of length. I believe it indicates just how much Macneil wanted to make something of a fresh start that he was enthusiastic about this suggestion: IR Macneil, *The Relational Theory of Contract* (Sweet & Maxwell 2001) ix–x.

missteps had been largely unavailing,[91] and, with the greatest respect, this was not only because these efforts did not receive the attention they should have, but because Macneil's normative schemas were unfortunately over-ambitious. Macneil had always seen the relational theory of contract as part of a—one hesitates but it seems right to say universal[92]—social theory, the 'relational theory of exchange',[93] applicable 'to all choice situations,[94] in which all human action, by no means just economic exchange, was understood as 'exchange'.[95] I am afraid that this theory lost sight of the specifics of market exchange as rational economic action,[96] and so Macneil's contribution to the analysis of legal doctrine became unclear, as the persistence of what we have seen he called a 'misconceived perception' of his argument evidenced. Beyond a general level, Macneil's schemas are difficult—I have found it impossible—to map onto the legal doctrines they are meant to explain.

Though it is the case that both Macneil's demonstration of the relational constitution of all contracts and, as will be argued in Chapter 10, the distinction he then drew between discrete and relational contracts in light of this general constitution are essential foundations of an adequate understanding of the law, it is necessary to move away from Macneil's schemas and restate the relational critique of the very idea of a discrete contract in a way which more effectively disrupts the claim of the classical law to be adequate even to the discrete contract. The unquestionable shortcomings of this claim, the exposure of which gave rise to Gilmore's death of contract, cannot lead to the abandonment of the classical law unless there is a superior general alternative to which to move, the foundation of which alternative Macneil certainly wanted, but it must be conceded failed, to lay. The argument of this book is that the adequate understanding of the market economy, and therefore of both the classical law and the rejection of that law by welfarism, must be *drawn from* the existing economics and law of that economy, and, paradoxically enough, this is best undertaken by consideration of the only argument that that economy should be completely abandoned that requires sustained attention because of its merits as an argument; that of Karl Marx. It is very instructive to now begin to describe what we have seen is the necessary relational constitution of contract by drawing on Marx.

[91] Macneil, 'Reflections' (n 21).

[92] Macneil, *New Social Contract* (n 86) 3.

[93] IR Macneil, 'Exchange Revisited: Individual Utility and Social Solidarity' (1986) 96 Ethics 567.

[94] IR Macneil, 'Political Exchange as Relational Contract' in B Marin (ed), *Generalised Political Exchange* (Campus Verlag 1990) 154. Macneil goes on, ibid 154–55, to affirm some of the examples of exchange ('slavery in an Arabian satrapy', 'Stalin's labour camps', etc) which had startled the readers of Macneil, 'Many Futures' (n 18) 703–704.

[95] Macneil, 'Many Futures'(n 18) 700:

> 'Exchange' ... does not necessarily require measurement of reciprocity or conscious desires to gain by exchange ... Nor ... the use of money.

[96] D Campbell, 'The Social Theory of Relational Contract: Macneil as the Modern Proudhon' (1990) 18 International Journal of the Sociology of Law 75.

Exchange and Contract as Mutual Recognition

The various non-communist criticisms of the market economy, such as the liberal socialism advocated in this book, are based on a range of claims that that economy does not work as well as what is now known as Pareto optimisation requires. Though Marx himself made much use of such criticisms in his political activity and writing,[97] and his theoretical economic works are replete with evidence for them,[98] they were ultimately unimportant to him.[99] Marx's fundamental criticism of the market economy was of the alienation of human labour he believed was intrinsic to that economy, and Pareto optimisation is irrelevant to this criticism, which would apply with full force even to a Pareto equilibrium. This was never made more clear than in Marx's comments on the political programme adopted by what was to become the German Social Democratic Party at its 1875 Congress which we know as *The Critique of the Gotha Programme*:

> *equal right* ... is still in principle *bourgeois right* [and] this *equal right* is still constantly encumbered by a bourgeois limitation. The right of the producers is *proportional* to the labour they supply; the equality consists in the fact that measurement is made with an *equal standard*, labour. But one man is superior to another physically or mentally and so supplies more labour in the same time, or can work for a longer time; and labour, to serve as a measure, must be defined by its duration or intensity, otherwise it ceases to be a standard of measurement. This *equal* right is an unequal right for unequal labour. It recognises no class distinctions, because everyone is only a worker; but tacitly recognises the unequal individual endowment and hence productive capacity as natural privileges. *It is, therefore, a right of inequality in its content, like every right* ... To avoid ... these defects, right would have to be unequal rather than equal.
>
> But these defects are inevitable in the first phase of communist society as it is when it has just emerged after prolonged birth-pangs from capitalist society. Right can never be higher than the economic structure of a society and its cultural development which this determines.

[97] K Marx and F Engels, *Manifesto of the Communist Party* in *Collected Works*, vol 6 (Lawrence and Wishart 1976) 491 (emphasis added):

> No sooner is the exploitation of the labourer by the manufacturer [in the production process] at an end, and he receives his wages in cash, than he is *set upon* by the other portions of the bourgeoisie, the landlord, the shopkeeper, the pawnbroker, etc.

[98] Eg 'the series of more enduring consequences' which in Victorian times were made possible by the way in which wages were paid, which included workers' 'acceptance' of adulterated goods and the truck system, noted in K Marx, *Capital*, vol 1 in K Marx and F Engels, *Collected Works*, vol 35 (International Publishers 1996) 184 (hereafter Marx, *Capital*, vol 1). It is significant that Marx put this extension of 'credit' by the labourer to the capitalist aside in his basic analysis of the labour process.

[99] K Marx, *Value, Price and Profit*, in K Marx and F Engels, *Collected Works*, vol 20 (Lawrence and Wishart 1985) 148 (hereafter, Marx, *Value*):

> [Ought] the working class ... renounce their resistance against the encroachments of capital and abandon their attempts at making the best of occasional chances for their temporary improvement. If they did, they would be degraded to one level mass of broken wretches past salvation [Nevertheless, instead] of the *conservative* motto '*A fair day's wage for a fair day's work!*' they ought to inscribe on their banner the *revolutionary* watchword '*Abolition of the wages system!*'.

We shall return to this passage in the conclusion of this book.

> In a higher phase of communist society, after the enslaving subjugation of the individual to the division of labour, and thereby the antithesis between mental and physical labour, has vanished; after labour has become not only a means to life but life's prime want; after the productive forces have also increased with the all-round development of the individual, and all the springs of common wealth flow more abundantly—only then can the narrow horizon of bourgeois right be crossed in its entirety and society inscribe on its banners: From each according to his abilities, to each according to his needs![100]

'From each according to his abilities, to each according to his needs' is not an egalitarian principle. It is a principle in which equality and inequality have no relevance to a distribution, if indeed this itself is an opposite term, made by unconstrained human beings able to consciously direct their labour as they wish.

The very act of exchange, Marx argued, prevents economic actors from consciously understanding and controlling their economic relations, producing 'a state of society in which the process of production has the mastery over man instead of being controlled by him'.[101] As part of his acknowledgement of the sense in which humanity experiences nature as refractory discussed in the previous chapter, Marx allowed that all economies must have, as one of a set of 'general conditions',[102] production for the sake of consumption,[103] and the capitalist economy is in this respect no different to its predecessors.[104] But the capitalist economy is based on the general separation of the use-value and the exchange-value of economic goods,[105] and for Marx the direction of the production by consumers' choice of use-values is completely subordinated to the production of exchange-value[106] in the capitalist pursuit of profit.[107] I shall expand this discussion of Marx's disregard of the economic significance of consumer choice in the conclusion of this book, but the point to be made here is that the core of his argument

[100] K Marx, *Critique of the Gotha Programme* in K Marx and F Engels, *Collected Works*, vol 24 (Lawrence and Wishart 1989) 86–87.

[101] Marx, *Capital*, vol 1 (n 98) 92.

[102] K Marx, 'Economic Manuscripts of 1857–8 [*Grundrisse*]' in K Marx and F Engels, *Collected Works*, vols 28–29 (Lawrence and Wishart 1986–87) vol 28, 26 (hereafter Marx, *Grundrisse*).

[103] Marx, *Capital*, vol 1 (n 98) 194:

> The labour-process ... human action with a view to the production of use-values, appropriation of natural substances to human requirements ... is the everlasting Nature-imposed condition of human existence.

[104] ibid 187:

> The fact that the production of use-values, or goods, is carried on under the control of a capitalist and on his behalf, does not alter the general character of that production.

[105] ibid 46. The exposition of Marx's economics which briefly follows and which will be taken up at length in the conclusion of this book will elide certain distinctions central to those economics, notably those between exchange-value and value and between surplus value and profit.

[106] ibid 196 and K Marx, *Capital*, vol 3 in K Marx and F Engels, *Collected Works*, vol 37 (Lawrence and Wishart 1998) 45.

[107] Marx, *Capital*, vol 3, 194:

> capitalist production is itself indifferent to the particular use-value and distinctive features of any commodity it produces. In every sphere of production it is only concerned with producing surplus value.

is that under capitalism production is fundamentally misdirected as it is governed by the 'external, coercive laws'[108] of exchange-value and profit:

> capital contains a particular restriction of production [the] restriction of the production of use-values by exchange value [such that] real wealth has to take on a specific form distinct from itself, a form not absolutely identical with it, in order to become an object of production at all.[109]

Marx conceived of capitalism as a 'restless, never-ending process of profit-making *alone*'[110] which has as its only commandment, as he unforgettably put it: 'Accumulate, accumulate! That is Moses and the Prophets.'[111] In this book I hope to show that this claim, decoupled from its theoretical base, is the 'principle' of the maximalist welfare state and the welfarist law of contract. But Marx himself believed that rational production could take place only in a 'higher economic form of society'[112] in which exchange is replaced by 'The life-process of society ... consciously regulated ... by a settled plan.'[113]

A criticism of the market economy as radical as this allows, and indeed paradoxically requires, that exchange will normally take place according to its own criteria (and still be subject to absolute criticism). Though the 'exploitation'[114] of labour involved in the creation of surplus value and profit, and the way this would lead to 'immiseration',[115] are central to Marx's economics, this is so in a way wholly different to any sense of exploitation as swindling made possible by inequality of bargaining power,[116] which is irrelevant to the structural exploitation which Marx believed must be a feature of the alienated sale and purchase of labour-power at its correctly determined exchange-value.[117] 'The sphere of circulation or commodity exchange, within whose boundaries the sale and purchase of labour-power goes on is', Marx tells us:

> in fact a very Eden of the innate rights of man. It is the exclusive realm of Freedom, Equality, Property, and Bentham. Freedom, because both buyer and seller of a commodity, let us say of labour-power, are determined only by their own free will. They

[108] ibid 588.
[109] Marx, *Grundrisse* (n 102) vol 28, 342.
[110] Marx, *Capital*, vol 1 (n 98) 164 (emphasis added).
[111] ibid 591.
[112] Marx, *Capital*, vol 3 (n 106) 763.
[113] Marx, *Capital*, vol 1 (n 98) 89–90.
[114] ibid 221–229.
[115] ibid 634–640
[116] ibid 205:

> a surplus value ... has been created ... money has been transformed into capital ... while the laws that regulate the exchange of commodities have been in no way violated. Equivalent has been exchanged for equivalent. For the capitalist as buyer paid for [plant, raw material] and the labour-power at its full value ... and sells his [output at] its exact value.

[117] Marx, *Value* (n 99) 127:

> To explain ... the general nature of profits, you must start from the theorem that, on an average, goods are sold at their real value, and that profits are derived from selling them at their values ... If you cannot explain profit upon this supposition, you cannot explain it at all.

I have whenever possible replaced Marx's use of 'commodities' with 'goods'.

> contract as free persons, who are equal before the law. Their contract is the final result in which their joint will finds a common legal expression. Equality, because each enters into relation with the other, as with a simple owner of commodities, and they exchange equivalent for equivalent. Property, because each disposes only of what is his own. And Bentham, because each looks only to his own advantage. The only force bringing them together, and putting them into relation with each other, is the selfishness, the gain and the private interest of each. Each pays heed to himself only, and no one worries about the others. And precisely for that reason ... they all work together to their mutual advantage, for the common weal, and in the common interest.[118]

In another remarkable passage, Marx gives further detail of exchange by contract, in which the parties:

> must behave in such a way that each does not appropriate the [goods] of the other, and part with his own, except by means of an act done by mutual consent. They must, therefore, mutually recognise in each other the rights of private proprietors. This juridical relation, which thus expresses itself in a contract ... is a relation between two wills and is but the reflex of the real economic relation of the two. It is this economic relation that determines the subject matter comprised in each such juridical act.[119]

The, one has to say truly historical, significance of these two passages is that in them Marx gave as positive a description of contracting as can be found in all writing on the subject by those supporting the market economy, but that he set at far less than nought the positives he had described. In the conclusion of this book, the theory of alienation which led him to do this will be directly confronted in light of the account of the common law of contract's core doctrines to which we shall shortly turn. That account will itself be an overwhelmingly positive one, but it will also be an exploration of a defining contradiction *in those doctrines themselves* which Marx's description of contracting acutely expresses.

In the first of the two just-quoted passages, Marx describes the role of 'selfishness' and 'gain' in a way which, terminology aside, could readily have played roles in the classical law and neo-classical economics of exchange as discussed in the previous chapter.[120] However, the 'freedom' of exchange and contract insisted upon in the first quoted paragraph turns in the second quoted paragraph upon a distinction between 'appropriation' and an act by which economic actors may legitimately 'part' with goods which has two elements. The first element (the second as Marx presents them) is that initially economic actors 'must ... mutually recognise in each other the rights of private proprietors'. The second element (the first as Marx presents them) is that the transfer of goods must be 'by means of an act done by mutual consent'. The distinction between appropriation and legitimate parting, though both are motivated by

[118] Marx, *Capital*, vol 1 (n 98) 186.
[119] ibid 95.
[120] In those few works of Marxist analysis which have paid attention to the process of contracting and exchange, this is how Marx has been interpreted: A Sohn-Rethel, *Intellectual and Manual Labour* (Macmillan 1978) 41: 'commodity exchange impels solipsism between its participants'.

self-interest, is that in the latter the actors 'must behave' on the basis of 'mutual recognition' of each other as owners and consenters to transfer.

Though I am unaware of any direct textual warrant for this, it is undoubtedly the case that Marx derived his description of exchange from Hegel's various comments on contract, which make the necessity of consensual exchange,[121] and mutual recognition as the means of obtaining consent,[122] essential features of contract.[123] The concept of mutual recognition is the basis of Hegel's claim to have fundamentally added to the moral and political philosophy of Kant, and, though we shall return to the issues in the conclusion of this book, we are able to explore only in a limited way the implications of this most radically intersubjective analysis of human consciousness. Here we should note only that consciousness of mutual recognition in exchange transforms exchange's, if this language may be excused, ontological and therefore ethical character. Exchange conscious of mutual recognition is no longer exchange *only* between *two* self-interested parties but is always between two parties which must pursue their subjective self-interest by reference to a, to put it in a way which it is hoped is not misleading, *third* party to the contract. That third party is the relationship, made objective by the state in the law of contract, which stipulates that each contracting party must recognise the other as autonomous, and that persuading that party to enter into an agreement is the only legitimate way in which to pursue subjective self-interest. A party wishing to avail itself of the law of contract must frame its action by reference to this objective standard.

Exchange *is* based on self-interest, and shares this with mere appropriation. But whereas mere appropriation is a solipsistic exercise of self-interest, this is the last thing that can be said of exchange, which has the moral, other-regarding component of mutual recognition as an analytically essential feature. It is not only that an economy of exchange could not possibly be stable otherwise,[124] but that even a single act of exchange properly so-called—exchange as agreement motivated by mutual advantage—is not possible otherwise. Self-interested exchange that is fully self-conscious of its own nature, or is actual as Hegel would have put it, rejects solipsism in favour of mutual recognition.

Empirical instances of exchange will always have a tension between subjective, potentially solipsistic, self-interest and the objective requirement of mutual recognition at their heart. The 'crooked timber' of humanity[125] will always fall short of a state of 'moral … perfection of which no rational being in the sensible world is capable'.[126]

[121] GWF Hegel, *Philosophy of Mind* (Clarendon Press 1971) s 492.

[122] GWF Hegel, *Elements of the Philosophy of Right* (CUP 1991) s 71.

[123] P Benson, 'Abstract Right and the Possibility of a Non-distributive Conception of Contract: Hegel and Contemporary Contract Theory' (1989) 10 Cardozo Law Review 1077; Benson, *Justice* (n 61) 413–21; and M Rosenfeld, 'Hegel and the Dialectics of Contract' (1989) 10 Cardozo Law Review 1199.

[124] JA Schumpeter, *Capitalism, Socialism and Democracy* (5th edn, George Allen & Unwin 1976) 423–24:

> no social system can work which is based exclusively upon a network of free contracts between (legally) equal contracting parties and in which everyone is supposed to be guided by his own (short-run) utilitarian ends.

[125] I Kant, 'Idea for a Universal History With a Cosmopolitan Intent' in *Anthropology, History, and Education* in *The Cambridge Edition of the Works* (CUP 2007) 113. Professor Wood's translation has 'crooked wood'.

[126] I Kant, *Critique of Practical Reason* in *Practical Philosophy* in *The Cambridge Edition of the Works* (CUP 1996) 238.

But the presence of this tension in the doctrines of the classical law of contract themselves is a very different matter. For reasons which follow from commitment to autonomy in exchange and which we therefore must allow are, indeed must celebrate as, in themselves good, the classical law is based on solipsistic self-interest. On the basis of only this, however, it cannot perform its basic function of institutionalising the objective relationship of mutual recognition. It is therefore impossible that the classical law could ever have been constituted only of solipsistic self-interest. That law has always expressed the necessity of exchange being more than solipsistic self-interest, either through what is understood as the flat imposition of 'external' limits to freedom of contract or by intimations of an 'internal' morality in contract which yields action based on mutual recognition.

From at least the time of *Carter v Boehm*,[127] the famous insurance case so often cited in connection with Lord Mansfield's reference to a 'governing principle applicable to all contracts and dealings',[128] intimations of 'good faith' as an internal morality which some way questions and departs from solipsistic self-interest have been identified throughout the history of the common law of contract.[129] I have no competence to review the entire history of good faith, but a history of explicit (or near-explicit) references to good faith would, in any case, entirely cut across the argument I seek to make. In Part 2, I analyse the basic contractual doctrines of agreement, bargain, and remedy (and their background economic and social theory), and show that the law of contract analytically requires a concept of good faith. This requirement is not a call for the desirable imposition of an exogenous moral standard upon a refractory classical law, for this is the core of welfarism. The requirement will be shown to be immanent in the positive law, and its satisfaction will make actual the moral standard within the classical law of which that law is inadequately unconscious, the standard of mutual recognition.

An argument to this effect must, of course, immediately run up against the obstacle presented to the recognition of good faith by what is generally regarded as the definitive modern statement on the issue: the House of Lords judgment in *Walford v Miles*, in which Lord Ackner (with whom all their Lordships concurred) said that:

> the concept of a duty to carry on negotiations in good faith is inherently repugnant to the adversarial position of the parties when involved in negotiations. Each party to the negotiations is entitled to pursue his (or her) own interest, so long as he avoids making misrepresentations.[130]

I do not wish to anticipate the argument of Part 2, but I do think it would be helpful to show at the outset that even this obstacle is not an obstacle to good faith but an obstacle to our self-consciousness of good faith, for in the general sense of relational which has been identified in this chapter, *Walford v Miles* itself is a relational contract.[131]

[127] (1766) 3 Burr 1905; 97 ER 1162.

[128] ibid 1910; 1644.

[129] JF O'Connor, *Good Faith in English Law* (Dartmouth 1990) ch 2.

[130] *Walford v Miles* [1992] 2 AC 128 at 138E (HL) (hereafter *Walford v Miles* (HL)).

[131] I believe that the analysis I put forward of the particular issue in *Walford v Miles* could be traced back to *Hillas and Co Ltd v Arcos Co Ltd* (1932) 147 LT 503 (HL) and *May and Butcher Ltd v R* [1934] 2 KB 17n (CA), and from this to the treatment of 'selfishness' in numerous important cases of the period, eg *North*

Conclusion: *Walford v Miles* as a Relational Contract

In *Walford v Miles*, the defendants wished to sell their photographic processing company, PNM Laboratories Ltd. On their own behalf, the defendants' longstanding accountants, who previously had tried to buy the business, made an offer of £1.9 million. The claimants made an offer of £2 million, and this was accepted subject to contract. The defendants immediately told their accountants of this development, and continued negotiations with them which led to the accountants increasing their own offer to £2 million, and to the defendants accepting this offer. The claimants regarded this as a breach of contract.[132] The claimants did not dispute that the conveyance itself was subject to contract, and the breach they alleged was not of this agreement but of a collateral contract which stipulated certain conditions under which negotiation of the main contract was to have been conducted.

It was clear at the outset that this negotiation would take some time, not least because the defendants sought an assurance of the claimants' ability to pay the price offered, and a comfort letter was obtained from the claimants' bankers. But, aware of the defendants' relationship with their accountants, the claimants were extremely insistent that they would provide this letter, and otherwise commit themselves to the negotiation, only if the defendants agreed to negotiate with them exclusively.[133] It was not disputed that the relevant terms under which the comfort letter was provided were set out in a letter from the claimants to the defendants' solicitor:

> [the defendants] agreed that if [the comfort] letter were in [their] hands by close of business on Friday of this week [they] would terminate negotiations with any third party or consideration of any alternative with a view to concluding agreements with [the claimants,] and [they] further agreed that even if [they] received a satisfactory proposal from any third party before close of business on Friday night [they] would not deal with that third party and nor would [they] give further consideration to any alternative.[134]

The alleged breach was of this contract, which purported to 'lock out' other potential buyers of PNM, including, of course, the accountants who did eventually buy it.

Without going fully into the commercial background which certainly can justify the use of a lock-out agreement in appropriate circumstances,[135] it is necessary here only to say that it was not really argued that a potential offeror cannot in principle protect the expenditure it must make in drawing up its offer by seeking a period of exclusivity in negotiations, and this was allowed by Lord Ackner.[136] Confirming the

Western Salt Co Ltd v Electrolytic Alkali Co Ltd (1912–13) 107 LT 439 (CA) 444 (Farwell LJ), citing *Mogul Steamship Co v McGregor, Gow and Co* (1889) 23 QBD 598 (CA) 614–15 (Bowen LJ).

132 In the interests of brevity, a claim for misrepresentation, though of significance, will not be discussed. This claim was not the occasion of the reference to misrepresentation in Lord Ackner's famous *dictum*.

133 *Walford v Miles* [1990] 1 EGLR 212 (QB) 214D–E (hereafter *Walford v Miles* (QB)).

134 *Walford v Miles* (HL) (n 130) 133E.

135 BJ Davenport, 'Lock-out Agreements' (1991) 107 Law Quarterly Review 366.

136 *Walford v Miles* (HL) (n 130) 139D–E.

Court of Appeal's reversal of the trial judge's verdict for the claimants, Lord Ackner found, however, that the particular lock-out agreement relied on by the claimants was an 'agreement to agree', and as such unenforceable in English law for want of certainty. Lord Ackner believed the law about agreements to agree to have been settled over 15 years previously in *Courtney and Fairbairn v Tolaini Brothers (Hotels) Ltd*,[137] and he approvingly cited the reasoning there of Lord Denning MR:

> If the law does not recognise a contract to enter into a contract (when there is a fundamental term yet to be agreed) it seems to me it cannot recognise a contract to negotiate. The reason is because it is too uncertain to have any binding force ... It seems to me that a contract to negotiate, like a contract to enter into a contract, is not a contract known to the law ... I think we must apply the general principle that where there is a fundamental matter left undecided and to be the subject of negotiation, there is no contract.[138]

In *Courtney and Fairbairn v Tolaini*, negotiations had been started about the development of a building site, but the term which remained to be agreed, about which it was argued there was an agreement to agree, was in essence the price of the extensive works still to be undertaken. Though the case does, in fact, give rise to some concern,[139] it is submitted that it is correct to refuse to enforce an agreement of this nature.[140] But the fundamental reason this is so is, not a want of certainty, but that the voluntary, persuasive nature of any *main* agreement which would be reached in the circumstances of the works contract in *Courtney and Fairbairn v Tolaini* or the sale of PNM in *Walford v Miles*, would very likely or even certainly be undermined were the *collateral* contract enforceable.

Discussion of the agreement to agree is in general undermined by confusion over the concept of the want of certainty. It is not that performance of the principal obligations under any main contract would need an undesirable or indeed impossible level of court supervision in order to be performed.[141] It is that, were an agreement to agree enforced, then, fearing a substantial damages award reflecting lost expectation on the main contract,[142] the defendants would be effectively obliged to reach an agreement (or pay for release), and such constraints obliging the defendants to agree

137 [1975] 1 WLR 297 (CA) (hereafter *Courtney and Fairbairn v Tolaini*).

138 ibid 301H–302; cited in *Walford v Miles* (HL) (n 130) 136H–137A.

139 The decision in the case allowed the defendant to benefit from work the claimant did in arranging finance for the works without the claimant deriving any of the benefit of the consideration of carrying out the works itself.

140 The pricing of complex works and the like, as a whole or substantial part of a contract, must be distinguished from the pricing of standard goods or goods about which a price can be ascertained by reasonable inquiry, which, of course, are dealt with under The Sales of Goods Act 1979, s 8(2). Even more significant is the distinction between possible gap-filling in basic agreement and gap-filling in performance after, *ex hypothesi*, basic agreement has been reached. Lord Ackner was anxious to draw this distinction when commenting on the idea of 'best endeavours': *Walford v Miles* (HL) (n 130) at 138B–C.

141 There could be no question of specific performance and I am unaware of any authority in relevant circumstances leading to, as it were, indirect specific performance by means of prohibitory injunction.

142 The question whether an expectation award may be made these cases of this nature was famously answered in the affirmative by Lord Wright in *Hillas v Arcos* (n 131) 515 col 2, 516 col 2. The judgment at first instance in *Walford v Miles* (QB) (n 133) at 214E–F would lead one to think such an award would have been made, but the parties had agreed that quantum would be determined by a higher court. The matter was

would unacceptably undermine the persuasive, voluntary nature of that agreement. I repeat that, whilst it is entirely conceivable that a party would agree to conduct its negotiations under certain restrictions of its freedom to contract (such as an exclusivity agreement), it is not reasonably conceivable that a party would objectively intend to curtail its capacity to choose whether or not to agree a main contract in the drastic fashion of agreeing to agree.

As much commentary has indicated,[143] *Walford v Miles* can readily be distinguished from *Courtney and Fairbairn v Tolaini*. A lock-out agreement *qua* lock-out agreement is not an agreement to agree. It rather obliges the defendants to negotiate exclusively with the claimants for the agreement's duration. As we have seen, Lord Ackner himself allowed such agreements in principle. The issue is why the lock-out agreement in *Walford v Miles* was viewed differently.

Lord Ackner regarded it as very important that this particular lock-out agreement did not specify its duration.[144] It may have been wiser for the claimants to have specified a date by which agreement should have been reached, and after *Walford v Miles* one would be inclined to take this into account when giving advice.[145] But it is hard to maintain this position in regard of *Walford v Miles* itself, for one can readily see why the parties instead saw the matter as one of the agreement lasting for a 'reasonable time',[146] which, by avoiding a specific date, or by being usefully relaxed about any such date,[147] would itself have minimised one source of pressure to agree. In the Court of Appeal, Bingham LJ, dissenting, had little problem implying the necessary term,[148] and it is not necessary to go into the considerable authority which may be marshalled in justification of his doing so because it is, I believe, generally agreed that, had the lock-out agreement been seen only as a negative exclusivity agreement rather than a positive agreement to agree, it would have been enforceable,[149] and the defendants' breach of it, though it was the principal issue of fact to be decided at first instance, should then have been unarguable.[150]

It was very largely some unwisely over-ambitious pleading by the claimants in response to the perceived difficulty of the exclusivity agreement's having no specific duration that led Lord Ackner to formulate the *dictum* which has led to *Walford v Miles* becoming so influential.[151] The lock-out agreement detailed in the claimants' letter

discussed by Bingham LJ in *Walford v Miles* [1991] 2 EGLR 185 (CA) 188G, 189G–J (hereafter *Walford v Miles* (CA)) and *en passant* in *Walford v Miles* (HL) (n 130) 137B–C, but, of course, these discussions were *obiter*.

[143] Most of the issues are canvassed in JW Carter and MP Furmston, 'Good Faith and Fairness in the Negotiation of Contracts' (1994) 8(1) Journal of Contract Law 1; (1995) 8(2) Journal of Contract Law 93, and in commentaries on this paper in (1995) 8(2) Journal of Contract Law.

[144] *Walford v Miles* (HL) (n 130) 136D–E.

[145] *Pitt v PHH Asset Management Ltd* [1994] 1 WLR 327 (CA) 332–33.

[146] *Walford v Miles* (HL) (n 130) 136D.

[147] I am at a loss to explain why the trial judge's finding that the claimants specified that the exclusivity agreement was agreed 'with a view to concluding the deal as soon as possible after April 6' did not play a larger part in the appeals: *Walford v Miles* (QB) (n 133) 214E.

[148] *Walford v Miles* (CA) (n 142) 188F–G.

[149] P Neill, 'A Key to Lock-out Agreements' (1992) 108 Law Quarterly Review 405.

[150] Evidence that the defendants and the eventual buyers of PNM did not in fact continue to negotiate was not believed by the trial judge: *Walford v Miles* (QB) (n 133) 214F–215B.

[151] *Walford v Miles* (HL) (n 130) 140D.

quoted above[152] was made the basis of the statement of claim, but that statement was amended so that the following was added:

> It was a term of the [lock-out] agreement necessarily to be implied to give business efficacy thereto that, so long as they continued to desire to sell the said property and shares, the [defendants] would continue to negotiate in good faith with the plaintiff.[153]

The purpose of this was to show that the negotiations could not, in the absence of a date for their conclusion, go on forever, but this particular way of doing so purports to transform the negative agreement not to negotiate with others into a positive agreement to agree with the claimants if PNM was to be sold at all, and as such it was rightly rejected by Lord Ackner.[154] Lord Ackner claimed that there was a want of certainty because the main contract was still subject to contract, and so literally had not been agreed,[155] but an air of casuistry about this arises from its being an indirect way of referring to the real mischief, which is that enforcing this specific collateral contract as it emerged from the claimants' pleadings would tend to push the defendants into an agreement in an unacceptable way. The vital clause was not 'negotiate in good faith' but 'so long as they continued to desire to sell'.

If this was not enough, when further pressed on the, as it were, variant point of how the defendants were to end the negotiations if an agreement to sell was not concluded, the claimants suggested that 'a term was to be implied giving the [defendants] a right to determine the negotiations, but only if they had "a proper reason"'.[156] Lord Ackner rightly was unprepared to countenance the burden he saw this imposing on the courts of deciding whether or not any reason given was proper,[157] and this was the precise occasion for his famous comments on good faith:

> uncertainty is demonstrated in the instant case by the provision which it is said has to be implied in the agreement for the determination of the negotiations. How can a court be expected to decide whether ... a proper reason existed for the termination of negotiations? The answer suggested depends upon whether the negotiations have been determined 'in good faith'. However the concept of a duty to carry on negotiations in good faith is inherently repugnant to the adversarial position of the parties when involved in negotiations. Each party to the negotiations is entitled to pursue his (or her) own interest, so long as he avoids making misrepresentations. To advance that interest he must be entitled, if he thinks it appropriate, to threaten to withdraw from further negotiations or to withdraw in fact, in the hope that the opposite party may seek to reopen the negotiations by offering him improved terms.

It can be seen that, Lord Ackner's famous comments on good faith are barely connected with the issue *Walford v Miles* actually presented. In defence of an agreement to

[152] See the text accompanying n 134.
[153] *Walford v Miles* (HL) (n 130) 135B–C.
[154] ibid 139G–H.
[155] ibid 137H–138A.
[156] ibid 136F.
[157] ibid 138D.

provide a period of exclusive negotiations with the defendants, the claimants unwisely argued for an agreement that the defendants agree to sell to the claimants, or give a proper reason why it did not do so to the court. But there is no necessary connection between an undertaking to negotiate exclusively with a party for a fixed or a reasonable period and an undertaking to reach agreement with that party. Lord Ackner followed the claimants in eliding these undertakings and rejected the resultant view of the agreement. He specifically did not believe it possible to 'sever' the exclusivity agreement.[158] Claiming that the agreement the parties had reached was an agreement to agree, and following the claimants in describing such an agreement as a 'good faith' commitment to agree, Lord Ackner held that good faith should have no part in negotiations. He had, with respect, no need to do this, and by doing it his rejection of the agreement to agree as unacceptably resting on good faith blurred his rejection of what precisely was unacceptable about the agreement in dispute.

That agreement was found unenforceable, not because it involved good faith, but because, in the circumstances of the case, it would have extinguished or unacceptably undermined the persuasive, voluntary quality of the agreement it was to facilitate. In those circumstances, and in further response to the claimants' pleadings, Lord Ackner sought to preserve the defendants' right to withdraw from negotiations as protection from an agreement to agree. If his interpretation of the agreement in dispute was correct, then he was right to do this. Rather than the defendants' being bound to agree, Lord Ackner wanted the position to be that, in order to press negotiations to what they regarded as a successful conclusion, the claimants would have had to persuade the defendants by 'offering him improved terms'.

Lord Ackner's approach to the particular facts of *Walford v Miles* is far from clear, and it has been unhelpful to the subsequent development of the law of exclusivity agreements in particular, and of good faith, and therefore agreement, in general.[159] His Lordship was obliged to reject Bingham LJ's reasoning which, though Bingham LJ did not himself use the term, was based on 'severance' of the exclusivity agreement,[160] but one does, I am afraid, get the impression that, focusing on good faith and a proper reason, he talked past Bingham LJ. The significance of the way that Bingham LJ had to distinguish *Walford v Miles* by identifying precisely what was objectionable about the agreement in *Courtney and Fairbairn v Tolaini*—'the terms of the transaction were almost entirely at large'[161]—is not fully appreciated. However, whether Bingham LJ was justified, not in generally distinguishing lock-out agreements from agreements to agree, but in severing a lock-out agreement from the actual collateral agreement reached in *Walford v Miles*, are two different things. If what was agreed was an agreement to agree, Lord Ackner's rejection of this in the circumstances of *Walford v Miles* is, it is submitted, the preferred view.[162] But this rejection was, with respect, the opposite of lucid.

[158] ibid 139C. One of the majority in the Court of Appeal, Stocker LJ, also advanced a substantial argument that an exclusivity agreement could not be 'compartmentalised' or 'severed': *Walford v Miles* (CA) (n 142) 190F, 191B.

[159] DW McLauchlan, 'The Justiciability of an Agreement to Negotiate in Good Faith' (2003) 20 New Zealand Universities Law Review 265.

[160] *Walford v Miles* (CA) (n 142) 190E and *Walford v Miles* (HL) (n 130) 139C.

[161] *Walford v Miles* (CA) (n 142) 188H.

[162] *Walford v Miles* (HL) (n 130) 138H–140D.

Where the line between an enforceable exclusivity agreement and an unenforceable agreement to agree should be drawn need not be discussed here.[163] I can only repeat that, as Lord Ackner himself allowed, some agreements which impose bargaining restrictions serve a valuable commercial purpose, and it is regrettable that the way he phrased his argument would seem to have led his judgment to obstruct the development of the law of such agreements. But this is not at all the point I am trying to make here. The crucial point here is that, far from legitimating the exercise of solipsistic self-interest, Lord Ackner was seeking, in the circumstances of *Walford v Miles*, to preserve the persuasive, voluntary nature of any possible agreement between the parties for the sale of PNM. He may have been wrong in the way he went about this, but, however this is, his motivation in reaching his conclusion is the opposite of what it is generally taken to be.

One intent on underwriting solipsistic self-interest could hardly have found the claimants' position in *Walford v Miles* unattractive, for their self-interest is a prominent feature of the case. We do not know how the claimants learned of PNM's being put up for sale, but, though they knew nothing of photographic processing and one imagines would quickly have sold on the business, they believed the offer price 'dramatically undervalued' PNM,[164] and indeed the claimants' quantification of loss was based on the difference between their £2 million offer and the £3 million which they believed was the market value of the company.[165] In addition to the favourable price, in the negotiations the claimants secured, not only the purported lock-out agreement, but a guarantee of PNM's profitability which it was so very unwise of the defendants to agree that it stretches credulity, but which, if it was an agreement, nevertheless should itself have been enforceable.[166] The claimants evidently entered into these negotiations in the correct belief that the default rules of contractual negotiation impose no barrier to, indeed facilitate, seeking to gain an advantage from what a contracting party believes is the superiority of its acumen over that of the other party. Had they clearly confined themselves to a lock-out agreement as a negative exclusivity agreement, the claimants' further exercise of their self-interest would still have been found acceptable to the law of the contract. But when they very arguably tried to interpret the lock-out agreement as a positive agreement to agree, they pushed their self-interest too far, and their conduct no longer was found acceptable by Lord Ackner, who sought to prevent the unacceptable undermining of the persuasive, voluntary nature of any resultant main agreement. If it were legitimate to pursue self-interest in any way other than by making misrepresentations, on what ground could Lord Ackner have objected to the claimants putting pressure on the defendants by an agreement to agree? He nevertheless found the collateral agreement to be illegitimate and therefore unenforceable.

Lord Ackner's famous *dictum* is, in the end, a very confusing, indeed, with respect, flatly contradictory attempt to state the *ratio* of his judgment. This follows from

[163] DW McLauchlan, 'Rethinking Agreements To Agree' (1998) 18 New Zealand Universities Law Review 77.

[164] *Walford v Miles* (HL) (n 130) at 132G–H.

[165] ibid 135D.

[166] ibid 132H. Apart from the relationship between the defendants and the eventual buyers, their seeking to avoid this guarantee may be the explanation of the defendants not concluding an agreement with the claimants, though they certainly feared that to do so was likely to lead to dispute: ibid 134A, 134D.

a misconception about the nature of, not only economic exchange, but also of contractual agreement. One is obliged to state that this *dictum* is simply wrong about the law. It is not the law that parties to a negotiation may pursue their self-interest in a way which is limited only by the necessity of avoiding misrepresentations. As will be shown particularly in chapter four, in which we will return to Lord Ackner's *dictum*, the English law of contract contains a large number of doctrines which confine self-interest to legitimate courses. Misrepresentation is indeed one of these doctrines, but so is the agreement mistake discussed in the previous chapter, and so is the aversion towards agreements to agree upon which Lord Ackner himself insisted! An adequate understanding of how all this developed out of the positive law has to focus on a concept of good faith.

It is a sign of our current confusion that Lord Ackner's attempt to preserve the persuasive, voluntary nature of agreement has been interpreted as a defence of the solipsistic self-interest which he himself in fact rejects, and His Lordship no doubt understood the issue in this mistaken way himself. Whilst Lord Ackner was in a most important sense right to describe contract negotiations as 'adversarial', and one can appreciate the air of certainty he therefore gave to his statement of the point he was trying to make, he omitted very important features of what he was trying to describe. It is, of course, pure speculation, but perhaps Lord Ackner's real meaning can be understood only by taking into account the extremely elaborate system of rules and courtesy that govern, and so make possible, the legal proceedings that his Lordship, formerly a very distinguished advocate, may have had in mind when choosing the word 'adversarial' to describe a case which sought to insist upon the conditions of proper agreement.

We must, in sum, come to terms with the fact that *Walford v Miles*, like all contracts, is a relational contract. In Part 2 of this book, to which we now turn, I shall claim that a developing self-consciousness of this, centred on the concept of good faith, is the key to understanding the common law of contract's basic doctrines of agreement, consideration, and remedy.

PART 2
THE RELATIONAL CONSTITUTION OF THE LAW OF CONTRACT

3

The Relational Constitution of Agreement (1)

From *Caveat Emptor* to *Caveat Venditor*

Introduction: The Voluntariness of Agreement

As we have seen in chapter 1, it is inevitable and, within its proper confines, correct, that economic exchange and contractual agreement should initially be understood as matters of the subjective intentions of the contracting parties. If the conditions established in neo-classical economics for the existence of general equilibrium obtain in an economy, that economy will be Pareto optimal. Such an economy is perfectly efficient in that goods are allocated entirely in accord with economic actors' subjectively determined choices, and the economy is therefore justified as a system of perfect autonomy. This fundamentally moral justification lies behind the doctrine of freedom of contract, which seeks to legally institutionalise economic actors' power of autonomous, subjectively determined choice.

For general equilibrium to carry this positive welfare implication, however, the fundamental neo-classical assumption that 'each [economic actor] acts so as to maximise his utility'[1] requires that the utility is indeed *his*. That the economic actor 'reveals his preference pattern' 'by his market behaviour'[2] is a condition of ever regarding an economy as efficient.[3] But, far from being able simply to make this

[1] KJ Arrow and G Debreu, 'Existence of an Equilibrium for a Competitive Economy' in KJ Arrow, *Collected Papers*, vol 2 (Belknap Press 1983) 59 (hereafter Arrow and Debreu, 'Equilibrium').

[2] PA Samuelson, 'Consumption Theory in Terms of Revealed Preferences' in *Collected Scientific Papers*, vol 1 (MIT Press 1966) 64.

[3] M Friedman, *Capitalism and Freedom* (University of Chicago Press 1982) 13:

> Fundamentally, there are only two ways of co-ordinating the economic activities of millions. One is central direction involving the use of coercion … The other is voluntary co-operation of individuals—the technique of the market place. The possibility of co-ordination through voluntary co-operation rests on the elementary … proposition that both parties to an economic transaction benefit from it, *provided the transaction is bilaterally voluntary and informed.*

Contractual Relations. David Campbell, Oxford University Press. © David Campbell 2022.
DOI: 10.1093/oso/9780198855156.003.0003

assumption,[4] the law of contract has as one of its most important functions the regulation of economic exchange so that it does indeed reveal preferences. Contract performs this function by requiring that an enforceable contract be an agreement,[5] a voluntary acceptance by one party of a voluntary offer by the other, which expresses the intentions of both. In the previous chapter we noted that Sir George Jessell MR told us that it is essential to freedom of contract that 'contracts when entered into freely and voluntarily shall be held sacred and shall be enforced by courts of justice'.[6] The obverse of this doctrine of the sanctity of contract is that it is a possible defence to contractual liability for a party to show that its contract was not 'entered into freely and voluntarily', and so to deny that the ostensible contract was actually agreed.[7]

Evaluating the reality, if it may be put this way, of the preferences revealed by choice in order to judge whether a market economy is just has, when considered as an abstract matter of political philosophy, given rise to an enormous number of issues, ranging from the absolutely fundamental to the utterly chimerical. A point should be made about the selection of the issues which will be addressed here. Anyone familiar with the practical difficulties of the legal regulation of economic activity in general, and of regulating exchanges by means of the law of contract in particular, can find it difficult not to assume a superior attitude when reading much of the political philosophical literature gathered around the concept of 'complex equality'.[8] In that literature, all sorts of desirable 'end-states' and reallocations of 'resources' are set out, often in the most careful detail, drawing the nicest distinctions, but this effort seems rather wasted as it is quite impossible to conceive how those states and resource allocations might, as a practical matter, be established. It is surely significant that, though elaborately refined proposals to move the law in the direction of the philosophy abound, reference is rarely made to how the positive law of contract has itself actually addressed these issues.[9]

> Exchange can therefore bring about co-ordination without coercion. A working model of society organised through voluntary exchange is a *free enterprise exchange economy*... competitive capitalism.

[4] In itself, the language of the 'revelation' of preferences has a mysterious quality which the distinguished Cambridge economist Dennis Robertson memorably parodied by imagining the revelation being made to 'some latter-day saint [Samuelson], in some new Patmos off the coast of Massachusetts': DH Robertson, 'Utility and All That' in *Utility and All That and Other Essays* (Allen and Unwin 1952) 19.

[5] Offer and acceptance analysis is discussed only incidentally in this book. In ch 2 it was noted that in his early work Macneil exposed the doctrinal incoherence of, *inter alia*, offer and acceptance in a manner reminiscent of Atiyah, and there must be a question whether offer and acceptance as it has been developed now serves its basic purpose: S Bayern, 'Offer and Acceptance in Modern Contract Law: A Needless Concept' (2015) 103 California Law Review 67. The essence of what I would wish to say about that purpose, with particular reference to objectivity as discussed in ch 2, is set out in P Benson, 'The Unity of Contract Law' in P Benson (ed), *The Theory of Contract Law* (CUP 2001) 138–49 and P Benson, *Justice in Transactions* (Belknap Press 2019) 102–17.

[6] *Printing and Numerical Registering Co v Sampson* (1875) LR 19 Eq 462 (Ch) 465.

[7] B Bix, *Contract Law* (CUP 2012) 43:

> If one starts with freedom of contract as a strong principle underlying the formation of contract law, the [formation-based defences to] enforcing agreements seem to follow naturally.

[8] M Walzer, *Spheres of Justice* (Blackwell 1983) 17–20.

[9] R Powell, 'Good Faith in Contracts' [1956] Current Legal Problems 16, 38:

If we use the positive law of contract as an Ockham's razor with which to trim away most of these issues, we may say that contract has had to address two major problems in the regulation of exchange so as to ensure that exchange actually does, as a practical matter, express economic actors' preferences. As they arise from the first principles of the analysis of economic action, these are problems of consumer sovereignty and inequality of bargaining power. They are addressed in the legal doctrines of agreement and consideration. This chapter and Chapter 4 discuss consumer sovereignty and agreement. Chapters 5, 6, and 7 address consideration and inequality.

Consumer Sovereignty

One aspect of the welfare justification of the market economy that requires particular attention when evaluating the contractual doctrine of agreement emerges from the claim that that economy is a system of 'consumer sovereignty'.[10] In Chapter 1 when this claim was first raised and traced to Smith, we saw that Menger distinguished between first order consumption goods and second order capital goods in order to identify in both the essential quality of being used to satisfy consumer wants. This is a sort of dissolving of consumer sovereignty into the broad concerns of neo-classical economics, and though 'consumption units' and 'production units' ('individuals', 'families', 'firms', etc) are distinguished even in as abstract an approach as the theory of general equilibrium,[11] the 'ultimate sovereignty'[12] of consumers over business organisations does not naturally emerge from that theory. General equilibrium theory is focused on economic actors' (ie business organisations as well as natural persons) ordinal ordering of their choices according to their preferences in given circumstances, and is incurious about the questions of, as it were, the social formation of the choices that are to be given effect by consumer sovereignty.[13]

It is unarguable that such incuriosity places a strict limit on the depth of economic explanation, and for this reason neo-classical economics have been subject to intendedly withering 'sociological' criticism. Though this book concludes on a strong note of agreement with this criticism, at this point in the argument it should be said that, once the proper nature of exchange and of the law of contract seeking to institutionalise exchange is acknowledged along the lines set out in Chapter 1, then it is essential to take this incurious approach. In general, this approach is required by the liberal respect for

> When I read of a lawyer trying to tread daintily in the china shops of ethics, I wish that someone would lead him back to the streets where walk all manner of men.

[10] WH Hutt, *Economists and the Public* (Transaction Publishers 1990) ch 16 (hereafter Hutt, *Economists and the Public*).

[11] Arrow and Debreu, 'Equilibrium' (n 1) 61, 63.

[12] Hutt, *Economists and the Public* (n 10) 258–59.

[13] EH Chamberlin, 'Product Heterogeneity and Public Policy (Welfare Economics)' in *Toward a More General Theory of Value* (OUP 1957) 94:

> Granted that the techniques of modern advertising are an affront to good taste, or objectionable on other grounds, it remains true ... that whether advertising is ... a misallocation of resources, simply cannot be answered by any criteria derived from ... the conventional [welfare economic] analysis of the subject.

the *de gustibus* principle which we saw in Chapter 1 is essential to freedom of choice and of contract. But, with reference to the specific concerns of this chapter, treating the actions of natural persons and business organisations as similar in principle generates a ready appreciation that both face the same informational and computational problems of bounded rationality when making choices, and this remains the case even though business organisations may well apply enormously greater resources to the process of choosing than are available to consumers. The development of 'transaction cost' or 'new institutional' economics has greatly deepened our understanding of the context of economic action, and has done so in a way largely consistent with an overall unified approach to choice within bounded rationality.

Allowing liberal respect for the *de gustibus* principle, an economy nevertheless must exhibit consumer sovereignty in order to be justified, for *de gustibus* can be actual only if consumer sovereignty obtains. If the sovereignty of consumers over producers did not obtain, economic activity would in general be pointless or, if directed to some other purpose such as infinite accumulation by business organisations (to which consumers therefore are subject), worse than pointless, and the direction of economic activity by pursuit of profit could have no welfare justification. We saw in the previous chapter that the core of Marx's criticism of capitalism was that, on the basis of the separation of use-value and exchange-value, capitalist production was a 'restless, never-ending process of profit-making *alone*'.[14] Given this, far from promoting welfare, the function of liberal economics would, as Offe has very tellingly put it, be that of 'ideologically screening out the numerous and clear indications that many consumer choices have nothing to do with the satisfaction of [real] needs',[15] obscuring the fact that needs are 'structurally imposed' by 'modern social structures [which] restrict the development of the capacity of choosing, establishing and questioning needs'.[16] It is very instructive to contrast Marx's complete disregard of the significance of consumers' choices about use-values on a market economy directed by profit with one of the most influential assertions of the moral and political, as aspects of the economic, value of that economy, that of Ludwig von Mises,[17] which turns on the strongest claim for consumer sovereignty as the equivalent in economics (indeed far superior in effectiveness) of universal suffrage in politics.[18]

As was immediately recognised by William Harold Hutt, who coined the term 'consumer sovereignty' in the 1930s,[19] preferences are not formed solispsistically by the consumer but rather are the product of the consumer's personality as it is formed

[14] K Marx, *Capital*, vol 1 in K Marx and F Engels, *Collected Works*, vol 35 (International Publishers 1996) 164 (hereafter Marx, *Capital*) (emphasis added).

[15] C Offe, 'Alternative Strategies in Consumer Policy' in *Contradictions of the Welfare State* (Hutchinson 1984) 226.

[16] ibid 225–26.

[17] L von Mises, *Socialism* (Liberty Classics 1981) 400:

> The lord of production is the consumer. From this point of view the capitalist society is a democracy in which every penny represents a ballot paper. It is a democracy with an imperative and immediately revocable mandate to its deputies.

[18] The converse account of democracy as 'a competitive struggle for the people's vote' is due to JA Schumpeter, *Capitalism, Socialism and Democracy* (5th edn, George Allen & Unwin 1976) 269 (hereafter Schumpeter, *Capitalism*).

[19] Hutt's principal discussion was that in *Economists and the Public* to which I have referred. This book was published in 1936, but WH Hutt, 'The Concept of Consumers' Sovereignty' (1934) 50 Economic Journal 66, 66 n 2, tells us that he actually coined the term in 1931, and first used it in a published paper in 1934. Though von Mises' use of the concept, if not the term, can be traced to 1922, the specific term and a number of

and exercised in a social situation which has clear influences upon that personality.[20] Obviously, this ultimately raises the most general and profound issues of the social formation of the individual will which it would be inappropriate to discuss here even were I able productively to do so, which I am not,[21] though I do think I can say that it is merely platitudinous to claim that social formation, which is after all an existential given, in itself undermines the autonomy of will in general,[22] or of desire for economic goods in particular.[23] If we press our acknowledgement of the social formation of desire and therefore choice as far as it could go, 'the self dissolves',[24] and whatever interest this may have for some types of philosophy, it can have none whatsoever for the law of contract. We must be more precise than this if we are to call into question the autonomy of the economic actor institutionalised in contract on which the legitimacy of the market economy ultimately rests. The specific problem that the law of contract has been obliged to confront is whether business organisations are actually subject to the sovereign consumer in the requisite way or whether, amongst other ways of escaping that sovereignty, they play an unacceptably active role in the formation of consumers' preferences, with advertising and other sales practices being an obvious point of difficulty. As Hutt put it:

interesting refinements which have valuably influenced the discussion are due to Hutt, who appears to have been unaware of Mises' formulations.

[20] Hutt, *Economists and the Public* (n 10) ch 17.

[21] With the aim only of clarifying the position taken in this book, let me say that, for what my opinion is worth, that I think it very significant that Parsons' immense efforts to theorise, to his standards, 'institutionalised individualism' ended on the vaguest of notes. There is, indeed, an element of bathos. At the conclusion of a chapter of a book left incompletely revised at his death (T Parsons, 'Individuality and Institutionalised Individualism' in *American Society: A Theory of the Societal Community* (Paradigm Publishers 2007) 459), Parsons told us that:

> I see the possibility that, in the great struggles over emphases on subjectivity and objectivity . . . there may emerge a new synthesis, which is neither objective nor subjective, but in some sense both.

Though N Elias, *On the Civilising Process* in *Collected Works* (University College Dublin Press 2012) 499 is but one particularly distinguished instance of many arguments that Parsons creates the problem by initially conceiving of 'individual' and 'society' as 'existing separately', that subsequent social theory has yielded no advance at Parsons' level would seem to be evidence that, *inter alia*, Kant has said all that we can fundamentally say about the possibility of apprehending (and responding to the awareness of) the 'supersensible' faculty of freedom discussed in ch 1.

A remarkable account of the historical formation of economic action in terms of this conclusion about human volition as causality is given (without reference to Kant) in TL Haskell, 'Persons As Uncaused Causes: John Stuart Mill, the Spirit of Capitalism, and the "Invention" of Formalism' in TL Haskell and RF Teichgraeber III, *The Culture of the Market* (CUP 1993).

[22] GH Mead, 'The Philosophy of John Dewey' (1935) 46 International Journal of Ethics 64, 70:

> the individual is no thrall of society. He constitutes society as genuinely as society constitutes the individual.

[23] FA Hayek, 'The *Non Sequitur* of the "Dependence Effect"' (1961) 27 Southern Economic Journal 346: 'To say that a desire is not important because it is not innate is to say that the whole cultural achievement of man is not important', and FH Knight, 'The Ethics of Competition' in *The Ethics of Competition*' (Transaction Publishers 1997) 43 n:

> One cannot condemn advertising and salesmanship out of hand unless one is prepared to repudiate most of education, and of civilisation in general; for most of the desires which distinguish men from the brutes are artificially created.

[24] Y Mounk, *The Age of Responsibility* (Harvard University Press 2017) 17.

> Our practical problem arises from the fact that individuals cannot be trusted not to usurp, on behalf of the investors to ... whose interests they are formally pledged, the power that society in its sovereign role expressing consumers' will has granted to them as entrepreneurs.[25]

There is a simply immense literature which regards this point as seriously or even fatally undermining the welfare claims of the market economy. Though the historically unprecedented wealth of the market economies has led to them long being described as economies of (some synonym of) 'abundance',[26] a major theme of the economics of abundance has been the criticism of it as not being correlated with, or even opposed to, consumer welfare. One of the most successful, in terms of immediately influencing public opinion, economics books ever written, JK Galbraith's *The Affluent Society*, first published in 1958, emphasised the importance of consumer sovereignty to the legitimacy of the market economy, but went on to argue that consumer demand was 'dependent' on the 'vested interest' in expanding 'output'[27] of what Galbraith elsewhere called the 'technostructure' of contemporary capitalism.[28] The atmosphere captured by *The Affluent Society* strongly influenced the emergence of the 'consumer protection' lobby which addressed a perceived want of consumer sovereignty caused by the ability of producers to exercise an unacceptable degree of control over consumers' choices.[29]

Recognising that consumers' choices are in part determined by actions of producers has led to two main strands of consumer policy: first, a criticism of consumers' tastes, and, secondly, an evaluation of consumers' competence to choose in line with their tastes. It is difficult to imagine that a more theoretically sophisticated criticism of the first kind will ever be mounted than that of Adorno,[30] the central feature of whose Marxist 'critical theory' was a depiction of 'the culture industry' as 'mass deception',

[25] WH Hutt, 'Co-ordination and the Size of the Firm' (1934) 2 South African Journal of Economics 383, 392. In a note to this passage, Hutt rightly enlarges his statement of the practical problem so as to include the possibility which arises from the separation of ownership and control that the managers of a company may act so as to themselves benefit from defeating the interests of both consumers and investors.

[26] S Chase, *The Economy of Abundance* (Macmillan 1934).

[27] JK Galbraith, *The Affluent Society* (40th Anniversary edn, Penguin 1998) chs 10–12. Galbraith's criticism of consumer choice required a rejection of what he saw as an economic methodology which, for reasons of ideology in the bad sense, blocked such criticism:

> The theory of consumer demand ... is based on two broad propositions ... both extremely important for the present value system of economists ... The second [of which] is that wants originate in the personality of the consumer, or, in any case ... are given data for the economist. The [economist's] task is merely to seek their satisfaction. He has no need to inquire how these wants are formed. His function is sufficiently fulfilled by maximising the goods that supply the wants (ibid 117).

[28] JK Galbraith, *The New Industrial State* (4th edn, Princeton University Press 2007) chs 6–8.

[29] RS Lynd, 'The Consumer Becomes a "Problem"' (1934) 173 *Annals of the American Academy of Political and Social Science* 1. The views of both Galbraith and Lynd (RS Lynd and HM Lynd, *Middletown* (Harcourt, Brace, Jovanovitch 1956) pt 4) were formed within an American strand of criticism of 'mass society', including mass consumption, which drew its inspiration, not from Marx, but from de Tocqueville: WM McClay, 'The Strange Career of *The Lonely Crowd*' in TL Haskell and RF Teichgraeber III, *The Culture of the Market* (CUP 1993).

[30] Whilst it would be wrong to deny the sophistication of the learning in the background of Marcuse's criticism of consumerism, its incredible success in the 1960s must very largely be attributed to what are now embarrassing period features: H Marcuse, *One-dimensional Man* (Beacon Press 1964) 23 (emphasis added): 'Those whose life is the *living hell* of the Affluent Society'.

a gross debasement of the entire aspiration of the Enlightenment,[31] which was supported by many vehement attacks upon specific mass cultural practices, such as listening to popular music[32] or reading newspaper horoscopes.[33] Such attacks have undeniable purchase, but though in line with Marx's own disregard of consumer choice, those attacks display a completeness of *contempt* for such choice which characterises the broad attitude of 'western Marxism'.

I do not believe that Adorno's attitude is, in fact, a good, or to be frank even plausible, explanation of consumers' actions, for its contempt for consumer choice of other than 'elevated' goods arises from a very much greater concern to condemn than to understand.[34] Adorno exemplified both the 'Gifted Europeans, horrified at the alleged vulgarisation of taste brought about by industrialisation' and the 'left-wing critics in the [tradition] of Marx who see popular culture as an anti-revolutionary narcotic' criticised by David Reisman for having an 'interest in popular culture [which] springs from the motives … of dismay and dislike'.[35] Informed critics believe that Adorno's opinions about jazz display a snobbishness based on ignorance—Eric Hobsbawm famously stated that 'Adorno wrote some of the most stupid pages ever written about jazz'[36]—and Adorno's explanation of astrology as a psychological comfort to the powerless actually seems to involve claiming that horoscopes normally are literally believed.[37] Adorno's attitude takes for granted, and so gives no value to, the production of wealth in accord with consumers' preferences that is the core of the legitimacy of the market economy,[38] and Adorno was entirely prepared to regard belief in such legitimacy as completely illusory. The 'materially respectable … rise in the living standard of the lower classes' was 'socially deplorable' because, 'In an unjust state of life, the impotence and pliability of the masses grow with the quantitative increase in commodities allowed them.'[39]

[31] T Adorno and M Horkheimer, *Dialectic of Enlightenment* (Verso 1979) 120–67 (hereafter Adorno and Horkheimer, *Dialectic*).

[32] T Adorno, 'On Jazz' (1989) 12 Discourse 45 and T Adorno, 'Perennial Fashion: Jazz' in *Prisms* (MIT Press 1989).

[33] T Adorno, 'The Stars Down to Earth' in *The Stars Down to Earth* (Routledge 1994) (hereafter Adorno, 'Stars').

[34] Adorno, to my mind unconvincingly, responded to criticisms like the one I am making here in T Adorno, 'Culture Industry Reconsidered' in T Adorno and JM Bernstein, *The Culture Industry* (Routledge 1991).

Orwell, who once enjoyed a reputation of being 'capable of breath-taking Marxist paradoxes and epigrams' (R Rees, *George Orwell: Fugitive from the Camp of Victory* (Secker and Warburg 1961) 147) that was meretricious if by 'Marxist' one means derived from a knowledge of the thought of Karl Marx, is an ignoramus over matters of theory in comparison to Adorno. Various of his writings on popular culture demonstrate, however, an appreciation of the range of legitimate human interests, including 'lowness', which inform consumption choices which is a miracle of humane wisdom by comparison to Adorno: eg G Orwell, 'The Art of Donald McGill' in *All Propaganda is Lies* in *Collected Works*, vol 13 (rev edn, Secker and Warburg 2001).

[35] D Reisman, 'Listening to Popular Music' in *Individualism Reconsidered* (Free Press 1954) 183.

[36] E Hobsbawm, 'Playing for Ourselves' in *The Jazz Scene* (Faber and Faber 2014) 300. Hobsbawm had two periods of writing a regular jazz column, during the first pseudonymously, and became a respected jazz critic.

[37] The comments in Adorno, 'Stars' (n 33) 49, on an 'absence of ultimate "seriousness"' are a mere equivocation.

[38] PL Berger, *The Capitalist Revolution* (Basic Books 1986) ch 2.

[39] Adorno and Horkheimer, *Dialectic* (n 31) xv.

It is only if one gives weight to Marx's views of capitalism's historical achievement that his criticism of what he argued was a process of 'immiseration' inherent in capitalist development, which would, if allowed to run its course, cut short that improvement, makes sense.[40] But when maintaining 'the immiseration thesis' became less than implausible in the face of facts undeniable to those capable of facing them,[41] western Marxism bathetically substituted *Kulturkritik* for revolution, and, derived from this, though largely divorced from the profound social thought which gave rise to it, the disparagement of mass consumer tastes is now characteristic of left-wing thought, including consumer policy.

A policy which, starting from the indisputable truth that economic actors' choices are influenced by business organisations, concludes that the state can and should *generally* allocate goods, is, of course, politically self-defeating in a liberal democracy. With the collapse in the credibility of communism, no one explicitly seeks to implement such a general policy, and, in light of what we now know of the satisfaction of consumer demand by the actually existing planned economies compared to the market economies, this is particularly so in regard of issues of consumer sovereignty.[42] But much sophisticated consumer policy and law actually is motivated by a wish generally to second-guess consumers' choices, its disparagement of consumer taste unknowingly reproducing the criticism of false consciousness which is the most odious Marxist concept that can with at least some justice be laid at the door of Marx himself.[43] This second-guessing is, however, perforce carried out only in a piecemeal way, the selection for the occasions of which it is impossible coherently to specify for they depend on the politics of the time.

The fundamental issue is not that general second-guessing is impossible but that it is wholly undesirable. It is, to be frank, merely ridiculous to fail to acknowledge the 'Great Fact'[44] of the immense welfare gains furnished by the mass consumer economy,[45] but even if, pressed to take a position, no credible commentator would outright do so, the problem remains that in the left-wing approach that broadly underpins consumer policy such an acknowledgement would be only grudging.[46] Such an

[40] Marx, *Capital*, vol 1 (n 14) ch 35.

[41] Adorno and Horkheimer, *Dialectic* (n 31) 38:

> gone are the objective laws of the market which … tended toward catastrophe … the standard of living of those who are still employed to service the machines can be assured … the superfluous remainder … are fed and quartered as the army of the unemployed.

[42] As even JK Galbraith, *The Culture of Contentment* (Penguin 1993) 7–8, grudgingly acknowledged.

[43] G Lukács, *History and Class Consciousness* (Merlin Books 1971) 70–81, is the real source of false consciousness. But Lukács undoubtedly is Marx's most profound interpreter, and false consciousness can be traced to eg K Marx, *The Poverty of Philosophy* in K Marx and F Engels, *Collected Works*, vol 6 (Lawrence and Wishart 1976) 211.

[44] DN McCloskey, *Bourgeois Dignity* (University of Chicago Press 2010) ch 6.

[45] On Galbraith, B Loasby, *Choice, Complexity and Ignorance* (CUP 1976) 180, says:

> Consumer manipulation is … a standard theme in Galbraith's writings: since they are formed by the technostructure, consumers' preferences are irrational, and therefore no basis for a properly run society. Fortunately, this irrationality is not complete; there remain enough pockets of rationality to ensure a good sale for the writings of JK Galbraith.

[46] There are, of course, important exceptions. Though Joan Robinson was to the fore of those who argued that Pareto optimality is faced with 'formidable objections … which the orthodox theory has never succeeded in meeting', or have been very ready to advocate intervention in order to meet those perceived

acknowledgement can play no integral part in consumer policy, because there is no actually positive theory of the market in that policy. The theory is all market failure. But the law of contract must reject an attitude like Adorno's because it flatly contradicts freedom of contract in what is a particularly stark rejection of Mill.[47] This is, in fact, rather easy to do if one keeps the achievements of the mass consumer economy in proper focus and respects choices with which one may disagree, for one's disagreement should not be taken as a warrant to deny the autonomy, as opposed to the advisability, of the choice.[48] The former, however, has the attraction of seemingly justifying using the law to second-guess in a way that the latter cannot.

It nevertheless must be said that, though acknowledging the legitimacy of the market economy on the basis of consumer sovereignty by no means rests on a fiction, and indeed the reality of consumer sovereignty is the background of all the most influential defences of that economy,[49] including Hutt's own, consumer sovereignty does rest on a distinct narrowing of focus. *De gustibus non disputandum est* is essential to freedom of contract. Whatever the value of attempts to *persuade* consumers to alter their tastes, perhaps by reference to the way those tastes were formed, the basis of legal policy should not be the *coercive* second-guessing of consumer choice but the actualisation of freedom of choice. There is a great deal of scope for criticism of mass consumer choice on this basis, but such criticism, if it is to be consistent with the values of exchange and contract, must reject direct and indirect authoritarian improvement upon such choice.

Even mass consumer advertising, which certainly poses particular problems, cannot possibly be divorced from the essential function it must be acknowledged to play, if one gives the matter serious thought, in the provision of necessary information,[50] and

objections (J Robinson 'Consumer Sovereignty in a Planned Economy' in *Collected Economic Papers*, vol 3 (Blackwell 1965) 77), she nevertheless insisted that:

> there is a solid justification for the market as a method of distributing consumer goods in the fact that it regulates itself. The task of choosing what to buy is thrown on the consumer, and he, or rather she, feels this not to be a burden but a pleasure and a privilege ... by and large, the freedom of the consumer to spend his money as he chooses may be accepted as the concept of a rational price system.

[47] JS Mill, *On Liberty* in *Collected Works*, vol 18 (University of Toronto Press 1977) 223–24:

> [a] member of a civilised community ... cannot rightfully be compelled to do or to forebear because it will be better for him to do so.

[48] The disparagement of consumers' tastes in consumer policy is a contemporary version of the attitude which Mill, ibid 298–99, described as being:

> suited only to a state of society in which the labouring classes are avowedly treated as children or savages ... This is not the principle on which the labouring classes are professedly governed in any free country, and no person who sets due value on freedom will give his adhesion to their being so governed.

[49] EA Young, 'Increasing Returns and Economic Progress' (1928) 38 Economic Journal 527, 536:

> It is sometimes said [that] since the rise of 'industrial capitalism' ... commerce [is] now merely the servant of industry. If this means that the finding of markets is one of the tasks of modern industry, it is true. If it means that industry imposes its will upon the market, that whereas formerly the things which were produced were the things that could be sold, now the things that have to be sold are the things that are produced, it is not true.

[50] GJ Stigler, 'The Economics of Information' in *The Organisation of Industry* (University of Chicago Press 1968) 182–87.

so cannot be simply eliminated.[51] Adorno was, of course, wholly critical of mass consumer advertising, describing it as the provision of 'information when there is nothing to choose from, when the recognition of brand names has taken the place of choice'.[52] One surmises that at the back of Adorno's mind will have been some nostalgic regret at the eclipsing of the small, independent retailing by mass, standardised retailing.[53] This will resonate with any cultivated person.[54] But, not only is the picture it paints of the organisation of retailing very inaccurate,[55] it simply fails to acknowledge that, as an aspect of what Schumpeter called the 'democratisation' of consumption,[56] standardised retailing is the basis of the affluence of the modern consumer. Standardised retailing makes possible standardised manufacture, and branding, with corollary advertising, plays an essential role in this, allowing the manufacturer to make large-scale plans in reliance on customer goodwill in the form of brand allegiance.[57]

[51] I do not deny, indeed I urge, that certain forms of advertising should be completely eliminated, most unambiguously television and online advertising directed at children. Whilst there are obvious difficulties, such as in this case even determining the age of minority, in principle this policy naturally emerges from the position which this book attempts to state because, in this case, children, of course, do not have contractual capacity and so, in the terms of modern political philosophy, this policy involves 'soft', not 'hard' or 'legal', paternalism: J Feinberg, 'Legal Paternalism' (1971) 1 Canadian Journal of Philosophy 105. A very thought-provoking evaluation of the possible role of paternalism in the law of contract informed by Feinberg's views is put forward in P Cserne, *Freedom of Contract and Paternalism* (Palgrave Macmillan 2012) ch 5.

The pursuit of very fine points in much sophisticated consumer policy debate as much more obvious abuse receives less attention because its elimination, though it would involve smaller moral difficulty, currently is a political impossibility, does make one wonder about the nature of the 'consumer interest' for the benefit of which that debate is being conducted. Even I Ramsey, *Advertising Culture and the Law* (Sweet & Maxwell 1996) 118, is sceptical about regulation specific to advertising to children because 'The myth of childhood as a separate sphere filled with innocents is primarily a Northern European creation of the nineteenth-century middle-class', and 'The issues raised by children's advertising may therefore not be dissimilar from cultural questions about advertising and the dominance of commercial values.' This general issue is briefly discussed in ch 6.

[52] T Adorno, 'The Schema of Mass Culture' in *The Culture Industry* (n 34) 73.

[53] Adorno's nostalgia could find remarkable expression. '[E]arlier popular culture … during the eighteenth century', escaped the strictures he in 1954 levelled at contemporary mass culture in T Adorno, 'How to Watch Television' in *The Culture Industry* (n 34) 140, and so he found it possible to praise *Manon Lescaut* and *Die Zauberflote* for 'striking a balance between the "high" and the popular style almost unthinkable today'.

[54] In perhaps the most eloquent literary lament for the *Mitteleuropean* culture which was the background of Adorno's thought, F Zweig, *The World of Yesterday* (Puskin Press 2009) 8, factory machinery which 'gave the workers power and social advancement' is criticised because:

> it threatened small crafts. Huge department stores and mass production were the ruin of the lower middle classes and small master craftsmen who were still plying their old trades.

[55] I have chosen 'eclipse' in the previous sentence in order to emphasise that small retailing has not, of course, disappeared, and the retail market is made up by a range of sellers providing a range of services the demand for which will vary, in part depending on the nature of the good sold: PWS Andrews, 'Some Aspects of Competition in Retail Trade' in *The Economics of Competitive Enterprise* (Edward Elgar 1993) 247, 258 (hereafter Andrews, 'Some Aspects'):

> the consumer *has* the choice of many different kinds of retailing, including the cash-and-carry multiple store, at lower prices. If he chooses to go to a more expensive type of retailer it is because he thinks the extra service worth the extra cost, and it will be a rational choice … the relative success of … standardised methods [has left] room for the satisfaction of unstandard wants where sufficient people have them to make this worthwhile.

[56] Schumpeter, *Capitalism* (n 18) 160 n 3.

[57] Andrews, 'Some Aspects' (n 55) 253–54:

Within the parameters of mass production, branding performs an indispensable function for the consumer by allowing her or him, initially at least, to focus, amongst the 'literally bewildering variety'[58] of the rival consumer goods now available were each considered individually, upon a segment of those goods to which the consumer has learned to 'come back and ask for more of what he finds satisfactory at its price'.[59] This is an instance of what later in this chapter is called the 'bracketing' of certain possibilities as an essential component of choice.[60] Placed in the context of the range of choice made possible by the mass production that is the basis of affluence, consumer choice is largely situationally rational, and an attitude like Adorno's merely demonstrates that 'One of the things we have to guard against is that we may not recognise rational conduct when we meet it.'[61]

The common law of contract correctly has had little concern with mass consumer advertising, but it is right to say this only if one is precise about what one means.[62] The basic stance has been to leave the credence given to merely vague and emotive statements such as are typical of mass advertising messages, which are classed as 'mere puffs',[63] to the judgement of the consumer,[64] whilst regulating statements, including advertising statements, which, even if subjectively intended otherwise, objectively

> many … consumers' goods … now cost a lot less than they used to, and are much better goods, because they are produced in a modern mass-production fashion. That, in turn, has been possible just because of the orderly development of retail markets on the basis of the preferences and conveniences of consumers … The branding of consumers' goods is a natural complement of this development.

58 ibid 251.

59 ibid 255. 'Or equally', Andrews adds, ibid 258, 'shun what disappointed him'.

60 It has been mentioned that, in principle, business organisations and consumers face the same problem of bounded rationality, and the 'solution' of the problem by the law of contract set out in this and the next chapter applies, *mutatis mutandis*, to both. In particular, business 'character' or 'reputation' normally serves a similar function for business organisations as branding does for consumers: FA Hayek, 'The Meaning of Competition' in *The Market and Other Orders* in *Collected Works*, vol 15 (Routledge 2014) 109:

> the explicit and complete exclusion of from the theory of perfect competition of all personal relationships existing between the parties [is especially remarkable]. In actual life the fact that our inadequate knowledge of the available commodities or services is made up for by our experience with the persons or firms supplying them—that competition is in a large measure competition for good will—is one of the most important facts which solves our daily problems.

Though business reputation cannot be treated in detail in the argument now focused on consumer sovereignty, it is discussed with regard to non-legal remedies in ch 8 and with regard to relational contracting in ch 10.

61 PWS Andrews, *On Competition in Economic Theory* (Macmillan 1964) 100.

62 An aspect of branding that has generated a substantial body of common law is the intellectual property law of passing off, where what seemed to be attempts to obtain excessive protection of brands were rejected because the 'infringement' complained of would confuse only a consumer who was 'a moron in a hurry': *Morning Star Co-operative Society Ltd v Express Newspapers Ltd* [1979] FSR 113 (Ch D) 117 (Foster J). Distaste for this unpleasant phrase, the aggressively anti-competitive efforts of some trademark holders, and a greater emphasis on consumer protection has led to a considerable weakening of this stance in subsequent law.

63 Reading around its period features, the distinguishing of statements intended to induce a very substantial purchase of land which did not ground liability ('a mere flourishing description') from those which did ('calculated to mislead, and … not prepared with the good faith which is requisite in conditions of sale') in *Dimmock v Hallett* (1866) LR 2 Ch App 21, 27, 31 is exemplary.

64 GJ Stigler, 'Can Regulatory Agencies Protect the Consumer?' The Citizen and the State (University of Chicago Press 1975) 178:

amount to contractual statements as, precisely, terms.[65] This approach is, I suggest, far more sensible than is usually allowed, and is to be credited for placing a much higher value on responsibility than paternalism. Such credit will be given, however, only if it is appreciated that the common law of contract *does* have the capacity readily to create liability for statements that, because a reasonable person would consider them to have contractual significance, *are* terms: 'puffery cannot deceive. If it deceives, it is not within the legal concept of puffery!'[66]

It may well be argued that this regulatory capacity of the common law has been much less developed than it should and could have been had its possibilities been more actively pursued,[67] and public regulation certainly has been found to be necessary to fill the gap that is perceived to have been left.[68] But as statute of this sort is *by definition* distanced from contractual values, it will tend to assume an authoritarian aspect, and this becomes clear when a core of paternalist measures, to which the reasonable person undoubtedly would find it awkward to oppose, expands into its, itself thereby expanded, penumbra as political circumstances allow. To take two examples which allow me to make the point sharply, the statutory conditions under which cigarettes are now sold are wholly inconsistent with respect for freedom of contract in respect of a good the sale of which it has not proven possible to make illegal. So ingrained is welfarist paternalism in attempts to influence policy over this issue that there is remarkable frankness about what is an attempt to correct the criminal position by surreptitious means which run counter to economic and political freedom.[69] It is not merely that failure to comply with the regulations for labelling[70] a product it is legal to sell can lead to imprisonment for two years,[71] but that those regulations are so convoluted as to show they have no basis in common morality.

> For the long centuries during which the state concerned itself little with such problems, the consumer had two main resources in dealing with the possible vicissitude of purchasing … The first … was his own intelligence.

[65] *Carlill v Carbolic Smokeball Co* [1893] 1 QB 256 (CA).

A *Carlill* argument was dismissed in an instructively abrupt fashion in a 1981 commercial case, though the *ratio* is difficult to perceive because a grossly excessive number of arguments in misrepresentation, contract, and tort were raised as a consequence of the extent of the welfarist confusion of the law at the time: *Lambert v Lewis* [1978] 1 Lloyd's Rep 610 (QBD) 628; affd [1982] AC 225 (CA) 261F–263C. On *Carlill* in a consumer context, see the 1995 divided judgment of the Court of Appeal in *Bowerman v Association of British Travel Agents Ltd* [1996] CLC 451 (CA).

[66] JI Richards, 'A "New and Improved" View of Puffery' (1990) 9 Journal of Public Policy and Marketing 73, 78.

[67] MJ Trebilcock, 'Private Law Remedies for Misleading Advertising' (1972) 22 University of Toronto Law Journal 1 and JM Feinman and SR Brill, 'Is an Advertisement an Offer? Why It Is, and Why It Matters' (2006) 58 Hastings Law Journal 61.

[68] AWB Simpson, 'Quackery and Contract Law: *Carlill v Carbolic Smokeball Company (1893)*' in *Leading Cases in the Common Law* (reprinted edn, OUP 2001) 288–90.

[69] All Party Parliamentary Group on Smoking and Health, *Delivering a Smokefree 2030* (June 2021) <APPGTCP2021.pdf (ash.org.uk)> (23 December 2021) is a compendium of measures designed to eventually produce the desired outcome in light of the impossibility of passing primary legislation publicly recognised to do so.

[70] The Tobacco and Related Products Regulations 2016, SI 2004/3166, Pt 2. See also Department of Health and Social Care, *Tobacco Packaging Guidance* (19 April 2021) <Tobacco packaging guidance: guidance for retailers, manufacturers and distributors of tobacco products, enforcement agencies and the public on tobacco packaging in Great Britain (publishing.service.gov.uk)> (23 December 2021).

[71] The Tobacco and Related Products Regulations 2016, cls 48(a)(i), 51(b).

The Advertising Standards Authority is a self-regulatory body[72] established by the advertising industry in 1962 to obviate the necessity of direct governmental regulation in the consumer interest which, as part of the growth of consumer legislation which is discussed in Chapter 6, was then being considered.[73] In 2017, the Authority proposed banning 'gender stereotypes', which 'have the potential to cause harm by inviting assumptions about adults and children that might negatively restrict how they see themselves and how others see them'.[74] A rule that 'Marketing communications must not include gender stereotypes that are likely to cause harm, or serious or widespread offence'[75] was introduced into the Authority's Advertising Codes in 2019, the amended guidance to which is composed of masterpieces of cant such as: 'Where an ad features a person with a physique that does not match an ideal stereotypically associated with their gender, the ad should not imply that their physique is a significant reason for them not being successful, for example in their romantic or social lives.'[76] The fearful difficulties regulation of this sort obviously will encounter if seriously enforced follow from its assertion of a mandatory view of things about which, beyond a small core, reasonable persons can disagree. Such regulation is simultaneously vague to the point of nonsense because the disagreement persists in the interpretation of the regulation even as fear of failing to anticipate the interpretation that will be found right pervades the entire exercise. Any possible justification of this must refer to the authoritarian paternalism of a superior vanguard, honestly giving this justification is precisely what regulation of this nature seeks to avoid doing. Leaving aside the public law dimension, regulation of this sort shrinks the Pareto domain which can properly be regulated by the law of contract.

Instead of such explicitly or implicitly radical critique of consumer choice, it is possible to frame the discussion of consumers' sovereignty in such a way as to throw up problems which are of practical importance to the law of contract based on autonomy because they run counter to what that law requires of a voluntary agreement. The second approach consumer policy has taken towards consumers' choices has been to evaluate the competence with which those choices are made in terms of what is now called the economics of information. Granting the potential freedom of consumers' choice, it has been asked whether, in a specific case, the consumer can be thought to be possessed of sufficient information and sufficient computational power to make that freedom actual?

[72] The Authority can, if it believes it necessary to obtain compliance, make reference to the statutory regulators: National Trading Standards and Ofcom.

[73] Committee on Consumer Protection (Chairman (Mr JT Molony QC), *Final Report* (Cmnd 1781, 1962) para 794 (hereafter Molony Committee, *Report*).

[74] Advertising Standards Authority, *Depictions, Perceptions and Harm* (nd [July 2017]) 2–3 <https://www.asa.org.uk/asset/2DF6E028-9C47-4944-850D00DAC5ECB45B.C3A4D948-B739-4AE4-9F17CA2110264347/> (23 December 2021).

[75] Advertising Standards Authority, *The [Committee of Adverting Practice] Code* (12 edn, nd) rule 4.9 <The-Cap-code.pdf (asa.org.uk)>(23 December 2021).

[76] Advertising Standards Authority, *[Committee of Advertising Practice] Advertising Guidance on Depicting Gender Stereotypes Likely to Cause Harm or Serious or Widespread Offence* (nd) 5 <guidance-on-depicting-gender-stereotypes.pdf (asa.org.uk)> (23 December 2021).

The Welfare Implications of Expanding a Consumer's Knowledge

The principal theme of the analysis of consumer choice as a problem of information economics has been the criticism of 'asymmetric information'. As has been mentioned, the consumer will, of course, normally be able to apply less resource to the acquisition and computation of information relevant to a choice than the business organisation with which it typically agrees a contract. This specific issue is one aspect of inequality of bargaining power, and I therefore reserve it for the discussion of such inequality in Chapter 6. However, behind asymmetric information lies the evaluation of consumers' information as such, and to this I now turn.

The issues as they bear on the general principles of contract have been valuably discussed by Professor Bar-Gill in his tellingly entitled *Seduction by Contract: Law, Economics and Psychology in Consumer Markets*. His examination of the operation of the markets in three important products—cell (mobile) phones, credit cards, and mortgages—powerfully argues that consumers make costly, sub-optimal choices in these markets. The transaction costs of gathering information about and then comparing an overwhelmingly large number of alternative products make the idea that the consumer is choosing in conformity with the perfect rationality of general equilibrium nothing more than a poor joke. Bar-Gill relates an industry estimate that there are more than 10 million different mobile phone 'plans' on the market,[77] to which the consumer cannot, of course, possibly respond in a perfectly rational manner. The provision of such a number of alternatives is shown to be a calculated business strategy of generating a complexity the consumer cannot handle in order to exploit sub-optimal choice:

> A main theme of this book is that the design of consumer contracts can be explained as the result of the interaction between market forces and consumer psychology. We consumers are imperfectly rational, our decisions and choices influenced by bias and misperception. Moreover, the mistakes we make are systematic and predictable. Sellers respond to those mistakes. They design products, contracts, and pricing schemes to maximise not the true (net) benefit from their product, but the (net) benefit as perceived by the imperfectly rational consumer. Consumers are lured, by contract design, to purchase products and services that appear more attractive than they really are. This *Seduction by Contract* results in a behavioural market failure.[78]

It is argued that the main regulatory response to this situation should be disclosure rules which will increase the amount of information available to consumers, enabling them to make better choices:

> The interaction between consumer psychology and market forces creates a behavioural market failure. This failure reduces welfare and hurts consumers. Market

[77] O Bar-Gill, *Seduction by Contract* (OUP 2012) 208.
[78] ibid 2.

> solutions exist, but their reach is limited. They mitigate the problem but cannot ameliorate it. The persistence of a market failure opens the door for considering the potential role of legal intervention. The policy [suggested] focuses on disclosure regulations ... [which,] when optimally designed, directly target the mistakes and misperceptions at the core of the behavioural market failure.[79]

Surely one has to recognise a paradox here once one appreciates the precise nature of the problem exposed by the penetrating empirical studies in *Seduction by Contract*. What in essence is exposed is, not exploitation by fraud or misleading statements akin to fraud,[80] but exploitation by the excessive provision of accurate information. The consumer is not misled by inaccurate but by accurate information. How can it possibly be a sensible response to this to mandate the provision of further accurate information? The 'behavioural market failure' is a failure of the consumer to be perfectly rational, which is to be addressed by supplying more information. But the behavioural economics premise of *Seduction by Contract*, and in this it is, of course, perfectly right, is that the consumer can never be perfectly rational. As with much criticism of the operation of the law of contract in consumer policy, *Seduction by Contract* both insists that perfect rationality is unavailable, and then 'pathologises' consumer choice that is boundedly rational because it is not perfectly rational.[81] Policy prescriptions made on this paradoxical basis will tend to fail, or enjoy only limited success.[82] Whatever the disclosure rules, the consumer's information will, of course, always remain imperfect, and the establishment of a realistic bargaining context must be pursued in ways other than the provision of more information. How can this be done?

The particular aspect of the theory of general competitive equilibrium which renders Bar-Gill's disclosure suggestion paradoxical is the infinite complexity bound up in that theory's definition of a 'commodity' as 'a good or service completely specified physically, temporally, and spatially'.[83] A good in the legal sense has a number of readily appreciated physical properties—size, weight, colour, texture, etc—which may be one of the bases of the sale as they are described by the seller. But, in principle, the number of such properties if one includes more recondite but nevertheless possibly vitally important properties such as chemical composition or heat capacity (of the constituent parts if it is a composite good) is very large. Additionally, two physically identical commodities may have importantly different properties arising from their spatial location with regard to the buyer. To the buyer, a locally available commodity may be significantly different from a remotely available one, and the number of intermediary positions also is in principle very large.

[79] ibid 32.

[80] One distinguished member of an earlier generation of US critics of standard form contracting called the mischief he perceived 'lawful fraud': WD Slawson, 'Mass Contracts: Lawful Fraud in California' (1974) 48 Southern California Law Review 1.

[81] J Mehta, 'The Discourse of Bounded Rationality in Academic and Policy Arenas: Pathologising the Errant Consumer' (2013) 37 Cambridge Journal of Economics 1243.

[82] H Collins, 'Review of O Bar-Gill, *Seduction by Contract*' (2014) 77 MLR 1030, 1034 (hereafter Collins, 'Review').

[83] G Debreu, *Theory of Value* (Wiley 1959) s 2.5 (hereafter Debreu, *Value*).

This multiplication of the properties of a commodity is rendered infinite if one takes into account temporal issues. A good will have different values depending on when it is utilised or consumed over its lifetime, a good available now being significantly different to a physically identical one which one may want in the future.[84] In the theory of general competitive equilibrium, all the temporal properties of otherwise physically identical goods are known so that the commodity is 'completely specified',[85] or, as it is more generally put, fully 'contingent'.[86] The allocation of a good which is fully contingent will be Pareto optimal for every relevant temporal state: if we 'assume that the consumers and producers forecast future prices perfectly ... then as the economy passes through successive dates, it will find at each one of them that supplies and demands are in fact equilibrated at the anticipated prices'.[87]

Perfectly rational choice requires an apprehension of the 'state of the world'—'a description of the world so precise that it completely defines all initial holdings of goods and all technological possibilities'[88]—in which all the properties which define a good are known. It must be realised that this extremely abstract concept is of no value to the analysis of empirical economic choice, for the state of the world in this abstract sense cannot be known. In statements of the theory of general equilibrium, a fully contingent good's properties are not, of course, actually exhaustively listed, but are abstractly denoted in a mathematical metalanguage.[89] This cannot without absurdity be thought to be translatable into an actual specification of those properties in any way relevant to policy. Given that the range of possible characteristics of a fully contingent good are infinite, it does not make sense to single-mindedly seek the expansion of knowledge of the state of the world as a way of optimising choice. The expansion will always be inadequate and the computational burden imposed by that expansion will quickly exhaust computational capacity. This is, in fact, what Bar-Gill shows to be characteristic of the markets in the products he examines. If we are to optimise choice of those products within parameters relevant to the empirical world, our first task must be, not to expand knowledge with the aspiration of making the good fully contingent, but to drastically *limit* the knowledge which is necessary in order to make an optimising choice.

If a consumer is to make an optimising choice, that choice must be made from within a range of possibility very much smaller than the range of 'all alternative logically possible decisions' contemplated in general equilibrium theory,[90] with much of that range 'bracketed'[91] in order to allow a workable Pareto domain in which

[84] In this sense, an identical physical good at a range of spatial and temporal locations constitutes a range of different goods: ibid s 2.3. The treatment is, of course, intended to be applied, not just to legal goods, but to all economic goods in an economy, though Debreu does distinguish between goods and services in a way which connotes the commonsense aspect of the legal distinction: ibid ss 2.3–2.4 and Arrow and Debreu, 'Equilibrium' (n 1) 61.

[85] Debreu, *Value* (n 83) s 2.5.

[86] KJ Arrow, 'General Economic Equilibrium' in *Collected Papers*, vol 2 (n 1) 221 (hereafter Arrow, 'General Equilibrium').

[87] KJ Arrow, 'The Future and the Present in Economic Life' in *Collected Papers*, vol 2 (n 1) 277.

[88] Arrow, 'General Equilibrium' (n 86) 221.

[89] Debreu, *Value* (n 83) s 2.5.

[90] KJ Arrow, 'Utilities, Attitudes, Choices: A Review Note' in KJ Arrow, *Collected Papers*, vol 3 (Belknap Press 1984) 56.

[91] I take 'bracketing' from eg E Husserl, *Ideas* (Collier Macmillan 1962) s 31, but do so more than a little shamefacedly and without, of course, making any pretence to replicate Husserl's analysis or, indeed, ambition.

optimising choices may, as a practical matter, be made. Bracketing, not expansion of knowledge of the state of the world, is the absolute necessity for optimising choice, for, as Professor Loasby acutely put it in an important British contribution to institutional economics: 'restraints on free choice are the conditions for any intelligent choice at all'.[92] The impossibility of knowing more than a miniscule fraction of the processes which go into the production of almost any good can, we saw in Chapter 1, be said to be the foundation of Smith's economics, and we should now add is the jumping off point[93] for Hayek's analysis of 'discovery' as the function of competition.[94] Once one acknowledges the number, indeed the infinitude, of the properties of existing and potential economic goods, then this essential implicit bracketing must be acknowledged to be always present in contracts, otherwise exchanges of those goods could never take place. As Black has wisely told us, 'It is not . . . a requirement of economics that the people concerned should be fully acquainted with the commodity that they buy and sell'.[95] The fundamental problem in economics as Hayek saw it is, not the impossible one of obtaining complete knowledge of economic processes, but explaining how it is that rational decisions (and market order) are possible given general ignorance of those processes:

> the task of economic theory [is] to explain how an overall order of economic activity was achieved which utilised a large amount of knowledge which was not concentrated in any single mind but existed only as the separate knowledge of thousands or millions of individuals.[96]

The most important issue which bracketing raises for the law of contract is the formulation of the requirement of agreement in such a way as to accommodate the fact that only a very small fraction of the typical contract can possibly be 'agreed' in any active manner.[97] If it is valuable to say that contract is the result of agreement, as this book turns on believing is the case, this can only be so if we do not fail to see that two radically different meanings of 'agree' are always simultaneously at work in a legitimate contract.[98] It is essential to distinguish what we might call the 'active' from

[92] B Loasby, *The Mind and Method of the Economist* (Edward Elgar 1989) 91.

[93] FA Hayek, 'A New Look at Economic Theory' in *The Market and Other Orders* (n 60) 407:

> it is because a modern economy is so complex that nobody can know all the facts that it could not effectively be guided by a central plan but must be conducted on the basis of decentralisation of decisions.

[94] FA Hayek, 'Competition as a Discovery Procedure' in *The Market and Other Orders* (n 60).

[95] D Black, *The Theory of Committees and Elections* (CUP 1958) 13.

[96] FA Hayek, 'Kinds of Rationalism' in *The Market and Other Orders* (n 60) 50.

[97] E Durkheim, *The Division of Labour in Society* (Macmillan 1984) 161:

> Undoubtedly the initial action is always a contractual one. But it entails consequences, even immediately, that more or less go beyond the limits of the contract itself. We co-operate because we have wished to do so, but our voluntary co-operation creates for us duties that we have not desired. Viewed in this light, the law of contract appears very differently. It is no longer a useful supplement to individual agreements, but their basic norm. It imposes itself upon us with the traditional authority of experience; it constitutes the foundation of our contractual relationships.

[98] And so the principal account of the law of contract in terms of consent in recent times, RE Barnett, 'A Consent Theory of Contract' (1986) 86 Columbia Law Review 269, has, as its author on occasion seems largely to acknowledge, to stretch the meaning of 'consent' so that it encompasses eg, not merely silence, but

the 'habituated' components of choice and agreement.[99] When a consumer chooses to buy, he or she will actively focus on a number of properties of the good that he or she believes 'really matter',[100] normally at a minimum on parts of its express description and its price, but, of course, in differing circumstances the focus can shift. The evaluation and possible improvement of the adequacy of the available information is entirely apposite to the active component of choice. It is the consumer's form of what Macneil called, as we saw in Chapter 2, presentiation. But active choice is possible only because the consumer can rely on other properties of the good (and the nature of the sales process) being consistent with the actively considered properties, and that reliance will normally be unconscious; a matter of habit.[101]

The issue emerges very clearly from another of the leading contributions to the upsurge of interest in standard form (consumer) contracting in the US following the judgment of Easterbrook J in *ProCD v Zeidenberg*,[102] Professor Radin's *Boilerplate*. Radin is exceedingly critical of the absence of agreement in standard form contracts, which she sees as often 'deleting rights' without actual consent in the mere name of contractual agreement. To this she contrasts the 'agreement [which is] the traditional basis of contract'.[103] Let us consider the hypothetical example of an agreement she puts forward:

also ignorance about that to which consent is silently given. A valuable retrospective account of Barnett's views, RE Barnett, 'Contract is Not Promise; Contract is Consent' (2012) 45 Suffolk University Law Review 647, 647, expresses the nub of the argument thus:

> By remaining silent [the parties] have consented to whatever term the law supplies as gap-filler ... Parties who do not contract around these default rules can realistically be said to have objectively manifested their consent to them.

This certainly is so if we can say that the parties reasonably should have known of the gap-filler, and this is indeed essential to the concept of agreement. But using the language of consent to specify reasonable knowledge puts great demands on that language if 'consent' it is to retain its core meaning, and, it is submitted, can obscure the very important point Barnett sought to make. It is very significant that RE Barnett, 'Conflicting Visions: A Critique of Ian Macneil's Relational Theory of Contract' (1992) 78 Virginia Law Review 1175 does not deny the existence of the 'relational' phenomena to which Macneil wished to draw attention, but Barnett's methodologically individualist approach, itself a corollary of a libertarian reluctance to acknowledge the social foundations even of liberal forms of action, requires him to misdescribe social relations in (as close as possible to) individualist terms.

[99] I take this use of the term 'habituation' from T Veblen, 'The Limitations of Marginal Utility' in *The Place of Science in Modern Civilisation* (Transaction Books 1990) 243. Directed at the marginal revolution of the late nineteenth century, Veblen contributed to the criticism of general competition used as a direct guide to policy towards exchange put forward in this chapter.

[100] G Katona, *Psychological Economics* (Elsevier Scientific 1975) 218:

> a human being ... is apt to prefer short cuts, follow rules of thumb, and behave in a routine manner. But he is also capable of acting intelligently. When he feels it really matters, he will deliberate and choose to the best of his ability.

[101] FA Hayek, *The Constitution of Liberty* in *Collected Works*, vol 17 (University of Chicago Press 1989) 128:

> in order to make ourselves act rationally we often find it necessary to be guided by habit rather than reflection.

[102] 86 F 3d 1447 (US 7th Cir 1996).

[103] M Radin, *Boilerplate* (Princeton University Press 2013) xiii.

> Sally says to John, 'I really like your bicycle. Will you sell it to me for $100?' John says, 'Well, I couldn't part with it for $100, but how about $125.' Sally says, 'OK, I really do like it, so how about $120?' John says, 'It's a deal, I'll go get the bike.' Then Sally hands over $120. But John never delivers the bike. After John fails to perform his side of the bargain, Sally can bring John to court . . . and ask that John be found in breach of contract. If the court finds that John breached a contract with Sally, John will be ordered to compensate Sally. Probably John will be ordered to pay Sally what amount she lost by not receiving the bicycle, which could include not only the amount it would cost her to buy an equivalent bicycle from someone else, but whatever amounts she has lost as a consequence of the broken contract, such as being unable to deliver her packages of handmade chocolates to her customers, and having her customers go to other chocolate sellers.[104]

With all respect, this is a highly misleading account. The express description of the good which is the subject matter of the contract and the statement of the price to be paid for it do not begin to capture the content of the contract, for those terms would be valueless were it not for contractual guarantees of very numerous other potential issues.[105] Just to look at things from the perspective of the buyer, and confining ourselves to the physical properties of the good, the strength of the steel from the which the frame of the bicycle was made, the resilience of the rubber from which the tyres were made, etc, all have to be bracketed if the bicycle can ever possibly actually be the subject matter the buyer intends to buy, and the price paid for it the price she intends to pay. At the cost of dwelling on the point, bracketing a property of the good does not mean that that property is unimportant to the buyer, though it might be. Rather, it is certain that some bracketed properties will be vitally important. The issue is to allow the buyer to buy in reliance on these properties, which it cannot reasonably be required to actively know.

This illustration taken from Radin emphasises that the best regulatory strategy in the cases Bar-Gill analyses would be, in light of the realistic scope of their possible understanding of the issues, to limit consumers' choice to a workably limited number of contracts.[106] This does not mean that additional knowledge relevant to the active component of choice may not feature in the regulatory strategy, but it would always have to be couched within bracketed terms which would allow the consumer to utilise the additional knowledge in a welfare enhancing way. A range of more clearly set out phone charging plans could be valuable, but only if the number of alternatives and the grounds on which each of the alternatives comes into effect are so limited as to remain comprehensible. Such a strategy would run entirely counter to approximating to general equilibrium. But it will be the best possible strategy, not because it is a paternalistic

[104] ibid.

[105] It is furthermore the case that the remedy provided will not have been expressly agreed by John and Sally, and indeed is very unlikely to be the compulsory performance that, as discussed in ch 8, is commonly ascribed, though not by Radin, to the intentions of contracting parties.

[106] J Davis, 'Protecting Consumers from Over-disclosure and Gobbledygook: An Empirical Look at the Simplification of Consumer-Credit Contracts' (1977) 63 Virginia Law Review 841 remarkably anticipated the debate occasioned by Bar-Gill and, having acutely weighed the issues, powerfully argued for 'The need for legislative regulation of seller-drafted clauses' (ibid 900) to promote an essential 'simplification'.

imposition of the right outcome, but because, by facilitating agreement in an achievable manner, it is the optimal competitive outcome.

Accepting the thrust of this argument, it is then natural to think of, say, a restricted number of contracts being designed by trade associations in participation with consumer organisations and sanctioned by the state.[107] The very valuable core of this way of thinking is that it shows that, in principle, there is nothing wrong with the standard form contract as such, and, really, once one has taken a sensible attitude towards the development of mass consumer affluence, the recognition of this rather compellingly follows.[108] The standard form, making its own contribution to standardised production, is an indispensable foundation of that affluence;[109] indeed, one can think of no legal device which has done more to enhance welfare. The standard form is not a 'psuedo-contract'[110] but is a perfectly normal contract, not only in the sense that has been stressed in socio-legal studies of contract,[111] that it is of overwhelming prevalence and importance, but that, even in the sense of the degree to which it is express, it is not in principle different from other contracts, for no other contract is fully express or even remotely fully express.

The problems with the standard form arise, not from its bracketing of certain possibilities, which is an indispensable response to an ineliminable feature of contracting which mass contracting emphasises,[112] but from the way that the process of its drafting can obviously invite abuse, which raises the quite distinct problem of abuse of bargaining power, to which problem and its solution we return in Chapters 6 and 7.[113] Publicly approved design of standard forms intended to increase their legibility may be a valuable response. There nevertheless are drastic limitations on the possible value of public involvement of this sort even if one does not question that it is intended to be welfare-enhancing,[114] for, of course, these contracts themselves cannot be fully contingent. Such design can possibly enhance welfare only because the contractual

[107] Collins, 'Review' (n 82) 1035.

[108] DG Baird, *Reconstructing Contracts* (Harvard University Press 2013) ch 8.

[109] T Rakoff, 'Contracts of Adhesion: An Essay in Reconstruction' (1983) 96 Harvard Law Review 1173, 1220–30.

[110] RB Kar and Radin, 'Pseudo-contract and Shared Meaning Analysis' (2019) 132 Harvard Law Review 1135.

[111] W Friedmann, *Law in a Changing Society* (2nd edn, Penguin 1972) 129–32.

[112] RA Posner, *ProCD v Zeidenberg* and Cognitive Overload in Contractual Bargaining' (2010) 77 University of Chicago Law Review 1181.

[113] In perhaps the most radical criticism of the standard form contract ever made, F Kessler, 'Contracts of Adhesion: Some Thoughts About Freedom of Contract' (1943) 43 Columbia Law Review 629, 632, the point was put this way:

> The use of standard contracts has, however, another aspect which has become increasingly important. Standard contracts are typically used by enterprises with strong bargaining power. The weaker [party's] contractual intention [may actually be] but a subjection more or less voluntary to terms dictated by the stronger party, terms whose consequences are often understood only in a vague way, if at all. Thus, standardized contracts are frequently contracts of adhesion; they are *à prendre ou à laisser*.

[114] I put to one side the question of satisfying the demands such design would make of the informational and computational competences of the designer, particularly when, *ex hypothesi*, competition, which is normally the principal source of information about optimal design, has been limited. Leff's important and, in itself telling, criticism of common law regulation of standard forms is, in my opinion, overall undermined by a failure to squarely address such problems as they would be faced by the governmental regulation of 'deal quality regardless of [consumer] information' he (sometimes) advocated: AA Leff, 'Unconscionability

doctrine of agreement, which it is essential not to undermine, continuously accomplishes the bracketing I have argued is necessary for welfare optimising choice by use of the devices of the implied contract and the requirement that parties negotiate in good faith. I now discuss the former in the remainder of this chapter, and the latter in Chapter 4.

The Implied Term

In all ostensibly express contracts, the express terms are in fact necessarily bracketed within implied terms which give the express terms their meaning.[115] If we take Radin's intendedly simple hypothetical example of Sally's purchase from John, in the UK the vital issues concerning the physical properties of the bicycle which have been mentioned would, if John acted in the course of a business, be dealt with by the Sale of Goods Act 1979, s 14(2).[116] This of course provides that 'there is an implied term that the goods supplied under the contract are of satisfactory quality', and this allocates to John the risk that the bicycle is unsatisfactory, however that risk becomes manifest. On the other hand, if, as seems more consistent with Radin's example, John did not act in the course of a business, then no general term allocating this risk to John would be implied, and Sally would bear the risk, the natural construction of a sale between two consumers being that the seller buys in reliance on her or his own judgement as to quality, and this is, of course, the default position under s 14(1) of the 1979 Act. But even in this case, not only is any promise about the satisfactoriness of the bicycle which John makes an actionable express term, but the general conduct of the bargaining process is itself extensively regulated, and I return to these issues in Chapter 4.

A seller in the course of business almost always sells by 'description' under s 13(1) of the 1979 Act, which reads: 'Where there is a contract for the sale of goods by description, there is an implied term that the goods will correspond with the description'. On a first look this provision amounts to an implied requirement that the goods will correspond with the express terms of the contract under which they are sold, and so the drafting appears to create a redundancy, the implied term apparently merely restating the express undertaking to sell the good described. But, though the great difficulties to which this drafting have given rise are examined in Chapter 4, it is essential to see that something like s 13(1) is analytically essential to the law of sales, and so to the law of contract. I will not discuss here the Victorian sales practices which gave sale by description its original meaning, principally seeking to distinguish it from a sale on the

and the Crowd: Consumers and the Common Law Tradition'(1970) 31 University of Pittsburgh Law Review 349, 352.

[115] CJ Goetz and RE Scott, 'The Limits of Expanded Choice: An Analysis of the Interaction Between Express and Implied Contract Terms' (1985) 73 California Law Review 261, 283:

> implied terms expand contractors' choices by providing standardised and widely suitable 'pre-formulations', thus eliminating the cost of negotiating every detail, of the proposed arrangement.

[116] And, if Sally were a consumer, by the Consumer Rights Act 2015, s 9(1). Unless a point specific to the 2015 Act is at issue, I refer only to the 1979 Act in the remainder of this chapter.

basis of the buyer's direct acquaintance with the goods.[117] Even though the legacy of these practices is to be found in a number of regrettable intricacies in the current law of specific goods,[118] it is now clear, if this is the right way to put it, that it is perfectly normal to sell specific goods by description,[119] and I discuss the current law only as it relates to the point that it is sought to make here: the role of the s 13(1) implied term in agreement. For it is vitally important whether 'there is a contract for the sale of goods by description', ie whether the goods are sold by description at all.

It is settled, as both logic and policy would seem to demand save for the intricacies just mentioned, that when the physical goods are unseen by the buyer,[120] the sale must be by description.[121] But a sale by description has the paradoxical quality that, as is now expressly stipulated by s 13(3),[122] it is by description even if the buyer has inspected or even selected the goods.[123] In *Morelli v Fitch and Gibbons*,[124] the claimant bought ginger wine from the defendant licensee of a public house, responding to a question about the price he wished to pay by specifically requesting by proprietary name a particular brand and correctly identifying the more expensive price at which that brand was sold. This nevertheless was a sale by description of a bottle of that brand of ginger wine, which placed the burden on the defendant to supply a conforming physical good, not a sale of a particular bottle of ginger wine which the claimant had, relying on his own judgement, selected and bought as that particular bottle. I shall return to the consequences of this.

The essential feature of the sale by description perhaps more clearly emerges if we consider a sale other than by description. In *Harlingdon and Leinster Enterprises v Christopher Hull Fine Art Ltd*,[125] an art dealer offered for sale to another art dealer two paintings which the offeror stated were by Gabriele Münter, a German expressionist artist of renown. The offeree inspected the paintings and then bought them.[126] When

[117] SJ Stoljar, 'Conditions, Warranties and Descriptions of Quality in Sale of Goods: I' (1952) 15 MLR 425, 441 (hereafter Stoljar, 'Quality').

[118] These intricacies now raise 'the whole question: what exactly do we mean by specific goods?': E McKendrick, *Goode and McKendrick on Commercial Law* (6th edn, Penguin Books 2020) para 11.35 (hereafter McKendrick, *Goode*).

[119] MG Bridge, *The Sale of Goods* (4th edn, OUP 2019) para 7.06 (hereafter Bridge, *Sales*). The tendency of some older authorities to assert that a sale of specific goods is not a sale by description is a clear example of *caveat emptor* thinking, and such authorities should therefore be treated with caution.

[120] And no reasonable opportunity to inspect has been given.

[121] *Varley v Whipp* [1900] 1 QB 513 (DC) 516: 'The term "sale of goods by description" must apply to all cases where the purchaser has not seen the goods, but is relying on the description alone.' *Varley v Whipp* arose because, though unseen by the buyer, the reaping machine which was the subject of the contract was a particular second-hand machine.

[122] The reasoning behind the insertion of sub-s 3 is set out in Molony Committee, *Report* (n 73) paras 426–36 and Law Commission and Scottish Law Commission, *Exemption Clauses in Contracts: First Report, Amendments to the Sale of Goods Act 1893* [1969] EWLC 24, paras 23–25 (hereafter Law Commissions, *Exemption Clauses*).

[123] *Grant v Australian Knitting Mills Ltd* [1936] AC 85 (PC) 100 (Lord Wright) (hereafter *Grant* (PC)):

> there is a sale by description even though the buyer is buying something displayed before him on the counter: a thing is sold by description, though it is specific, so long as it is sold not merely as the specific thing but as a thing corresponding to a description.

[124] [1928] 2 KB 636 (DC).

[125] [1991] QB 564 (CA).

[126] The trial judge had found that, in fact, the buyer did not rely on the description: ibid 570E–H. This is, it is crucial to realise, not determinative of whether the sale was by description, though it may very well be important evidence as to whether it was: ibid 574F–G.

the paintings subsequently proved to be forgeries, the buyer claimed breach of s 13(1). By a majority, the Court of Appeal held this was not a sale by description. The dissent of Stuart-Smith LJ received much support in the academic literature because the, in lay terms, description of the paintings as by Münter undoubtedly was at the heart of the sale. But, it is submitted, the majority was correct because the fundamental issue is, not description in any literal sense, but whether the buyer's reliance on the description is reasonable. It is only when the buyer may rely on the description that the sale is by description. In the business of art dealing, it is by default, and almost always in fact the case, that a buyer must rely on its own judgement.[127] This is also the case in sales of art by auction and, indeed, in most forms of auction.

The issue, then, in deciding whether a sale of goods is subject to the implied term that it is a sale by description is whether the buyer may rely on the seller to guarantee that the delivered good corresponds with its description, and in all but a small number of cases when a seller acts in the course of a business, the buyer may so rely. When the buyer may not so rely, it is because, in the terms of the Sale of Goods Act, the sale is not by description. In a most important sense, the buyer buys, not the physical good, but a description of the good, and the seller's duty is to supply a good conforming to the description. The paradigm exchange is not then, fundamentally an exchange of a physical good but a purchase of a legal duty to supply a good which conforms to its description. A further crucial point about this is that the seller's duty is to supply a good which conforms to, not merely any express words of description, but to what a reasonable party could expect a good of that description to be in all respects.

The relationship of description and quality

Though there are, of course, cases where the buyer wishes to reject goods because they do not conform with description by being, for example, the wrong colour, the most important issue that lies behind disputes whether goods were or were not sold by description is whether they are goods of a quality the buyer could reasonably expect. Recalling what has been said of the fully specified economic good, we could, for the purposes of argument, allow the theoretical possibility of so fully describing a legal good that the good as described would necessarily be a satisfactory good. All the properties essential to the buyer's voluntary agreement to buy the good would be known and agreed. The breach in *Morelli v Fitch and Gibbons* was that the bottle in which the ginger beer was contained was defective and broke as the claimant tried in a reasonable way to open it, injuring him. A description of the ginger beer which included 'in a bottle which will not break when being opened in reasonable way' would, let us allow for the purposes of argument, ground the requisite liability.[128] But the problem really was that the

[127] ibid 574G–H: 'there cannot be a contract for the sale of goods by description where it is not within the reasonable contemplation of the parties that the buyer is relying on the description'.

[128] And so when the buyer cannot rely on s 14(2) because of what in the circumstances of the case before them courts regard as mere technicalities arising from the wording of The Sale of Goods Act, what really is a s 14(2) argument has been allowed to be grounded in s 13(1). In *Beale v Taylor* [1967] 1 WLR 1193 (CA), a motor car was advertised as a '[Triumph] Herald ... 1961' when it actually was an unroadworthy welded composite of the halves of two cars, only one of which originally was from a 1961 Herald. The seller was not fraudulent and s 14(2) was unavailable to the buyer as the sale was private, but the advertised words were

good was not of satisfactory quality (as would also have been the case if, for example, the beer itself was contaminated) because the bottle in which the beer was supplied was defective, which is why we would like to read 'in a bottle which will not break when being opened in reasonable way' back into the description.

Recognition of this relationship between implied terms of description and quality lies behind the following highly perceptive *dictum* of the newly formed Court of Appeal in *Randall v Newson*,[129] an 1877 case decided, of course, on the common law prior to description and quality's codification in 1893:

> In some contracts the undertaking of the seller is said to be only that the article shall be merchantable; in others that it shall be reasonably fit for the purpose to which it is to be applied. In all, it seems to us, it is either assumed or expressly stated, that the fundamental undertaking is *that the article offered or delivered shall answer to the description of it contained in the contract*. That rule comprises all the others; they are adaptations of it to particular kinds of contract of purchase and sale. You must, therefore, first determine from the words used, or the circumstances, what, in or according to the contract, is the real mercantile or business description of the thing which is the subject-matter of the bargain of purchase or sale, or, in other words, the contract. If that subject-matter be merely the commercial article or commodity, the undertaking is that the thing offered or delivered shall answer to that description, that is to say, shall be that article or commodity, saleable or merchantable.[130]

This is profoundly correct. The most important point is that, by default, the implied terms as to quality must be read into sales by description or sale as the basis of a general market economy is impossible. But, despite the many criticisms that have been made of Mackenzie, later Sir Mackenzie, Chalmers' drafting at this crucial point of the Sale of Goods Act 1893, his distinguishing of ss 14 and s 13(1), and adding the former to the latter, turns on a perceptive recognition that the best basic approach was to address quality directly.[131] This is because seeking to create liability for defects of quality by an ever more precise express description is, first, a practical impossibility, and, secondly, a merely tangential, and, as I shall argue, actually misleading response to the problem which it is trying to address.

found to be part of the description, allowing nonconformity to justify rejection. This was done at some cost to the construction of s 13(1) and to the common law distinction between representations and terms, and is not ultimately defensible save in terms of the court's evident belief that doing it was necessary to do justice in the case before it. The reasoning in *T and J Harrison v Knowles and Foster* [1918] 1 KB 603 (CA), which was not cited in *Beale v Taylor*, is, it is submitted, to be preferred.

129 (1877) 2 QBD 102 (CA).

130 ibid 109.

131 The distinguishing of s 13(1) and s 14 allows sales to be by description but not to have guarantees of quality and, of course, the latter are implied only into commercial sales by ss 14(1)–(3). Conversely, it allowed description to be added to quality, and so a satisfactory good which is not in conformity with description may be rejected, such an in itself satisfactory ginger beer in an in itself satisfactory bottle which was incorrectly labelled and not the brand the claimant in *Morelli v Fitch and Gibbons* offered to buy. This 'additionality' has been the occasion of much difficulty, discussed in ch 4.

Some perception that the ever more precise approach is a practical impossibility lies behind the disdain for the 'Aristotelian' or 'metaphysical' or 'philosophical' problems said to be involved in the concepts of 'attribute', 'identity', 'substance', etc involved in completely accurately describing a good, or any other object, in much judicial *dicta* and distinguished commentary.[132] We have seen that, in terms of general equilibrium theory, the properties to be described are infinite, and so an attempt to improve the description by accumulation of detail is in principle futile.[133] Such an accumulation can, to repeat, be of value only in the context of the bracketing of the remaining infinite number of properties, and this is exactly what the common law of description and the interpretation of s 13(1) does.[134] This law provides a different principle to guide the adequacy of description, replacing mere accumulation of detail with a 'test of a mercantile character'. In the famous words of Lord Wilberforce:

> I do not believe that the Sale of Goods Act was designed to provoke metaphysical discussions as to the nature of what is delivered in comparison with what is sold. The test of description ... is intended to be a broader, more common sense, test of a mercantile character. The question is whether that is what the buyer bargained for has to be answered according to such tests as men in the market would apply, leaving more delicate questions of condition, or quality, to be determined under other clauses of the contract or sections of the Act.[135]

And so, in one case which has found a place in the authorities, a delivery of the industrial chemical oxalic acid which contained 10% of sulphate of magnesium was found not to be 'oxalic acid' because the admixture changed the good's commercial character, ie the uses to which it could be put.[136] In contrast, a delivery of 'Argentina Bolita beans', which are white, that contained a small (1.8%) but, it was argued, 'commercially significant' proportion of coloured beans, was referred back to an Umpire to clarify whether this delivery would still be regarded in the trade as properly described.[137] Mustill J observed, with reference to the *dicta* of Lord Wilberforce, that 'the question of compliance with description [was] one for the "men in the market"', and not for the Court.[138] The Umpire found for the sellers.[139] The mercantile character of

[132] Eg McKendrick, *Goode* (n 118) paras 11.36–11.40.

[133] See text accompanying n 85.

[134] This issue is distinct from, though obviously intimately connected to, the problem with the perfect tender rule discussed in ch 9.

[135] *Ashington Piggeries Ltd v Christopher Hill Ltd* [1972] AC 441 (HL) 489F–G.

[136] *Josling v Kingsford* (1863) 13 CB(NS) 447; 143 ER 177.

[137] *Gill and Duffus SA v Berger and Co Inc* [1981] 2 Lloyd's Rep 233 (Com Ct). The beans also showed signs of insect infestation. There being no argument that the seller had breached a warranty of quality, the issue was whether the defendant buyer, the remedies of which in regard of quality were limited, ibid 235, could reject the entire consignment under s 13.

[138] ibid 236 col 2.

[139] *Gill and Duffus SA v Berger and Co Inc* [1983] 1 Lloyd's Rep 622 (CA) 623 col 1. The value of the Umpire's finding and of Mustill J's wise observation was undermined in the case by the apparent incompetence of an arbitral Board of Appeal, which reversed the Umpire on grounds which never became clear. This incompetence was perhaps the most important of a number of regrettable factors which led to very protracted and in part meretricious litigation which Lord Roskill, *Berger and Co Inc v Gill and Duffus SA* [1984] AC 382 (HL) 388D, described as 'a disgrace to the judicial system'. During this litigation, the case 'managed

description provides the necessary narrowing of the range of choices which allows exchanges to be made. An unhelpful expansion of that range, either intentionally by business organisations seeking to defeat choice in the way criticised by Bar-Gill, or inadvertently by pursuing an increase in information as an attempt to approximate to full contingency in the way that lies behind Bar-Gill's thinking, will decrease the power of welfare-enhancing choice.

The morality of the implied term

Not only is the general approach of increasing information futile but the second criticism that may be made of it is that it is merely tangential to the problem at issue. The implied term does not work by providing information about the content of a contract in any direct way, and in this sense it can be quite misleading to think of the issue of being one of the 'incompleteness' of contracts, for this naturally lead one to think of completing the contracts, when, as discussed in Chapter 4, contracts can never be complete in this 'informational' way. This is by no means to deny that there is indeed much 'gap-filling' to do,[140] for all contracts are almost all gaps, but the gaps are filled, not by directly supplying an extra piece of information, but by specifying a moral rule of legitimate conduct in contract in a way which I describe in the remainder of this chapter and in Chapter 4.

The legal reasoning involved in the process I am trying to set out was described, though not with specific reference to contract, by Hayek:

> There never has been and there never can be a 'gap-less' system of formulated rules . . . not only has no made law ever succeeded in replacing the already recognised rules of justice which it presupposes or even succeeded in dispensing with explicit references to such unarticulated conceptions of justice, but the whole process of development, change and interpretation of the law would become wholly unintelligible if we closed our eyes to the existence of a framework of such unarticulated rules from which the articulated law receives its meaning.[141]

It being impossible exhaustively to specify all the potentially relevant characteristics of (to remain focused on sales) the quality of a legal good by expressly stating them as terms of a contract, the commercial seller undertakes to provide a good which is satisfactory (or fit for purpose). This is a general, open-ended duty[142] to sell a good

to acquire a deceptive appearance of complexity', ibid, and it was ultimately decided on a ground at some distance from the instructive s 13 point.

[140] I Ayres and R Gertner, 'Filling Gaps in Incomplete Contracts: An Economic Theory of Default Rules' (1989) 99 Yale Law Journal 87.

[141] FA Hayek, 'The Results of Human Action but Not of Human Design' in *The Market and Other Orders* (n 60) 299.

[142] To those familiar with the discussion of 'rules' and 'principles' in legal philosophy and regulatory theory, this use of 'duty' seems inappropriate, because it is normally taken in that discussion that 'Rules prescribe relatively specific acts; principles prescribe highly unspecific actions' (J Raz, 'Legal Principles and the Limits of the Law' (1972) 81 Yale Law Journal 823, 838), and it will be seen that I am arguing that, in this sense, the quality duties are principles. It would, of course, be the merest affectation to seek to use

which meets, as the Sale of Goods Act 1979, s 14(2A) now has it, 'the standard that a reasonable person would regard as satisfactory, taking account of any description of the goods, the price (if relevant) and all the other relevant circumstances'. The work of identifying the duty is done, not by fruitless pursuit of detail, but by use of the concept of reasonableness. It is perfectly right to say that interpretation of s 14(2), as always with interpretations of reasonableness, initially seems to be merely circular,[143] satisfactory being, as we have seen, meeting 'the standard that a reasonable person would regard as satisfactory'. But it is wrong to say that this definition is circular in the sense that it actually lacks content. The point is that the content is furnished, not by *ex ante* provision of detailed information, but by the *ex ante* recognition of a general, open-ended duty.

The quality duty certainly will not have a completely expressly specified content at the time of the sale, or how could disputes ever arise? Content relevant to any dispute which may arise (most of the content of the sale never becomes explicit in any dispute) is supplied by (to take the paradigm case) the claimant buyer when in possession learning of and complaining about a characteristic of the good of importance to it about which, *ex hypothesi*, it had no knowledge at the time of sale. The decision in such a case then turns on whether, focusing on the characteristic previously unknown but now specified by being complained about, the good should have been regarded as satisfactory when sold.

In an influential formulation, Dixon J defined merchantable quality thus:

> The condition that goods are of merchantable quality requires that they should be in such an actual state that *a buyer fully acquainted with the facts* and, therefore, knowing what hidden defects exist and not being limited to their apparent condition, would buy them without abatement of the price obtainable for such goods if in reasonably sound order and condition and without special terms.[144]

The wide endorsement of this definition, despite its turning on hidden defects which are known and an appearance which is penetrated, shows the extent of the difficulties that have been encountered.[145] It would, with respect, have been much better if the crucial part of the definition, which has been emphasised in the quotation above, had read 'a buyer, *if* fully acquainted with the facts'. To do this requires us to acknowledge that the decision in important quality cases, as with all disputes over implied terms,[146]

'principles' for what in the usage of the law of contract and sales is a duty, and it is incidental to the point I seek to make here. I seek to point to the other-regarding, relational content of a legal duty that the classical law tries to treat in a way consistent with solipsistic self-interest.

[143] C Twigg-Flessner and R Canavan, *Atiyah and Adams' Sale of Goods* (14th edn, Pearson 2021) 141 (hereafter Twigg-Flessner and Canavan, *Sale of Goods*). Putting aside the merits or otherwise of replacing 'merchantable' with 'satisfactory', these criticisms may, of course, be levelled at merchantable quality under the Sale of Goods Act 1893.

[144] *Australian Knitting Mills Ltd v Grant* (1933) 50 CLR 387 (HCA) 418 (emphasis added).

[145] The confusion in what are analysed as 'hidden defects' has, accordingly, often been lamentable: eg the imputation to the buyer of 'full knowledge', including circumstances it could not *ex ante* reasonably expect to have arisen, in *(Henry) Kendall and Sons (A Firm) v William Lillico and Sons Ltd* [1969] 2 AC 31 (HL) 55B.

[146] *Phillips Electronique Grand Public SA v British Sky Broadcasting* [1995] EMLR 472 (CA) 481 (Lord Bingham MR): 'the court comes to implication with the benefit of hindsight'. Lord Bingham's specific

is in an undeniable sense retrospective, and as retrospective adjudication as such is unjust, to be clear about how reaching a decision in this way can be justified.[147]

The seller knows *ex ante* it has a duty to provide a satisfactory good, but *precisely* how it should perform this duty cannot be fully specified *ex ante*. This is instead a question of the seller trying to anticipate and meet the buyer's standards in order to persuade it to buy. Striving to do this is, as a matter of economic or business understanding, how a commercial seller may *legitimately* attempt to gain a buyer's custom, and this is a vital aspect of consumer sovereignty as a justification of the market economy. Analysing competition as involving the *three* roles of two competing suppliers and a buyer, Simmel tells us that:

> The aim for which competition occurs ... is ... the favour of one or more third persons. Each of the competing parties therefore tries to come as close to that third one as possible ... competition ... has [an] immense sociating effect. Competition compels the wooer who has a co-wooer ... to go out to the wooed, come close to him, establish ties with him, find his strengths and weakness and adjust to them, find all bridges, or cast new ones, which might connect the competitor's own being and doing with his ... Innumerable times [competition] achieves what usually only love can do: the divination of the innermost wishes of the other, even before he himself becomes aware of them. Antagonistic tension with his competitor sharpens the businessman's sensitivity to the tendencies of the public ... Modern competition is described as the fight of all against all, but at the same time it is the fight of all *for* all.[148]

The implied term as to quality institutionalises this economic practice as a legal duty. It is, of course, impossible to grasp this if one believes that the legitimate standard of contracting behaviour is the narrow pursuit of solipsistic self-interest rather than open ended-respect for (the standard necessary to satisfy) the other party. Such a belief is unable to distinguish between the legitimate and the illegitimate pursuit of self-interest, and thus finds the seeming restriction of self-interest by the law of contract rather a puzzle, though this restriction is actually regulatory facilitation, without which standard sales could not take place.

The, as it were, technical, legal issues could not be better analysed than they were by Rougier J in *Bernstein v Pamson Motors (Golders Green) Ltd.*[149] A brand new car completely broke down, with much consequent inconvenience, after only 140 miles of use, and the consumer buyer wished to reject it, despite the defect, though it had had serious consequences on this occasion, being trivial and easily repaired. Whether one agrees with the finding that the car was unmerchantable is of less importance than the

concern in this discussion of implied terms was not with retrospectivity as such but with welfarist rewriting of the contract with the benefit of hindsight, which is, as he wisely said, 'Tempting, but wrong'.

[147] LL Fuller, *The Morality of Law* (rev edn, Yale University Press 1969) 44 was most acutely aware that, whilst it was 'one of the most obvious seeming demands of legality', avoiding retrospectivity 'turns out to present some of the most difficult problems of the whole internal morality of law'.

[148] G Simmel, 'Conflict' in *"Conflict" and "The Web of Group Affiliations"* (Free Press 1955) 61–62.

[149] [1987] 2 All ER 220 (QB).

way in which the decision was reached.[150] Having been told that the case was of public importance because the car trade was desirous of 'some more specific guidance and definition as to what makes a motor car merchantable', Rougier J declined to proffer such guidance because he 'very much [doubted] whether any all-embracing definition of a car of merchantable quality could ever be made'. The drafter of the 1893 Act had left merchantable quality 'undefined, merely to be understood in the ordinary commercial sense in which commercial men would interpret it', and the drafters of the 1979 re-enactment also 'left [it] in the widest possible terms in order to cater for the great variety of situations which may occur'. This was wise because:

> Any attempt to forge some exhaustive, positive and specific definition of such a term, applicable in all cases, would soon be put to mockery by some new undreamt of set of circumstances.[151]

Though the most important thing to note is the continued immense utility of Chalmers' essential achievement, the call for greater *ex ante* definition of merchantable or satisfactory quality has, of course, often been repeated.[152] But the concession to this call represented by the insertion into the 1979 Act of what is now s 14(2B),[153] which lists five illustrative aspects of quality such as 'appearance and finish', 'safety', 'freedom from minor defects', and 'durability', is (ignoring the difficulties it might actually introduce which are, with respect, obvious) instructively fruitless. In what material sense are any of these aspects of satisfactory quality more precisely defined than satisfactory quality itself? The attitude Chalmers took towards defining 'merchantable' endorsed by Rougier J is much to be preferred.[154]

As the case law develops, an increasing number of examples of what has been found to be satisfactory or otherwise will, of course, accumulate for the future guidance of the seller. But, at the cost of repetition, it is not so much that any such accumulation cannot possibly approximate to the general equilibrium condition of full contingency, but that *ex ante* accumulation of specific information is not the principal issue. In all disputes, the facts can come to be objectively known only *ex post*. The retrospectivity of reaching a decision on these facts is, however, not merely unavoidable but, when properly understood, normally unproblematic.

[150] ibid. The issue was whether it is reasonable to reject a brand new car for any defect, or at least any defect that has led to a breakdown as in the case itself, for of course the buyer's satisfaction from new ownership will be appreciably diminished, and though the issue is difficult and I personally do not agree with Rougier J's decision, that decision is at least defensible once this is understood. The later legislative identification of 'Freedom from minor defects' which is to be discussed shortly surely could not have been intended to allow rejection just for a slight, easily repairable defect without the context, such as that which Rougier J addressed, being taken into account. Any intention to do so, without which these refinements are hard to understand, will therefore be contradicted by limits on the rights to reject and replace under the new legislation in ways which deplorable drafting makes too complicated to set out at proportionate length here.

[151] This and the previous 4 quotations are at ibid 222c–h.

[152] J Morgan, 'Compulsion, Choice and Statutory Intervention in Contract' in TT Arvind and J Steele (eds), *Contract Law and the Legislature* (Hart 2020) 166–77 (hereafter Morgan, 'Compulsion').

[153] Sale and Supply of Goods Act 1994, s 1. See also Consumer Rights Act 2015, s 9(3).

[154] MG Bridge, 'The Evolution of Modern Sales Law' [1991] Lloyds Maritime and Commercial Law Quarterly 52.

It is impossible to specify the precise content of the commercial seller's duty to meet 'the standard that a reasonable person would regard as satisfactory' *ex ante*. But the seller knows perfectly well *ex ante* that it has to conduct itself so as to perform this duty *in the precise circumstances as they should come to be known to the seller in course of performance*, given that the parties 'must be credited with knowledge of the transaction and its background'.[155] The buyer's coming to believe that there is a lack of quality and the court's objective verdict about this are indeed retrospective because the precise circumstances can come to be known to the buyer and the court only *ex post*. But this does not at all effect the *ex ante* obligation of the seller, and should give rise to no concern in the normal case when it is settled that the failures of quality are those about which a seller should have known (or even did know, though there is no need to prove this to ground liability).

Concern understandably arises, however, because, regrettably but inevitably, reasonable disputes about what quality is will arise at the margin, and the settling of these disputes by the courts will require retrospective adjustment of one of the parties' formerly held opinions.[156] This, however, is not a problem about s 14(2) as such but about the openness of the meaning of the reasonable standard and, indeed, about the nature of the adjudication of 'hard' cases.[157] To the extent that the court's decision about what is satisfactory captures, as it should, the parties' intentions, these problems will be minimised. But the existence of hard cases at the margin should not be denied.

In deciding cases under s 14(2), the reasonable person can, of course, be a consumer, but this should mean a reasonable consumer, one cognisant of the relevance of price when set in the context of the sale[158] and not insistent upon a standard of quality regardless of these factors. Of course, in the age of consumer rights, a tendency of consumers to want to stand on rights for which they have not paid,[159] and to be encouraged to do so by those promoting those rights, can be an important issue.[160]

155 *Bramhill v Edwards* [2004] EWCA Civ 403; [2004] 2 Lloyd's Rep 653 [41] (Auld LJ).

156 I do not wish to further complicate the discussion so will merely state that I regard this argument as essentially reconcilable with Hayek's Diceyan insistence that just laws must be stipulated in advance. What is being stipulated is, as Hayek required, the rule for 'general types of situations' rather than its precise application (FA Hayek, *The Road to Serfdom* in *Collected Works*, vol 2 (University of Chicago Press 2007) 114). I do, however, think that Hayek failed to appreciate the inevitability of retrospectivity.

157 ML Friedland, 'Prospective and Retrospective Judicial Law-making' (1974) 24 University of Toronto Law Journal 170.

158 Sale of Goods Act 1979 s 14(2A) and Consumer Rights Act 2015 s 9(2)(b).

159 Bridge, *Sales* (n 119) para 7.03:

> there exist commonplace misunderstandings that ... buyers may freely return goods to retail sellers for no other reason than a change of mind.

160 In respect of the fundamental concepts of the law of contract, the most significant recent issue has been the provision of more extensive consumer rights, effectively wider rights to forms of literal enforcement, initially under a new Pt 5A of the Sale of Goods Act 1979. As is now all but customary when altering the general principles of the contract in this way, the revised legislation was slipshod, and, following criticism in Law Commission and Scottish Law Commission, *Consumer Remedies for Faulty Goods* [2009] EWLC 317, Pt 5A was replaced by the Consumer Rights Act 2015, s 19. Leaving aside the continuing shortcomings of drafting as too tedious to discuss, these new remedies continue to fail to conceptually grasp the function of the requirement of inadequacy of damages in the previous law of literal enforcement. The issue will be briefly discussed in ch 9.

Implication in law and fact

If we distinguish terms implied in fact and terms implied in law by describing the latter as terms mandatorily incorporated into contracts regardless of the intentions of the parties, how should we classify the implied terms of description and quality? I believe that, though they are statutory, the implied terms of quality and fitness are not a state intervention but were fundamentally derived from the spontaneous economic action of contracting parties as it could be known from existing commercial practice, and so should be classified as terms implied in fact. The original Sale of Goods Act, the long title of which was 'An Act for codifying the Law relating to the Sale of Goods', was understood by its drafter to be a codification of commercial practice which 'endeavoured to reproduce as exactly as possible the existing law',[161] and, without going into a complex matter,[162] which includes instances of frustration of the draftsman's intent during Parliamentary debate, I would say that the subsequent case law has very largely confirmed that this was so.[163] The terminology in the cases is so inconsistent

[161] MD Chalmers, *The Sale of Goods Act 1893* (2nd edn, William Clowes and Sons 1894) iv–v tells us that the Bill he drafted 'endeavoured to reproduce as exactly as possible the existing law' and that 'the conscious changes' introduced in the course of the extensive Parliamentary debate were only 'very slight'. On Chalmers' more general views on the Parliamentary hazards of codification see MD Chalmers, 'Experiment in Codification' (1886) 2 Law Quarterly Review 125 and MD Chalmers, 'Codification of Mercantile Law' (1903) 19 Law Quarterly Review 10.

The common law of merchantable quality was influentially stated in *Jones v Just* (1868) LR 3 QB 197 (QB), discussed in Chalmers, *Sale of Goods Act 1893*, ibid 20–23. I cannot here address claims that this statement's unequivocal rejection of a law based on *caveat emptor* is contradicted by the actual decision in the case. It is more germane to note that, with respect, Professor Stapleton overemphasises the absence of an opportunity to inspect when, citing *Jones v Just*, she says inspection being '*impossible* . . . became a precondition of the implied warranty of merchantability at common law', going on then to say that, by phrasing inspection as an exception to general implied liability, s 14(2) allowed 'a remedy for commercial buyers' to become 'the warranty which later proved to be of most importance to consumers': J Stapleton, *Product Liability* (Butterworths 1994) 14. What Stapleton says is, of course, right in itself, but the 'mystery' (ibid 67) of the apparent transformation is largely resolved if it is realised that her point carries a different burden if, for the reasons set out in this chapter, inspection in the sense of the buyer being responsible for the quality of the goods is usually impossible for both consumers and business organisations, and inspection (if this is the right word) properly understood has and must have a minimal role in sales by description (see the text accompanying n 123). Chalmers was of the view that s 14 'probably narrows somewhat the already restricted rule of *caveat emptor*': Chalmers, *Sale of Goods Act 1893*, ibid 30.

I say, not in criticism but from a belief that to say nothing would be unfair, that the value of Stapleton's own grasp of the 'economic efficiency' argument (Stapleton, *Product Liability*, ibid 12) is curtailed because she identifies such efficiency with Posnerian wealth maximisation (ibid ch 5), though it actually is a form of welfare economics entirely opposed to Pareto optimisation: D Campbell, 'Welfare Economics for Capitalists: The Economic Consequences of Judge Posner' (2012) 33 Cardozo Law Review 2233.

[162] P Mitchell, 'The Development of Quality Obligations in Sales of Goods' (2001) 117 Law Quarterly Review 645, 663 (hereafter Mitchell, 'Quality Obligations') is but one of a number of highly interesting claims that, despite Chalmers' own opinion, in effect, it was 'impossible' for the Act 'to do justice to the law as it stood', giving interesting detail about the Parliamentary debate in support of this. But, with great respect and with considerable hesitancy given the limits of my knowledge of the legal history, I do not think that, given the account here of what is involved in description, any of these claims essentially disturb Chalmers' own view of his achievement.

[163] *Lister v Romford Ice and Cold Storage Co Ltd* [1957] AC 555 (HL) 594 (Lord Tucker):

> Some contractual terms may be implied by general rules of law. These general rules, some of which are now statutory, for example, Sale of Goods Act, Bills of Exchange Act, etc, derive in the main from the common law by which they have become attached in the course of time to certain

as to invite misunderstanding however it is used, but ss 13 and 14 are in the most important sense of a piece with common law terms implied in fact (or by custom or usage), for they state (in their case codify) the objective intentions of the parties, and this, I submit, is the most useful meaning of the category of terms implied in fact.

I fully acknowledge that this use cuts across other usage of the highest authority in case law[164] and theory,[165] indeed it is intended to do so, and in particular to cut across the distinction between statutory implied terms and common law implied terms because, of course, it is perfectly possible for a court prepared to embark upon judicial legislation to incorporate a term into a contract which cannot plausibly be related to the intentions of the parties.[166] Such a term constitutes a welfarism which it is not possible to justify by reference to the values of contract, and, when applied to the facts of the particular instant case, are an example of unjustifiable intervention. On the other hand, that a term is implied by statute does not necessarily mean that that term is a mandatory imposition, and the Sale of Goods Act 1893 made an exceptional success of, in this sense, mere codification.[167]

The term implied in fact as the category is being understood here establishes a default rule out of which parties can contract.[168] This power to contract out was generally recognised under the Sale of Goods Act as originally enacted,[169] and has been

> classes of contractual relationships, for example, landlord and tenant, innkeeper and guest, contracts of guarantee and contracts of personal service.

[164] *Luxor (Eastbourne) Ltd v Cooper* [1941] AC 108 (HL) 137 (Lord Wright):

> The expression 'implied term' is used in different senses. Sometimes it denotes some term which does not depend on the actual intention of the parties but on a rule of law, such as the terms, warranties or conditions which, if not expressly excluded, the law imports, as for instance under the Sale of Goods Act.

[165] H Collins, 'Implied Terms: The Foundation in Good Faith and Fair Dealing' [2014] *Current Legal Problems* 297, 301–06.

[166] *Liverpool City Council v Irwin* [1976] QB 319 (CA); [1977] AC 239 (HL). Such were the difficulties left by the judgments that I do not think it would be productive to discuss the detail of this case here, but it should be noted that it would be naïve and callous to ignore the, in fact, impossible position in which this case placed the courts. However, the point remains, and is tacitly accepted, I think, even in the majority of sympathetic commentary, that a coherent law cannot be based on judgments of this nature. If we leave aside the unresolved conflicts over 'reasonableness' in general, even the clearest point to emerge from those judgments, the 'continuous spectrum' (ibid HL 254A (Lord Wilberforce)) between generally or widely implied terms at one end and terms implied in particular contracts in the other, is not clear at all. E Peden, 'Policy Considerations Behind the Implication of Terms in Law' (2001) 117 Law Quarterly Review 459, 461 tells us that:

> there is much flexibility for the courts to exploit in order to achieve a result they think is just. Courts are able to define the type of contract broadly, or more narrowly, and then either to refuse implication on the basis that the term would not sit properly with all contracts of this type, or to imply a term on the basis that the type of contract is small enough to avoid problems.

One can only say that if this is an approving comment, one would not like to see a criticism.

[167] Stoljar, 'Quality' (n 117) 434 describes many cases which I would classify as cases of implication of terms in fact as instances of the courts having 'pretended that they were merely giving effect to the "contractual intention" of the parties'. But, once one appreciates the objectivity of intention, this is indeed what the parties themselves intended to do, which may have been Stoljar's point.

[168] Morgan, 'Compulsion' (n 152). Dr Morgan is right to insist on the strength Chalmers' approach gained from making this possibility intrinsic to s 14, but for reasons which are clearly implied in the argument of this chapter I think he overemphasises the point when he claims it 'the main reason for the endurance' of s 14 (ibid 176).

[169] Sale of Goods Act 1893, s 55.

substantially retained when both parties act in course of business.[170] The issue really is one only for commercial parties as sales when both parties are consumers are, as I have mentioned, not by default sales by description with guarantees of quality. More relevant to the argument here, however, is that the effective position that contracting out is impossible when only one of the parties is a consumer does rest on a statutory intervention. The conclusion was reached, as is discussed in chapter 7, that the common law could not satisfactorily regulate exemptions from liability, including liability for breach of the ss 13 to 15 terms.[171] The legislation which culminated in The Unfair Contract Terms Act 1977 therefore mandatorily limited the possibility of ss 13 and 14's exclusion. When both seller and buyer act in course of business, exclusion of ss 13 and 14 is subject to evaluation by the court according to a statutory requirement of reasonableness.[172] Exclusion of ss 13 and 14 by a seller acting in course of business against a consumer was effectively made impossible,[173] and this position has been if anything strengthened in the subsequent legislation.[174] It is argued in Chapter 7 that the conclusion that statutory intervention was necessary to bring about this situation was mistaken, and for the moment I merely assert that the position established by the apparent ousting of the common law accomplished by the 1977 Act is one that is essentially consistent with regarding ss 13 and 14 as terms implied in fact (though the law has been made unnecessarily complicated).

The seller may modify s 14(2) by drawing the attention of even a consumer buyer to a defect[175] or by extending to the buyer an, in the context, reasonable opportunity to examine the goods, though any defect must be reasonably discoverable by such examination.[176] I have described this as modification because I do not think it would be right to call it ousting s 14(2). Once it is recognised that of its nature it is of limited application in sales by description,[177] this identification is an essentially unproblematic corollary of s 14(2).

170 Sale of Goods Act 1979, s 55(1).

171 Molony Committee *Report* (n 73) paras 426–36 and Law Commissions, *Exemption Clauses* (n 122) paras 64–113.

172 Now Unfair Contract Terms Act 1977, s 6(1A)(a), as amended by the Consumer Rights Act 2015, Sch 4 para 8(2). There was, of course, an override in respect of negligence leading to personal injury or death under s 2(1) of the 1977 Act which must be accounted for, not in terms of the law of contract, but in terms of the status given to personal injury by the tort of negligence.

173 Unfair Contract Terms Act 1977, s 6(2)(a), now repealed by the Consumer Rights Act 2015, Sch 4 para 8(3).

174 Consumer Rights Act 2015, s 9(1). It is significant that important commentary is so out of sympathy with the common law that it now bemoans that the legislative tendency expressed in the quality provisions of this Act (and elsewhere) has not been carried through to the point where these provisions have been placed on a 'fully statutory' basis: Twigg-Flessner and Canavan, *Sale of Goods* (n 143) 475, 501.

175 Sale of Goods Act 1979, s 14(2C)(a).

176 ibid s 14(2C)(b).

177 The use of 'in the course of a business' in the wording of s 14(2) unarguably creates difficulties which are not discussed here.

The Relational Nature of the Implied Term

The burden of the foregoing argument is that sales by commercial parties in contemporary market economies are not *caveat emptor* but, it may be said, *caveat venditor*,[178] and this is not fundamentally because of statutory intervention in the market economy, but because this is the nature of any possible general market economy in which sale by a business organisation is the principal means of allocation of economic goods.[179] The typical sale is one in which the seller in the course of business is obliged to anticipate and satisfy the buyer's demand for a described, satisfactory good. The seller self-interestedly pursues a profit, but must do so in a way framed by the buyer's demand. The implied terms as to description and quality are in this way the fundamental legal foundations of the buyer's ability to choose in the market economy, not merely in the way they apply to consumers but as they apply to business organisations. In Chapter 4, I argue that *caveat emptor* in a pure sense is actually impossible, but a workable and very useful concept of *caveat emptor* as encompassing sales other than by description, which are sales in which the buyer must rely on its own judgement (save in the case of fault by the seller), should be retained. The usefulness of this concept turns, however, on it being clearly understood that sales of this type, exemplified by various types of auctions of goods,[180] are exceptional, their principal doctrinal significance being their exceptionality.

These issues are the background to a case which is still widely used to illustrate the narrowness of a seller's duties when, it is submitted, it rather illustrates their width: *Horsfall v Thomas*.[181] I have so far considered only the implied term of

[178] Though the point is made by other authorities (eg McKendrick, *Goode* (n 118) para 11.07), all thinking on this point is indebted to Atiyah's work on the sale of goods, and, behind this, PS Atiyah, *The Rise and Fall of Freedom of Contract* (pbk edn, Clarendon Press 1985) 464–79. The subheading 'From *caveat emptor* to *caveat venditor*?' in the chapter on 'The Duty to Supply Goods of the Right Quality' in Atiyah's book on sales was not introduced until PS Atiyah, *Sale of Goods* (9th edn, Pitman 1995) 111, the first edited by the late Professor Adams (see now Twigg-Flessner and Canavan, *Sale of Goods* (n 143) 113, in which the question mark is omitted). The idea had, however, clearly been there from the start: PS Atiyah, *Sale of Goods* (1st edn, Pitman 1957) 61.

[179] *Grant* (PC) (n 123) 98:

> it has been said the old rule [of *caveat emptor*] has been changed to the rule of *caveat venditor*: the change has been rendered necessary by the conditions of modern commerce and trade.

[180] On the effect of the implied term of description in auctions, see BW Harvey and F Meisel, *Auctions Law and Practice* (OUP 2006) 207–13. In appropriate auctions, the seller has, of course, to exercise great care over express words of description, but that is not the point I am seeking to make here. On the sale of goods implied terms generally see ibid 193–98.

[181] (1862) 2 F and F 784; 175 ER 1284 (NP (London Assizes)) (hereafter *Horsfall* (NP)) and (1862) 1 H and C 90; 158 ER 813 (Court of Exchequer) (hereafter *Horsfall* (Exchequer).

The analysis about to be put forward would also apply to the similarly famous *Hopkins v Tanqueray* (1854) 15 CB 130; 139 ER 369, in which a non-fraudulent statement about the soundness of a horse bought at Tattersalls was found not to be a warranty because sales there were known, by default which it would take clear words to oust even were it possible to do so, to be in reliance on the buyer's own judgement: DK Allen, *Misrepresentation* (Sweet & Maxwell 1988) 104. (*Hopkins v Tanqueray* itself is unclear about the possibility of ouster, but Mitchell, 'Quality Obligations' (n 162) 645–50, though it emphasises the unusual, unwarranted nature of horse sales, shows that it was possible to pay a larger price, in horse sales in general and at Tattersalls in particular, to oust the default in what therefore was a 'stratified market'). This essential context went unappreciated as *Hopkins v Tanqueray* was used as authority for a generalisation of *caveat*

satisfactory quality under The Sale of Goods Act 1879, 14(2) but, of course, in a more restricted set of cases the relevant term may be that of fitness for purpose under s 14(3), which, despite its familiarity, it is as well to set out:

> Where the seller sells goods in the course of business and the buyer, expressly or by implication, makes known … to the seller … any particular purpose for which the goods are being bought, there is an implied term that the goods supplied under the contract are reasonably fit for that purpose, whether or not that is a purpose for which such goods are commonly supplied, except where the circumstances show that the buyer does not rely, or that it is unreasonable for him to rely, on the skill or judgement of the seller.

Though *Horsfall v Thomas* was handed down in 1862, and so decided on the common law to be codified only some 30 years later, it allows us to apply the argument made here to the concept of fitness.

The defendant bought a gun (ie a military cannon) which it hoped in its turn to sell to what is now the Ministry of Defence. As it would seem is timelessly the case with defence procurement of this type, the gun was meant to be technologically superior to existing guns, and it had been manufactured by the claimant seller to the original specification of the defendant buyer, an inventor of military armament. After delivery, the defendant carried out six initial trials of the gun at which it did perform in a superior manner, firing successively heavier shells propelled by successively larger charges of gunpowder further and more accurately than previously had been possible with guns of this size. On the seventh trial with an even larger charge, the gun burst. The claimant brought the action after the defendant refused to pay the agreed price.

This case is generally cited in support of the claim that a fraud which did not influence the choice of the buyer is not actionable. On inspecting the pieces of the burst gun, the defendant claimed to have found part of the gun to have been made of flawed steel and a plug to have been inserted to mask the flaw. It is submitted that this evidence was not accepted, though the case as reported does not allow one to be certain about this. This apparently vital point could be left unclear by the reporter because the defendant had not taken the opportunity to inspect the gun upon delivery, and as it has since been generally believed that the consequence of this was that, even if the insertion of the plug was fraudulent, it could not have had any effect upon the sale and so was not actionable. But even if this is right in itself as a point about the law of misrepresentation, it does not adequately address the nature of the claimant's duties in this case. These were more fully examined by the trial court than at the appeal, which was entirely occupied with the possible fraud.[182]

For it was by no means inevitable that the defendant had to inspect the gun, and if it did not have to, then the point about what is needed to make a fraud actionable would

emptor which was even in its own terms incoherent, creating particular difficulties for the understanding of representations.

[182] The report of the appeal does, however, have a far more ample account of the correspondence between the parties which evidences the claimant's duties: *Horsfall* (Exchequer) (n 181) 90–94; 813–15.

not arise. The claimant was a commercial steel fabricator, The Mersey Steel and Iron Company, and as such it normally would have to deliver what we would now call a satisfactory gun, ie one fit for ordinary use. This was the first plea advanced by the defendant and, in principle, it was accepted by the trial court:

> there is an implied warranty of soundness, by the maker of anything, and against flaws he knows of . . . The flaw ordinarily would sustain an action for a breach of warranty, apart from fraud, if it made the gun unfit for ordinary use; for there is always a warranty by a maker, that the article is sound and fit for ordinary use.[183]

But *Horsfall v Thomas* was not an ordinary case in this sense. The gun was manufactured to the defendant's innovative specification, and in this sense this was not even a case of fitness for purpose, for the claimant did not undertake to deliver a gun fit for the defendant's purpose. It undertook to deliver a gun manufactured to the defendant's specification, and that the gun burst only when being pushed to the edge of the technological frontier is highly significant. In essence, this was as far from a sale, not merely on the basis of fitness, but by description as one can envisage. If it had been a sale by description, with consequent guarantees of quality, the point about fraud would be irrelevant. The claimant would have been liable without any need to show fraud, for the claimant would be in breach of a term of the sale.

If we expand the previous discussion based on sales to apply to the general principles of contract,[184] we should say that, in a most important theoretical, if not doctrinal, sense, there is no such thing as an express contract. In order to recognise the role of the implied term in constituting agreement, we cannot conceive of contracts as normally express agreements to which implied terms are inessential but sometimes highly valuable additions. We must conceive of the express terms of contracts as always situated within implied terms which give the express terms their meaning. These are one of the essential 'implicit dimensions' of contract.[185]

The best way to comprehend the significance of this is to recognise that the implied term, a basic component of the classical doctrine of agreement, is inherently relational. The implied terms of description and quality which impose active duties of recognition of the buyer's autonomy of choice on the seller (I have only occasionally looked at the reciprocal duties of the buyer) are indispensable to contractual agreement in all save exceptional sales, the theoretical significance of which is that they are exceptional. The relations institutionalised in the implied terms make the general market economy possible by putting sales on the basis, not of *caveat emptor*, but of *caveat venditor*, without which basis that economy could not exist. The point is generalisable

183 *Horsfall* (NP) (n 181) 786 n (a); 1285 n (a).

184 In a contract for services, the supplier must by default 'carry out the service with reasonable care and skill': Supply of Goods and Services Act 1982, s 13. Without for a moment wishing to claim to be describing legal doctrine through this analogy, I would hope it is now clear the buyer buys a 'description' of the service, including all its aspects, not merely the actively considered ones, and there is a consequent guarantee of 'quality'. Section 13 codified the common law position in eg *Harmer v Cornelius* (1858) 5 CB(NS) 235.

185 D Campbell and H Collins, 'Discovering the Implicit Dimensions of Contracts' in D Campbell, H Collins, and J Wightman (eds), *Implicit Dimensions of Contracts* (Hart 2003) 33–37.

to all terms implied in fact in the sense used here, that is to say, to contracts other than sales.

Ronald Coase's criticism of what is 'often supposed by economists' is certainly applicable to much theoretical commentary on law:

> what are traded on the market are not, as is often supposed by economists, physical entities but the rights to perform certain actions, and the rights which individuals possess are established by the legal system ... As a result the legal system will have a profound effect on the working of the economic system and may in certain respects be said to control it.[186]

Both the informational problems discussed in this chapter and institutional responses to it have been productively discussed at length in the 'new institutional economics'.[187] But even such economics remain focused on solipsistic self-interest in economic action, and thus find it difficult to come to terms with the intrinsically relational nature of those rights which makes a welfare-enhancing general market economy possible only by basing it on a self-interest which intrinsically recognises moral duties towards others. That the market economy's paradigm exchange is not, adequately understood, a sale of a physical good but a sale of a description open-endedly guaranteed by the seller, with consequent open-ended, and so inherently other-regarding, guarantees of quality, is not, I believe, ultimately comprehensible unless exchange is seen as constituted by a moral relationship of mutual recognition.

I expand on these issues in Chapter 4 in the course of locating the implied term within a general understanding of the nature of agreement. For the implied term is by no means the only legal doctrine relationally constituting agreement, and in that chapter I shall turn to the others governing all sales, including the exceptional sales outwith the implied terms of description and quality, and indeed governing all contracts.

Conclusion

In my analysis of the doctrine of agreement so far, I hope to have established that, though criticisms of market failure—such as Bar-Gill's—valuably identify issues which must be addressed by any purportedly welfare maximising economics and law, especially when they address issues of consumer sovereignty, a *general* strategy of optimising welfare by further approximating to the informational conditions of competitive equilibrium is bound to have worse than no success. But this criticism is not at all intended to be a counsel of despair. It is intended to establish that the idea that a legitimate contract must be based on the parties' express agreement is wrong

[186] RH Coase, 'The Institutional Structure of Production' in *Essays on Economics and Economists* (University of Chicago Press 1994) 11. See also RH Coase, 'The Problem of Social Cost' in *The Firm, the Market and the Law* (University of Chicago Press 1988) 155.

[187] Eg the discussion of 'measurement' in DG North, *Institutions, Institutional Change and Economic Performance* (CUP 1990) 28–30.

in principle, and a regulatory response to perceived market failure which seeks to approximate to general equilibrium also is wrong in principle.

But, despite the classical legal understanding, this is not, I submit, the concept of agreement with which the law of contract works. In this chapter I hope to have shown the vital role the implied term plays in all contracting as a facilitative structure which makes express agreement possible. The essential point is that a contractual agreement simply is not possible between two parties acting from solipsistic self-interest. Without the moral rule furnished by implied terms, the parties would be faced with an infinite task of active negotiation. In the most important case of a sale of goods by a commercial party, this has led to the development of a default law of *caveat venditor*, without which the developed market economy also would be impossible. To complete this argument I shall in Chapter 4 generalise the discussion of the problems which the law of contractual agreement encounters in its attempt to institutionalise voluntary exchange. We will see that the general response to these problems has been the development of the concept of good faith.

4

The Relational Constitution of Agreement (2)

Business Efficacy and Good Faith

Introduction: Implied Terms, the Old Legal Baggage, and Interpretation

Without denying the challenge which understanding and evaluating the claims made in the previous chapter imposes on the reader, important relatively recent developments in the law of interpretation have reduced that challenge by indicating what we must now do in order to coherently integrate the implication of terms into the general law of agreement. Though, as we shall see, his actual decision in the case is an example of just what we should not do, the law has been very much improved by Lord Hoffmann's attempt in 1997 in *Investors Compensation Scheme Ltd v West Bromwich Building Society (No 1)* to set the seal on discarding 'almost all the old intellectual baggage of "legal" interpretation'[1] in order for interpretation to take place with awareness of 'all' relevant context:

> Interpretation is the ascertainment of the meaning which the document would convey to a reasonable person having all the background knowledge which would reasonably have been available to the parties in the situation in which they were at the time of the contract.[2]

This principled statement of contextual openness is the main service Lord Hoffmann rendered the law of contract; it is certainly one welcomed by the generation—to which this writer belongs—which previously had to work hard against the positive law to ensure that carrying the old intellectual baggage did not frustrate parties' journeys to

[1] [1998] 1 WLR 896 (HL) 912H (hereafter *Investors* (HL)).
[2] ibid.

Contractual Relations. David Campbell, Oxford University Press. © David Campbell 2022.
DOI: 10.1093/oso/9780198855156.003.0004

clearly intended destinations.[3] In *nuce*, *Investors* is the principal Commonwealth authority rendering otiose any basic argument about the desirability of the 'new contextualism' in interpretation.[4] But desirability is not entirely the right word. The reason the new contextualism is fundamentally correct is, not that it is desirable in the sense that it is an approach one chooses to take when one could choose otherwise, but that it is essential because, if interpretation is to give effect to the voluntary exchange expressed in the intentions of the parties, there is no alternative.[5]

As there is no possibility of a fully specified exchange, there is no possibility of a fully express contract. When, after the agreement is reached, a particular liability or lack of liability of one of the parties which *ex hypothesi* was not adequately specified is called into question by the unfolding of events, inquiry must be made into the commercial context needed to ascertain objective meaning, and there is no possibility of *ex ante* setting a coherent limit to what is relevant context, save relevance itself. There is no 'unambiguous' 'natural (or many synonyms of natural) language' to be contrasted to contextual interpretation, for it is context that in one case makes language appear natural and in another makes it appear ambiguous.[6] The real issue at the heart of the 'neo-formalist' response to contextualism[7] is not a return to what present themselves as hard and fast constraints on interpretation, much less a recovery of an actual formalism that never could exist nor ever has existed,[8] but the handling of the responsibilities of contextualism in a way which, by not going beyond the point where elucidation of context *must* turn into interventionist elaboration of that context,[9] respects sanctity of contract.[10]

[3] J Wightman, 'Contract in a Pre-realist World: Professor Macaulay, Lord Hoffmann and the Rise of Context in the English Law of Contract' in J Braucher, J Kidwell and WC Whitford (eds), *Revisiting the Contracts Scholarship of Stewart Macaulay* (Hart 2013).

[4] R Brownsword, 'After *Investors*: Interpretation, Expectation and the Implicit Dimension of the "New Contextualism"' in D Campbell, M Collins and J Wightman (eds), *Implicit Dimensions of Contracts* (Hart 2003).

[5] I do not wish to relate the argument to the law which constituted the old legal baggage, but I was struck by the way one commonly finds statements of that law to be nuanced, or it might be said contradictory. Tindal CJ's famous insistence that an 'instrument . . . always . . . be construed according to the strict, plain, common meaning of the words themselves', but only when instruments 'are free from ambiguity in themselves, and external circumstances do not create any doubt or difficulty', is but one, admittedly striking, example: *Attorney General v Shore* (1843) 11 Sim 592, 631; 59 ER 1002, 1021.

[6] *Investors* (HL) (n 1) 913C–914G. Perhaps the starkest illustration of this in the case law following *Investors* is the dispute over a calendar date in *Mannai Investment Co Ltd v Eagle Star Life Assurance Co Ltd* [1997] 3 All ER 352 (HL). This case also illustrates the difficulties of relating interpretation and rectification that have persisted after *Investors*.

[7] L Bernstein, 'The Questionable Empirical Basis of Article 2's Incorporation Strategy: A Preliminary Study' (1999) 66 University of Chicago Law Review 76; R Scott, 'The Case for Formalism in Relational Contract' (2000) 94 Northwestern University Law Review 847; R Scott and A Schwarz, 'Contract Theory and the Limits of Contract Law' (2013) 113 Yale Law Journal 541, and A Schwartz, 'Relational Contracts in the Courts: An Analysis of Incomplete Contracts and Judicial Strategies' (1992) 21 Journal of Legal Studies 308.

[8] D Kennedy, *A Critique of Adjudication (Fin de Siècle)* (Harvard University Press 1997) 105: Langdellian formalism is 'a theory with no known American proponents'.

[9] R Craswell, 'Do Trade Customs Exist?' in J Kraus and S Walt (eds), *The Jurisprudential Foundations of Corporate and Commercial Law* (CUP 2000).

[10] J Morgan, *Contract Law Minimalism* (CUP 2013) (hereafter Morgan, *Minimalism*).

I have said Lord Hoffmann set the seal because, as he acknowledged,[11] *Investors* pulled together and rationalised many previous attempts, which can be traced far back into the historical case law, to discard particular items of old intellectual baggage. Lord Hoffmann did not, indeed could not if he was to act productively, do something radically new, but rather he made us conscious of the best parts of what had previously been done, which should, of course, allow it to be done better in future. Two particular items of baggage had to be discarded. The first (Lord Hoffmann's second principle) was any fixed restriction on our ability to take into account 'absolutely anything which would have affected the language of the document would have been understood by a reasonable man', a background which had been 'famously referred to by Lord Wilberforce as the "matrix of fact"'.[12] The second item to be discarded (Lord Hoffmann's fifth principle) was literal interpretation claiming to rest on 'natural and ordinary meaning'[13] when it frustrated the objective intentions the parties could be seen to have as a matter of, as Lord Diplock had previously put it, 'business common sense':

> The 'rule' that words should be given their 'natural and ordinary meaning' reflects the common sense proposition that we do not easily accept that people have made linguistic mistakes, particularly in formal documents. On the other hand, if one would nevertheless conclude from the background that something must have gone wrong with the language, the law does not require judges to attribute to the parties an intention which they plainly could not have had. Lord Diplock made this point more vigorously when he said ... 'if detailed semantic and syntactical analysis of words in a commercial contract is going to lead to a conclusion that flouts business common sense, it must be made to yield to business common sense'.[14]

[11] *Chartbrook Ltd v Persimmon Homes* [2009] UKHL 38; [2009] AC 1101 [37] (hereafter *Chartbrook*). This acknowledgement was in response to Lord Bingham's eloquently entitled 'A New Thing Under the Sun? The Interpretation of Contract and the *ICS* Decision' (2008) 12 Edinburgh Law Review 374.

[12] *Investors* (HL) (n 1) 912G; quoting *Prenn v Simmons* [1971] 1 WLR 1381 (HL) 1383H-1384A (Lord Wilberforce):

> The time has long passed when agreements, even those under seal, were isolated from the matrix of facts in which they were set and interpreted purely on internal linguistic considerations.

[13] *Reardon Smith Line Ltd v Yngvar Hansen Tangen, The Diana Prosperity* [1976] 1 WLR 989 (HL) 995H–996A (Lord Wilberforce):

> one must [not] be confined within the four corners of the document. No contracts are made in a vacuum: there is always a setting in which they have to be placed. The nature of what is legitimate to have regard to is usually described as 'the surrounding circumstances' but this phrase is imprecise: it can be illustrated but hardly defined. In a commercial contract it is certainly right that the court should know the commercial purpose of the contract and this in turn presupposes knowledge of the genesis of the transaction, the background, the context, the market in which the parties are operating, etc.

[14] *Investors* (HL) (n 1) 913D-E; quoting *Antaios Compania Naviera SA v Salen Rederierna AB, The Antaios* [1985] AC 191 (HL) 201ED. As an indication of the argument to be put forward in this chapter, it should be noted that Lord Diplock preceded the quoted *dictum* by saying, ibid, that he 'deprecat[ed] the extension of the use of the expression "purposive construction" from the interpretation of statutes to the interpretation of private contracts'.

In subsequent cases, Lord Hoffmann drew the conclusion that including everything potentially relevant and avoiding literalness meant that the implication of terms could be seamlessly assimilated into interpretation, culminating in a statement of the position in 2009 in *Attorney General of Belize v Belize Telecom Ltd*:

> It follows that in every case in which it is said that some provision ought to be implied in an instrument, the question for the court is whether such a provision would spell out in express words what the instrument, read against the relevant background, would reasonably be understood to mean.[15]

One must begin a discussion of interpretation after *Investors* by saying that it is logically entailed in the *Investors* approach that the implication of terms in fact should be understood simply as part of the general work of interpretation of contract.[16] What could be more 'contextual'? What is more, discussing interpretation in terms which drew on Lord Diplock's stress on business common sense allowed Lord Hoffmann to draw authority from one of the most valuable doctrines in the law of contract. That the reasonable person whose understanding is to be liberated by discarding the old baggage is cognisant of the commercial nature of the intentions of the parties to the contract is, *mutatis mutandis*, the core theme of the case law on the implication of terms as an interpretative device, which focuses on legitimate implication being confined to the 'business efficacy' of the exchange. Without trying to close off the issue of the relationship of 'interpretation' and 'implication', which will be discussed at some length, when we shall see that Lord Hoffmann mishandled it, I shall normally use 'business efficacy' to denote the contextual objective intention which it is the goal of interpretation to elucidate.[17] Acknowledging the essential moral basis of exchange described in this book as mutual recognition, it will be argued that this is entirely the correct way to proceed and, in order to do so it will be convenient, despite their extreme familiarity, to quote the two most influential *dicta* on implication in commercial cases; the first, of course, being Bowen LJ in *The Moorcock*:

> The implication which the law draws from what must obviously have been the intention of the parties, the law draws with the object of giving efficacy to the transaction and preventing such a failure of consideration as cannot have been within the contemplation of either side ... In business transactions such as this, what the law desires to effect by the implication is to give such business efficacy to the transaction as must have been intended at all events by both parties who are business men; not to impose on one side all the perils of the transaction, or to emancipate one side from all the chances of failure, but to make each party promise in law as much, at all events, as it

[15] [2009] UKPC 10; [2009] 1 WLR 1988 [21].

[16] Arguments to this effect before and after *Belize Telecom* (but before the main criticism it received) were made in A Kramer, 'Implication in Fact as an Instance of Contractual Interpretation' [2004] Cambridge Law Journal 384 and R Hooley, 'Implied Terms after *Belize Telecom*' [2014] Cambridge Law Journal 315.

[17] I intend this term to include contracts involving consumers, for I do not believe there should be, indeed cannot be, a consumer law distinct from commercial law, and the undeniable differences of interpretative attitude which inequality of bargaining power necessitates be taken towards (negotiation, drafting and) interpretation is discussed in chs 6 and 7.

must have been in the contemplation of both parties that he should be responsible for in respect of those perils or chances;[18]

and the second, equally of course, being Scrutton LJ in *Reigate v Union Manufacturing Co (Ramsbottom) Ltd*:

> A term can only be implied if it is necessary in the business sense to give efficacy to the contract; that is, if it is such a term that it can confidently be said that if at the time the contract was being negotiated someone had said to the parties, 'What will happen in such a case,' they would both have replied, 'Of course, so and so will happen; we did not trouble to say that; it is too clear.' Unless the Court comes to some such conclusion as that, it ought not to imply a term which the parties themselves have not expressed.[19]

Why Is Interpretation Necessary and How Does the Law of Contract Do It?

It is, of course, not uncommonly the case that the test for implication derived from *The Moorcock* and *Reigate v Union Manufacturing* has been applied using Mackinnon LJ's later description of the person asking the otiose question as 'an officious bystander'.[20] Mackinnon LJ's famous *dictum* is a quotation from a lecture he had given, whilst a High Court judge, at the LSE in 1926, in which problems of interpretation are considered widely, and are ultimately ascribed to a failure to fully specify the meaning of the contract:

> if every commercial contract were fully and clearly written out, there would be no problems of law for the Commercial Court to decide . . . when the Court knows clearly the meaning of all parts of the contract it has solved all the problems it provides.[21]

This very practically focused lecture concentrates on some of the old baggage particular to commercial law that prevents this desirable clarity, but the thought that ultimately motivated the developments on which *Investors* set the seal is that the basic problems of interpretation, following from some given features of any use of language, including but by no means confined to the legal, are 'intractable'.[22] It is crucial to realise, however, that we are not only always beset by these problems, but that we also normally solve them.[23] The impression one gains from some despairing

[18] (1889) LR 14 PD 64 (CA) 68 (hereafter *The Moorcock*).
[19] [1918] 1 KB 592 (CA) 605 (hereafter *Reigate v Union Manufacturing*).
[20] *Shirlaw v Southern Foundries (1926) Ltd* [1939] 2 KB 206 (CA) 227.
[21] Sir Frank Mackinnon, *Some Aspects of Commercial Law* (Humphrey Milford for OUP 1926) 13 (hereafter Mackinnon, *Some Aspects*).
[22] Lord Steyn, 'The Intractable Problem of the Interpretation of Legal Texts' in S Worthington (ed), *Commercial Law and Commercial Practice* (Hart 2003).
[23] A Kramer, 'Common Sense Principles of Contract Interpretation, And How We've Been Using Them All Along' (2003) 23 Oxford Journal of Legal Studies 173.

commentary—which curiously mixes the rhetorics of commercial hardheadedness and postmodern irrationalism[24]—that interpretation is doomed, does not capture the nature of the interpretative task. That task is not, at root, an hermeneutic one in the sense of ascertaining meaning by the application of linguistic technique. At root, it is a question of applying our linguistic technique with the correct moral attitude.

In what surely is the most important modern jurisprudential contribution to handling the task posed by 'open texture' as 'a general feature of human language', Hart advised us that 'we should not cherish, even as an ideal, the conception of a rule so detailed that the question whether it is applied or not to a particular case was always settled in advance':

> Put shortly, the reason is that we are men, not gods. It is a feature of the human predicament ... that we labour under two connected handicaps whenever we seek to regulate ... The first ... is our relative ignorance of fact; the second is our relative indeterminacy of aim. If the world in which we lived were characterised only by a finite number of features, and these together with the modes in which they could combine were known to us, then provision could be made for every possibility ... Plainly, this world is not our world ... This inability to anticipate brings with it a relative indeterminacy of aim [We may] frame some ... rule of conduct ... and certain clear examples of what is certainly within its scope may be present to our minds. These are the paradigm clear cases ... On the other hand, until we have put the [rule] ... into conjunction with those cases we did not, or perhaps could not, initially envisage ... our aim is ... indeterminate. We have not settled, because we have not anticipated, the question which will be raised by the unanticipated case when it occurs ... When the unenvisaged case does arise, we confront the issues at stake and then settle the question by choosing between the competing interests in the way which best satisfies us.[25]

The rejection even as a goal of a rule so detailed that questions of its application are settled *ex ante* leads Hart to conclude that what fundamentally is needed is, not technical refinement *ex post*, but taking the correct moral attitude towards settling the question. I cannot hope that it goes without saying, for I spend much of the rest of this chapter in various ways saying, that skill in (negotiation, drafting and) interpretation exercised at the level (which may include an exceedingly complex level requiring familiarity with specialist usage) appropriate to the commercial context of the contract, are of indispensable value in the law of contract. Nevertheless, it is the moral attitude of the (drafters and) interpreters (including judges) that is the essence of the matter.

Hart's argument was, of course, focused on general legislation, and the way of choosing 'which best satisfies us' in this context is a balance between the plurality of concerns which constitutes the public 'interest of all who will be effected'.[26] To say that the parallel 'private interest' in the law of contract is business efficacy seems straightaway to jar, for does not 'business' carry some connotation of an absence of morality

[24] F Nietzsche, *The Will to Power* (Random House 1967) ss 1, 13, 540, 616: 'All interpretations of the world are false ... There is no truth'.

[25] HLA Hart, *The Concept of Law* (3rd edn, Clarendon Press 2012) 128–29.

[26] ibid 205.

in the negotiation of contracts by the self-interested parties to exchange? One does not have to look far into the business and economic literature to find statements to this effect, and though these typically are so risible—at the level of the TV programme *The Apprentice*—they do express an understanding of the 'economic motive' described by Macneil:

> An individual utility maximiser may be perfectly well aware of the fact that the deal ... creates [a] surplus [utility], but his *sole* concern about that utility is to grab as much of it for himself as he can. He will feel nothing but regret at whatever amount is snared by the other party and nothing but happiness that the other failed to secure more of it.[27]

Macneil is describing parties who pursue solipsistic self-interest rather than self-interest based on mutual recognition, but whilst there are, of course, such parties, their action cannot generate legitimate exchange and contract. The classical law of contract does not clearly grasp that it is essential to refuse to acknowledge the legitimacy of the actions of such parties if contractual interpretation is even to be possible, for their subjective intentions would prevent business efficacy being a valuable guide at all. Let us imagine that a party, in its subjective, solipsistic self-interest, would prefer interpretation X, and that the other party, also taking this attitude, would prefer interpretation non-X. If solipsism is legitimate, how can we choose? Each solipsism is as little or as much legitimate as the other. The entire point of reference to 'what must obviously have been the intention of the parties' is to refer to an objective standard, and the entire point of business efficacy is to recognise that contracts, or, to put it this way, contracts that merit being upheld as legitimate, are the products of agreement. There is, or should be, no clash between *business* efficacy and respecting the intentions of the parties, for both are approaches towards determining agreement (or its legitimate absence).

I later address the margin of advantage a party may gain relative to the other in the process of competitive negotiation, but the point to note here is that there is a limit to this, for no objective interpretation can allow that a term was incorporated if it is impossible that a reasonable person would think a party would have agreed to that term. There can be no question of *ex ante* closing all gaps. When the gap is exposed *ex post*, we must settle the question on the basis that, when the parties manifested agreement, they did so in possession of all reasonable opportunities to actually agree. It should be fruitless for a party to obtain the manifestation of the incorporation of a term by negotiating conduct which does not respect, or indeed intentionally negates, the autonomy of the other party, for the court should not give the term effect. An interpretation which would yield such a term defeats the business efficacy of the contract; for, to repeat, business efficacy is a matter of mutual agreement which rests on the moral relationship of mutual recognition.

[27] IR Macneil, 'Exchange Revisited: Individual Utility and Social Solidarity' (1986) 96 Ethics 567, 578–79.

To illustrate the relationship of solipsistic self-interest, mutual recognition, and business efficacy, I will turn to *Arcos Ltd v EA Ronaasen and Sons*,[28] notoriously the paradigm of a rigidly formal interpretation of contract terms absurdly and unfairly trumping a sensible and fair contextual interpretation of those terms; just the sort of thing, in fact, that should no longer be possible after *Investors*. By focusing on *Arcos*, we may contrast the argument of this book to the particularly insightful explanation of *Arcos* as the result of the buyer's unacceptably selfish attitude being endorsed by courts applying a classical sympathy to that attitude which can be drawn from the work of Professors Adams, Brownsword, and MacQueen.[29]

In 1929, Arcos Ltd, a commercial agency of the Government of the USSR, agreed to sell a large consignment of wooden staves to an English buyer, EA Ronaasen, to be shipped in 1930 cif Archangel to London. Though it does not seem that the written contracts made reference to this, the buyer made it known to the seller that the staves were to be used to manufacture cement barrels, and it was never challenged that the sellers had an obligation under what was then the Sale of Goods Act 1893, s 14(1) to ensure the staves were fit for this purpose, nor that the seller satisfied that obligation.[30] The contract also described the staves in various respects, such as the type of timber from which they were to be cut and, in particular, their sizes. The entire consignment of staves was rejected for breach of the s 13 implied condition of conformity with the description of size.

Though, it is submitted correctly, certainly as the law then stood, the lack of conformity could not be disregarded as *de minimis*,[31] *Arcos* is a notorious case because that lack nevertheless was negligible, and rejection was possible only because under the 1893 Act a breach of s 13 was mandatorily a breach of condition.[32] One consignment of the delivery was, for example, to consist of '135 to 180 standards [of staves] ½ in [thick] by 28 in [long] by 2 in [wide]',[33] but it was found that '[n]one are less than ½ in. 4.3% are ½ in. 85.3% are more than ½ in but not more than 9/16ths in. 9.4% are more than 9/16ths in and not more than 5/8ths in. 1% are more than 5/8th in and not more than ¾ in. None are over ¾ in.'[34] This lack of conformity did not, as has been mentioned, effect fitness for purpose. Had it been an issue, though it was not, the goods were also perfectly merchantable under s 14(3).[35]

[28] *Ronaasen and Son v Arcos Ltd* (1932) 42 Ll L Rep 163 (KB) (hereafter (*Arcos* (KB)); *Ronaasen and Son v Arcos Ltd* (1932) 43 Ll L Rep 1 (CA) (hereafter *Arcos* (CA)) and *Arcos Ltd v EA Ronaasen and Son* [1933] AC 470 (HL) (hereafter *Arcos* HL).

[29] References to Atiyah's textbook on sales are to the last edition by the late John Adams and Hector MacQueen: JN Adams and H MacQueen, *Atiyah's Sale of Goods* (12th edn, Pearson 2010). I do not discuss Atiyah's own previous formulations of similar arguments, nor do I refer to the handling of the issues under the book's current editors.

[30] *Arcos* (KB) (n 28) 167 col 2, 168 cols 1–2 and *Arcos* (HL) (n 28) 480.

[31] *Arcos* (KB) (n 28) 170 col 1.

[32] Drawing on the common law reform of the condition and warranty dichotomy initiated in *Hong Kong Fir Shipping Co Ltd v Kawasaki Kisen Kaisha Ltd, The Hong Kong Fir* [1962] 2 QB 26 (CA), an, it is submitted, incoherent attempt to address this by amendment of the 1979 Act has not stopped calls of the highest scholarly authority being made for complete repeal of what was s 13 of the 1983 Act. In light of what has been said in the previous chapter of the function of description, it is clear that this would involve great difficulty. The issues will be discussed in connection with termination in ch 8.

[33] *Arcos* (KB) (n 28) 166 col 2. A standard was the 'St Petersburg standard' common to the timber trade, a 165 cubic foot bundle of lengths of timber.

[34] ibid 166 col 2, 167 col 2.

[35] ibid 168 col 2, 170 col 1.

It is scarcely possible to overstate the malign influence *Arcos* has had on a number of very important sales concepts. But we shall focus on the main mischief with which *Arcos* has been identified throughout the general law of contract. By apparently requiring that 'duties must be strictly complied with and that any breach of these conditions, however trivial, *prima facie* justifies the buyer in refusing to accept the goods', *Arcos*, Adams and MacQueen tell us, 'permitted rejection on capricious and technical grounds' 'for many breaches of no serious import at all'.[36]

In this instance, however, 'capricious' is not really apt. The buyer had a motive which cannot better express solipsistic self-interest. *Arcos* is all but universally believed to be perhaps the leading example of those cases in which 'the buyer's real motive in rejecting the goods was that market prices had fallen since the contract was made'.[37] There is no actual evidence about the movement of timber prices in *Arcos*, and this motive is nowhere set out in so many words. But the time at which this dispute took place—at the onset of the Great Depression—and the facts—a rejection of (merchantable) goods fit for purpose for a breach which had no effect on fitness—make this explanation of the buyer's conduct overwhelmingly likely. And if this was the case, it has been also all but universally believed that acting with such a motive is unacceptable: by making it possible 'to be able to escape from the contract in order to take advantage of falling prices on the timber market',[38] *Arcos* is 'a blatant example of … economic opportunism'.[39] It is not legitimate 'to play the market', for when 'economic self-interest prevails' 'over contractual commitment' in this way, it is an instance of 'bad faith'.[40] The buyer, Adams and Brownsword complain, was 'not actually rejecting *for breach* (except in the technical legal sense); the seller's breach was merely a pretext for getting out of the bargain'.[41] The fundamental shortcoming of *Arcos* is that it gives expression to 'the classical view … that where one party is in breach of contract, then the innocent party may legitimately take up any of the legally available options irrespective of whether this is for self-serving economic advantage'.[42]

I would be the last to deny that there is an important set of contracts based on flexible obligations which require conscious co-operation over adjustment conducted in what is often described in the case law as good faith. These are the earlier Macneil's relational contracts, introduced in Chapter 2 and to be discussed at length in Chapter 10. This is a specialised concept of good faith derived from but very importantly distinct from the general concept of good faith at which I am now trying to drive. For *Arcos*, and all the cases addressed in the treatment of agreement in this and the previous chapter, were what Macneil called discrete contracts based on presentiation. And for such contracts to work, the presentiated obligations must stick; which is to say these contracts absolutely require respect for sanctity. Interpretation identifies the

[36] J Adams and H MacQueen, *Atiyah's Sale of Goods* (12th edn, Pearson 2012) 86, 499, 87.

[37] ibid 499.

[38] J Adams and R Brownsword, *Key Issues in Contract Law* (Butterworths 1995) 226–27 (hereafter Adams and Brownsword, *Key Issues*).

[39] *Arcos* (KB) (n 28) 170.

[40] ibid 226.

[41] ibid 171–72.

[42] R Brownsword, '*Suisse Atlantique Société d'Armament SA v NV Rotterdamsche Kolen Centrale* (1967)' in C Mitchell and P Mitchell (eds), *Landmark Cases in the Law of Contract* (Hart 2008) 307 (hereafter Brownsword, *Suisse Atlantique*).

intentions of the parties that must be given that respect, but does so correctly only if it is itself objectively based on that respect.

As a matter of interpretation, *Arcos* seems, to a degree which at first strains credulity, to turn on taking the description of the sizes literally; one is tempted to say literally literally. If this was so, it was not consistent with other aspects of the approach taken towards other issues by all the courts and tribunals that heard the case, which was entirely open to what we would now call contextual reading.[43] The problem in regard of the sizes was that the courts believed that if the seller wanted a margin of deviation from the description, it had to expressly provide for it: '[i]f the seller wants a margin he must ... stipulate for it'[44]. The goods had to correspond with the description, and so the seller should have changed the description. If the word 'about', for example, had been included, then the seller would not have been in breach.[45] This sets up an interpretation of s 13 which is often called the 'perfect tender rule', where a description is by default (subject to *de minimis*) to be read literally, unless the parties specify otherwise.

Arcos did not, however, turn on some absurd denial of the commercial realities of the case but on an anxiety to take them into account. If the market had not fallen, the goods would have been accepted and all would have been well. But by securing the incorporation of the description in the way it was when it is inconceivable that the goods would conform—I know nothing of the matter but I assume that planning thousands of cubic feet of timber to *de minimis* tolerances is a vastly expensive undertaking—the seller was bound to be in breach just by delivering. The buyer effectively secured an all but universal right to reject, which it could exercise for whatever reason it wished, with a falling market being, indeed, a very good example of such a reason. Lord Atkin was fully conscious of this:

[43] In the Lords, for example, Lord Atkin acknowledged that 'by recognised trade usage particular figures may be given a different meaning, as in a baker's dozen' (*Arcos* (HL) (n 28) 479), and an actual instance of this was central to the dispute. Before, it seems, the goods had been landed, the buyer rejected the shipping documents on the ground that the contract provided for 'shipment during the summer', but the goods had not been shipped until on or about 9 October. A previous arbitral award, confirmed in an unreported King's Bench judgment, found that, in the timber trade, October deliveries could be regarded as summer deliveries, and dismissed rejection on this basis. In the *Arcos* litigation we are discussing, Wright J let this pass without any criticism (*Arcos* (KB) (n 28) 167 col 1), as did Lord Atkin (*Arcos* (HL) (n 28) 478), and it was enthusiastically affirmed, *obiter*, by Scrutton LJ: *Arcos* (CA) (n 28) 5 col 2.

It is inappropriate here to go into the background interpretive stances of the three distinguished judges on whom my discussion of *Arcos* concentrates, but the remarkable events in the career of Wright J around the time he heard this case demand some comment. (Some relevant comments on Scrutton LJ are also made in ch 7). In April 1932, less than two months after Wright had heard *Arcos*, Sankey LC took the remarkable step of appointing him directly to the House of Lords as Sankey felt there was a desperate need to strengthen the quality of the Lords of Appeal. Within three months of his appointment to the Lords, Lord Wright gave a speech in *WN Hillas and Co Ltd v Arcos Ltd* (1932) 43 Ll L Rep 359 (HL) which is now generally regarded as an exemplary instance of taking a sensibly contextual approach to the interpretation of contracts. In sum, Wright J was not a formalist: N Duxbury, 'Lord Wright and Innovative Traditionalism' (2009) 59 University of Toronto Law Journal 265.

[44] *Arcos* (HL) (n 28) 479.

[45] *Arcos* (KB) (n 28) 168 col 2–170 col 1. It will be recalled that the consignment we are discussing was to be of '135 to 180 standards', and Scrutton LJ was reported to be of the opinion this meant that 'the seller is given liberty to deliver either 135 or 180 standards' (*Arcos* (CA) (n 28) 5 col 1). I think it more likely that Scrutton LJ read the term as allowing a delivery of any number between 135 and 180, but the point is that flexibility, when expressly provided for, was in principle accepted readily enough in *Arcos*.

> the right view is that the conditions of the contract must be strictly performed. If a condition is not performed the buyer has a right to reject ... No doubt, in business, men often find it unnecessary or inexpedient to insist on their strict legal rights. In a normal market if they get something substantially like the specified goods they may take them with or without grumbling and a claim for an allowance. But in a falling market I find that the buyers are often eager to insist on their legal rights as courts are ready to maintain them ... Buyers are not, as far as my experience goes, inclined to think that the rights defined in the [Sale of Goods Act] are in excess of business needs.[46]

Adams, Brownsword, and MacQueen could, and as we have seen did, criticise this in terms drawn from the influential distinction between market individualism and consumer welfarism which was discussed in Chapter 1. But in a most acute way Adams and Brownsword came to see that this analysis is lacking when it is acknowledged that Lord Atkin 'perfectly well understood [and] saw nothing wrong with the buyers taking advantage ... in this way',[47] for this was legitimate commercial practice in his classical view of the buyer's conduct,[48] and 'sellers who failed to deliver goods corresponding precisely to the contractual description had no cause for complaint if buyers then rejected the goods purely for their own economic advantage'.[49] What is more, in light of this, the criticism of want of good faith becomes very problematic, for if the Lords:

> had employed the concept of good faith ... the question would have been whether the relevant commercial community would have regarded the buyers' rejection as a bad faith withdrawal—and, on the evidence of Lord Atkin's judgment, we can take it that the answer would have been in the negative, with the result that a good faith requirement would not have altered the outcome of the case.[50]

It would seem that we are left with the dead end of a mere clash of the values of the classical law and welfarism described in Chapter 1.

But is, as Adams', Brownsword's, and MacQueen's criticism requires, what the courts did in *Arcos* defensible as an interpretation of the contract in terms of business efficacy? The timber was fit for purpose (and merchantable). Is it consistent also to require it to be in conformity in the literal sense we have seen; that is to say, is it right to regard the s 13 obligation as or 'cumulative'[51] with or 'additional'[52] to the s 14 obligation?[53] As a matter of interpretation based on business efficacy, it is preposterous to do so. To deliver timber fit for purpose at a competitive price, the seller has to deliver

46 *Arcos* (HL) (n 28) 480.
47 Adams and Brownsword, *Key Issues* (n 38) 172.
48 ibid 226.
49 R Brownsword 'General Considerations' in MP Furmston (ed), *The Law of Contract* (6th edn, LexisNexis 2017) para 1.23 n 8.
50 Adams and Brownsword, *Key Issues* (n 38) 227.
51 *Arcos* (KB) (n 28) 167 col 2.
52 *Arcos* (HL) (n 28) 480.
53 The attempts made within the sale of goods to deal with this will be ignored.

timber which is not in literal conformity. The case could never have arisen had the seller intended to deliver conforming goods, for the buyer would never have bought them as they would have been astronomically expensive. The seller intending to perform its function as seller could not reasonably be expected to put in 'about', as this was a paradigm instance of what is too obvious to need saying.

The effect of the contract as interpreted was that the buyer got both the goods at a competitive price, and also a more or less complete discretion to reject. Whether this should be possible raises the issue of the parties being able to provide for 'certainty' that has been discussed *ad infinitum* after *The Hong Kong Fir* made substantial performance the default position, and the penetrative criticism of Adams, Brownsword, and MacQueen has come to allow that this should be possible because 'self-reliance might be the appropriate ethic in some markets',[54] even though, as the 'default provisions are set on the basis of a robust individualistic ethic',[55] this would seem to involve sacrificing 'the modern counter-culture of co-operation in commercial contracting'.[56]

This is, with respect, wrong in a precise and instructive way. It should be possible to have terms which create either possibility: flexibility which requires a reasonable margin, or (let us use the language) certainty which eliminates it. But such terms must be the result of an agreement, and for this to be the case the default interpretation, based on business efficacy, *has* to be flexibility. A party delivering normal commercial goods to the tolerances that make them satisfactory or fit for purpose cannot be expected to have agreed the drastic implications of an *Arcos* interpretation of s 13 (and any analogue provision in any contract).[57] But if language sufficiently clear to manifest the contrary intentions of the parties ousts the default, it should be allowed to do so, though this writer finds it hard to conceive of an actual exchange on this basis. More importantly, he finds it impossible to conceive of a provision to this effect being legitimately incorporated as a sidewind of a delivery obligation which makes no mention of it.

And yet we see in *Arcos*, Scrutton LJ, who was responsible for the famous *dictum* in *Reigate v Union Manufacturing* on which this chapter is substantially based,[58] forcefully stating his opinion that:

> The commercial mind and the legal mind are quite at variance as to the obligations of a seller and a buyer, the seller having undertaken to supply described 'goods' [so that] 'the commercial man says: "I have undertaken to deliver a particular size, but it is reasonable that I should be allowed to deliver a certain percentage which is not that

[54] Brownsword, *Suisse Atlantique* (n 42) 320.

[55] ibid.

[56] ibid 309.

[57] *Cehave NV v Bremer Handellsgesellschaft mbh, The Hansa Nord* [1976] QB 44 (CA) 71A (Roskill LJ):

> In principle contracts are made to be performed and not to be avoided according to the whims of market fluctuation and where there is a free choice between two possible constructions I think the court should tend to prefer that construction which will ensure performance and not encourage avoidance of contractual obligations.

[58] And the subject of extraordinary praise by Llewellyn(!) in a 'dedication' to 'On Warranty of Quality, and Society', which appeared shortly after Scrutton's death. According to Llewellyn, Scrutton was 'a matchless commercial lawyer, indeed 'a greater commercial judge than Mansfield': KN Llewellyn, 'On Warranty of Quality, and Society' (1936) 36 Columbia Law Review 699, 700, 701.

> size"' [whereas the] court says ... "[y]ou must deliver what you have agreed to deliver, and if you have agreed to deliver something without giving yourself any option of variation, then the inevitable consequence follows that the buyer may reject"'.[59]

I cannot pretend fully to explain the inconsistency of these views with the approach expressed in *Reigate v Union Manufacturing*.[60] I can only point to it as a very telling example of the contradictions of the classical law's acceptance of solipsistic self-interest in a contracting party's conduct of its affairs.[61] With respect and indeed hesitation, it is submitted that Scrutton LJ's distinction between the commercial mind and the legal mind completely misconceives their proper relationship.[62] For it cannot be legitimate to say, as if this were ethically acceptable, that when a party that, judged objectively, did not agree, then that party should just accept it has been bettered, as it has to do when solipsistically competitive efforts are legitimate, in a battle of legal champions seeking to incorporate terms and obtain interpretations (and thus performances) by any means other than those which, as is appropriate to the circumstances, give each party a reasonable opportunity to agree. It is right to observe what in the end are, in a sense, artificial legal devices, such as canons of construction or even ostensibly idiosyncratic meanings of standard terms, when they are conventionally accepted in various walks of commercial life, for these are in principle defensible as ways of minimising transaction costs, and could constitute the best attempt to give effect to the intentions of the parties.[63] But this reasoning cannot apply when those devices, having no such defence, do quite the opposite, and a truly artificial reification of those devices can serve no useful purpose.[64]

If, with requisite legal assistance, a party can negotiate and interpret terms that will confer advantages to which the other party cannot be said to have agreed save in a *Bleak House* sense, and for which advantages that party therefore will not have been paid, the law of contract should not endorse an interpretation that will give effect to this advantage. No doubt such practices will always be found in this vale of tears, and

[59] *Arcos* (CA) (n 28) 4 col 2, 6 col 1, 6 col 2.

[60] To which we return in connection with *L'Estrange v Graucob* [1934] 2 KB 394 (KB) in ch 6.

[61] No doubt there are other issues at work as well. In his LSE lecture that he repeated in *Shirlaw v Southern Foundries*, Mackinnon J attributed persistence with 'the difficulty or obscurity' of some 'traditional forms of commercial contracts' to, precisely, 'the provision of further litigation', and hence the 'further enrichment' of the 'deserving class' of 'commercial lawyers': Mackinnon, *Some Aspects* (n 21) 16.

[62] The range of issues involved in, to quote the book's subtitle, *Bridging the Gap Between Legal Reasoning and Commercial Expectation*, are authoritatively reviewed in C Mitchell, *Contract Law and Contract Practice* (Hart 2013) A striking feature of the enormous literature Mitchell discusses is the number of contributions by current and former senior judges, more common now but going back at least a century, which are strongly critical of the privileging of the 'legal mind'.

[63] *Investors* was all but immediately met by Evans LJ saying that the old intellectual baggage had merely 'been replaced by airline suitcases, the contents [of which] are much the same': *BOC Group v Centeon LLC* 979B [1997] 1 All ER (Comm) 970 (CA); see further G McMeel, *The Construction of Contracts* (2nd edn, OUP 2017) para 1.124.

[64] It is on this basis that Lord Bridge gave his wise advice about how to deal with incompetence in *Mitsui Construction Co Ltd v Attorney-General of Hong Kong* (1986) 10 Con LR 1 (PC) 41:

> the poorer the quality of the drafting, the less willing any court should be to be driven by semantic niceties to attribute to the parties an improbable and unbusinesslike intention, if the language used, whatever it may lack in precision, is reasonably capable of an interpretation ... on a sensible and businesslike basis.

no hermeneutic device, not even business efficacy in all its various forms as an interpretive device, though these are essential, will ultimately prevent them, for the fundamental issue is not hermeneutic but moral. Legitimate interpretation cannot accept the results of the exercise of solipsistic self-interest in pursuit of business advantage. Legitimate interpretation can, nevertheless, be based on business efficacy because business efficacy is not a licence to solipsistic self-interest but expresses a moral commitment to the values of the law of contract. Business efficacy is a constraint on the exercise of power in self-interest.[65] In commercial cases, the 'us' which has to be best satisfied when dealing with Hart's unenvisaged case is the 'us' of parties which reach their contractual agreements on the basis of mutual recognition.

Investors and the Restatement of the Law of Interpretation

Even though the argument of this book is that adequately understood self-interest is the basis of welfare-enhancing economic action, it may still be feared that the argument about interpretation is undermined by its potential to substitute welfarist outcomes for the intentions of the parties. For it cannot be denied that, though the *Investors*' approach has so far been warmly approved here,[66] *Investors* itself has given considerable grounds for such a fear. I argue that this happened because the decision reached by Lord Hoffmann and others involved the abandonment of business efficacy which the *Investors*' approach had confirmed to be the proper basis of the law. Not only were, as there were bound to be, good as well as bad objections raised about the detail of the *Investors*' approach, but criticism at a basic level was stimulated by the unwelcome welfarism of what Lord Hoffmann did in the very first application of that approach.

Though there can be very few if any better known modern cases than *Investors*, it is necessary to describe the crucial aspect of the case in some detail. In order to deal with numerous deplorable cases of retail investors being given very poor advice to mortgage their homes in order to generate funds for investments which then performed badly, the government agency then at the time overall responsible for financial regulation set up the Investors Compensation Scheme to manage the claims process. Investors wishing to avail themselves of the Scheme had to assign their claims to the Scheme. When certain investors who had assigned their claims formed the opinion that the Scheme had adopted a policy which meant that they would receive less from the Scheme than private claims for damages against the culpable institutions could be

65 H Havighurst, *The Nature of Private Contract* (Northwestern University Press 1961) 91:

> If ... the legal enforcement of contract is a tenet of individualism ... it might seem that enforcement must serve the interests of the stronger ... But what individualism really meant when it said that contracts should be enforced, was that enforceable contracts should be enforced only in strict accordance with the terms to which the parties had agreed.

66 The balance of the reception generally of Lord Hoffmann's 'principles' was markedly positive. In the edition which appeared since those principles were stated, a leading authority on interpretation was begun with a long quotation of them, then (after brief mention of another case) saying: 'The lazy reader may stop here [on page 3 of an 862 page book]': Sir Kim Lewison, *The Interpretation of Contracts* (5th edn, Sweet & Maxwell 2011) para 1.01 (hereafter Lewison, *Interpretation*).

expected to realise,[67] they brought such claims directly against the defendant, even though the defendant was in process of reaching a settlement with the Scheme. The litigation in effect sought to establish whether the defendant's liability was to the investors directly or to the investors via the Scheme.

As the argument was developed, the main issue was whether the investors' claims were what were called 'third party claims', and this largely turned on s 3(b) of their contract with the Scheme, which provided:

> [The Scheme] agrees that the following claims shall not be treated as a 'third party claim' (as defined in section 4 of this form) for the purposes of this agreement and that the benefits of such claims shall enure to [the investor] absolutely: Any claim (whether sounding in rescission for undue influence or otherwise) that you have or may have against the West Bromwich Building Society in which you claim an abatement of sums which you would otherwise have to repay to that society in respect of sums borrowed by you from that society in connection with the transaction and dealings giving rise to the claim (including interest on any such sums).[68]

On the accepted basis that a claim for damages was, as a set-off, a claim for abatement of sums,[69] the investors had argued that such a claim fell under 'Any claim (whether sounding in rescission for undue influence or otherwise)', and so was not an assigned third party claim, leaving the investors free to pursue their claims outside of the Scheme. Lord Hofmann held, however, that 'Any claim (whether sounding in rescission for undue influence or otherwise)' should be read as 'Any claim sounding in rescission (whether for undue influence or otherwise)'. The effect of this was to acknowledge that claims for rescission were not assigned, but that all other claims, including claims in damages such as the ones at issue, were.

Their Lordships, save Lord Lloyd in a powerful dissent, agreed with Lord Hoffmann, reversing the unanimous judgment of the Court of Appeal delivered by Leggatt LJ.[70] Leggatt LJ had concluded that the interpretation of 3(b) eventually approved by Lord Hoffmann was 'not an available meaning of the words', and so there was 'simply no warrant for limiting the rights retained to claims for or consequent upon rescission'.[71] Lord Lloyd was 'in complete agreement' with this.[72] How could this very troubling divergence of view arise? The fundamental answer has to lie, not in hermeneutic technique, but in the economic and legal values that guide the application of any such technique.

Lord Hoffmann's insistence that the interpretation he advanced was essential to avoid 'alleged commercial nonsense'[73] is persuasive only on the condition that, as

[67] *Investors* (HL) (n 1) 909C.
[68] ibid 900E.
[69] ibid 911F.
[70] I shall not attempt to discuss the complications of relating the appeal courts' judgments to the first instance decision on 3(b).
[71] *Investors Compensation Scheme Ltd v West Bromwich Building Society (No 1)* [1998] 1 BCLC 493, 521 (CA) 527h–i.
[72] *Investors* (HL) (n 1) 902A.
[73] ibid 912F.

he evidently believed was the case, his task was to give effect to what he believed to be the purpose of the Scheme intended by the regulatory body, which could work only if the assignment was generally effective. But it was not Lord Hoffmann's task to make the Scheme work in this way when interpretation of the parties' objective intentions showed that the regulatory body had itself failed to make the Scheme work in this sense by negotiating appropriate wording; its, as Lord Lloyd put it, 'slovenly' drafting creating a 'needlessly confusing and obscure' situation which prejudiced the investors' interests?[74] Even Lord Hoffmann acknowledged that he was 'dealing with one badly drafted clause which is happily no longer in use'.[75] It was quite wrong of Lord Hoffmann to apparently equate 'avoiding commercial nonsense' with preventing the Scheme's failure, for, of course, failure is integral to business efficacy because it is integral to economic action: 'what the law desires to effect . . . is to give . . . business efficacy to the transaction . . . not to emancipate one side from all the chances of failure'.[76] There really is no contractual defence of Lord Hoffmann giving effect to what he thought were the subjective intentions of the Scheme because he approved of them. In simply supplying what he thought was the best outcome, Lord Hoffmann just did what he should not have done, and over the subsequent decade he went on doing it, culminating in a disturbing exploitation of implication in *Belize Telecom*.

A number of important cases backed by a very large amount of judicial and academic commentary have in various ways criticised Lord Hoffmann's overriding of the parties' objective intentions in order to supply what was believed to be a superior outcome to that expressed in those intentions. In particular, after a number of effective refusals to follow *Belize* in which the judgment of Andrew Phang JA, an outstanding academic authority on implied terms,[77] in the Singaporean case of *Foo Jong Peng v Phua Kiah Mai* was, as it were, substantively damning,[78] the Supreme Court spoke of *Belize* in terms of not tremendously well disguised contempt in *Marks and Spencer plc v BNP Paribas Securities Services Trust Co (Jersey) Ltd*.[79] In the course of this criticism, every one of *Investors'* valuable formulations has been at one time or other cast into doubt, not least by inconsistent things Lord Hoffmann himself has said in purported justification of doing just what he should not have done,[80] and 'natural words', 'ambiguity', 'relevance', 'rectification', 'implication', etc have all been worked over again[81] as,

[74] ibid 899B.

[75] ibid 913F.

[76] *The Moorcock* (n 18) 68.

[77] A Phang, 'Implied Terms, Business Efficacy and the Officious Bystander: A Modern History' [1997] Journal of Business Law 1.

[78] *Foo Jong Peng v Phua Kiah Mai* [2014] 4 SLR 1267; (2013) 149 Con LR 117 (Singapore Court of Appeal) [34]–[36]; approved in *Marks and Spencer plc v BNP Paribas Securities Services Trust Co (Jersey) Ltd* [2015] UKSC 72; [2015] 3 WLR 1843 [24] (hereafter *M and S v BNP Paribas*).

[79] *M and S v BNP Paribas* (n 78) [31] (Lord Neuberger).

[80] In particular, so unwise was Lord Hoffmann's couching of his welfarist intervention in defence of a public initiative in terms of avoiding 'commercial nonsense' that it has led to a revival of 'natural meaning' which should not be overridden by commercial common sense, as if the appearance of natural meaning could ever be other than the result of words read in a particular context: *Skanska Rasleigh Weatherfoil Ltd v Somerfield Stores Ltd* [2006] EWCA Civ 1732; [2007] CILL 2449 [22] (Neuberger LJ).

[81] The words of caution sounded in D MacLauchlan's 'The New Law of Contract Interpretation' (2000) 19 New Zealand Universities Law Review 147 have proven prescient and have led to Professor MacLauchlan's substantial body of work charting with some despair the regrettable twists and turns: D MacLauchlan, 'A Better Way of Making Sense of Contract Law' (2016) 132 Law Quarterly Review 577 and D MacLauchlan,

in sum, what had been gained for conscious contextualism seemed to be in danger of being lost.[82] And though it is right that they should be lost if the cost of keeping them was interpretation (including implication) normally leading to results like *Investors* and *Belize Telecom*, there is no necessity for this to happen. Ultimately it was not the *Investors'* or even the *Belize* approach to interpretation which was at fault, for in the end there was nothing new under the sun,[83] but what Lord Hoffmann did in the name of that approach, and about this no guidance, no matter how valuable, on how to interpret the intentions of the parties can prevail if doing this is not the intention of the court.[84]

Though one acknowledges there is some weight in the argument that the openness of the *Investors'* approach gave Lord Hoffmann a latitude he would not have enjoyed when burdened by the old baggage,[85] it surely is less weight than has sometime been thought, for it can hardly be maintained that, had he had to do so, Lord Hoffmann would not have been able to carry that burden where he wished to go. It is impossible to read *Investors* and not think of Lord Denning's judgments in, well, a great many cases. Indeed, Professor Atiyah was able to base his unforgettable conclusion that Lord Denning did 'a great deal of good' in the law of contract although it was 'a good thing there was only one Lord Denning'[86] in large part on Lord Denning's handling of the baggage in cases which needed dexterity to establish what would now be (and should then have been) regarded as the intentions of the parties.[87] That, as we shall see particularly in our discussion of consideration and inequality of bargaining power in the following chapters, Lord Denning often saw the issues in terms of welfarist improvement which trumped business efficacy,[88] and so did not give effect to the intentions of the parties at all, cannot be doubted, and certainly should not be approved,[89] but the point is that the baggage by no means completely hampered him.

The argument I am seeking to make cannot be made by sole reference to so extraordinary a figure as Lord Denning but the case law of the time of his first period in the Court of Appeal yields overwhelming evidence for that point. *Shanklin Pier Ltd v Detel*

'The *ICS* Principles: A Failed "Revolution" in Contract Interpretation?' (2016) 27 New Zealand Universities Law Review 263.

[82] J NcCunn, '*Belize* It or Not: Implied Terms in *Marks and Spencer v BNP Paribas*' (2016) 79 Modern Law Review 1090.

[83] Lord Bingham, 'A New Thing Under the Sun: The Interpretation of Contract and the ICS Decision' (2008) 12 Edinburgh Law Review 374.

[84] I would hope my inability to let go of a good phrase does not lead the reader to think my use of the court's 'intention' implies that the court's choice is deliberate in other than unusual cases.

[85] In *Investors* (HL) (n 1) 904D itself Lord Lloyd had, of course, cautioned against the possibility that 'purposive interpretation' could 'shade' into 'creative interpretation'.

[86] PS Atiyah, 'Lord Denning's Contribution to Contract Law' (1999) 14 Denning Law Journal 1, 11.

[87] This is discussed in relationship to Lord Denning's handling of exclusion clauses in ch 6.

[88] In *Liverpool City Council v Irwin* [1976] QB 319 (CA) 329E–330G, Lord Denning dismissed the famous *dicta* of business efficacy as 'old cliches' which 'do not truly represent the way in which the courts act', for the courts were seeking to imply what was 'reasonable'.

[89] In *British Movietone News v London and District Cinemas* [1951] KB 190 (CA) 201–202 Denning LJ declared his intention not to let the 'words' in which contracts 'happen to be phrased' become 'tyrannical masters' because 'The day is done when we can excuse an unforeseen injustice by saying to the sufferer "It is your own folly. You ought not to have passed that form of words. You ought to have put in a clause to protect yourself"'. This case, and its reversal in the Lords, is discussed in connection with frustration in ch 10.

Products Ltd,[90] a Commercial Court judgment which once drew considerable comment though is now obscure, demonstrated the welfarist approach behind the result in *Investors* almost half a century earlier. The claimant, wishing to have its pier, which had fallen into disrepair, repainted as part of the pier's restoration, made inquiry of the defendant about a suitable paint, and the defendant recommended one of its products. When entering into a contract for the painting with third party contractors, the claimant stipulated use of the defendant's product. When that paint proved so unsuitable that the claimant was put to great extra expense, it sought damages from the defendant for breach of the warranty of (one concludes from the brief report, but it is irrelevant if the warranty was of merchantability) fitness for purpose which the court accepted the defendant had given by its recommendation. The main contract made no reference to the defendant's recommendation; nor, indeed, if it had could the contractors be held liable in respect of a stipulation by the claimant. But by use of what *Investors* should have, but certainly has not, made redundant, the implied 'collateral' contract or warranty, McNair J was able to imply the requisite basis of liability:

> I am satisfied that, if a direct contract of purchase and sale of the [paint] had ... been made between the plaintiffs and the defendants, the correct conclusion on the facts would have been that the defendants gave to the plaintiffs ... warranties [of fitness].[91]

The particular significance of *Shanklin Pier* is that it recognised what Wedderburn, in an influential paper advocating the use of the collateral contract—'this weapon of justice'[92]—in fulsome terms, classified as a 'three party collateral contract'.[93] *Shanklin Pier* therefore had the potential to generate a wide ranging exception to privity, but although it did lead to a way of dealing with a privity problem inherent in consumer hire-purchase contracts which was then of considerable importance,[94] this general potential was not realised.[95] In substantial part this will have been due to its being thought unnecessary after the emergence of the tort of negligent misstatement, and the relationship of contract and negligence is discussed in the next chapter,[96] but we shall return to the contractual aspects below. For the moment we should note the items of old baggage *Shanklin Pier* seemed to indicate should be discarded even were it a 'two party' case.

The 'warranty' was bogged down in antediluvian notions of the limits to a seller's liability which turned on distinctions between representations and warranties in a

[90] [1951] 2 KB 854 (KB) (hereafter *Shanklin Pier*).

[91] ibid 856.

[92] KW Wedderburn, 'Collateral Contracts' [1959] Cambridge Law Journal 58, 85 (hereafter Wedderburn, 'Collateral Contracts').

[93] ibid 68–69.

[94] In the leading case, *Andrews v Hopkinson* [1957] 1 QB 229 (QB) 235, McNair J followed his own decision in *Shanklin Pier*.

[95] JE Stannard, 'The Road to Shanklin Pier, or the Leading Case that Never Was' (2006) 57 Northern Ireland Legal Quarterly 375 (hereafter Stannard, 'Shanklin Pier').

[96] It is, however, of interest to note here that it was McNair J who in 1960 handed down the first instance judgment in *Hedley Byrne*. Unreported and previously effectively not publicly available, this judgment is now reproduced as an appendix to K Barker, R Grantham, and W Swain (eds), *The Law of Misstatements: 50 Years On from Hedley Byrne v Heller* (Hart 2015).

way the contemporary reader would find very hard to understand. Even were this not the case, the parol evidence rule would at least have hindered the incorporation of the warranty into the main contract.[97] The point here, however, is that discarding the old baggage was entirely possible, even though this required the acquisition of further baggage, for the implied collateral contract is a mere fiction with no possible justification other than the, to recall Wedderburn, justice of its results.

Once one has determined to find a collateral contract in the absence of a 'direct', ie a real, contract, one can find the necessary consideration for the warranty in 'the plaintiffs specifying that the contractors should use for repainting the pier two coats of [the] paint'.[98] No biting hermeneutic constraint can be placed on this. The constraint has to be respect for the value of sanctity, but this is what was missing from McNair J's approach, which sought to improve on the contractual outcome by providing a remedy for the claimant regardless of what had been agreed, and regardless of the claimant's problem being entirely caused by its own negotiating incompetence. Not only did it fail to enter into any 'direct' contract with the defendant, but, by specifying the paint, it made it impossible to avail itself of the warranty of the quality of the paint the defendant would have made when 'transferring' goods it had selected under what is now The Supply of Goods and Services Act 1982, s 4(2) (or s 4(4)).[99]

Why should the courts invent a contract, or rewrite a contract, in order to protect a claimant from its own incompetence in this way? Whilst no-one but a misanthrope can celebrate the visiting of the adverse consequences of mistakes upon those making those mistakes, that those consequences should be visited upon them is essential to contractual justice (and behind this Pareto optimality). And, of course, the interests of the other party are prejudiced by courts acting in this way. This was blatant in *Investors*. It is significant that the interests of the defendant were not even discussed in *Shanklin Pier*, but it cannot have had in its reasonable contemplation that, by recommending its own product to a potential buyer, it was assuming the liability of the paint not working after being applied by a third party. This is simply not the same as recommending one's product.[100] Who could be thought to, by default, assume the uncontrollable risks of assuming such liability?

Even those arguing, with good reason, that the collateral contract or warranty could have performed a valuable function given the law of interpretation at the time (particularly the parol evidence rule as it then stood), acknowledged that it opened attractive but therefore hazardous vistas of judicial creativity, and its use should, in the famous words of Lord Moulton, be 'viewed with suspicion by the law'.[101] To read *Investors* and its aftermath with some knowledge of cases like *Shanklin Pier* gives rise to a feeling of déjà vu, and this is because the basic moral issue has never been adequately addressed. Welfarism which seeks to improve upon parties' agreements raises a moral

[97] Stannard, 'Shanklin Pier' (n 95) 376–79.

[98] *Shanklin Pier* (n 90) 855.

[99] The common law position in 1951 was to be found in *Watson v Buckley, Osborne, Garrett and Co Ltd* [1940] 1 All ER 174 (Manchester Assizes).

[100] The statement of the facts seems to show that the defendant tried but failed to secure the contract for the painting work.

[101] Wedderburn, 'Collateral Contracts' (n 92) 77 quoting *Heilbut, Symonds and Co Ltd v Buckleton* [1913] AC 30 (HL) 47.

question for those who have the power and for whatever reason the belief that they have the competence to (leaving aside legislation) adjudicate for such improvements. What weight do they put on Sir George Jessell MR's 'paramount public policy'; are they committed to sanctity in difficult cases? Much of the answer to this lies not in no sophisticated ratiocination but in frankly facing the moral issues, but there is an aspect that has particular interest for the theoretical and doctrinal development of the law of contract.

Business Efficacy and Necessity in Interpretation

Welfarism may be described as an attack on the values institutionalised in sanctity of contract,[102] and the actual decision in *Investors* does illustrate, if in the form of an unsubtle exaggeration, a tension in adjudication of the law of interpretation acutely described by Macaulay more than 50 years ago. Macaulay identified policies in the law of contract which 'support the market system', including 'the dogma that courts do not make contracts for parties', with policies which 'promote general economic welfare', including a 'case by case' 'relief of hardship policy' which 'is based not on considerations of market functioning but on ethical ideals and emotional reactions to the plight of the underdog', and claimed that adjudication in contract turns on the 'problem of proportioning' these policies.[103] Although Macaulay describes a tension which has as a matter of fact been central to post-war contract adjudication,[104] the alternatives have not been, with respect, quite as he says. Given a proper understanding of Pareto optimality, the opposition of 'ethical ideals and emotional reactions to the plight of the underdog' to the results of interpretation which 'support[s] the market system' fails to give proper weight to the 'ethical ideals' of the 'market system' and its outcomes. A reorientation of our attitude to the way these outcomes are generated allows a very considerable reduction of the unproductivity of the tension.[105]

Lord Hoffmann's opening of interpretation up to 'absolutely anything which would have affected the way the language of the document would have been understood by a reasonable man' was, of course, made subject to the explicit exception that 'The law excludes from the admissible background the previous negotiations of the parties and

[102] JE Baker, 'From Sanctity of Contract to Reasonable Expectations' (1979) 32 Current Legal Problems 17; H Collins, 'The Sanctimony of Contract' in R Rawlings (ed), *Law, Society and Economy* (Clarendon Press 1997) and SM Waddams, *The Sanctity of Contracts in a Secular Age* (CUP 2019).

[103] S Macaulay, 'Justice Traynor and the Law of Contracts' (1961) 13 Stanford Law Review 812, 813.

[104] It is this fact that provides a ground for the argument that contract adjudication should adopt a 'principled pluralism': N Oman, 'Unity and Pluralism in Contract Law' (2005) 103 Michigan Law Review 1483. In addition to the criticisms that have been made of the unwelcome consequences for legal reasoning of this acceptance of inconsistency or incoherence within contract (R Kreitner, 'On the New Pluralism in Contract Theory' (2012) 45 Suffolk University Law Review 915, 923), the argument here is that the pluralism is based on a misconception of the moral nature of freedom of contract.

[105] It would be otherworldly to deny that what Macneil calls proportioning plays its part in the exercise of a, to put it this way, ineliminable discretion to balance the outcomes of certain cases as they are pleaded in the lower courts, and one can see the force of an argument that it may be ineliminable because there is some value in it. An example would be the award of small sums, unjustifiable in principle, to consumers suffering a disappointment with which it is impossible not to have some sympathy (Macaulay's 'emotional reactions') in the practical circumstances of the proceedings: D Harris, D Campbell, and R Halson, *Remedies in Contract and Tort* (2nd edn, CUP 2005) 596–97.

their declarations of subjective intent.'[106] The reason initially given for this was 'practical policy',[107] giving an impression of a wish to avoid being deluged with Brandeis briefs of material even if that material was potentially relevant, and, of course, even more so if it was not.[108] But as the difficulties of defending it have shown,[109] this reason does not squarely address the issue, which is the binding character of objective intentions is something to which subjective intentions are irrelevant, as is the material 'drenched in subjectivity'[110] which might be used to establish those intentions.

It is the duty of economic actors wishing to make their exchange legally enforceable to turn their subjective intentions into the objective intentions expressed in the terms of a contract, and contracting parties can legitimately require that the contract alone (though within its context) is taken to be the expression of their intentions.[111] Criticisms of the exclusion of evidence of previous negotiations which claim that it may be possible to more accurately revise the contract by using that evidence are no doubt right in the hermeneutic sense.[112] But, unlike in personal life,[113] where a failure to make oneself understood should not normally prevent an attempt at clarification, even including reference back to earlier subjective intention—I am sorry. What I meant to say was—subjective intention is irrelevant to legal enforceability.[114] The contract is not, in a very important sense, directly addressed to the parties themselves.[115] It is addressed to the position in which the parties themselves stand when interpreting the legal significance of their contract, that of the objective third party, and the institutionalisation of the interpretation of that party is work of the court.[116] The objective position the parties' actions created *is* their contract. Fully understanding

[106] *Investors* (HL) (n 1) 912H–B.

[107] ibid.

[108] Sir Christopher Staughton was amongst many who feared that openness to context would have deplorable practical consequences: 'How Do Courts Interpret Commercial Contracts?' [1999] Cambridge Law Journal 303, 307: 'It is hard to imagine a ruling more calculated to perpetuate the vast cost of commercial litigation.' Apart from the problem mentioned in the main text, Sir Christopher was concerned that parties might not take too scrupulous a view of what constituted the 'potentially relevant', and, though the size of the problem is uncertain, one understands there have been numerous cases which ground his concern. But parties seeking to introduce (large volumes of) this evidence are trying tendentiously to force their subjective understanding on the court, when the point should be to assist the court to ascertain the objective understanding established by reasonable attempts to persuade the other party to agree, not to bury it in arcana during negotiation or surprise it with arcana during litigation: *Chartbrook* (n 11) [38]. Material which legitimately might be regarded as potentially relevant must itself be confined within the restrictions imposed by business common sense.

[109] See the reference to the merely 'pragmatic' in *Chartbrook* (n 11) [27]–[42] (Lord Hoffmann).

[110] ibid [38].

[111] *(L) Schuler AG v Wickman Machine Tool Sales Ltd* [1974] AC 235 (HL) 261A-C (Lord Wilberforce):

> the parties' intentions must be ascertained, on legal principles of construction, from the words they have used. It is one and the same principle which excludes evidence of statements, or actions, during negotiations, at the time of the contract, or subsequent to the contract, any of which to the lay mind might at first sight seem to be proper to receive.

[112] Lord Nicholls, 'My Kingdom for a Horse: The Meaning of Words' (2005) 122 Law Quarterly Review 577.

[113] Lewison, *Interpretation* (n 66) para 1.03.

[114] It is not irrelevant to the practice of contracting, and indeed one assumes it is extremely important in that practice, for the party advancing an interpretation which would be regarded as objectively correct may allow, as it were, the other party to amend that meaning. But the crucial word is allow.

[115] A Berg, 'Thrashing Through the Undergrowth' (2006) 122 Law Quarterly Review 354, 359.

[116] *Davis Contractors Ltd v Fareham UDC* [1956] AC 696 (HL) 728 (Lord Radcliffe):

this requires us to recognise that the relationship between the parties, irreducible to their two subjective wills, is the essence of agreement and contract.

How a party goes about incorporating a term into a contract is firstly a question of its negotiating competence, which it may legitimately exercise in its own self-interest with ignorance or disregard of the ultimate interest of the other party. If, after negotiation, a buyer pays a price it subsequently regrets, it would simply run counter to the freedom of choice of both the seller which obtained the price and the buyer itself, and so to the working of the price system, for the state to revise the exchange. To point out the obvious, sanctity of contract allows one to claim the benefit of negotiating well, and requires one to bear the consequences of doing the other thing.

But the exercise of negotiating skill which led to that choice of price must display respect for the buyer's autonomy, so that the buyer's choice must be shown to have been obtained by agreement. When it comes to asking whether there has been agreement at all, say in the case of an over-assertive claimant not extending a reasonable opportunity to accept or reject an offer in *Harvey v Facey*,[117] or of an incompetent defendant not utilising a sufficient opportunity to formulate its purchase offer in *Tamplin v James*,[118] the basic issue of objectivity of intention seems clear. It is this issue that underpins interpretation.[119] When the unenvisaged case calls for interpretation in terms of business efficacy, the question properly posed and answered is 'could the parties reasonably have agreed this term?' The 'business' of business efficacy is what economic actors both believe is an advantageous exchange, and does not endorse the solipsistic assertion of self-interest but endorses only meanings which it is plausible to say could have been agreed. Cases such as *Arcos* seem pathological because it is impossible to conceive of them involving an agreement, as indeed *Arcos* did not.

It certainly follows that interpretation based on (obvious) business efficacy must of its nature be confined to doing only that which is 'necessary' for such efficacy.[120] No

> the spokesman of the fair and reasonable man, who represents after all no more than the anthropomorphic conception of justice, is and must be the court itself'.

This case is discussed in connection with frustration in ch 10.

[117] [1893] AC 552 (PC).

[118] (1880) LR 15 Ch D 215 (CA).

[119] H Collins, 'Objectivity and Committed Contextualism in Interpretation' in S Worthington (ed), *Commercial Law and Commercial Practice* (Hart 2013) 189–90.

[120] *Ilyssia Compania Naviera SA v Bamaodah (The Elli 2)* [1985] 1 Lloyd's Rep 107, 115 col 2 (May LJ):

> no ... contract should be implied on the facts of any given case unless it is necessary to do so: necessary, that it to say, to give business reality to a transaction and to create enforceable obligations between the parties who are dealing with one another in circumstances in which one would expect that business reality and those enforceable obligations to exist.

In what is, with the work of John Gava, one of the two best Commonwealth statements of the argument for neo-formalism, Dr Morgan calls this approach 'minimalism': Morgan, *Minimalism* (n 10) ch 6. Without wishing to let questions of mere terminology override the substance of what Morgan argues, I do not think this is entirely right, for it implies keeping things to a minimum when, as Morgan perfectly well realises, adequate interpretation, even when kept, as it should be, to what is necessary, can be rather extensive. It is significant that, as Morgan notes (J Morgan, *Great Debates in Contract Law* (3rd edn, Macmillan 2020) 136) that in KN Llewellyn, 'Review of O Prausnitz, *The Standardisation of Commercial Contracts in English and Continental Law*' (1939) 52 Harvard Law Review 700, 703, interpretation is said to involve determining the '*minimum decencies* ... essential to [or] inherent in a bargain of that type', when no-one would maintain that Llewellyn's approach to interpretation was based on, as it were, a principle of minimalism. The issue has to be traced to determining the nature of the appropriate extent of regulation even when one is determined to facilitate voluntary choice which was discussed in chs 1 and 2.

word can actually govern, but it is submitted that some evidence that necessity has exercised desirable constraint may be found in attempts, not to expand the 'necessary', but to dispense with the use of 'necessity' when one seeks 'reasonableness, fairness and the balancing of ... policy'.[121] It is submitted that the foundational implied terms authorities quoted above sought to show that implication was necessary, but that legitimate implication was of *only* what was necessary. Obviously they not uncommonly failed in both respects, though the failure in respect of the latter is now by far the more important, with the, as it were, rhetorical emphasis of, in particular, 'purposive interpretation' going in just the wrong way.[122]

It was in this vein that in his criticism of *Belize Telcom* Lord Neuberger said that:

> Lord Hoffmann suggested that the process of implying terms into a contract was part of the exercise of the construction, or interpretation, of the contract ... There are two points to be made about that observation ... First, the notion that a term will be implied if a reasonable reader of the contract, knowing all its provisions and the surrounding circumstances, would understand it to be implied is quite acceptable, provided that (i) the reasonable reader is treated as reading the contract at the time it was made and (ii) he would consider the term to be so obvious as to go without saying or to be necessary for business efficacy.[123]

It was certainly necessary for something like this criticism of *Belize* to be made, but it would be unfortunate if this criticism were to have excessive and retrograde consequences by leading to strong distinctions being drawn between interpretation and implication,[124] which would run against *Investors*.[125] There are, of course, differences between the approaches that should be taken to these tasks, but giving those differences an unhelpful rigidity or fixity is just what the essential sense of the new contextualism of *Investors* tells us not to do. All this is much clearer to grasp if the minimal ambition[126] bound up in the very concept of business efficacy is acknowledged.[127] The linguistic burden of purposive interpretation itself, but also of other terminology to

[121] *Crossley v Faithful and Gould Holdings Ltd* [2004] EWCA Civ 293; [2004] 1 All ER 447 [36] (Dyson LJ).

[122] The most important modern failure in the first respect, *Baird Textiles Holdings Ltd v Marks and Spencer plc* [2001] EWCA Civ 274; [2002] 1 All ER (Comm) 737, discussed at length in ch 10.

[123] *M and S v BNP Paribas* (n 78) [22]–[23].

[124] This claim must, of course, be understood in light of the definitions I put forward in Chapter 3 of terms implied in fact and in law. On those definitions, terms implied in law are not implied by reference to business efficacy.

[125] *Mutatis mutandis*, I would also say this of the distinction between interpretation and relatively minor doctrines such as rectification.

[126] Which should survive Lord Neuberger's in itself correct rejection of 'absolute necessity' in *M and S v BNP Paribas* (n 78) [21] but, with respect, may not survive in Lord Neuberger's resultant formulation of a 'lack of commercial or practical coherence'.

[127] R Austen-Baker, *Implied Terms in English Contract Law* (2nd edn, Edward Elgar 2017) para 7.12 interestingly suggests that some perception of this minimal aspect explains why the *dicta* of Bowen LJ in *The Moorcock* (n 18) have been so influential, overshadowing Lord Esher MR's 'broader' formulations in what was after all the leading judgment by the senior judge.

similar effect, of which 'reasonable expectations' as they are now principally understood is the most influential, leads in the wrong direction.[128] For it is not, or should not be, a question of determining the optimal agreement; finding what Lord Hope recently called 'the centre line marking on the … rope' in 'the tug'o'war of commercial negotiation'.[129] It is a question of ruling out what could not have been agreed in order to leave what could have been agreed by reference to 'obvious' 'efficacy' with the aim of, as it was put in *The Moorcock*, 'preventing such a failure of consideration as cannot have been within the contemplation of either side'.[130]

Some order might be brought to the very considerable number of reformulations of this point in the case law by considering some of the reflections on 'bargaining' or 'recontracting' by FY Edgeworth, an important pioneer of marginalist (and indeed of mathematical) analysis in economics. Though his attitude towards what became the theory of general competition was in a sense the opposite of Hayek's, Edgeworth was for a considerable time regarded as an anomalous figure in the history of that theory because he was intent on explaining equilibrium prices 'perhaps not so much as axiomatic as deducible from the process of competition in a perfect market'.[131] In the conditions prior to equilibrium which Edgeworth called the 'indeterminateness' of contract, there is a range of points, which he called the 'contract curve', at which economic actors might voluntarily agree to exchange, believing that they have reached the achievable optimal position given the constraints of imperfect information and other transaction costs of negotiation. Further investment in negotiation could produce movement along this curve, as one actor improves its position and the other, its position not worsening, is still prepared to agree, with the 'final settlement' of the exchange emerging when no further mutually agreed movement is possible (when what we would now call the conditions of general equilibrium have been established because all possible exchanges have been explored).[132]

This is, of course, the essence of negotiation, and it must be appreciated that, in addition to the law of contract acknowledging that a party can improve its negotiating position by, for example, investing in the acquisition of superior knowledge of the subject

[128] Lord Steyn, 'Contract Law: Fulfilling the Reasonable Expectations of Honest Men' (1997) 113 Law Quarterly Review 433. See further C Mitchell, 'Leading a Life of Its Own? The Roles of Reasonable Expectation in Contract Law (2003) 23 Oxford Journal of Legal Studies 639.

[129] *Wood v Capita Insurance Services Ltd* [2017] UKSC 24; [2017] AC 1173 [28].

[130] *The Moorcock* (n 18) 68.

[131] FY Edgeworth, 'On Some Theories Due to Pareto, Zawardski, WE Johnson and Others' in *Papers Relating to Political Economy*, vol 2 (Macmillan 1925) 450, 453. Edgeworth's views were particularly directed against those of his contemporary Léon Walras, arguably, with Pareto, the most important economist between Smith and Keynes, to whom the mathematically acceptable attempt to state general equilibrium is traced. Walras' model of equilibrium required a special assumption about the formation of prices which need not be discussed here (but which has generated an entire library of commentary from subsequent mathematical economists who have not the slightest concern with its empirical plausibility) which Edgeworth regarded as not 'after all, a very good idea' (FY Edgeworth, 'Review of L Walras, '*Élements d'economie Politique Pure*, 2nd edn' in FY Edgeworth, *Mathematical Psychics and Further Papers on Political Economy* (OUP 2009) 556), but rather as a 'laboured description … calculated to divert attention from a sort of higgling which may be regarded as more fundamental than [Walras'] description, the process of [recontracting]': FY Edgeworth, 'On the Application of Mathematics to Political Economy' in *Papers Relating to Political Economy*, ibid, vol 2, ibid 311.

[132] FY Edgeworth, *Mathematical Psychics* in *Mathematical Psychics and Further Papers on Political Economy* (OUP 2009) 19–30.

matter of the exchange,[133] one of the legitimate determinants of the final settlement is the relative negotiating skill of the parties, which includes ascertaining the other party's negotiating parameters. It has been right of the argument for neo-formalism to maintain that there is no realistic possibility of the courts having the information or competence to improve upon the parties' agreement; but, much more importantly, there is no legitimate basis on which they can do so consistent with the values of exchange and contract, in which handling the transaction costs of exchange is of the essence of contractual competence. Edgeworth seeks to drive home his argument by quoting from one of the founding texts of marginalist economics, WS Jevons' *Theory of Political Economy*, the relevant passage in the original being:

> The result of the bargain will greatly depend upon the comparative amount of knowledge of each other's position and needs which either bargainer may possess or manage to obtain in the course of the transaction. Thus the power of reading another man's thoughts is of high importance in business, and the art of bargaining mainly consists in the buyer ascertaining the lowest price at which the seller is willing to part with his object, without disclosing if possible the highest price which he, the buyer, is willing to give.[134]

Though the theory of general competition posits a unique equilibrium to which exchange tends, Pareto-optimising exchange involves a range of agreements, arrived at through competitive bargaining in empirical situations, which are optimal for those situations. It accordingly is no business of the law of contract generally to seek to pass judgement on contracting parties' comparative success and failure in negotiation *of agreements*. If an agreement is one which reasonable parties could have reached, ie an objective agreement is shown, it should be enforced even if one of the parties, in light of subsequent knowledge, may wish to set the agreement aside because, if it had that knowledge, it could have achieved a better position on the contract curve. Business efficacy must treat this as irrelevant if interpretation is to give effect to the dimension of sanctity of contract which institutionalises legitimate differences of bargaining competence.

This all, of course, assumes that the exercise of contracting competence is based on securing the agreement of the other party through negotiating conduct which evidences mutual recognition. Advantage secured by the illegitimate exercise of 'competence' should not be acknowledged by the law of contract. The problem of interpretation in a sense amplifies the basic problem of ensuring that a contract is an agreement because the range of unenvisaged cases is infinite. For reasons of economic theory, Edgeworth and Jevons examined the issues in terms of the price of a good viewed as an homogenous unit. But the meaning of the terms, and therefore the

[133] AT Kronman, 'Mistake, Disclosure, Information and the Law of Contracts' (1978) 7 Journal of Legal Studies 1, 15:

> One (seldom noticed) way in which the legal system can establish property rights in information is by permitting an informed party to enter and enforce contracts which his information suggests are profitable, without disclosing the information to the other party.

[134] WS Jevons, *The Theory of Political Economy* (Penguin 1970) 159.

(non-)performance of the obligations under those terms, determines the true significance of price (in some cases it is the price terms themselves that give rise to unenvisaged cases). Our discussion of the impossibility of dealing with the illegitimate exploitation of the unenvisaged case by making all terms clear, and the consequent necessity of contextual interpretation based on the moral standard of business efficacy may be concluded by placing it in the context of the general recognition in economic theory of the necessity of trust, and in legal doctrine by the recognition of the necessity of good faith.

Conclusion: Moral Hazard, Trust and Good Faith

The way the law of implied terms makes possible reliance on the quality of goods despite the impossibility of making a commodity fully contingent, or a contract fully presentiated, examined in Chapter 3, can now be placed in the general context of the way that the law of interpretation makes economic exchange possible despite it being impossible ever to fully specify an agreement. The relevant way in which we are 'men, not gods' is that we are always faced with transaction costs as an aspect of economic scarcity. Making a contract involves an expenditure of resource and contracting parties' resources are, to differing degrees but always, finite. Having demonstrated that the allocation even of economic goods such as the harms of pollution then, very largely as now, thought not to be amenable to market organisation would be optimal at general competitive equilibrium, Coase observed that this demonstration turned on 'the assumption that there [are] no costs involved in carrying out market transactions', and that '[t]his is, of course . . . very unrealistic':

> In order to carry out a market transaction, it is necessary to discover who it is that one wishes to deal with, to inform people that one wishes to deal and on what terms, to conduct negotiations leading up to the bargain, to draw up the contract, to undertake the inspection needed to make sure that the terms of the contract are being observed, and so on. These operations are often extremely costly.[135]

The empirical existence of transaction costs inevitably posits the 'bounded rationality' of economic action,[136] and the consequent inevitability and ubiquity of incomplete contracts: 'complete contracts . . . are contracts where everything that can ever happen is written into the contract . . . Actual contracts are not like this, as lawyers have realised for a long time. They are incomplete'.[137] The myriad transaction costs of entering into an exchange have been classified in very many ways, and in some influential contributions 'negotiating costs' have played a central part. Were this not enough, however, the existence of these costs, coupled to a neo-classical economic

[135] RH Coase, 'The Problem of Social Cost' in *The Firm, the Market and the Law* (University of Chicago Press 1988) 114.

[136] HA Simon, *Administrative Behaviour* (4th edn, Free Press, 1997) 88: 'in the real world . . . human behaviour is *intendedly* rational but only *boundedly* so'.

[137] O Hart, 'Incomplete Contracts and Control' (2017) 107 American Economic Review 1731, 1732.

concept of self-interest, gives rise to the further problem which, though the term is paradoxical,[138] is in the commonest usage described as 'moral hazard'. In the concept of moral hazard, the continuous, general re-evaluation of one's exercise of one's agency which classical sociology identified as the 'reflexivity' unique to the way the human self or mind chooses its courses of action, and thus as the basis of the differentiation of social from physical science, is drastically narrowed to an economic conception of 'self-interest seeking with guile'[139] to which 'calculativeness'[140] is central. When a party enters into a contract, it *thereby* creates the possibility of being taken advantage of by the other party, in the most blatant case by fraud but obviously also by less blatant cases such as the solipsistically self-interested interpretation (and therefore performance or non-performance) of contractual obligations.

The natural solution which economics proposes to this problem, very often viewed in terms of some metaphorical 'principal-agent' relationship, is 'monitoring' the other party.[141] It is, of course, not at all my intention to deny the significance of the real law of agency or other fiduciary relationships, nor to deny the value of literal monitoring in some forms of exchange governed by the law of simple contract, and the legal design of complex contracts as monitoring devices is discussed in Chapter 10. But at the fundamental level at which we are now addressing the problem, there is no monitoring, because there is no solipsistically self-interested solution to the general problem of moral hazard in contracting. Ultimately for the reason Hart identified, contracts cannot be so closely specified as to provide for every contingency and, a derived but also *sui generis* (a sociologist would say emergent) point, cannot provide against the action described as moral hazard which reflexively takes advantage of this. There is not merely a problem of initial complexity but a problem of infinite regression which amounts to, to adapt a coinage of the late Niklas Luhmann,[142] an insoluble 'hypercomplexity'.[143]

[138] MV Pauly, 'The Economics of Moral Hazard' (1968) 58 American Economic Review 531.

[139] OE Williamson, *Markets and Hierarchies* (Free Press 1975) 26.

[140] OE Williamson, *The Mechanisms of Governance* (OUP 1996) 250–56.

[141] MC Jensen and WH Meckling, 'Theory of the Firm: Managerial Behaviour, Agency Costs and Ownership Structure' (1976) 3 Journal of Financial Economics 305, 308:

> The *principal* can limit divergences from his interest by establishing appropriate incentives for the agency and by incurring monitoring costs designed to limit the aberrant activities of the agent.

[142] N Luhmann, *Social Systems* (Stanford University Press 1995) 471.

[143] It is impossible to conceive of a more stark illustration of this than the initial statement of game theory, in which the important identification of the irreducible social element of exchange noted in ch 1 is followed by the discussion of the pursuit of optimisation by what remain solipsistically self-interested actors, who, however, have to deal with each other: J von Neumann and O Morgenstern, *The Theory of Games and Economic Behaviour* (60th anniversary edn, Princeton University Press 2004).

It is of course no criticism whatsoever of von Neumann and Morgenstern to say that that, beyond a vestigial level, I cannot understand their mathematical reasoning, but it is a criticism of their claim to develop a general theory of the economy that it is inconceivable that economic actors understand their own conduct in the way they describe, save in specially devised situations. Game theory, many strains of which are highly critical of von Neumann and Morgenstern, may very well have certain productive uses, not only in economics (K Binmore, *Game Theory* (OUP 2008) but in law (DG Baird, RH Gertner, and RC Picker, *Game Theory and the Law* (Harvard University Press 1994), but this categorically does not include the general understanding of economic action; an issue which overlaps, but certainly is not congruent with, the mathematicisation of economic theory. It is not in any approving manner that the leading historian of economics, Philip Mirowski, has predicted that von Neumann 'will come to be regarded as the single

Responses have been made to this problem which have sought to raise fundamental questions about the social foundations of market order in ways critical or highly critical of neo-classical economics. But the solution, or rather dissolution, of this problem lies, it is submitted, in the proper understanding of the moral nature of contracting parties' economic action, for economic self-interest involves trust.[144] It preserves a valuable focus on self-interest to turn to handling of the problem by the late Kenneth Arrow, who has already repeatedly been cited as one of those most responsible for identifying the conditions of existence of general competitive equilibrium. Arrow was nevertheless under no illusion about the extreme abstraction of that equilibrium, and he posed in an acute way some of the difficulties of relating that possibility to the analysis and guidance of empirical economic action. He was in particular perfectly aware that transaction costs, in particular what he called 'communication and information costs',[145] meant that 'there is no way to ensure complete enforceability' of contracts,[146] and that '[b]ecause of moral hazard, complete reliance on economic incentives does not lead to an optimal allocation of resources'.[147]

I believe Arrow was here acknowledging the explanatory, because normative, limitations of the solipsistic concept of self-interest, and he sought to supply the normative lack by reference to 'norms of social behaviour', for '[t]here is a whole set of customs and norms which might be ... interpreted as agreements to improve the efficiency of the economic system ... by providing commodities to which the price system is inapplicable'.[148] Arrow recognised that 'ethical elements enter in some measure into every contract: without them no market could function',[149] and he repeatedly described these elements as trust: 'in the absence of trust, it would become very costly to arrange for alternative sanctions and guarantees, and many opportunities for mutually beneficial cooperation would have to be foregone'.[150] In particular, Arrow believed that, as 'it would be too costly to draw up contracts which would cover every contingency, some aspects have to be left for interpretation when needed [with it being] implicitly understood that it will be possible to agree on the meaning of the contract',[151]

most important figure in the development of economics in the twentieth century': P Mirowski, *Machine Dreams: Economics Becomes a Cyborg Science* (CUP 2002) 94.

144 G Simmel, *The Philosophy of Money* (3rd edn, Routledge 2011) 191:

> Without the general trust that people have in each other, society itself would disintegrate, for very few relationships are based on what is known with certainty about another person, and very few relationships would endure if trust were not as strong as, or stronger than, rational proof or personal observation. In the same way, money transactions would collapse without trust.

145 KJ Arrow, 'The Organisation of Economic Activity: Issues Pertinent to the Choice of Market Versus Non-market Allocation' in *Collected Papers*, vol 2 (Belknap Press 1983) 149 (hereafter Arrow, 'Organisation of Economic Activity').

146 KJ Arrow, 'Limited Knowledge and Economic Analysis' in *Collected Papers*, vol 4 (Belknap Press 1984) 163.

147 KJ Arrow, 'The Economics of Moral Hazard: Further Comment' in *Collected Papers*, vol 4 (Belknap Press 1984) 104 (hereafter Arrow, 'Moral Hazard').

148 Arrow, 'Organisation of Economic Activity' (n 145) 151, 152.

149 KJ Arrow, Information and Economic Behaviour' in *Collected Papers*, vol 4 (Belknap Press 1984) 150 (hereafter Arrow, 'Information').

150 Arrow, 'Organisation of Economic Activity' (n 145) 151.

151 Arrow, 'Information' (n 149) 150.

and that in 'a successful economic system ... relations of trust and confidence between principal and agent are sufficiently strong that the agent will not cheat even though it may be "rational economic behaviour" ' to do so'.[152]

The limitations of the economic concepts with which Arrow struggled to capture the indispensability of—in this theoretical context a complete oxymoron—'commodities to which the price system is inapplicable' indicates the significance of that struggle: a historically significant economist starting from as pure an understanding of economic action as self-interest as has ever been expressed had to acknowledge the inadequacy of that understanding in order to retain self-interest at all. Trust does not have to denote, though it has often been used to denote, even, as we saw in Chapter 2, in seminal contributions to the relational theory, a 'sociological' rejection of self-interest in our understanding of economic action. But, derived as a condition of our understanding of economic action, trust can denote a moral structure which makes self-interested economic action possible, and this, I believe, is the defensible sense in which Macaulay,[153] in what I hope is now seen as a striking parallel to Arrow, told us that trust 'is necessary to make any economic system work'.[154] To the extent that the classical law of contract regards contract as turning on parties' solipsistic self-interest, it will itself tend to reject or marginalise any notion of trust. But if it is right that trust is necessary, the law of contract has always had to accommodate it, and it has in fact done so in doctrines which turn on a recognition that 'good faith' is indispensable and integral to agreement; and in this sense good faith analytically is, and so has always been, contract's 'core value', as Markovits has put it.[155]

It will be recalled that in Chapter 2 *Walford v Miles* was analysed as a case which contradictorily combined an apparent insistence on solipsistic self-interest with a most determined attempt to prevent an illegitimate imbalance of negotiating power between the parties, and that this extreme confusion was expressed by Lord Ackner in terms of a rejection of a doctrine of good faith which, for convenience, will be repeated here:

> the concept of a duty to carry on negotiations in good faith is inherently repugnant to the adversarial position of the parties when involved in negotiations. Each party to the negotiations is entitled to pursue his (or her) own interest, so long as he avoids making misrepresentations.[156]

But, far from always being celebrated, the absence of good faith has, of course, also been widely deplored, described by Sir Roy Goode as 'at once the most remarkable and

[152] Arrow 'Moral Hazard' (n 147) 104.

[153] The other, 'sociological' as opposed to 'economic', sense of trust which may be found in Macaulay's work is discussed in ch 10.

[154] S Macaulay, 'Relational Contracts Floating on a Sea of Custom: Thoughts About the Ideas of Ian Macneil and Lisa Bernstein' (2000) 94 Northwestern University Law Review 775, 804.

[155] D Markovits, 'Good Faith as Contract's Core Value' in G Klass, G Letsas, and P Saprai (eds), *Philosophical Foundations of Contract Law* (OUP 2014).

[156] *Walford v Miles* [1992] 2 AC 128 (HL) 138E.

the most reprehensible feature of the English law of contract'.[157] How is it possible that such divergent evaluations can be reached?

I am obliged to repeat one of the conclusions of the analysis of *Walford v Miles* in Chapter 2: Lord Ackner's famous *dictum* is simply wrong about the law. It is not the law that parties to a negotiation may pursue their self-interest in a way which is limited only by the necessity of avoiding misrepresentations. For, as Byron is reported to have said of the word '*ennui*', whilst we in England may not have a general doctrine of good faith, we have the thing in abundance, and the English law of contract has always contained a large number of doctrines in addition to misrepresentation which, confining self-interest to legitimate courses, together amount to an ample obligation of good faith.[158] One mentions, purely illustratively, fraud about terms, agreement mistake, duress, estoppel, and various disclosure requirements. I myself attempted to classify these doctrines a quarter of a century ago.[159] The most important point is to relate the general interpretation of contract on the basis of business efficacy to the concept of good faith. And this, of course, is just what Leggatt J (as he then was) did in *Yam Seng Pte Ltd v International Trade Corporation Ltd*, underpinning his judgment with by reference to, if I may put it this way, some issues identified in the social theoretical account of legitimate self-interest in negotiation which has, I think, no equivalent in the Commonwealth law:

> The modern case law on the construction of contracts has emphasised that contracts, like all human communications, are made against a background of unstated shared understandings which inform their meaning. The breadth of the relevant background and the fact that it has no conceptual limits have also been stressed . . . Importantly for present purposes, the relevant background against which contracts are made includes not only matters of fact known to the parties but also shared values and norms of behaviour. Some of these are norms that command general social acceptance; others may be specific to a particular trade or commercial activity; others may be more specific still, arising from features of the particular contractual relationship. Many such norms are naturally taken for granted by the parties when making any contract without being spelt out in the document recording their agreement. A paradigm example of a general norm which underlies almost all contractual relationships is an

[157] RM Goode, *Commercial Law* (rev 1st edn, Penguin Books 1985) 117; see now E McKendrick, *Goode and McKendrick on Commercial Law* (6th edn, Penguin Books 2020) para 3.113.

[158] *Carter v Boehm* (1766) 3 Burr 1905; 97 ER 1162 is not, it is submitted, itself consistent with the understanding of agreement advanced here (S Watterson, '*Carter v Boehm* (1766)' in C Mitchell and P Mitchell (eds), *Landmark Cases in the Law of Contract* (Hart 2008)), though Lord Mansfield's famous reference to a 'governing principle applicable to all contracts and dealings' (*Carter v Boehm*, ibid 1910; 1644) certainly could be read in that way.

[159] D Campbell, 'The Relational Constitution of the Discrete Contract' in D Campbell and P Vincent-Jones (eds), *Contract and Economic Organisation* (Dartmouth 1996) (hereafter Campbell, 'Relational Constitution'). I would not now bother either to defend or to repent of this specific classification, but mention of one of its defects may usefully illustrate a perennial problem in the analysis of good faith. Is it necessary or productive to distinguish between good faith at different stages of the contracting process? From my classification I omitted the general disclosure obligation recognised in *Hadley v Baxendale* (1854) 9 Ex Ch 341; 156 ER 145, surely the most important such obligation in the law of contract. I did so because I took too literally the distinction between agreement and remedy. But should not all good faith obligations, including during performance and during pursuit of remedy, be capable of being traced to the agreement?

> expectation of honesty. That expectation is essential to commerce, which depends critically upon trust ... The central idea [behind fidelity to the parties' bargain] is that contracts can never be complete in the sense of expressly providing for every event that may happen. To apply a contract to circumstances not specifically provided for, the language must accordingly be given a reasonable construction which promotes the values and purposes expressed or implicit in the contract.[160]

Leggatt J's reflections on good faith are, of course, *a tour de force*, and it has been tellingly argued that they were not required in order to reach a decision in the case.[161] Whilst acknowledging the point, this is not, it is submitted, entirely correct. *Yam Seng* involved a requirements contract; a relatively simple[162] instance of one of Macneil's relational contracts.[163] As we shall see in Chapter 10, the existing law did deal with these cases, as indeed it did deal with good faith, but in a theoretically incoherent way which prevented self-awareness of what the law was doing.[164] It is the development of self-awareness of the nature of the existing law, and eschewing any doctrinal addition to good faith, that is the nature of Leggatt J's achievement, and indeed makes it not merely defensible but very valuable. It is not an attempt to impose an exogenous standard; it is an attempt to elucidate the endogenous standard. One can, in fact, lament the way that having to step off from a requirements contract allowed *Yam Seng's* broadly unfavourable initial reception to confine good faith to express terms which might be incorporated into that type of contract. Especially as this was all couched in terms of a distinction between the 'interpretation' of a good faith term and the 'implication' of such a term derived from *Marks v Spencer v BNP Paribas*, Leggatt J's truly fundamental point did not even register. One felt the feeling of déjà vu all over again,[165] though this has thankfully been much lessened by the number of cases approving *Yam Seng* which, as we saw in Chapter 2, allowed Fraser J to claim, on the basis of a review of those cases in *Bates v The Post Office (No 3)*,[166] that 'the concept of relational contracts is an established one in English law'.[167]

Let us put aside the wrong tack taken of thinking this is a matter of recognising a particular 'specie' of contract,[168] which has been discussed in Chapter 2 and to which we shall return in Chapter 10, and focus on the fundamental significance of recognising the relational contract for the doctrine of agreement. That doctrine (to which implication and interpretation are integral) cannot acknowledge a subjective

160 *Yam Seng Pte Ltd v International Trade Corporation Ltd* [2013] EWHC 111 (QB); [2013] 1 All ER (Comm) 1321 [133]–[135], [139] (hereafter *Yam Seng*).

161 JW Carter and W Courtney, 'Good Faith in Contracts: Is There an Implied Promise to Act Honestly? (2016) 75 Journal of Contract Law 608 (hereafter Carter and Courtney, 'Good Faith in Contracts').

162 D Campbell, 'Good Faith and the Ubiquity of the "Relational" Contract' (2014) 77 Modern Law Review 460, 480–81.

163 *Yam Seng* (n 161) [142].

164 As a judgment of the House of Lords, *Walford v Miles* had to be manoeuvred around carefully: *Yam Seng*, ibid [123].

165 *Mid Essex Hospital Services NHS Trust v Compass Group UK and Ireland Ltd (t/a Medirest)* [2013] EWCA Civ 200, [2013] BLR 265 [105] and *Globe Motors Inc v TRW Lucas Varity Electric Steering Ltd* [2016] EWCA Civ 396; (2016) 168 Con LR 59 [67]–[68].

166 [2019] EWHC 606 (QB); [2019] All ER (D) 100 (Mar) [702]–[768].

167 ibid [705].

168 ibid [703].

attitude of solipsistic self-interest. It must impose an objective morality which in the case law has been called good faith.[169] Though it has of course been put to welfarist purposes, the requirement of good faith is not a relatively recent welfarist innovation. As a general concept of an implied undertaking not to take opportunistic advantage in ways that could not have been contemplated, and therefore provided for, at the time of negotiation, good faith is inherent in contract as such.[170] In a sense, the entire argument here seeks only to place on a firmer footing the view expressed by Sir Frederick Pollock in 1885:

> The law of contract may be described as the endeavour of the state ... to establish a positive sanction for the expectation of good faith which has grown in the mutual dealings of men of average right mindedness.[171]

If we may transplant the legal terminology, good faith is inherent in market exchange, and to understand why this is so is to become conscious of the necessity of mutual recognition.

Though, perhaps inevitably, there is abiding confusion about this, it is submitted that Leggatt J did not wish to advocate a general doctrine of good faith,[172] and in taking this position Leggatt J was very wise.[173] Of course, many other national legal systems,[174] including the common law system of the US,[175] and many international trade agreements and model laws,[176] do recognise a general principle of good faith, and the projected unified EU contract law certainly would have done so.[177] But though it is unhelpful to deny that there is a doctrine—unless one is rather inflexible in what one means by doctrine—of good faith in English law, whether this should take the form of a *general* doctrine inviting reasoning from first principles or a *piecemeal* doctrine requiring the incremental accumulation of precedents is a question which cannot be given an, as it were, technical answer on the basis of juristic technique. The piecemeal

169 *Yam Seng* (n 161) [144].

170 *Market Street Associates Ltd Partnership v Frey* 941 F 2d 588, 595 (US 7th Cir 1991) (Posner J).

171 F Pollock, *Principles of Contract* (4th edn, Stevens and Sons 1885) 9. I discuss Sir Frederick's views on good faith as they relate to consideration in detail in ch 5.

172 *Yam Seng* (n 161) [147]. As with so much other case law and comment (including my own (Campbell, 'Relational Constitution' (n 160), 62–63), Leggatt J (*Yam Seng* (n 161) [122]) was clearly influenced by the judgment of Bingham LJ in *Interfoto Picture Library Ltd v Stiletto Visual Programmes Ltd* [1989] QB 433 (CA), but the former sets out in clearer terms than the latter the way in which 'a result not very different from the civil law principle of good faith' (ibid 445C) should be obtained.

173 E McKendrick, 'Good Faith in the Performance of a Contract in English Law' in LA DiMatteo and M Hogg (eds), *Comparative Contract Law* (OUP 2016) 209.

174 B Nicholas, *The French Law of Contract* (2nd edn, OUP 1989) 153–54. My knowledge of civilian systems is vestigial and—I believe I am by no means alone in this—the greatest influence they have had on my thinking is via F Kessler and E Fine, '*Culpa in Contrahendo*: Bargaining in Good Faith and Freedom of Contract: A Comparative Study' (1964) 77 Harvard Law Review 401, which is discussed in ch 5.

175 Uniform Commercial Code § 1-304 and Restatement (Second) Contracts s 205.

176 UNIDROIT General Principles for International Commercial Contracts art 1.7.

177 O Lando and H Beale, *The Principles of European Contract Law* (Kluwer 2000) art 1:201 and C von Bar and others (eds), *Draft Common Frame of Reference (Outline Edition)* (Sellier 2009) Princ 42. I briefly discuss one instance when civilian good faith did in fact penetrate the law of England and Wales when discussing unfair terms in ch 6.

doctrine follows from the moral character of good faith appropriate to a law which respects the intentions of the parties, and the juristic issues are secondary to grasping that character.[178] These issues have been authoritatively set out in Professor Summers' account of the 'exclusionary' approach.[179] As interpretation is of its nature open to allowing welfarist intervention, taking the exclusionary approach of the common law when it conforms to what Llewellyn called the formal style is, it is submitted, not preferable but essential.[180] It is hoped that this, and the preceding, chapter show that this requires no retreat from, or improvement upon, an approach that intrinsically requires respect for the interests of both parties when determining their intentions expressed in their agreement. One seeks self-consciousness of what the law necessarily does in order to improve our ways of doing it.[181]

This and the preceding chapters of this part of this book have sought to show that contractual agreement has to be based on mutual recognition. Agreement of this sort is legitimate because, by legally actualising autonomy in Pareto optimising economic action, it institutionalises freedom in the market economies of liberal democracy. But it will immediately be asked whether the distribution of economic goods yielded by a general market economy based on such agreement satisfies the liberal democratic standard of equality. Behind this question lies, of course, the further question whether an illegitimately inegalitarian distribution of economic goods is consistent with a general economy of freedom. Such answer as the law of contract has given to these questions is expressed in the doctrine of consideration.

[178] H Collins, 'Implied Terms: The Foundation in Good Faith and Fair Dealing' [2014] Current Legal Problems 297, 331: 'the polarised positions developed in the English scholarly literature for and against a duty to perform a contract in good faith are beside the point'.

[179] RS Summers, '"Good Faith" in General Contract Law and the Sales Provisions of the Uniform Commercial Code' (1968) 54 Virginia Law Review 195 (hereafter Summers, '"Good Faith"') and RS Summers, 'The General Duty of Good Faith: Its Recognition and Conceptualisation' (1982) 67 Cornell Law Review 810. On the application of this approach to the English law: M Clarke, 'The Common Law of Contract in 1993: Is there a General Doctrine of Good Faith?' (1993) 23 Hong Kong Law Journal 318, 340–41.

I should stress that Summers himself came to see the fundamental issue as one of the 'contractual morality' (Summers, '"Good Faith"', ibid 811) that is 'the unspecified inner logic of contract': RS Summers, 'The Conceptualisation of Good Faith in American Contract Law: A General Account' in R Zimmerman and S Whittaker (eds), *Good Faith in European Contract Law* (CUP 2000) 136.

[180] MG Bridge, 'Doubting Good Faith' (2005) 11 New Zealand Business Law Quarterly 430, 450. Without going into the way that Professor Bridge's argument about technique involves, in my opinion, a failure to recognise that there is a necessity 'to stitch [together] an ethical backcloth' within the law itself, he has never denied that 'a preoccupation with [good faith] is useful in articulating contract theory and in defining the goals that our contract law is harnessed to serve': MG Bridge, 'Does Anglo-Canadian Contact Law Need a Doctrine of Good Faith?' (1984) 9 Canadian Business Law Journal 385, 409, 426.

[181] And so, with respect, much criticism of Leggatt J is misplaced, pointing to the virtue of what he did as a defect because the value of expressly stating the ethical underpinning of the law is not acknowledged: Carter and Courtney, 'Good Faith in Contracts' (n 162) 608:

> Like many other *obiter* discussions extolling the virtues of good faith as a concept and lamenting the absence of a common law rule of good faith, Leggatt J succeeded in *Yam Seng* in proving that the same result is achieved by the orthodox processes [of] construction and implication.

Leggatt J did not lament this absence but went a long way towards making us conscious of what the orthodox processes do.

5

The Relational Constitution of Bargain (1)

Formalism, Substance, and Good Faith in Consideration

Introduction: The 'Strange Paradox' of Consideration

The most curious feature of our understanding of consideration is that it generally[1] gives little weight to an all but unparalleled regulatory success. It instead focuses on doctrinal *conundra* which are indeed themselves perplexing.[2] And though the key to understanding these *conundra* is to see that they are, in a way described in this chapter, largely just ignored in the practical conduct of business, this can be carried only up to a certain point, for the *conundra* themselves continue to give rise to significant specific problems,[3] and, what is more, they are generally illustrative of the basic misunderstanding of the ethical nature of consideration which has opened contract to vehement attack. The resolution of these *conundra* very largely follows, however, from placing them in the proper context of the practical achievement of the law.

Let us trace the modern law of consideration to 1875, and to the wide acceptance of core ideas about the doctrine expressed by Lush J in *Currie v Misa*:

[1] A notable exception is KO Shatwell, 'The Doctrine of Consideration in the Modern Law' (1954) 1 Sydney Law Review 289 (hereafter Shatwell, 'Consideration').

[2] Consideration is that part of classical commercial law that on its doctrinal face gives most colour to Weber's 'England problem': M Weber, *Economy and Society* (rev edn, University of California Press 1978) 814: 'it may indeed be said that England achieved capitalistic supremacy among the nations not because but rather in spite of its judicial system.'

[3] KN Llewellyn, 'What Price Contract?' (1931) 40 Yale Law Journal 704, 741 (emphasis added):

> In purpose consideration surely [has to provide a] sufficient justification for court-enforcement. *In broad effects, that purpose is accomplished.* In detail, however, the machinery is embarrassed by a number of rules not too well designed to meet the purpose, yet sufficiently crystallized to make continuous trouble in such cases as involve them.

Contractual Relations. David Campbell, Oxford University Press. © David Campbell 2022.
DOI: 10.1093/oso/9780198855156.003.0005

> A valuable consideration, in the sense of the law, may consist either in some right, interest, profit, or benefit accruing to the one party, or some forbearance, detriment, loss, or responsibility, given, suffered, or undertaken by the other.[4]

If this dating is accepted, then it is unarguable that the modern law has existed coextensive with fundamental criticism of that law,[5] reaching its apogee in England and Wales with the damning 1937 verdict of the Law Revision Committee: 'today in very many cases the doctrine of consideration is a mere technicality which is irreconcilable either with business expediency or common sense'.[6] This, however, led, not to the abolition which I think the Committee, and certainly its Chair Lord Wright,[7] accepted in principle, but to some timid suggestions for reform.[8] Thankfully, given that the task of abolition, should it ever be undertaken,[9] requires legislation if any private law matter ever has,[10] subsequent declarations of an intention to judicially visit the fundamentals have come to nothing.[11] I have no wish to deny the difficulties of our understanding of the doctrine and the inevitably serious shortcomings of a law which

[4] (1875) LR 10 Ex 153 (Ex Ch) 162. Coleridge CJ, dissenting, agreed with this definition: ibid 169. The definition itself has clear pre-modern antecedents, and indeed was acknowledged by both Lush J and Coleridge CJ to be directly drawn from *Comyn's Digest*, a work of similar ambition to *Blackstone*, first published a century prior to the case.

[5] GC Cheshire and CHS Fifoot, *The Law of Contracts* (Butterworths 1945) 69 (hereafter Cheshire and Fifoot, *Contracts*):

> Professional reactions to the doctrine of consideration have oscillated in the course of its history between the extremes of complacency and disgust.

[6] Law Revision Committee, *Sixth Interim Report: Statute of Frauds and the Doctrine of Consideration* (Cmd 5449 1937) para 25 (hereafter Law Revision Committee, *Report*).

[7] Writing in his personal capacity during the Committee's deliberations, Lord Wright was explicit: 'Ought the Doctrine of Consideration Be Abolished from the Common Law?' (1936) 49 Harvard Law Review 1225, 1253. Acknowledging that the 'dead weight of legal conservatism' prevented 'the English law being completely changed in so vital respect', he nevertheless concluded:

> I see no practical objections to the abolition of the doctrine to counterbalance the reasoning on which I have advocated that it should be abolished.

[8] Cheshire and Fifoot, *Contracts* (n 5) 72:

> So lame a conclusion can only be explained, as the Committee indeed admit, on the assumption that they lacked the courage of their convictions.

[9] As will be discussed below at paras 73–78, I accept that The Contracts (Rights of Third Parties) Act 1999 addressed a form of promise that in principle should be severed from the doctrine of consideration because that form of promise is non-contractual. I am less able to accept the sympathetic view of one distinguished commentator that the 1999 Act was 'carefully tailored to leave the consideration rule in place ... and so is unlikely to have a radical or detrimental impact on the operation of the law of contract': Sir Anthony Mason, 'Privity: A Rule in Search of a Decent Burial' in P Kincaid (ed), *Privity* (Ashgate 2001) 103.

[10] Criticising, as he wrote, Denning LJ for having in *Central London Property Trust Ltd v High Trees House Ltd* [1947] KB 130 (KB) (hereafter *High Trees*) done what would have surprised the Law Revision Committee by introducing far-reaching reform 'without recourse to legislation at all', FAR Bennion, 'Want of Consideration' (1953) 16 Modern Law Review 441, went on to say that: 'what Lord Mansfield was too late to achieve in the eighteenth century cannot be achieved in the twentieth century otherwise than by legislation' But what of the twenty first century?'

[11] The most chilling of these was that of Lord Steyn in *Williams v Natural Life Health Foods Ltd* [1998] 1 WLR 830 (HL) 837F, which actually seemed to maintain that the law of contract should more fully aspire to the 'principle' of negligent misstatement, which is discussed below at para 57. The latest declaration of intent is *MWB Business Exchange Centres Ltd v Rock Advertising Ltd* [2018] UKSC 34; [2018] 2 WLR 1606 [18], [20].

has been developed on the basis of that understanding,[12] not least by offering, as the Law Revision Committee went on to say, 'a loophole' to be exploited by sufficiently adroit and opportunistic parties.[13] Properly understood, however, the doctrine can be seen to contain within itself the possibility of overcoming those shortcomings, and in the one very important case in which this is not so, dealing with the adjustment of existing obligations, which are discussed in Chapter 10, the difficulties are not traceable to the requirement of consideration but to our prior understanding of the nature of the obligations to be supported by consideration.

The doctrine of consideration's core task is the hugely—no word is strong enough—important one of determining when an agreement should be contractually enforceable, and in the overwhelming number of cases consideration does this unproblematically. The recognition that the doctrine accomplishes the greatest part of the work it is called on to do has been impeded because this work is intrinsically ethical and a classical understanding of the doctrine based on solipsistic self-interest has been unable to come to terms with this; indeed it has been obliged largely to ignore what we will see is the 'strange paradox' to which that understanding reduces the doctrine. One reason why consideration has failed to do its proper work is that it has undeniably often been called on to do the inappropriate,[14] to the point where it has become a 'scrap-collector' of awkward jobs of 'doing justice'.[15] But a second, more important, reason is that the outcomes the doctrine *correctly* produces tend to run against welfarism, and to the extent that the law has become welfarist, this has involved the criticism or ousting of the doctrine.[16] What, then, is the ethical basis of the doctrine of consideration?

Exchange and the substance of consideration

Though it would be uncharitable to completely deny that the most important of the core ideas about consideration which Lush J attempted to capture was what Holmes[17]

[12] D Campbell, 'The Undeath of Contract' (1992) 22 Hong Kong Law Journal 20.

[13] Law Revision Committee, *Report* (n 6) para 25.

[14] HG Beale, WD Bishop, and MP Furmston, *Contract: Cases and Materials* (5th edn, Butterworths 2008): 'The other great source of difficulties over consideration is cases that are "marginal" in relation to normal contracts.'

[15] JP Dawson, *Gifts and Promises* (Yale University Press 1980) 207 (hereafter Dawson, *Gifts*):

> much loose talk [fails to] draw the essential distinction between contract formation and the other functions that have been brought under the rubric 'consideration'. It is in the performance of these extraneous functions that [consideration] has become a scrap-collector.

[16] This and the following chs 6 and 7 are in a sense a response to Professor Fried's seminal formulation of the claim that the doctrine of consideration (and therefore a law of contract ultimately based on economic exchange) is so 'contradictory' and 'internally incoherent', and has generated so many irreconcilable exceptions, that it would be better 'to stigmatise certain promises as unfair or unconscionable and to deny enforcement on that ground rather than on the ground of insufficient consideration': C Fried, *Contract as Promise* (2nd edn, OUP 2015) 29, 35, 39.

[17] OW Holmes, *The Common Law* (Little, Brown and Co 1881) 293–94:

> it is the essence of consideration [as ground of enforceability] that, by the terms of the agreement, it is given and accepted as the motive or inducement of the [allegedly breached] promise. Conversely, the promise must be made and accepted as the motive or inducement for furnishing the consideration. The root of the whole matter is the relation of reciprocal inducement, each for the other, between consideration and promise.

was far more firmly grasping as 'reciprocity',[18] one is obliged to say that Lush J's attempt was not a distinguished one.[19] There may be 'either' a benefit or a detriment, and not only have neither been analytically tied to promisor or promisee (the difficulty being exaggerated because it seems often to be ignored that the labels promisee and promisor are not *ex ante* but depend on the *ex post* determining of the parties' legal positions when one party claims the other has breached), but whether only benefit or detriment, and if so which one, is necessary, or whether both are, is unclear. The various debates over these points around the turn of the nineteenth century are now seen to be of little or no value.[20] Their eventuation in some distinction between 'legal' as opposed to 'actual' benefit or detriment, though we shall see it does obliquely express a vital point,[21] was itself a failure, for if the aim was to identify a criterion of enforceability, not much was gained as, other than by circular reasoning, it was not possible to show why what was 'legal' was indeed legal.[22]

The interesting question is how those debates could simultaneously be prodigiously elaborate about enforceability in doctrine and yet simplistically at odds with enforceability in common sense. This was in part the result of an understandable anxiety to accommodate a (too often not merely historical but ancient) case law that, viewed retrospectively, went off at many tangents, but was much less excusably the result of a preoccupation with the classification of juridical categories,[23] in the rococo results of which the core idea of reciprocity, in this context fundamentally an economic idea, was submerged.[24]

Once it is acknowledged that the legal contract has the purpose of facilitating economic exchange, then the concurrence of benefit and detriment simply follows. Recalling what was said in Chapter 1 of the necessity of mutual advantage for voluntary exchange to take place, it can be seen that both the promisee and the promisor must each gain a benefit *as they themselves define benefit* (we return to this crucial point below)[25] or there is no possibility of agreement and therefore of a legitimate

[18] G Gilmore, *The Death of Contract* (2nd edn, Ohio State University Press 1995) 19–23.

[19] KCT Sutton, *Consideration Reconsidered* (University of Queensland Press 1974) 14 (hereafter Sutton, *Consideration*).

[20] PS Atiyah, 'Consideration: A Restatement' in *Essays on Contract* (rev edn, Clarendon Press 1990) 187–99 (hereafter Atiyah, 'Restatement').

[21] See the text accompanying n 78.

[22] Sutton, *Consideration* (n 19) 19–20.

[23] A Leff, 'Contract As Thing' (1970) 19 American University Law Review 131,133:

> It is, of course, exceedingly rare, especially in legal classification, most especially when the classification is at the level of generality that the 'contract [or] not contract' decision represents, to classify by only one resemblance. But there is a very sharp limitation upon the number of classificatory things one can formally use ... things can pretty quickly get out of hand when great refinement of classification is attempted.

[24] EW Patterson, 'An Apology for Consideration' (1958) 58 Columbia Law Review 929, 963:

> this defence of the doctrine of consideration has rejected as not necessarily a part of the doctrine some supplementary rules that have supplied critics with most of their horrible examples. The 'legal detriment' concept of consideration was a spurious simplification that over-emphasized the role of consideration as a merely accidental element of a transaction, one that was used as a formal justification of the enforceability of a promise, and in this way it obscured the important economic and social functions of reciprocal exchanges.

[25] See the text accompanying n 76.

contract. And as we are dealing with economic goods, ie goods which are scarce in the way also discussed in Chapter 1, conveying a benefit necessarily involves incurring a detriment. One party must incur the detriment of transferring what the other party defines as a benefit in order to receive what the first party itself defines as a benefit. Reciprocity is central to this because exchange is an agreement of a unique kind, motivated by self-interest when dealing with scarce goods under a system of transfer that requires mutual recognition. Neither party wishes to convey a benefit on the other with the ultimate purpose of benefitting that party.[26] As each party nevertheless *must* convey a benefit to the other in order to receive a benefit in return, this exercise of self-interest is intrinsically not solipsistic.[27] In sum, consideration is, in the words of Sir Frederick Pollock, 'the price for which the promise of the other is bought'. It will be convenient to quote the famous passage in which this is found, to which I repeatedly return:

> An act or forbearance of the one party, or the promise thereof, is the price for which the promise of the other is bought, and the promise thus given for value is enforceable.[28]

What must be said, but what is very insufficiently said, is that as the way of distinguishing which promises or agreements should be enforceable as contracts from those which should not, consideration, as analysed in the 'bargain theory'[29] resting on Holmes' understanding of reciprocity, works.[30] I shall return to the obvious counter-evidence to this claim. We saw in Chapter 1 that Adam Smith sought to identify

[26] See the text accompanying n 73.

[27] G Simmel, *The Philosophy of Money* (3rd edn, Routledge 2004) 314 (hereafter Simmel, *Philosophy of Money*):

> Exchange … is the first, and in its simplicity really wonderful, means for combining justice with changes in ownership. Insofar as the receiver is, at the same time, the giver, the mere one-sidedness of advantage that characterises changes of ownership dominated by [pure] egotism or altruism disappears.

[28] F Pollock, *Principles of Contract* (3rd edn, Stevens & Sons 1881) 179. In *Dunlop Pneumatic Tyre Co Ltd v Selfridge and Co Ltd* [1915] AC 847 (HL) 853 (hereafter *Dunlop v Selfridge*) Viscount Dunedin LC quoted from the 8th edn ((1911) 175) when giving this statement merely the first of numerous high judicial endorsements. Sir Frederick noted that his statement had been 'adopted' in *Dunlop v Selfridge* in the 9th edn ((Stevens and Sons 1921) 177 n (b)) (hereafter Pollock, 9th edn). In *Dunlop v Selfridge*, Lord Dunedin also adopted Pollock's definition, but he did so perforce, in the context of an express condemnation of the doctrine (*Dunlop v Selfridge*, ibid 855).

[29] The word 'bargain', the general use of which in this context derives from the nineteenth century, is in a sense unfortunate, and one might prefer the use of 'exchange' if this did not create a confusing duplication of usage and were there, as I doubt, any point in having a preference. A bargain now often connotes some unusual advantage, even perhaps one tinged with illegitimacy, and this runs counter to the proper relationship of exchange and contract.

[30] EA Farnsworth, 'Comparative Contract Law' in M Reimann and R Zimmerman (eds), *The Oxford Handbook of Comparative Law* (OUP 2006) 909:

> The requirement of consideration took care of the bulk of economically vital commercial agreements, and found easy acceptance in a society entering a commercial age. In view of the difficulty that other societies have had in developing a general basis for enforcing promises, it is perhaps less remarkable that the basis developed by the common law is flawed than that the common law succeeded in developing any basis at all.

persuasion as the basis of legitimate exchange, and 'the one central and essential idea'[31] of consideration, that the way for an economic actor to persuade another actor to transfer goods is to pay for them (and so in the absence of payment no-one has an entitlement to those goods which contract should enforce),[32] is an 'overwhelmingly … normal' idea.[33] And as this normality is absolutely necessary for the general formation of money prices, and therefore rational economic calculation by natural and legal persons,[34] it is an essential foundation of the market economy and liberal democracy. In a society which is free because it makes its collective principle the normal refusal to form collective goals, competitive claims over economic goods can be productively resolved, or even sensibly formulated,[35] only in terms of their autonomous exchange, and the necessary legal institutional form of autonomy in this material world is the reciprocal furnishing of consideration:

> The tasks of all economic activity is to reconcile … competing ends by deciding for which of them … limited means are to be used. The market order reconciles the claims … by the only known process that benefits all for the simple reason that there can exist in such a system no single ordering of needs [and goods are allocated] solely on the basis of a principle of reciprocity though which the opportunities of a person are likely to be greater than they otherwise would be.[36]

It is at this very point, however, that the attempt to legally express the nature of exchange in the doctrine of consideration appears, not merely to have some inconsistencies, or even bad inconsistencies, over the range of situations which it properly should cover, but to completely collapse at its core.[37] Pollock began his famous statement by distinguishing between 'An act or forbearance of the one party, or the promise thereof'; in effect distinguishing between an executed and an executory contract. In using this distinction to make my argument understood, I am anxious not to be drawn

[31] Dawson, *Gifts* (n 15) 198.

[32] R Nozick, *Anarchy, State and Utopia* (Basic Books 1974) 151, 157:

> The legitimate means of moving from one distribution to another are specified by the principle of justice in transfer. The means of change specified by the principle of justice in transfer preserve justice … most people most of the time choose to transfer some of their entitlements only in exchange for something from them.

[33] Dawson, *Gifts* (n 15) 221.

[34] L von Mises, *Human Action* (4th edn, Fox and Wilkes 1996) 230:

> Monetary calculation is the main vehicle for planning and acting in the social setting of a society of free enterprise directed and controlled by the market and its prices … Our civilisation is inseparably linked with our methods of economic calculation. It would perish if we were to abandon this most precious intellectual tool of acting.

[35] RG Collingwood, 'Economics as a Philosophical Science' (1926) 36 International Journal of Ethics 36:

> A just price, a just wage, a just rate of interest, is a contradiction in terms. The question what a person ought to get in return for his goods and labour is a question absolutely devoid of meaning. The only valid questions are what he can get in return for his goods or labour, and whether he ought to sell them at all.

[36] FA Hayek, *Law, Liberty and Legislation*, vol 2 (rev edn, Routledge & Kegan Paul 1982) 113.

[37] R Bronaugh, 'A Secret Paradox of the Common Law' (1983) 2 Law and Philosophy 193; N Duxbury, *Frederick Pollock and the English Juristic Tradition* (OUP 2004) 201–15 (hereafter Duxbury, *Pollock*) and Sutton, *Consideration* (n 19) ch 2.

into a general discussion of the concept of the executed contract,[38] which I believe has long served no purpose except other than assisting in the development of the, for certain, limited circumstances, valuable device of the unilateral contract accepted by performance.[39] For the purposes of argument, let us allow that in an executed contract consideration is already furnished. It is easiest to think of the physical subject matter of the contract having been transferred—the buyer has title and possession of legal goods and has paid the price—but the general point is that the primary obligations have been performed. In an executory contract, however, only the promises of performance are furnished, and how can either be a ground for enforcing the other? Such a promise is binding only if we assume that promises made in this situation are binding. The *petitio principii* is unavoidable and radical, and we find that, having perforce put aside the subject matter and the executed performance, we are left with nothing at all—consideration without substance. This was, Pollock said *en passant* in a very brief review of a book now forgotten, 'one of the Secret Paradoxes of the Common Law'.[40] The point has since been put at much greater length by numerous others, but all to the same effect: Pollock was right to say he could not find 'any *logical* reason why mutual promises are sufficient consideration for each other'.[41] It comes as little surprise that, shortly before he died, Pollock agreed with Lord Wright's personal view that the doctrine should be abolished.[42]

Consideration and Good Faith

Faced with a stark contrast between the undoubted overwhelming common sense to which consideration was attempting to give expression and the theoretical emptiness resulting from the attempt, it was inevitable and in a strong sense defensible that direct recourse was had to the empirical in order to dispose of what was regarded as theoretical in the bad sense. Pollock had a low regard for any theory or even law of consideration that could not just accommodate this common sense, which is, of course, better

[38] All discussion of this topic must, of course, take account of PS Atiyah, *The Rise and Fall of Freedom of Contract* (pbk edn, Clarendon Press 1985) 419–48 (hereafter Atiyah, *Rise and Fall*), and much other of Atiyah's work. A valuable indirect lesson of that work, however, is that the welfarism of surely one of the greatest of commentators led Atiyah to have great difficulty with the general enforceability of the executory contract, and in particular with the protection of pure expectation loss, ie, as he in a sense recognised, with the very basis of his subject: PS Atiyah, 'Executory Contracts, Expectation Damages and the Economic Analysis of Contract' in *Essays on Contract* (n 20) 178.

[39] Of course, difficulties arise even here in the absence of understanding the good faith in which a unilateral promise is objectively given, and so this potentially useful doctrine seems to generate its own specific absurdities: K Llewellyn, 'Our Case Law of Contract: Offer and Acceptance II' (1938) 48 Yale Law Journal 779, 785:

> it may even be urged that safe conclusions as to business cases of the more ordinary variety cannot be derived from what courts or scholars rule about the idiosyncratic desires of one A to see one B climb a fifty foot greased flagpole or push a peanut across the Brooklyn Bridge.

[40] Anon [F Pollock], 'Review of JG Pease and AM Latter, *The Student's Summary of the Law of Contract*' (1914) 30 Law Quarterly Review 128, 129.

[41] Letter from Frederick Pollock to Oliver Wendell Holmes (16 October 1908) in F Pollock and OW Holmes, *The Pollock-Holmes Letters*, vol 1 (CUP 1942) 170.

[42] Letter from Frederick Pollock to AL Goodhart (16 June 1936) in Duxbury, *Pollock* (n 37) 204.

than letting oneself be bewildered by inadequate theory, but is not the development of adequate knowledge.[43] In a review of a textbook by Clarence Ashley of New York University School of Law,[44] Pollock responded to Ashley raising the conundrum of the sufficiency of an existing obligation to a third party[45] by saying:

> Both the plain man and the average lawyer will say that, whatever Prof Ashley's logic may be, the law really cannot be so absurd as that; and they will be right, and, what is more, any rational court before whom such a question is moved will surely find a way to make them so ... Prof Ashley's besetting temptation is to forget that law exists for the convenience of mankind and not for the training of logicians. What logical justification is there for holding mutual promises good consideration for each other? None, it is submitted. But the contrary doctrine would only have led to cumbrous fictions, and our seventeenth century ancestors rightly took the illogical course and said very little about it ... in dealing with the particular question whether a promise to do something one is already under contract to do is consideration for a new promise by a stranger ... Ashley ... concludes that the strict doctrine of consideration is inapplicable. We agree with him so far as this, that if it cannot be applied here it is not good for much anyhow.[46]

In addition to noting the depressing contemporary feel of Pollock's views, there is little to be gained from dwelling on the shortcomings of theory. It should be noted how much this recourse to the empirical may be identified in the modern English case law.[47] One very extensively discussed form of this has been the way in which the appeal courts have countered attempts to exploit the loophole identified by the Law Revision Committee with *tours de force* of ingenuity.[48] Just to select from post-war cases, past consideration has had its *Pao On v Lau Yiu Long*;[49] existing obligations

[43] Nothing, I think, could more show the desperation to which our understanding of consideration has reduced us that Pollock, a man capable of theoretical engagement at an extremely high level, even the author of a work on Spinoza which, though of course obsolete now, has a creditable place in the history of Spinoza scholarship, took this line.

This point is quite different from the line which Pollock believed legal reasoning should in principle draw between itself and ethical and political philosophy. Professor Gordley is, with respect, ungenerous to Pollock about this: J Gordley, *The Philosophical Origins of Modern Contract Doctrine* (Clarendon Press 1991) 216–17.

[44] More than 20 years earlier than Lord Wright, Ashley had also argued for the abolition of the doctrine in pages of the *Harvard Law Review*: CD Ashley, 'The Doctrine of Consideration' (1913) 26 Harvard Law Review 429.

[45] See n 59.

[46] FP [F Pollock], 'Review of CD Ashley, *The Law of Contracts*' (1912) 28 Law Quarterly Review 100, 101.

[47] AG Chloros, 'The Doctrine of Consideration and the Reform of the Law of Contract' (1968) 17 International and Comparative Law Quarterly 164:

> in the large majority of cases in which the courts are called upon to discuss consideration, every effort is made to avoid its pernicious effects.

[48] Lord Stewart's determination (*J Dykes Ltd v Littlewood's Mail Order Stores Ltd* 1982 SC(HL) 157 (CS(OH)) 166) not to let a meritorious claim 'simply [disappear] into some legal black hole' has been taken up as an alternative, vivid metaphor.

[49] [1980] AC 614 (PC) 628F–631C (hereafter *Pao On*). In this way their Lordships were able to avoid the consequence of their statement, ibid 628E, that 'If the law really compels [the] conclusion [that the defendant is not liable] one may be forgiven for thinking that the time has come to re-consider it'. See further the text accompanying n 154.

its *Central London Property Trust Ltd v High Trees House Ltd*[50] and *Williams v Roffey Bros and Nicholls (Contractors) Ltd*;[51] and privity its *New Zealand Shipping Co Ltd v AM Satterthwaite and Co Ltd, The Eurymedon*[52] and *Beswick v Beswick*.[53] But all of these cases, though the last perhaps even more than the others, make it abundantly clear that admiration of the instant result has to be tempered by the obvious unworthiness of the ingenuity,[54] and the equally obvious likelihood of most unwelcome consequences down the line.

For perfectly understandable reasons, *tours de force* of this nature seize our attention,[55] but it is more important by far to note that on the very small number of occasions on which consideration issues are raised, they are typically just dismissed. This is so even in the highest courts. In *Woodhouse AC Israel Cocoa Ltd SA v Nigerian Produce Marketing Co Ltd*,[56] the Lord Chancellor cut through a tangled attempt to elide the necessity of furnishing consideration for an agreement which it was only common sense to enforce by merely saying that 'I imagine that a modern court would have no difficulty in discovering consideration for such a promise ... I do not think there would have been insuperable difficulty in spelling out consideration from the [parties'] correspondence'.[57] It may be of more practical importance that this sort of thing can be found in lower courts. When in 1977 dismissing a defence of want of consideration which he, it is submitted correctly, found of no merit at all, but long discussion of which could have drawn him into the 'mutuality of obligations' in something like a 'requirements contract', Donaldson J was forthright:

> A defence of lack of consideration rarely has merit. This case is certainly no exception. The realities of the dispute were always known to both parties and they did not include the question of whether there was consideration for the contract [It] is a highly technical matter which rarely, though occasionally, has any substance from the point of view of determining the rights of the parties.[58]

[50] *High Trees* (n 10).

[51] [1991] 1 QB 1 (CA) (hereafter *Williams v Roffey*). *High Trees* (n 10) and *Williams v Roffey* will be discussed at length in ch 10.

[52] [1975] AC 154 (PC).

[53] [1966] Ch 538 (CA) 555E–F; affd on this point [1968] AC 58 (HL).

[54] Somewhat supererogatorily, two further clouds hang over *Beswick v Beswick*. First, it is unclear, though of course one can imagine reasons (GH Treitel, *Some Landmarks of Twentieth Century Contract Law* (Clarendon Press 2002) 84–87 (hereafter *Treitel, Landmarks*)), why the seemingly blatant errors that put Mrs Beswick in her plight did not lead to a then surely very attractive negligence action against the solicitor that advised Mr Beswick and his nephew (ibid 88–89). However this is, one has to agree with Treitel that *Beswick v Beswick* does not appear to represent an optimum use of legal aid funds: ibid 85. Secondly, it may have been unfortunate that war time emergency prevented (assuming it was otherwise possible) the passage of the tenth item of legislation recommended in Law Revision Commission, *Report* (n 6) para 50. Even bearing The Law Reform (Frustrated Contracts) Act 1943 in mind, one finds it hard to think that the resulting law would have been worse than that created by *Beswick v Beswick*. On The Contracts (Rights of Third Parties) Act 1999 Act, see the text accompanying n 170.

[55] It was with 'decision after decision' of this nature uppermost in his mind that Atiyah, 'Restatement' (n 20) 179 told us in 1970 that 'the conventional account of the "doctrine of consideration" no longer accords with the law actually enforced in the courts'.

[56] [1972] AC 741 (HL) (hereafter *Woodhouse v Nigerian Produce Marketing*).

[57] ibid 757H–758A (Lord Hailsham LC).

[58] *Thoresen Car Ferries Ltd v Weymouth Portland BC* [1977] 2 Lloyd's Rep 614 (QB Comm) 619 col 2, 622 col 1. To be precise, Donaldson J saw the matter as so 'immensely technical' in the bad sense that, even if want of consideration had been successfully pleaded in the defendant's favour, he 'should have wanted a lot

I am in complete sympathy with the motivation of such attempts to close the loophole, and behind this to have simple recourse to common sense, but, with of course some trepidation, I submit that there is no reason for any of these forms of theoretical or doctrinal surrender, and therefore for the continuous patching up. Great doctrinal clarification may be achieved if the form of common sense is, as it surely should be, identified as giving effect to the obviously legitimate intentions of the parties, but this requires that those intentions are identified, not with the emptiness of 'agreeing' anything with a solipsistically self-interested party, but with the substance of an agreement made in good will.

Of the famous post-war cases mentioned above, let us put aside *High Trees* and *Williams v Roffey* until existing obligations are considered in Chapter 10. Who does not doubt that there were legitimate agreements in *Pao On*, *The Eurymedon*, and *Beswick v Beswick*? What on earth has happened so that trying to put those agreements in the form of a contract is the reason *not* to perform the obligations they create? This can happen only because, on the classical understanding of exchange and contract as motivated by solipsistic self-interest, it seems that by moving into the domain of contract, one moves into an area free of moral compulsion.[59] If one promises to do something outside of contract, one is, let us allow, under a compulsion to perform. If one puts that very promise into the form of a contract, one is not under such a compulsion! One can imagine no more absurd position for one of the three principal doctrines of the law of contract to articulate.

It is this that robs executory promises of any substance and leads to the strange paradox and all its paraphernalia. It is certainly right—uncountable works of fiction tells us so—that if one receives a promise from a perfectly self-interested person, one gets nothing. In the case of contract, it seems that the performance of the promise cannot be traced to the bindingness of the promise; it is wholly contingent on the pragmatic circumstances of performance being in the promisor's purest self-interest. Mutual promises by two such persons are equally wholly without substance and cannot yield consideration. This conclusion is surely right on its assumption, which is why it has never been able to be dealt with in the doctrine of consideration, save by

of persuading that the law required me to reach that conclusion': ibid 622 cols 1–2. Donaldson J's determination of the 'factual matrix' was exemplary: ibid 618 col 1–619 col 2.

In a 1971 case which it could be argued (but not by this writer) was confined to particular practices of the insurance industry, Donaldson J had, again in an exemplary way, disregarded the 'absurd consequences' which would follow from recognising 'nice points founded upon the ancient doctrine of consideration which I am sure the market would disdain to take': *Jaglom v Excess Insurance Co Ltd* [1972] 2 QB 250 (QB) 257F–258A.

[59] Some perception that this cannot be the case underlies all the law I am about to discuss, but for reasons of length I shall not discuss the specific doctrine in connection with which some apparent heightening of that perception runs through a substantial case law and an enormous academic discussion at the end of the nineteenth century: the enforceability of promises of an obligation already owed to a (private) third party. This exception, which 'is not very easy to understand on principle', was given, by comparison to other topics, long discussion in the first edition of *Anson*: WR Anson, *Principles of the English Law of Contract* (Clarendon Press 1879) 80–81. The passage of the years has not diminished the unease, and indeed has merely led to the additional citation of cases which increase it: A Burrows, J Beatson, and J Cartwright, *Anson's Law of Contract* (31st edn, OUP 2020) 108–10.

being to some degree evaded or ignored. But why on earth should we think this assumption is correct?

I have tried to argue that Pollock's description of consideration as 'the price for which the promise of the other is bought' is correct. But in the light of Pollock's own views, his description looks impossibly naïve. For what do the parties pay to buy in light of the strange paradox save nothing? Surely this involves claiming that solipsistically self-interested contracting parties are not merely immoral but also fools. What is the point of contracting if contract yields nothing except what would anyway follow without it: performance by the other party so long, and only so long, as performance was in that party's solipsistic self-interest? This cannot possibly describe the real nature of exchange or contract.[60] In previous chapters we have seen that an agreement to exchange is impossible in the absence of good faith. This is also the basis of the law of bargain. When a party makes an executory promise in order to receive an executory promise, the motivation is economic exchange, but economic exchange is not possible on the basis of solipsistic self-interest; it must have a basis in the relation of mutual recognition legally recognised as good faith. Executory promises exchanged are promises to perform in good faith, and these are consideration justifying enforceability because, far from having no substance, such promises have so definite an ethical content that it is able to support the market economy as the most legitimate and stable general economy of which it has been possible to conceive. The consideration for an executory contract (and all contracts) is a promise to perform made in good faith.[61]

I used a quotation from Pollock's *Principles* in the conclusion of the previous chapter explicitly on good faith but made no further reference to him in that chapter. I believe Pollock had a workable idea of good faith (and reasonable expectation)[62] as it bears on agreement, but shortcomings in the way in which he expressed it would mean that defending this belief would have involved a lengthy distraction from the main theme of this book. But though we have already noted that Pollock had a low opinion indeed of the legal doctrine of consideration, I believe understanding consideration requires

[60] AWB Simpson, *A History of the Common Law of Contract* (pbk edn, Clarendon Press 1987) 488:

> the view that the law of contract is the handmaid of commerce seems to me to be mistaken if it is opposed to the view that the law of contract expresses, in a form thought appropriate (bearing in mind the practicalities of litigation), moral ideas. For commerce, like other areas of life, must be conducted morally if the general good is to be furthered ... The doctrine of consideration is indeed intensely moralistic, and we may disagree with some of its judgements; what is mistaken is to fail to see that a good law of contract has as its function in relation to the commercial world the imposition of decent moral standards.

[61] I have made no attempt to follow up Professor Ibbetson's fascinating line of thought in a paper on *Coggs v Barnard*: D Ibbetson, '*Coggs v Barnard* (1703)' in C Mitchell and PO Mitchell (eds), *Landmark Cases in the Law of Contract* (Hart 2008). Playing on the narrowly legal and the more general sense of 'trust', he tells us, ibid 21, that:

> Hobbes' treatment of contracts in his *Elements of Law* is shot through with the language of trust. Whenever there was a contract which was not immediately executed, the party or parties who had not yet performed were said to be trusted to perform their obligations.

[62] Pollock, 9th edn (n 28) viii:

> in all contracts the promisee's rights and remedies are founded on and measured by his reasonable expectation, and the purpose of the law is to protect and forward reasonable men's business.

engagement with Pollock's views. Let us repeat and expand upon the quotation from the *Principles* in the last chapter:

> The law of contract may be described as the endeavour of the State ... to establish a positive sanction for the expectation of good faith which has grown in the mutual dealings of men of average right mindedness. Accordingly, the most popular description of a contract that can be given is also the most exact one, namely that it is a promise or set of promises which the law will enforce ... He who has given the promise is bound to him who accepts it, not merely because he had ... expressed a certain intention, but because he so expressed himself as to entitle the other party to rely on his acting in a certain way.[63]

This appears to be a species of that variant of the 'reliance theory' of liability in which it is not the promise, or promise as consideration, that gives rise to enforceability, but the promisee's detrimental (let us momentarily put aside the implications of this adjective) reliance.[64] This is not, I submit, what Pollock means. The promisee can rely because the law will enforce. But it will only enforce if there is a contract, and when deciding whether this is the case, one must note the executory nature of Pollock's language. It is not that the promisee has relied in the sense of the reliance theory, ie done some act 'in reliance' on the contract, but that he is 'entitled to rely'. The entitlement arises because the promises are from the time of the agreement mutually binding as consideration as they are not the empty promises of solipsistically self-interested parties but are promises replete with 'the expectation of good faith which has grown in the mutual dealings of men of average right mindedness'. The promisor and promisee both undertake to do in good faith what is required of them by the terms of their agreement. Though I use this language at this stage of the argument only to relate my point to my anticipated audience, good faith makes this undertaking a benefit and a detriment of substance.[65]

[63] F Pollock, *Principles Contract* (4th edn, Stevens & Sons 1885) 9.

[64] By this I mean the thinking analysed in Atiyah, *Rise and Fall* (n 38) 184–89 which, of most importance here, grounded Atiyah's own approach to the current law and its reform: PS Atiyah, 'Contracts, Promises and the Law of Obligations' in *Essays on Contract* (n 20) 33–36.

[65] The principal obstruction to seeing this is the way that, without at all going into wide consideration of the 'promissory morality' of contract, 'promise' is typically understood in this context. A promise is taken to be a promise to perform the primary obligation specified. This is, of course, so, but the entire point of it being a contractual promise to exchange is missed. I shall extremely briefly summarise an argument that will be made at length in chs 8 and 9. We have seen that the very point of the law of contract is to deal with the risk of non-performance that is inevitable given bounded rationality. It must follow from this that a promise to perform in contractual good faith has to allow for the possibility of breach in good faith. There are extremely common circumstances in which breach becomes unanticipatedly costly and a legitimate question arises whether the defendant agreed to absorb all those costs.

The answer given by the modern positive law of remedies for breach of contract, institutionalising commercial practices basically settled in the nineteenth century, is to allow breach and in the overwhelming majority of cases hold the defendant liable only to compensate the claimant's lost profits, or expectation. Of course, despite its commonness, breach must be a marginally occurring event, both in particular cases—a contracting party frequently in breach would eventually be unable to agree new contracts—and in general. But obligations under the law of contract countenance breach and give very considerable latitude to breach. I must admit I am very untroubled about the role the term 'promise' should play in our understanding of contract. But I do find it essential that if we use 'promise', we should clearly identify the specific quality of the contractual promise, which does not merely encompass but has as an essential feature allowing legitimate breach, though this is exactly what does not happen in theories of promissory liability.

The particular form of misunderstanding of the nature of economic action at work here is the very common deprecation of 'the economic motive' which PH Wicksteed, an important contributor to the dissemination of the marginalist economic theory of particularly WS Jevons, had seen as long ago as 1910 as 'one of the most dangerous and indeed disastrous confusions that obstruct the progress of Economics'.[66] We have seen that a contracting party conveys a benefit to the other party, not because it is its intention to improve the situation of that party, but because it intends to improve its own situation by itself receiving a benefit in return. The entire economy is driven by self-interest, and, once again, it is best to quote one of those famous passages in which Smith did so much to make the nature of exchange clear:

> In civilised society [man] stands at all times in need of the co-operation and assistance of great multitudes [and] has almost constant occasion for the help of his brethren, and it is in vain for him to expect it from their benevolence only. He will be more likely to prevail if he can interest their self-love in his favour ... and it is in this manner that we obtain from one another the far greater part of those good offices which we stand in need of. It is not from the benevolence of the butcher, the brewer, or the baker, that we expect our dinner, but from their regard to their own interest. We address ourselves, not to their humanity but to their self-love, and never talk to them of our own necessities but of their advantages.[67]

This book is an attempt to explain the part the law of contract plays in the transformation of self-interested action into a stable market economy, and we have seen that this is both a matter of establishing an external framework for action, and of the internalisation of the values of the framework. Mutual recognition will ultimately be imposed, but this has to be seen only as the reinforcement of an attitude which normally spontaneously obtains because parties actively embrace mutual recognition in the form of good faith. But at the very point where the doctrine of consideration should be able to make the legitimacy of an exchange intrinsic to the criteria of the enforceability of a bargain, our understanding, indeed our very perception, of good faith in consideration collapses, and economic action seems to be motivated by solipsistic self-interest.[68]

It is impossible to over-estimate the significance of our failure to be conscious that the economic exercise of self-interest does not mean disregarding the interests of the other party. In part, this has happened because it is profoundly true that what might be called 'depersonalisation' is an indispensable core feature of the market economy. Unless economic actors can sever the benefit they expect to receive from exchange

[66] PH Wicksteed, *The Commonsense of Political Economy* (rev edn, Routledge & Kegan Paul 1933) 163 (hereafter Wicksteed, *Commonsense*).

[67] A Smith, *The Wealth of Nations* in *The Glasgow Edition of the Works and Correspondence*, vol 2 (Clarendon Press 1976) 26–27. I treat Smith's usage 'self-love' as synonymous with 'self-interest'.

[68] I Kirzner, 'Altruism, Social Responsibility and the Market Economy' in *Reflections on Ethics, Freedom, Welfare Economics, Policy and the Legacy of the Austrian Economists in Collected Works* (Liberty Fund 2018) 237:

> To the extent that market exchanges are conducted within the given framework of private rights, they provide no room within which egoistic market participants might inflict harm on others.

from the identity of other actors, be they natural persons or business organisations, and so regard those actors as interchangeable potential sources of those benefits, general freedom of choice and competition cannot work.[69] Such interchangeability requires indifference towards the consequences of one's choice for the potential sources. Competition *must* involve the systemic disappointment of the hopes of some economic actors,[70] and what is more, failure in competition may well be for reasons which it is the case the actor is not 'responsible'—a change in technology, a change in fashion, etc—because the forces involved are, precisely, beyond their control.[71]

Depersonalisation is, however, too wide a term. As a matter of fact, identity is often very important, for as we saw in Chapter 3, reputation (including branding and business character) rightly play an important role in many exchanges. What precisely is at issue in depersonalisation is that exchange turns each actor not being ultimately concerned to confer an advantage upon the other party, a stance which Wicksteed called 'non-tuism'.[72] One party confers a benefit on the other actor, thereby itself sustaining a detriment, not directly to benefit the other party, but only because this is necessary to persuade that party to confer a benefit in return. Though we shall examine the very important class of non-standard cases which Macneil described as 'relational' in Chapter 10, in the standard case of a party entering into a simple contract (ie leaving aside fiduciary relationships), that party *should* be (and in the overwhelming majority of cases will be) indifferent to the welfare of the other party.

Depersonalisation, nevertheless, cannot mean the reduction of the other party to nothing. Consideration can exist only if it is acknowledged that agreements to perform obligations must be made in good faith, and non-tuistic indifference towards the welfare of the other party does not sanction conduct which undermines the other party's autonomous capacity to agree. Though we shall turn to other aspects of this in the discussion of adequacy in Chapter 6, the core of depersonalisation is mutual

[69] Simmel, *Philosophy of Money* (n 27) 321–22:

> though we are ... dependent on the whole of society through the complexity of our needs ... and the specialisation of our abilities ... we are remarkably independent of every *specific* member of this society, because his significance for us has been transferred to the one-sided objectivity of his contribution, which can be just as easily produced by any number of other people with different personalities with whom we are connected only by an interest that can be completely expressed in money terms.

[70] In a passage simultaneously both commonsensical and acutely perceptive, *Hamble Fisheries Ltd v L Gardner and Sons, The Rebecca Elaine* [1999] 1 Lloyd's Rep 1 (CA) 8 col 2 (hereafter *Hamble Fisheries*), Mummery LJ recognised:

> the inevitability (and acceptability) of widespread and uncompensatable financial loss in a free market economy, in which even intentional infliction of substantial financial loss (eg by one trade competitor on another) does not normally attract legal liability.

[71] FA Hayek, 'Competition as a Discovery Procedure' in *The Market and Other Orders* in *Collected Works*, vol 15 (Routledge 2014) 311:

> all economic adjustment is made necessary by unforeseen changes ... Adaptation of the whole order of activities to changed circumstances rests on the remuneration derived from different activities being changed, without regard to the merits or faults of those affected.

[72] Wicksteed, *Commonsense* (n 66) 170–83. Wicksteed was anxious to insist that non-tuism carries no implication that the substantive desires of the natural legal person *qua* economic actor be venal, though they may be. What benefit the actor seeks may lie anywhere on the, as it were, spectrum of (legally permitted) moral quality.

recognition in good faith agreement, and behind this autonomy. For the indifference of the parties allows each to define the substance of the benefit which one party requires be provided so as to be persuaded to provide a benefit, as defined by the other party, in return. The opprobrium with which self-interested exchange is regarded that lies behind our failure to reach a proper evaluation of the doctrine of consideration is, it is submitted, a mistake about the morality of indifference. It is radically insufficient to say that 'We enter into business relations with others ... because our purposes are selfish'.[73] We do so:

> because those with whom we deal are ... indifferent to [our purposes] but are (like us) keenly interested in purposes of our own, to which we in our turn are ... indifferent ... There is surely nothing degrading or revolting to our higher sense in this fact of our mutually furthering each other's purposes because we are interested in our own. There is no taint or presumption of selfishness [ie as opposed to self-interest] in the matter at all.[74]

The exchange will not take place unless it is mutually advantageous, but mutual advantage does not mean that there is an overall, or perhaps better joint, benefit which the parties are united in identifying and which they share after it is realised, in which sense of benefit the power of *each* party to define its *own* benefit is lost.[75] In exchange, each party realises a benefit *as it defines it*, and this is the point of first importance that the distinction between actual and legal detriment, putting the substance of actual benefit aside as irrelevant, tries to capture.[76] As Pollock put it: 'what a man chooses to bargain for must be conclusively taken to be of some value to him'.[77] Even if a party is itself of the subjective opinion that the benefit the other party has agreed the exchange

[73] ibid 179.

[74] ibid.

[75] One of the ways in which T Nagel, *The Possibility of Altruism* (Princeton University Press 1970) 79 (emphasis added) tried to describe altruism was as 'behaviour which has as its *object* the benefit of others'. In regard of economic goods, this must involve what Nagel called 'serious self-sacrifice', and so the provider must either just accept and satisfy, ie subsume her or himself to, the recipient's wishes or, more commonly, provide the goods on the terms the provider defines best for the recipient. The latter, more a matter of political than personal morality, requires brief comment here.

Accepting that a planned intervention is predicated upon altruism, and leaving aside the question of the competence to effect the intervention, the formation and execution of the plan has to unite the wills of providers and recipients, changing some or all of those wills, and such unity, its concrete form determined by the planning authority, analytically rests on (the threat of) coercion backed by the monopoly of violence. Political altruism of this sort has, of course, a vital place in liberal democratic societies, but this cannot be as the means of generally allocating of economic goods, and this is so as a matter of principle and of practice, for 'When the collectivist abolishes the market place, all he really does is locate it in the brains of his planning board': W Lippmann, *The Good Society* (Transaction Publishers 2005) 175.

[76] I am anxious not to be drawn into a discussion of authorities which I think can now be properly comprehended by, and need be properly comprehended by, only the legal historian, but the famous disdain of Lord Denman CJ for ascertaining the value the defendant found in weighing the boilers in *Bainbridge v Firmstone* (1838) A and E 743, 744; 112 ER 1019, 1020 does, I think, illustrate the point. The consideration found by Patteson J, to support taking the same line, is manifestly contrived.

[77] Pollock, 9th edn (n 28) 186. Duxbury, *Pollock* (n 37) 210 draws our attention to F Po [F Pollock], 'Contract' in *Encyclopaedia Britannica*, vol 7 (11th edn 1910) 37:

> consideration for a promise ... need not be anything which is obviously for the promisor's benefit. His acceptance shows that he set some value on it.

in order to obtain does not justify the detriment the second party has agreed to suffer, that is none of the first party's business, so long as the exchange is indeed an agreement. The general possibility of freedom of choice and contract depends on each party respecting, which requires being objectively indifferent about, the other's valuations.[78]

The immense body of criticism of depersonalisation will never, one assumes, be more powerfully expressed than it was by Engels and Marx in *The Communist Manifesto*: 'The bourgeoisie … has left remaining no other nexus between man and man than naked self-interest, than callous "cash payment"'.[79] Though neither really maps onto the fundamental criticism Engels and Marx sought to make of bourgeois society, this criticism has often been seen as having two aspects. First, there is a criticism of inappropriate commodification. The only nexus is cash payment, and this is so even in regard of relationships which should rest on another nexus, the obvious example being sexual relationships.[80] For whatever this writer's opinion is worth, this can be a telling criticism, but the second aspect, that all action within the market sphere is based on 'naked self-interest' is just wrong. We have seen in Chapter 2 that Marx himself described exchange as based on mutual recognition. Action on this basis is not naked self-interest. A discussion of Marx's views in light of this contradiction, and the immense influence of those views on the criticism of exchange and contract, form the conclusion of this book.

Contractual and pre-contractual agreements

With non-tuism wrongly seen as solipsistic self-interest, the furnishing of consideration has appeared a moral empty space, giving rise to the strange paradox which really, were it not ignored, would undermine the entire law of contract. How far things have gone awry is vividly illustrated by really rather absurd divergence between the way that 'pre-contractual' agreements are treated in the classical doctrine of consideration, as opposed to the way those agreements are treated in business practice and in the case law which gets around that doctrine. These agreements were identified as 'residual categories' in Kessler and Fine's seminal paper,[81] in the sense that they are collateral to but definitely outside of a core contract which would be enforced because of consideration on the price of the promise definition as it is normally understood,

[78] The US case of *Hamer* v *Sidway* 124 NY 538; 27 NE 256 (1891) (Court of Appeals of New York) seems to be an illustration of this which was heaven sent to law teachers. However, not only is the interpretation of the case bogged down in the distinction between legal and actual detriment, but the *ratio* is muddled by the strong sense in which the case was one of gratuitous transfer, motivated, indeed, by the promisor altruistically wishing to control the behaviour of the promisee.

[79] K Marx and F Engels, *Manifesto of the Communist Party* in *Collected Works*, vol 6 (Lawrence and Wishart 1976) 486–87.

[80] K Marx, *Economic and Philosophical Manuscripts of 1844* in K Marx and F Engels, *Collected Works*, vol 3 (Lawrence & Wishart 1975) 324:

> I am ugly, but I can buy for myself the most beautiful of women. Therefore I am not ugly, for the effect of ugliness—its deterrent power is nullified by money.

[81] F Kessler and E Fine, '*Culpa in Contrahendo*: Bargaining in Good Faith and Freedom of Contract: A Comparative Study' (1964) 77 Harvard Law Review 401, 449.

but are rightly found to be enforceable despite it seeming that no such consideration has been furnished because 'bargaining in good faith' requires it.

Let us focus on the 'firm offer', in which an offer is coupled with a statement, not supported by independent consideration, of a period of time in which the offer will not be (varied or) withdrawn, and accept for the moment that this device, unarguably prior to a 'main' contract which may be agreed, is therefore pre-contractual and so unenforceable. Richard Lewis' empirical study of the practice over firm offers in the Cardiff construction industry showed them to be, on occasions which it is very important to precisely identify, binding, despite not, of course, ever being so on a classical legal analysis.[82] This study was conducted against the background of the Law Commission[83] having taken up the disquiet about such offers registered by the Law Revision Committee in 1937, which, long anticipating Kessler and Fine, noted that civil systems required no payment and that it was 'particularly undesirable that ... the English law should accept a lower *moral* standard'.[84] It is remarkable that a body concerned with the reform of the law of contract should regard enforcing a promise unsupported by consideration as involving a higher morality than a promise supported in that way, but complexities abounded.

A number of judgments have sought to enforce firm offers in the absence of consideration,[85] but recourse to the courts runs against Lewis' main finding that commercial parties were largely uninterested in such recourse, and 'the potential which exists for making use of the legal system has not been exploited'.[86] For Lewis showed that both main or general contractors and sub-contractors saw little or no prospect of a reform which would substantially improve commercial practices which already acceptably distinguished firm offers which should, and were, respected from both an opportunistic withdrawal of a firm offer and from 'bid shopping', in which a main contractor used a submitted bid to bargain with other potential bidders. Lewis' point, in the tradition of Macaulay, was that non-legal strategies had been used to improve on the formal law, and of course he was right, but, as was argued in Chapter 2, it is always the case with Macaulay's non-use that one must be precise in identifying what it is about the formal law that drives the parties into apparently 'non-contractual relations'. The formal law of consideration was not of much help, or much consequence, to the parties. But their basic practice turned on good faith acknowledgement of liability for actual benefit and detriment as determined by the parties' commercial understandings. Enforcement could well not involve litigation, for of course the formal law obstructed this. But the legitimacy of self-help enforcement, and perhaps legal enforcement, of good faith practice was general.

The parties Lewis surveyed did not question either that a firm offer should, in good faith, be kept open when this served business efficacy, or that it could, in good faith, be

[82] R Lewis, 'Contracts Between Businessmen: Reform of the Law of Firm Offers and an Empirical Study of Tendering Practices in the Building Industry' (1982) 9 Journal of Law and Society 153 (hereafter Lewis, 'Firm Offers').

[83] Law Commission, *Firm Offers* [1975] EWLC C60. The doctrinal crux of the matter as it was understood at the time was set out in Sutton, *Consideration* (n 19) 174–82.

[84] Law Revision Committee, *Report* (n 6) para 38 (emphasis added).

[85] See n 89.

[86] Lewis, 'Firm Offers' (n 82) 170.

departed from when, in different circumstances, this also served the same end. That what was at issue *was* business efficacy as good faith, ie the legitimate, but not the illegitimate, pursuit of self-interest, was undoubted, and in this sense the idea behind consideration obtained. But a doctrine of consideration that could not accommodate good faith within its formal categories consequently could not capture the variety of what business efficacy required, which did not admit of 'a simple yes or no answer' to the questions as they could be posed by the formal law of consideration.[87] A law of consideration which did turn on good faith could easily do so, and with this the whole problem of pre-contractual expenditure would disappear. The expenditure would never be pre-contractual. A bid would be submitted in conformity with the intentions of the parties understood in the context of the practices of their industry (perhaps a firm offer would be involved), and in return would receive an appropriate level of evaluation.[88] This sort of arrangement, based on interpretation of the good faith conduct required for business efficacy, is called a contract.

The strange paradox of consideration is taken to a new level when the 'moral' obligation to protect pre-contractual expenditure is enforced in the absence of consideration because the positive work of consideration, of requiring payment to make obligations enforceable, is seen only in a negative light. I will not review the various authorities which have enforced firm offers, but merely assert that all of them work by what I have called recourse to the empirical.[89] There is a background perception that the doctrine of consideration is simply inappropriate, and rather than recognise the loophole, there is a feeling that something should be done to protect the promisee's reliance, which boils down to determining the reasonableness of that reliance. But when is reliance reasonable? The answer consideration gives to this question is 'when a party has paid for it'. The entire problem over consideration has been a failure to see that this is not an answer based on solipsistic selfishness, but a morally correct answer that enjoys almost universal acceptance—it takes considerable doctrinal learning to find fundamental difficulty with it.[90] In this situation, space for the regrettable exercise of welfarism has been created. In the Commonwealth,[91] this has reached its highest

[87] ibid 169.

[88] This is to say that the analysis of the firm offer applies equally to, or should embrace, the obligation to properly evaluate tenders in accord with the obvious intention of the parties, to which 'The law would ... be defective if it did not give effect': *Blackpool and Fylde Aero Club v Blackpool BC* [1990] 1 WLR 1195 (CA) 1202E (Bingham LJ).

[89] Treitel's attempt to classify these cases, which would seem to be as good as the material admits, is retained in H Beale (ed), *Chitty on Contracts*, vol 1 (34th edn, Sweet & Maxwell 2021) para 6.203 n 1124 (hereafter Beale (ed), *Chitty*).

[90] G Orwell, 'Notes on Nationalism' in *I Belong to the Left* in *Complete Works*, vol 17 (rev edn, Secker and Warburg 2001) 154:

> One has to belong to the intelligentsia to believe a thing like that; no ordinary man could be such a fool.

[91] In the US, the formal position is that a doctrine of promissory estoppel runs largely parallel—one does not know the precisely correct word, which would have to embrace both 'parallel' and 'tangential'—to consideration: R2d Contracts § 90. As the views it is wished to express here may now be advanced through discussion of *Waltons Stores*, discussion of the very large and unrewarding subject of the attempt to prefer 'reliance' over 'consideration' in the US law is unnecessary. It is highly instructive to examine the reasons for Professor Knapp's growing disillusionment with § 90: CL Knapp, 'Reliance in the Revised Restatement: The Proliferation of Promissory Estoppel' (1981) 81 Columbia Law Review 52 and CL Knapp, 'Rescuing Reliance: The Perils of Promissory Estoppel' (1998) 49 Hastings Law Review 1191.

possible point short of the abolition of the doctrine of consideration in the famous Australian case of *Waltons Stores (Interstate) Ltd v Maher*.[92]

The claimants in *Waltons Stores* had entered into negotiations to lease commercial premises to the defendant. The successful conclusion of the negotiations was dependent on the claimants replacing existing buildings on their site. The defendant unarguably made statements during the negotiations which anticipated the successful conclusion of the negotiations, but when the claimants' solicitors submitted formal documents for exchange, no reply was made. In order to move negotiations along in line with the defendant's stated timetable, the claimants, as the defendant knew, demolished the existing buildings, and had made considerable progress on the new ones when the defendant, having changed its mind, withdrew. The defendant was estopped from denying that it was bound,[93] and in my view the best, as it were composite, reading of the judgments is that this was because the defendant's statements of future intention, or its not notifying the claimants of its change of mind, had inequitably (or unconscionably) induced detrimental reliance. The overwhelmingly important point is, of course, that 'enforcing directly in the absence of a pre-existing relationship [a] non-contractual promise' was to 'drive promissory estoppel one step further'[94] than the 'shield not a sword'[95] interpretation of the English law. An attempt was made to deny that, as Brennan J put it, the doctrine of consideration [had been] 'blown away by a side-wind'[96] because 'equitable estoppel does not elevate non-contractual

A truly fascinating debate between Professors Macaulay and Whitford and Professor Scott over one of the most celebrated US cases, *Hoffman v Red Owl Stores* 26 Wisc 2d 263; 133 NW 2d 267 (Supreme Court of Wisconsin 1965) is reviewed with the intention of describing the opposed values that guide the application of the doctrine in D Campbell, What Do We Mean By the Non-use of Contract?' in J Braucher, J Kidwell, and WC Whitford (eds), *Revisiting the Contracts Scholarship of Stewart Macaulay: On the Empirical and the Lyrical* (Hart 2013) 175–76.

The most authoritative Commonwealth review of the US law, written when its author so shared Knapp's initial enthusiasm that the adoption of § 90 was enthusiastically advocated, is Sutton, *Consideration* (n 19) ch 7,

92 (1988) 164 CLR 387 (HCA) (hereafter *Waltons Stores*).

93 More settled lines of argument of which the claimant might have availed itself other than the one for which *Waltons Stores* now is taken to stand were on the facts not available, or were not pursued as strenuously as they might have been or actually were not available.

94 *Waltons Stores* (n 92) 400 (Mason CJ and Wilson CJ).

95 *Combe v Combe* [1951] 2 KB 215 (CA) 224 (Birkett LJ).

96 The 'side-wind' of course refers to Denning LJ's own important attempt in *Combe v Combe*, ibid 220, to apply the brakes when even he was abashed to see just what juggernaut he had set rolling in *High Trees* (n 10).

When in 1979 he began his autobiographical writings, Lord Denning, *The Discipline of the Law* (Butterworths 1979) 223 (hereafter Lord Denning, *Discipline*) pointed to the dearth, indeed Lord Denning thought complete absence, of decisions on consideration whilst he was Master of the Rolls, which he explained by saying that:

> The effect of [promissory estoppel] has been to do away with the doctrine of consideration in all but a handful of cases [and to replace it with] the better precept: 'My word is my bond', irrespective of whether there is consideration to support it.

Leaving aside the difficulty of reconciling this with *Combe v Combe* (and *Tool Metal Manufacturing Co Ltd v Tungsten Electric Co Ltd Engineering* [1955] 1 WLR 761 (HL) 764 (Lord Simonds), mentioned in Lord Denning, *Discipline*, ibid 764), I am unaware of anything I have read on the law of contract more clearly displaying the effects of a scarcely credible belief that 'cases' say all that there is to say about the law and action based on it. Inside its own legal sphere, Lord Denning's view is wrong; outside that sphere, it is delusional.

promises to the level of contractual promises'.[97] Of its nature, estoppel could protect only reliance, not the expectation that would be protected by contract proper, and so the claimants should have been limited to recovering their wasted expenditure and not the profit from the lease.[98] This has certainly left its legacy in the Australian law of remedies,[99] but this legacy is, with respect, a complicated refinement of a distinction that should not have been drawn in the first place.

No *ratio* can be derived from the judgment of the High Court, and this no doubt has played its part in the uncertainty of the resulting law, which stops short of abolishing consideration, but how far short is unknown.[100] Far from claiming to engage with the detail of the resulting law, I wish to address a crucial, as it were, prior point. The overwhelming tenor of the reception of *Walton Stores* is that some extension of liability by *Waltons Stores*, whatever it is, represents a valuable 'moralisation' of commercial relationships.[101] But this is quite wrong, for the defendant's conduct was entirely legally and morally justifiable. *Walton Stores*' failure to assist in the consolidation of a 'unifying purpose'[102] for estoppel is the result of the case's failing to recognise the value of requiring consideration appropriate to the circumstances.

Though of course it is recognised, commentary has placed insufficient weight on the negotiations in *Waltons Stores* being for the disposition of an interest in land, and therefore governed by the Conveyancing Act 1919, s 54A (NSW), which provides that no action in relationship to such a disposition may be brought unless the necessary formalities have been completed.[103] The position was, I understand, the same as then and now prevails in England and Wales. It is one thing to, as I, for whatever my opinion is worth, do, believe that the system of conveyancing is open to radical reform, and therefore to be concerned about the conduct of the legal and related professions which

[97] *Waltons Stores* (n 92) 427. It is, of course, perfectly easy to find *dicta* which can be read to the contrary throughout the judgment. Deane J indeed seems to have believed he was strengthening the doctrine of consideration: ibid 453.

[98] The actual remedy granted at first instance and affirmed by the New South Wales Court of Appeal and the High Court actually was damages in lieu of specific performance: ibid 393, 433. The first instance judgment referred quantification to a Master (*Maher v Waltons Stores (Interstate) Ltd*, Kearney J, NSWSC, 8 August 1984, unreported but available via Lexis (hereafter *Maher v Waltons Stores*)), and the complete absence of discussion of this matter on appeal (*Waltons Stores (Interstate) Ltd v Maher* (1986) 5 NSWLR 407 (NSWCA)) means that one can merely speculate, but it is hardly conceivable in the circumstances that such damages would not have fully compensated reliance loss, and it is likely they would have included a further small (following settled practice under Lord Cairns Act) sum in partial 'compensation' of expectation loss. This is to say, the damages awarded would not have fitted into the distinction between expectation and reliance.

[99] *Commonwealth of Australia v Verwayen* (1990) 170 CLR 394 (HCA) and *Giumelli v Giumelli* (1999) 196 CLR 101 (HCA).

[100] Though the book is of course now outdated, the basic tension emphatically emerged, despite the author's favourable view of developments, from M Spence, *Protecting Reliance* (Hart 1999).

[101] As the then Professor Finn put it, *Waltons Stores* represented a 'flowering' of this tendency: P Finn, 'Commerce, the Common Law and Morality' (1989) 17 Melbourne University Law Review 87, 96.

[102] A Robertson, 'Towards a Unifying Purpose for Estoppel' (1996) 22 Monash University Law Review 1.

[103] I am anxious to avoid venturing deeply into the *Walton Stores* labyrinth, but must point out that extensive questioning whether an 'exchange' had taken place was, so far as one can say, resolved in the defendant's favour (*Waltons Stores* (n 92) 395–97). Finding otherwise would, of course, make the subsequent reasoning even less secure, were that possible.

seems to obstruct such reform.[104] It is quite another to require commercial parties negotiating a conveyance to comply with anything other than the position defined by statute.[105] Until the formalities were completed, neither party had any legal assurance in respect of anything whatsoever. The atmosphere of much commentary on the case is that Mr and Mrs Terrence and Patricia May Maher were the 'Mom and Pop' beloved of critics of franchise law.[106] But the case arose because claimants, who were in receipt of very extensive legal advice, hoped to lease land they had recently purchased for the very purpose of commercial development for *circa* A$5 million in present values.[107]

It was wholly within the competence of far less agile minds than those of the judges of the appeal courts of Australia to get around the obstacle presented by the statute,[108] but why would they want to do so? Mason CJ and Wilson J were surely right when they 'conceded' that

> The application of [estoppel] principles to the facts of the present case is not without difficulty. The parties were negotiating through their solicitors for an agreement for lease to be concluded by way of customary exchange. [One of the authorities discussed in their judgment][109] illustrates the difficulty of establishing an estoppel preventing parties from refusing to proceed with a transaction expressed to be 'subject to contract'. And there is the problem identified in [another authority discussed][110] that a voluntary promise will not generally give rise to an estoppel because the promisee may reasonably be expected to appreciate that he cannot safely rely upon it. This problem is magnified in the present case where the parties were represented by their solicitors.[111]

I have argued that, if the promises which constitute consideration were seen as promises in good faith, then the problems of pre-contractual expenditure would simply disappear. The promise on reliance on which the expenditure was made would be contractual. The reaction to the facts of *Waltons Stores* arises from some recognition of this, for the case turned on statute law which it is very hard to believe agreement in the normal course of business could yield. It should, of course, be possible for the parties to agree that their promises do not have contractual effect in the way for which

[104] Possible movement over residential conveyancing in England and Wales is reviewed in H Cromarty and L Abreu, *Improving the Home Buying and Selling Process in England*, HC Library Briefing Paper 06980 (27 February 2019).

[105] The English case of *Lane v O'Brien Homes Ltd* [2004] EWHC 303 (QB) went even further in this respect, ignoring a specific statutory prohibition. This case did not reach the appeal courts and is little discussed, but its excess was representative of developments in the law of damages at the time and it is noted in ch 8.

[106] The first paragraph of Kearney J's judgment, in which Mr Maher is described as 'a builder and a property developer in a small way', is to this effect: *Maher v Waltons Stores* (n 98) BC8411369 at 1. Deane J's finding it appropriate to mention that the Mahers 'were not lawyers' in the course of trying to distance them from the advice they received is, with respect, preposterous: *Waltons Stores* (n 92) 438.

[107] *Maher v Waltons Stores* (n 98) BC8411369 at 2.

[108] The nub of what was argued throughout the judgment may be found at *Waltons Stores* (n 92) 464 (Deane J).

[109] *Attorney General of Hong Kong v Humphrey's Estate (Queen's Gardens) Ltd* [1987] 1 AC 114 (PC) 121B.

[110] *Amalgamated Investment and Property Co v Texas Commerce International Bank Ltd* [1982] 1 QB 84 (CA) 107B.

[111] *Waltons Stores* (n 92) 406.

Rose and Frank Co v JR Crompton and Bros Ltd is often cited as authority.[112] This is, in fact, a difficult case which it is not proposed to discuss,[113] but it is evidence that that which should in principle be possible can be awkward to execute, and whilst this is part reflects doctrinal shortcomings,[114] it is right that parties must express themselves 'so precisely that outsiders may have no difficulty in understanding what they mean'[115] so that it would require 'clear words' to rebut the 'heavy' onus of the contractual default presumption of liability.[116] The most important legal device negating contractual intention is, of course, the phrase 'subject to contract' in a disposition of an interest in land, by which statute reverses the liability default. This reversal had happened in *Waltons Stores*, and it was, with respect, quite wrong of the courts which heard the case to, leaving aside the disrespect of statute, undermine the contractual intentions formed on the basis of the position described by Mason CJ and Wilson J.

Even the best of our commentators have not been precise enough in their analysis of *Waltons Stores*.[117] It is not a question of contract based on consideration, or rather the absence of contract based on the absence of consideration, versus protection of reliance made in, to use the term which draws the argument of this chapter together, good faith. The defendant's withdrawal was made in good faith, given the statutory position. It may, to repeat, speak against the statutory law of conveyancing that it allows default conduct approximating to solipsistic self-interest in a way it is impossible to conceive of the common law contract doing, but this is hardly a matter which should concern the court when interpreting intentions formed on the basis of that law. The most important general point is, however, that it was only because consideration was seen as devoid of moral substance that it could be thought necessary to support, or in my view supplant, it with moralistic estoppel. Recognition of good faith in consideration will solve problems of unenforceability in line with the intentions of the parties in a way which the welfarist bringing in of the endogenous device of estoppel cannot possibly, because it is not intended to, do.

[112] [1923] 2 KB 26 (CA) (hereafter *Rose and Frank* CA); reversed on other grounds [1925] AC 445 (HL). The honour clause, described by Lord Phllimore as a 'remarkable' one for which 'there was no explanation' on the record nor offered by counsel, is set out at [1925] AC 451 (HL).

[113] Intention to create legal relations is discussed in the text accompanying n 158.

[114] B Rudden, 'The Gentleman's Agreement in Legal Theory and in Modern Practice' (1999) 7(2) European Review of Private Law 199.

[115] *Rose and Frank* CA (n 112) 288.

[116] *Edwards v Skyways* [1964] 1WLR 349, 354–55 (QB). The interpretation of '*ex gratia*' to mean only no prior legal obligation to pay was, it is submitted, on the facts of the case correct.

[117] JW Carter, 'Contract, Restitution and Promissory Estoppel' (1989) 12 University of New South Wales Law Journal 30 (1989) 42:

> In a society where contract is seen as the basis for enforcing promises, it will normally be perfectly legitimate for a person to withdraw a non-contractual promise. But the circumstances were that detriment to the Mahers would result from that course of action. Therefore, Waltons had engaged in unconscionable conduct and was precluded from contradicting its promise.

This is, of course, much more wise than the enthusiastic rush—only held back on the occasions when it perforce has to confront what it is doing—to abolish consideration. Nevertheless, Professor Carter himself does not sufficiently penetratingly ask why Waltons' conduct could be held to be unconscionable.

Negligence liability

Though the significance of *Waltons Stores* is that it is an a potentially radical restriction on the application of the doctrine of consideration, and therefore on the Pareto domain of the law of contract, it is of far less significance than the restrictions which have been applied through the law of negligence. Though I am most reluctant to depart from the law of contract, the argument that is being made about that law at this point requires some discussion of these restrictions, for the welfarist revision of the law of contract itself is situate within the general attitude towards social regulation which informs the maximalist welfare state. Particularly in regard of personal injury, which is at the greatest distance from the direct concerns of this book, this discussion is not an argument as such but a synopsis of views expressed elsewhere, to which the reader is referred for such an argument supported by authority.[118]

The most important circumscription of the market sphere is the provision of what I shall persist in calling social security, which in the modern liberal democracies now turns on a collective decision with incontestable democratic legitimacy that the distribution of economic goods cannot be determined by the operation of the market alone. As discussed at greater length in subsequent chapters, the form which welfare was intended to be given in the UK by the post-war creation of the universal welfare state was uniform provision against want by ensuring an agreed minimum standard of living when disability or age reduce or eliminate income. It is important to realise that, not only is it arguable (this writer is convinced of it) that the stability of a market economy requires the provision of this social security floor, but such provision is intended to be, not merely supportive of the market economy and consistent with the liberal democratic rule of law, but very acceptably reconciled with that economy when confined to a floor of the prevention of want.

The general argument that it was never going to be possible to make the universal welfare state keep to the essentially Beveridgean bounds within which it is legitimate need not be considered here. What must be considered is the effect of the welfare state, not merely initially failing to abolish the private action for personal injury caused by negligence, but indeed eventually allowing and supporting the almost complete imposition of third party liability by the state. This so 'chills' as to nullify the market contractual possibility of widespread use of first party insurance. What is called 'full compensation' of the loss (including non-pecuniary loss) attributed to this particular cause of claimed disability is in principle and even more in practice irreconcilable with

[118] On personal injury see D Harris, D Campbell, and R Halson, *Remedies in Contract and Tort* (2nd edn, CUP 2005) ch 24; D Campbell, 'Interpersonal Justice and Actual Choice as Ways of Determining Personal Injury Law and Policy' (2015) 35 Legal Studies 430 and D Campbell, 'The *Heil v Rankin* Approach to Law-making: Who Needs a Legislature?' (2016) 46 Common Law World Review 340. On negligent misstatement see D Campbell, 'The Curious Incident of the Dog that Did Bark in the Night-time: What Mischief Does *Hedley Byrne and Co Ltd v Heller and Partners* Correct?' in K Barker, R Grantham, and W Swain (eds), *The Law of Misstatements: 50 years on from Hedley Byrne v Heller* (Hart 2015) 111 (hereafter Campbell, 'Curious Incident'); D Campbell, 'The Absence of Negligence in *Hedley Byrne v Heller*' (2016) 132 The Law Quarterly Review 266 and D Campbell, 'The Consequences of Defying the System of Natural Liberty: The Absurdity of the Misrepresentation Act 1967' in TT Arvind and J Steele (eds), *Contract Law and the Legislature* (Hart 2020) 127.

uniform provision against want, and the mechanism of its provision has inevitably been a mockery of the rule of law, both in terms of the routinisation of claims at the bottom end, and of the nonsense of legal argument at the top end.

The most important mischief is the annihilation of the moral atmosphere of responsibility engendered by the law of contract. Even setting aside the particular incentive third party insurance gives to fraud, the 'compensation culture' is a disgusting strain of mendicancy which undermines the welfare state, fostered by and pandered to by the legal profession, which has received much but not nearly sufficient criticism over its role as the principal gatekeeper to the resources the state commands be spent on the personal injury system. The argument for provision of a social security floor should not, and in an important sense cannot, be modified so as to be carried over to the personal injury system. Though provision of the floor, which of its nature the market cannot and should not provide, is essential in a liberal democratic society. But the provision of full compensation goes beyond the prevention of want, and so involves transfers which should be a matter of market choice. Full compensation provided by third party insurance is so bad because it rests on a general avoidance of requiring consideration for insurance against disability, and so of the test by which transfers of economic goods are normally deemed legitimate, that of choosing to pay for them.

The avoidance of this test is central to the legal reasoning behind negligent misstatement, for 'assumption of responsibility' is a grossly misleading way to describe the extension of imposition of liability by the state from personal injury to pure economic loss. In order to remedy a situation, to which we shall return, in which 'the country [was thought] not in a state of civilisation',[119] liability is, not bought by its beneficiary, but forced upon parties said by Lord Devlin to be in relationships ' "equivalent to contract", that is, where there is an assumption of responsibility in circumstances in which, but for the absence of consideration, there would be a contract'.[120] This formulation was intended 'to settle the law so that the presence or absence of consideration makes no difference'. But, of course, a contract without consideration is not a contract at all, and negligent misstatement is not equivalent to contract but is its very antithesis. That there is a positive significance in parties not choosing to create liability by contract has been but a very minor theme of the huge literature generated by *Hedley Byrne*. The fatuity of the House of Lords unthinking confidence that it could improve welfare by substituting its choice of the pattern of liability for the results of the choices of economic actors has principally been demonstrated by legal reasoning over proximity in misstatement that, addressing economic loss but dispensing with an anchor in economic rationality is even more absurd than the law of proximity in personal injury.

[119] *Candler v Crane, Christmas and Co* [1951] 2 KB 164 (CA) 176 (hereafter *Candler v Crane, Christmas*); quoting *Slim v Croucher* (1860) 1 De GF and J 518; 45 ER 462, 466 (Knight Bruce LJ).

[120] *Hedley Byrne and Co Ltd v Heller and Partners Ltd* [1964] AC 465 (HL) 529 (hereafter *Hedley Byrne*). Lord Devlin derived the phrase 'equivalent to contract' from the speech of Lord Shaw in *Nocton v Lord Ashburton* [1914] AC 932 (HL) 972. Lord Shaw, ibid 971, had himself noted the use of the phrase 'equivalent to a contract' in the argument of Sir Roundell Palmer QC in *Peek v Gurney* (1871–72) LR 13 Eq 79 (Ch) 97. By this route, Chancery arguments exploring the limits and potentials of contractual (including fiduciary) liability have become a pillar of the law of negligent misstatement which in principle sets those limits and potentials at nought.

The further one's view of the law of contract is removed from the voluntary economic exchange which it is the law's function to institutionalise, the more one will tend to substitute one's exogenous goals set by contract's endogenous goals of the parties' intentions. Seeing the absence of consideration as merely something to be got round has been very much intertwined with denying that contract has a distinct domain at all, focusing on, sometimes not merely very old but ancient, legal history, and on legal doctrine formalistically understood to describe contract as a 'wrong' the fundamental nature of which is akin to other wrongs in the law of obligations, and in particular to regard contract as a tort.[121] This is not the place to repeat the, as it were, 'methodological'[122] argument against doing this which I have made extensively elsewhere.[123] That argument turns on the specific legal form contract is claimed to take as a result of its economic function which runs throughout this book. A discussion focused on showing the indispensable value of the core of the doctrine of consideration to the performance of that function can, however, usefully focus on the consequences of attempting to decide cases on the basis of negligence liability when, under a contractual 'scheme' or 'structure', the claimant has not paid for such liability and the defendant would have it imposed upon it by the court. From a number of other notorious cases,[124] I am selecting the one which yields the most instruction to be derived from what Mummery LJ rightly called 'the dubious and lethal colonisation by

[121] PBH Birks, 'The Concept of a Civil Wrong' in D Owen (ed), *Philosophical Foundations of Tort Law* (OUP 1995) 51:

> the correct conclusion must be that for most purposes the common law approaches contract through the wrong of breach of contract. In effect it adds breach of contractual duty to the list of torts.

[122] I adopt this term from its surprising use in A Burrows, *Remedies for Torts, Breach of Contract, and Equitable Wrongs* (4th edn, OUP 2019) 21. Burrows' version of the relationship of contract to other obligations and in particular to tort is unusual in that it involves an explicit recognition of the voluntary nature of contractual obligations (ibid 8), which is then overwhelmed by an approach dominated by what are understood to be mandatory rules: D Campbell, 'Our Obligations to the Common Law (Review of A Burrows, *Remedies for Torts, Breach of Contract and Equitable Wrongs*)' [2020] Lloyd's Maritime and Commercial Law Quarterly 149, 166–69.

[123] Citations may be found in ch 8 in the course of a criticism of the argument about remedies that led to *Attorney General v Blake (Jonathan Cape Ltd Third Party)* [2001] 1 AC 268 (HL).

[124] I would not dream of defending the distinction I am drawing amongst cases of which I believe incoherence is the defining feature, but I am trying to exclude from this discussion of a contractual structure the flat imposition of liability which previously was unheard of. The set of cases which arose from the inappropriate imposition of negligence liability in *Scruttons Ltd v Midland Silicones Ltd* [1962 AC 446 (HL) (hereafter *Midland Silicones*) just disregarded the important acceptance of 'vicarious immunity' based on commercial parties' clear choice not to have contractual liability: PS Atiyah, 'Lord Denning's Contribution to Contract Law' (1999) 14 Denning Law Journal 1, 6–8 (hereafter Atiyah, 'Lord Denning'). (Not properly dealing with this point undermines the, in itself exemplary, defence of 'Dixonian strict legalism' in the treatment of privity, one of a number of defences of similar quality of the contract jurisprudence of Sir Owen Dixon, in J Gava, 'Dixonian Strict Legalism: *Wilson v Darling Island Stevedoring* and Contracting in the Real World' (2010) 30 Oxford Journal of Legal Studies 519). By no means do the well-known drafting contrivance or the statutory provision addressed to the problem eliminate the difficulty (Treitel, *Landmarks* (n 54) 64–82), but, much more than this, neither even make any basic sense unless it is, as it were, unconsciously allowed when interpreting them that avoiding the negligence liability is perfectly legitimate.

All that therefore can be learned from this deplorable episode, which is 'don't do it!, can equally be said of the comparable approach to concurrent liability exemplified by the even worse *Henderson v Merrett Syndicates Ltd* [1995] 2 AC 145 (HL).

the tort of negligence of the conceptual territory of contract'[125] when I now turn to *Junior Books Ltd v Veitchi Co Ltd*.[126]

The pursuer in *Junior Books* engaged a main contractor to construct a factory. The main contractor sub-contracted the laying of the some of the factory flooring to the defender. *Junior Books* looks even less like proper litigation than *Donoghue v Stevenson*,[127] for it was entirely argued by abstract reference to tort proximity at the time when *Anns v Merton LBC*[128] was in its ascendancy rather than on what the parties had agreed, about which no evidence whatsoever was presented.[129] The argument was whether liability could be found in principle, and proceeded on the assumption that the flooring had defects caused by the negligence of the defender which caused very considerable loss.[130] I shall entirely put aside the distinctions between the types of loss for which the defender might have been held liable, which were but some of the absurdities of the law of pure economic loss emerging at the time, and allow for the purposes of argument that there would have been no issue of proximity in contract relating to the expenses incurred in replacing the floor.[131]

But this leaves the finding of any liability at all. There was, of course, no privity between the parties, which were linked only through a chain of contracts including the main contractor. But there was found to be a special relationship between the parties which justified liability in negligence, and the main ground for this was that the pursuer had nominated the defender. In the, with respect, wrong-headed view of Lord Fraser, the floodgates argument was no barrier in *Junior Books* because:

> The [defender satisfies] most, if not all, of the ... tests that have been suggested as safeguards against opening the floodgates. The proximity between the parties is extremely close, falling only just short of a direct contractual relationship. The injury to the [pursuer] was a direct and foreseeable result of negligence by the [defender]. The [pursuer or its] architects, nominated the appellants as specialist sub-contractors and they must therefore have relied upon their skill and knowledge. It would surely be wrong to exclude ... a claim which is so strongly based, merely because of anxiety about the possible effect of the decision upon other cases where the proximity may be less strong.[132]

By floodgates Lord Fraser understood problems in tort. What he, of course entirely representatively, did not realise at all was that *Junior Books* opened an even potentially

[125] *Hamble Fisheries* (n 70) 8 col 2.

[126] [1983] 1 AC 520 (HL Sc) (hereafter *Junior Books*).

[127] [1932] AC 562 (HL Sc).

[128] [1978] AC 728 (HL).

[129] *Junior Books* (n 126) 538D–G. Concluding his criticism of this manufactured approach, Lord Roskill pointed out that at least *Donoghue v Stevenson* reached the Lords '3¾ years only' after the sale of the bottle of ginger beer, with or without the snail, whereas the Lords heard *Junior Books* only after a gap of 12 years: ibid 538G. Though it contains a bizarre amount of detail about the claimed, but not proven, defects in the flooring, *Junior Books v Veitchi Co Ltd* [1982] SLT 333 (IH 2D) also has nothing about the nature of the contract.

[130] The total losses averred, about which surely something had been done during that time, were £207,000 (over £2.25 million in 2021): *Junior Books* (n 126) 548B–G.

[131] *Circa* £60,000 (almost £950,000 in 2021) of the losses averred were of this nature: ibid.

[132] ibid 533B–C.

wider set of floodgates,[133] for *Junior Books* would in principle have led to the haplessness of pure economic loss in tort being extended over the sphere proper to contract.[134] The reason Lord Fraser would have held the defender liable was, so far the reported facts allow one to say, just the reason he should not have done so. Complex construction works are, of course, based on contractual chains of liability because—the point should be unarguable—this is what parties have chosen.[135] As part of the absence of evidence of what actually happened, no explanation was given why the pursuer had not brought a contractual action against the third party, which was not joined to the proceedings.[136] This may have been just because the entire point of the case was to extend pure economic loss, but if we look at the case contractually it is safe to assume that by nominating the defender the pursuer undermined liability through the chain. It is very difficult indeed to think a main contractor should have been liable for a fault that became manifest only after two years had passed since the installation[137] when a client had nominated the sub-contractor in reliance on its (the client's) belief in the sub-contractor's abilities.

Junior Books still remains with us but only in a vestigial way.[138] In the course of it becoming recognised that pure economic loss in tort had been taken so far as to threaten a very serious mischief and absolutely had to be reined back, *Junior Books* was so repented of that it was continually distinguished, with Dillon LJ doing much to airbrush it from legal history in a manner most unusual if not unique by effectively overruling it in the Court of Appeal.[139] *Junior Books* is now taken to exemplify the sort of contractual structure which should not be undermined by negligence.[140] However welcome in itself, this, as it were, treating of a contractual structure as an exception to a general sense—one cannot find a less vague word—of the existence of negligence

[133] JC Smith and P Burns, '*Donoghue v Stevenson*: The Not So Golden Anniversary' (1983) 46 Modern Law Review 147, 153: 'The implications of this case for the law of contracts and products liability are staggering to say the least'. The implications are set out ibid 159–60.

[134] Lord Keith's refusal in *Junior Books* (n 126) 537A to use the case 'To introduce a general liability [which] would be disruptive of commercial practice' was, in retrospect, one important beginning of the retreat from *Anns*. His wisdom in seeing, ibid 537C, that 'The policy considerations ... involved [were] such as a court of law cannot properly assess, and ... much better left for the legislature', has not had such impact.

[135] W Hughes, R Champion, and J Murdoch, *Construction Contracts: Law and Management* (5th edn, CRC Press LLC 2015) sec 19.3 (hereafter Hughes and others, *Construction Contracts*).

[136] *Junior Books* (n 126) 538F.

[137] ibid 534F.

[138] Beale (ed), *Chitty* (n 89) para 20.021 has a description of these vestiges after noting 'that later decisions have taken a highly restrictive view of the scope of the ... case'. At ibid para 17.059 n 384, we are advised that *Junior Books* 'must now be regarded as an exceptional, if not heretical, case'.

[139] *Simaan General Contracting Co v Pilkington Glass Ltd (No 2)* [1988] QB 758 (CA) 784: 'I find it difficult to see that future citation from *Junior Books* can ever serve any useful purpose.'

[140] Understandably alarmed by some expressions of the Law Commission's intentions (Law Commission, *Privity of Contract: Contracts for the Benefit of Third Parties* [1991] EWLC C121 paras 4.12–4.14 and Law Commission, *Privity of Contract: Contracts for the Benefit of Third Parties* [1996] EWLC 242 para 1.2 (hereafter Law Commission, *Privity*)), the construction industry remained very concerned that the operation of what was to become The Contracts (Rights of Third Parties) Act 1999, s 1(1)(b) should not undermine the chain (HL Deb 2 February 1999, vol 596, cols 1423–24), and the Law Commission eventually accepted that *Junior Books* should not give a client a direct action against a sub-contractor: Law Commission, *Privity*, ibid paras 7.47, 7.18(iii), 7.38. It is inconceivable that reasoning on the basis of s1(1)(b) could be adequate to the range of positions parties might choose to adopt, but the exclusion of s1(1)(b) has continuously caused difficulty: PS Davies, 'Excluding the Contracts (Rights of Third Parties) Act 1999' (2021) 137 Law Quarterly Review 101. On the 1999 Act see the text accompanying n 170.

liability is the wrong approach which follows from placing no weight on the presence or absence of consideration, so that it seems that liability does not need to be paid for. In an ill-fated article,[141] Professor Markesinis saw *inter alia Junior Books* as evidence that negligence was expanding to fill gaps in liability caused by English contract law being too 'rigid'.[142] This fear of rigidity is possible only if it is generally assumed that there should be liability, an assumption that is irreconcilable with freedom of contract. Leaving aside the chain, it was perfectly possible that the client and the defender could have brought themselves into privity through the common device known in the construction industry as a 'collateral warranty', used precisely when parties wish to avoid the chain,[143] but one is entitled to believe that they did not choose to do so; ie that the client did not value the benefit highly enough to pay for it. It is of significance that a case in which no evidence was given about the parties' contractual position has been used to illustrate the belief that contract law is too rigid because what drove the preference for negligence liability were, not specific defects in the law of contract, but a belief that the law of contract *tout court* is defective, resting as it does on consideration's insistence, fundamental to the market economy, that to acquire an economic good one must pay for it.

Insufficiency and the Formalism of Consideration

As the modern doctrine of consideration has had the effect of reducing the good faith bargain which is its basic subject matter to the nullity of a strange paradox, it is wholly unsurprising that the two main ways in which the doctrine has been elaborated—adequacy and insufficiency—are beset by difficulty. The doctrine of adequacy of consideration is analytically essential to the concepts of exchange and contract, and it is discussed at length in Chapter 6. The doctrine of sufficiency, in sharp contrast, has been a most unfortunate, *purely* doctrinal development which clouds our understanding of those concepts, and it will now be dealt with briefly in order to round off the criticism of the lack of substance at the heart of the classical understanding of consideration. The specific grounds of insufficiency themselves have substance. The attempt to bring them together into an overall doctrine of insufficiency does not do this, for it is a spurious formalism, and it should be abandoned. This argument will be made with reference to past consideration and the requirement that consideration move from the promisee. Though this argument encompasses the insufficiency of existing obligations, this ground of insufficiency raises other issues of the greatest importance and is the entire subject of Chapter 10.

[141] Markesinis' arguments that contract could be made more flexible were lost in the enthusiasm of the idea of initial rigidity. Lord Steyn, for example, was of the view that Markesinis had 'convincingly argued that a contractual as opposed to a tortious solution is the preferable one'. But where was this view expressed? In *White v Jones*!, where it was of course completely discounted, not least by Lord Steyn: *White v Jones* [1995] 2 AC 207 (HL) 236H–237B.

[142] BS Markesinis, 'An Expanding Tort Law: The Price of a Rigid Contract Law' (1987) 103 Law Quarterly Review 354.

[143] Hughes and others, *Construction Contracts* (n 135) sec 19.7. Both parts of this term obviously could generate misunderstanding, but by collateral is meant only that the warranty was given as one of the contracts governing the works, being legally separate from the main contract.

That the rule that past consideration is inadequate is aimed at denying contractual enforceability to gratuitous promises is now so well established as to need no argument here. Gratuitous promises are in some sense altruistic and therefore precisely not made on the basis of self-interest. Even if it is appropriate to use the law to enforce gratuitous promises,[144] and even if self-interest is properly understood as an entirely moral stance, it is inappropriate to require or allow parties to use the law of contract in order to secure the enforcement of gratuitous promises. The moral atmosphere of gratuitous promising and contract law are inimical.[145] It is a corollary of this that the remedies for breach of contract, which, as we shall see in Chapter 8, are focused, not on the performance of primary obligations but on the claimant's expectation of an advantage derived from such performance, must be bent out of their proper shape in order to serve the beneficiary's interest.[146]

My overriding concern being to give coherence to the law of contract as the institutionalisation of exchange,[147] and believing that Fuller's seminal identification of where we have gone so wrong remains essentially sound, it is my concern to distinguish peripheral issues of insufficiency from the core of consideration.[148] Though my opinion is formed on the basis of an only superficial knowledge of the practicalities of possible reform, I would require all gratuitous promises to comply with an appropriate set of

[144] AS Gold, 'Consideration and the Morality of Promising' in JW Neyers, R Bronaugh, and SGA Pitel (eds), *Exploring Contract Law* (Hart 2009). Even if enforceability is allowed in principle, the, as it were, degree of flexibility about it remains a vexed question to which contractual strict liability would seem to be no answer.

[145] MJ Eisenberg, 'The World of Contract and the World of Gift' (1997) 85 California Law Review 821, 847:

> the world of gift is driven by affective considerations like love, affection, friendship, gratitude, and comradeship. That world would be impoverished if it were to be collapsed into the world of contract.

[146] The terminology used by Professor Trebilcock to describe a gratuitous promise under seal (MJ Trebilcock, *The Limits of Freedom of Contract* (Harvard University Press 1993) 170) is, with respect, misleading:

> the law traditionally enforces such a promise as if it were a contract. That is, it is assumed that the promisor intended to be legally bound and the full expectancy interest of the promisee is protected.

By protection of the full expectancy interest is meant literal enforcement, but this is precisely what a contract does not normally provide.

[147] M Chen-Wishart, 'Consideration and Serious Intention' [2009] Singapore Journal of Legal Studies 434, 455: 'The consideration doctrine is not simply a proxy for serious intention to be bound'. Consideration is, rather, the legal institutionalisation of the *reason* that a party is bound, ie that the other party has paid to bind it. See further the text accompanying n 167.

[148] LL Fuller, 'Consideration and Form' (1941) 41 Columbia Law Review 799, 824:

> It has sometimes been proposed that the doctrine of consideration be 'abolished'. Such a step would, I believe, be unwise, and in a broad sense even impossible. The *problems* which the doctrine of consideration attempts to solve cannot be abolished. There can be little question that some of these problems do not receive a proper solution in the complex of legal doctrine now grouped under the rubric 'consideration'. It is equally clear that an original attack on these problems would arrive at some conclusions substantially equivalent to those which result from the doctrine of consideration as now formulated. What needs abolition is not the doctrine of consideration but a conception of legal method which assumes that the doctrine can be understood and applied without reference to the ends it serves. When we have come again to define consideration in terms of its underlying policies the problem of adapting it to new conditions will largely solve itself.

formalities in order to be enforceable. The point on which I wish to dwell is the disruption to the law of contract caused by dealing with gratuitous promises in terms of past consideration. The 'pastness' of consideration does indirectly identify the altruistic motivation of a gratuitous promise made in some circumstances that, let us allow, look like an exchange.[149] But the indirect approach is too broad, and it catches consideration which can be depicted as past though it formed part of what was certainly an economic exchange.

In *Re Casey's Patents*,[150] the claimants sought to recover a one third interest in two of their patents which they had granted to the defendant 'in consideration of your services' in promoting the use of the patents.[151] The letter specifying the grant of the one third interest was sent after the relevant services had been performed, but it was, of course, inconceivable that those services were rendered for anything other than commercial reasons in exchange for an expected benefit; ie the defendant' implicit commercial intention to perform the services for payment was itself executory consideration. Though it does not emerge in a case preoccupied with the registration of patents, it is readily conceivable why an initial undertaking to pay was not formalised until after the results of the defendant's efforts, on which the patents' success depended, became known. On the reported facts, this does appear, in terms of contract, to be merely a loophole case, and the manoeuvring needed to produce the correct outcome is an unfortunate cost of the inaptness of past consideration to its task.

In *Casey's Patents*, Bowen LJ recognised that a correct decision about the contractual enforceability of the transfer of the interest in the patents could be based on the reasoning associated with *Lampleigh v Braithwait*.[152] But, in a judgment handed down as early as 1891, Bowen LJ was scornful of this 'answer' to a 'question' of 'great interest' only to 'scientific students of law', and rather than waste 'perhaps [a] week' on it he chose to give direct effect to what is obvious:

> the fact of a past service raises an implication that at the time it was rendered it was to be paid for, and, if it was a service which was to be paid for, when you get in a subsequent document a promise to pay [it] may be treated ... as a positive bargain which fixes the amount of that reasonable remuneration on the faith of which the service was originally rendered.[153]

Some 80 years later, the Privy Council believed itself to be obliged in *Pao On* to formalise *Lampleigh v Braithwait*,[154] and whilst one can see why the circumstances of

149 Though it contains substantial elements which make it inappropriate for the use to which it is commonly used in undergraduate teaching, *Re McArdle* [1951] 1 Ch 669 (CA) does illustrate the point. The document at the heart of the case, in the names of all the testator's children but drawn up by the only one of them who wished the claimant to be paid, began by saying 'IN CONSIDERATION of [the claimant] carrying out certain alterations and improvements ... We ... hereby agree, etc': ibid 675. Though the works had been executed, this certainly could be read as, and it seems was intended to be read as, an executory, ie unproblematically enforceable, contract.

150 [1892] 1 Ch 894 (CA) (hereafter *Casey's Patents*).

151 ibid 115.

152 (1615) Hob 105; 80 ER 255.

153 *Casey's Patents* (n 150) 115–16.

154 *Pao On* (n 49) 629G.

this extremely high value loophole case gave rise to this belief, and admire *Pao On* as a leading example of the 'adroit' judicial closure of the loophole, this approving attitude does not survive mature reflection on this sort of ingenuity being necessary. Bowen LJ's direct recourse to the empirical is the more instructive position.[155] But even this is not, of course, an acceptable general position. If the law addressed gratuitous promises directly, pastness simply would not pose a problem for a doctrine of consideration recognised to be addressed to bargains.

It is now generally held that the 1919 judgment of Atkin LJ in *Balfour v Balfour*[156] consolidated the Victorian development, itself delving back into an 'obscure' legal history, of a requirement of a distinct 'intention to create legal relations' in order to create liability,[157] in response to the perception that consideration did not adequately manage to distinguish gratuitous from exchange promises.[158] Without at all going into the detail of the matter, this device was always fundamentally ill-conceived. Considered on its own rather than as a *deux ex machina*, it is without basic content. One does not need a separate doctrine to base enforceability on the intentions of the parties.[159] This is what enforceability would always have been based on in a law of contract which could recognise the good faith substance of consideration. It is irrelevant to claim that parties as a matter of fact often have no subjective intention regarding enforceability.[160] Leaving aside domestic arrangements,[161] even if non-performance, much less actual disputes, are not at all the things commercial parties want to happen

[155] A striking recourse to the empirical from, as it were, the other direction may be found in Parke B just stating, in response to an attempt to enforce a promise that a father should effectively pay his son to stop complaining about his prospective inheritance, that 'there was no binding agreement at all': *White v Bluett* (1853) 23 LJ Ex 36. This avoided the difficulty which Pollock CB and Alderson B encountered by ever engaging with consideration (W Swain, *The Law of Contract 1670-1870* (CUP 2015) 189–90), though Pollock CB's dismissal of the consideration argument as a 'ridiculous' 'absurdity'—'a bubble blown until it bursts' made *White v Bluett* a noted case (*White v Bluett* 37).

[156] [1919] 2 KB 571 (CA) 578–80.

[157] D Ibbetson, *A Historical Introduction to the Law of Obligations* (OUP 1999) 233–34, 247–48.

[158] AWB Simpson, 'Innovation in Nineteenth Century Contract Law' (1975) 91 Law Quarterly Review 247, 263–65.

[159] Amongst a number of commentators who have made this point authorities, I refer again to Shatwell, 'Consideration' (n 1) 314–15.

[160] S Hedley, 'Keeping Contact in Its Place: *Balfour v Balfour* and the Enforceability of Informal Agreements' (1985) 5 Oxford Journal of Legal Studies 391 was an early and influential criticism, based on a correct understanding of contractual intention (ibid 399–401), of the intention to create legal relations doctrine as inviting, not the enforcement or non-enforcement of contracts on the basis of the parties' intentions, but on the basis of the court's 'own view of whether the agreement *ought* to be enforced': ibid 393.

[161] In the wake of Hedley's analysis, *Balfour v Balfour* has been subject to sometimes very strongly worded, as it were, political criticism which cuts across that analysis in order to condemn the content of objective contractual intention then and now: O Gan, 'Anti-Stereotyping Theory and Contract Law' (2019) 42 Harvard Journal of Law and Gender 83, 101–102. On the known facts, *Balfour v Balfour* undoubtedly was a very difficult case, perhaps wrongly decided: SJ Stoljar, 'Enforcing Benevolent Promises' (1989) 12 Sydney Law Review 17, 22–23. But it seems to me that Lord Atkin did give general expression to the objective intention of contemporaneous reasonable persons.

I would not maintain this about the overall legacy of the noted cases which have challenged *Balfour v Balfour*. The thinking behind these cases, turning on the truisms that private action is influenced by social relations and law, and that private actions will have public consequences, does not see the value of an in principle private sphere from which it is very important that purposive law is excluded: M Freeman, 'Contracting the Haven: *Balfour v Balfour* Revisited' in R Halson (ed), *Exploring the Boundaries of Contract* (Dartmouth 1986) 74 and P Saprai, '*Balfour v Balfour* and the Separation of Contract and Promise' (2017) 37 Legal Studies 468.

or even in any concrete sense envisage as a result of entering into legal contracts, such parties enter into them, as opposed to just making an economic exchange, because they always have enforceability as an objective intention in a way at least as clear as any other non-express term necessary for business efficacy. Why else do they enter into a contract? How else could the law of contract perform its function?[162] This is the point at the core of consideration, and it is only because the law has so badly struggled to acknowledge the moral substance of the self-interest motivating exchange that this has remained of any difficulty.

I shall make no attempt to keep the requirement that consideration move from the promisee (ie claimant) separate from reflections on privity of agreement, but distinguish two proscriptions that the, as it were, combined doctrine of privity establishes. That no third party should be placed under an obligation by a simple contract between others is obviously analytically essential to the claim about the legitimacy of contract resting on autonomy that underpins this book—a 'corollary' of contract rather than a separate rule, as Kincaid aptly puts it[163]—and I shall say nothing about the core of this. The very important systems of commercial law such as agency and assignment which might be described as involving exceptions can indeed be properly regarded as exceptions to the law of simple contract,[164] and the vestigial residuum of other cases are, from the point of view of doctrine and theory, mere curiosities.[165]

In contrast, a clear perception that certain intended beneficiaries should have an enforceable right runs through the history of the law of the agreement by two parties to provide a benefit to a third,[166] and the formalism of the combined doctrine of privity would sweep too wide and proscribe this. The common law attempts which have been made to give effect to this perception need not be discussed as, for our purposes, the problem is similar, or in one sense, identical to that of gratuitous promises in general.[167] It is therefore again suggested that the necessary reform is to require that promises intended to benefit a third party comply with an appropriate set of formalities, and behind the formalities there should be clarity about the character of the promise that should make it both unenforceable as simple contract and enforceable in other ways.[168] This former at least would have been the essential effect of The

[162] It is submitted that the position over collective agreements is a political exception that proves the economic rule. That the common law expressed a 'political' position was sufficiently conveyed by a number of Geoffrey Lane J's remarks in *Ford Motor Co v Amalgamated Union of Engineering and Foundry Workers* [1969] 2 QB 303 (QB) 330H: 'background of opinion adverse to enforceability'. But unfortunately it was perhaps naïve of Professor Hepple (BA Hepple, 'Intention to Create Legal Relations' [1970] Cambridge Law Journal 122, 137) to expect a serviceable formula to be abandoned by statute merely in the interests of facilitating public debate about what was being done.

[163] P Kincaid, 'The UK Law Commission's Privity Proposals and Contract Theory' (1995) 8 Journal of Contract Law 51.

[164] M Furmston and GJ Tolhurst, *Privity of Contract* (OUP 2014) chs 3 and 4.

[165] ibid ch 7.

[166] R Flannigan, 'Privity: The End of an Era (Error)' (1987) 103 Law Quarterly Review 564.

[167] This is to say that Kincaid's powerful criticism of the focus on 'the abstract enforceability of the promise', rather than on bargain and reciprocity, that lies behind much argument for third party beneficiary rights, can be extended to all gratuitous promises: P Kincaid, 'Third Parties: Rationalising a Right to Sue' [1989] Cambridge Law Journal 243, 258.

[168] Though the distinction between rights *in rem* and *in personam* seems to be central to Lord Haldane's famous statement about privity in *Dunlop v Selfridge* (n 28) 853, and perhaps was what his Lordship had in mind, it is submitted that this proposal would merely extend the grounds on which Lord Haldane would

Contracts (Rights of Third Parties) Act 1999, s 1(1)(a), were it not for the enactment of s 1(1)(b), both of which are quoted together with s 1(2):

> 1(1) Subject to the provisions of this Act, a person who is not a party to a contract (a 'third party') may in his own right enforce a term of the contract if:
> (a) the contract expressly provides that he may, or
> (b) subject to subsection (2), the term purports to confer a benefit on him.
> 1(2) Subsection (1)(b) does not apply if on a proper construction of the contract it appears that the parties did not intend the term to be enforceable by the third party.

Though the enactment of only s 1(1)(a) would not, of course, have ended the difficulties of determining the class of third party beneficiaries, the enactment of s 1 (1)(b), which works in an open, informal way opposed to the closed formality of s 1(1)(a), was bound to lead to an exaggeration of those difficulties, with s 1(2) a despairing recognition of this. Leaving aside issues of drafting,[169] it would seem that the main reason for this was an uncertainty about the Law Commission's goal.[170] Were that goal the protection of the third party's interest, to which the existence of a contract between other parties is in principle irrelevant,[171] then s 1(1)(a) could have been sufficient. But if, as overall was the case,[172] the goal was to give effect to the intentions of the contracting parties, then, though not actually essential, s 1(1)(b) was very likely to be thought so, for to do otherwise would be to impose formality on simple contract in just the way the Commission thought it was avoiding. Insufficient thought was given to the way that the very concept of a third party beneficiary runs against the requirement of paying for a contractual benefit, for that requirement was given no weight by an approach which saw privity, consideration, and in the end contract, as mere obstructions to 'moral' enforceability which should not be limited by having to pay for it. The lack of concern for the integrity of the law of contract that allowed consideration to become a scrap-collector in the first place persists through consideration's statutory reform. It is striking to once again find the common law functions of the Law Commission being carried out in a way which cannot see the specific moral value of exchange and contract, but in this the Commission was merely representative of the stance of many of those who have exercised the highest influence on the post-war development of the law of contract. We return to this in Chapter 6.

have thought a *jus quaesitum tertio* legitimate, for surely his example of property (and so not eg agency or assignment) cannot be regarded as exclusive.

169 JN Adams, D Beyleveld, and R Brownsword, 'Privity of Contract: The Benefits and the Burdens of Law Reform' (1997) 60 Modern Law Review 238, 249–55. On the more recent case law see Beale, *Chitty* (n 89) paras 20.094–20.099.

170 Law Commission, *Privity* (n 140) paras 3.1–3.28.

171 C Mitchell, 'Privity Reform and the Nature of Contractual Obligations' (1999) 19 Legal Studies 229, 241.

172 Law Commission, *Privity* (n 140) para 1.8

Conclusion: The Fallacy of the Privity of Contract Fallacy

During the Second Reading in the Lords of the Contracts (Rights of Third Parties) Bill, Lord Meston offered the Bill as an early present to Lord Denning, then 12 days short of his 100th birthday. In claiming that 'in the Bill we reach fulfilment of something tenaciously advocated for many years by the noble and learned Lord, Lord Denning',[173] Lord Meston not only was too sanguine about the prospects of the legislation but did not really capture Lord Denning's attitude to privity. Lord Denning did, of course, make repeated onslaughts on privity,[174] and it should be noted that one of these made even less sense, and has led to enormously more mischief, than *Beswick v Beswick*. In *Candler v Crane, Christmas*, Lord Denning, as we have noted, claimed the absence of what was to become the tort of negligent misstatement represented the absence of 'a state of civilisation'.[175] This absence was a consequence of an 'error ... which appears time and time again in nineteenth century thought, namely, that no one who is not a party to a contract can sue on it or on anything arising out of it'.[176] But it was not really 'the privity fallacy' which Lord Denning had in his sights; it was consideration,[177] and therefore, though this was—representatively—but dimly perceived, contract. Lord Denning was right to claim that *Hedley Byrne* made his dissent in *Candler v Crane, Christmas* into law,[178] and, as we have seen, *Hedley Byrne* was a rejection of contract *tout court*.[179] Lord Denning saw privity only as a bar to liability he thought should be imposed for his own moralistic reasons exogenous to contract, and stopped only when the disruption within the law of contract his reasoning would cause became too blatant for him to disregard.[180]

The point that must be made about the general alternatives to contract set up by *Donoghue v Stevenson* and *Hedley Byrne*, that once the euphoria of doing something for a particular claimant by discarding limits to liability connected with privity and contract wears off one has to find substitute limits, must also be made about Lord Denning's interventions within contract. He sometimes valuably hit the mark, but that even *High Trees* is so wholly dubitable that Denning LJ himself quickly resiled from its implications is very significant. In addition to public encomia and his own extra-judicial expressions of his views, there is a literature extolling the 'jurisprudence' of Lord Denning.[181] But, quickly passing over Lord Denning's general views,[182] and

[173] HL Deb 11 January 1999, vol 596, col 29.

[174] Lord Denning's dissent in *Midland Silicones* (n 124) 481–92 can hardly be read as support for privity, or even contract, or even law (ibid 467–68 (Lord Simonds)), but it did very knowledgeably consider the legal history and, one occasion of Lord Denning's remarkable saving grace, produce the right outcome.

[175] See n 119.

[176] *Candler v Crane, Christmas* (n 119) 177.

[177] It is unsurprising that Lord Denning tells us in his autobiography that he had consideration in his sights long before he was elevated to the Bench: Lord Denning, *Discipline* (n 96) pt 5.

[178] ibid 237: 'Fourteen years later my dissent in *Candler v Crane, Christmas* was approved by the House of Lords'.

[179] Both *Candler v Crane, Christmas* and *Hedley Byrne* could have been easily handled by a properly understood law of contract, but this would have led to results which completely ran against the belief in the necessity of what was to become negligent misstatement: Campbell, 'Curious Incident' (n 118) 129–30.

[180] See n 96.

[181] C Stephens, *The Jurisprudence of Lord Denning*, 3 vols (Cambridge Scholars 2009).

[182] Lord Denning, *The Family Story* (Butterworths 1981) 174:

seeking to confine myself to private contract (and to the elements of tort to which contract supposed deficiencies have been linked, not least by Lord Denning), the point precisely is that Lord Denning's judgments display immense cleverness, but do not express a jurisprudence in the sense of coherent, systemic thought.[183] There are only *ad hoc* interventions in an actual system, of which consideration is a key aspect, which Lord Denning simply took for granted as something in which he could meddle only for the better because he did not begin to understand it as a system.

The closest Lord Denning came to this understanding was in his views on inequality of bargaining power, which are discussed at length in Chapter 6, and inevitably the paradox emerged that the closer he came to such an understanding, the more manifestly unsatisfactory his views became. The entire argument of this book is that the law of contract needs to be much modified if it is to enhance welfare as it could and should. But to enhance welfare it has to survive, and it is by no means idle to ask how far welfarism has shrunk the actual Pareto domain of contract.[184] Though his overriding commitment to 'justice' was the foundation of the esteem in which he was held, Lord Denning's welfarist *ad hocery* was in principle a threat to contract. How far the threat was executed was, as we discuss in Chapters 6 and 7, a matter of Lord Denning encountering barriers rooted in the nature of exchange which he could not remotely comprehend, and so put down to a sad want of the commitment to justice in others. It does, however, show how often Lord Denning actually did hit the mark that Professor Atiyah's verdict, which should be damning, is never read (not even by this writer) without sympathy: although 'Lord Denning did a great deal of good to the law of contract ... it is a good thing there was only one Lord Denning'.[185]

Whatever Lord Denning's thought about contract in general may have been, one thing it would not involve would be discussion of the privity fallacy in terms of the 'modern ideas of economic efficiency' which, as Professor Stapleton has told us,[186] are the 'jargon' in which another important rejection of privity is largely

> My root belief is that the proper role of the judge is to do justice between the parties before him. If there is any rule which impairs the doing of justice, then it is the province of the judge to do all he legitimately can to avoid that rule ... He need not wait for the legislature to intervene because that can never be of any help in the instant case. I would emphasise, however, the word 'legitimately': the judge is himself subject to the law and must abide by it.

No accurate appreciation of Lord Denning's achievement can take this at face value.

[183] PS Atiyah, 'Contract and Tort' in JL Jowell and JPWB McAuslan (eds), *Lord Denning: The Judge and the Law* (Sweet & Maxwell 1984) and Atiyah, 'Lord Denning' (n 124).

[184] J Gava and P Kincaid, 'Contract and Conventionalism' (1996) 10 Journal of Contract Law 141, 142:

> there has been a revolutionary change in the trajectory of contract law in Australia ... Contemporary law has moved a significant way from will-based [ie based on the intentions of the parties] contract towards a regime where contractual obligations are better understood as imposed by the courts according to notions of fairness and community expectations ... The destruction of will-based contract may represent a well-intentioned but ultimately dangerous manoeuvre which slides too easily into a functionalist view which sees the primary role of law as the satisfaction of an ever-increasing economy of needs.

John Gava's subsequent body of criticism of the economic and social consequences of welfarism and its effect on the quality of legal reasoning has long deserved, but unfortunately has not adequately received, sustained evaluation as a Commonwealth parallel to the very influential US statements of neo-formalism.

[185] Atiyah, 'Lord Denning' (n 124) 11.

[186] J Stapleton, *Product Liability* (Butterworths 1994) 12.

discussed: product liability.[187] I do not wish to discuss product liability as such, for as I am of the opinion that no rational policy or just legal grounding[188] has ever been provided for identifying this form of liability,[189] my discussion would superfluously repeat with reference to a different terminology my criticism of *Donoghue v Stevenson* in order to say that, viewed as a product liability case, *Donoghue* is even worse than it is when viewed as a general principle of negligence case. I want here to examine the economic justification now typically claimed for product liability,[190] which tries to give theoretical strength to the rejection of privity by claiming that product liability addresses a very important market failure.

In the first UK attempt to state in a manner similar to *Chitty* or *Clerk and Lindsell* the law of product liability after the Consumer Protection Act 1987, Professor Howells, in his capacity as the book's general editor, put the point this way under the heading 'Free market':

> Coase had shown that where transaction costs were insignificant, the market mechanism would produce the optimum mix of costs [of prevention and of harm] ... This market based solution was, however, shown to be unrealistic. In the real world transaction costs place barriers in the way of individuals bargaining for their rights and where the impact is on third parties or on the general welfare there is little incentive for a consumer to bargain over such externalities. Moreover ... consumers are often poor at assessing risks and therefore are unable to effectively participate in the bargaining process. The dangers of letting the market regulate product safety [are] fairly well recognised in the modern legal framework protecting consumers ... However, in US writings there has been a move back to contract. This is based on a belief that the individual should be free to choose which products suit him best and to accept risks in return to access to products at cheaper prices. This is dressed up as a policy of concern for the poor, who are forced to contribute to a third party insurance system (reflected in the price of the product) which has a regressive aspect ... This seems an unrealistic policy because of the individual's inability to assess risk and ensure that adequate first party insurance is taken ... [There is] too much faith in an individual's ability to negotiate the best deal for himself.[191]

[187] Consumer Protection Act 1987 (c 43).

[188] As with personal injury generally, I do not, of course, deny the valid (and, a different point, the invalid) political motivations behind the creation of product liability, which for the US in 1955 were summed up in the following way: RG Wilson, 'Products Liability II: The Protection of the Producing Enterprise' (1955) 43 California Law Review 809:

> Within a society that has no universal and comprehensive social insurance for all injuries, a law of products liability must balance the twin objectives of achieving minimum legitimate compensation (or loss distribution) and of achieving minimum conditions under which the enterprise can perform its service to the community.

The assistance this gives us in understanding the EU and UK position is, however, limited, and indeed it is largely ignored in the European literature.

[189] R Epstein, 'The Unintended Revolution in Product Liability Law' (1989) 10 Cardozo Law Review 2193.

[190] On the parallel, at least equally as spurious, justification claimed for harmonisation of contract law see D Campbell and R Halson, 'Harmonisation and Its Discontents: The Transaction Cost Argument for the European Contract Code' in J Devenney and M Kenny (eds), *The Transformation of European Private Law* (CUP 2013).

[191] G Howells (ed), *The Law of Product Liability* (Butterworths 2000) para 1.54 (see now 2nd edn (2007) para 1.54).

This passage is a clear example of the way that product liability and consumer law generally gives the 'central' but 'wholly unfortunate' role to the externality that Ronald Coase argued it played in leading to an extremely extensive perception of market failure.[192] Coase's central achievement lay in the persuasiveness of his demonstration that the assumption of zero transaction costs was 'very unrealistic'[193] as there is always 'a cost of using the price mechanism',[194] and of his insistence that such an assumption should play no direct role whatsoever in policy formulation, its use in this way being 'pernicious'.[195] We return to these arguments in the conclusion of this book, but the point to note here is that Coase then moved the argument on in a way that the previously quoted passage, and in this is it representative of welfarism, just does not comprehend.[196]

For if there is 'a cost of using the price mechanism', there is also a cost of using government or interventionist courts, and the beginnings of a sound approach to regulation should have a concept of 'government failure' to balance the appreciation of market failure.[197] Leaving aside other issues, to claim to be able to identify a market failure is not logically to demonstrate the necessity of a non-market solution, for that 'solution' may not improve welfare; it perfectly well may reduce it.[198] In order to formulate welfare-enhancing policy, it is necessary to replace 'blackboard economics'[199]

[192] RH Coase, 'The Firm, the Market and the Law' in *The Firm, the Market and the Law* (University of Chicago Press 1988) 26.

[193] RH Coase, 'The Problem of Social Cost' in *The Firm, the Market and the Law*, ibid 114 (hereafter Coase, 'Social Cost').

[194] RH Coase, 'The Nature of the Firm' in *The Firm, the Market and the Law*, ibid 38.

[195] RH Coase in EW Williams and RH Coase, 'The Regulated Industries: Discussion' (1964) 54 The American Economic Review (Papers and Proceedings) 192, 195 (hereafter Coase, 'Regulated Industries').

[196] After decades in which the Coase Theorem as it was first all but universally understood had been subjected to profound criticism, not least by Coase himself, it was, with respect, by 1994 questionable and by 2007 just not good enough to make the claim about the Coase theorem made in the quoted passage; Coase had long made it himself: D Campbell and M Klaes, 'What Did Ronald Coase Know About the Law of Tort?' (2016) 39 The Melbourne University Law Review 793, 825; discussing the most substantial version of this claim made by a Commonwealth legal scholar: AWB Simpson, 'Coase v Pigou Re-examined' (1996) 25 Journal of Legal Studies 53; revised as AWB Simpson, 'The Story of *Sturges v Bridgman*: The Resolution of Land Use Disputes Between Neighbours' in G Korngold and AP Morriss (eds), *Property Stories* (2nd edn, Foundation Press 2009).

In the 1960s and 1970s, however, discussion of the Coase Theorem in this way could play a more positive role because the argument for the inevitable existence of positive externalities, which the Coase Theorem undermined, was then regarded as theoretically unchallengeable, and the contemporaneous discussion of product liability partook of this quality, a noted example being the important joint American Association of Law Schools and American Economic Association symposium on product liability published in the 1970 University of *Chicago Law Review*, the core paper of which was RN McKean, 'Products Liability: Economic Analysis and the Law' (1970) 38 University of Chicago Law Review 3.

[197] Coase, 'Regulated Industries' (n 195) 195.

[198] Coase, 'Social Cost' (n 193) 117–18:

> It is clear that the government has powers which might enable it to get some things done at a lower cost than could a private organisation ... But the governmental administrative machine is not itself costless. It can, in fact, on occasion be extremely costly ... From these considerations it follows that direct governmental regulations will not necessarily produce better results than leaving the problem to be solved by the market or the firm. But equally there is no reason why, on occasion, such governmental regulation should not lead to an improvement in economic efficiency ... All solutions have costs and there is no reason to suppose that governmental regulation is called for simply because the problem is not well handled by the market or the firm.

[199] Coase, 'Regulated Industries' (n 195) 195.

policies which simply assume that interventions will optimise welfare with a realistic evaluation of what can be done to improve things,[200] which itself requires a rigorous evaluation of the capacity of the government or interventionist courts to improve welfare before making a non-market policy proposal.[201]

In the just quoted passage, however, (potential) contractual ways of making the consumer's choice real and welfare-enhancing in the absence of unbounded rationality are simply dismissed in favour of—what? It is just assumed that the government and interventionist courts can determine 'the optimum mix', 'adequate' insurance, and 'the best deal'. It is surely not necessary for the reader to fully share this writer's opinion that product liability is even more of a pointless and lawless costly levy on UK citizens than third party insurance against personal injury to see that without comparing the detailed (potential) law of product liability with the detailed (potential) law of contract, the argument against the privity fallacy, against the doctrine of consideration generally, and ultimately against exchange and contract, can have little value.[202]

It is not to deny that good cases for non-market interventions could be made to deprecate the failure to see any real moral value in the working of exchange and contract that can yield things such as the law of product liability. In some way, the existence of the background system of contract is both indispensably taken for granted and yet

[200] Coase, 'Social Cost' (n 193) 154:

> very little analysis is required to show that an ideal world is better than a *laissez faire* world ... But the whole discussion is largely irrelevant for questions of economic policy since, whatever we may have in mind as out ideal world, it is clear we have not yet discovered how to get to it from where we are. A better approach would seem to be to start our analysis with a situation approximating to that which actually exists, to examine the effects of a proposed policy change, and to attempt to decide whether the new situation would be, in total, better or worse than the original one. In this way, conclusion for policy would seem to have some relevance to the actual situation.

[201] ibid 118–119:

> Satisfactory views on policy can only come from a patient study of how, in practice, the market, firms, and governments handle the problem ... It is my belief that economists, and policy-makers generally, have tended to overestimate the advantage which comes from governmental regulation. But this belief, even if it is justified, does not do more than suggest that governmental regulation should be curtailed. It does not tell us where the boundary line should be drawn. This, it seems to me, has to come from a detailed investigation of the actual results of handling the problem in different ways.

[202] Though I believe Professor Howells representatively takes a completely wrong, perpetually dissatisfied approach because, in the way generally discussed in ch 3, he does see how the market normally can make available the information necessary for Pareto optimising exchanges (G Howells, 'Information and Product Liability: A Game of Russian Roulette?' in G Howells, A Janssen, and R Schulze (eds), *Information, Rights and Obligations* (Ashgate 2005), it would be wrong of me to imply that Howells has not been aware from an early stage of many of the shortcomings of the UK law of product liability (G Howells, 'Product Liability in the UK' (1994) 2 European Review of Private Law 255), to which law he has continually proposed modifications. In the way that all of its leading advocates openly lament its shortcomings, product liability is, in fact, one of the best examples of a sort of refinement of blackboard economics which I have called the '*ceteris paribus*' approach to regulation. Lamentation of the inevitable shortcomings of *any* policy, including the one to be adopted, has a ritual cleansing function, allowing one to proceed with effectively the blackboard proposals originally intended: D Campbell, 'Of Coase and Corn: A (Sort of) Defence of Private Nuisance' (2000) 63 Modern Law Review 197, 203–206 and D Campbell, 'The Sense in Coase's Critique of Pigou' (2017) 13 The Journal of Law, Economics and Policy 39.

given no weight. One really does have to ask why the argument is not fully rolled out and the consumer always beset by bounded rationality is not completely replaced by an allocation of goods by law. And, as we will see in Chapter 6, these welfarist 'economics' of consumer law are merely the language *de nos jours* of a criticism of failure of the doctrine of adequacy of consideration that indeed has no other stopping point.

6
The Relational Constitution of Bargain (2)
Procedure and Fairness in Consideration

Introduction

In Chapter 5 it has been argued that the shortcomings of our doctrine of agreement, which turn on a lack of self-consciousness of the necessity of agreeing in good faith in order to agree at all, have taken an even more radical form in the doctrine of consideration. When consideration's constitution by good faith is denied, the doctrine is reduced to a strange paradox lacking moral substance and therefore legal sense. The besetting incoherence of the doctrinal attempt to recognise the truly fundamental practice of economic exchange as legally enforceable bargains, though such recognition is a normal feature of contracting, is the remarkable result. I sought to distinguish the successful way in which consideration performs its overwhelmingly most important task of making the necessity of paying in order to legitimately obtain the transfer of an economic good from the unsuccessful way it addresses other, far less important tasks, most, arguably all, of which it should not even attempt to perform. Though in this connection I have been extremely critical of the 'formalism' of the doctrine of insufficiency, in this chapter I want to argue that the shortcomings of insufficiency should not prevent us from seeing that, in a most important sense to be described, consideration *should be* purely formal.

Exchange, Adequacy and Consideration as Procedure

Fairness in exchange and contract

The reason that consideration should be purely formal is implicit in the commitment to a market economy within liberal democracy which is the foundation of this book.

Contractual Relations. David Campbell, Oxford University Press. © David Campbell 2022.
DOI: 10.1093/oso/9780198855156.003.0006

We have seen in Chapter 5 that the general possibility of freedom of choice and contract depends on each party respecting the other's valuations of the terms of their exchange, which respect the doctrine of consideration expresses in the distinction between 'actual' and 'legal' benefit and detriment. This distinction is an aspect of the general requirement, first set out in Chapter 1, that the law must not second guess the substance of exchange, both in the *de gustibus* sense that a consumer's choice of what to buy should not be overridden, and also in the sense that such overriding would make it impossible to form prices on the basis of competition between business organisations, utilising their differing knowledges and opinions about how to respond ultimately to consumers' preferences.

Even if all this is accepted, it seems a mere affectation not to allow that the law of contract must ensure that transfers of economic goods are 'fair',[1] for general belief that this is in some sense the case unarguably is a condition of the operation of the market. It may be the case would be preferable to follow Nozick and speak of transfers which take place in accord with the endogenous criteria of the law of contract as being 'just',[2] but in order to do this we cannot simply ignore the very widely held sense that fairness connotes substantive fairness,[3] and a statement of contractual justice must acknowledge this connotation in order to argue against it, or at least place it in its proper context.[4] The law necessarily must ask of all transfers that they conform to the values of freedom of contract institutionalised in the enforceability only of voluntarily agreed bargains, and distinguish between those transfers which it will and will not support, support being no merely passive, matter. The converse of the law of contract's active role in enforcing legitimate bargains[5] is that it must not enforce illegitimate

[1] E Durkheim, *The Division of Labour in Society* (Macmillan 1984) 316–18 (hereafter Durkheim, *Division of Labour*):

> If contracts were observed only by force or the fear of force, contractual solidarity would be in extremely parlous state ... for the obligatory force of the contract to be [reliable], it ... must ... be fair.

[2] R Nozick, *Anarchy, State and Utopia* (Basic Books 1974) 150–53 (hereafter Nozick, *Anarchy*).

[3] E Durkheim, *Professional Ethics and Civic Morals* (new edn, Routledge 1992) 209–10:

> there exists a vague but lively sense of the value of the various services used in society, and of the values, too, of the things that are the subject of exchange ... there is ... in every social group a state of opinion that fixes [a scale of ... normal value[s] at least roughly ... All sorts of causes enter into the way it has evolved [but what] alone matters to us ... that this ... scale is certainly a real one, and that it is the touchstone by which the equity of ... exchanges is to be judged.

The defects of a highly interesting attempt to base a general theory of contract on treating substantive fairness as a 'variable' distinct from 'voluntariness', so that 'Voluntariness x Fairness = Contract', are instructive: J Levin and B McDowell, 'The Balance Theory of Contracts: Seeking Justice in Voluntary Obligations' (1993) 29 McGill Law Journal 25, 26.

[4] L Kaplow and S Shavell, *Fairness Versus Welfare* (Harvard University Press 2002) ch 4. The essential point is argued from, as it were, the opposite direction in L Kaplow and S Shavell, 'Why the Legal System Is Less Efficient than Income Tax in Redistributing Income' (1994) 23 Journal of Legal Studies 667 (hereafter Kaplow and Shavell, 'Legal System').

[5] MR Cohen, 'The Basis of Contract' (1933) 46 Harvard Law Review 553, 585:

> The cardinal error of the traditional individualistic theories of contract is their way of speaking as if the law does nothing but put into effect what the contracting parties originally agreed on ... It is an error ... then to speak of the law of contract as if it merely allows people to do things. The absence of criminal prohibition will do that much. The law of contract plays a more positive role in social life, and this is seen when the organized force of the state is brought into play to compel the loser of a suit to pay or to do something.

ones,[6] and must whenever necessary undo (or even prevent) them. Making particular reference to implied terms and business efficacy, we have already seen in Chapters 3 and 4 that the agreement of economic actors consistent with consumer sovereignty rests on a social framework which facilitates the exercise of self-interest conscious of mutual recognition. To repeat, this social foundation cannot justify a general second guessing of the choices of those actors. If, however, an argument is successfully made that an apparent agreement were but agreement's sham, then the sham agreement should not be enforced. In regard of this crucial issue, we must acknowledge the task identified by John Rawls:

> Suppose we begin with the initially attractive idea that the social process should be allowed to develop overtime as free agreements fairly arrived at and fully honoured ... Straightaway we need an account of when agreements are free and the conditions under which they are reached are fair.[7]

In this chapter it is argued that in order to institutionalise freedom of contract consideration must, to adopt Rawls' term which now dominates discussion of the background political philosophy,[8] be a 'purely procedural'[9] test of the enforceability of agreements. If one is to retain the use of fairness in discussion of contract, as one must, this should not be substantive fairness but procedural fairness. If a transfer is made through an agreed bargain, the resulting contract should be enforced because it is in the correct form of a voluntary exchange to which the substantive terms are in principle irrelevant. The doctrine of consideration institutionalises this pure procedure in its most important rule, refusing to inquire into adequacy. Though there is a principled limit to this refusal which shall be mentioned shortly,[10] I will argue that are no plausible general arguments against it.

Though I shall make important reference to *dicta* drawn from an eighteenth century case made famous, I believe, by Atiyah, I have no capacity to comment on the way that the refusal to inquire into adequacy emerged as a rejection of the idea that the law of contract could set the substantively 'fair' or 'just' price of economic goods,[11] which

[6] D Kimel, 'The Morality of Contract and Moral Culpability for Breach' (2010) 21 King's Law Journal 213, 230 states the point and rightly develops the corollary:

> When [the law of contract] recognises and enforces ... morally tainted [contracts] it actively partakes in enabling them and securing their ends.

[7] J Rawls, 'A Kantian Conception of Equality' in Collected Papers (Harvard University Press 1999) 257.

[8] P Benson, *Justice in Transactions* (Beknap Press 2019) (hereafter Benson, *Justice*) attempts to provide a 'public basis for justification' of the law of contract which satisfies in some detail Rawls' requirements for any justification of a political arrangement, its quality lying in what one is now more than a little hesitant to call the dialectic of the political philosophy and the juridical categories which adds great interest to both. Nevertheless, Professor Benson's discussion does in part display what it emerges in this chapter is a defect of modern political philosophy of equality, even of Rawls—though one that, even if I am right, cannot possibly diminish the core of Rawls' thought—that its refinements are too elaborate to inform, if it can be put this way, legal decision-making as opposed, to legal philosophy.

[9] Rawls, *Justice*, ibid s 14.

[10] See the text accompanying n 24.

[11] PS Atiyah, The *Rise and Fall of Freedom of Contract* (pbk edn, Clarendon Press 1985) 162–77 (hereafter Atiyah, *Rise and Fall*). Atiyah's views were in general developed through a detailed engagement with the earlier historical material, and he is generous in his acknowledgement of his reliance on Simpson: ibid viii. Simpson was, of course, highly critical (AWB Simpson, 'The Horwitz Thesis and the History of Contracts'

rejection brought about a 'revolution' in the legal institutionalisation of commercial life.[12] The criticisms of the substantive outcome of a contract discussed in this chapter are treated as responses to a positive law based on the refusal to inquire into adequacy. We saw in Chapter 5 that the doctrine of consideration is beset by serious misunderstandings and vehement criticism, and this *a fortiori* has been the case regarding the refusal to inquire into adequacy,[13] respect for which in the legal doctrine of sanctity has become precarious, so that, as Professor Ibbetson describes it:

> by the end of the Twentieth Century [it could no] longer ... be said that contract law was based on the assumption that effect should be given to the agreement of the parties [and] ideas of fairness were simply grafted onto the classical model of contract.[14]

Considerations of substantive fairness based on an inchoate rejection of the refusal to inquire into adequacy have played a large part in the way that a number of factors have been recognised at common law to vitiate contracts claimed to be reduced to sham by unconscionability, undue influence, and inequality of bargaining power.[15] The essential tendency of consumer law seems now to have reached its apogee as the Consumer Rights Act 2015, s 62 on its face potentially lays all terms of a consumer contract open to review for unfairness, s 62(4) telling us that 'A term is unfair if, contrary to the requirement of good faith, it causes a significant imbalance in the parties' rights and obligations under the contract to the detriment of the consumer'. If one interprets this literally or even seriously as a general principle of substantive unfairness, it leads to an abyss, and it was reined in by s 64 which purports to exclude from the assessment of fairness what has come to be known as the 'core' of the contract,[16] including 'appropriateness of the price',[17] which obviously allows the refusal to inquire into adequacy right back in. When faced with a flat choice between avoiding the abyss

in *Legal Theory and Legal History* (Hambledon Press 1987)) of the romantic (my word) account of 'the equitable conception of contract' and its rejection in MJ Horwitz, *The Transformation of American Law 1780–1860* (Harvard University Press 1977) ch 6.

[12] W Swain, *The Law of Contract 1670–1870* (CUP 2015) ch 8.

[13] MA Eisenberg, 'The Bargain Principle and Its Limits' (1982) 95 Harvard Law Review 741 and SM Waddams, 'Unconscionability in Contracts' (1976) 39 Modern Law Review 369.

[14] DJ Ibbetson, *A Historical Introduction to the Law of Obligations* (OUP 1999) 261.

[15] An argument of particular note because of the distinction of those making it has been put forward that we should greatly extend the legal doctrine of incapacity along lines indicated by Amartya Sen's 'capabilities approach' so that it will serve the 'consumerist' aspiration we are here discussing in the vitiating factors cases and in consumer law: SF Deakin and A Supiot (eds), *Capacitas: Contract Law and the Institutional Preconditions of a Market Economy* (Hart 2009). At one level this argument is but a variant of the questioning of the consumer's ability to make choices in his own interest which was criticised in ch 3 and is criticised in this chapter and ch 7. But it is the nature of Sen's approach that this argument develops this questioning into a thoroughgoing authoritarianism quite out of line with the intention with which the argument was made: D Campbell, 'The Law of Contract and the Limits of the Welfare State' in M Del Mar and C Michelon (eds), *The Anxiety of the Jurist: Themes from the Work of Professor Zenon Bańkowski* (Ashgate 2013).

[16] *Director General of Fair Trading v First National Bank plc* [2001] UKHL 52, [2001] 1 AC 481 [12] (hereafter *Director General v First National Bank*).

[17] Consumer Rights Act, s 64(1)(b). Under s 64(2), s 64(1) comes into play only when a term is 'transparent and prominent', a provision which would appear from ss 64(3), (4) to be based on a procedural test of objective agreement which is advocated in this chapter but is hardly consistent with s 62(4).

to which applying s 62(4) leads, and of leaving a 'gaping hole in the system of protection',[18] the Supreme Court did the former.[19] Whatever one feels about the reasoning involved in this, it has, it is submitted, had the great virtue of demonstrating the unworkability as *principle* of the common law and statutory interventions, which, at the level of legal doctrine, arises because those interventions are motivated by nothing more concrete than an antipathy against the refusal to inquire into adequacy, from which they inevitably must in an inchoate manner resile.[20] As a criticism of the current situation, there seems nothing to add to what Lord Eyre CB said in 1787 in *Griffith v Spratley*, which Atiyah thought 'may well have been' 'the decisive case in Equity' which 'repudiated the eighteenth century ideas about the fairness of an exchange'.[21] On facts which led him to say 'he could have wished to found a ground for giving relief to the [promisor]', Lord Eyre could not have done so 'without establishing [a principle] which would shake the commercial intercourse of the nation' by making 'inadequacy of consideration of itself a distinct principle of relief in equity':

> I know of no such principle; the common law knows of no such ... Common sense knows no principle. The value of a thing is what it will produce, and admits of no precise standard. It must be in its nature fluctuating, and will depend on ten thousand different circumstances. One man in the disposal of his property may sell it for less than another would; he may sell it under pressure of circumstances, which may induce him to sell it at a particular time. Now ... to unravel all these transactions ... would throw everything into confusion and set afloat all the contracts of mankind. Therefore I never can agree that inadequacy of consideration is in itself a principle upon which a party may be relieved from a contract which he wittingly and willingly entered into.[22]

Inequality of bargaining power

It would be most undesirable, and as a matter of the jurisprudence of the English law of obligations it is inconceivable, that there should be no residual equitable discretion to intervene in contracts that for exceptional reasons have unacceptable outcomes

18 *Director General v First National Bank* (n 16) [34].

19 *Office of Fair Trading v Abbey National Bank plc* [2009] UKSC 6, [2010] AC 696. This case interpreted The Unfair Terms in Consumer Contracts Regulations 1999, SI 1999/ 2083, reg 4, a predecessor of s 62.

20 R Bigwood, 'Exploitation' in W Swain and D Campbell (eds), *Reimagining Contract Law Pedagogy* (Routledge 2019) 61:

> hoping for a more nuanced and complete account of victimisation in transactional settings may ultimately be to cry for the moon; for there is little evidence that courts think deeply about the inner logic of exculpatory categories in contract law and the exact relationship and interplay (if any) between them ... it is becoming increasing difficult to provide a coherent descriptive and normative account of the law in this area—the more so if one attempts a cross-jurisdictional approach in comparative perspective. This ... does not augur well for the teacher or (worse) the student of modern contract law. Certainly, the exploitation concept is not capable of rescuing the situation. On the contrary, it is possibly partly to blame for the present state of the law.

21 Atiyah, *Rise and Fall* (n 11) 448–49.

22 *Griffith v Spratley* (1787) 1 Cox Ch 383, 388–39; 29 ER 1213, 1215.

(both 'exceptional' and 'unacceptable' being understood in very demanding senses). Because of the (still poorly understood) role it came to play in *White and Carter (Councils) Ltd v McGregor*,[23] and so in the development of the concept of the 'legitimate interest', arguably the most important influence on the exercise of such discretion has been *Grahame v Swan and others (Magistrates of Kirkaldy)*,[24] though, as will be discussed in Chapter 9, that case itself took the requirement that the exercise of discretion be 'exceptional' very seriously. The core of the vitiating factor cases is a weakening of this requirement to the point where really quite normal situations have been embraced, making it necessary to then rein back the interventions the incoherence of which was thereby exposed, culminating in the equivocation at the heart of Lord Denning's attempt to state a general principle of inequality of bargaining power in *Lloyd's Bank Ltd v Bundy*:

> There are cases in our books in which the courts will set aside a contract, or a transfer of property, when the parties have not met on equal terms—when the one is so strong in bargaining power and the other so weak—that, as a matter of common fairness, it is not right that the strong should be allowed to push the weak to the wall. Hitherto those exceptional cases have been treated each as a separate category in itself. But I think the time has come when we should seek to find a principle to unite them. I put on one side contracts or transactions which are voidable for fraud or misrepresentation or mistake. All those are governed by settled principles. I go only to those where there has been inequality of bargaining power, such as to merit the intervention of the court.[25]

Lord Denning presented the cases from which he sought to derive his principle as 'exceptions to [a] general rule' which provided that 'No bargain will be upset which is the result of the ordinary interplay of forces'.[26] The particular contradiction involved in this is, not that the exceptions are themselves hard to define, but that, for a reason shortly to be set out, the more one moves away from exceptions towards a uniting principle, the more one *must* increase one's difficulties. Some recognition of this underlies the flat rejection of inequality of bargaining power as a principle of the contract law of England and Wales.[27] Lord Scarman's criticism of Lord Denning's 'general principle' in *National Westminster Bank plc v Morgan* has been telling: 'even in the field of contract I question whether there is any need in the modern law to erect a general principle of relief against inequality of bargaining power'.[28]

It has been authoritatively argued that the elements of substantive fairness in the vitiating factors cases lead to radical incoherence,[29] and the most plausible attempts to provide such coherence as can be given to those cases have been based on the procedural argument 'that the law's desire to protect the integrity of contractual consent

[23] [1962] AC 413 (HL Sc) 430.
[24] (1882) 7 App Cas 547 (HL Sc).
[25] [1975] QB 326 (CA) 336H–37A.
[26] ibid 336H, 336F.
[27] N Andrews, *Contract Law* (2nd edn, CUP 2015) 316: 'Lord Denning's lead balloon'.
[28] [1985] AC 686 (HL) 708A, 708C (hereafter *National Westminster Bank v Morgan*).
[29] R Bigwood, *Exploitative Contracts* (OUP 2003) 157 (hereafter Bigwood, *Exploitative Contracts*):

> because all end-state theories must ultimately incorporate externalist or objective standards against which the fairness of the transaction is to be assessed—that is they must subsume

is a central concern of each of the general vitiating factors'.[30] But such plausibility is obtained by abandoning the substantive fairness the argument is supposed to rationalise, and the valuable general conception of fairness which lies behind what is a procedural argument[31] can be stated in terms of the moral relationship of mutual recognition which is the basis of the legal contract's institutionalisation of economic exchange.

Inequality of bargaining power in the market economy

It is unarguable that inequality of bargaining power is a ubiquitous feature of the market economy which we cannot eradicate. But the formulation of policy towards such inequality has to have at its centre a recognition that we *should not* attempt to eradicate it. Business organisations investing in the development of entrepreneurial competence in negotiating sales with their various customers, on which their competitive performance will in part be based, are almost bound to have markedly superior bargaining power over (smaller businesses)[32] and consumers, but this power is an important reason why those organisations are able to increase consumer welfare by providing goods and services which could not possibly be provided if those organisations had only the competence of a typical consumer. The always half-heartedness of the criticism of standard form contracting, which with varying degrees of clarity has always been expressed with some perception that, as was discussed in Chapter 3, the standard form is essential to the vast increase in welfare through mass consumer contracting,[33] is the main way in which

> standards or principles of fair division—such theories are insupportable if we to maintain the liberal (hence internalist, content-independent) conception of contract.

[30] G Spark, *Vitiation of Contracts* (CUP 2013) 1. See also 'disturbs the balance of negotiations' in J Cartwright, *Unequal Bargaining* (Clarendon Press 1991) 231 and 'constrained decisional autonomy' in M Moore, 'Why Does Lord Denning's Lead Balloon Intrigue Us Still? The Prospects of Finding a Unifying Principle for Duress, Undue Influence and Unconscionability' (2018) 134 Law Quarterly Review 257.

[31] Benson, *Justice* (n 8) 20: 'purely representational medium of the parties' mutual assents'; Bigwood, *Exploitative Contracts* (n 29) ch 5: 'a purely processual conception' and AA Leff, 'Unconscionability and the Code: The Emperor's New Clause' (1967) 115 University of Pennsylvania Law Review 485, 489–508: 'procedural unconscionability'.

[32] I put to one side the policy success, especially at EU levels, of the argument that opposing inequality of bargaining power and unfairness in the dealings of large business and small to medium enterprises requires the extension of 'consumer' legislation to those enterprises: Law Commission and Scottish Law Commission, *Unfair Terms in Contracts* [2005] EWLC 292, pt 5.

[33] What in ch 3 was described as perhaps the most radical criticism of the standard form contract ever made, F Kessler, 'Contracts of Adhesion: Some Thoughts About Freedom of Contract' (1943) 43 Columbia Law Review 629 (hereafter Kessler, 'Contracts of Adhesion'), was based on so severe a view of the monopolisation of the US economy (see n 37) that it was essentially right, if exaggerated, of FH Buckley, *Just Exchange* (Routledge 2005) 153 to claim that 'Kessler thought that, in moving from Nazi Germany to the US, he had simply traded off one form of tyranny for another'. Nevertheless, Kessler saw the part the standard form played in the reduction of the costs of production, and of this he said (Kessler, 'Contracts of Adhesion', ibid 632):

> In so far as the reduction ... is reflected in reduced prices, society as a whole ultimately benefits from the use of standard contracts. And there can be no doubt that this has been the case to a considerable extent.

this has been, albeit most inadequately, recognised in contract law, and this is taken up in the discussion of exclusion clauses in Chapter 7.

It is of course true that no empirical pattern of industrial organisation can conform to the conditions of general competition, one of which logically is an extreme divisibility which would allow competition over the recombination of all technologically conceivable components of output.[34] It is unarguable that what are by this standard indivisibilities in the production process inevitably are ubiquitous,[35] and indeed increasingly characterise that process as scales of production increase.[36] This obviously is one of those 'realities' which raises the fundamental questions whether general competitive equilibrium should, and if so how it can, play a role in our understanding of the empirical operation of the market economy. Certain aspects of these questions that directly relate to inequality of bargaining power must be addressed here.

General competitive equilibrium may be regarded as akin to what Kant called a 'regulative principle', such a principle arising from 'the interest of reason in . . . a . . . possible perfection of the cognition of [an] object'.[37] That we are able to clearly conceive of a criterion of welfare which is entirely based on voluntary choice, and absolutely divorced from the substance of that choice, is, in my opinion, the result of the pure analytic demonstration that a generally competitive economy is stable at a Pareto optimum. But relating the purely theoretical model of general competition, particularly as a demonstration of the properties of a stable, ie achieved, equilibrium, to the analysis of, and the formulation of policy towards, any possible empirical situation has of course been, and of course is, beset by difficulty. To the extent that such difficulty arises from some, indeed to my outsider's view most, of the ways that mathematics and extreme abstraction have come to be used in the practice of intellectual and, even more, applied economics,[38] they can be set aside. Nor is the postulation of the 'perfection' of an optimal state of which we can never have experience in itself a difficulty. If one believes that ultimate values are in principle open to rational determination, then all moral human action, of which exchange is a most important example, requires such postulation,[39] even though progress towards the optimal state will be

See further n 46.

[34] KJ Arrow and L Hurwicz, 'Decentralisation and Computation in Resource Allocation' in RW Pfouts (ed), *Essays in Economics and Econometrics* (University of North Carolina Press 1960) 34:

> For a given technology, the . . . problem of optimal resource allocation is to choose among all the feasible combinations of production processes that combination which maximizes the utility achieved by the economy.

[35] RF Fowler, *The Depreciation of Capital* (PS King 1934) 107:

> Capital once invested in durable instruments is sunk, and cannot be wholly transferred until the investment is used up.

[36] JA Schumpeter, *Capitalism, Socialism and Democracy* (5th edn, George Allen & Unwin 1976) 105–06:

> the bulk of what we call economic progress is incompatible with [perfect competition, which] is impossible under modern industrial conditions [and indeed] has always been impossible.

[37] I Kant, *Critique of Pure Reason* in *The Cambridge Edition of the Works* (CUP 1998) 603.

[38] The distinguished historian of economics, the late Mark Blaug, argued that the Arrow-Debreu model marked the onset of 'what has since become a cancerous growth in the very centre of microeconomics': M Blaug, 'Disturbing Currents in Modern Economics' (1998) 41(3) *Challenge* 11, 13.

[39] I Kant, *Groundwork of the Metaphysics of Morals* in *Practical Philosophy* in *The Cambridge Edition of the Works* (CUP 1996) 62:

endless.[40] Though it takes place in relationship to humankind's natural environment in a way which gives it a specific character at once both exhaustively analysed and inadequately understood, exchange is moral action which should be approached in this way. It both postulates an optimum, general competitive equilibrium, and it *must* denote the existence of a tendency towards that optimum, or general competitive equilibrium is irrelevant to the empirical world, not in the sense that it can never exist, but in the sense that it gives no guidance to action in that world:

> [Regarding] our concern with the admittedly fictitious state of equilibrium ... there seems to be no possible doubt that the only justification for this is the supposed existence of a tendency towards equilibrium. It is only by the assertion that such a tendency exists that economics seeks to be an exercise in pure logic and becomes an empirical science ... [This assertion] can hardly mean anything but that, under certain conditions, the knowledge and intentions of the different members of society are supposed to come more and more into agreement.[41]

In the simplest statement of the conditions of general competitive equilibrium of which I am aware, Arrow reduced them to two: convexity and the existence of all relevant markets.[42] Convexity is the graphical property displayed by consumption and production vectors under what would seem to be the weakest possible assumptions about the form of economic action that will make that action yield general equilibrium. It boils down to action which rationally maximises the ownership of economic goods so as to maximise the actor's satisfaction (including the profit of business organisations), so that, for example, the non-transitive set of preferences revealed when an actor prefers good A to good B and good B to good C, but also prefers good C to good A, is not analysable within neo-classical economics. At general equilibrium such action cannot take place, but, in the empirical world, the equilibrium statement of an optimum translates into the *maxim*: if an economic actor wishes to maximise its satisfaction, it *should* seek to maximise the rationality of its action. The natural economic

> One need not be an enemy of virtue but only a cool observer ... become doubtful ... whether any true virtue is to be found in the world [But] even if there have never been actions arising from such pure sources, what is at issue here is not whether this or that happened [and] accordingly, actions of which the world has perhaps so far given no example, and whose very practicability might be very much doubted by one who bases everything on experience, are still inflexibly commanded by reason.

[40] Kant, *Critique of Practical Reason* in *Practical Philosophy* in *The Cambridge Edition of the Works* (CUP 1996) 238:

> The production of the highest good in the world is the necessary object of a will determinable by the moral law. But in such a will the *complete conformity* of dispositions with the moral law is the supreme condition of the highest good ... Complete conformity with the will of the moral law is, however, *holiness*, a perfection of which no rational being in this sensible world is capable at any moment of his existence. Since it is nevertheless required as practically necessary, it can only be found in an endless progress toward that complete conformity.

[41] FA Hayek, 'Economics and Knowledge' in *The Market and Other Orders* in *Collected Works*, vol 15 (Routledge 2014) 67–68. By this 'pure logic', Hayek meant a system of pure tautology.

[42] KJ Arrow, 'Pareto Optimality with Costly Transfers,' in *Collected Papers*, vol 2 (Belknap Press 1983) 291 (hereafter Arrow, 'Pareto Optimality').

actor whose philosophic anthropology is given in Chapter 1 will normally seek to do this. But how this is done in the empirical world is, not merely not entailed in the model of general competitive equilibrium which postulates the optimum, but, as a matter of principle,[43] our empirical policy should not just unidirectionally seek to *replicate* the equilibrium model, which, of course, is extremely likely to have perverse effects.[44]

Empirical policy must seek *progress towards* general competition given the empirical constraints which obtain, but given those constraints this may very well involve steps which in themselves *appear* anti-competitive, for the good reason that, if one takes general competitive equilibrium to be a description of an empirically achievable state, they indeed are anti-competitive. It is hoped that the demonstration in Chapter 3 of the necessity of limiting choice in order to expand the rationality of choice will serve as an example of the argument. Looked at actively, the limitation of the information needed for rational choice is a question of the regulatory establishment of markets which, cognisant of the bounds (and the possibilities of expanding these) of the rationality of the relevant actors, will provide information in a way which will enhance welfare, and in the empirical world this cannot possibly be a question of the provision of all information, though it is informative that this is a condition of general competitive equilibrium.

The condition of the existence of all relevant markets can be addressed by generalisation of this example. An acknowledgement of an inevitable 'degree of monopoly' must inform our policy towards an economy we nevertheless should seek to make optimally, because 'workably', competitive.[45] As EH Chamberlin, one of the principal contributors to the theory of 'imperfect' or 'monopoly competition', put it:

[43] RG Lipsey and K Lancaster. 'The General Theory of Second Best' (1956) 24 Review of Economic Studies 11:

> given that one of the Paretian optimum conditions cannot be fulfilled, then an optimum situation can be achieved only by departing from all the other Paretian conditions. The optimum situation finally attained may be termed a second best optimum because it is achieved subject to a constraint which, by definition, prevents the attainment of a Paretian optimum.

[44] Responding to arguments for literal deregulation, whilst it has been necessary (D Campbell, 'The "Market" in the Theory of Regulation' (2018) 27 Social and Legal Studies 545, 554), has but a poor theoretical yield as those arguments are so foolish. Though a proper discussion of this aspect of Coase's views must await the conclusion of this book, it is to avoid a possible misunderstanding at this point of our argument that I refer to Coase's own explicit attempts to dissociate himself from this conception of deregulation: RH Coase, 'Social Cost and Public Policy' in GA Edwards (ed), *Exploring the Frontiers of Administration* (Bureau of Research, Faculty of Administrative Studies, York University, Toronto 1970) 40: 'A call for sensible regulation is not a call for no regulation'.

[45] JM Clark, 'Towards a Concept of Workable Competition' (1940) 30 American Economic Review 241. Clark later shifted his terminology, for reasons which need not be discussed, to 'effective' competition: JM Clark, *Competition as a Dynamic Process* (Brookings Institution 1961) ix. As is indicated by Clark taking the term 'effective' from B Smith, 'Effective Competition: Hypothesis for Modernising the Antitrust Laws' (1951) 26 New York University Law Review 405, Clark's position, and the position throughout in this book, is not to deny 'monopoly' may capture 'real and serious defects' in any empirical market, but these must be distinguished, as they overwhelmingly are not, from 'failures to attain an unreal "perfection" nor with those "imperfections" that actually serve a useful competitive purpose': Clark, *Competition as a Dynamic Process*, ibid 482.

> Now if pure competition is the ideal, the direction in which we should move is very clear. For it is easy enough to show that the actual economy is shot full of monopoly elements, and hence that any move to get rid of them or diminish their importance is in the right direction. But … the welfare ideal itself (as well as the description of reality) involves a blend of monopoly and competition and is therefore described as one of monopolistic competition. If this is true, it is no longer self-evident which way we should move, for it is no longer self-evident on which side of the ideal lies the actuality for which policy is sought. It is possible that the economy should be made 'more competitive'; but it is also quite possible that it should be 'more monopolistic' instead. Or perhaps, if there are faults to be found with it, it should simply be changed, towards something else which again involves both monopoly and competition.[46]

Any empirical competitive economy must be characterised by inequality of bargaining power as one dimension of the degree of monopoly in all patterns of industrial organisation.[47] As with the attack on the privity of contract fallacy discussed in Chapter 5, the principle of inequality of bargaining power intended to unify the vitiating factor cases and the concept of unfairness in consumer law rest on some general idea—the terminology would of course have been anathema to Lord Denning—that a departure from perfect competition represents a market failure justifying intervention. The paradoxical situation[48] has arisen that, as we saw in Chapter 5 with reference to Coase, though the informed institutional economics of market allocation are based on an insistence that general competitive equilibrium can never possibly occur, and that economic theory that believes that it can is worse than worthless as

[46] EH Chamberlin, 'Product Heterogeneity and Public Policy (Welfare Economics)' in *Towards a More General Theory of Value* (OUP 1957) 93.

The point I am trying to stress emerges even more strongly from the criticism of Chamberlin's 'imperfect' or 'monopoly competition' approach in GJ Stigler, 'Monopoly Competition in Retrospect' in *The Organisation of Industry* (University of Chicago Press 1968) 321:

> the predictions of [the] model of monopolistic competition differ only in unimportant respects from those of the theory of competition.

[47] The standard form played a major part in Kessler's claim that the corporate capitalist economy is monopolistic as 'one of the many devices to build up and strengthen industrial *empires*': Kessler, 'Contracts of Adhesion' (n 33) 632 (emphasis added). Kessler's views certainly accorded with much contemporary left-wing American thought, but though this is not discussed in his article, those views will, I surmise, have been formed by reference to important German neo-Marxist arguments that 'nineteenth century free trade and free enterprise are on their way out … gradually destroyed by … private monopolies and government interference': F Pollock, 'State Capitalism: Its Possibilities and Limitations' in A Arato and E Genhardt (eds), *The Essential Frankfurt School Reader* (Blackwell 1978) 72–73. As his article (Kessler, 'Contracts of Adhesion', ibid 629–31), but even more his casebook (F Kessler and M Sharp, *Contracts: Cases and Materials* (1st edn, Prentice-Hall 1953) pt 1) clearly show, Kessler had a clear grasp of the role of competition in a 'free enterprise system', and his enormous over-estimation of the powers of even giant firms to oust this system must be referred to the then lack of appreciation of the transaction costs of planning by firms (and governments), which led to a tendentious focus on returns to scale. As discussed in ch 10, Coase had in 1932 formed the argument which led to the 1937 publication of 'The Nature of the Firm' on the basis of believing Lenin's proposal to run the USSR economy 'like a single factory' under 'complete planning' to be plausible.

[48] GB Richardson, 'Price Notification Schemes' in *The Economics of Imperfect Knowledge* (Edward Elgar 1998) 127:

> It is a curious paradox that opposition to the effective working of the private enterprise sector of the economy comes, not only from its avowed opponents, but also from those who seek to force it to conform to their own mistaken conception of the ideal.

a guide to policy, the economic and legal criticism of market allocation that has culminated in the Consumer Rights Act, s 64 is a constant lament about departures from 'perfect competition' as a desirable goal, which of course sanctions all sorts of interventions actually motivated by inchoate concerns about substantive fairness.[49]

The doctrinal unworkability of inequality of bargaining power and of unfairness as general principles, which boils down to a romantic misunderstanding of the inevitable scarcity of the 'resource' of 'bargaining power',[50] in itself provides no means whatsoever of specifying the grounds for intervention, with the result that such interventions constitute the purest *ad hocery*.[51] The very idea that there is or should be a distinct consumer law in the sense that the law of contract is now or should be composed of two bodies of doctrine, commercial law and consumer law, is, in my opinion, essentially meaningless.[52] As the way the Sale of Goods Act features in the Consumer

[49] The aspect of the welfare economics of consumer behaviour of relevance here has been described by JR Hummel, 'Toward a Libertarian Reconstruction of Neo-classical Welfare Theory' (2008) 24 Journal of Private Enterprise 1, 5:

> A dubious development ... is the theoretical work attempting to show, with such concepts as merit goods and others, that much blatant government redistribution or paternalism in fact corrects some hitherto unnoticed market failure.

[50] IR Macneil, 'Political Exchange as Relational Contract' in B Marin (ed), *Generalised Political Exchange* (Westview Press 1990) 154 (hereafter Macneil, 'Political Exchange'):

> Neither [duress nor inequality of bargaining power] copes adequately with the fact that the exercise of choice is never voluntary, but always compelled by circumstances. The important compelling circumstances in exchange relations in this society are that everyone has property and liberty rights, and that everyone making an exchange is motivated to do so to secure a surrender of such rights in her or his favour. These rights in others create 'duress' in every exchange, and, since these rights are both unequally distributed and of differing value to different people, they create 'unequal bargaining power' in most if not all exchanges. Because of this, these neoclassical concepts either eliminate legal contract altogether or must be narrowly defined. In the latter case, they are simply empty buckets collecting instances of particular kinds of behaviour which will result in the law suspending the consent principle.

[51] That the selection of specific issues for campaigns by consumer groups and their advisers inevitably is a matter of politics, and sometimes 'politics' in the bad sense, is not properly confronted by the claim to identify a 'consumer interest': RH Coase, 'Discussion of CE Warne, 'The Muted Voice of the Consumer in Regulatory Agencies' in WJ Samuels and HM Trebing (eds), *A Critique of Administrative Regulation of Public Utilities* (Michigan State University 1972) and GJ Stigler, 'Can Regulatory Agencies Protect the Consumer' in *The Citizen and the State* (University of Chicago Press 1975). The part consumer advice can play in providing 'access to justice' in cases of breach is, in principle, far more sound, though it is essential that 'justice' is not conceived as a matter of the vindication of consumer 'rights' but of the satisfactory resolution of inevitable complaints: H Collins, *Regulating Contracts* (OUP 1999) 350–55.

[52] In the course of advocating a 'radical' or 'critical' form of 'consumerism' which 'reject[s] the existing market structure' and sees 'the contractual process' and 'contract doctrine based on notions such as freedom of contract' as 'weighted against consumers' and supportive of 'inherently unequal bargaining structures', Professor Howells acutely acknowledges the point: 'And yet critical lawyers cannot simply forget the existence of contract and contract law for the contractual relationship rests at the centre of their discipline': GG Howells, 'Contract Law: The Challenge for the Critical Consumer Lawyer' in T Wilhelmsson (ed), *Perspectives of Critical Contract Law* (Dartmouth 1993) 328. Having rejected the existing market and freedom of contract, what, then, is the principle radical consumerism should adopt when it is obliged to address the contractual relationship? '[T[he work of the critical consumer lawyer', we are told, must be underpinned by a vision of social justice': ibid. Howells further acutely recognises that this poses the problems of 'whether a consensus can legitimately be arrived at as to what terms should replace those determined by market outcomes' (ibid 337) and 'of establishing who, if not the consumer, has the right to decide what is in the consumer's best interest' (ibid 338). It must be allowed that a problem of *inequality* of bargaining power is unarguably solved if the right to decide *at all* what bargains are in the best interest of the consumer

Rights Act could not more amply demonstrate, the basic structure of what is or would be consumer law will always remain the market order of choice in exchange and of freedom of contract, in which consumer law then continually intervenes whilst taking that order for granted. The issue I wish to explore here is an atmosphere of general disregard for the reproduction of the order of both the market economy and of the law of contract that can make *ad hocery* of this sort appear to be a desirable syncretism.[53]

This disregard has become very influentially expressed in a highly misleading distinction between the common law and the statutory law of contract. Though the vitiating factors remain largely a matter of common law, ie equity, consumer law is largely a matter of statute. This is overwhelmingly the case since the passage of the Consumer Rights Act, but this should also be said of a body of law leading up to that Act which, as will be discussed in Chapter 7, can be traced back to the Hire Purchase Act 1938. We have seen that Lord Scarman rejected a general common law principle of inequality of bargaining power in *National Westminster Bank v Morgan.* He did, however, readily acknowledge that 'Parliament has undertaken the task—and it is essentially a legislative task—of enacting such restrictions upon freedom of contract as are in its judgement necessary to relieve against the mischief', and cited the principal statutes going back to the 1938 Act.[54]

In putting the point this way, Lord Scarman is in one sense merely saying what is unarguable. It has become the dominant view of the relationship of common law and statute in regard to fairness—in the edition of *Anson* published in 2020 it is called the 'traditional position'[55]—that a 'commercial' area of contract, identified by conscious adherence to 'freedom of contract' in the case law, can and should[56] be distinguished from a 'consumer' area identified by overwhelmingly statutory restrictions on this

formerly afflicted by that problem resides in an authority placed in a position unambiguously superior to the consumer.

[53] D Kimel, *From Promise to Contract: Towards a Liberal Theory of Contract* (Hart 2003) 119:

> on the descriptive level it can easily be concluded that the rigid conception of freedom in contract is highly unrealistic. Even more damaging, however, is the normative facet of the charge against this conception . . . suffice it to say that many, probably most, of the instances of intervention in freedom of contract that are found in modern legal systems appear to be justified. They often fit neatly into desirable social, economic, and legal policies—for vulnerable individuals, for social justice, for individual and public well-being.

[54] *National Westminster Bank v Morgan* (n 28) 708C–D.

[55] J Beatson, A Burrows, and J Cartwright, *Anson's Law of Contract* (31st edn, OUP 2020) 403. *Times Travel (UK) Ltd v Pakistan International Airlines Corp* [2019] EWCA Civ 828; [2020] Ch 98 [40] (Richards LJ) is cited as a recent statement of the traditional position. In this statement it is claimed that 'Commercial dealings have been largely untouched by statute', and whilst one can see the way in which this is right, it does require a particular understanding of the great codifying statutes exemplified by the Sale of Goods Act 1893.

[56] In the course of deciding an issue which turned on the use of an existing obligation as consideration (which is discussed in ch 10) in *Pao On v Lau Yiu Long* [1980] AC 614 (PC) 634C–D, Lord Scarman addressed the argument that 'public policy' should be allowed to invalidate a contract when there has been 'an unfair use of a dominating bargaining position'. Putting, as it were, the other side of the views he had set out in *National Westminster Bank v Morgan* (n 28), his Lordship said:

> where businessmen are negotiating at arm's length it is unnecessary for the achievement of justice, and unhelpful in the development of the law, to invoke such a rule of public policy . . . It is unnecessary because justice requires that men, who have negotiated at arm's length, be held to their bargains unless it can be shown that their consent was vitiated by fraud, mistake or duress.

freedom in the pursuit of substantive fairness.[57] I have argued that this is wrong in one way in that it is impossible to give coherence to the 'consumer' area. In the remainder of this chapter it is argued that it is wrong in a second way. Though 'fairness' must play a role in the commercial area because, as a matter not only of political philosophy or sociology but of the positive law, the law of contract *tout court* must depend on the 'justice of exchange' which cannot be equated with freedom of contract understood, as it were, pejoratively.[58] The *entire* law rests on a moral foundation, but it is in procedural, not substantive, fairness. The criticism I have made of inequality of bargaining power and unfairness is not a criticism of the idea of a principle regulating the justness of a bargain. I believe that requiring just transfers to be agreed bargains is itself that principle, for though it is based on the indispensability of the refusal to inquire into adequacy, it nevertheless allows the welfare optimising regulation of the issues which have given rise to the criticism of that refusal.[59] The point is that it has been possible to think that the 'bargain principle' is opposed to fairness, or in a sense deny the existence of a principle as such, because the principle's purely procedural moral basis in a relationship of mutual recognition has been only very inadequately institutionalised in the classical law of contract.

Exchange, Adequacy, and Distribution

Inequality and the refusal to inquire into adequacy

The refusal to inquire into adequacy has long been seen as the main and most objectionable way in which the law of contract, by not intervening in economic exchange,[60] systematically enforced illegitimately unequal bargains and therefore contributed to

[57] In *Erven Warnink BV v J Townend and Sons (Hull) Ltd* [1979] AC 731 (HL) 742H–743D Lord Diplock took the distinction further than it will be pursued here, other than by referring the reader back to ch 3, by arguing that, as Parliament had:

> progressively intervened in the interests of consumers [by imposing] on traders a higher standard of commercial candour than the legal maxim *caveat emptor* calls for ... the common law ... ought to proceed upon a parallel rather than a diverging course.

[58] H Collins, *The Law of Contract* (1st edn, Weidenfeld and Nicolson 1986) 8:

> We shall call the dominant ideal behind the classical law 'the justice of exchange'. Often the governing ideal is described as 'freedom of contract' but, though this terminology captures part of the spirit of the classical model, it is incomplete and ultimately misses the principal virtues of the justice of the market order as they were conceived.

The point was retained but rephrased in subsequent editions: (4th edn, Lexis Nexis UK 2003) 22.

Professor Collins tells us that 'justice of exchange' is an unattributed borrowing from F Kessler, G Gilmore, and AT Kronman, *Contracts: Cases and Materials* (3rd edn, Little, Brown and Co 1986) 533: H Collins, 'Friedrich Kessler 1901–1998' in J Goudkamp and D Nolan (eds), *Scholars of Contract Law* (Hart forthcoming).

[59] Cartwright, *Unequal Bargaining* (n 30) 231:

> once it is realised that there are common links between [the] vitiating factors, and that these are themselves linked to the basic rules for the formation of the contract and the establishment of its terms, the general approach of the English law in relation to the negotiations leading up to a contract can be seen to have a coherent basis which can be used as a guide for the future development of the law.

[60] LM Friedman, *A History of American Law* (2nd edn, Simon & Schuster 1985) 532–33:

illegitimately unequal distributions of wealth. This criticism of the refusal is, in the general sense discussed in Chapter 1, traceable to at least Anatole France, but the specific criticism made in the advanced legal theory of the law of contract (and regulation generally) has been that not intervening makes the claim that exchange is based on voluntary agreement fundamentally misleading. As Robert Hale put it:

> The practical function of economic theory is merely to prove to statesmen ... that they should make no effort to control the working of economic events ... But ... the systems advocated by professed upholders of *laissez-faire* are in reality permeated with coercive restrictions of individual freedom, and with restrictions, moreover, out of conformity with any formula of 'equal opportunity' or of 'preserving the equal rights of others'.[61]

In the 'supposedly' free situation criticised by Hale, a party seeking to drive a bargain will minimise what it offers in order to secure what it wants, the end-point being to offer as little as possible, or even nothing if it is possible to get away with it.[62] Hale's criticism is of a failure of the law to take steps to prevent the consequences of the 'economic motive' as he understood it, which it is convenient to illustrate by returning to the quotation from Macneil given in Chapter 4, which will be discussed at length in Chapter 10:

> An individual utility maximiser may be perfectly well aware of the fact that the deal he makes creates exchange-surplus, but his *sole* concern about that utility is to grab as much of it for himself as he can. He will feel nothing but regret at whatever amount is snared by the other party and nothing but happiness that the other failed to secure more of it.[63]

The criticism of the refusal to inquire into inadequacy is, then, rooted in the equation of contractual action with solipsistic self-interest, and this chapter applies the concept of legitimate self-interest generally advanced in this book to argue that this equation is quite wrong. Exploitative contracting is, of course, an ineliminable feature of the market economy, but the very substantial shortcomings of the law of contract's response to this are the consequence of a failure to actualise the relationship of mutual recognition which is central to contracting. For, despite the recent deep penetration of the general principles of contract by consumer law, the refusal is of a piece with consideration generally in that, as was claimed in Chapter 5, it is 'overwhelmingly

> The concrete body of law *called* contract ... hardly seemed worthy of ... fuss. The law of contract was essentially negative. Its doctrines gave more or less free play to individual choice. What people voluntarily agreed on courts would enforce.

[61] R Hale, 'Coercion and Distribution in a Supposedly Non-coercive State' (1923) 38 Political Science Quarterly 470.

[62] Macneil ruled out the possibility of offering nothing, but this is for reasons deriving from the 'social theory of exchange' which he saw as underlying but distinct from his theory of capitalist contract, and these reasons are different, in fact opposed, to the ones advanced in this chapter: Macneil, 'Political Exchange' (n 50).

[63] IR Macneil, 'Exchange Revisited: Individual Utility and Social Solidarity' (1986) 96 Ethics 567, 578.

[accepted as] normal' by the citizens of liberal democracies.[64] The outcomes of contracts are normally held to be legitimate even though contracts are motivated, and their outcomes determined, by the parties' self-interest. As a matter of legal doctrine, the rule that a court will not 'enter into an inquiry into the adequacy of consideration' is, as Pollock put it, simply a 'deduction'[65] from the concept of consideration when the proper relationship of bargain and exchange is grasped.

For this reason almost all of the modern case law relating to adequacy is not to the point,[66] and the vanishingly small amount that is can hardly be said to make that point clearer. The principal modern case used in teaching, *Chappell and Co Ltd v Nestlé Co Ltd*,[67] if it is comprehensible at all, is comprehensible only as a case on the interpretation of a copyright statute difficult to apply to the facts, to which interpretation the doctrine of consideration was curiously bent. I can recall no contract undergraduate I have taught ever receiving a benefit from trying to ascertain the *ratio* of this case before I acquired sufficient confidence in my own judgement to normally confine my teaching of the case just to some apposite *dicta*.[68] In these circumstances, the refusal, even more than other core doctrines of the law of contract, is known from the textbooks, and in the last edition of his textbook under his own hand the late Sir Gunter Treitel told us that:

> the courts do not, in general, ask whether adequate value has been given, or whether the agreement is harsh or one-sided. The reason for this is not that the courts *cannot* value the promise of each party; they have to do that when assessing damages. It is rather that they should not interfere with the bargain actually made by the parties. The fact that a person pays 'too much' or 'too little' for a thing ... does not of itself affect the validity of the contract.[69]

In order to explain the acceptance of the refusal as a normal belief resting on a general if inadequate perception of the relationship of mutual recognition which is institutionalised in the contractual bargain, it is first necessary to look again at the welfare claim stated as Pareto optimality.

[64] JP Dawson, *Gifts and Promises* (Yale University Press 1980) 221.

[65] F Pollock, *Principles of the Law of Contract* (9th edn, Stevens & Sons 1936) 186.

[66] GH Treitel, *The Law of Contract* (11th edn, Sweet & Maxwell 2003) 73–74 (hereafter Treitel, 11th edn):

> [The vitiating factor cases are exceptions to the refusal which] indicate that the courts are (even when legislation has not intervened) by no means insensitive to the problems raised by unequal or unfair bargains; but in none of them is a promise held invalid *merely* because adequate value for it has not been given. Some additional factor is required to bring a case within one of the exceptions.

Treitel had taken this line since 1979 when he first made the exceptions integral to the definition of adequacy in his 5th edn: (Sweet & Maxwell 1979) 57.

[67] [1960] AC 87 (HL) (hereafter *Chappell v Nestlé*). The confusion about the value of the 'themselves valueless' (ibid 104) chocolate bar wrappers was repeated, this time over physical gaming chips, in *Lipkin Gorman v Karpnale Ltd* [1991] 2 AC 548 (HL), the foundational unjust enrichment case which is best explained as not being about unjust enrichment at all: G Virgo, 'Note on *Macmillan Inc v Bishopsgate Investment Trust plc (No 3)*' (1996) 10 Trust Law International 24.

[68] *Chappell v Nestlé* (n 67) 114 (Lord Somervell).

[69] Treitel, 11th edn (n 66) 73–74.

Pareto optimality and justice

In Chapter 1 I argued that justifying the law of contract as an attempt to institutionalise Pareto optimisation required the recognition that the establishment of a competitive equilibrium did not imply approval of the moral substance of that equilibrium. A competitive equilibrium is entirely the product of voluntary choices, and as a matter of legal command contract must be neutral about the substance of the choices. *De gustibus non disputandum* is a foolish guide to making a choice to exchange. It is essential to the enforcement of contracts.

The existence of a competitive equilibrium also does not imply that the equilibrium is just. It will be recalled that in Chapter 1 the relationship of competitive equilibrium to Pareto optimality was stated by reference to Kenneth Arrow's 'First theorem of welfare economics: every competitive equilibrium is Pareto efficient'. Arrow's second theorem states that:

> For every Pareto efficient allocation of resources, there is a redistribution of the endowments such that the given Pareto efficient allocation is a competitive equilibrium for the new endowment distribution.[70]

An economy may be Pareto optimal, but the optimality follows the initial distribution of endowments, and this may not be just. We saw in Chapter 1 that Pareto used the term 'ophelimity' rather than 'utility' in order to stress that general equilibrium conveyed no implication about the substantive moral worth of an economy, and we can now see that Arrow used the term Pareto 'efficiency' rather than 'optimality' because 'the latter term conveys more commendation than the concept should bear, since a Pareto efficient allocation ... might not be optimal in any sense in which distributional ethics are involved'.[71] One need not agree with Arrow over terminology to acknowledge his indication of a further limit to the legitimacy that a competitive equilibrium may claim because it is the product of voluntary choices: 'General competitive equilibrium ... teaches that not only can an allocation be achieved, but the result will be Pareto efficient. But ... there is nothing in the process which guarantees that the distribution be just'.[72]

Though it should do so, this way of approaching justice has not prevented those who appear to have elevated what they understand to be 'economic efficiency' to the *summum bonum* from making indefensible claims for the results of the market economy.[73] Dismissing those claims must not stop us recognising that Arrow's 'two stage' approach carries a political implication of the first importance. That approach:

[70] Arrow, 'Pareto Optimality' (n 42).

[71] KJ Arrow and FH Hahn, *General Competitive Analysis* (Holden-Day 1971) 91. Pareto efficiency was and is a common usage, and Arrow was not alone in using it for this reason.

[72] KJ Arrow 'General Economic Equilibrium' in *Collected Papers*, vol 2 (n 42) 222–23. Rawls accepted this argument for 'efficiency': Rawls, *Justice* (n 9) 58, citing the authority of the important contributor to general equilibrium theory Tjalling Koopmans: TC Koopmans, *Three Essays on the State of Economic Science* (McGraw-Hill 1957) 49.

[73] Though he fully accepted the theoretical statement of general competitive equilibrium, the scorn the great socialist economist Evan Durbin felt for apologists for capitalism who read far too much into Pareto

> implies problems of equity can be separated from those of efficiency; if the existing distribution of welfare is judged inequitable, rectification should proceed by redistributing endowments . . . and then allowing the market to work unimpeded.[74]

The two stage approach allows of redistribution at the first stage, but then strongly separates 'equity', the concern of 'distributive justice', from 'efficiency' (ie optimality), the concern of market allocation, which latter it is the function of the separation to preserve. But though this separation is essential to the operation of contractual justice, it cannot be understood in a literal way. First, as any redistribution of initial endowments *must* involve differential taxation[75] and *must* itself alter economic conditions in the subsequent economy,[76] we are dealing with a separation that can only be a matter of degree.[77] The huge questions which attend the relationship of the desirability and the possibility of redistributions of endowments will, save in one sense to be discussed, be put to one side.

Secondly, though we must be committed to neutrality between economic actors and their choices, such neutrality carries a very clear economic and political burden.[78] Even if we accept the workability of the separation of the stages of the two stage approach, the allocation at a competitive equilibrium under that approach nevertheless *is* a distribution,[79] and one of a specific sort which inevitably involves an acceptance in

optimality emerged from his own definition of it: E Durban, *The Politics of Democratic Socialism* (William Pickering 1994) 354 (emphasis added):

> I think no one who has studied the logic of the theory of value carefully now disputes the validity of [its] formal conclusion . . . It . . . shows that if a number of . . . conditions are assumed the distribution of real economic resources will possess one rational characteristic. It will satisfy the most urgent desires of *the existing owners of income.*

[74] Arrow, 'Pareto Optimality' (n 42) 290.

[75] G Myrdal, *The Political Element in the Development of Economic Theory* (Routledge & Kegan Paul 1953) 170:

> Since taxation necessarily alters incomes and property in some way, the problem consists in changing them 'equally' . . . But this condition is highly ambiguous.

[76] T Scitovsky, 'A Note on Welfare Propositions in Economics' in KJ Arrow and T Scitovsky (eds), *Readings in Welfare Economics* (George Allen & Unwin 1969) 393.

> a change in economic institutions or policy . . . will no longer mean a mere redistribution of income . . . but may also involve a change both in the total quantity of resources available to the community and in the degree of their utilisation.

[77] JE Meade, *Planning and Price Mechanism: The Liberal Socialist Solution* (William Pickering 1994) 37:

> what further steps could wisely be taken to reduce inequalities in the distribution of income and property? At the outset it must be realised that this is essentially a matter for compromise. It is not even theoretically, much less practically, possible to find a solution in which there is full economic efficiency and freedom on the one hand . . . and a perfectly just distribution of income and property on the other.

[78] B Barry, *Justice as Impartiality* (Clarendon Press 1995) 133:

> There is a distinctively liberal individualist second-order conception of the good from which can be derived the idea of neutrality between substantive conceptions of the good.

[79] H Collins, 'Distributive Justice Through Contracts' [1992] Current Legal Problems 49 (hereafter Collins, 'Distributive Justice') and H Collins, 'Social Market and the Law of Contract' (1992) 49 Archives for Philosophy of Law and Social Philosophy 85, 85–88.

principle of inequality as a systemic feature of the economy. The second stage *must* be a stage of distribution by desert.

Liberal democratic societies are of course inegalitarian, and as contract is the principal institutional mechanism of economic exchange in those societies, contract must be the principal medium by which that inequality is reproduced. The market gives effect to voluntary choices, but as human beings are so disparate in their possession of natural gifts, this inevitably will mean that allocations through contract will systemically lead to inequality. It is crucial, however, that no *pattern*[80] of inequality is systemic,[81] save the patternless pattern of desert yielded by the operation of the invisible hand:

> To give different people the same objective opportunities is not to give them the same subjective chance. It cannot be denied that the Rule of Law produces economic inequality—all that can be claimed for it is that this inequality is not designed to affect particular people in a particular way.[82]

In essence, persons will get their desert through the operation of the market,[83] and in the work which brought his views to such prominence, Nozick expressed this in a deliberately provocative[84] maxim: 'From each as they chose, to each as they are chosen'[85] which condenses his 'entitlement conception of justice'.[86] On this basis, one accepts the consequence of exchange that distribution will take place according to the maxim:

> From each according to what he chooses to do, to each according to what he makes for himself (perhaps with the contracted aid of others) and what others chose to do

[80] The particular resonance of Nozick's position can be traced to his telling criticisms of what he called 'patterning' discussed in ch 1: Nozick, *Anarchy* (n 2) 155–60.

[81] FA Hayek, *Law, Legislation and Liberty* (corr edn, Routledge 1982) vol 2, 64 (hereafter Hayek, *Law*):

> the manner in which the benefits and burden are apportioned by the market mechanism would in many instances have to be regarded as very unjust if it were the result of a deliberate allocation to particular people. But this is not the case. Those shares are the outcome of a process the effect of which on particular people was neither intended nor foreseen by anyone.

[82] FA Hayek, *The Road to Serfdom* in *Collected Works*, vol 2 (University of Chicago Press 2007) 117. For reasons that cannot be gone into at proportionate length, Hayek himself, in a way which I believe was a serious mistake, strongly opposed describing the market as distributing by desert: Hayek, *Law* (n 81) 72.

[83] Consumer sovereignty as discussed in ch 3 brings the interests of consumers and business organisations into line in a way which was forthrightly expressed in L von Mises, *The Ultimate Foundation of Economic Science* (Sheed, Andrews, and McMeel 1978) 112:

> One of the characteristics of the market economy is the specific way in which it deals with the problems offered by the biological, moral, and intellectual inequality of men ... In the market economy, the better people are forced by the instrumentality of the profit and loss system to serve the concerns of everybody, including the hosts of inferior people. In its frame the most desirable situations can be attained only by actions that benefit all the people. The masses, in their capacity as consumers, ultimately determine everybody's revenue and wealth. They entrust control of capital goods to those who know how to employ them for their own, ie the masses', best satisfaction.

[84] It is an obvious play on Marx's 'From each according to his abilities, to each according to his needs!': K Marx, *Critique of the Gotha Programme* in K Marx and F Engels, *Collected Works*, vol 24 (Lawrence and Wishart 1989) 87, discussed in ch 2, and to which we return in the conclusion of this book

[85] Nozick, *Anarchy* (n 2) 160.

[86] ibid 150–53.

> for him and choose to give him of what they've been given previously (under this maxim) and haven't yet expended or transferred.[87]

The passages just quoted make it particularly clear that the two stage approach to justice will have no appeal to those who do not accept some inequality of outcome. We return to this in the conclusion of this book. What is more important for our concerns at this point, however, is that casting profound doubt on desert has been the foundation of welfarism in the law of contract. The point could not be better expressed than it was by Atiyah in *The Rise and Fall of Freedom of Contract*:

> Promise-based liability rests upon a belief in the traditional liberal values of freedom of choice. Many still admire these values but they bring with them, inescapably, many other consequences which are today less admired, especially in England. They bring, in particular, the recognition that some individuals are better equipped to exercise free choice than others, through natural aptitude, education, or the possession of wealth. And the greater is the scope for the exercise of free choice, the stronger is the tendency for those original inequalities to perpetuate themselves by maintaining or even increasing economic inequalities.[88]

The liberal socialism advocated in this book, however, does accept distribution by desert, and therefore inequality of outcome, as a, not only integral, but also invaluable aspect of, to cite Sir George Jessell MR yet again, the 'paramount policy'[89] to which we should be committed of pursuing freedom of contract. The essential point is that such acceptance is, of course, conditional on it being possible to give effect to distribution by desert with welfare optimising results. The question which must be addressed here, applied by Collins to the law of contract as 'The Claim of Neutrality',[90] is whether exchange and contract can be 'neutral', not in the sense of value neutrality as a purely negative liberty (though we saw in Chapter 1 that this is necessary), but in the specific sense, at variance with much use of neutrality in political philosophy,[91] of actually

[87] ibid 160.

[88] Atiyah, *Rise and Fall* (n 11) 6. Anxious as I am to avoid discussion of the distribution of initial endowments, I cannot forebear remarking just how much Atiyah's account of the consequences of free choice exemplifies the 'misdirected' criticism of market order described in J Buchanan, 'Fairness, Hope and Justice' in *Collected Works*, vol 17 (Liberty Fund 2001) 326 (a revised version of this 1983 paper appeared as *Liberty, Market and State* (Harvester 1986) chs 12 to 13, with the quoted passage at 137):

> The institutions of the market have been criticised for their failure to produce distributive results that meet stated normative objectives when, in fact, the results are more closely related to disparities in pre-market endowments and capacities.

[89] *Printing and Numerical Registering Co v Sampson* (1875) LR 19 Eq 462 (Ch) 465.

[90] Collins, 'Distributive Justice' (n 79) 49–53.

[91] It might indeed be said that the preponderant theme of the at all recent political philosophy of distribution has been, after Rawls had made it impossible for the other than extreme left to argue against inequality as such, to accept inequality of outcome, but then seek to so skew what is called the 'equality of resources' as to produce equality of, however defined, end-states of welfare, ie outcomes. In a vast literature, the contributor closest to the concerns of legal theory is Ronald Dworkin (R Dworkin, *Sovereign Virtue* (Harvard University Press 2001)), but this closeness does not make Dworkin's proposals generally more realistic. If they worked, these liberal egalitarian arguments would be pointless, for by working they would extinguish the basic acceptance of contractual justice that made it seem necessary to take them up in the first place. But these arguments need not be considered here because their indirect way of pursuing their

effecting distribution through desert. If it is not possible to answer yes to this question, then the two stage approach falls, and with it the possibility of contractual justice.

The work of neutrality

As with other aspects of negative liberty, neutrality requires continuous, active steps be taken to realise it. Regarding distribution, this requirement asserts itself as soon as we clearly grasp just what it is we are to be neutral about. For distribution by desert and its resultant inequality can be just only if each actor's relative social position actually is her or his desert; that is to say, her or his position reasonably accurately reflects the value of her or his efforts. That a distinction must be drawn between 'natural' and 'social' powers has been a defining feature, traceable at least to Hobbes,[92] of all the major contributions to the political philosophy of liberal democracy,[93] and a distribution by desert must be neutral in the sense that the distribution is the product of differences in natural power alone. But giving such a role to natural power is something that only the institutions of social power can do.[94] Even in Rawls himself, not to speak of others, the possible refinements of the distinction between natural and social powers are, in my opinion, often pursued well beyond the point where they can have a bearing on practical policy-making, and amidst the elephantine elaboration of these discussions we shall focus on the essential point for the working of the law of contract, put this way by GA Cohen: 'it is scarcely intelligible that one should be interested in how much freedom people have in a certain form of society without being interested in how readily they are able to exercise it'.[95] Access to the 'major institution' of 'competitive markets'[96] may be a primary good in Rawls' sense, essential to the citizens of liberal democratic society 'carrying out their intentions and advancing their ends, whatever these ends may be',[97] but if economic actors can only 'supposedly', as we have seen Hale put it, conclude the bargains they choose, then freedom of contract is indefensible, for

goal so complicates 'complex equality' that, as was noted in ch 3, they can have little relationship to what it is actually possible to put into practice, certainly through the law of contract: Kaplow and Shavell, 'Legal System' (n 4).

It is significant that these arguments have embraced attempts to correct for luck, not merely in the sense of the luck of eg having been born with advantaged life chances, but of 'brute' luck (GA Cohen, 'On the Currency of Egalitarian Justice' in *On the Currency of Egalitarian Justice and Other Essays in Political Philosophy* (Princeton University Press 2011)), for serious, general attempts to correct for luck must encounter such overwhelming problems of practical implementation that they are bound to be a cure that is far worse than the problem.

92 T Hobbes, *Leviathan* (CUP 1991) 62.

93 Rawls, *Justice* (n 9) 54.

94 ibid 55, 79:

> Whether men are free is determined by the rights and duties established by the major institutions of society. Liberty is a certain pattern of social forms ... liberties and opportunities are defined by the rule of major institutions and the distribution of income and wealth is regulated by them.

95 GA Cohen, 'Illusions About Private Property and Freedom' in J Mepham and D-H Ruben (eds), *Issues in Marxist Philosophy*, vol 4 (Harvester Press 1981) 231.

96 Rawls, *Justice* (n 9) 6.

97 ibid 79.

'a fair procedure translates its fairness to the outcome only when it is actually carried out'.[98]

Criticism of the law of contract for not satisfying this condition must be put in the wider context of the criticism of nineteenth century liberalism[99] as a, to use the extremely influential terms of TH Marshall, merely 'political freedom' based on 'civil' and 'political' 'rights'[100] which 'it would be absurd to contend were as egalitarian in practice as they professed to be in principle', with the result that, except in a sham sense, 'Equality before the law did not exist'.[101] In the late nineteenth century and in the twentieth century, fundamental social policy has been the provision of 'social rights' 'of a different order from the others' in that they are the rights necessary to give effect to civil and political rights, and so to actualise 'citizenship'.[102] Though in the end social rights are of course a matter of law, and as a matter of fact access to the legal system was a particular concern of Marshall's,[103] the more than legal nature of the social rights of citizenship has been definitively conveyed in Rawls' conception of primary goods. What Marshall and other contributors to the idea of social citizenship capture in a way that modern political philosophy's predominantly abstract argumentation does not, however, is the historical process of these developments,[104] of which developments in the law of contract discussed in this chapter and Chapter 7 are a central part.[105] It is possible to understand the modern history of the law of contract only in terms of an emerging background perception of the social inadequacy of the operation of the classical law.

[98] Ibid.

[99] HJ Laski, *The Rise of European Liberalism* (Unwin Books 1962) 15:

> Like all social philosophies, [liberalism] contained in its birth the conditions of its own destruction ... It never understood, or was never able to fully admit, that freedom of contract is never genuinely free until the parties thereto have equal bargaining power.

[100] TH Marshall, *Citizenship and Social Class* in TH Marshall and TB Bottomore, *Citizenship and Social Class* (Pluto Press 1992) 8.

[101] ibid 21–22.

[102] ibid 8.

[103] ibid 29–31.

[104] TH Marshall, *Social Policy* (1st edn, Hutchinson 1965). The last edition for which Marshall himself was responsible was the 4th of 1975.

[105] Perhaps the most important 'new' or 'social' liberal comment on the law of contract intended to actualise citizenship by criticism of merely legal right is TH Green, 'Liberal Legislation and Freedom of Contract' in *Lectures on the Principles of Political Obligation and Other Writings* (CUP 1986) (hereafter *Lectures*). This famous lecture in truth says very little about the law of contract as opposed to labour law in a wide sense, and its significance is that, given in 1881, it did much to set a pattern for the approach to welfarist legislation criticised in this chapter.

It would be preposterous to purport to adequately criticise Green here, but it is instructive to draw attention to the ambiguity of 'freedom' from 'compulsion' in TH Green, 'On the Different Senses of "Freedom" as Applied to Will and to the Moral Progress of Man' in *Lectures*, ibid 234.

> 'freedom' according to the primary meaning of the term [expresses] that relation between one man and others in which he is secured from compulsion. All that is ... implied is that a man should have the power to do what he wills or prefers.

Moved by a truly liberal impulse, Green was trying to identify what he called 'the juristic sense' of (negative) liberty (ibid), but whilst from the very outset he saw that the necessary use of 'power to do what he wills' cannot be contained within this sense, his 'positive' philosophy was, in my opinion, inevitably not essentially liberal but a form of the 'ethical socialism' associated with RH Tawney discussed in the conclusion of this book.

I have already said that this book on the law of contract will not address the huge questions of determining which redistributions of initial endowments are desirable and feasible. I must, however, briefly say that, the general market economy would never have been possible at all without some form of what I will persist in calling 'social security', with Polanyi's influential demonstration of this being noted in Chapter 1. Nor would the liberal socialist defence of the market economy advocated here be possible were it not for the provision by the welfare state of certain public goods, notably school education, basic health care, and a minimum income which prevents want, which limits the effects of competitive distribution in what is thereby a 'social market'.[106] This implies, as indeed is the case, that though desert may and should be the main, it cannot and must not be the only principle which guides the allocation of goods.[107] The contractual justice of the 'market sphere'[108] must be supported by the public altruism of welfare, and should be supported by the private altruism of charity,[109] both of which are based on the abandonment of market neutrality.[110]

Leaving aside the fundamental questions which such proposals raise about the limits of 'monism'[111] in political choice,[112] there are two, as it were, practical things that can go wrong with such proposals. First, it may be impossible to secure the provision of the public goods.[113] It is not to detract from the importance of this concern

[106] The 'idea behind the social market economy [of] market freedom combined with social balance' was definitively set out in A Müller-Armack, 'The Meaning of the Social Market Economy' in A Peacock and H Willgerodt (eds), *Germany's Social Market Economy: Origins and Evolution* (Macmillan 1989) 82–83:

> The advocates of a social market economy share with neo-liberalism the conviction that while the functional importance of competition was recognised under the 'Old Liberalism', nevertheless insufficient attention was paid to social and sociological problems. In contrast to 'Old Liberals', neo-liberals do not wish to restore a *laissez faire* economy; their goal is a new kind of synthesis. The concept of a social market economy differs just as widely from an interventionist economic policy ... The advocates of a social market economy believe that there is good reason to doubt whether a central control system, once created, would be able to resist the temptation to intervene in free consumer choice ... The concept of a social market economy may therefore be defined as a regulative policy which aims to combine, on the basis of a competitive economy, free initiative and social progress.

[107] D Miller, *Principles of Social Justice* (Harvard University Press 1999) ch 7.

[108] M Walzer, *Spheres of Justice* (Basil Blackwell 1983) 108–10.

[109] D Miller, *Market, State and Community* (Clarendon Press 1989) ch 4.

[110] ibid ch 3.

[111] ibid 3–4.

[112] L Kolakowski, 'My Correct Views About Everything' [1974] Socialist Register 1, 20:

> when I say 'socialism' I do not mean a state of perfection but rather a movement trying to satisfy demands for equality, freedom and efficiency, a movement that is worth trouble only as far as it is aware not only of the complexity of problems hidden in each of these values separately but also of the fact that they limit each other and can be implemented only through compromises. We make fools of ourselves ... if we think ... otherwise.

[113] The variety and profundity of failures in this respect are extremely marked, but one example that can be mentioned here because of its immediate relevance to the defence of contractual justice in this book is the failure to eliminate inequality of educational provision. Sidgwick is a principal representative of 'the liberal interpretation' of equality of opportunity upon which Rawls sought to improve: Rawls, *Justice* (n 9) 63 n 11. But one has to ask how far, despite its achievements, the welfare state has managed to act even upon as basic a matter as Sidgwick's suggestion, made in 1874, that 'it would be possible to remove, to some extent, the inequalities that are attributable to circumstances by bringing the best education within the reach of all classes': H Sidgwick, *Methods of Ethics* (7th edn, Hackett 1981) 285 n 1. The disparity between much political philosophical discussion of welfare provision and the real world of that provision is often extreme.

to focus in this book on problems of a second, different sort. There is no difficulty in principle with extensive welfare provision so long as it is confined to the prevention of want.[114] Whilst it is of course Beveridge's conception of the bounds to the ambition of the welfare state, mentioned in Chapter 1, that has been the focus of debate, the essential point has been made by Hayek:

> There is no reason why in a free society government should not assure to all protection against severe deprivation in the form of an assured minimum income, or a floor below which nobody need to descend. To enter into such an insurance against extreme misfortune may well be in the interest of all, or it may be felt to be a clear moral duty of all to assist, within the organised community, those who cannot help themselves. So long as such a uniform minimum income is provided outside the market to all those who, for any reason, are unable to earn in the market an adequate maintenance, this need not lead to a restriction of freedom, or conflict with the rule of law.[115]

A struggle between conceptions of a 'minimalist' welfare state conceived as a necessary complement to the market sphere and a 'maximalist' state which seeks to supplant, or certainly sees no principled reason to acknowledge the continuance of, that sphere,[116] has from the outset been a defining feature of 'the social citizenship state'.[117] The very undesirable consequences of the success of the maximalist view for the rule of law in the conduct of government[118] are paralleled in the law of contract[119] by the flat incoherence of the common law of the vitiating factors and of largely statutory consumer law, which, in their substantive aspect, cannot possibly be regarded as general systems of the regulation of exchange but are inchoate interventions. No amount of concern over inequality can justify ineffectual contractual doctrines which undermine the law of contract's integrity.[120] But, conscious of the necessity of actualising social citizenship, in order to make progress we should ask *precisely* what has been found so wrong with the common law of contract, and in particular with the refusal to inquire into the adequacy of consideration, that it has been thought necessary to

[114] Sir William Beveridge, *Social Security and Allied Services* (Cmd 6404, 1942) paras 12–16. Beveridge also, of course, spoke specifically of 'physical want' as one of 'five giant evils', together with disease, ignorance, squalor, and idleness: ibid para 456.

[115] Hayek, *Law* (n 81) vol 2, 87. It is perhaps particularly significant that, although it is my opinion that the arguments against it are overwhelming, it has been strongly maintained that commitment to the market sphere involves no principled objection to a minimum wage: P van Parijs, *Real Freedom for All* (Clarendon Press 1995).

[116] N Barry, *Welfare* (Open University Press 1990) 104–07.

[117] G Esping-Anderson, *Politics Against Markets* (Princeton University Press 1985) 145–49.

[118] D Campbell, 'Gathering the Water: Abuse of Rights After the Recognition of Government Failure' [2010] The Journal Jurisprudence 487, 507–34.

[119] The point refers to the private law generally and I refer the reader to the discussions of negligence in ch 5.

[120] J Gava, 'Contract Law and Inequality: A Reply to Frank Carrigan' (2013) 13 Oxford University Commonwealth Law Journal 9.

improve upon that law by the *ad hocery* we have discussed? In Chapter 7 we can explore what has gone wrong by turning to the detail of the treatment of agreement in what have proven to be the foundations of modern consumer legislation: the law of hire purchase, and the attempt to curb exclusion clauses under the Unfair Contract Terms Act 1977.

7

The Relational Constitution of Bargain (3)

Fairness in Legislation and Common Law

The Hire Purchase Contract

Though still used to finance sales to consumers, especially of cars, the far greater availability to consumers of other forms of credit, and, as we shall see, the extensive legislative steps taken to eliminate the objectionable legal characteristics of the hire purchase contract mean that hire purchase does not now have nearly the importance that it previously had.[1] But between, say, 1877, the year of the formation of the first company with the specific object of financing credit sales of furniture, and 1974, the year of the passage of The Consumer Credit Act, hire purchase was the principal means of financing sales of relatively high value, 'durable' goods to consumers—sewing machines and pianos featured prominently in the late Victorian era but cars were the most important twentieth-century example—so that hire purchase came to stand a similar relationship to such sales as the mortgage to house purchases.[2]

The hire purchase contract was the result of innovation in the appellate courts in the second half of the nineteenth century which radically altered the objective intentions regarding a sale which were codified in the Sale of Goods Act 1893. The aim of this innovation was to give the seller of consumer durables on credit an all but absolute legal security in the goods. But the specific contract which was devised contained great potential for unfairness and the infliction of hardship,[3] and the realisation of

[1] Department of Trade and Industry, *Fair, Clear and Competitive: The Consumer Credit Market in the 21st Century* (Cm 6040, 2003) paras 1.1–1.36 (hereafter Department of Trade and Industry, *Fair, Clear and Competitive*).

[2] Committee on the Working of the Monetary System (Chairman Lord Radcliffe), *Report* (Cmnd 827, 1959) para 205.

[3] I focus only on transfer of property, but hire purchase transactions which came normally to involve credit companies distinct from the supplier also allowed particular possibilities of misleading consumers about the price and of evading the implied terms as to quality in sales of goods, and these also have been found to require statutory remedies: Sale and Supply of Goods (Implied Terms) Act 1973, ss 9–10.

Contractual Relations. David Campbell, Oxford University Press. © David Campbell 2022.
DOI: 10.1093/oso/9780198855156.003.0007

this potential is a most instructive example of the shortcomings of the classical law of contract, specifically of its failure adequately to institutionalise contract's relational character of mutual recognition. This unfairness and hardship gave rise to great public concern, and eventually led to extensive legislative intervention beginning with the Hire Purchase Act 1938,[4] and this legislation specifically for hire purchase set a pattern for consumer credit regulation and consumer protection generally established under the Consumer Credit Act 1974 which has now led to Consumer Credit Act 2006 and the Consumer Rights Act 2015.

Though it would be the merest affectation to argue that the legislative regulation of hire purchase as a form of consumer credit was unnecessary or has not markedly increased welfare, it is wrong to say that legislation was necessary to correct market failure. What failed was a law of contract which, as we shall see, specifically did not attempt to institutionalise the values of exchange and agreement. A market properly regulated by the private law of contract would not have given rise to hire purchase in the specific form which caused such concern.

The function of the hire purchase contract

Hire purchase was devised in response to a 'contract of sale' being a transfer or an agreement to transfer 'the property in goods' from a seller to a buyer in return 'for a ... price'.[5] For by the exercise of sufficient legal ingenuity a distinction can be drawn between sales and cognate transactions in which the transfer of property is in some way reserved.

It is part of the definition of a 'sale' that the transfer of property takes place at the time of the agreement of the contract.[6] But in an 'agreement to sell', the transfer of property 'is to take place at a future time or subject to some condition later to be fulfilled'.[7] The agreement to sell is in this sense 'conditional',[8] and the term 'agreement to sell' has never been as widely used as the terms 'conditional sale' or, latterly, 'conditional sale agreement'.[9] But the conditions, including the eventuation of the future time, in a conditional sale are specified in the contract, and in this sense the transfer of property, though it is delayed, is completed by such a sale as much as by a sale proper, and this creates some rights of ownership, including some right of alienation, in the conditional sale buyer at the time of the agreement.

However, in a hire purchase transaction the supplier (seller) transfers possession but retains property until the hirer (buyer) exercises an option to purchase (buy) towards the end of the hire term, probably at the time of the payment of the final instalment of the hire charge (price), because the requirement that an option actively be

[4] The Hire Purchase Act 1938 was preceded by the Hire Purchase and Small Debt (Scotland) Act 1932.

[5] Sale of Goods Act 1893, s 1(1) (1979 Act, s 2(1)).

[6] 1893 Act, s 1(3) (1979 Act, s 2(4)).

[7] 1893 Act, s 1(3) (1979 Act, s 2(5)). Under the 1893 Act, s 1(4) (1979 Act, s 2(6)) 'An agreement to sell becomes a sale when the time elapses or the conditions are fulfilled.'

[8] 1893 Act, s 1(2) (1979 Act, s 2(3)).

[9] A 'conditional sale agreement' has a specific meaning which emerged from legislative regulation of hire purchase and consumer credit generally: 1979 Act, s 25 (2)(b).

exercised prevents the hire purchase agreement being an agreement to sell. However merely formal it actually is,[10] the option gives the hirer a legal choice whether to make the purchase or not, and so is not a condition in the terms needed to create an agreement to sell. The process of innovation which created the hire purchase contract culminated in the House of Lords' 1895 decision in *Helby v Matthews*,[11] a case about a piano brought by a claimant financially supported by the then Hire Traders Protection Association, which held that a hirer under a hire purchase contract had not, by entering into that contract, agreed to buy. This was then supported by many instances in the lower courts of disputed enforcement action being resolved in favour of the supplier.[12] Without this specific, one can say *sui generis*, or more precisely *sui iuris*,[13] device, the contract itself would give the seller little security against unauthorised disposition by a consumer buyer paying by instalment, who could transfer property to a third party before paying the total price. Given the statutory protection of buyers in good faith,[14] the seller could well have no legal rights against the third party, nor have a real remedy against the very likely impecunious buyer. But under hire purchase, the consumer was not a buyer until the option was exercised, merely a strangely hybrid form of buyer and hirer.

A normal sale was governed by the Sale of Goods Act 1893, s 12(1) (1979 Act, s 12(1)), which provided that: 'In a contract of sale ... there is an implied term on the part of the seller that in the case of a sale he has a right to sell the goods'. It is vital to

[10] See the text accompanying n 18.

[11] [1895] AC 471 (HL) (hereafter *Helby v Matthews*); distinguishing *Lee v Butler* [1893] 2 QB 318 (CA). The relationship of these cases, and the Hire Purchase Act 1965, to the law of passage of property in the Factors Act 1889 and the Sale of Goods Act 1893 is clearly set out in GC Cheshire and CHS Fifoot, *Law of Contract* (7th edn, Butterworths 1969) 151–56, the first edition after the passage of the 1965 Act.

[12] The law up to the passage of the Hire Purchase Act 1938 may conveniently be approached by consulting E Holroyd Pearce and R Ormrod, *Dunstan's Law Relating to Hire Purchase* (4th edn, Sweet & Maxwell 1939).

[13] JK Macleod, *Consumer Sales Law* (2nd edn, Routledge-Cavendish 2006) (hereafter Macleod, *Consumer Sales Law*) para 1.20.

[14] The Sale of Goods Act 1893, s 25(2) (1979 Act, s 25) and the Factors Act 1889, s 9 drastically curtailed the *nemo dat* rule in respect of buyers in good faith. I focus on the relationship of the supplier and the hirer, but the development of hire purchase was, as the corollary of the way it conceived of that relationship, also intended to defeat the expectations engendered by statute of good faith third parties who had paid the hirer for a transfer of ownership which, with unauthorised disposition coming to be regarded as it was under hire purchase, counted for little or nothing: *Whiteley Ltd v Hilt* [1918] 2 KB 115 (DC) (hereafter *Whiteley v Hilt*). The problem of unauthorised disposition of consumer durables, especially cars, obtained on hire purchase led to much litigation and statute seeking to explore the limits of the, as it were, hire purchase reassertion of *nemo dat*: Law Reform Committee, *Twelfth Report*: *Transfer of Title to Chattels* (Cmnd 2958, 1966) (hereafter Law Reform Committee, *Twelfth Report*), The at the time still significant case of sale in market overtly recognised under the 1893 Act, s 22 (1979 Act, s 22) fell into desuetude and was repealed by the Sale of Goods (Amendment) Act 1994 s 1, despite the fascinating suggestion of the Law Reform Committee, ibid paras 30-35 that it be generalised.

Of the way that hire purchase was created by evasion of very important statute—including the Bills of Sale Acts and the Moneylenders Acts as well as Acts already mentioned—the Committee on Consumer Credit (Chairman Lord Crowther), *Report* (Cmnd 4596, 1971) vol 1, para 2.1.45 (hereafter *Crowther Report*) said:

> There can be little doubt that [the hire purchase contract's] by-passing [of legislation which would have made hire purchase impossible] has been in the interests of consumers as a class, since otherwise the great extension of credit to ordinary households, and the higher material standards of living based on it, would not have been possible. But the inevitable corollary was that the individual consumer was deprived of the protection the [legislation was] designed to afford, and it soon became apparent that other remedies against abuses were necessary.

realise that this implied term institutionalises a relation of mutual recognition. In a sale, the seller's legal right to sell is both an acknowledgement of the seller's initial ownership of the goods, and a contractual duty that the seller owes to the buyer, a failure to perform which is a fundamental breach of the contract. Ownership by the seller is respected by others, but the seller agreeing to sell has to, by providing the conditions of objective agreement necessary in the circumstances, guarantee the buyer that it has the requisite alienable interest in the goods. This active duty of the seller is an essential part of the legal framework by reference to which the buyer forms its intentions. It is a natural expression of the essence of exchange. This becomes very clear when one considers the consequences of the legal departure from this duty in the hire purchase contract.

One cannot explain, and therefore justify, the specific form of the hire purchase contract as an attempt to give suppliers security in the goods. It must be explained as an attempt to give the supplier so *absolute* a security that it defeated the objective intentions a consumer had regarding what he saw as a sale.[15] It should be possible to oust such intentions (treating them as a default rule), but doing so could possibly be justified as the outcome of an agreement only by the clearest words made in the course of the frankest negotiations. However, the entire history of hire purchase, as revealed in recurrent noted *dicta*,[16] and in a number of important official reports into a form of sale that gave rise to such great concern, is evidence that it is preposterous to claim that such words were ever remotely sufficiently used in promotional[17] and negotiating practices which the contemporary sensibility would regard as unacceptable.

The most striking aspect of the 'artificial' or 'fictional' character of hire purchase is that consumer hirers normally did not at all understand the option which was the entire point of the contract, even as they exercised it! The final instalment was believed just to be the last payment of a total price which the consumer thought her or himself to have always been entirely liable to pay. Whereas a commercial party buying on hire purchase might legitimately be regarded as being aware of the implications of the transaction it had entered into, the application of this reasoning to consumers entering into hire purchase contracts as they were given their *sui iuris* form was always

[15] Committee on Consumer Protection (Chairman Mr JT Molony QC), *Final Report* (Cmnd 1781, 1962) para 437 (hereafter *Molony Report*):

> The broad and powerful justification for equating the law on sale and the law on hire-purchase is that the customer does not appreciate the legal distinction between the two types of transaction. For him they are the means of getting the goods he wants when he wants them and the only difference he knows is that he pays cash down in one case and by instalments in the other;

and ibid para 503:

> It may be doubted whether the average consumer appreciates the important difference in legal character between a credit sale and a hire purchase. For him they are both forms of buying on credit and the vital questions are how much he has to pay 'cash down' and how long he will be given to pay the rest.

[16] Eg *Bridge v Campbell Discount Co Ltd* [1962] AC 600 (HL) 627 (Lord Denning), which was immediately taken up in Parliamentary debate which ultimately led to the passage of the Hire Purchase Act 1965: eg HC Deb 20 February 1962, vol 654, col 191 (Mr George Darling).

[17] The objectionable features of sales practices involved in making the contract were, if anything, even worse in respect of advertising and other forms of solicitation of business: *Molony Report* (n 15) pt VI. The use of unarguably misleading statements to advertise hire purchase was first addressed by specific legislation in The Advertisements (Hire Purchase) Act 1957.

'an absurd legal fiction'.[18] The whole problem was clearly expressed by Atiyah who, when he began to devote a separate part of his book on sales to hire purchase after the passage of the Hire Purchase Act 1965, began that part by saying:

> Contracts of hire purchase are treated by the man in the street as contracts of sale in which the price is to be paid in instalments. In law, however ... contracts of hire purchase are very different from contracts of sale. In fact the whole *raison d'être* of hire purchase contracts was that they should not be contracts of sale.[19]

Totally nullifying any ownership interest the hirer would naturally have believed itself to have acquired by part-payment, which normally included a substantial deposit, of a price which was out of all proportion to an actual hire charge, hire purchase allowed repossession and resale by the seller in addition to retention of the part-payment, even if that part-payment approached the total price,[20] for the outstanding part of which the hirer remained liable.[21] The common practice of repossessing in such circumstances, which came to be called 'snatching-back', was the focus of the Parliamentary debate that led to the Hire Purchase Act 1938,[22] but it may be seen at least as early as the Court of Appeal's 1884 decision in *Cramer and Co v Carlton*,[23] an example of a type of case which became notorious.[24] In this case, the defendant had paid 50 guineas of the 60 guinea (now *circa* £7,000) hire charge for a piano, but

[18] *Crowther Report* (n 14) vol 1, para 2.1.45:

> what was, even as late as 1895, an understandable form of contract in which the hirer had a genuine option to terminate the hiring without further monetary liability is now a complicated legal fiction.

In debate on the *Crowther Report*, Viscount Hanworth, HL Deb 28 June 1972, vol 332, col 941, emphasised the point:

> Our hire purchase system ... developed out of an absurd legal fiction whereby a person takes goods in theory on hire and after he has had them on hire for a certain time and paid the hiring charges he has the option to buy them at a nominal sum. In other words, the reason for this was not logical; it was purely from the point of view of producing a convenient legal fiction. Nobody thinks of it as being a hire agreement or an option purchase; it is in reality a system for buying goods by instalments.

[19] PS Atiyah, *The Sale of Goods* (3rd edn, Pitman 1966) 240. Atiyah had always seen that 'the ultimate sale of the goods is the real object of the transaction: and that the hire purchase agreement was 'artificial': PS Atiyah, *The Sale of Goods* (1st edn, Pitman 1957) 4, 5; see now C Twigg-Flesner and R Canavan, *Atiyah and Adams' Sale of Goods* (14th edn, Pitman 2021) 14–15 (hereafter Twigg-Flessner and Canavan, *Sale of Goods*).

[20] This was not merely in contradiction of reasonable intentions regarding a sale of goods but at variance with other laws of borrowing on security such as mortgage where, after sale or foreclosure, the value of the security normally is deducted from the amount of the debt.

[21] The hirer was also liable for any damage to the goods caused by a breach of the underlying bailment.

[22] The Hire Purchase Act 1938 was principally the work of Miss Ellen Wilkinson, Labour MP for Jarrow, who had been successful in the ballot for Private Members' Bills. When moving the Commons Second Reading of her Bill she gave some pathetic examples of snatch-back (including of a 'linked-on agreement' which had made it even possible to repossess goods for which a sum greater than the price had been paid), and called the underlying legal device—the very point of the hire purchase contract—'the cancer in the whole system': HC Deb 10 December 1937, vol 330, col 730.

[23] *The Times*, 9 May 1884 (CA).

[24] The type of case of which *Whiteley Ltd v Hilt* (n 14) is an example is, in my opinion, even worse, for the very similar facts and result arose even though the defendant was in effect a purchaser in good faith who could not possibly know of the circumstances in which she obtained possession of the piano.

then did not pay on time the two remaining quarterly installments due in January and April. Despite the defendant tendering the outstanding 10 guineas in May, the supplier, in addition to retaining the 50 guineas, repossessed, and no doubt resold, the piano!

The legislative response to hire purchase

As a response to unfairness and hardship of the sort displayed in *Cramer and Co v Carlton*, hire purchase has been subject to statutory regulation since the Hire Purchase Act 1938, and the rules governing termination following breach by the consumer hirer[25] and its consequences[26] came to be closely prescribed by the legislation consolidated under the Hire Purchase Act 1965, which, as I have mentioned, set a pattern for general consumer credit legislation under The Consumer Credit Act 1974, into which the 1965 Act was subsumed.[27] The history of hire purchase between *Helby v Matthews* and the 1974 Act is generally regarded as one of market failure eventually requiring extensive government intervention. The most eminent authorities are united in this view. JK Macleod describes the present law of hire purchase as a set of now '(largely theoretical?) Victorian *laissez-faire* arrangements ... mostly reversed by detailed statutory provisions',[28] the reversal being necessary because those arrangements typify 'the nineteenth century attitude of freedom of contract [or] *laissez faire*'.[29] And Atiyah himself observed that 'Freedom of contract ... was ... absolute',[30] and 'so long as total freedom of contract prevailed, much hardship to the consumer resulted'.[31] Such intervention led to even the greatest critics of hire purchase at common law to think it had been made 'respectable' under statute.[32]

It is a central aim of this book to argue that, with the greatest respect to views like these which are part of the foundation of our understanding of the modern development of the English law of contract, this sort of approach is wrong, both because its belief in what regulation based on administrative and criminal law can do always was, and certainly has proven to be, excessive, but more because it is, paradoxical as it initially seems to say, insufficiently critical of the way the common law was developed.

25 Consumer Credit Act 1974, s 99.

26 ibid s 100.

27 In an attempt to quell undeniable difficulties in regarding hire purchase as credit which need not be discussed here, hire purchase agreements are expressly stated to be a form of credit under ibid s 9(3), and so could be regulated credit agreements.

28 Macleod, *Consumer Sales Law* (n 13) para 1.26.

29 ibid.

30 PS Atiyah, *The Rise and Fall of Freedom of Contract* (pbk edn, Clarendon Press 1985) 696 (hereafter Atiyah, *Rise and Fall*).

31 PS Atiyah, *Sale of Goods* (5th edn, Pitman 1975) 10 (see now Twigg-Flessner and Canavan, *Sale of Goods* (n 19) 17).

32 AL Diamond, *Commercial and Consumer Credit* (Butterworths 1982) vii (hereafter Diamond, *Credit*) 94. The much improved conduct of trade associations, which conduct previously had often been quite the other thing, once the framework for competition over the terms of hire purchase had been shifted by the (threat of) legislation, is celebrated by the authors of a rare overall warm endorsement, rather than the usual contempt for, or resigned acceptance of, hire purchase published by the Institute for Economic Affairs: R Harris, M Naylor, and A Selden, *Hire Purchase in a Free Society* (3rd edn, Hutchinson 1961) 27 (hereafter Harris, Naylor, and Selden, *Hire Purchase*).

But before turning to this second point, let us look at the legislative intervention that was made.

The Consumer Credit Act 1974 sought to regulate the hire purchase contract[33] in the interests of the consumer in a way which explored the limits of the refusal to inquire into adequacy. The 1974 Act as originally passed[34] empowered a court to 're-open' an 'extortionate' hire purchase agreement (as a credit agreement) if it found that agreement to be extortionate because it involved 'grossly exorbitant' payments or 'grossly contravenes ordinary principles of fair dealing'.[35] However, it is of the first importance to note that the regulatory technique adopted to prevent this was to mandate negotiating procedures intended to ensure that that contract was actually the result of an agreement by the consumer. The aim is eloquently captured in the title of The Truth in Lending Act, passed into law in 1968 as part of the US forerunner of the 1974 Act.[36] The broad requirement which it has been found necessary to impose by statute on a hire purchase agreement as a 'regulated' 'consumer credit agreement'[37] is that there should be a written document embodying all the express terms of that agreement in such a way that all those terms are readily legible.[38] Regulations may specify what in detail has to be done to ensure that a consumer 'is made aware of . . . the rights and duties conferred or imposed on him by the agreement'.[39] The sanction for non-compliance was that the agreement was regarded as being improperly executed, and therefore enforceable only by court order which could be made only within limits the Act stipulated.[40]

The form of pre-contractual negotiations was prescribed under ss 55–59, and the making of the actual agreement under ss 60–66. These provisions were modelled on The Hire Purchase Act 1965. These sections of the 1974 Act were, it is submitted,

[33] I will, somewhat artificially, put to one side regulation not directed at the contract itself, such as the creation of the (now replaced) regulatory agency the Office of Fair Trading and the licensing of providers of consumer credit. These measures were, of course, ultimately intended to effect the form of the contract.

[34] The Consumer Credit Act 1974's powers in regard of extortionate credit agreements were replaced by powers to 'set aside' and 'alter' an agreement arising from an 'unfair credit relationship' under the Consumer Credit Act 2006, ss 19–22, the 2006 Act being passed as a response (Department of Trade and Industry, *Fair, Clear and Competitive* (n 1), para 3.30), albeit after a period of 15 years, to a really rather critical 1991 review of the operation of ss 137–40 of the 1974 Act by the Office of Fair Trading: *Unjust Credit Transactions* (OFT 1991 (available via the British Library)). I regard it as evidence for a point I am trying to make about consumer legislation that the principal feature of this response was neoteristic logomachy, and I am, of course, barely touching upon all the relevant changes that have been made: Financial Conduct Authority, *Review of Retained Provisions of the Consumer Credit Act: Final Report* (FCA March 2019).

[35] Consumer Credit Act 1974, ss 137(1), 138(1).

[36] Consumer Credit Protection Act of 1968, Title I (82 US Stat 146). The similarity of the substance of the US and UK Acts—striking in respect of the Regulations passed under the Acts—also extends to their legislative history of their implementation and the evaluation of their effectiveness: E Durkin and G Elliehausen, *Truth in Lending* (OUP 2011) and S Aveyard, P Corthorn, and S O'Connell, *The Politics of Consumer Credit in the UK 1938–92* (OUP 2018) ch 7 (hereafter Aveyard, Corthorn, and Connell *Consumer Credit*).

[37] Consumer Credit Act 1974, s 8. Identifying which agreements were regulated under or were exempt from the 1974 Act was itself a matter of considerable intricacy: ibid ss 8, 16. The classification of regulated agreements also is difficult: ibid pt II, Sch 2. There were, in addition, what might be called partially regulated agreements under ibid ss 17 ('small agreement'), 189(1) ('non-commercial agreement').

[38] ibid s 61(1).

[39] ibid s 60(1)(a). Under Pt 5 generally, these provisions about the agreement itself are supported by requirements about pre-contract negotiations and a proper opportunity for consideration supported by provisions for withdrawal and cancellation.

[40] ibid ss 65, 127.

merely an exercise is spelling out the obvious, with s 61(1) requiring, for example, a document be (a) signed; (b) to contain all the express terms; and (c) be readily legible. Such spelling out has an overblown quality, and so s 61(1)(b), requiring the document to contain all express terms, specifically provided that: 'A regulated agreement is not properly executed unless ... the document embodies all the terms of the agreement, other than implied terms'.[41]

But the definition of 'embodies' under s 189(4) was that 'A document embodies a provision if the provision is set out either in the document itself or in another document referred to in it', so s 61(1)(b) actually allows reference to another document which the debtor could very well never consult. The relationship of terms to representations and devices such as collateral warranties could not be settled by this language, nor could the effect of later 'modifying agreements'. The regulations which the Secretary of State was obliged to make under s 60 to concretely specify what is needed under s 61 are, in my view, outright comical in their elaborateness,[42] and, not only did this invite cheese-paring dispute about the precision of compliance, but the inevitably repeated amendment[43] of such narrowly drafted requirements added a serious degree of complication to what, if it is to be any good, had to be simple. Most importantly, even if s 61(1)(b) could be justified if its effect was to make the creditor put in all the terms, what about the possibility that this does not happen? Section 61 had to strengthen the presumption that the written document contains the relevant terms. But in circumstances, surely not inconceivable in the context of a regulated credit agreement, especially in light of what had become notorious about hire purchase selling practices, effectively strengthening this exclusion of a *debtor's* evidence that the written agreement was not what orally had been agreed was of questionable wisdom.

The market, the common law, and the interests of the consumer

That the results of the 1974 Act and the previous hire purchase legislation were very disappointing was, I think it fair to say, acknowledged in all academic commentary on that legislation.[44] Leaving aside all problems of enforcement, let us just take up the problem of the complexity of the legislation, which one is obliged to say raises the question of how many of Fuller's ways not to make law were brought into play.[45] Though the achievement of the Crowther Committee and the Parliamentary draftsman in placing the Consumer Credit Act 1974 on the statute book even in so good a form as

[41] I put it to one side that there is a to some extent overlapping requirement in ibid s 61(1)(a).

[42] The Consumer Credit (Agreements) Regulations 1983, SI 1983/1553, regs 2–3. It is essential to read their Schedules to appreciate the character of these Regulations.

[43] Westlaw allows us quickly to identify that there are 111 differences between these two regs as made and as they are now in force.

[44] D Kraft, 'Private Law Control of Consumer Credit in the UK' in C Twigg-Flessner, D Parry, G Howells, and A Nordhausen (eds), *The Yearbook of Consumer Law 2008* (Ashgate 2007) 403:

> There is a widespread consensus that the extortionate credit provisions have failed to provide adequate protection for consumers in unfair credit relationships ... due to, first, the wording of the provisions, the courts' restrictive interpretation of them, and third, issues of access to justice.

Kraft told us he had 'not been able to find a single scholar who takes the opposite view'.

[45] LL Fuller, *The Morality of Law* (rev edn, Yale University Press 1969) 33–38.

it was given has been widely applauded,[46] that Act is manifestly unsatisfactory as law, and not only, or even principally, because the extraordinarily protracted time which the Government took to draft, pass, and even then implement merely those parts of the *Crowther Report* it adopted has provided an excellent illustration of the wisdom of the comparison of making law and making sausages attributed, wrongfully it seems, to Bismarck.[47]

Even after it had been substantially implemented, the complexity of the Consumer Credit Act 1974 became a central theme of commentary on that Act, even of the most sympathetic kind. Diamond prefaced the book which, principally by dealing with the 1974 Act, revived what had been his textbook on hire purchase, by saying that the first of two problems he had encountered when making his very substantial revisions was 'the complexity of the Act':

> Despite its skilled and masterly arrangement, I sometimes felt that, like Hermann Melville in *Moby Dick*,[48] I could claim that 'The classification of the constituents of a chaos, nothing less is here assayed'.[49]

When it became no longer arguable that the 'social' cost of hire purchase in the form it was given could be justified by the 'social' benefit of expanded sales of consumer durables, legislation was passed. I do not think, however, that the case for intervention in hire purchase, and by extension consumer credit and consumer law more widely, has ever been properly made out. One might say that the legislation sought to do what the classical case law did not: balance the interests of the consumer and the supplier. But that the means of arriving at a balance are legislative does not grant a magical power to strike it, and the complexity of the 1974 Act is more than sufficient evidence of this. I am anxious not to be carping about the 1974 Act, but I do think it is an inadequate response to its gross complexity to say that one is bound to encounter this problem with legislation of this ambition. This is indeed so, but surely that gives rise to the further question whether one should attempt to legislate in this way.

The precise question to ask surely is whether the 1974 Act is an improvement, not on what the courts did, for that this is the case is unchallengeable, but on what the courts would have done if they had done as they should and sought to actualise the relation of mutual recognition as the general structure facilitating the *agreements* of contracting parties.[50] In the case of hire purchase, this would have required a refusal to enforce, much less devise, agreements in which the quality of being a bargained-for

[46] RM Goode, *The Consumer Credit Act* (Butterworths 1979) ix, 37. This applause must be put in context. Shortly after the passage of the 1974 Act, Professor Goode, who had been a member of the Crowther Committee, gave an account of the way that that Committee had wished to bring the hire purchase legislation into a general structure for credit and security in personal property, and of how its wish was but partially realised by the 1974 Act, the provisions of which were themselves implemented in a so 'painfully slow' fashion that the Hire Purchase Act 1965 remained the basis of the law of hire purchase for a decade after 1974, and this remains of great interest: RM Goode, *An Introduction to the Consumer Credit Act 1974* (Butterworths 1974) 4–13; revised as Goode, *The Consumer Credit Act*, ibid 5–10.

[47] The seventh edition of the *Oxford Dictionary of Quotations* lists this in its section on misquotation.

[48] ch 32, 'Cetology'.

[49] Diamond, *Credit* (n 32) vii.

[50] L Friedman, *Contract Law in America* (2nd edn, Quid Pro Quo Books 2011) 154:

agreement was, in fact, spurious. I am of the opinion that this question has never seriously been asked, because the issue has never been seen as one of comparison of the effectiveness of the common law and legislative methods of pursuing the same goal.[51] The common law has been taken to, because it did, give effect to the dominance of the hire purchase owner, and behind this capitalist business interests, whereas legislation has been taken to have striven to balance the interests of business with those of the consumer. That the limits of regulation by legislation have become manifest is, to be truthful, neither here nor there when the issue is seen in this way. Caught between what are understood as capitalist exploitation of the market and welfarist paternalism even with its shortcomings, one cannot be surprised if the collective election is of the latter, even if the cost is loss of freedom of contract.[52] But the issue should not been seen in this way. It is right that the positive common law of contract should be condemned for institutionalising injustices such as hire purchase. But it is not right to see this as anything other than an abnegation by the classical law of contract of the common law's function of institutionalising exchange.

The common law, it is submitted, could and should have been used to address issues that had, in a way inevitably inferior to that which would have been possible through the common law, to be addressed by statute. We are confronted with an instance of the contradiction by experience of the theoretical case for the intrinsic superiority of the common law in refining, if not establishing, legal principles.[53] The common law of contract should work itself pure,[54] but its defects, very markedly after the successful establishment of mass consumer contracting,[55] have overwhelmingly been thought to call for legislative intervention.[56] It is submitted, however, that this has not

> a tissue of extremely detailed rules follow from a grant of power to make such rules; and the grant of power to make detailed rules is a denial that the subject to be regulated is susceptible of governance by grand and generalised propositions … a judgement that the market was a failure.

[51] The authoritative review of the common law of hire purchase in JWA Thorneley, 'Hire-purchase Hardships and Hopes' [1962] Cambridge Law Journal 39 ends in advocacy of further legislation after the imminent appearance of the *Molony Report*. I wish to stress the quality of this authoritative account when I point to it as exemplifying the, in the end, mistaken approach I am criticising.

[52] A MacIntyre, 'Breaking the Chains of Reason' in EP Thompson (ed), *Out of Apathy* (Stevens 1960) 201–2:

> In the name of positive freedom men have been called free so long as they are being tyrannised over for their own good. In the name of negative freedom men have been called free when enclosed by ignorance in their natural situation, provided that nobody else was actively coercing them. Certainly belief in negative freedom is less obviously vicious than belief in positive freedom, but so long as the choice is between these two, one can understand … why belief in freedom is not an active inspiration in much of our social life.

[53] C Menger, *Investigations into the Method of the Social Sciences with Special Reference to Economics* (New York University Press 1985) 233.

[54] This claim is discussed in ch 8.

[55] W Friedmann, *Law in a Changing Society* (2nd edn, Penguin 1972) 132–35.

[56] Atiyah's criticisms of hire purchase should, of course, be located within his general view of the growth of welfarist because, although up to 1870 the classical law 'still corresponded substantially with the reality of the law which was being applied', 'the arrival of democracy … spelled the doom of arguments based on *laissez faire* and freedom of contract': Atiyah, *Rise and Fall* (n 30) 693, 589. The background economic and social theory of these views, that led Atiyah to say in 1981 that 'liberal theory seems unlikely to carry the day in a democratic society' (PS Atiyah. 'The Liberal Theory of Contract' in Essays on Contract (rev edn, Clarendon Press 1988), and the remarkable and instructive *volte face* Atiyah performed over this seven years later (PS Atiyah, 'Freedom of Contract and the New Right' in *Essays on Contract*, ibid), are discussed

predominantly been because of defects in the practice of common law reasoning, but because the classical common law of contract has failed to adequately articulate the relational constitution of contract, and so has inconsistently privileged a solipsistic self-interest which cannot be justified by reference to the values of exchange and contract.

Hire purchase has been an acute example. One has to ask how a process of legal innovation by courts committed to freedom of contract could have yielded a form of contract which attained enormous economic, legal, and social importance whilst being so defective as to eventually call forth this sort of legislative intervention. A contract is a bargained-for agreement. But the common law hire purchase agreement typically was not understood by one of the parties, and typically made that party subject to the strong possibility of what statute came to call extortion. It should not have been regarded as a contract. And yet the courts overwhelmingly affirmed that it was, and the potential for striking down those features which should not have been said to be part of an agreement or part of a bargain, that is to say should not have been said to be part of a contract, was not exploited,[57] save it would seem in exceptional cases.[58]

The irony which one assumes would be entirely lost on those who were in the position of the hirer in *Cramer and Co v Carlton* is that, given proper consideration of the legal alternatives in the light of the experience particularly of the legislative intervention, influential opinion on consumer law came to widely believe that there was 'hardly ... any need for the development of the system of hire purchase'.[59] But this belief assumes that the hire purchase contract should balance the interests of the parties, whereas the assumption that informed its historical development was that the contract should enforce the result of the solipsistic pursuit of self-interest by legal means. The common law hire purchase contract was not an attempt to institutionalise a market; it was, in the respects fundamental to its specific legal identity, an attempt to do quite the opposite.

It has been argued that the nineteenth century cases in which the specific features of hire purchase were devised gave the law of contract a shape which tendentiously

in D Campbell, 'The Undeath of Contract: A Study in the Degeneration of a Research Programme' (1992) 22 The Hong Kong Law Journal 20.

[57] I do not purport to convey the detail of the case law but I can point to exemplary judgments showing what could have been done, eg in *Muirhead and Turnbull v Dickson* (1905) 7 F 686 (IH) 695 a contract's clearly referring to instalment payments was interpreted to convey the way a price for a sale was to be paid, and not to convey the specific option aspect of hire purchase:

> The plain lesson to be derived I hope from the judgment is this, that when parties wish to bind persons to a contract with unusual stipulations they must bring that contract clearly to their knowledge, and that, on the other hand, if they use words which are capable of ordinary interpretation, they must expect the persons who hear them to take them up in their ordinary significance.

Leaving aside wider issues, an irresolvable lack of clarity about the facts of this case will have undermined its value as authority.

[58] After a certain point, of course, hire purchase, even if seen as unfair, had become so important that judicial insistence that it fundamentally display the contractual characteristics of agreement and bargain would have been unwise as the basic reform this implied could be undertaken only by Parliament. In his book on consumer credit, Professor Diamond maintained his long held view that 'it may be that the whole subject was created by a legal misapprehension; but whether or not this is so, it is too late to turn back the clock': Diamond, *Credit* (n 32) 95.

[59] Law Reform Committee, *Twelfth Report* (n 14) para 23 n.

reflected the interests of the commercial supplier. But a tendentious contract does not actualise the relational essence of the law of contract. Though I have acknowledged the indeed undeniable justification of hire purchase as security for the hirer, this specific form of security, which was bound to catch a good faith consumer who had got into financial difficulty, an inevitable situation to which that security allowed a completely unfit response,[60] cannot be explained as a *necessary* provision against unauthorised disposition, save insofar as the supplier's interests enjoyed such overwhelmingly greater recognition than the hirer's as to defeat the justification of exchange and contract. Unauthorised disposition was, after all, breach, and was also conversion (and, with the requisite intent, could be fraudulent conversion and larceny).[61] The point of hire purchase was, not to provide security, but to extend security beyond that which the laws reflecting objective expectations about ownership and sale anchored in business efficacy already provided.

This is insufficiently appreciated because the evaluation of the benefit of hire purchase tends to focus exclusively on the consumer. Though hire purchase came to have some importance for commercial parties, its overwhelming significance was its role in the growth of mass consumer contracting, by which goods not previously available to common citizens were brought within their reach, an instance of the market economy's civilising augmentation of the wealth, not merely of an elite, but of a greatly widening proportion of all citizens. The enormous use of hire purchase from the later nineteenth century onwards is more than sufficient evidence that it was a response to a widespread consumer demand to buy relatively expensive durable goods on credit, and so have use of them prior to paying their price.[62]

But whilst it was a method of financing the consumer's use prior to payment of the price, the corollary of this is that it was also a method of financing sales by suppliers which, as it was put by Goddard LJ in the first case to come up under the 1938 Act: 'also could not afford to wait for their money. When one is considering … hire purchase finance one has to remember that the whole object of the business is to finance the dealer'.[63] Remedies for breach of contract or tort are of little value against an impecunious buyer, and the precise purpose of hire purchase was, by giving tantamount to an absolute remedy against the goods, to allow sales to those one might well fear were not sufficiently creditworthy, without the seller having to guard against the likelihood of

[60] It was unfit on the assumption that such financial difficulty was to be avoided. But, of course, it was perfectly fit if the aim actually was to encourage hiring by those who were likely to encounter such difficulty in order to snatch back the subject matter, retaining the payments made. The authors of the Institute of Economic Affairs' study mentioned above, Harris, Naylor, and Selden, *Hire Purchase* (n 32) 26, commendably objectively tell us that they had heard

> of examples, some well vouched for, of traders who came into the business with the object of allowing customers to fall into arrears (preferably towards the end of the contract but before the hirer could become the legal owner) and then suddenly foreclosing the contract and snatching back the goods under the guise of repossession.

[61] *R v Wynn* (1887) 56 LT 749 (Crown Case Reserved). It seems highly likely that almost all consumer hirers will have subjectively believed that they could legally sell the goods if they kept up the instalments.

[62] P Johnson, *Saving and Spending: The Working Class Economy in Britain 1870–1939* (Clarendon Press 1985) 155–62.

[63] *Menzies v United Motor Finance Corporation* [1940] 1 KB 559 (CA). I refer the reader back to the wider criticism of the role of consumer debt in determining the size of the capitalist economies discussed in ch 3.

default, not least by assessing the buyer's actual ability to pay, when such assessment has not only since been made a feature of consumer credit,[64] but which would always be commonplace when extending commercial credit.[65]

The specific form of the hire purchase contract entirely privileged the interests of the supplier which had transferred possession without full payment but wanted to avoid the obvious risks of doing so, and it was because it was so tendentious that hire purchase could and did lead to great unfairness. An explanation of the 'emergence' of a law of this nature must in the first instance be based on the influence of sellers organised in powerful trade associations which backed the litigation in which hire purchase was developed, and prior to 1938 prevented legislation intended to protect the consumer.[66] But legal emergence of this sort, whilst it may reflect the power of certain business interests, does not reflect the values of freedom of contract.[67]

It is only if freedom of contract is regarded as the exercise of solipsistic self-interest that the emergence of hire purchase can be explained as the result of freedom of contract. This is, of course, quite wrong, but the classical law of contract did regard freedom of contract in just this way. In *Cramer and Co v Carlton*, the Court of Appeal insisted that the agreement 'must be construed according to its plain words', and concluded that the contract 'required punctual payment' so that the hirer's argument 'that an unpunctual payment was sufficient' was regarded as wholly unpersuasive. This strikes us now, not merely as deplorably callous in such a period manner as to evoke passages in Dickens, but to be so crudely formalistic as to be very poor law because it assumes that the intentions of the parties were expressed in the 'plain words' when this is the last thing one should assume.

Those plain words were in complete contradiction, not only of what consumers subjectively thought, but of what interpretation which placed proper weight on objective intentions about what is involved in a sale, particularly in light of the size of the 'price' stipulated in hire purchase contracts, should have yielded. Sir Gordon Borrie was right in his noted Hamlyn Lectures to argue that the courts had been far too 'timorous' in

[64] The stated goal of the current mandatory requirements could not be more different to the one behind the law which allowed snatch-back: Financial Conduct Authority, *Assessing Creditworthiness in Consumer Credit*, PS18/19 (FCA 2018) para 1.14:

> We want firms to make a reasonable assessment, not just of whether the customer will repay, but also of their ability to repay affordably and without this significantly affecting their wider financial situation. This should minimise the risk of financial distress to customers.

[65] The *Crowther Report* has a fascinating discussion of forms of instalment selling to consumers which depended 'on the collector knowing the households he calls on well enough to assess the upper limit of their creditworthiness': ibid para 2.1.55.

[66] M Lobban, 'Consumer Credit and Debt' in W Cornish, S Anderson, R Cocks, M Lobban, P Polden, and K Smith, *The Oxford History of the Laws of England*, vol 12 (OUP 2010) 869–76.

[67] Though Smith gave little weight to what would now be seen as consumer problems (A Smith, *The Wealth of Nations* in *The Glasgow Edition of the Works and Correspondence*, vol 2 (Clarendon Press 1976) 362), his contempt for 'the mean rapacity [and] the monopolising spirit . . . of merchants and manufacturers' (ibid 493) was part of a generally critical view of capitalists when competition was insufficiently well organised (ibid 163–64) as to align their action with the system of natural liberty (ibid 687) that passes unnoticed in most theoretical criticism of the market economy. Capitalists were:

> an order of men whose interest is never exactly the same with that of the public, who generally have an interest to deceive and even to oppress the public, and who accordingly have, upon many occasions, both deceived and oppressed it (ibid 267).

using the resources of the common law to recognise the interests of consumers.[68] But even this does not go far enough in capturing the way that the classical law, in not even pursuing the institutionalisation of the relational essence of contract, actively worked against such recognition. As a bargain for an actual hire, the price under a hire purchase contract was almost always exploitative. The consideration furnished by the consumer could be justified only because the contract was, in fact, interpreted as a sale. But when the payment conditions were breached, in however minor a way, the interpretation of the contract reverted to its being a hire! It is entirely right that courts which 'failed to realise … the true intention' of the parties to hire purchase contracts because they 'took the terms of the agreement literally' as if it genuinely was a hiring when it certainly was understood by the consumer to be a sale came to be regarded as in a 'major respect … open to censure'.[69] The question is how a 'contract' of this sort could ever have been a 'contract' at common law when it was institutionalised in flat defiance of the relational nature of contract expressed in legitimate intentions about what was involved in the exchange.

Though I have mentioned that legislation was passed only in 1938, public concern about hire purchase certainly can be traced back prior to *Helby v Matthews*, and whilst, as I have also mentioned, the role of the actions of organised business interests such as those that funded that case played in opposing regulation is highly significant, that opposition was successful only because of a contradiction in the criticism of hire purchase. Perhaps the most important *dictum* in *Helby v Matthews* is the following by Lord Macnaghten:

> The learned counsel for the respondents spoke of dealings of this sort with an air of righteous indignation as if they were traps for the extravagant and the impecunious—mere devices to tempt improvident people into buying things which they do not want and for which at the time they cannot pay. I think that is going too far.[70]

And the point is that even those highly critical of hire purchase accepted this. Hire purchase was justified because it was thought economically efficient to do so. After pointing out some of the shortcomings of the judgments which created hire purchase, Atiyah went on to say:

> I do not wish to imply that, as a matter of public policy, these decisions were necessarily undesirable; nor that, as a matter of economic efficiency, they may have been unsound. My point is the simpler one that the Courts did not see any question to be discussed here as a matter of common law.[71]

The problem as it was understood by Atiyah was, as I have mentioned above, that 'Freedom of contract, by this time, was … absolute'.

[68] G Borrie, *The Development of Consumer Law and Policy: Bold Spirits and Timorous Souls* (Stevens & Sons 1984). For Sir Gordon's view of the law of hire purchase see G Borrie, *Commercial Law* (6th edn, Butterworths 1988) ch 3.

[69] Diamond, *Credit* (n 32) 95.

[70] *Helby v Matthews* (n 11) 482.

[71] Atiyah, *Rise and Fall* (n 30) 696.

This, from certainly one of the greatest post-war books written on the common law of contract, *The Rise and Fall of Freedom of Contract*, shows the depth of our confusion. Hire purchase was developed in the way it was because of the mistaken identification of economic action with solipsistic self-interest characteristic of the classical law. Solipsistic self-interest may be deplored, but unless this identification is broken, it is ultimately justified because the economic benefits of 'the market' are thought to depend on allowing such action. In the case of hire purchase, the cost of making durable goods available to a mass consumer market was that many of the consumers were subjected to a hardship about which no reasonable person could feel other than grave disquiet, but, with various degrees of reluctance, it was concluded that the cost was worth paying.[72]

This conclusion has real substance and cannot be dismissed. The all but absolute reservation of title by hire purchase did serve a valuable purpose in giving the supplier a security in the goods without which, let us allow because it must to some degree be right, credit sales of consumer durables would have been more restricted. The absoluteness of the reservation of title by hire purchase would, let us again allow because it must be right, expand the number of credit sales beyond the number that would have been made were that security not absolute in this way. But what is the right number of such sales, and how can we come to identify it? It simply is not a Pareto optimisation argument to claim that the size of the expansion of the mass consumer market made possible by hire purchase was economically efficient because it promoted such a degree of growth. Though it is bound up in this, let us leave aside criticism of the 'consumerism' made possible by hire purchase. If one seeks to use the market to determine the right number of such sales through Pareto optimisation, one must try to establish the conditions for exchanges that are as close as possible to voluntary choices to be made about those sales; that is to say, one must try to ensure contracts are agreed bargains.[73]

Such bargains will not be made if the hire purchase market is based on a law which militates against them. We encounter again the fundamental misunderstanding about the nature of economic action that underpins the classical law of contract. The solipsistic self-interest of the commercial supplier is thought to be efficient because it expands the volume of hire purchase business. But in the sense of efficiency which is central to exchange properly understood, this is flatly a mistake. An optimising market balances costs and benefits in line with voluntary choice. A market cannot be optimising if the conditions of making a voluntary choice are not institutionalised in contract. The welfarist response to the failure of the classical law of contract turns on believing that this is the, not universal but common (the occasions cannot be coherently specified), result of the solipsistically self-interested conduct of parties, especially business organisations enjoying typically superior bargaining power, which is regarded as intrinsic to exchange and contract.

[72] Harris, Naylor, and Selden, *Hire Purchase* (n 33) 254–57.

[73] This is precisely *not* the swinging between left-wing 'controlling' and right-wing 'liberalising' ideologies authoritatively, if in my view ultimately uncomprehendingly, described in Aveyard, Corthorn, and Connell, *Consumer Credit* (n 36) 151–52.

This misrecognition of the ethical basis of exchange and contract can be discussed in a more general way if we turn to the attempt to handle, saving some specifically identified exceptions, another legal device fundamental to mass contracting: the exemption clause as it was used in standard forms generally.

How Are Exclusion Clauses Ever Agreed?

Striking down under statute and at common law

That the Unfair Contract Terms Act 1977[74] is misleadingly entitled because it does not address 'unfair terms' as a general category but only exclusion (or exemption) and limitation clauses has been a point of criticism since the Act was passed. One form of this criticism is, as it were, technically indisputable, though some such criticism can be made of all regulatory legislation, in that, despite the steps that were taken to curtail this,[75] the Act inevitably gave an incentive to devising ways of doing just what the Act purported to prevent by escaping the Act's scope.[76] But it was asked more generally why only these clauses are singled out when it can be said of all sorts of terms that they are unfair? In the first edition of his contract textbook after the passage of the Act, Atiyah wrote:

> It should first perhaps be stressed that the Act deals only with exemption clauses as that term is commonly understood. It does not, despite its title, deal with the whole subject of unfair contracts. Contracts can, in a broad way, be said to be unfair as a result of one [of] two causes: either the contract may impose an excessive burden on one party or it may impose too light a burden on the other party—for example by exclusion clauses. The 1977 Act does not in general have anything at all to say on contracts which impose too heavy a burden on one party, and it only deals with one of the ways in which too light a burden may be imposed on the other.[77]

This criticism became of great salience as an important driver of the subsequent attempt to address unfairness generally in consumer law which was examined earlier

[74] Hereafter UCTA. The prior legislation on which UCTA builds, with particular reference to hire purchase, was reviewed in the course of the argument for 'extending control' in Law Commission and Scottish Law Commission, *Exemption Clauses: Second Report* [1975] EWLC 69 (hereafter Joint Law Commissions, *Second Report*) paras 12–31. The link to the *Molony Report* is stressed in PKJ Thompson, *The Unfair Contract Terms Act 1977* (Butterworths 1978) 2–4.

[75] UCTA s 3(2)(b) and ss 4 (now repealed), 10, 13, and 25(1B) explicitly extend the Act's scope beyond terms which purport to 'exclude or restrict' liability for breach. That lacunae remained in the Act was quickly shown in A Nicol, 'How Potent Is the Magic of a Signature?' [1979] Cambridge Law Journal 273. The devices used to indirectly to effect exclusion were reviewed in D Yates, *Exclusion Clauses in Contracts* (2nd edn, Sweet & Maxwell 1982) 33–44 (hereafter Yates, *Exclusion Clauses*).

[76] B Coote, 'Unfair Contract Terms Act 1977' (1978) 41 Modern Law Review 312. Coote's argument is framed in terms of his 'definition of rights' view of exclusions which will be discussed, and rejected, in the text accompanying n 134. But even if one accepted Coote's view, it would not avoid creating the perverse incentive but merely alter its form.

[77] PS Atiyah, *An Introduction to the Law of Contract* (3rd edn, Clarendon Press 1981) 171. I have inserted 'of' where the text has 'or'. The text was amended to 'of' in the next edition: (4th edn, 1989) 323.

in this chapter, and though the extensive out of phase duplication of the controls upon exclusion clauses in consumer contracts which was a regrettable feature of the legislative history of that attempt[78] are now of much reduced importance, the incoherence of two regimes of differing scope and intent ultimately cannot be eliminated.[79] Although the Consumer Rights Act, s 62(8) seeks to integrate the wide ranging mandatory prohibitions of exclusion under ss 31, 47, 57, and 65 with the test of unfairness in s 62, what can be the rationale of the mandatory prohibitions if the exclusions they cover would not fall foul of s 62, given the general nature of that section? The issue is not at all the same as mandatory prohibition in some cases and the requirement of reasonableness in other cases under UCTA. The point of relevance here, however, is that the failure of the attempt to address unfairness generally follows from an antecedent failure to recognise why, though I would be the last to claim it was the result of a choate decision, the singling out of exclusion clauses, in both consumer and business-to-business contracts, is not merely legitimate but essential if we are to understand how to deal with those clauses properly.

UCTA was famously intended to obviate the necessity which the courts had felt to decide cases on incorporation[80] and interpretation[81] in such a way as to defeat exclusion clauses believed to be objectionable in substance but which, it was believed, had been agreed and did cover the breach. Lord Denning's attempt to aggregate to the courts a common law power to strike down exclusion clauses[82] for want of reasonableness, audaciously conceived as a counterpart to a legislative 'test of reasonableness',[83]

[78] Law Commission and Scottish Law Commission, *Unfair Terms in Contracts* [2002] EWLC 166 CP, para 2.22.

[79] I leave aside, first, the, one assumes now not of general significance, consequences for contracts entered into before 1 October 2015 of the partial duplication of what was called the 'old' and the 'new' laws in H Beale (eds), *Chitty on Contracts* (33rd edn, Sweet & Maxwell 2018) para 15-065; secondly, the consequences of the decision to provide private 'rights to redress' for loss caused by an 'aggressive commercial practice' under the Consumer Protection from Unfair Trading Regulations 2008 Pt 4A, SI 2008/1277 (as amended); and thirdly legislation directed at specific contracts, eg for package holidays: Package Travel and Linked Travel Arrangements Regulations 2018, SI 2018/634, reg 30.

[80] In *McCuthcheon v David MacBrayne Ltd* [1964] 1 WLR 125 (HL(Sc)) (hereafter *McCutcheon v MacBrayne*), the pursuer was able to use to his advantage the fact that his agent had never, during a long course of dealing, read a reasonably placed notice or a document he had repeatedly signed. In a judgment which raised the possibility of overruling *L'Estange* (ibid 134), Lord Devlin explicitly made the issue one of 'actual and not constructive' knowledge (ibid). Despite the resonance of His Lordship's observations about the 'world of make-believe which the law has created' as opposed to 'the real world in which transactions of this sort are done' (ibid 133), this approach simply is not compatible with the real world of standard form contracting, ie with the basis of consumers' affluence.

[81] In *Wallis, Son and Wells v Pratt and Haynes* [1911] AC 394 (HL), on facts which made it perverse to read 'warranty' as anything other than 'term creating liability for', the House of Lords held that a provision that the 'Sellers give no *warranty* expressed or implied' (emphasis added) did not cover a failure of the goods to correspond with description, ie a mandatory *condition*, which, to rub it in, the buyer could then elect to treat as a breach of warranty.

[82] Lord Denning MR made a particular attempt to integrate exclusions into his wider view of inequality of bargaining power in *Levison v Patent Steam Carpet Cleaning Co Ltd* [1978] QB 69 (CA) 78H–80A (hereafter *Levison v Patent Cleaning*).

[83] Having drawn a parallel to the *Working Paper* that led to Joint Law Commissions, *Second Report* (n 74) in *Gillespie Brothers and Co Ltd v Roy Bowles Transport Ltd, Rennie Hogg Ltd (Third Party)* [1973] QB 400 (CA) 416C (hereafter *Gillespie Brothers v Bowles* (CA)), Lord Denning went further in *Levison v Patent Cleaning* (n 82) 79E, which was handed down on 22 April 1977:

> there is a Bill now before Parliament which gives effect to the test of reasonableness. This is a gratifying piece of law reform: but I do not think we need wait for that bill to be passed into law.

was, in his remarkable way,[84] described in *Gillespie Brothers v Bowles* as merely frankness about these exercises in judicial ingenuity:

> The judges have, then, time after time, sanctioned a departure from the ordinary meaning. They have done it under the guise of 'construing' the clause. They assume that the party cannot have intended anything so unreasonable. So they construe the clause 'strictly'. They cut down the ordinary meaning of the words and reduce them to reasonable proportions. They use all their skill and art to this end ... I know that the judges hitherto have never confessed openly to the test of reasonableness. But it has been the driving force behind many of the decisions.[85]

Even if one accepts, as one should not, an argument that, because of the nature of its own conduct,[86] the *proferens* is not treated unjustly when this sort of thing is done,[87] the problem, of course, is the precedent set. Lord Denning was himself a leading force in the creation of the major source of such trouble, the 'rule of law' doctrine of 'fundamental breach',[88] which is, as it was intended to be, quite at odds with a coherent law of termination.[89] It was concluded that UCTA's passage has made the 'strict' laws of incorporation and interpretation of exclusion clauses, including in this sense fundamental breach as a rule of law, redundant in cases where the exclusion clause was objectionable, and therefore it had become possible to take a proper interpretative attitude to such clauses generally.[90]

Setting the irredeemable error of fundamental breach aside, it has to be said that Lord Denning's bark was generally worse than his bite. I have just quoted a passage from *Gillespie Brothers v Bowles*, one of Lord Denning's cases which became notorious for what I have called the audacity of his statements about what he was doing with

> You never know what may happen to a Bill. Meanwhile the common law has its own principles ready to hand.

[84] Similarly, in Lords debate on the Misrepresentation Bill Lord Denning told us that one reason he welcomed the Bill was that it would render supererogatory the effort that 'we have tried [to make] quite often in the Court of Appeal to get round [the] old law ... We have often said [in eg *Dick Bentley Productions Ltd v Harold Smith (Motors) Ltd* [1965] 1 WLR 623 (CA)] that these representations are really warranties [and so] have managed to make [sellers] liable': HL Deb 17 May 1966, vol 274, col 940.

[85] *Gillespie Brothers v Bowles* (CA) (n 83) 415D–E, 416C.

[86] It absolutely was not accepted in the rejection of fundamental breach about to be discussed, because it was not accepted that the *proferens*' conduct was objectionable according to the basic doctrine of interpretation of agreement.

[87] This attitude towards interpretation is an acute example of the problem of, in effect, all the forms of the criticism of the refusal to inquire into adequacy noted in MJ Trebilcock, *The Limits of Freedom of Contract* (Harvard University Press 1993) 249:

> singling out [a] particular contracting party or class of contracting party to bear a disproportionate share of the burden of some larger community commitment to distributive justice values, simply by virtue of the relative fortuity of their interaction with victims of inequality, itself offends a sense of justice.

[88] *Photo Production Ltd v Securicor Transport Ltd* [1978] 1 WLR 856 (CA) 863F–864B; rvsd [1980] AC 827 (HL).

[89] ibid (HL) 844E–G, 844A–845D.

[90] ibid 845B–E and, on the situation as things have developed, *Persimmon Homes Ltd v Ove Arup and Partners Ltd* [2017] EWCA Civ 373, [2017] 2 CLC 28 [56]–[57] (Jackson LJ).

'reasonableness'. But were it not for these audacious statements, I do not think the exclusion aspect of *Gillespie Brothers v Bowles* would be thought to pose a particular problem.[91] In that case, the claimant watch sellers bought three expensive watches from a continental manufacturer for immediate resale to an overseas buyer, transit to be arranged by a forwarding agent, which engaged a third party carrier to transport the watches. After the watches were permitted to be stolen in transit by the negligence of the carrier's employee, the claimant successfully claimed in tort against the carrier, with which it was not in privity. The matter of relevance here, the subject of third party proceedings, was whether the forwarding agent was obliged to indemnify the carrier under the Road Haulage Association's Conditions of Carriage (1967) which were found to be incorporated into their contract, clause 3(4) of which provided that 'The [forwarder] shall save harmless and keep the carrier indemnified against all claims or demands whatsoever by whomsoever made in excess of the liability of the carrier under these conditions'.

Browne J at first instance[92] and the Court of Appeal rightly saw this indemnity as calling for the same approach as an exclusion, and both courts also rightly relied heavily on *Canada Steamship Lines Ltd v The King*[93] when deciding whether clause 3(4) provided for an indemnity against a party's own negligence. Basing their decisions on a distinction which was described as 'a fine one',[94] Brown J found that it did, and the Court of Appeal unanimously found that it did not. The point, however, is that the matter was treated as one of interpretation of the clause. Now, because Buckley LJ[95] and Orr LJ[96] confined themselves to this whilst Lord Denning MR expressed himself, as we have seen, in terms of common law 'reasonableness' understood in a way similar to the rule of law view of fundamental breach, his judgment seems quite apart from those of his brethren.[97] This was not really so.

Lord Denning's judgment could in fact readily be expressed in terms of interpretation without any recourse to his audacious views about departing from 'ordinary meaning' when 'reasonableness' required it. Having set out those views, Lord Denning then said that:

[91] This case was one of those caught up in the meddling in the carriage of goods by the law of negligence discussed in ch 5. It is of considerable interest, but the detail of it is only an aspect of matters addressed in that discussion, that a limitation clause in the contract between the claimant and forwarding agent led the claimant to bring its claim against, not the forwarder, but the defendant carrier with which the claimant was not in privity.

[92] *Gillespie Bros and Co Ltd v Roy Bowles Transport Ltd, Rennie Hogg Ltd (Third Party)* [1971] 2 *Lloyd's Law Reports* 521 (QBD).

[93] [1952] AC 292 (PC) (hereafter *Canada Steamship v The King*).

[94] *Gillespie Brothers v Bowles* (CA) (n 83) 421F.

[95] ibid 417G, 420II:

> The decision of this case depends, in my opinion, on the proper interpretation to be given to one word, 'whatsoever' ... In my judgment, it signifies that the indemnity is intended to extend to all claims and demands of whatsoever kind, that is to say, without exception.

[96] ibid 421E-F:

> this appeal should be allowed on the ground that the words 'all claims or demands whatsoever' constitute ... an agreement in express terms to indemnify the carrier against all claims or demands without exception and therefore including those arising from the negligence of the carrier or his servants.

[97] I put to one side the detail of the Court of Appeal's treatment of *Canada Steamship v The King* (n 93).

> none of that applies to the present case, because [clause 3(4)], as I see it, when given its ordinary meaning, is perfectly fair and reasonable. When a clause is reasonable, and is reasonably applied, it should be given effect according to its terms.[98]

But what determined that the test of reasonableness need not be applied? It is that, in the context of the business relationship at issue, reasonable parties could have agreed it:

> It is perfectly fair to put the responsibility on to the forwarding agents. They have been employed by the owner of the goods to make the necessary arrangements for him. They should see that the owner of the goods has insured the goods (as he probably has) or they themselves should take out an insurance to cover the goods. But all we have to decide is whether the indemnity clause avails the carriers against the forwarding agents. I think it does.[99]

By this sort of, with respect, non-argument, an indemnity against one's own negligence, ie the sort of thing Lord Denning would never normally countenance, became ordinary meaning. One can see why Lord Denning reached his conclusion. The difficulty is that he cannot himself explain why, certainly not nearly as well as his brethren explained the interpretation of the contract by which they arrived at the same outcome.[100] In one of those instances when Lord Denning strains the belief one normally holds in his complete frankness, he concluded by saying that he was 'glad to find' authority for what he did in the 1961 judgment of Paull J in *Harris (L) (Harella) Ltd v Continental Express Ltd, and Burns Transit Ltd*.[101] The precedent is, indeed, four square, except insofar as Paull J did not, of course, make any reference to the possibility of reasonableness trumping ordinary meaning but simply interpreted the contract.

Obtaining agreement

The main reason why Lord Denning argued in this way emerges from consideration of what remains, even now, the most instructive case on exclusion clauses: *L'Estrange v F Graucob*.[102] The claimant, the sole proprietor of a small café business conducted on premises in which she also lived, bought an automatic cigarette dispensing machine from the defendant, a much larger business manufacturing and selling automatic vending machines. The machine never worked satisfactorily and after a month the claimant sought to reject it as, *inter alia*, unfit for purpose under the Sale of Goods Act 1893 s 14(1),[103] and sought to recover the payments she had so far made.[104] The

98 *Gillespie Brothers v Bowles* (CA) (n 83) 416B–C.
99 ibid 417E–F.
100 Orr LJ's judgment adds a brief supplement to his basic agreement with Buckley LJ.
101 [1961] 1 Lloyd's Rep 251 (QBD).
102 [1934] 2 KB 394 (KBD) (hereafter *L'Estrange*).
103 1979 Act, s 14(3). It is immaterial to the discussion here that the breach would appear to sound better as one of merchantability or satisfactory quality.
104 There is difficulty about the various sums awarded as reported, and in particular the sum the claimant was awarded by the County Court seems to be incomprehensible: *L'Estrange* (n 102) 401, 404.

defendant, which had installed and sought to repair the machine, did not accept this ground of rejection, but was eventually obliged to rely on an exclusion of liability for breach stated in the written sales agreement, which provided that 'any express or implied condition, statement, or warranty, statutory or otherwise not stated herein is hereby excluded'. The claimant had not read the clause, but this did not avail her, in fact it ultimately had quite the opposite effect, the Divisional Court unanimously finding against her, with Scrutton LJ famously saying:

> In this case the plaintiff has signed a document headed 'Sales Agreement', which she admits had to do with an intended purchase, and which contained a clause excluding all conditions and warranties. That being so, the plaintiff, having put her signature to the document and not having been induced to do so by any fraud or misrepresentation, cannot be heard to say that she is not bound by the terms of the document because she has not read them.[105]

The result was a disaster for the claimant personally, for, in addition to the costs of the action, her liability under accelerated instalment payment provisions in the contract would seem to have made her overall liable to pay the entire price of, I believe, £81 19s 6d (now *circa* £6,000) for a machine she did not want.[106] But the case has also been a disaster for the law of contract.

For *L'Estrange* has led to the law of incorporation by signature being understood to be one of almost absolute imposition of an austere objective standard, the acknowledged exceptions to 'the rule in *L'Estrange v Graucob*' being marginal.[107] In a recent, in this respect entirely representative, statement, *L'Estrange* was cited as authority for the statement that:

> The usual test for contract formation, as for construction of legal documents, is an objective one. In the normal case, the outward appearance of agreement ... by signature on a document ... will be sufficient, regardless of the parties' subjective states.[108]

The absoluteness of our understanding of the rule in *L'Estrange v Graucob* is in sharp contrast, however, to the ambivalence of the atmosphere of the case itself.[109] The case

[105] ibid 404. This view was essentially repeated by Maugham LJ: ibid 406.

[106] ibid 404.

[107] JR Spencer, 'Signature, Consent and the Rule in *L'Estrange v Gaucob*' [1973] Cambridge Law Journal 104 (hereafter Spencer, 'The Rule'). The argument here draws heavily on this outstanding paper, seeking, however, to press further than Spencer the change from an inadequate concept of agreement plus exceptions into an adequate concept of objective agreement implicit in this generalisation: RA Samek, 'The Objective Theory of Contract and the Rule in *L'Estrange v Garucob*' (1974) 52 Canadian Bar Review 351.

SA Boosen, 'Rethinking the Signature Rule' [2013] Lloyd's Maritime and Commercial Law Quarterly 21 places the Singaporean case *Als Memasa v UBS AG* [2012] SGCA 43; 4 SLR 992 in the context of other relatively recent English and Commonwealth decisions which broadly develop Spencer's line.

[108] *Green Deal Marketing Southern Ltd v Economy Energy Trading Ltd* [2019] 2 All ER (Comm) 191 [95]. I have omitted Judge Keyser QC's general reference to offer and acceptance which, though right in itself, detracts from the specific issue about signature after *L'Estrange*.

[109] The contested nature of what now is typically presented a monolithic law is very strikingly conveyed in the seminal O Prausnitz, *The Standardisation of Commercial Contracts in English and Continental Law* (Sweet & Maxwell 1937). *L'Estrange* is discussed at 28, 41, and 86.

was regarded as deplorable at the time,[110] Maugham J began his judgment by saying 'I regret the decision to which I have come',[111] and, if my understanding of the then procedure is not at fault, that a Divisional Court of this composition was felt necessary surely shows that there was an awareness of the sensitivities involved in reversing what seems to be, from the Divisional Court's account of it, an exemplary County Court judgment for the claimant on liability.[112] The forthrightness of Scrutton LJ's language was perhaps a response to this particular ambivalence, but it undoubtedly indicated a general cast of mind,[113] and it has not aged well. Though he cites another of Scrutton's cases in support of his view,[114] it was no doubt with *L'Estrange* also in mind[115] that Atiyah said that Scrutton:

> had a high reputation as a commercial lawyer ... But ... was unable to see the point of view of the consumer in contractual relationships. His long experience as a commercial barrister, almost invariably acting on behalf of commercial clients, combined with the general traditions of English contract law, made him see all consumers in the same light as the classical economists had done a hundred years previously. He was certainly not the kind of man who would have signed a contract without reading it, and he had no sympathy with the consumer who did so.[116]

Atiyah's criticism is, with respect, wrong from, as it were, two opposite directions. Sir Thomas Scrutton may in his personal affairs never have signed a document without reading it, though I very much doubt it, but if he, for example, ever had water in his house, not to speak of ever having got on a train, he certainly contracted on terms he had not read. That one could think that the solution to the problems of exclusion clauses is the actual negotiation of those clauses is, as Atiyah would, of course, generally insist, actually part of the problem.[117] Looking at the matter the other way, Scrutton LJ undoubtedly was addressing a very serious problem, and the position he took was a rational one. In *Blay v Pollard and Morris*,[118] he had rightly told us that 'It would be very dangerous to allow a man over the age of legal infancy to escape from the legal effect of a document he has, after reading it, signed, in the absence of an express misrepresentation by the other party of that legal effect.' How much more dangerous would it be to let a party use not reading the document as a defence?

But though Scrutton LJ's response was rational, it was not, it is submitted, remotely adequate. Maugham LJ told us that he 'could wish that the contract had been in a

[110] PA L[andon], 'Note on *L'Estrange v Graucob*' (1935) 51 Law Quarterly Review 272 (hereafter Landon, 'Note'): 'The decision ... is a menace to the community'.

[111] *L'Estrange* (n 102) 405.

[112] But see n 104.

[113] Which has been discussed in ch 4 as it was evidenced in Scrutton LJ's judgment in *Ronaasen and Son v Arcos Ltd* (1932) 43 Ll L Rep 1 (CA).

[114] *Newsholme Bros v Road Transport and General Insurance Co Ltd* [1929] 2 KB 356 (CA). The facts of this case manage to exaggerate the questionable aspects of *L'Estrange*.

[115] D Foxton, *The Life of Thomas E Scrutton* (CUP 2013) 278.

[116] Atiyah, *Rise and Fall* (n 30) 663–64.

[117] In Landon, 'Note' (n 110) 273 this, I am afraid unavailing, advice is given: 'we, the public, must learn the lesson, and must resolutely refuse to sign contracts excluding liability on the part of the seller'.

[118] [1930] 1 KB 628 (CA) 633.

simpler and more usual form',[119] and indeed the clause was presented in small print, on brown paper, in a document signed at the initial sales meeting and separate from later important documents, with the defendant's sales representatives' oral guidance, whilst not being actively misleading, being the opposite of fulsome. In light of this, the County Court had found for the claimant because, as Scrutton LJ told us:

> the learned judge asked himself the three questions appropriate to these cases, and in answering them has found as facts: (i) that the plaintiff knew that there was printed material on the document which she signed, (ii) that she did not know that the document contained conditions relating to the contract, and (iii) that the defendants did not do what was reasonably sufficient to bring these conditions to the notice of the plaintiff.[120]

The three questions had been laid down by Lord Herschell LC in *Richardson, Spence and Co v Rowntree*,[121] a railway case, and Scrutton LJ readily distinguished *L'Estrange* from such cases because of the signature. But Scrutton LJ was by no means closed to the sort of argument broadly implied in Lord Herschell's questions. In *Roe v RA Naylor Ltd*,[122] he had been a member of a Court of Appeal which, referring to those questions, unanimously affirmed two decisions below[123] which found for a claimant in a similar position to *L'Estrange*. The difference between the cases[124] was that in *Roe v Naylor* the clause was even more awkwardly presented, being contained in a document which it was much more problematic to claim was part of an initially oral contract, whereas it will be recalled that in *L'Estrange* Scrutton LJ placed great emphasis on the 'plaintiff [having] signed a document headed 'Sales Agreement', which she admits had to do with an intended purchase, and which contained a clause excluding all conditions and warranties'.

It was not, then, that Scrutton LJ himself took what has become the absolute view of signature for which *L'Estrange* is now generally taken to be authority. But, to go straight to the point, Scrutton LJ had a very limited concept of what a *proferens* had to do to assist the other party to understand the agreement, that concept seeming to require an active step which, intentionally or otherwise, misled the other party in order to come into play.[125] But this, with respect, is a very inadequate approach to take towards determining what, as Scrutton LJ insisted, not merely in cases like *Roe v Naylor*[126] but in *L'Estrange* itself, is the basic issue, expressed in the third of Lord Herschell's questions: did the *proferens* 'do what was reasonably sufficient to bring

[119] *L'Estrange* (n 102) 407.
[120] ibid 402.
[121] [1894] AC 217 (HL) 219.
[122] (1918) 87 LJKB 958 (CA) 963–65 (hereafter *Roe v Naylor*).
[123] The County Court judgment was, of course, unreported, but the judgment of a Divisional Court composed of Bailhache and Atkin JJ is reported at [1917] 1 KB 712 (KBD).
[124] Scrutton LJ did not discuss the case in *L'Estrange*, but Maugham LJ distinguished it on the ground of the initially oral contract: *L'Estrange* (n 102) 406.
[125] The approach Scrutton LJ took is analysed in terms of the decided law on what became the rule and its exceptions in Spencer, 'The Rule' (n 107).
[126] *Roe v Naylor* (n 122) 965: 'the question in my view is one of fact: [has] the [*proferens*] taken reasonable care, taken reasonable precautions, to bring [the exclusion] to the notice of the other party?'.

these conditions to the notice of the plaintiff'. Scrutton LJ's approach applied generally to incorporation and interpretation of exclusions was bound to lead to ingenious judicial attempts to avoid the consequences of what appeared to be the absolute rule, and so to the apparent necessity of passing UCTA. But how much more doctrinally economical it would be to have a common law which simply asks what could be reasonably required of the *proferens* in the circumstances, including where necessary taking active steps to make objective agreement actual.[127] It would be, it is submitted, preposterous to think the way the defendant in *L'Estrange* conducted negotiations satisfied this test.

What is required is to reinterpret the *entire* law on the agreement[128] of exclusion clauses[129] in the light of Denning LJ's famous *dictum*

[127] The first, as it were, technical obstacle one encounters is the, if not unnuanced (B Nicholas, 'The Pre-contractual Obligation to Disclose Information: English Report' in D Harris and D Tallon (eds), *Contract Law Today* (Clarendon Press 1989)), then certainly general antipathy to disclosure which follows from seeing competition in terms of solipsistic self-interest, of which A Leff, 'Contract as Thing' (1970) 19 American University Law Review 131, 156–57 said:

> attempts *not* to regulate quality, but instead to increase the availability and quality of information upon which buying (market) decisions are based, have good sense behind them ... viewing ... disclosure not in the old contract-interpretation terminology but in a more realistic context, more attuned to what happens at retail, to the ultimate production of more *actual* information disclosure ... fuller *message* disclosure, at relatively small information cost ... might increase the power of the market itself to control the price-quality mix.

I cannot develop the argument at this point but this approach to agreement surely gains strength from the, in terms of the principle of requiring that active steps be taken, completely unproblematic, disclosure requirements for an effective ouster of default reasonable contemplation under the second limb of *Hadley v Baxendale* (1854) 9 Exch 341, which is examined in the course of the discussion of remedies in ch 8.

[128] M Chapman, 'Common Law Contract and Consent: Signature and Objectivity' (1998) 49 Northern Ireland Legal Quarterly 363. Behind the issue of incorporation by notice, the argument for making actual the conditions of objective agreement by notice should, as Chapman does, be extended to encompass the basic principles of all common law interpretation: J McCunn, 'The *Contra Proferentem* Rule: Contract Law's Great Survivor' (2019) 39 Oxford Journal of Legal Studies 483.

[129] I have no competence to look at the entire history of the exclusion clause, but the cases I have read lead me to the belief that, not merely that scrutiny of the conditions of objective agreement in the sense of Lord Herschell's questions, but even of what Lord Denning in this *dictum* indicates may be necessary, was common in cases prior to *L'Estrange*: eg in *Crooks v Allan* (1879) 5 QBD 38 (QBD) 40 Lush J held that a party which wanted to rely on:

> a clause which not only deprives the shipper of an ancient and well understood right, but which might avoid his policy and deprive him also of recourse to the underwriter, [that party] ought not only to make it clear in words, but also to make it conspicuous by inserting it in such type and in such a part of the document as that a person of ordinary capacity and care could not fail to see it.

L'Estrange, and all cases in this area, were of course, decided in the shadow of *Parker v South Eastern Railway Co* (1877) LR 2 CPD 416 (CA) (hereafter *Parker*), but it is hard to think that what CJ Slade, 'The Myth of Mistake in the English Law of Contract' (1954) 70 Law Quarterly Review 385, 388 called 'The celebrated test laid down by Mellish LJ [in *Parker*, ibid 424]: "Did the [*proferens*] do what was reasonably sufficient to give the plaintiff notice of the conditions"', has been read as it should in the modern law. However, of the Victorian history of exclusions by railway companies, RW Kostal, *Law and English Railway Capitalism 1825–75* (OUP 1997) 319 tells us that:

> When in the 1850s railway companies began to experiment with contractual ... conditions exonerating companies['] liability [to passengers] for loss or injury ... they were soon made to realise that the experiment would not be permitted to succeed. Sensing the extreme hostility of the judges to the inclusion of express waivers and exculpatory clauses in railway ticket contracts, the companies appear to have quickly abandoned the initiative.

regarding one of those circumstances, the nature of the clause, in *J Spurling Ltd v Bradshaw*:[130]

> I quite agree that the more unreasonable a clause is, the greater the notice which must be given of it. Some clauses which I have seen would need to be printed in red ink on the face of the document with a red hand pointing to it before the notice could be held to be sufficient.

This 'red hand' or 'red ink rule'[131] approach is quite distinct from Lord Denning's test of substantive reasonableness, which there was not merely no reason to employ, but every reason not to employ. That the *Spurling v Bradshaw* clause would be 'unreasonable' is not an internal property of the clause itself, as Lord Denning effectively admitted when allowing the clause *could* be incorporated, but is the result of the *proferens* (to a marked degree) ousting the default and not doing nearly enough to make this clear.[132] For what is always involved in an exclusion is an ousting of a reasonable belief in the availability of remedies for breach of contract. There is, it is submitted, no problem in principle with setting such active requirements as are necessary for a *proferens* to effect that ouster by conducting negotiations in a way which allows it to be other than a joke to say there was objective agreement.[133] A common law which gave full weight to these requirements would, it is submitted, itself have rendered unnecessary the unsatisfactory reasoning to which UCTA was a legislative response, and

[130] [1956] 1 WLR 461 (CA) 466.

[131] S Kapnoullas and B Clarke, 'Fine Print in Contracts: From "Invisible Ink" Cases to "Red Ink" Rules' (1993) 19 Melbourne University Law Review 92 and S Kapnoullas and B Clarke, 'Incorporation of Unreasonable Terms into Contracts: The Red Hand Rule and Signed Documents' (2006) 11 Deakin Law Review 95.

[132] In E McDonald, 'The Duty to Give Notice of Unusual Contract Terms' [1988] Journal of Business Law 375, 385 it is regretted that a red hand rule 'cannot prevent [the *proferens*] having a very unusual or unreasonable clause in any contract he makes'. But it cannot be the legitimate purpose of such a rule to mandatorily prevent incorporation of such a clause, save in the sense that one can ask whether, with appropriate notice, the clause could remain 'very unusual or unreasonable'.

[133] I do not for a moment deny two extremely important points. First, a common law which still is classical in the sense that it in part regards negotiation based on the stronger negotiating party as, up to a remote point, legitimate is bound to continually yield undesirable outcomes, and Professor McMeel is to be congratulated on being to the forefront of those seeking to draw our attention to an egregious modern example in the 'doctrine of contractual estoppel', a deplorable development traceable to an innovation first endorsed by the Court of Appeal as recently as 2006: *Peekay Intermark Ltd v Australia and New Zealand Banking Group Ltd* [2006] EWCA Civ 386; [2006] 2 Lloyd's Rep 511; rvsg [2005] EWHC 830 (Comm); [2005] 2 CLC 111, which has led to a flood of disputed case law: G McMeel, 'Documentary Fundamentalism in the Senior Courts: The Myth of Contractual Estoppel' [2011] Lloyd's Maritime and Commercial Law Quarterly 185 and G McMeel, *The Construction of Contracts* (3ed edn, OUP 2017) paras 25.52–26.76.

Secondly, one must recognise the general point that the practical determination of the necessary requirements for negotiating conduct is inherently difficult, even if one believes the common law enjoys an inherent advantage over legislation in doing this, and the point could not be more graphically illustrated than it has been in the surety cases following *Barclays Bank plc v O'Brien* [1994] 1 AC 180 (HL) culminating in *Royal Bank of Scotland v Etridge (No 2)* [2001] UKHL 44, [2002] AC 773. I must say, however, that a great deal of the difficulty stems from a lack of clarity about what precisely was objectionable about the 'undue' influence in these cases and so about the aim of the advice required. The extent to which this lack was dispelled by what I would call the business efficacy approach taken in the Court of Appeal's judgment in *Etridge* is highly instructive: [1998] 4 All ER 705 (CA).

would have rendered unnecessary the legislative setting of standards for incorporation which generate their own difficulties.

Exclusion clauses are, in sum, not a subset of the set of substantively unfair clauses. Exclusion clauses have the specific procedural form of being an ouster of the default law, and as such can and should merit specific attention. It was some recognition of this that led Adams and Brownsword to firmly dismiss Coote's 'definition of rights' view of exclusions[134] as 'elegantly formalistic[, ignoring] both the historical development of the problem and the realities of the situation'.[135] Coote argued that exclusions did not work as exclusions of liability for breach, ie as a matter of the secondary obligations which the *proferens* undertook, but defined the primary obligations the *proferens* undertook: a sale of a horse with an exclusion of liability for soundness was never a contract to sell a sound horse.

Now, of course, a contract may be drafted specifically to try to avoid (statutory) limitations on exclusion of liability by defining primary obligations in this way. But as a matter of the general nature of exclusions, even when the drafting just mentioned has been attempted, Coote is, with respect, seriously wrong. For the great bulk of any contract is not expressly defined. It is a matter of an underlying relationship, parts of which the law sometimes fixes as required as implied terms, which, when it can be varied, can be varied only by agreement.[136] The most important term, if it can be put this way for the purposes of argument, of all contracts is the secondary obligation to provide a remedy. As we have seen in Chapter 1, the reason parties enter into a contract is to thereby create legally enforceable expectation interests in the improvements of their positions. As will be seen in Chapter 8, in the standard case they intend to perform, and by default to be awarded compensatory damages if the other party does not perform. It is right that this can be varied or waived by agreement, but this must be by objective agreement which does enough to make the ouster of the default clear. Coote's definitional view must obscure this fundamental understanding because it is, with respect, a legalistic caricature of contracting which simply does not grasp that exchange and contract are possible only because they are grounded in a relationship of mutual recognition, of which the default provision of an adequate compensatory remedy is part.

[134] B Coote, *Exception Clauses* (Sweet & Maxwell 1964) 7–11. Coote's view was taken up by another leading commentator on exclusions, David Yates: *Exclusion Clauses* (n 75) 123–33 and N Palmer and D Yates, 'The Future of the Unfair Contract Terms Act 1977' [1981] Cambridge Law Journal 108. The drafting of UCTA s 3(2) is, of course, an attempt to deal with draftsmen's specific attempts to give effect to this approach.

[135] JN Adams and R Brownsword, 'The Unfair Contract Terms Act: A Decade of Discretion' (1988) 104 Law Quarterly Review 94, 95–96.

[136] E Durkheim, *Division of Labour* (Macmillan 1984) 161–62:

> contractual law exists to determine the legal consequences of those of our acts that we have not settled beforehand. It expresses the normal conditions for attaining equilibrium, as they have evolved gradually from the average case ... what we could not regulate is regulated, and this regulation is mandatory upon us, although it is not our handiwork but that of society and tradition ... Viewed in this light, the law of contract ... is no longer a useful supplement to individual agreements., but their basic norm ... We can only depart from it in part ... In particular cases we can renounce some rights and relieve ourselves of some duties. Both nevertheless represent the normal type of rights and duties that the circumstances entail, and deliberate action must be taken if we wish to modify them ... The law of contract ... is a law that can be changed only by the agreement of the parties concerned.

The moral stance of the *proferens*

I have claimed that there is no problem in principle with setting extensive, active requirements which a *proferens* must satisfy to secure incorporation. What clearly is a problem is putting the agreement between the parties into the context of their contractual relationship.[137] Behind Scrutton LJ's inadequately limited view of the legal demands that should be made of the *proferens* lies an inadequately limited view of the economic relationship of the *proferens* and the other party. It is ultimately thought legitimate that the *proferens* should do only so much as it is compelled to do because its basic motivation is taken to be a solipsistic self-interest which posits, as we have seen, doing as little as possible. It is only on this basis that the conduct of the *proferens* in *L'Estrange* can be found acceptable. *L'Estrange* in fact offers us a remarkable and instructive illustration of the point.

In the Court of Appeal hearing of *L'Estrange*,[138] the leading counsel for the appellant *proferens* was AT Denning. Mr Denning enjoyed a particular professional success as a consequence of establishing the rule in *L'Estrange v Graucob*, but when some 43 years later, as the Master of the Rolls debating the Second Reading of the Unfair Contract Terms Bill, he looked back upon this success, he did so with the opposite of equanimity:

> I was engaged in a case many years ago which exemplified the old law as it existed. It was a case in which a salesman went to a little shop in North Wales and induced the shopkeeper, a lady, to buy an automatic machine from him, the price to be paid by instalments. He produced a long brown printed form and asked her to 'sign here', which she did without reading it. The automatic machine was delivered. It did not work. Mechanics were sent down three times. Still it did not work, and finally she said, 'I cannot pay the instalments'. So the company took her to the county court. There she said that the machine did not work. The company said, 'Look at the clause'. There it was in small print on the back of the form, 'Any condition or warranty, express or implied by Statute or by common law is hereby excluded'. The county court judge managed to get round this and found for the lady and I was instructed for the company in the Court of Appeal. At the Bar, I was concerned to win the case. I was not concerned with what was right or wrong. I said to Lord Justice Scrutton, producing some old cases, 'Look at this, she signed it. It doesn't matter that she didn't read it; it doesn't matter if she couldn't read it because the print was too small; it doesn't matter if it was most unreasonable. She is still bound.' Lord Justice Scrutton said, 'Yes, in the absence of fraud or misrepresentation she is bound to pay these instalments.' There she was, bound to pay the instalments for the machine that would not work.

[137] IR Macneil, 'Bureaucracy and Contracts of Adhesion' (1984) 22 Osgoode Hall Law Journal 5, 20–21. Macneil's takes as its starting point the—my word—impossible situation in which Lord Devlin found himself in *McCutcheon v MacBrayne* (n 80).

[138] From his speech on the Unfair Contract Terms Act which is about to be discussed, it would seem that Mr Denning did not appear for the defendant in the County Court.

> To tell you the sequel, my Lords, [the] reporter in the courts did not report the case at once. He did not think so much of it, but my company had it privately printed and I went round the county courts of England winning case after case, most unrighteously. That was the law as laid down in 1934 and it has remained so ever since.[139]

Lord Denning's claim that he was 'not concerned with what was right or wrong' encapsulates the issue at which this book is trying to drive. It cannot be taken literally, and yet it unarguably does describe an understanding of the moral quality of economic and contractual action definitive of the classical law that must be rejected. The professional lifetime which Lord Denning spent in repentance of this aspect of his career at the Bar shows the defectiveness of his self-understanding. The criticism which it is most appropriate and useful to make of Lord Denning is that in contract he rarely did what he believed he was doing. Although, as was discussed in Chapter 5, he had remarkable success, particularly in *Candler v Crane, Christmas and Co*,[140] in actually narrowing the contractual sphere, his contract judgments, though fundamental breach is a gross exception, were predicated on the basic values of an exchange economy, with which he tinkered in ignorance of the role those values have in making that economy work, and complacent disregard of the damage which might be done to those basic values. One might even allow that, with the passage of UCTA, his test of reasonableness was made into law, save that the test of reasonableness, as applied by himself as well as by others, is actually a poorly expressed test of agreement. The inevitable welfarist *ad hocery* caused by approaching the issues in terms of applying an exogenous standard to a system believed to be fundamentally defective, in which the concern to do justice undermines the uncomprehended system, has been described in Chapter 6.

Conclusion: The Substance and Form of Adequacy

It is essential not to conceive of the preceding argument as requiring the *proferens*, and by extension parties which in the circumstances enjoy a superiority in bargaining power, to act as the other party's fiduciary, and to conceive of the law behind this as the law of a 'fiduciary state'.[141] This is precisely not the argument's objective. Of its nature, a fiduciary relationship entails the fiduciary identifying with the interest of the principal in the outcome *for the principal*, indeed in many cases it is the agent which identifies the principal's interests, and this 'single-minded loyalty'[142] is inimical to the autonomy which simple contract seeks to institutionalise. Though such loyalty is, of course, required in the 'peculiar',[143] if commonplace, circumstances of a fiduciary contract

[139] HL Deb 23 May 1977, vol 383, col 1120.
[140] [1951] 2 KB 164 (CA).
[141] MJ Radin. 'The Fiduciary State and Its Ordering' in PB Miller and AS Gold (eds), *Contract, Status and Fiduciary Law* (OUP 2016).
[142] *Bristol and West Building Society v Mothew* [1998] Ch 1, 18B. In this definition of a fiduciary, Millett LJ uses 'good faith' in a restricted sense divorced from simple contracting which, whilst quite right in itself, is being criticised in this book.
[143] ibid 18A.

proper, we should say, drawing on our discussion of non-tuism in Chapter 5, that it is one thing to identify and seek to realise an outcome for a contractual party, but quite another to work to realise the conditions of mutual recognition which will allow that party to identify that outcome for itself by agreeing a contract.[144]

As was discussed in Chapter 6, inequality of bargaining power is ubiquitous. It is worse than pointless, then, to purport to isolate a contract unaffected by such inequality and identify and remedy the 'unreasonable' results of the cases claimed to be exceptional which are, in fact, if it is really inequality of bargaining power that we are objecting to, the norm. But it is not inequality of bargaining power to which we are objecting.[145] It is a failure to respond to circumstances which convey superiority of bargaining power in such a way as to make actual the conditions of objective agreement in those circumstances. It can seem plausible to endorse such a failure by enforcing its results if one believes economic action is based on solipsistic self-interest. Though I have tried to give a ground in the law of contract to Nozick's theory of just transfer, it must be said that this requires considerable labour against Nozick himself. His way of putting things, which could take the form of Gradgrindian or Smilesian rhetoric,[146] is not without an other-worldly dimension[147] which badly failed to capture the nature of the empirical contractual relationship, and the empirical legal framework, ie the state action, which institutionalises it.[148] Nozick himself came to realise this up to a

[144] It was argued in ch 2 that viewing relational contracts as a 'specie' of contracts detracts from the ability to recognise that all contracts are in a fundamental sense relational. The way that 'discrete' and 'relational' contracts should nevertheless be distinguished in light of this recognition is set out in ch 10. This should be taken into account when considering the way Leggatt LJ, as he then was, acutely identified the main point about fiduciary obligations in *(Al) Nehayan v Kent* [2018] EWHC 333 (Comm); [2018] 1 CLC 216 [167]:

> 'relational' contracts involve trust and confidence but of a different kind from that involved in fiduciary relationships. The trust is not in the loyal subordination by one party of its own interests to those of another. It is trust that the other party will act with integrity and in a spirit of co-operation.

[145] J Cartwright, *Unequal Bargaining* (Clarendon Press 1991) 218:

> [Lord Denning's] choice of 'inequality of bargaining power' ... is unfortunate. It can suggest that the courts will give relief simply on the basis of the unequal position of the parties, rather than on an *abuse* of that position.

[146] Nozick's attempt to explain what he believes is a general commitment to wealth maximisation, described as an economist's 'standard assumption' instead of as the peculiarly Posnerian rejection of Pareto optimality which it is (D Campbell, 'Welfare Economics for Capitalists: The Economic Consequences of Judge Posner' (2012) 33 Cardozo Law Review 2233), is an outré but nevertheless instructive example. Apparently, those having a 'genetically based heritable psychological predisposition to be (more) concerned with wealth' are able 'to produce more offspring', and so 'A heritable disposition to desire and strive for wealth would have been selected for': R Nozick, *The Nature of Rationality* (Princeton University Press 1993) 126–27.

[147] HLA Hart, '1776–1976: Law in the Perspective of Philosophy' in *Essays in Jurisprudence and Philosophy* (OUP 1983) 151:

> [the conditions under which ultra-minimal state] could be justified ... are conditions produced out of Nozick's lively imagination which are highly unlikely to be satisfied in the real as contrasted with the imaginary world.

[148] Nozick's most famous example of legitimate wealth is of the income of the great basketball player Wilt Chamberlain: R Nozick, *Anarchy, State and Utopia* (Basic Books 1974) 161–64. Nozick focuses on large crowds being prepared to pay to attend games to watch Chamberlain. But, of course, even in Chamberlain's

point, but his repentance of 'The libertarian position which I once propounded'[149] in truth detracted rather than added to what went before because it was a purely conventional recognition of certain social consequences of individual action, consequences which he might well have thought of previously, which did nothing to revise the basic understanding of that action. The principle which allows parties to identify their own legitimate interest is not solipsistic self-interest but self-interest actualised in mutual recognition, and legally institutionalised in good faith as the basis of the agreement of simple contracts.

To some extent, the issues discussed in this chapter arise because the nature of a claimant's concerns after what it believes is a breach inevitably gets our attitude towards adequacy off on the wrong foot. For those concerns *are* based on perceived substantive inadequacy as the claimant believes it has not obtained a benefit which justifies the detriment it suffered. No one is ever directly concerned about a want of correct procedure but rather is always directly concerned about a discrepancy between actual, ie substantial, benefit and actual detriment. The unworkability of a doctrine of consideration which inquires into adequacy and into the substance of benefit and detriment nevertheless shows that if the conditions of objective agreement were actually established, a party complaining of a want of substantial adequacy should be bound. If these conditions were not established, and the want of substantial adequacy may very possibly be evidence of this,[150] that party should not be bound. The test of being bound should be purely procedural.

It is at just this point, however, that the doctrinally sophisticated law of contract has dreadfully wavered over sanctity, even though the law of contract in practice has unproblematically regarded sanctity as normal. It is essential to the law of contract as a system of autonomy that a party which has made, let us allow for the purposes of argument, an inadequate bargain must take responsibility for it if that party could have objectively agreed it. And yet the substantive aspects of the common law of the vitiating factors and of unfairness in consumer law repeatedly pick away at this. It has been argued that it is acceptance of the inadequate concept of solipsistic self-interest which has played the major part in the belief, in doctrine at least, that large exceptions are required to be made to the law of exclusions in particular, and to the refusal to inquire into adequacy in general; a belief which has reached the absurd point where consumer law (legislation) itself seems to be a, to put it this way, general exception to the (common) law of contract. A law fashioned on an adequate conception of self-interest

day the main sources of professional sports revenue was not ticket receipts but broadcasting and merchandising, and these revenues were obtained under the protection of intellectual property rights. This famous example of what the ultra-minimal state would allow is, then, based on monopolies supported by an elaborate and extensive system of criminal sanctions and draconian civil remedies, both of which are intended to oust market competition.

[149] R Nozick, *The Examined Life* (Touchstone 1990) 286.

[150] GH Treitel, *The Law of Contract* (11th edn, Sweet & Maxwell 2003) 74:

> The fact that a person pays 'too much' or 'too little' for a thing may be evidence of fraud or mistake, or it may induce the court to imply a term as to the quality of the subject-matter ... But it does not of itself affect the validity of the contract.

This possibility was acknowledged in *Griffith v Spratley* (1787) 1 Cox Ch 383, 389; 29 ER 1213, 1215.

as mutual recognition would naturally incorporate all these exceptions,[151] for they would be integral to the institutionalisation of exchange as a mutually advantageous relation, ie of exchange which satisfies its own claim to legitimacy, by a law of contract which made actual the requirement that bargains be agreed.

[151] The reader is referred back to the discussion in ch 1 of IR Macneil, 'Review of H Shepherd and BD Sher, *Law in Society: An Introduction to Freedom of Contract*' (1960) 46 Cornell Law Quarterly 176, 177.

8

The Relational Constitution of Remedy (1)

Performance and Expectation

Introduction: The Holmesian Choice

Contracting parties' misunderstanding of the ethical nature of their exchange relationships is central to the remedies which the positive English law provides for non-performance of contractual obligations. It is necessary to distinguish two sets of remedies. The first is addressed to what familiar but, as we shall see, inaccurate usage calls the 'impossibility' of performance, and is composed of the doctrines of common mistake and frustration which excuse the non-performing party from liability, and therefore seek to apportion loss between the parties. Though the explanation of its existence is of great historical and theoretical interest, this set of remedies, which has always been wholly inappropriate to the law of contract, and is now of minor practical significance, is discussed in Chapter 10.

The second set is of the final remedies proper which a defendant may be required to furnish the claimant after the defendant has breached a primary obligation which it was strictly liable to perform. The explanation of these remedies in terms of providing legal security for those entering into an economic exchange, the essential function of contract, was set out in Chapter 2. In this chapter and Chapter 9, I examine and assess the various ways in which this set of remedies performs this essential function.

These remedies can initially be divided into compensatory damages and literal enforcement. It is argued that, despite the basic difference between damages and literal enforcement, all the remedies proper seek to make the defendant compensate the claimant for lost expectation, and in the course of doing so attempt, with very mixed degrees of success (which themselves will be explained), to establish a framework for co-operation over dealing with the consequences of non-performance by breach. The key to understanding the law, once again, lies in consciousness of its recognition of the

Contractual Relations. David Campbell, Oxford University Press. © David Campbell 2022.
DOI: 10.1093/oso/9780198855156.003.0008

mutual interests of, not only the claimant, but of both parties to the contract. When applied to what will be called the standard case of breach of contract, the law understood in this way is highly commendable. The undoubted shortcomings of the law, which are very much greater when dealing with the non-standard cases focused upon in Chapter 9, arise, once again, from solipsistic self-interest being mistakenly regarded as a legitimate motivation of economic action. Legitimate contractual action must pursue self-interest through a relationship of mutual recognition.

It is as well to start with the, to the classical view, paradoxical[1] and unacceptable permission to breach generally known as the 'Holmesian choice' because the most celebrated formulation of it was due to OW Holmes, which is the heart of the law of remedies. Compensatory damages are overwhelmingly the most common remedy for breach, with literal enforcement being exceptional.[2] As a matter of the positive law, compensatory damages are the 'default' remedy for breach, available as of right, and a claimant seeking literal enforcement must successfully make an argument which 'ousts' the default. This being so, then '[t]he only universal consequence of a legally binding promise is that the law makes the promisor pay damages if the promised event does not come to pass', and therefore the law of contract leaves the promisor 'free to break his contract if he chooses'.[3]

To those who maintain the classical position that a contractual promise *is* a promise of performance,[4] the Holmesian choice has always been anathema, but this anathema has been strongly emphasised in an important line of Commonwealth[5] remedies case law and scholarship reaching back over the last half-century in which a number of ways have been devised of responding to a belief that the existing law offers manifestly weak protection of a claimant's supposed interest in performance.[6] This 'performance interest' criticism reached its zenith in *Attorney General v Blake (Jonathan Cape Ltd Third Party)*, in which the most senior courts of England and Wales described the existing law as 'seriously defective',[7] and the attempt in *Blake* to address this subsequently was welcomed as a necessary 'new start in this area'.[8] One of the earliest and most

[1] Atiyah called it 'a joker in the pack': PS Atiyah, *The Rise and Fall of Freedom of Contract* (pbk edn, Clarendon Press 1985) 429 (hereafter Atiyah, *Rise and Fall*).

[2] This is not so if, as we should, we regard debt as a literal enforcement remedy. The issue is addressed in ch 9.

[3] OW Holmes, *The Common Law* (Little, Brown and Co 1881) 301.

[4] *Tilley v Thomas* (1867) LR 3 Ch App 61 (CA) 72 (Sir John Rolt LJ):

> Contracts ought to be performed. To break them, and to propose compensation for the breach by damages, is not complete justice.

For a US equivalent see *Union Pacific Railroad Co v Chicago, Rock Island and Pacific Railway Co* 133 US 564, 600 (US Supreme Court 1986) (Fuller J).

[5] The principal US contribution has been the inclusion of § 39 in the new Restatement (Third) Restitution and Unjust Enrichment, which drew heavily on Commonwealth sources. See D Campbell, 'A Relational Critique of the Restatement (Third) of Restitution § 39' (2011) 68 Washington and Lee Law Review 1063 (hereafter, Campbell, 'Restatement').

[6] D Friedmann, 'The Performance Interest in Contract Damages' (1995) 111 Law Quarterly Review 628 (1995) 632. '[t]he expectation interest is simply an inappropriate term describing the performance interest'.

[7] [1998] Ch 439 (CA) 457E and [2001] 1 AC 268 (HL) 277F (hereafter *Blake* (HL)).

[8] *Experience Hendrix LLC v PPX Enterprises Inc, Edward Chalpin* [2003] EWCA Civ 323; [2003] 1 All ER (Comm) 830, [16].

prominent contributors to the criticism, to whose magisterial 1966 work on restitution with Lord Goff the criticism might be traced,[9] put the point this way in 1983:

> [the Holmesian choice] would frustrate the natural and reasonable commercial expectations of the contracting parties. In Buckland's graphic sentence: 'One does not buy a right to damages. One buys a horse'.[10]

I believe nothing more wrong could be said about remedies for breach of contract, unless it is many things later said in the same vein on the basis of far less learning. Two things which raise the same difficulty from, as it were, opposing directions have to be noted. First, the Holmesian choice *is* the positive law, and so it certainly is the case that if one believes the function of remedies is to ensure performance, then that law is extraordinarily unfit for its purpose.[11] But, secondly, this law—we focus on *Robinson v Harman*,[12] *Hadley v Baxendale*,[13] *British Westinghouse Electric and Manufacturing Co Ltd v Underground Electric Railways Co of London Ltd (No 2)*,[14] and the Sale of Goods Act 1893—has been a principal foundation of the success of the market economy.[15] Could a law which frustrated 'the natural and reasonable commercial expectations of the contracting parties' possibly do this?

It is argued that, in fact, the positive law of remedies has been the legal foundation of the extremely successful handling by the market economy of an inevitable and major problem of economic action: that economic actors make errors when making the choices they embed in contracts. The law of contract should deal with these errors at least cost, and the law of remedies indeed takes its basic shape from the attempt to do just this. This is an acute illustration of the argument stated in Chapter 2 that understanding that law turns on acknowledging that it is contract's primary function to legally facilitate economic exchange.

[9] RLA Goff and GH Jones, *The Law of Restitution* (1st edn, Sweet & Maxwell 1966).

[10] GH Jones, 'The Recovery of Benefits Gained from a Breach of Contract' (1983) 99 Law Quarterly Review 443, 454, quoting from the criticism of Holmes in WW Buckland, 'The Nature of Contractual Obligations' (1944) 8 Cambridge Law Journal 247. Buckland's sentence was itself derived from *The Digests* (Paulus D.18.4.21), of which he had produced an edition.

[11] And so Friedmann has had to introduce the completely equivocatory—one has to say it is theoretically unscrupulous—concept of 'tolerated' breach to try to preserve his criticism of breach in face of its ubiquity: D Friedmann, 'Economic Aspects of Damages and Specific Performance Compared' in D Saidov and R Cunnington (eds), *Contract Damages* (Hart 2008) 74–82.

[12] (1848) 1 Ex 850; 154 ER 363 (hereafter *Robinson v Harman*).

[13] (1854) 9 Exch 341; 156 ER 145 (hereafter *Hadley v Baxendale*).

[14] [1912] AC 673 (HL) (hereafter *British Westinghouse*).

[15] One does not wish to overwhelm the performance interest argument by drawing the parallel, but one does again think of the 'Max Weber problem', mentioned in ch 5, for Weber's enormous contribution to the explanation of capitalist growth did encounter the problem that his emphasis on technical rationality made it very difficult for him to acknowledge any strength in the common law: Max Weber, *Economy and Society* (University of California Press 1978) 814: '[I]t may indeed be said that England achieved capitalistic supremacy among the nations not because but rather in spite of its judicial system'.

The Expectation Interest and the First Rule of Remedies for Breach of Contract

Our understanding of remedies for breach of contract remains dominated to a remarkable degree by Fuller and Perdue's 1936–37 three interests model.[16] Though the enormous criticism it has received is principally a reflection of how stimulating a contribution it has been, it cannot be denied that this model displays marked shortcomings, and only the basic concepts of the expectation, reliance, and restitution interests will be taken from it here, and indeed those concepts will not be used in line with Fuller and Perdue's intention in two important ways. First, the remedies of *quantum meruit* and recovery which they saw as protecting the restitution interest have always been an uncomfortable, 'quasi-contractual' graft onto the law of contract, and I have argued elsewhere that they no longer have a useful place in that law.[17] I shall mention the quasi-contractual remedies only when this is necessary in connection with other issues. Secondly, on what seems the best interpretation of their intention, Fuller and Perdue wished to place 'primary emphasis' on reliance 'as a possible measure of recovery',[18] and so the overwhelming emphasis which will be placed here on expectation cuts against the 'scale of enforceability'[19] which Fuller himself had in mind.[20]

Fuller and Perdue tell us that when a remedy intended to protect the expectation interest is awarded 'our object is to put the plaintiff in as good a position as he would have occupied had the defendant performed his promise', and in contrast when a remedy intended to protect the reliance interest is awarded 'our object is to put him in as good a position as he was in before the promise was made'.[21] In Chapter 2, we saw that the attempted realisation of a surplus—unless otherwise stated the discussion of remedies in this and Chapter 9 will focus on business organisations' profit—is the driving force of exchange in a market economy. When an exchange is given the form of a contract, this attempted realisation is legally institutionalised as the expectation interest, and it is recognition and protection of the claimant's interest in the future state it would be in after performance that distinguishes expectation from reliance, the latter describing an interest in restoring the claimant to a state prior to the agreement.

As was mentioned in Chapter 2, the basic relationship of the exchange and the contract is expressed in the distinction between the 'primary' and 'secondary' obligations under a contract.[22] The primary obligations of a contract are the (express and implied) terms of the exchange agreed by the parties. This is essentially an economic matter, but

[16] LL Fuller and WR Perdue Jr, 'The Reliance Interest in Contract Damages I' (1936) 46 Yale Law Journal 52, 53–57 (hereafter Fuller and Perdue, 'Reliance Interest').

[17] D Campbell, 'Better Than Fuller: A Two Interest Model of Remedies for Breach of Contract' (2015) 78 The Modern Law Review 296.

[18] Fuller and Perdue, 'Reliance Interest' (n 16) 53.

[19] LL Fuller, 'To KN Llewellyn, 8 December 1938' in RS Summers, *Lon L Fuller* (Edward Arnold 1984) 133.

[20] WD Slawson, 'Why Expectation Damages for Breach of Contract Must Be the Norm: A Refutation of the Fuller and Perdue "Three Interests" Analysis' (2003) 81 Nebraska Law Review 839.

[21] Fuller and Perdue, 'Reliance Interest' (n 16) 54.

[22] *Photo Production Ltd v Securicor Transport Ltd* [1980] AC 827 (HL) 848B–49B (hereafter *Photo Production*).

by giving their exchange the form of a legal contract the parties also create a secondary obligation, arising at the time of the agreement but, as it were, at that time latent, to provide a remedy in the event of breach. This secondary obligation crystallises into a remedy when a breach occurs. Though as formulated by Lord Diplock,[23] the distinction between primary and secondary obligations had a period basis in responding to the always problematic and now obsolete doctrine of 'fundamental breach' discussed in Chapter 7, that distinction is central, indeed it is analytically essential, to the law of contract,[24] for it creates the doctrinal space in which it is clear that there is no need to equate the provision of a remedy with the (compulsory) performance of a primary obligation.

As was discussed in Chapter 5, contracting parties of course normally attempt to realise their expectation by actually performing the exchange legally expressed in their primary obligations, and we shall return to this. But when, after breach, the matter turns to the claimant seeking to realise its expectation through obtaining a legal remedy, things are completely different in a way that remains, to an extraordinary degree, but poorly understood. The focus on expectation means that the remedy need not be compulsion of performance of the primary obligation but may be what Lord Diplock called a 'substituted' obligation,[25] of which compensatory damages were so much the most common case that in his formulations Lord Diplock called them 'the general secondary obligation'.[26] In theory, we could always make literal enforcement the remedy, but that is precisely what we do not do.

Lord Diplock's analysis is almost startlingly pellucid by the standards of much recent commentary, but, with respect, to move from secondary obligation to compensatory damages is to create a difficulty by missing a step in the argument, and the difficulty is compounded by the use of the word 'substituted'. For whilst there is an obvious and undeniable sense in which Lord Diplock was right to see the secondary obligation as a substitute for the primary performance, compensatory damages are never, for commercial parties, a substitute for performance. For performance is not what is essential. Those parties are focused, not on performance, but on the expectation of profit, which it therefore would be more precise to call, though I shall continue to talk of expectation as such, net expectation.[27] The actual performance of the contract is but the means of obtaining of the profit, indeed it is a cost of obtaining that profit, and an understanding of contract remedies turns on seeing that expectation is what commercially matters, not actual performance of the obligation. The law of contract remedies takes its basic shape by not normally protecting an interest in performance but an expectation interest in profit. We shall see that this is the expectation interest's enormous virtue, but at this point it merely should be stressed that this is and has been

[23] The first formulation was in 1965 in the Court of Appeal: *Hardwick Game Farm v Suffolk Agricultural Poultry Producers Association Ltd* [1966] 1 WLR 287 (CA) 341E–G.

[24] The distinction may be found in Pothier, the translation of which by WD Evans first appeared in 1806: RJ Pothier, *A Treatise on the Law of Obligations, or Contracts* (Lawbook Exchange 2000) pt II, ch I, s 5 (hereafter Pothier, *Obligations*). Even were it not for the historical work of Atiyah to which I am about to refer (leaving aside the comparable work of others), I have not the slightest doubt that there were important distinctions between what Evans sought to connote and what is argued here.

[25] *Photo Production* (n 22) 848H.

[26] ibid 849D.

[27] DW Barnes, 'The Net Expectation Interest in Contract Damages' (1999) 48 Emory Law Journal 1143.

the positive law, as the greatest of authorities laboured, it would seem to some considerable extent in vain,[28] to point out:

> The extraordinary thing which happened to contract theory in the mid-nineteenth century was contracts came to be protected as expectation rights in all circumstances ... Because even an executory contract might be treated as 'binding', even though mere expectations were protected, the new rules about expectation damages protected only the plaintiff's expectation of net profit ... The reality is that the bindingness of executory contracts protects[,] not the expectation of performance, but the expectation of profit.[29]

That this is the case may be seen from *Robinson v Harman*, the occasion of Parke B's statement of what is acknowledged throughout the Commonwealth as the 'first rule' of remedies for breach of contract: 'where a party sustains a loss by reason of a breach of contract, he is, so far as money can do it, to be placed in the same situation, with respect to damages, as if the contract had been performed'.[30] The obvious similarity between Parke B's *dictum* and Fuller and Perdue's definition of the expectation interest and its distinction from reliance, is, in fact, illustrated by the facts of *Robinson v Harman* in a particularly clear way.

Robinson v Harman concerned the lease of a dwelling for a term of 21 years at an annual rent of £110, which the vendor breached when it emerged that his interest in the property was not sufficient to allow of this disposition of it. Speaking more than a little anachronistically, the initial significance of *Robinson v Harman* was that it followed one of the exceptions to the then obtaining rule in *Bain v Fothergill*,[31] which limited to reliance loss the liability of vendors who failed to complete sales of interests in land because of defects in title. By not normally compensating the purchaser for lost expectation, the conveyancing practice of the time was to in this way share the risks of establishing title, which, prior to general land registration, were unavoidably considerable, often requiring investigation of documents which were, in the famous words attributed to Lord Westbury, 'difficult to read, disgusting to touch, and impossible to understand'.[32] But in *Robinson v Harman* the defects in title, arising from the terms on which the defendant had recently inherited an interest in the property, were of a sort that the defendant should reasonably have known and the claimant could not reasonably know, and the rule in *Bain v Fothergill* was not applied. One imagines that the

[28] I cannot here dwell on Atiyah's difficulties with the 'pure expectation' award of damages into which he was led by Fuller's ranking of reliance and expectation: PS Atiyah, 'Contracts, Promises and the Law of Obligations' in *Essays on Contract* (rev edn, Clarendon Press 1990) 33–34. The issues are effectively dealt with in SJ Stoljar, 'Promise, Expectation and Agreement' [1988] *Cambridge Law Journal* 193, 209–12.

[29] Atiyah, *Rise and Fall* (n 1) 428–30. Atiyah goes on to say that even then expectation 'was only protected so long as the promisee cannot secure it elsewhere', and we shall, of course, discuss mitigation below.

[30] *Robinson v Harman* (n 12) 855; 365.

[31] *Bain v Fothergill* (1874) LR 7 HL 158 (HL). In *Bain v Fothergill*, the Lords restated a rule traceable to cases then a century old, and so the name of the rule is in a sense misleading. In the course of this restatement, the Lords probably overruled *Robinson v Harman* in its specific connection with the rule. Though the older cases are discussed in *Robinson v Harman* in this specific connection, I avoid full treatment of an issue which is tangential to the argument here and must now be of only vanishingly small practical importance, the rule in *Bain v Fothergill* having been statutorily abolished for prospective cases in 1989.

[32] *Wroth v Tyler* [1974] Ch 30, 56C (Megarry J).

mellifluousness of Parke B's phraseology has played its part in subsequent case law and commentary generalising this into the first rule, but let us look back at the case itself.

The defendant did not dispute liability but, no doubt with the rule in *Bain v Fothergill* in mind, paid £25 into court, which would have met the reliance loss represented by the claimant's legal expenses, which were found (the facts are unclear) to be something over £15. But in the event £200 beyond the payment into court was awarded, which, deducting the £15 which will have been paid in addition to expectation, meant that expectation damages were *circa* £210. Although liability for expectation at all was the crux of the case, we cannot directly know from the case itself how these damages, once they were to be awarded, were quantified, which was not raised as an issue. But one can be as certain as one can be absent direct evidence that the difference in the value of the property at the intended time of completion and the market value of a similar property, ie market damages, were awarded. £210 cannot have been only what would now be called a reliance award in respect of a year's rent which had been advanced. In other authorities of the time, of which *Engell v Fitch* was the most important,[33] this market damages measure was adopted explicitly in order to give effect to Parke's B's rule.[34] Alderson B's speaking of damages in *Robinson v Harman* having 'been assessed according to the general rule of law that where a person makes a contract and breaks it he must pay the whole damage sustained'[35] is now taken as axiomatic of the necessity of putting the claimant in the position it would have been in had the contracted been performed, as of course it is. But it is rarely adequately realised that in *Robinson v Harman* this meant protection of expectation, and even less that this was done by payment of market damages.

The question which now arises, of course, is why the positive law of remedies for breach is focused in this way, not on performance, but on lost expectation of surplus, and to this we now turn.

Breach and the Second Rule of Remedies for Breach of Contract

Though of course all who study contract must acknowledge that breach is a common event, if one regards primary obligations as essentially legal—'promise' has carried a particularly unfortunate linguistic burden here[36]—one will tend to see breach as a pathology, the general response to which by the law of remedies based on the Holmesian choice is perverse. The criticism of expectation culminating in *Blake* was based on some idea that breach was one form of (civil) wrong[37] which (it was acknowledged this was not always possible) should be prevented.[38] But breach normally is a

[33] (1869) LR 4 QB 659 (Ex Ch) 665–66.

[34] Having in previous editions distinguished two 'normal' measures of damages for failure to complete depending on whether the case came within or outside the rule in *Bain v Fothergill*, after the statutory abolition of the rule in 1989 *McGregor* described market damages as *the* normal measure: H McGregor, *Damages* (16th edn, Sweet & Maxwell 1997) para 964.

[35] *Robinson v Harman* (n 12) 855–56; 365.

[36] See n 161.

[37] P Birks, *Introduction to the Law of Restitution* (rev edn, Clarendon Press 1989) 39.

[38] ibid 25.

wrong only in a technical sense which does not convey condemnation, and the general goal of preventing it is wholly inappropriate. Starting from recognising that primary obligations are economic, it will be argued that breach is morally legitimate, serves an essential purpose, and its prevention should not, and indeed if freedom of economic choice and of contract prevail cannot, be set as a goal.

If we set aside intentional breach by those who entered into a contract with fraudulent purpose, the ultimate cause of breach is the bounded rationality of economic actors in the inevitably empirically obtaining circumstances of positive transaction costs. When a defendant undertakes a primary contractual obligation, it does so holding a certain view of the state of the world which leads it to believe that performance of that obligation will cost a certain amount. The inevitable risk that this estimate of cost is wrong may become manifested in a perceived rise in the cost the defendant would incur in performing.[39] Any rise in the cost of complete performance above the defendant's original estimate will reduce the defendant's expected profit margin, and thus the defendant's own expectation interest, and beyond a certain point the rise will extinguish that margin completely (leaving the defendant in a 'break-even' contract, where receipts equal costs), or make the margin negative (leaving the defendant in a 'losing contract', where receipts are lower than costs).[40] The enormous variation in the empirical circumstances which give rise to these outcomes—unanticipated shortage of raw materials, destruction of premises by fire, etc—should not obscure the fact that it is an unforeseen rise in the cost of performance gives the good faith defendant an incentive to breach.

It is not logically possible for any increase in the costs of performance to lead to breach[41] unless the cost of breach is lower than the anticipated costs of performance. This is possible only if remedies are normally focused on expectation, and precisely not on performance. The defendant's costs of breach will be its own wasted reliance and its own lost expectation, plus the claimant's wasted reliance and lost expectation. Let us treat the first three as liquidated sums. Breach can make sense only because the claimant's lost expectation will normally be remedied by compensatory damages quantified as net profit, for it is only this that can possibly allow a defendant to choose breach as a less expensive alternative to performance. There can be no doubt that many, perhaps most, defendants facing unanticipated costs do not immediately

[39] For ease of exposition a single contract with a lapse of time between agreement and performance is discussed. In contracts with no such lapse of time in which the seller finds it has been unable to deliver or to deliver non-breaching goods, the considerations about to be discussed in the single contract case will be taken into account when the seller considers the terms on which it will enter into future agreements. I do not think it is necessary to go into the considerable economic literature on 'multi-period' contracting, which is tangential to our purpose, for the reader to make the necessary extension of the argument. It seems plausible to assume that a former defendant deciding whether to enter into a new contract on the terms that previously led to breach will consider the option of seeking to revise those terms in a more deliberate manner than might in many cases be exhibited by a defendant during the process of 'managing' the breach of an existing contract.

[40] See the text accompanying n 90.

[41] There are ultimate caps to liability set by common mistake and frustration and by personal bankruptcy and company insolvency. For reasons already mentioned, the former two are not discussed here, their discussion reserved until ch 10. The latter two are fundamental to the understanding of the operation of the market economy overall but unfortunately cannot be discussed here.

perceive matters in this way,[42] but nevertheless even they eventually must fall back on rationality in order to make a choice to breach or perform in a way which is beneficial to them. Calling breach 'deliberate', or one of many synonyms or intensifiers of deliberate, as a way of criticising it when, in all good faith cases, deliberate means only 'clearheaded', has been one of the terminological symptoms of the lack of clear headedness that has attended the attack on expectation.[43]

If the damages system works in the sense that damages actually are adequate, the claimant should in any particular case be indifferent whether the defendant pays damages or performs.[44] The issue should be whether the defendant be made to perform or to pay compensatory damages when *both* protect the claimant's expectation; and, if the defendant decides that breach is a less costly way of doing this than performance, then the defendant should be allowed to breach. To compel the defendant to perform will protect the claimant's expectation, but *ex hypothesi*, damages will do this more cheaply than literal enforcement. As no benefit will be conferred by making the defendant protect the claimant's expectation by the more expensive method of literal enforcement, the defendant should be allowed to elect the cheaper method.

Nor is this a matter of being unilaterally generous to the defendant. As rational pricing requires the parties to include the cost of potential liability for breach, the claimant will benefit from a price lowered because expectation lowers the cost of liability. I will argue that it is competition over this aspect of contracting that has made contracts which minimise liability the norm, and therefore why compensatory damages are the default rule of remedies. To do otherwise than adopt what Goetz and Scott have called the 'principle of joint-cost minimisation'[45] of loss would be to impose pointless waste on the parties which they themselves normally avoid.

In a contract which is performed, expectation is protected by performance. In a contract which is breached in good faith, something has happened to make performance more costly, and though the overriding goal remains protection of the claimant's expectation, this should be done as cheaply as possible, and for this to be possible, the alternatives to compulsory performance opened up by distinguishing between primary and secondary obligations should be considered by the parties. The law of contract's remedial focus on expectation can be explained only by the parties doing just this being the norm. In sum, we might say that the fundamental goal of the law of contract is to put the claimant in the position it would have been in had the contract

[42] IR Macneil, 'Contract Remedies: A Need for a Better Efficiency Analysis' (1988) 144 Journal of Institutional and Theoretical Economics 6, 15 (hereafter Macneil, 'Contract Remedies'):

> What does happen in the world of contracts—often in clear violation of legal rules of contract remedies—is that people get themselves into trouble in an incredible variety of ways, both ingenious and disingenuous, and are unable or at the very least think themselves unable to perform.

[43] RA Posner, 'Let Us Never Blame a Contract Breaker' in O Ben-Shahar and A Porat (eds), *Fault in American Contract Law* (CUP 2010).

[44] MA Eisenberg, 'Actual and Virtual Specific Performance, the Theory of Efficient Breach, and the Indifference Principle in Contract Law' (2005) 93 California Law Review 975.

[45] CJ Goetz and RE Scott, 'The Mitigation Principle: Toward a General Theory of Contractual Obligation' (1983) 69 Virginia Law Review 967, 972–73 (hereafter Goetz and Scott, 'Mitigation Principle').

been performed, the first rule of remedies, *but by the means which imposes least cost on the defendant*, the second rule.[46] As it has been put by Andersen:

> remedies for breach of contract ... attempt to accommodate two competing goals ... (1) securing to the injured party the benefit of the bargain, (2) without imposing unnecessary costs on the breaching party.[47]

To explain why these *two* rules have been developed, and in particular why the second complements the first, we must more deeply consider why contracts are breached. At considerable risk of exposing my ignorance,[48] in a previous statement of the argument now being made here I drew a parallel to an aspect of John von Neumann's work which has proved to be one of the foundations of modern computing,[49] which I attempted to read when trying to come to terms with game theory. Most of this is incomprehensible to me, but insofar as I understand the matter, one of von Neumann's contributions to the conceptualisation of computing problems was to recognise that error is ineliminable,[50] and that the goal of eliminating error from calculation was illusory. One should first be aware of this, and so not put excessive faith in one's results, and then try to manage the inevitable failure. In computing, von Neumann's basic strategy was to duplicate the calculation on various computers (or parts of computers), and work from some sample of the multiple results.

Without wishing to too much weight on what is intended purely as a heuristic device, I submit that an analogue to this happens in the market economies. It is obvious that in those economies, composed of countless numbers of exchanges of varying degrees of complexity, dealing with those inevitably occurring contracts in which one party finds its costs during performance growing in an unanticipated way (telling it it had made a mistake (in the lay sense) by agreeing this contract), is a major problem. The mechanism for handling this problem is central to the efficiency of the market economy. The fundamental mechanism is adjustment of obligations by the parties without recourse to legal action, but this is encouraged by limiting the extent to which performance can legally be insisted upon in the way we have seen. Breach allows flexibility into the system of exchanges, allowing parties relief from unanticipatedly expensive obligations when further performance would be pointless as the claimant can be compensated in damages. In this sense, *a major function of the law of contract is to allow breach*, but only on the right occasions, and only on the right terms. In the

[46] Having referred to *Robinson v Harman* as the 'foundation of the measure of damages for breach of contract' and quoted the *dictum* of Parke B, in *Ruxley Electronics and Construction Ltd v Forsyth* [1994] 1 WLR 650 (CA) 660D Mann LJ went on to say that 'This very general principle is shadowed by another', identifying this second principle with mitigation in a general sense.

[47] EG Andersen, 'Good Faith in the Enforcement of Contracts' (1983) 73 Iowa Law Review 299, 306.

[48] D Campbell, 'The Relational Constitution of Remedy' (2005) 11 Texas Weslyan Law Review 455.

[49] J von Neumann, 'Probabilistic Logics and the Synthesis of Reliable Organisms from Unreliable Components' in CE Shannon and J McCarthy (eds), *Automata Studies* (Princeton University Press 1956) 43:

> Error is viewed ... not as an extraneous and misdirected or misdirecting accident, but as an essential part of the process under consideration—its importance ... being fully comparable to that of the factor which is normally considered, the intended and correct logical structure.

[50] The mechanical reliability of the computing machines available to von Neumann was very much poorer than that of contemporary computers, but the basic point still of course holds.

standard case, the right occasions and the right terms are when the claimant is able to obtain a substitute legal good or service and the defendant compensates any damages the claimant incurs in doing so. And so the structure of Pt V of the Sale of Goods Act 1893,[51] codifying Victorian commercial practice and adopted throughout the common law world, was to '*prima facie*' assess what we will see are *Hadley v Baxendale* first limb 'damages directly and naturally resulting, in the ordinary course of events' as the difference between the contract price and the price of obtaining a substitute sale, and to stipulate that obtaining other remedies required an ouster of this default of market damages, specifically in order to claim consequential losses as 'special damages' under s 54.[52]

The law of England and Wales does not know the term, but the principal remedy provided by Pt V is, in fact, not the market damages themselves but the, to use the language of the Uniform Commercial Code § 2-712(1),[53] 'cover' of purchasing 'goods in substitution' that the claimant can take with the assurance provided by the availability of those damages that no net cost will be incurred:

> the buyer ... is entitled to recover the expense *of putting himself* into the position of having those goods, and this he can do by going into the market and purchasing them at the market price. To do so he must pay a sum which is larger than that which he would have had to pay under the contract by the difference between the two prices. This difference is, therefore, the true measure of his loss from the breach, for it is that which it will cost him *to put himself* in the same position as if the contract had been fulfilled.[54]

Properly regulated breach will, then, incentivise claimants to cover in the knowledge that the defendant will, because cover is in its own as well as the claimant's interest, compensate lost expectation, and this is normative contractual action based on mutual recognition of those interests.

All this, of course, assumes that it normally is possible to take cover, but for commercial parties this normally is possible because the market economies are characterised by the ready availability of goods in competitive supply,[55] including a margin of excess capacity which allows a buyer faced with breach to take cover by finding a substitute. Nothing is more important than to recognise the ultimate scarcity of economic

[51] Now Sale of Goods Act 1979, Pt VI (as amended). Remedies under the Consumer Rights Act 2015 cannot be discussed in this chapter and receive only the briefest mention in ch 9.

[52] Bruce J was right to say in *Bostock and Co Ltd v Nicolson and Sons* [1904] 1 KB 725 (KB) 735–36 that whilst s 53(2), and, we should add ss 50(2) and 51(2), adopted the language of *Hadley*, s 54 did not. But, whilst s 54 'special damages' are therefore very wide, there can be no doubt they encompass consequential loss which is subject to second limb requirements, as *Bostock v Nicolson* itself shows.

[53] The seller's equivalent remedy is available under Uniform Commercial Code § 2-708. For reasons which are of the highest interest but which cannot be discussed here, the Code also has, under § 2-713(1), provided for market damages as an alternative to cover. For an explanation of this, and the corollary issue which arises under the Sale of Goods Act, see D Campbell, 'Market Damages and the Invisible Hand' in LA DiMatteo and M Hogg (eds), *Comparative Contract Law: British and American Perspectives* (OUP 2016) (hereafter Campbell, 'Market Damages').

[54] *William Bros v ED T Agius Ltd* [1914] AC 510 (HL) 530–31 (emphases added).

[55] One of the founding works of economics, D Ricardo, *On the Principles of Political Economy and Taxation* in *Collected Works*, vol 1 (CUP 1951) 12, begins by identifying this central feature of market economy, telling us that goods of which there truly 'is a very limited quantity' such as 'Some ... statues ... pictures, books and coins':

goods, but it is part of the achievement of the market economies that they can nevertheless be regarded, to use the concept discussed in another connection in Chapter 3, as economies of 'abundance', insofar as they are characterised by the normal, ready availability of substitute economic goods. This is in contrast to all other economies that have ever existed, not only other states of society prior to what Smith called commercial society, but including actually existing communist economies, which are characterised by 'shortage'.[56] Abundance in this connection does not signify an absence of scarcity; indeed its significance is that it describes a very important aspect of the way in which the market economies, by making substitutes available, deal with scarcity under the universal condition of bounded rationality. The ready availability of substitutes is the principal means by which inevitable misallocations of resources through contract are adjusted through breach.[57] Much economic theory which views 'excess capacity' in the economy as a sign of 'a wasteful anomaly' simply fails, because it has a wildly optimistic view of the possible perfection of planned arrangements, to take onboard the vital function of such capacity in making the taking of cover widely possible.[58] This mistake is greatly exaggerated by legal theories of the performance interest, which simply have no inkling of the economic difficulties which their pursuit of general literal enforcement would involve.

The point of relevance to us is that cover is both efficient and co-operative in a way that undercuts the typical opposition of these qualities. It is efficient because it is co-operative. In circumstances when the claimant can be compensated in damages, cover obviously is efficient, for insisting upon anything else would be to satisfy the claimant's expectation at a higher cost to the defendant than the cost of the cover, and what would be the point of that? The breach is efficient in this case because it minimises *the defendant's* loss. But this efficiency emerges only because the claimant co-operates by taking cover. Allowing the defendant to breach and placing the burden of mitigation on the claimant enlists the claimant's co-operation in dealing with the defendant's problems, one aspect of this co-operation being that it makes legal action unnecessary in cases where compensation is adequate.

> form a very small part of the mass of commodities daily exchanged in the market. By far the greatest part are of those goods which are the objects of desire ... may be multiplied, not in one country alone, but in many, almost without assignable limit, if we are disposed to bestow the labour necessary to obtain them.

[56] J Kornai, *The Socialist System* (Clarendon Press 1992) 233. The difficulty the shortage economies encounter with remedies based on cover is discussed in D Campbell, 'Breach and Penalty as Contractual Norm and Contractual Anomie' [2001] Wisconsin Law Review 681.

[57] FA Hayek, 'The Use of Knowledge in Society' in *The Market and Other Orders* in *Collected Works*, vol 15 (Routledge 2014) 97:

> Is it true that, with the elaborate apparatus of modern production ... once a plant has been built the rest is all more or less mechanical ... leaving little to be changed in adapting to the ever-changing circumstances? ... The continuous flow of goods and services is maintained by constant deliberate adjustments ... made every day in the light of circumstances not known the day before, by B stepping in at once when A fails to deliver. Even the large, mechanised plant keeps going largely because of an environment on which it can draw for all sorts of unexpected needs ... and all the thousand and one kinds of equipment in which it cannot be self-contained and which the plans for the operation of the plant require to be readily available on the market.

[58] JM Clark, *Competition as a Dynamic Process* (Brookings Institution 1961) 59.

If we recall the argument in Chapter 2, it can be seen that the writing of this chapter can be particularly directly traced to the appearance in 1963 of the two articles by Stewart Macaulay on 'non-use' and 'non-contractual relations' which are the empirical foundation of the relational theory.[59] But though we shall see in Chapter 10 that Macaulay's findings do show, in relationship to the complex contracts discussed in those chapters, a profound and vexed divergence between the formal law of contract and parties' action when contracting, and so non-use of the former and the use of 'non-contractual relations' in the latter, this absolutely is not the case in regard of the standard breach discussed so far. The parties' response to the standard case which we are now discussing ultimately does not support Macaulay's claim that 'there is little evidence that ... today's businessmen would use the courts to settle disputes',[60] for that response is legal at its core, and cannot be understood otherwise.

However, Macaulay is of course right in that this legal quality is manifested in actual recourse to legal advice or litigation becoming exceptional, but that is because the formal law is so good that parties spontaneously frame their actions within it. In the standard case, the claimant covers and the defendant unproblematically compensates any loss without use of formal legal processes; indeed without a 'dispute' in any real sense of the term arising.[61] In the shadow of this law, the parties may, in various circumstances, spontaneously devise other ways of reaching the same result, such as the defendant itself providing a substitute or a repair. Though the Uniform Commercial Code attempts to identify these other steps, I am of the opinion, which I shall not defend here, that there is no need for this, and the more elaborate identification of remedies can itself create legal difficulties which leaving the parties to work around the basic default cover rule would avoid.[62]

As one whose professional life has been substantially occupied with the now preponderantly dismal science of regulation, I am pleased to be able to say that this account of the practice of cover under the law of England and Wales, and in particular the Sale of Goods Act, is one of an extraordinary regulatory success. Indeed, it meets the principal criterion of such success in that those subject to the regulation adopt it wholeheartedly, and so, in an extremely important sense, their economic action is spontaneously beneficent. The parties' each co-operate out of their own self-interest because the interests of both are united by the legal framework of market damages. The claimant's expectation is protected, and the defendant's interests are united with the claimant's as the protection is secured at least cost to the defendant. Of course, in any one instance the defendant would prefer simply to walk

[59] S Macaulay, 'The Use and Non-use of Contracts in the Manufacturing Industry' (1963) 9 Practical Lawyer 13 and S Macaulay, 'Non-contractual Relations in Business: A Preliminary Study' (1963) 38 American Sociological Review 55.

[60] Macaulay, 'Non-contractual Relations' ibid.

[61] OE Williamson, 'Transaction Cost Economics: The Governance of Contractual Relation' in *Economic Organisation* (Wheatsheaf Books 1986) 123:

> The reason why Macaulay observes so few litigated cases in business is because markets work well for non-specific transactions, while recurrent non-standard transactions are governed by bilateral or unified structures.

[62] Precisely the opposite is argued in respect of 'cure' under UCC § 2-508 in E McKendrick, *Goode's Commercial Law* (6th edn, Penguin 2020) s 12.29, but this is, with respect, not entirely consistent with what is said of the existing 'legal principle [and] commercial practice' following lawful rejection at ibid 12.17.

away, but walking away is inconsistent with maintenance of the law of contract as a system for facilitating contractual exchange and so, on the fundamental Kantian argument discussed in Chapter 1, is morally inconsistent with the defendant's participation in, and reproduction of, that system. As their being essentially a codification of Victorian commercial practice evidences,[63] market damages are, in fact, the product of the voluntary agreement of the claimant and the defendant, as I now propose to demonstrate.

Causation and the Agreement to Co-operate

This explanation of the remedies system deals with, I submit successfully, what was claimed at the start of this chapter to be the serious difficulty into which the performance interest argument must run: the positive law simply does not focus on performance; in fact it does the opposite, and for good reason. This explanation is, however, open to criticism of its 'efficiency' being bought at the cost of having to take an immoral attitude towards performance. This criticism gained enormous strength when it took the form of a response to the theory of 'efficient breach', which seemed a scandal that threatened to undermine the moral basis of contracting, and I conclude this chapter with a discussion of efficient breach. At this point, however, I want to argue that criticism of the immorality of the remedies system is wholly misplaced. The remedies for breach rest on the fundamental moral justification of exchange and contract: agreement by parties in a relationship of mutual recognition. This emerges from analysis of the doctrine of causation.

To claim its lost expectation, the claimant must satisfy the requirement of causation, tying the loss to the breach. At some considerable cost of simply cutting through the confused or even vexed quality of much of the relevant law, I will claim that there are three basic doctrines which constitute successive stages of the causation argument which the claimant must successfully make in order to be awarded substantial damages.[64] These doctrines are set out in the following table and will be discussed in turn:

Stage	Losses compensated	Losses not compensated
1 cause in fact	certain losses	uncertain losses
2 cause in law	proximate losses	remote losses
3 mitigation	unavoidable losses	avoidable losses

[63] The extent to which the 1893 Act was a 'pure' codification was discussed in relation to implied terms in ch 3.

[64] If one understands that by 'remoteness' Robert Goff J meant not only remoteness proper but also what here will be called certainty, then his statement of the position in *Koch Marine Inc v D'Amica Societa Di Navigazione ARL, The Elena D'Amico* [1980] 1 Lloyd's Rep 88 col 2 is the position I intend to argue.

Cause in fact and but-for

The claimant must prove that the loss for which compensation is sought was caused 'in fact' by the breach, but this is so in a specific sense which will be called the requirement of certainty, and there must be a serious question, to which I have no completely satisfactory answer, whether the law of contract has a 'but-for' requirement. Unlike in tort, but-for has given rise to little discussion in contract.[65] Indeed one finds it difficult to identify cases which clearly turn on the issue, which is very often confusingly discussed in a terminology of remoteness in the *Hadley v Baxendale*, or even tortious, senses, and is also very much overlapped by questions, leaving aside contributory negligence, of whether the defendant's actions or omissions amounted to a relevant breach or a relevant failure to mitigate.[66]

Though it anticipates the discussion of remoteness which will shortly follow, readers will of course be aware that in *Victoria Laundry (Windsor) Ltd v Newman Industries Ltd*[67] a refusal at first instance[68] to award consequential loss was in part reversed by the Court of Appeal. The claimant was a launderer and dyer which, seeking to expand both parts of its business, bought a boiler of much larger capacity than its existing boiler from the defendant, which had previously used the larger boiler in its own business. Damage to the boiler whilst it was being moved for which the defendant was liable caused installation to be delayed by five months, and the claimant claimed the loss of the extra profits it would have made from the expansion during this time. The complete refusal of consequential loss at first instance turned in part on complications in the facts of the case,[69] in part on some defunct reasoning which need no longer need be considered,[70] but mostly on a very narrow understanding of reasonable contemplation which it is the significance of *Victoria Laundry* to have dispensed with. It would seem that the Court of Appeal found the defendant to have had the broad nature of the claimant's business, its planned expansion, and the essential role of the new boiler in reasonable contemplation under the first limb of *Hadley v Baxendale*, and the claimant was awarded all its lost profits from laundering. But it was awarded only part of its lost profits from dyeing,[71] for a fascinating reason.

The lost profits from laundering were, if it can be put this way, purely a quantitative matter of the expansion of former business. But the lost profits from dyeing had a different qualitative dimension, for the claimants were about to take on dyeing contracts

[65] HLA Hart and T Honoré, *Causation in the Law* (2nd edn, OUP 1985) 308.

[66] *Borealis AB v Geogas Trading SA* [2010] EWHC 2789 (Comm); [2011] 1 Lloyd's Rep 482 [43]–[47] is an illustrative case. Despite Gross LJ's commendable attempt, *ibid* [42]–[50], to clarify 'the legal framework', especially in respect of 'causation' expressly distinguished from 'remoteness', it is, with respect, submitted that no real clarity about what was regarded as the central issue, whether the defendant had 'broken the chain of causation', emerges. It is no doubt significant that this does not seem to disturb the soundness of the overall decision reached by Gross LJ.

[67] [1949] 2 KB 528 (CA) 538–39 (hereafter *Victoria Laundry* (CA)).

[68] *Victoria Laundry (Windsor) Ltd v Newman Industries Ltd* [1948] 1 All ER 806 (KB).

[69] The defendant was an engineering firm not specifically engaged in laundering and dyeing, nor indeed in the making of boilers; the physical act that led to the breach was that of a third party, etc.

[70] J Edelman, *McGregor on Damages* (21st edn, Sweet & Maxwell 2021) para 25.047 (hereafter Edelman, *McGregor*, 21st edn).

[71] *Victoria Laundry* (CA) (n 67) 543.

from the government which were described as 'highly' or 'particularly lucrative',[72] and these were sufficiently unusual that they could be recovered only under the second limb. As it was found that no notice had been given, these losses were not awarded. But, a very important point rarely noted and even more rarely given sufficient weight, this did not mean that nothing was awarded in respect of these losses, for the Court of Appeal went on to say that, though damages would not be given for the unusual government contracts:

> It does not, however, follow that the plaintiffs are precluded from recovering some general (and perhaps conjectural) sum for the loss of business in respect of dyeing contracts to be reasonably expected, any more than in respect of laundering contracts to be reasonably expected.[73]

And indeed, though the quantification was referred to a referee so we cannot know what was awarded, it would appear that, though the claimants were awarded damages for the lost dyeing contracts, these did not amount to the full 'highly' or 'particularly lucrative' profits, but only the ordinary profits that would have been in reasonable contemplation under the first limb.

In light of this, it has been persuasively argued that, though second limb losses can be fully recovered only with second limb notice, even in the absence of notice second limb losses will be partially recovered up to a 'cap' set by the limits of first limb reasonable contemplation.[74] One must be very careful how one understands this. For the claimant in *Victoria Laundry* was not going to use the boiler in the ordinary way; it was going to use it in the unusual way. This must mean that the cap award was compensation for a loss that would not have taken place in fact!

The point seems to be rubbed home by the heavy reliance placed in *Victoria Laundry* on *Cory v The Thames Ironworks and Shipbuilding Co Ltd*,[75] a case then regarded as of impeccable authority[76] though, as with but-for as such, now neglected. In *Cory*, a loss in reasonable contemplation would have been that arising from using the hull of the former floating derrick which was delivered late as a coal store, whereas the claimant actually intended to put the hull to a much more profitable and physically entirely different 'special purpose', albeit one 'to the purpose of their trade', as a means of 'transhipping coals' without intermediate storage, which the court found to be 'exceptional and unnatural'.[77] The claimant was awarded the loss which would have been caused by an inability to use the hull for its ordinary purpose. But it does not appear that the claimant would ever have made this use of the hull, and so, even more clearly

[72] ibid 535, 543. It does not, of course, itself convey a full picture, but it is surely significant that the claimants assessed the lost laundering profits at £16/week and the lost dyeing profits at £262/week.

[73] ibid 543.

[74] M Stigglebout, 'Contractual Remoteness, "Scope of Duty" and Intention' [2012] Lloyd's Maritime and Commercial Law Quarterly 97, 99–102.

[75] (1867–68) LR 3 QB 181 (QB) (hereafter *Cory*).

[76] Edelman, *McGregor*, 21st edn (n 70) para 25.045.

[77] ibid 187, 190. In *Victoria Laundry* (CA) (n 67) 538 the situation was described as 'a quite unprecedented use for a chattel of this kind, one quite unsuspected by the sellers and one calculated to yield much higher profits'.

than in *Victoria Laundry*, the loss which was contemplated should not have survived the but-for test:

> the seller cannot be called upon to make good [the larger] loss if it was not within the scope of his contemplation that the thing would be applied to the purpose from which such larger profit would result ... [But] the buyer has lost the larger amount, and there can be no hardship or injustice in making the seller liable to compensate him in damages so far as the seller understood and believed that the article would be applied to the ordinary purposes to which it was capable of being applied.[78]

Of course, as the second limb losses have actually occurred, one might say the losses which are partially recovered were sustained in fact. And the most important point is that, in one sense, abstractly doctrinal questions about cause in fact are of subordinate importance. If the cap represents the liabilities the parties implicitly agree, as it seems that it does,[79] then of course one should not interfere with it. But the cap surely means that a but-for test of any definiteness actually plays no role in contract, for the *Cory* issue as it takes a less stark form in *Victoria Laundry* must commonly arise in remoteness cases, even though it gives rise to little discussion, seeming to be absorbed within remoteness itself so that a normal loss in reasonable contemplation will always be awarded, despite facts showing that a normal loss would not have been suffered. The real limitation which cause in fact places on claims would seem to arise from a quite different issue: certainty.

Cause in fact and certainty

Much more important than, as it were, pure but-for arguments is the very important indeed case law on the aspect of cause in fact which will, though it is by no means a universal usage, here be called 'certainty'[80] in order to convey that some, if not precision, then definiteness is demanded in quantification.[81] Some vague idea of but-for must lie behind the requirement of certainty, but the positive law of certainty very much departs from any strict idea. Though standard cases involving market damages should of their nature involve a liquidated or all but liquidated sum, and so should present no difficulty,[82] the idea of compensating consequential loss can give rise to an obvious

[78] *Cory* (n 75) 190.

[79] This possibility seems to have been recognised by Lord Rodger in *Transfield Shipping Inc of Panama v Mercator Shipping Inc of Monrovia, The Achilleas* [2008] UKHL 48, [2009] 1 AC 61 [58]–[59] (hereafter *The Achilleas* (HL)), where, at least in some cases, 'some general sum for loss of business somewhat along the line envisaged in [*Victoria Laundry*]' was explicitly contrasted to the damages which would be available had notice been given and so the second limb 'might well [have] come into play'.

[80] The late Dr McGregor long argued that if the equivocatory term 'reasonable certainty' was used, this would only mean that the burden was carried by the first word: Edelman, *McGregor*, 21st edn (n 70) para 10.002. It is submitted that certainty should be read so that reasonable is unnecessary as reasonableness in the relevant sense is intrinsic to certainty itself. See further n 141.

[81] Anon, 'The Requirement of Certainty in the Proof of Loss of Profits' (1950) 64 Harvard Law Review 317.

[82] There is an extremely important exception, if it is right to call something so important an exception, to this arising in quantification in the absence of an 'available market', which cannot be discussed here but is discussed in Campbell, 'Market Damages' (n 53).

difficulty: we must seek to quantify a future state of affairs that not merely does not obtain at the time of breach, but which that breach means will never obtain. This can give rise to difficult problems of quantifying complex consequential losses.[83] When profits are lost because a project has had to be abandoned because of the breach, it might be possible that, for example, lost sales are readily provable because the claimant has a full order book. Even in the absence of such clear evidence, past records of trading either with established customers or even in general may provide grounds for quantification. The courts have by no means required standards of precision in the proof of consequential loss that go beyond those which, in the circumstances, would command acceptance in business circles, say by a bank considering an investment, and indeed a long line of cases can be easily identified which seem to apply more relaxed standards in their determination to ensure that the claimant receives compensation.[84]

Nevertheless, there has to be and there is a limit, which limit has sometimes been expressed in the claim that 'speculative' losses cannot be recovered. The term 'uncertain' rather than 'speculative' has, however, been used here, in part because it would seem that the term speculative losses is now more commonly, if inconsistently, used to denote that damages *will* be awarded when 'quantification … is necessarily speculative',[85] and 'the court simply does its best to assess the loss',[86] with the 'loss of chance' cases being the main example. I will discuss the leading case, *Chaplin v Hicks*,[87] shortly, though a different vocabulary was used there to capture the problem. Though the awarding of in principle arbitrary sums as damages for non-pecuniary loss is central to the operation of the law of tort, and though much the same must be said of the limited number of awards for distress and disappointment in contract, in standard commercial contracts arbitrary sums of damages which *ex hypothesi* cannot be traced to the parties' agreement to absorb risk will not be awarded. By entering into a contract, the parties undertook a secondary obligation to provide a remedy, and by default compensatory damages, for losses caused by breach. Though this is an agreement creating strict liability, the liability is for loss for which the defendant is responsible, which logically requires definite quantification of the loss, and it certainly is not an agreement to be arbitrarily mulcted in any sum.

Perhaps the cases in which the consequences of an inability to quantify loss have been most thoroughly discussed are those which compose the, as it were, 'losing contracts' canon, for in *Anglia TV v Reed Ltd*[88] and *CCC Films (London) Ltd v Impact Quadrant Films*[89] the claimants did not proceed with lost profits claims they feared

[83] PA Gaughan, *Measuring Business Interruption Losses and Other Commercial Damages*, (2nd edn, Wiley 2009) and H Roberts, *Riley on Business Interruption Insurance* (10th edn, Sweet & Maxwell 2016). Whilst I am in any case barely equipped to do so, going in any depth into the litigation technique of proving contested losses is inappropriate here. The unreported (an ancillary decision of the Court of Appeal on the procedure for appointing expert witnesses providing the evidence of lost profits is reported) *Vasiliou v Hajigeorgiou* [2010] EWCA Civ 1475 is, however, illustrative.

[84] MG Bridge, 'Expectation Damages and Uncertain Future Losses' in J Beatson and D Friedman (eds), *Good Faith and Fault in English Law* (OUP 1995).

[85] E Peel, *Treitel on the Law of Contract* (15th edn, Sweet & Maxwell 2020) para 20-064.

[86] ibid para 20.063.

[87] [1911] 2 KB 786 (CA) (hereafter *Chaplin v Hicks*).

[88] [1972] 1 QB 60 (CA) (hereafter *Anglia TV*).

[89] [1985] QB 16 (QB) (hereafter *CCC Films*).

they could not prove.[90] In Chapter 9 we shall see that, in contrast to the limited problem of relating expectation and reliance in 'losing contract' claims of this nature, there is an important class of cases in which the claimant, in order to obtain what it regards as adequate compensation of lost expectation, has sought to avoid the way in which the rules of causation, and in particular the requirement of certainty, quantify such loss. For the moment, it is enough to note that the certainty requirement follows from the nature of the secondary obligation the parties created, and that, therefore, its ultimate ground is in their agreement.

One advantage of describing the standard of quantification as certainty is that it allows a clearer sense of what is involved in cause in fact by contrasting the word certainty's connotation of definiteness with its connotation of inevitability, when inevitability is precisely what is not meant. Some idea of the but-for test taken literally preventing the award of other than nominal damages clearly lies behind the misguided claim that the loss of a chance poses any particular problem, for, of course, in such cases it is analytically the case that the claimant might not have suffered any loss at all if the chance had not materialised. The claimant in *Chaplin v Hicks*, a participant in effectively a beauty contest, obviously might not have won at all, and the basic 'reason' this might have been the case was hardly fit for judicial scrutiny.[91] Though, as the claimant was awarded £100, *Chaplin v Hicks* has been cited as authority for the claim that sometimes speculative losses might in fact be compensated,[92] this is of course quite incoherent, and it is submitted that this is not the basis on which the case rests.

The Court of Appeal distinguished between remoteness which, in a proper *Hadley v Baxendale* sense, was not really an issue, and what was described as the damages being 'unassessable' or 'incapable of being [calculated] with certainty or precision'.[93] But, especially as the Court of Appeal considered the matter when the claimant had reached a stage in the competition when she had become one of 50 with a chance of winning one of 12 'prizes',[94] the damages were readily assessable. The total value of the prizes, as may be determined from the headnote, was £13,104,[95] and quantification therefore is a matter of the fundamentally simple and perfectly acceptable arithmetic operation of dividing that total by 50, though it must be said that this yields a loss of *circa* £150

[90] These cases are put to one side here but are discussed in D Campbell and R Halson, 'Expectation and Reliance: One Principle or Two?' (2015) 32 Journal of Contract Law 231. The term 'losing contracts' does describe the problem but it is conceptually loose. It does not even capture the facts of *Anglia TV* (n 88) or *CCC Films* (n 89), and *Omak Maritime Ltd v Mamola Challenger Shipping Co Ltd* [2010] EWHC 2026 (Comm); [2011] 2 All ER (Comm) 155 of course raised an, in a sense, opposed problem.

[91] *Chaplin v Hicks* (n 87) 791–92.

[92] For which there is justification in the judgment, eg ibid 792:

> In [some cases] the jury must do the best they can, and it may be that the amount of their verdict will really be a matter of guesswork. But the fact that damages cannot be assessed with certainty does not relieve the wrongdoer of the necessity of paying damages for his breach of contract.

[93] ibid 790, 791.

[94] ibid 791, 796, 798–99.

[95] The 12 prizes were of three year theatrical engagements, the first four prizes at £5/week, the second four at £4/week, and the third four at £3/week.

which is at some distance from the, no doubt rough and ready and rounded, but not nearly sufficiently *outré* to justify its being set aside, £100 awarded.[96]

The vital point is that all consequential loss of profits cases involve an element of chance in the sense of it not being able to be said with certainty in the sense of inevitability that a future profitable state of affairs would come about. If we were to apply a truly exacting but-for test to consequential loss, there would be few successful contested claims. We do not do this. It is when it cannot be proven that *any* loss capable of the standard of reasonable definition I am calling certainty has been sustained that the nominal damages argued for by the defendant in *Chaplin v Hicks* should be awarded. The claimants in *Anglia TV* and *CCC Films* did not think they had suffered no loss; it was that they could not prove their loss to this standard. And the exotic features of these cases should not distract from the mundanity of the underlying problem, which is explored at length Chapter 9. What in fact distinguishes *Chaplin v Hicks*, in which the loss was a quantity clearly susceptible of measurement, from cases such as the, in this sense, ordinary business investment represented by *Anglia TV* and *CCC Films*, is that the loss in the former was much *more*, not much *less*, certain in the sense we mean here, the sense in which it is essential for parties to have a definite and therefore rational idea of their risks of liability, about which they can then negotiate and agree.

Remoteness

Though regarded as a crucial part, if not indeed the foundation, of the law of remedies, which of course it is, *Hadley v Baxendale* is an attempt, not to stipulate a remedy, but to regulate agreement over the allocation of risk in the face of a problem of asymmetric information.[97] It is perhaps the paradigm example of that aspect of the common law (of contract) which used to drive the late Professor Simpson to distraction that, were it not enough that Alderson B's *dicta* now regarded as axioms of the common law were derived from Pothier,[98] and that the crucial facts of the case remain unknown and no doubt unknowable, the subsequent employment of those *dicta* have been subject to interpretations so divergent as to raise issues of basic meaning.[99] Here we will take it

[96] Slightly more complicated quantifications involving differentiating between the different prizes could bring the figure closer to £100, but it is the roundness of £100 that is, one suspects, the most important thing about it.

[97] JH Barton, 'The Economic Basis of Damages for Breach of Contract' (1972) 1 Journal of Legal Studies 277, 296 and RA Posner, *Economic Analysis of Law* (1st edn, Little, Brown 1972) 61 (hereafter Posner, *Economic Analysis*). Though I will not describe this development here, Judge Posner's treatment of efficient breach has grown somewhat more sophisticated over successive editions of his textbook, and it is no longer, in fact, directly open to the criticisms made of its statements in early editions, with some distinction between being clearheaded about the decision to breach (see the text accompanying n 43) and acting from solipsistic self-interest (see the text accompanying n 156) emerging.

[98] Pothier, *Obligations* (n 24) pt I, ch II, art III:

> the debtor is only liable for the damages . . . which might have been contemplated at the time of the contract, for to such alone the debtor can be considered to have intended to submit.

[99] AWB Simpson, 'Innovation in Nineteenth Century Contract Law' in *Legal Theory and Legal History* (Hambledon Press 1987) 197–201.

that the first limb of *Hadley v Baxendale* provides that the defendant will be liable, not for loss in fact caused by the breach, but only for such of that loss as was in its reasonable contemplation at the time of the agreement, ie it imposes a proximity limit. To this must then be contrasted the second limb, which requires 'special circumstances [to be] known and communicated'[100] if the defendant is to be liable for unusual losses outside of its initial reasonable contemplation (subject to the cap discussed above in connection with but-for). This has come to be generally called giving notice. In *Hadley v Baxendale* itself, the consequential loss of profits caused by the delay in carrying the broken crankshaft would have been recoverable if such loss was in the reasonable contemplation of the defendant common carrier; or, if not originally in reasonable contemplation, as it were brought within it by notice given by the mill owner obviously in a superior position to know of that loss.

I will not even address the now simply immense literature which has argued that the 'policy' behind *Hadley v Baxendale* is either inconsistent with some superior notion of justice (perhaps not at all specific to contract) or with some more efficient economic outcome. The problem at the root of the case is that a party enjoying asymmetric information has a solipsistic incentive to negotiate in such a way as to lead the other party to absorb a risk it did not understand. In countering this, the rule in *Hadley v Baxendale* is one of the clearest articulations of requiring mutual recognition by the parties for their contracts to be justifiable as agreements, and so enforceable.[101] The virtue of *Hadley v Baxendale* is that it does not attempt to stipulate an allocation of risk. It attempts to ensure that the allocation made in the contract is the product of agreement, and whether that allocation is, *sub specie aeternitatis*, a wise allocation is neither here nor there. It is possible (if extremely hard to envisage) that a contracting party could agree to be liable for all the consequences caused by its breach; but it is impossible to think that this could legitimately be the default agreement. The default rule surely has to be proximity as reasonable contemplation, and any variation of this would have to be the product of a clear ouster.

It is in this sense that 'notice' is perhaps a misleading terminology, and certainly one is struck by the amount of unhelpful discussion it has occasioned. Consistent with the requirement that the absorption of risk be agreed, the giving of mere notice, as in the well-known hypothetical example of the taxi driver, obviously is insufficient. What must be given is an opportunity to negotiate:

> had the special circumstances been known, the parties might have specially provided for the breach of contract by special terms as to the damages in that case; and of this advantage it would be very unjust to deprive them.[102]

Notice must be understood as a general disclosure requirement the purpose of which is to allow informed negotiations about the allocation of unusual liability by

[100] *Hadley v Baxendale* (n 13) 356.

[101] L Friedman, *Contract Law in America* (Quid Pro Quo Books 2011) 100 (emphasis added):

> it would distort the market to allow [the party with the knowledge of the risk] to *cast* his losses upon another party.

[102] *Hadley v Baxendale* (n 13) 356.

countering the defendant's initial informational disadvantage. Though it is perhaps reckless to lay too much stress on the use of single words more than a century ago (even if they were correctly reported), Alderson B's use of 'contemplation' at least now carries, it is submitted, more of the necessary connotation of deliberate consideration of and negotiation about risk allocation than the alternate use of 'foreseeable'. This use is, of course, essential if one seeks to conflate contract and tort, though the entire point is that in the latter liability is directly imposed by the state, precisely what should not be the case in the former.[103]

In distinguishing reasonable contemplation and foreseeability, I am trying to drive at the necessity of providing an opportunity to negotiate, not at some refinement of the relevant definition of foreseeability as was attempted by the House of Lords in *Koufos v C Czarnikow Ltd, The Heron II*.[104] Though the significance of the possibility of negotiation central to contract but absent in tort was recognised,[105] it was rather submerged in an exercise in oblique logomachy (admittedly occasioned by previous such exercises) which failed to clearly identify that what was at issue was not whether the loss was, if I may again be allowed to use the term, *sub specie aeternitatis* foreseeable (or not remote, or not likely to occur, etc, etc), but what a reasonable person in the defendant's position objectively should have known.

It is submitted that the far preferable line is taken in *British Columbia and Vancouver's Island Spar, Lumber and Saw-mill Co Ltd v Nettleship*,[106] in which, though there is no great rigour in terminology, contemplation is rightly taken to connote, not what might be foreseen, but what the defendant had an opportunity to negotiate, something, of course, that is wholly irrelevant to the imposition of negligence liability by the state. *British Columbia Saw-mill* considers, not what the defendant could have known, but for what it 'intended to become responsible',[107] or, looking at the matter from the opposite viewpoint, what 'advantage [the claimant] has ... paid for':[108]

> the mere fact of knowledge cannot increase the liability. The knowledge must be brought home to the party sought to be charged, under such circumstances that he must know that the person he contracts with reasonably believes that he accepts the contract with the special condition attached to it.[109]

[103] A great deal of the deplorable confusion of *H Parsons (Livestock) Ltd v Uttley Ingham and Co Ltd* [1978] QB 791 (CA) turned on the then prevailing failure, discussed in ch 5, to keep separate contract and the tort of negligence. With respect to our particular concerns at this point, Scarman LJ's views (ibid 807B–C) epitomised everything that had gone wrong

> where the contract contains no term limiting the damages recoverable for breach, the amount of damages does not depend upon whether, as a matter of legal classification, the plaintiff's cause of action is breach of contract or tort ... the difference between 'reasonably foreseeable' (the test in tort) ... and 'reasonably contemplated' (the test in contract) is semantic, not substantial.

[104] [1969] 1 AC 350 (HL).
[105] ibid 385G–386A.
[106] (1867–68) LR 3 CP 499.
[107] ibid 506.
[108] Ibid 508.
[109] Ibid 509.

It should be recalled that, to be perfectly accurate, *Hadley v Baxendale* was a decision about the direction to be given to a special jury charged with deciding what was in the reasonable contemplation of a party in the defendant's position as a matter of fact. For reasons of the administration of justice which must be given great weight, English civil procedure has eschewed the use of a jury in contract cases. But this has turned contractual proximity decisions into a 'legal product',[110] which poses a particular question about judges' ability to enter into 'the lived world of contracts'[111] in order to take such decisions, and behind this a most important further question about the satisfactoriness of the product to the commercial world.[112] All this should not alter the nature of the decision which has to be reached. It is not merely that no nice refinement of legal terminology should govern decisions about proximity in contract cases; it is that, once the law is clarified in the way *Hadley v Baxendale* did, contractual proximity remains a question of fact (in answering which precedent can of course play a part). The court must decide upon the liability of a commercial party by determining its objective negotiating competence, taking into account any special knowledge it should possess by virtue of its particular business standing, at the time of agreement. The task is, in a most important sense, an interpretative one which must be considered in the light of the discussion of contextualism in Chapter 4.

But, as if to demonstrate just what should not be done, a rule which has played a leading role in facilitating the success of the market economies was, to the extent that the perspective of the appeal courts has so far fed into commercial life, rudely shaken in 2008 by *The Achilleas*. In part, *The Achilleas* merely restated what it has been argued here indeed is the basis of *Hadley v Baxendale*. It is impossible to derive a *ratio* from the judgment as a whole, and one is obliged to focus on Lord Hoffmann's speech, not only because it was essential to the outcome of the case, but because it has certainly been the speech which has since drawn the most attention. Lord Hoffmann found that: it 'is logical to found liability for damages upon the intention of the parties (objectively ascertained) because all contractual liability is voluntarily undertaken',[113] and so it is 'in principle wrong to hold someone liable for risks for which the people entering into such a contract in their particular market, would not reasonably be considered to have undertaken'.

But if such an 'agreement-centred approach' turning on determining the parties' intentions[114] was the jumping-off point for his Lordship's reasoning, this was all but

[110] R Danzig, '*Hadley and Another v Baxendale and Others*' in R Danzig and GR Watson, *The Capability Problem in Contract Law* (2nd edn, Foundation Press 2004) 79.

[111] L Mulcahy, 'Telling Tales About Relational Contracts: How Do Judges Learn About the Lived World of Contracts' in D Campbell, L Mulcahy, and S Wheeler (eds), *Changing Concepts of Contract* (Palgrave Macmillan 2013).

[112] M Galanter, 'The Vanishing Trial: An Examination of Trials and Related Matters in Federal and State Courts' (2002) 1 Journal of Empirical Legal Studies 459 and R Dingwall and E Cloatre, 'Vanishing Trials? An English Perspective' [2006] Journal of Dispute Resolution 51.

[113] *The Achilleas* (HL) (n 79) [12].

[114] ibid [11]. 'Agreement-centred' appeared in the title of one of the academic works so important to Lord Hoffmann's judgment: A Kramer, 'An Agreement-Centred Approach to Remoteness and Contract Damages' in N Cohen and E McKendrick (eds), *Comparative Remedies for Breach of Contract* (Hart 2005). No unified line can be derived from this and the other two articles (A Robertson, 'The Basis of the Remoteness Rule in Contract' (2008) 28 Legal Studies 172 and A Tettenborn, '*Hadley v Baxendale* Foreseeability: A Principle Beyond its Sell-by Date' (2007) 23 Journal of Contract Law 120), otherwise why would they all merit publication? So in J Beatson, A Burrows, and J Cartwright, *Anson on Contract* (30th edn, OUP 2016)

completely obscured by this approach being expressed, in a way that left leading commentators aghast that judicial legislation of such ambition could even be thought of,[115] in terms which definitely sought to alter the rule in *Hadley v Baxendale*.[116] Lord Hoffmann sought to introduce, at least into some 'unusual' cases,[117] an 'assumption of responsibility test' which must be traced to *Hedley Byrne and Co Ltd v Heller and Partners Ltd*,[118] but with an added degree of complexity introduced into the law of negligence by Lord Hoffmann himself in *South Australia Asset Management Corpn v York Montague Ltd*.[119] Taken on its face, assumption of responsibility is merely one way of stating the agreement-centred approach: parties should be liable only for responsibilities they assume. But assumption of responsibility in tort is a sort of abuse of language. It does not mean assumption determined by the party's intentions; it means imposition of responsibility by the court applying exogenous standards.[120] In this way, *The Achilleas* has been one of the unhappiest recent instances of the regrettable failure to distinguish the nature and function of contract as opposed to tort, which failure remains a characteristic of the law of, and even more of academic reflection on, remedies for breach.[121]

The issues, if there were any, that led to Lord Hoffmann's restatement were not raised or discussed by counsel,[122] and seem to be attributable to his Lordship having found assistance in three pieces of academic writing.[123] Early hopes that *The Achilleas* could and should simply be ignored have overall been disappointed,[124] but the very—I apologise for this word but can think of none more fit—perversity of the actual decision in *The Achilleas* invited, perhaps obliged, legal advisers to in future see if their clients, formerly perfectly reconciled to their position because of the recognised value of the *Hadley v Baxendale* rule producing it, could avail themselves of that decision. In a way which required a remarkable departure from the conditions which common law reasoning, particularly when it is being innovative,[125] requires for the law to work

580 the differences between the academic arguments is used to read agreement-centred in quite the opposite fashion than I claim Lord Hoffmann read it.

[115] H McGregor, *McGregor on Damages* (18th edn, Sweet & Maxwell 2009) para 6.173.

[116] *The Achilleas* (HL) (n 79) [66].

[117] ibid [11]. I confine to a footnote the incontestable point that what may constitute 'unusual' is irremediably vague and, for the reasons discussed in the main text, the decision in *The Achilleas* itself is worse than no guidance. McGregor could hardly contain his scorn: 'What then is an unusual case, a very special case, an extraordinary case, an exceptional case—word it as you will': H McGregor, *McGregor on Damages* (19th edn, Sweet & Maxwell 2014) (hereafter *McGregor* (19th edn)) para 8.170.

[118] [1964] AC 465 (HL).

[119] [1997] AC 191 (HL).

[120] D Campbell, 'The Curious Incident of the Dog that Did Bark in the Night-time: What Mischief Does *Hedley Byrne and Co Ltd v Heller and Partners* Correct?' in K Barker, R Grantham and W Swain (eds), *The Law of Misstatements: 50 Years on from Hedley Byrne v Heller* (Hart 2015) 116–19.

[121] D Campbell, 'Our Obligations to the Common Law (Review of A Burrows, *Remedies for Torts, Breach of Contract and Equitable Wrongs*)' [2020] Lloyd's Maritime and Commercial Law Quarterly 149, 158–59, 166–68.

[122] *The Achilleas* (HL) (n 79) [93].

[123] See n 114.

[124] Edelman, *McGregor*, 21st edn (n 70) paras 8.160–8.165.

[125] LL Fuller, *The Law in Quest of Itself* (Foundation Press 1940) 140 (hereafter Fuller, *Law in Quest of Itself*):

itself pure[126]—disputes worth solving have to be identified by the parties themselves, not by judges;[127] the focus should be on 'the specific facts of the case';[128] and judges should confine themselves to reasoning in what Llewellyn called the formal style[129]—the House of Lords handed down a judgment which is incomprehensible. I make no pretence of giving an overall account of the reasoning in *The Achilleas*, but wish to make the point that the decision the Lords reached is wholly inimical to the values of the law of contractual causation based on agreement.

If there was a breach,[130] then damages would be quantified under either the first or second limbs of *Hadley x Baxendale*. If, as it should have been and perhaps was the case, quantification was analysed under the first limb,[131] then the question was whether it was within reasonable contemplation that a shipowner would seek a follow-on fixture for its vessel after redelivery in a market a defining characteristic of which was volatility. This question should need only to be asked to be answered. To give the wrong answer, the House of Lords reversed all but one of the arbitrators and judges who had tried the matter closer to the facts.[132]

Lord Hoffmann in part rested his doing this on a claimed knowledge of 'a general understanding in the industry'[133] that liability was limited. It is submitted that, for the reasons discussed in Chapter 4, no fixed barrier to reliance on such contextual information should, nor indeed can, be erected, and we discuss an important legitimate reference to such an 'understanding' in Chapter 9. But, for reasons also discussed in

> The judge ... ought to be proud that his contribution is such that it cannot be said with certainty whether it is something new or only the better telling of an old story. This is the best possible guarantee that his work is at once creative and sound, and that he is playing his part in the eternal process by which the common law works itself pure and adapts itself to the needs of a new day.

126 *Omychund v Barker* (1744) 1 Atk 22, 34; 26 ER 15, 23 (Mr Solicitor-General Murray, later Lord Mansfield):

> A statute very seldom can take in all cases, therefore the common law, *that works itself pure* by rules drawn from the fountain of justice, is for this reason superior to an Act of Parliament.

127 PH Rubin, 'Why Is the Common Law Efficient?' (1977) 6 Journal of Legal Studies 51:

> the efficient rule situation ... is due to an evolutionary mechanism whose direction proceeds from the utility maximising decisions of disputants rather than the wisdom of judges.

128 RE Megarry, *Lawyer and Litigant* (Hamlyn Trust 1962) 120–21.

129 KN Llewellyn, *The Common Law Tradition* (Little, Brown 1960) 38: 'policy is for the legislature, not for the courts, and so is change, even in pure common law'.

130 There is unresolved confusion over the relevance of the question whether late redelivery after a 'legitimate last voyage' constituted breach at all (*Transfield Shipping Inc v Mercator Shipping Inc, The Achilleas* [2007] EWCA Civ 901; [2008] 1 All ER (Comm) 685 [61] (hereafter *The Achilleas* (CA)), which would seem to make the discussion of the principle of remoteness, indeed of quantification of damages, wholly *obiter*: VP Goldberg, '*The Achilleas*: Forsaking Foreseeability' in *Rethinking Contract Law and Contract Design* (Edward Elgar 2015) 132:

> Common standard time charter forms differed on whether the charterer would have to pay charter or market rates for late redelivery. None, however, go so far as to give the owner loss-of-fixture damages for a legitimate last voyage.

131 Lady Hale, Lord Rodger, and in part Lord Walker can be most clearly said to have done this, but how did they then reach their conclusion?

132 On the views of the minority arbitrator see *The Achilleas* (CA) (n 130) [73]–[77].

133 *The Achilleas* (HL) (n 79) [6]–[8]. The account by Lord Walker, ibid [65], conveys something of the requisite note of caution. The point is rather emphasised by the way that descriptions of shipping industry practice in the academic literature convey a very mixed picture indeed.

Chapter 4, an approach based on great caution about the court's capacity to obtain such information should be taken. Though determining what is regarded as business efficacy in the industry is right in principle, it is impossible to form a clear view of the 'general understanding' from what is said by Lord Hoffmann of the views of various participants' in the shipping industry, which is unsupported by evidence, and about which no prior clarification was available of a matter never previously litigated.[134]

One has to say that the account of this understanding is implausible as, for it to have the effect Lord Hoffmann claimed for it, it would have to represent a general abandonment (not a specific, second limb ouster) of the first limb of *Hadley v Baxendale*! Leaving aside this surprising concession of law-making power to the shipping industry,[135] this would, as Rix LJ incisively pointed out,[136] create an 'undesirable and uncommercial' default rule allowing a charterer to have scant regard to redelivery dates when the market is rising, for it could, to use the language of the Lords, overrun and retain the margin between 'fixture' and 'overrun' rates. Could this have occurred without occasioning some debate, perhaps controversy, perhaps litigation within, or political lobbying by, 'the shipping industry'? Leaving aside all the other issues raised by *The Achilleas*, the perverse conclusion Lord Hoffmann reached on a claimed but implausible knowledge of the shipping industry is *per incuriam*.

Of course, it is essential that parties can limit or expand their default liability. But the law of contract requires that this must be done by agreement, as we have seen Lord Hoffmann in a sense tried to stress. Expansion of liability is, of course, the very business of the second limb. Other devices are normally used for limitation.[137] But it is instructive to see the common issue, so let us talk of limiting liability as a second limb issue. The charterer in *The Achilleas* would have to oust the limit of reasonable contemplation by giving notice, by which is meant provide a clear opportunity for negotiation. There is simply no discussion of this as 'fixture' measures and 'overrun' measures are contrasted as alternative mandatory rules by a House of Lords which has lost all sense of what it should be doing.[138] If the charterer did not give objective evidence of an ouster being agreed, then it was not agreed, and a decision which gives

[134] ibid [10].

[135] *Transfield Shipping Inc v Mercator Shipping Inc, The Achilleas* [2006] EWHC 3030 (Comm); [2007] 1 All ER (Comm) 379 [67 n 7].

[136] *The Achilleas* (CA) (n 130) [119].

[137] A regrettable addition to the logomachy that characterises the judicial treatment of this subject may have taken place as some of Lord Hoffmann's language (ibid [21]) seems to have been elevated to a terminology one now may be forced to use to redescribe the obvious in terms of the 'inclusionary' and the 'exclusionary': *Supershield Ltd v Siemens Building Technologies* FE Ltd [2010] EWCA Civ 7; [2010] 1 Lloyd's Rep 349.

[138] Only three years previously, the House of Lords had refused to do precisely this on exemplary reasoning in *Jackson v Royal Bank of Scotland plc* [2005] UKHL 3; [2005] 1 WLR 377 [37]:

> The parties have the opportunity to limit their liability in damages when they are making their contract. They have the opportunity at that stage to draw attention to any special circumstances outside the ordinary course of things which they ought to have in contemplation when entering into the contract. If no cut-off point is provided by the contract, there is no arbitrary limit that can be set to the amount of the damages once the test of remoteness according to one or other of the rules in *Hadley v Baxendale* has been satisfied.

There is, of course, a cut-off point, when proof of further loss would become 'too speculative to permit the making of any award' (ibid); ie it is a question, not of remoteness, but of certainty.

effect to such an ouster cannot follow from a refinement, but only from a rejection, of the *Hadley v Baxendale* rules and the value of agreement which they institutionalise.

Mitigation

Though it dates from 1912, the leading statement of the doctrine of mitigation, by Viscount Haldane LC in the *British Westinghouse* case, is framed in terms of 'certain broad principles which are quite well settled':

> The first is that, as far as possible, he who has proved a breach of a bargain to supply what he contracted to get is to be placed, as far as money can do it, in as good a situation as if the contract had been performed. The fundamental basis is thus compensation for pecuniary loss naturally flowing from the breach; but this first principle is qualified by a second, which imposes on a plaintiff the duty of taking all reasonable steps to mitigate the loss consequent on the breach, and debars him from claiming any part of the damage which is due to his neglect to take such steps.[139]

With the very important exception of *White and Carter (Councils) Ltd v McGregor*,[140] which is discussed at length Chapter 9, the general principles of the law of mitigation as they institutionalise the moral basis of contract which this book seeks to describe have continued to be settled, and are capable of reduction to the clear principle that 'the claimant cannot recover for avoidable loss'.[141] But, as we shall see the exception strikingly illustrates, the very existence of mitigation, which it is not worth arguing contradicts the classical conception of solipsistic self-interest, is not understood. Why, to adopt Viscount Haldane LC's term, is compensation qualified by mitigation?

'Qualified' is, with great respect, the wrong term. Its connotation of opposition to compensation cannot convey the way that mitigation is in line with the way the entire 'system of legal remedies for breach of contract ... has shown a marked solicitude for men who do not keep their promises'.[142] Focused on expectation rather than performance, compensatory damages are themselves quantified according to causation rules of certainty and proximity which 'have the effect of restricting rather than enlarging

[139] *British Westinghouse* (n 14) 689.

[140] [1962] AC 413 (HL Sc).

I do not regard the doctrinal problems to which *Golden Strait Corp v Nippon Yusen Kubishika Kaisha, The Golden Victory* [2007] UKHL 12; [2007] 2 AC 353 gave rise as of sufficient interest as to merit discussion here; indeed they are entirely chimerical, though these problems have spread throughout the law of damages, indeed beyond contract: *Hooper v Oates* [2013] EWCA Civ 91; [2014] Ch 287. The chimericality follows from an in doctrinal terms unaccountable failure to grasp is obvious and necessary implications of the basic mitigation rule: A Dyson and A Kramer, 'There Is No Breach Date Rule"' (2014) 130 Law Quarterly Review 259. The real problem is the excessive ambition exhibited by recent courts determined to do justice, and I have nothing to add particular to this case to what is said of *The Achilleas* in J Morgan, 'A Victory for "Justice" Over Commercial Certainty' [2007] Cambridge Law Journal 263.

[141] *Thai Airways International Public Company Ltd v KI Holdings Co Ltd* [2015] EWHC 1250 (Comm); [2016] 1 All ER (Comm) 675 [31]–[33] (Leggatt J), quoting *McGregor* (19th edn) (n 117) para 9.004. Under its new editor, 'reasonably' has been inserted before 'avoidable' in Edelman, *McGregor*, 21st edn (n 70) para 9.004, in apparent defiance of the reasoning about 'certainty' discussed in n 80.

[142] EA Farnsworth, 'Legal Remedies for Breach of Contract' (1970) 70 Columbia Law Review 1145, 1216.

the responsibility of the party in breach'.[143] The explanation for this, it has been argued, is that the protection of the claimant's interest at least cost to the defendant provides a means—the best ever devised and the best of which, given the plausibly realistic philosophic anthropology of the economic actor with which this book tries to work, I can conceive—of dealing with inevitable error in economic allocation under positive transaction costs. But this so far has been a 'functional' explanation based on the rationality of the economic system, and in itself is at a 'structural' level difficult to relate to economic actors' motivations for, and understandings of, their actions. Consideration of mitigation now allows us to complement this explanation with an account of the system as the result of choices,[144] building upon what has so far been said of certainty and proximity as being necessary for parties to agree the risks they take by entering into a contract.

In the interests of brevity, let us focus on legal goods. The prices of such goods will reflect not only the cost of the, as it were, physical factors of their production but also the transaction costs of the sales process, amongst which we may distinguish the costs of the anticipated risks of the liabilities the parties undertake by creating secondary obligations. Let us call 'generic' that great majority of goods which are available in ready, competitive supply, and consider the position of a potential claimant buyer of such a good. A buyer buying on default terms will buy with the objective intention that compensatory damages which must be certain, proximate, and unavoidable are ultimately available against the seller. A failure to deliver or rejection therefore will lead the buyer to mitigate by obtaining a substitute (or to negotiations with the seller in the shadow of the law of causation leading to replacement, repair, etc).

All this is possible only because the Holmesian choice makes breach readily possible, and undeniably therefore reduces the likelihood of performance of the primary obligation, or, to put it the other way around, increases the risk of breach and non-performance. Setting aside until Chapter 9 any consideration of the doctrinal limits on its choice, a potential claimant buyer could oust the default and agree a remedy more likely to reduce the risk, say specific performance or disgorgement damages. *Ex hypothesi*, the risk now borne by the defendant seller must increase and, *ceteris paribus*, this will be reflected in the price. If the pricing of risk is accurate, the defendant should be indifferent about the extent of a liability for which it is paid. But the claimant will not pay for the defendant to take on the extra risk, because doing so confers no benefit on the *claimant*. The buyer's real security is the existence of markets in generic goods, for, faced with non-performance, the buyer can obtain a substitute, and, if necessary, claim market damages. The buyer will not pay for security from the defendant which is more expensive than the cost of the buyer availing itself of the security of the market, for, in other than exceptional cases, the buyer will be better able to take steps to obtain a substitute which is suitable to it (concerning delivery terms, payment schedule, confidence in the alternative seller, etc) than the seller.

The 1957 case of *Charter v Sullivan*,[145] which gave rise to considerable discussion because of the ground on which the Court of Appeal distinguished an apparently four

[143] ibid.
[144] Goetz and Scott, 'Mitigation Principle' (n 45) 981.
[145] [1957] 2 QB 117 (CA) (hereafter *Charter v Sullivan*).

square decision of Upjohn J only three years earlier in *Thompson (WL) Ltd v Robinson (Gunmakers) Ltd*,[146] is instructive in its perfect ordinariness.[147] Both cases were of car dealer's damages following a buyer's wrongful rejection of a generic motor car. In the former, mitigation by sale to another buyer at the contract price[148] meant that the loss was zero and damages were nominal. This is what will happen in the overwhelming majority of cases. *Charter v Sullivan* was brought only because damages had been substantial in *Thompson v Robinson*, but this was because it was accepted in the latter case that mitigation was not possible, though this was not obvious because the problem was, not an inability to return the particular car to the suppliers, for it was returned, but a loss of volume of sales in a market in which supply exceeded demand.[149] I shall not enter into the merits of claims for 'lost volume',[150] though I can briefly say that such a claim should fall under the second limb of *Hadley v Baxendale*, for it is *Charter v Sullivan's* rather striking combination of perfect ordinariness as a case decided under the positive law of expectation and its scandalousness—breach without cost!—viewed from the performance interest perspective to which I wish to draw attention.

I shall not extend this argument to breach of warranty, seller's remedies, and the corollary laws in sales of services (or land, etc); nor shall I attempt to explicitly bring in the number of minor contractual doctrines, such as the minimum legal obligation rule, which support the principal law. I believe all these doctrines turn on the point I have sought to make in connection with buyer's remedies: remedies for breach of contract cannot be understood as seeking to, in principle, ensure performance; in principle they do not. Compensation of lost expectation quantified according to rules of causation which minimise the defendant's liability, and which typically lead to mitigation which gives rise to no substantial damages at all, is the basis of remedies for breach of contract. The result is a system for dealing with unavoidable error in economic allocation which can be said to be efficient in a technical sense as it keeps the cost of remedying such error to a minimum, and efficient in the Pareto optimising sense because it represents the choices the parties make in their self-interest.

That this can be so requires that *both* the claimant's and the defendant's interests to be taken into account, and this is done by laws which work so well that the main empirical finding about them is that they are not used, though non-use is a misleading term, and it is better to say that the law normally remains latent in the sense of legal advice not being sought or acted upon whilst the law simultaneously actively channels the parties' conduct into co-operation based on mutual recognition. In order to

[146] [1955] Ch 177 (Ch) (hereafter *Thompson v Robinson*).

[147] Professor Stevens is to be congratulated on concluding his treatment of breach of contract by getting to some justification of awards of nominal damages: R Stevens, *Torts and Rights* (OUP 2007) 71–72. But that this conclusion is reached by a, with respect, tortuous route compared to the basic clarity of the positive law is indicative of the difficulties of the thinking behind his version of the concept of 'substitutive' damages (ibid 60). Stevens strains to unify breach and other wrongs rather than squarely address the specific features of contract that make such a use of 'wrong' problematic, and so he calls the Holmesian choice 'a reformulation' of the law because the existence of the positive law of contract is for him ultimately an incomprehensible mistake.

[148] *Charter v Sullivan* (n 145) 118.

[149] *Thompson v Robinson* (n 146) 187.

[150] JM Breen, 'The Lost Volume Seller and Lost Profits Under UCC 2-708(2)' (1996) 50 University of Miami Law Review 779.

conclude this defence of breach, I will distinguish it from a famous argument which has been used to criticise basing remedies on the expectation interest, and to argue for the superiority of the performance interest: 'efficient breach'.

Conclusion: Efficient Breach and the Efficiency of Breach

Though the term 'efficient breach' was, to my knowledge, coined in 1977,[151] and the first formal statement of a concept which, if its specific sense is to emerge has to be closely defined, was made as recently as 1970,[152] this controversial concept certainly is traceable to the Holmesian choice, for the breach it describes unarguably is made possible only by basing remedies on expectation, not performance. The theoretical model of efficient breach establishes certain conditions under which a defendant has a rational but, even though the claimant's lost expectation is adequately protected, *prima facie* objectionable incentive to breach. If the claimant's expectation is not protected in this way, the breach is not efficient, and much of the criticism of efficient breach misses the point of the concept.[153] The efficient breach proper contemplates a situation in which, after entering into an agreement but prior to performing its primary obligations, a defendant becomes aware of an alternative possible contract with a third party, which it can accept only if it reallocates the resources it had committed to the first contract to the second. These conditions can be stated in a simple (complicating refinements are, of course, always possible) formula, but, in essence, the incentive to breach arises when the profit the defendant will realise from the second contract will substantially exceed the total cost of relinquishing its own profit on the first contract and meeting its liability to the claimant arising from breach of that contract. The defendant improves its original position, but the point is that the position of the claimant, which is compensated on the terms of the first contract, is not worsened.

The lingering *prima facie* unattractiveness of the defendant's conduct is connected to what is most important about efficient breach: its main function has not been in the commercial[154] but the intellectual

[151] CJ Goetz and RE Scott, 'Liquidated Damages, Penalties and the Just Compensation Principle: Some Notes on an Enforcement Model and a Theory of Efficient Breach' (1977) 77 Columbia Law Review 554.

[152] R Birmingham, 'Breach of Contract, Damage Measures, and Economic Efficiency' (1970) 24 Rutgers Law Review 273.

[153] Macaulay has questioned how often the theoretical conditions will obtain and therefore, in a subtle refinement of the argument, asks how wise it is to base a law on the assumption that those conditions will obtain: S Macaulay, 'Relational Contracts Floating on a Sea of Custom? Thoughts About the Ideas of Ian Macneil and Lisa Bernstein' (2000) 94 Northwestern University Law *Review* 775, 782:

> in my experience, when relational concerns do not matter, many large corporations and their law firms do not efficiently breach. They do not seek to buy their way out of contracts for anything like the other party's expectation damages. They just breach, at best offer an insulting token settlement, and practice scorched earth litigation tactics, taken out of that unpublished but very real text, *Discovery Abuse for Fun and Profit*.

[154] Empirical study has shown that commercial parties believe that the conduct described as efficient breach would indeed be a breach of commercial ethics, a clear case of the difference between such ethics and their misdescription in the self-avowed economics of 'efficiency': D Baumer and P Marschall, 'Wilful Breach of Contract for the Sale of Goods: Can the Bane of Business Be an Economic Bonanza' (1992) 65 Temple Law Review 159 171 (hereafter Baumer and Marschall, 'Wilful Breach'):

world,[155] where it is used to strikingly illustrate the supposedly 'economic' idea of efficiency which it expresses, which is either extolled by those committed to such an idea,[156] or regarded as immoral or amoral in a way which undermines the moral basis of contractual promising by those repelled by it.[157] This polarity largely follows from allowing the efficient breach too general a significance. It is not so much that the empirical circumstances which can be said to conform to the theoretical conditions of the efficiency of efficient breach are rare,[158] but that those circumstances, when they do arise, as they certainly have,[159] are of a nature quite different to what we normally mean by breach, the difference emerging from the very distinction between primary and secondary obligations.

In their refinement of the Holmesian choice in the course of re-examining the very basis of 'the compensatory principle', Professors Scott and Triantis are amongst the many who have claimed that the Holmesian choice amounts to contracting parties creating 'options' to perform.[160] The rhetorical burden of this description is, with respect, misleading. It is right to say that when parties agree a contract they do promise *to perform* their primary obligations in the way we discussed in Chapter 5. But this promise is not unconditional.[161] By putting these promises in the form of a contract,

> survey respondents overwhelmingly rejected the notion that it is ethical for a trading partner to breach a contract deliberately because a better deal can be had elsewhere. Respondents also indicated that the wilful nature of a breach would ... substantially increase the probability of litigation.

155 RR Anderson, 'The Compensatory Disgorgement Alternative to Restatement Third's New Remedy for Breach of Contract' (2015) 68 Southern Methodist University Law Review 953, 957:

> In the forty-plus years since it first slithered into view, the efficient breach paradigm has been almost exclusively a creature of the academic literature and the law school classroom.

156 Posner, *Economic Analysis* (n 97) 57: 'it is clear that commission of the breach would be value maximising and should be encouraged'.

157 IR Macneil, 'Efficient Breach of Contract: Circles in the Sky' (1982) 38 Virginia Law Review 947, 968:

> the bias of the simple efficient breach theory ... is in favour of individual, unco-operative behaviour as opposed to behaviour requiring the co-operation of the parties. The whole thrust of the Posner analysis is breach first, talk afterwards.

158 Macneil, 'Contract Remedies' (n 42) 15:

> In the real world of commerce, opportunities for gain through 'efficient breach' of transactions in goods other than true futures deals are so rare as to be almost non-existent. There simply are not many chances for deliberate breaches of this kind, and general propositions about remedies based on them tell singularly little about efficiency in the real world.

159 After Treitel drew attention to it in the 1975 edition of his book, the first edition to pay sustained attention to damages, the formerly obscure Scots case of *Teacher v Calder* (1898) 25 R 661; affd on this point [1899] AC 451 (HL) 467, 462 became the leading Commonwealth authority for the proposition that 'damages are based on loss to the plaintiff and not on gain to the defendant. They are not, in other words, based on any profit which the defendant may have made out of the breach': GH Treitel, *Law of Contract* (4th edn, Sweet & Maxwell 1975) 618. Though there are significant complications, *Teacher v Calder* was at root a Posnerian efficient breach case, very instructively correctly decided in favour of the defender: D Campbell, 'The Treatment of *Teacher* v *Calder* in *AG* v *Blake*' (2002) 65 Modern Law Review 256.

160 R Scott and G Triantis, 'Embedded Options and the Case Against Compensation in Contract Law' (2004) 104 Columbia Law Review 1429. An earlier claim that Holmes himself saw the matter in terms of an option was made in CA Remington, 'Intentional Interference with Contract and the Doctrine of Efficient Breach. Fine Tuning the Notion of the Contract Breacher as Wrongdoer' (1999) 47 Buffalo Law Review 645, 647.

161 I very substantially disagree with Professor Hogg's claim that the concepts of promise and the performance interest derived from promise (M Hogg, *Promises and Contract Law* (CUP 2011) 335) can explain

the parties simultaneously agree secondary obligations which anticipate breach and make provision for its remedy. The defendant cannot properly be said to have an option in the sense of having a legitimately unfettered power to choose which obligation to perform, but nor can it be said that there is no power to choose. The primary and secondary obligations are in a sense 'dual',[162] but they are not entirely 'disjunctive'[163] because they are ranked. The defendant must make a good faith obligation to perform the primary obligation, but it is recognised that there are good faith reasons, arising from error caused by bounded rationality, which might lead the defendant legitimately to breach, and *both* parties to turn to the defendant's secondary obligation, Liability for non-performance is strict, but only in the sense that the liability is to provide a remedy, of which compulsory performance may be one, but compensatory damages are the default and by far the most important.

The role of non-legal sanctions and in particular of the maintenance of reputation has gained enormous significance in the study of the law of contract (and hence of industrial organisation) since Macaulay's 1963 articles.[164] But, as was mentioned in Chapter 3, maintenance of reputation is a necessary and ubiquitous response to bounded rationality, and the very idea of non-legal sanctions is based on a common understanding—traceable to at least Smith's association of the growth of commerce with the improvement of manners due to the necessity of maintaining reputation[165]—that parties monitor each other's contracting action in terms which cannot be reduced to, or go beyond, formal contract, and their choice of counterparties can turn on the views they form. A defendant in breach loses not only its own investment in and profit on the contract, but will place a question mark against its future reliability. A refusal (by a specific party or a group or an industry) to conduct further business with a party which has brought its reliability into question by breach may well be an important sanction.[166] It is in general the case that the understanding and assessment

and should guide much of the law of contract. The former has largely come to connote, and the latter has always embodied, the belief that our thinking should be, as it were, purely legal, certainly void of economic context. Hogg nevertheless valuably opens up the discussion because, attempting to put on a coherent basis what the bulk of performance interest reasoning perforce acknowledges *ad hoc*, he insists on putting the making of a promise in context (ibid 466–67):

> None of [what I have argued] is to say that promise needs to be recognised as the whole of the law of contract, as once might have been argued. Promises . . . have a place within the law of voluntarily assumed obligations, but promise is not the source of all such obligations; other normative and descriptive concepts have their proper place too. Even where promise is properly recognised as the most appropriate form for an obligation, or where the performance interest equating to promise is protected in some remedial way in contract law, the law may quite properly constrain the private promises of parties or the performance interest by reference to other considerations.

162 A Schwartz and D Markovits, 'The Expectation Remedy and the Promissory Basis of Contract' (2012) 45 Suffolk University Law Review 799, 808.

163 S Smith, *Contract Theory* (OUP 2004) 400.

164 The loss of reputation and therefore of repeat business specifically consequent upon efficient breach is stressed in Baumer and Marschall, 'Wilful Breach' (n 154).

165 A Smith, *Lectures on Jurisprudence* in *The Glasgow Edition of the Works and Correspondence*, vol 5 (Clarendon Press 1978) 538–39. Smith saw the possibility of a claimant entirely foregoing a claim rather 'than give any ground for suspicion'.

166 B Klein and KB Leffler, 'The Role of Market Forces in Assuring Contractual Performance' (1981) 89 Journal of Political Economy 615.

of doctrine can be much improved if the effect of the relationship between legal and non-legal sanctions on the parties' actions is properly taken into account,[167] and attempts to 'design' the former should do so.[168] The specific and crucial point which it has been sought to make here is, however, that the 'solicitous' formal law of remedies, its apparent 'non-use', and the importance of apparently 'non-contractual relations' has, without conscious design, constituted an extremely well-functioning remedial response to the standard case of breach, made possible because single incidents of breach are not normally regarded as wrongs in any substantial way (though they may be depending on the circumstances) because commercial parties acknowledge the possibility of legitimate error.

That parties normally do continue to contract after breach is possible because a breach which is caused by circumstances which are regarded as coming within an inevitable and therefore tolerated margin of error is not regarded as a deplorable wrong, but, though regretted by both parties, a matter to be treated as a cost minimisation problem. But a party which choses efficient breach proper cannot avail itself of such an attitude. Such breach is, to borrow words which have not played an entirely beneficent role in the development of the law, not merely 'deliberate' but 'cynical', and as such it must have a corrosive effect on the defendant's reputation for reliability.[169] Whether this effect is sufficient to stop other parties dealing with the defendant is, of course, a matter for them in a widely divergent range of circumstances, and this particular choice has been subjected to extensive theoretical analysis. But their 'calculative' process will be quite different to the 'co-operative' one taken to breach of the ordinary sort.

In Chapter 1 I argued that it is wrong to think the law of contract should be based on the assumption that, because they are self-interested, economic actors are knaves. By far the most discussed knave in twentieth-century legal theory is, of course, Holmes' bad man,[170] who has been particularly connected with efficient breach as just the sort of thing the bad man would do.[171] To the extent that the bad man is just the clear-headed man, he should not be criticised, and if, as is generally the case, the criticism incoherently takes in, not only the efficient breach proper, but the normal breach by which the defendant seeks to avoid costs of performance, then it should be insisted that the bad man's actions are laudable because he is participating in breach as a beneficent means of dealing with error.[172]

[167] D Charny, 'Non-legal Sanctions in Commercial Relationships' (1990) 104 Harvard Law Review 373.

[168] RJ Gilson, CF Sabel, and RE Scott, 'Braiding: The Interaction of Formal and Informal Contracting in Theory, Practice, and Doctrine' (2010) 110 Columbia Law Review 1377 and G Hadfield and I Brozovic, 'Scaffolding: Using Formal Contracts to Support Informal Relations in Support of Innovation' [2016] Wisconsin Law Review 981.

[169] RA Epstein, *Torts* (Aspen Law and Business 1999) 581:

> When breaches of this sort take place within the organized trades, the opportunist is drummed out of the business as unreliable for any future dealings.

[170] OW Holmes, *The Path of the Law*' (1897) 10 Harvard Law Review 457, 459 (hereafter Holmes, 'Path of the Law').

[171] The literature is authoritatively reviewed in the context of an explanation of what Holmes himself would have understood by a 'wrong' in JM Perillo, 'Misreading Oliver Wendell Holmes on Efficient Breach and Tortious Interference' (2000) 68 Fordham Law Review 1085.

[172] Campbell, 'Restatement' (n 5) 1093–1106.

Though no-one has more sought to place the subtleties of the relationship of formal and informal contractual sanctions on a coherent doctrinal basis than Llewellyn, the basic polemical thrust of realism has led to the misunderstanding of the bad man's attitude over (efficient) breach. As Holmes unforgettably put it: 'The prophecies of what the courts will do in fact, and nothing more pretentious, are what I mean by the law',[173] and so 'The duty to keep a contract at common law means a prediction that you must pay damages if you do not keep it, and nothing else.'[174] This is not the same as the statement of the Holmesian choice in *The Common Law*. Leaving aside the flat problem caused by not mentioning equity, the talk 'of what the courts will do' is the talk of formalism, ie of a 'non-ethical' common law, against which Holmes was straining by his use of 'prophecy'.[175] Such talk is particularly misdirected when it is applied to a remedies system the legitimacy of which means its main manifestation has been in its seeming non-use. If the bad man wants to be able to make a prophecy that if he does certain things he will be subjected to disagreeable consequences by way of imprisonment or compulsory payment of money',[176] he will find concentration on what the courts will do does not take him far in calculating the influence what it is nevertheless right to call his 'legal duty'[177] will have on his actions.[178] It is grossly unfair to Holmes to ignore the context of what he was polemically trying to do,[179] and the lesson to be learned from legal realism is still one for moderns, but that the bad man would not normally commit an efficient breach is an acute example of the moral nature of exchange and contract constituting the law of contract in a way quite opposed to the way, as it is normally understood, of the bad man.

If it is right that efficient breach is objectionable in a way that breach as such is not, it might well be thought that remedies for breach of simple contract should be devised which will prevent efficient breach, and, leaving aside what can be seen as various attempts of older vintage to do so,[180] it has recently proven a short step to maintain

173 Holmes, 'The Path of the Law' (n 170) 461.

174 ibid 462.

175 Fuller, *Law in Quest of Itself* (n 125) 94:

> [The bad man] must ask himself ... 'What are the chances that my conduct may lead to detrimental interference in my affairs by the courts?' ... This question he cannot answer by consulting the letter of the law, for he still does not know in what direction the letter will be strained in cases of doubt ... our bad man cannot escape having to decide a question of morality [in order to] calculate accurately the chances of judicial intervention in his affairs.

176 Holmes, 'Path of the Law' (n 170) 461.

177 ibid.

178 HLA Hart, *The Concept of Law* (3rd edn, Clarendon Press 2012) 40:

> The principal functions of the law as a means of social control are not to be seen in private litigation ... which [represents] vital but still ancillary provisions for the failures of the system. It is to be seen in the diverse ways in which the law is used to control, to guide, and to plan life out of court.

The 'new legal realism' being developed by Macaulay and others is an attempt to restate the indispensable core of realism in terms of a full awareness of broadly this consideration: S Macaulay, 'A New Legal Realism: Elegant Models and the Messy Law in Action' in E Mertz, S Macaulay, and TW Mitchell (eds), *Translating Law and Society for Today's Legal Practice* in *The New Legal Realism*, vol 1 (CUP 2016),

179 And so Holmes main point, that the Holmesian choice 'stinks in the nostrils of those who think it advantageous to get as much ethics into the law as they can' (ibid 462), is completely apposite now.

180 An attempt to focus the longstanding if diffuse US doctrine of 'wilful breach' on the specific mischief of efficient breach has been made in S Thel and P Siegelman, 'Wilful Breach: An Efficient Screen for Efficient Breach' in O Ben-Shahar and A Porat (eds), *Fault in American Contract Law* (CUP 2010).

that the performance interest should be better protected to stop this sort of thing happening,[181] and no step at all to subsume this within a general belief that breach of contract is a wrong from which the wrongdoer should not benefit.[182] The problem is the slippery nature of what is found objectionable. The efficient breach is a breach from which the defendant hopes to make an additional gain. It is a clear target for literal enforcement, or disgorgement damages, or whatever. Unfortunately, once one understands the matter, one sees that the entire purpose of breach of the standard type is also to make a gain, albeit a 'negative' gain in the sense of avoiding the loss that continued performance would cause. It simply is not possible practically to distinguish the two, even when the cynical element in efficient breach is present, and as it is overwhelmingly more important to preserve the possibility of the standard case of breach, the performance interest attempt to do so, could, until recently, have been said to be an all but complete failure.

The origin in the case law of what became the performance interest argument should be traced to the 1973 *Wrotham Park Estate Co Ltd v Parkside Homes Ltd*,[183] in which damages under Lord Cairns Act[184] for breach of restrictive covenant came to be interpreted as a response to the problem of, in the most common usage, a 'lost opportunity to bargain'.[185] Through a convoluted—this word isn't strong enough—legal process, the creative use of an equitable remedy which might have been said to have fallen into disuse[186] was transformed into an argument for the wide availability of 'partial disgorgement damages' which, complemented by the 'total disgorgement' made possible by *Blake*, at one time was thought to form a general 'sliding scale' of alternative, non-compensatory damages.[187] This, however, seemed to have been rendered a matter merely of legal history[188] as the potentially revolutionary *Blake* failed to gain much purchase, and indeed was seen to have been the dampest of squibs,[189] until that history was recently revived, in a way to which we shall shortly turn, by the Supreme Court.

In his dissent in *Blake*, Lord Hobhouse rightly said that:

> if some more extensive principle of awarding non-compensatory damages for breach of contract is to be introduced into our commercial law the consequences will be very far reaching and disruptive.[190]

[181] D Friedmann, 'The Efficient Breach Fallacy' (1989) 18 Journal of Legal Studies 1.

[182] At this point, the efficient breach loses all specificity and becomes equated with the Holmesian choice, which it, seemingly unproblematically, taints: J Edelman, *Gain-based Damages* (Hart 2002) 163:

> The doctrine of efficient breach ... seeks to justify the idea that a party has the right to break a contract and choose to pay compensatory damages instead of rendering performance.

[183] [1974] 1 WLR 798 (Ch D).

[184] Chancery Amendment Act 1858, s 2; now Senior Courts Act 1981, s 50.

[185] RJ Sharpe and SM Waddams, 'Damages for Lost Opportunity to Bargain' (1982) 2 Oxford Journal of Legal Studies 290, 292.

[186] JA Jolowicz, 'Damages in Equity: A Study of Lord Cairns' Act' [1975] Cambridge Law Journal 224, 252.

[187] Lord Nicolls, 'Breach of Contract, Restitution for Wrongs, and Punishment: Review of Discussion' in A Burrows and E Peel (eds), *Commercial Remedies* (OUP 2003) 129.

[188] This history up to *Blake* is set out in D Campbell and D Harris, 'In Defence of Breach: A Critique of Restitution and the Performance Interest' (2002) 22 Legal Studies 208.

[189] D Campbell and P Wylie, 'Ain't No Telling (Which Circumstances are Exceptional)' [2003] Cambridge Law Journal 605.

[190] *Blake* (HL) (n 7) 299D.

The fundamental reason this is so is that, behind all the abstruse reasoning, the performance interest argument is based on a visceral conviction that simple breach of contract is in some way a wrong in a substantial rather than a technical way, and so should in principle be prevented,[191] when breach is normally the core of a vital legal response to ineluctable error in economic choice that is of the very highest value. The wayward path taken to *Blake* followed a fundamental mistake about the nature of economic action and contract. That remedies are a system of morality based on a relationship of mutual recognition between both parties to a contract wholly escapes the performance interest argument. In a gross misinterpretation of the positive law, which therefore has to be seen as fundamentally 'defective', breach is seen as a substantial moral wrong committed by the defendant, which is understood to have promised to perform *simpliciter*, against the 'innocent' claimant. It is therefore sought to make a remedy which approximates to literal enforcement the default; a wholly inappropriate imposition of an outcome derived exogenously to the intentions of the parties.

Even as *Blake's* potential general impact foundered, under its influence partial disgorgement continued to have a particular influence on cases of breach of restrictive covenant, and it must, of course, be acknowledged that such breach can often have some of the colour of what is specifically objectionable about efficient breach, especially when normally quantified damages would be nominal, as indeed were both the case in *Wrotham Park* itself. There are, of course, many situations in response to which commercial law has developed and accommodated 'exceptional' remedies because the law of simple contract is inadequate to them. The point of *Blake* was to generalise the 'light sprinkling of cases where courts have made orders having the same effect as an order for an account of profits',[192] creating the problem of then having to limit the general remedy which would be created. In this way, Blake sought to do precisely the opposite of what was necessary, and indeed what the uncomprehended positive law had sought to do, which was to distinguish the exceptional situations in which normally quantified damages were inadequate from the overwhelming number of standard situations in which they were adequate when it was essential that the latter be left alone, even and especially when damages were nominal.

In 2018 in *One Step (Support) Ltd v Morris-Garner*,[193] a non-competition covenant case which could have been handled perfectly well without innovation, the Supreme Court renewed the effort to generalise the partial disgorgement argument. The Court concluded a long review of the history just discussed by strongly intimating that the total disgorgement and the sliding scale parts of that history should be confined to the dustbin of legal history,[194] but sought to reclaim partial disgorgement under the new name of 'negotiating damages'.[195] But though anathema was placed on all previous usage going back to *Wrotham Park*,[196] one is right to conclude from their name that

[191] D Campbell, 'The Defence of Breach and the Policy of Performance' (2006) 22 University of Queensland Law Journal 271.

[192] *Blake* (HL) (n 7) 284C.

[193] [2018] UKSC 20; [2019] AC 649 (hereafter *One Step*).

[194] ibid [81]–[82].

[195] ibid [3]: 'this judgment will use the expression "negotiating damages" introduced by Neuberger LJ in *Lunn Poly Ltd v Liverpool and Lancashire Properties Ltd* [2006] EWCA Civ 430; [2006] 2 EGLR 29, [22].

[196] *One Step* (n 193) [2]–[3].

the rationale of negotiating damages is the lost opportunity to bargain. Negotiating damages were declared to be compensatory—ie not any form of non-compensatory—damages,[197] but this will be fruitless as it does not, because it cannot, solve the problem that ran through all the reasoning set in motion by *Wrotham Park*, especially that which tried to keep to the goal of 'compensation', of how to tell apart breaches which are to be compensated on normal principles, with no negotiating damages, and breaches which are to be 'compensated' in a way quite opposed to those normal principles.[198]

After a seller of generic goods fails to deliver, is a buyer which buys a substitute at a higher cost to receive only market damages, and so be compensated for the loss represented by the difference between the sale and the substitute price, but to receive nothing for release itself, or is there instead to be negotiating damages linked to the gain (ie negative loss) that motivated the buyer to breach; or is there to be a combination of the two? The obvious—unchallengeable if the market system is to survive—answer is only market damages, but why? What distinguishes this case from a case where negotiating damages are thought appropriate? As *One Step* itself perfectly well shows, this has all been gone through *ad tedium* previously, and no amount of going through it again whilst just making assertions about the superiority of what is claimed to be a compensatory analysis will deal with this.

The problem is this. The new judicial vocabulary of negotiating damages talks of the claimant having a 'valuable asset' in 'the right to performance' of which it is deprived when the defendant breaches without having to furnish compensation for the breach itself, ie distinct from furnishing compensation for the loss quantified normally as 'the difference to the claimant between the outcome of performance and non-performance'.[199] From there, the visceral feeling that runs throughout the performance interest argument can be given vent: 'Put shortly, [the defendant] takes something for nothing, for which the [claimant] was entitled to require payment'.[200] But there is no such asset! At the cost of repetition, a party which agrees a contract does indeed agree to perform its primary obligation, but that performance is by default agreed to be subject to the possibility of breach and the provision of a remedy for breach, which by default will be compensatory remedies. The parties do, of course, have an opportunity to negotiate what we should now call negotiating damages, but this is not at the time of breach but—when else?—at the time of the negotiation of their agreement, and they did not do so. Why should the law of contract imply a term here?[201] The only legitimate reason is, as was discussed in Chapter 4, to promote business efficacy by supplying

[197] ibid [91].

[198] The response to the acute statement of this problem as it arose in regard to Lord Cairns Act in *Johnson v Agnew* [1980] AC 367 (HL), 400 is devoid of content: *One Step* (n 193) [47].

[199] ibid [76].

[200] ibid [30].

[201] Perhaps the most instructive, if the anachronistic terminology be allowed, negotiating damages case is *Lane v O'Brien Homes Ltd* [2004] EWHC 303 (QB). There was not even a restrictive covenant in this case, but liability was found for breach of a collateral contract. This was a particularly egregious defiance of the intentions of the parties. Without going into the detail that may be found in D Campbell, 'The Extinguishing of Contract' (2004) 67 Modern Law Review 817, this case took place in a situation where the civil law of England and Wales insisted as strongly as it possibly can, including by statute, that what was not in the written contract was out, and even this did not stand in the way of doing remedial justice according to an abstract juridical scheme.

something so obvious the parties did not make it express. It is indeed obvious that the performance interest thinking that lies behind negotiating damages believes that, by entering into a contract, one gains 'the right to performance'. But one can believe this only if, because one does not understand why it has the shape it has, thinks the whole of the law of remedies for breach of contract is fundamentally wrong.

In this chapter I have tried to explain, not only that to regard the positive law of remedies in this way involves an absurd denial of value to the common law of contract and the growth of the market economy it has facilitated, but in what this value lies. This book attempts to analyse and assess the law of contract in terms of its provision of the conditions of Pareto optimisation, not for any reason of technical efficiency in the production of a collectively determined set of goods, but because those conditions are the conditions of an economy composed of mutually beneficial, because voluntarily agreed, exchanges. And the co-operative law of remedies I have just sought to describe is the product of such optimisation. Contracting parties have agreed that their default liabilities are based on damages which aim to compensate lost expectation, and damages are quantified according to rules of causation which, because the parties conduct themselves within a relationship of mutual recognition, tend to lead the parties into an optimal, cost minimising response to unavoidable errors in economic allocation. This response is, in the standard case of generic goods and services where mitigation is possible, so satisfactory that one can believe that, within ineluctable conditions of positive transaction costs and bounded rationality, it is impossible to improve upon it, save only to ask that contracting parties become fully self-conscious of its co-operative nature arising from mutual recognition. Chapter 9 turns to the great strains which a lack of this self-consciousness places on the law of remedies when it is used to respond to other than the standard case.

9

The Relational Constitution of Remedy (2)

Literal Enforcement as a Substitute for Damages

Introduction: Literal Enforcement in Consumer and Commercial Cases

In Chapter 8 it was claimed that the positive law of remedies for breach of contract based on default compensatory damages is the best general approach of which it is possible to conceive for dealing with the errors, inevitable in all empirical economic action under positive transaction costs, made by boundedly rational parties entering into contractual agreements. This claim is, of course, subject to the qualification one always has to enter about the fallibility of all human institutions. But by exploring a qualification of a different nature which turns on avoidable shortcomings in the law, this chapter attempts to explain the commercial use of the final remedies which try to effect what may be called 'literal enforcement'.

Let us put aside disgorgement damages which, as they relate to simple contract, were in Chapter 8 explained as unwise judicial legislation inimical to the economic functioning of contract. The other literal enforcement remedies are specific performance, indirect specific performance by injunction, cost to complete damages, affirmation, and agreed damages.[1] It is obvious that this is a set of significantly disparate

[1] From the perspective of the analysis of the work of the civil legal system and that system's social significance, debt is by far the most important literal enforcement remedy, and the routinisation of the civil law of debt collection a most important phenomenon in itself: RA Kagan, 'The Routinisation of Debt Collection: An Essay on Social Change and Conflict in the Courts (1984) 18 *Law and Society Review* 323. Debt was treated as a separate literal enforcement remedy in D Harris, D Campbell, and R Halson, *Remedies in Contract and Tort* (2nd edn, CUP 2005) ch 10 (hereafter Harris and others, *Remedies*). But the legal doctrinal nature of debt 'hardly merits comment' (F Lawson, *Remedies of English Law* (2nd edn, Butterworths 1980) 50), and so debt will not be discussed in this book save as it relates to affirmation, which is examined later in this chapter.

The law of debt (not normally the law of debt collection!) is a matter of the negotiation about the event which makes the debt payable, and thus, as with a range of devices including deposit, forfeiture, penalties, etc, raises, though the law on the point is the opposite of clear, issues which should ultimately be seen as common to agreed damages *in toto*: R Halson, *Liquidated Damages and Penalty Clauses* (OUP 2018) ch 5.

Contractual Relations. David Campbell, Oxford University Press. © David Campbell 2022.
DOI: 10.1093/oso/9780198855156.003.0009

remedies, and they can be said to try to effect literal enforcement only in a difficult way which cannot be defended save at the length of this chapter. But these remedies may initially be said to be united in being responses to the very poorly understood but enormously important problem of the compensatory 'inadequacy' of damages, for the key to these responses is to grasp that the very last thing that should be said about them, though it is all but universally said,[2] is that they are not compensatory in aim.

It is, of course, jarring to first make the fulsome claim I have just made for the value of remedies based on compensatory damages, and then to go on to say that inadequacy of damages is a very important problem. But the type of breach about which the claim I have made is entirely justified is what in Chapter 8 was called the standard case, ie a breach which leads to a loss which can be quantified according to the rules of causation. The paradigm case is of a failure to deliver a conforming generic good for which a substitute can be obtained, when the remedy will be market damages, and under this may be subsumed for our purposes the variants—discount on price, repair, etc—which the parties may devise in the shadow of the law which would otherwise provide market damages. It is similarly correct to regard the situation in which a substitute is not available and a consequential loss is sustained as a standard case, if the consequential loss is quantifiable according to the rules of causation. Failure to deliver specially designed components for which there are no practicable substitutes may lead to a very large consequential loss of sales of the final product, but the claimant will nevertheless be compensated if those sales were certain and proximate. We shall now turn to the non-standard case in which 'idiosyncratic' loss cannot be quantified.[3]

The general principles of the law of contract[4] (and the historically preceding laws) have, of course, from time immemorial recognised that a claimant may have a significant non-commercial interest in the defendant's performance of its primary obligation, and that an award of damages therefore will necessarily be an inadequate remedy for breach, in the sense that money awards are simply not relevant to the nature of the loss caused, for which a final remedy of specific performance therefore is justified. I shall refer to this tightly defined justification, and to this only, as the existence of 'consumer surplus'.[5] If the apparent pedantry be allowed, it is analytically essential to this justification that it can apply only to cases in which the claimant is a consumer, that is to say, the claimant's interest is in the non-pecuniary benefit to be derived from the

[2] A recent authoritative example is the table of remedies and their functions in A Burrows, *Remedies for Torts, Breach of Contract, and Equitable Wrongs* (4th edn, OUP 2019) 10 (hereafter Burrows, *Remedies*).

[3] OE Williamson, *Economic Organisation* (Wheatsheaf Books 1986).

[4] So far as possible I do not address the 'exceptions' relating to particular subjects, of which sale of land is the most important. Though one can readily imagine many cases in which a purchaser's argument for specific performance should succeed, the argument on general principles made here calls into question the all but universal availability of specific performance even as a remedy for the purchaser (PJ Brenner, 'Specific Performance and Contracts for the Sale of Land Purchased for Resale or Investment' (1978) 24 McGill Law Journal 513), and *a fortiori* the intrinsically less strong argument for such availability to the vendor.

[5] D Harris, AI Ogus, and J Phillips, 'Contract Remedies and the Consumer Surplus' (1979) 95 Law Quarterly Review 581, 587–89 (hereafter Harris and others, 'Consumer Surplus'). Though the argument is not be made explicitly, it is the burden of this chapter that Harris, Ogus, and Phillips' attempt to develop a broader sense of consumer surplus is just what should not be done.

use of goods or services, and is not in the monetary value which may be derived from those goods or services.[6]

With, it will be argued, most undesirable consequences for the present law, this justification has been approached somewhat obliquely,[7] with the focus being on the 'uniqueness' of the subject matter of the contract. Even if we set aside much ratiocination about the relevant sense of unique, and immediately focus on what, as we saw in Chapter 8 is central to the law of remedies, the availability or otherwise of a reasonable substitute for that subject matter, a serious confusion remains, regardless whether the subject matter in question is or is not unique. In the well-known case of *Cohen v Roche*,[8] specific performance of a sale of a set of Hepplewhite chairs was denied because 'the goods in question were ordinary articles of commerce and of no special value or interest; and not alleged to be of any special value to the plaintiff'.[9] But although the approach based on uniqueness tends to obscure this, that there was 'no special value' was a function, not only of the nature of the subject matter, but also of the claimant's interest. He was an art dealer who had bought the chairs 'in the ordinary way of his trade for the purpose of ordinary resale at a profit',[10] and his interest in the monetary value of the chairs could be compensated in market damages, which were readily quantifiable on the known facts.

I believe *Cohen v Roche* is inexplicable unless the claimant's interest actually was a monetary one, but the reported facts make this difficult to argue at an appropriate length, and the issues may be made clear more readily if we turn to *Falcke v Gray*,[11] the source of the famous *dictum* of Sir RT Kindersley VC commonly cited as the basis of the law of specific performance, certainly relating to delivery of goods, which approaches uniqueness from the opposite direction. Though stressing the normal availability of a substitute, and therefore the normal adequacy of market damages, Kindersley VC told us that specific performance would be awarded when 'the contract is for the purchase of articles of unusual beauty, rarity and distinction, so that damages would not be adequate compensation for non-performance'.[12] In the case, however, the significance of these qualities was that they gave the two china jars which were the subject matter a 'value in the market', and this was found to be the very considerable one of at least

[6] A Smith, *The Wealth of Nations*, in *The Glasgow Edition of the Works and Correspondence*, vol 2 (Clarendon Press, 1976) 44:

> The word value, it is to be observed, has two different meanings, and sometimes expresses the utility of some particular object, and sometimes the power of purchasing other goods which the possession of that object conveys. The one may be called 'value in use'; the other 'value in exchange'.

[7] Cases which actually turn on whether the claimant had the interest of a consumer, as opposed to whether the subject matter was unique, the nature of the claimant's interest being assumed, seem to be rare to the point of non-existence. *Dowling v Betjemann* (1862) 2 J & H 544; 70 ER 1175, cited if not discussed in a number of much better known cases, may to some extent turn on this point, and the judgment does take as axiomatic, based on ancient authority, what may be a statement of the consumer surplus justification. But even this case is so convoluted on the point that its discussion at appropriate length here would not be worthwhile.

[8] [1927] 1 KB 169 (KB) (hereafter *Cohen v Roche*).

[9] ibid 181; quoting *Whiteley Ltd v Hilt* [1918] 2 KB 808 (KB) 819 (Swinfen Eady MR).

[10] *Cohen v Roche* (n 8) 179.

[11] (1859) 4 Drew 651; 62 ER 250 (hereafter *Falcke v Gray*)

[12] ibid 657–58; 252.

£200 (now *circa* £25,000).[13] No evidence was introduced of a non-monetary interest the claimant had in the jars, nor about the possible availability of substitutes for them.

The claimant was, in fact, an eminent dealer in *objets d'art* such as the jars, who had rented a furnished home from the defendant, the lease including an option to purchase certain of the furnishings, including the jars. The jars were valued at £40, the figure being supplied by an employee of the estate agent acting for the defendant, who professed to have no competence about such matters; acquiesced in by the defendant, who maintained she also had no competence; and agreed by the claimant, an expert. The jars being sold by the defendant at a price which amounted to only 20% of the lowest estimate of their market value as found by the court effectively would have meant that the claimant paid nothing net for a six month tenancy. Repenting of her agreement when she learned more about it, the defendant sought to defeat the claimant's attempt to take possession of the jars by means which add to the dubiety or even squalor of the case. She 'sold' the jars for £200 to a third party expert from whom she sought a belated, competent valuation, who backed his judgment with his own money, and thus came to be joined as a defendant.

The judgment contains some reflections on the claimant's and defendant's respective obligations when negotiating which may deserve greater attention than they have received,[14] or will receive here. But in sum, though acknowledging that his was 'not a court of honour', and that the claimant 'had done nothing he was legally bound not to do',[15] Kindersley VC refused to order specific performance of a 'hard bargain' characterised by 'a very inadequate price'. The case therefore is some authority for equity being more sensitive to such considerations than the common law,[16] for, crucially for our purposes, the contract was not set aside, and so the claimant continued to have a remedy in damages.

The reported facts do not say what eventuated, and one assumes steps were taken that effectively rescinded the original sale *ab initio*. For though his conduct in negotiations did not undermine the claimant's contract, his remedy was useless to him because of the nature of his interest in the jars. The jars had no personal interest for him. Had he obtained possession, one readily imagines he would have resold them. But how could he possibly claim substantial market damages? He would have had to introduce evidence of a market value of at least £200, to which the valuation of £40 in a document collateral to a lease which he, an expert, had agreed, would have been counter-evidence! The claimant was defeated, not because the jars were not in the relevant sense unique, but because he did not have the right consumer interest in them.

In cases in which a claimant consumer did have a consumer surplus, a focus on the uniqueness of the subject matter can do no harm, and may well represent a welcome narrowing of attention on the issue in dispute.[17] But a law effectively based on

[13] ibid 658–59; 253.

[14] The judgment is, however, accorded only marginal significance in JL Barton, 'The Enforcement of Hard Bargains' (1987) 103 Law Quarterly Review 118, 128.

[15] *Falcke v Gray* (n 11) 665; 255.

[16] ibid 659; 253.

[17] Having themselves noted that 'There is little overt awareness of [consumer surplus in the narrow sense used here] in the reported cases', Harris and others, 'Consumer Surplus' (n 5) 587 put the unproblematic recognition of it down to 'judges [having] an intuitive sense of the problem'.

uniqueness of subject matter opens the possibility that a claimant without a consumer surplus could seek specific performance on the basis of the subject matter being unique, and just this has given rise to what should be seen as a very serious shortcoming of the law, though on our current understanding this shortcoming is in fact generally welcomed. Specific performance is worthy of its place in a discussion of the general principles of the law of contract only because it has been sought as a final remedy by commercial parties, though this can only very incoherently be tied to the consumer surplus justification for specific performance as such parties cannot have a consumer surplus![18] This is no mere nice point of logic or doctrine. The serious shortcomings to which it has given rise are yet further consequences of the law failing to institutionalise the mutual recognition required of the parties, in this case regarding choice of remedy.

Idiosyncrasy, Compensation, and Literal Enforcement

Plucked from all but total obscurity by Treitel in 1966 to substantiate an argument that the English courts should 'recognise a concept of commercial uniqueness',[19] the 1927 case of *Behnke v Bede*,[20] and Treitel's treatment of it, encapsulate the problems to which the commercial use of specific performance gives rise. In *Behnke*, a claimant buyer of a merchant vessel was awarded specific performance under s 52 of the Sale of Goods Act 1893.[21] Treitel tells us that it would have been possible simply to award specific performance under a particular equitable jurisdiction which would not have required argument,[22] but this will not be discussed here. The interest of *Behnke* lay in Wright J,

[18] It is incidental to the argument that it is being sought to make here, but the passage of the Consumer Rights Act 2015, ss 19, 23, 42–43, 54–55, 58 goes a long way to accomplishing the, as it were, logically opposite mistake to the one discussed in this chapter. Instead of extending the consumer interest justification to cases where there is no consumer, the 2015 Act extends it to cases where there is no defensible sense of uniqueness, and so no inadequacy of damages. Without entering into detail (s 58 alone is too convoluted to be able to be discussed at the necessary length here), a consumer has been presumed to have a literal enforcement remedy whether or not damages are adequate. Though, of course, some cases where damages are inadequate and the trader is behaving oppressively will be caught, and though the 'proportionality' defences which were made necessary may operate to mitigate the mischief, the disregard of what businesses have done in the shadow of the existing law and of the perverse incentives offered to consumers is marked.

The unwisdom of generally making these remedies available was pointed out when the prior legislative steps that led to the 2015 Act were first taken: D Harris, 'Specific Performance: A Regular Remedy for Consumers?' (2003) 119 Law Quarterly Review 2015. It is perhaps not yet possible to form an opinion of the impact of this potentially fundamental (or potentially trivial) departure from an axiom of the English law, or, more precisely, to separate out this impact from the confused picture left by legislation of such naïve (my word) immensity of ambition: J Devenney, 'The Consumer Rights Act 2015 and Related Reforms' in R Halson and D Campbell (eds), *Research Handbook on Remedies in Private Law* (Edward Elgar 2019).

[19] GH Treitel, 'Specific Performance in the Sale of Goods' [1966] Journal of Business Law 211, 215 (hereafter Treitel, 'Specific Performance'). 'Commercial uniqueness' was introduced into the second edition of Treitel's book, which also appeared in 1966: GH Treitel, *The Law of Contract* (2nd edn, Stevens & Sons 1966) 690. Only the theoretical aspect of Treitel's argument is of interest here, but it should be noted that Professor Burrows, as he was then, who we will see is convinced by that argument, is frank about its very limited influence: Burrows, *Remedies* (n 2) 405–06.

[20] [1927] 1 KB 649 (KB) (hereafter *Behnke v Bede*).

[21] I put to one side the issue of some significance whether a ship should be regarded as a good under the Act, and with this the difficulties specific to remedies under the Act with which Treitel deals.

[22] Treitel, 'Specific Performance' (n 19) 215.

as he then was, justifying the award on the ground that the vessel possessed an unusual combination of features suitable for the waters in which she was to sail, which made her 'of peculiar and practically unique value' to the claimant. Implicit in this was, of course, the impossibility of mitigation. The vessel was needed for 'immediate use', and there was 'only one other comparable ship [which] may now have been sold'.[23]

In the relevant sense, then, the vessel was unique. This does not make the concept of commercial uniqueness any less of the oxymoron which it unarguably is. For the claimant shipowner had, of course, no consumer surplus, its interest in the vessel being the profits to be made from its employment. If non-delivery caused the loss of those profits, the claimant could, in principle, always be compensated in damages, or, to put it the other way around, the claimant should, in principle, never be able to make a case for specific performance. In proper cases of consumer surplus, regarding the issue as uniqueness of subject matter causes us to lose focus on the nature of the requisite claimant's interest. But in commercial uniqueness cases, regarding the issue as uniqueness of subject matter causes us to disregard the claimant certainly not having the requisite interest.

The unavailability of a substitute of course made a claim for market damages under s 51 of the 1893 Act irrelevant in *Behnke v Bede*. But consequential losses could have been claimed as special damages under s 54. Why did the shipowner instead turn to s 52? The reported case does not make this clear, and one is obliged to speculate a little, but it is submitted it must have been because, the losses from being unable to carry cargoes surely coming within reasonable contemplation under the first limb of *Hadley v Baxendale*,[24] the extent of those losses could not be proven. If, for example, the claimant had agreed contracts with shippers on its books, it is impossible to understand why it would not have brought a s 54 claim rather than a s 52 claim for, even leaving aside the doctrinal difficulties it had to overcome to successfully make the s 52 claim which the defendant 'strongly contested',[25] damages which actually compensated the claimant for lost profits surely would have been at least as good a practical remedy as specific performance. The s 52 claim was motivated by the claimant's fear that an award of damages would not, in fact, compensate the loss which it would suffer. Though the long acknowledgement of uniqueness in true consumer surplus cases was bound to be drawn on if one was to develop an argument for commercial uniqueness, the problem for which commercial uniqueness is but 'a form of shorthand'[26] is the claimant's fear of uncompensated (or under-compensated) loss.[27]

This fear runs through all the attempts by commercial parties to seek forms of literal enforcement of primary obligations. In addition to specific performance outside of sales, and those cases in which, to avoid equitable defences to specific performance, an injunction effectively leading to specific performance is sought,[28] these include

[23] ibid 650–61.

[24] (1854) 9 Ex Ch 341; 156 ER 145.

[25] *Behnke v Bede* (n 20) 660.

[26] R Austen-Baker, 'Difficulties with Damages as a Ground of Specific Performance' (1999) 10 King's College Law Journal 1, 11.

[27] AT Kronman, 'Specific Performance' (1980) 45 University of Chicago Law Review 351, 355–68.

[28] *Warner Bros Pictures Inc v Nelson* [1937] 1 KB 209 (KB). It is unarguable that this case is not now good law: *Warren v Mendy* [1989] 1WLR 853, 864H–866A. The issues were discussed with reference to *Behnke v Bede* in *Societé des Industries Mitallurgiques SA v The Bronx Engineering Co Ltd* [1975] 1 Lloyd's Rep 465.

affirmation of an anticipatorily repudiated contract and commercial uses of cost to complete damages, both of which are discussed below. But, even if we accept, as we should, that the fear of uncompensated loss often has a basis in the claimant's predicament, we should, after acknowledging that consumer surplus certainly cannot be such a justification, ask whether this use of specific performance can be justified.

Quantification and Adequacy of Damages

The key part of Treitel's justification of the commercial use of specific performance anticipated much of the later literature on the performance interest by at least a quarter of a century. After posing the question why damages are the default remedy which it is necessary to oust, rather than specific performance being the default, Treitel went on:

> This question becomes all the more insistent where the damages, though commonly described as 'adequate', do not in fact put the buyer in the position he would have been in had the contract been performed. He may be unable to obtain a precise or substantial substitute elsewhere. He may suffer consequential loss, some or all of which is too remote. Or the damages may be speculative in the sense that they cannot be calculated with precise accuracy—for example, where damages are claimed for loss of future profits.[29]

In a paper focused on some of the 'technical'[30] shortcomings of Sale of Goods Act particularly regarding the definition of ascertained or specific goods, Treitel did no more than suggest that the default rule should be reversed, and if it were reversed, he saw grounds on which the defendant could successfully raise a defence against specific performance. By far the most important of these was, as Treitel put it, that 'the defendant may lose the benefit of the mitigation rule'.[31] I do not, with respect, think Treitel expressed himself perfectly clearly. It is hard to conceive of a claimant not mitigating in the sense of preferring compensatory damages if it was satisfied those damages would actually compensate it. The issue is, when the claimant prefers specific performance in the circumstances we are considering is that the defendant may lose the benefit of the certainty and remoteness rules. Treitel's argument was that the claimant has suffered an uncompensated loss, and that specific performance should be made far more widely available so that this does not happen.

After labyrinthine detours though the performance interest and related innovations,[32] Treitel's argument is now more clearly being used to generalise a fundamental criticism of the positive law of specific performance, with that law being turned on its head as a failure of damages to fully compensate the claimant is now being said to be

[29] Treitel, 'Specific Performance' (n 19) 216.
[30] ibid 231.
[31] ibid 215.
[32] One very important reason for this journey was to avoid the more overt 'balancing of convenience' in awards of equitable remedies and replace this with remedies available 'as of right': D Campbell, '*Hamlet* without the Prince: How Leng and Leong Use Restitution to Extinguish Equity' [2003] Journal of Business Law 131.

an important ground of inadequacy. In the latest edition of his book on remedies, Burrows suggests that 'where there is grave doubt about whether the damages will put the claimant in as good a position as if the contract had been performed, specific performance is *prima facie* a better remedy'.[33]

As we noted in Chapter 8, all of pt V of the 1893 Act, including damages for consequential loss under s 54, codifies the common law principles of causation, so it is generally instructive to return to *Behnke v Bede*, and ask exactly what it was about inadequacy of which Treitel complained. Had the rules in some way gone wrong? Not a bit of it. Treitel's complaint actually is that the rules had been applied correctly! The loss being, as we have assumed, proximate, it must have been uncertain. This rule, as with remoteness and mitigation, serves a vital function in allowing the parties to determine what it is to which they have agreed. It was, by default, on the basis of this rule that the parties agreed the sale. Why should the defendant be deprived of the benefit of it?

The claimant in *Behnke v Bede*, knowing, as we assume, it had no full order book or other evidence of proof of future business that could satisfy the court, and knowing the vessel was unique, should have dealt with this when negotiating the sale. It evidently failed to do so. This is the reason damages are inadequate in Treitel's sense, and so he argues specific performance is called for. But by inadequate in Treitel's sense we should understand damages that were perfectly adequate in terms of the parties' objective intentions formed with knowledge of the doctrine of causation, but not at all adequate when the claimant subjectively came to realise the consequences of what it had negotiated. The claimant's mistake is highly representative. By agreeing a contract in ignorance of the Holmesian choice, the claimant believed it had secured a guarantee of performance of the primary obligation, when, by default, this is precisely what a claimant does not get in these circumstances. Devices such as agreed damages were available to the claimant, but it did not, it would appear, seek to use them (which would have involved in some fashion paying for them).

Realising it had failed to secure the remedy it wanted *ex ante*, the claimant then sought it *ex post*, and a court as much beset by a fundamental confusion about the nature of the remedies system as the claimant itself came to its rescue. Ultimately, the whole issue is generally misunderstood, and indeed the current[34] enthusiasm for a 'substitutionary' theory of damages[35] takes the firmest grip of the wrong end of the

[33] Burrows, *Remedies* (n 2) 408. Particular disappointment was occasioned by *Co-op v Argyll* because it seemed to reverse a former trend towards wider availability of specific performance, exemplified by the widely discussed *Sky Petroleum v VIP Petroleum* [1974] 1 WLR 576 (Ch), in which the Commercial Court seemed to have little difficulty asserting a greater knowledge of how to allocate petrol resources then in shortage than oil companies!

[34] To my knowledge, the terminology may be traced to Treitel's 1976 (the text was completed in 1972) contribution to *The International Encyclopaedia of Comparative Law*, now available as GH Treitel, *Remedies for Breach of Contract* (Clarendon Press 1988) ch 4.

[35] D Winterton, *Money Awards in Contract Law* (Hart 2015) 6:

> Substitutionary money awards aim to substitute for the performance promised irrespective of the factual detriment that breach has caused the innocent party. Compensatory awards aim to make good certain detrimental factual consequences that a breach has caused the innocent party.

stick.[36] In commercial uniqueness cases, compensatory damages are not being sought as a substitute for specific performance. Specific performance is being sought as a substitute for damages; or, more precisely, as a way of avoiding the correct result according to the rules of causation on which the contract was by default agreed,[37] and so erasing the defendant's agreed interests. There can be no possible justification for this consistent with our commitment to agreement on the basis of mutual recognition as the basis of legitimate exchange and contract.

It is not, of course, being denied that a failure to obtain specific performance will in these circumstances do anything other than leave the claimant with an uncompensated loss. The contrast between the result yielded when damages can be quantified, and therefore, as we saw in Chapter 8, the claimant's and the defendant's interests are, so far as the very nature of a failed exchange allows, both taken into account, and the result in cases like *Behnke v Bede* is stark. As the loss is idiosyncratic, it cannot be dealt with by quantification under the causation rules, and it must be borne by one or other of the parties. A loss-sharing result is replaced by the zero sum allocation to one party of an *ex ante* unquantifiable loss. The spontaneous generation of co-operation in what was in Chapter 8 called the standard case cannot take place, and we shall examine those complex contracts in which it is sought to plan for co-operation in response to the risk of idiosyncratic loss in Chapter 10. The contracts like *Behnke v Bede* we are dealing with here are fundamentally unsatisfactory contracts in which the risk of idiosyncratic loss has not been anticipated because the parties are subject to the delusion that agreement guarantees primary performance, and then the claimant seeks the aid of the court to shift the loss to the defendant by awarding specific performance or another form of literal enforcement, in defiance of the remedy which the parties had agreed by default.

How Can Literal Enforcement Be Justified?

In the cases discussed in Chapter 10, we will see that the doctrine of the insufficiency of existing obligations has placed considerable obstacles in the way of parties who wish to agree to expressly plan for co-operation. The problem we face in the remainder of this chapter is the opposite. Labouring under their belief that agreement guarantees performance, parties' contracts have given rise to significant litigation by failing to consider what to do when breach gives rise to idiosyncratic loss.[38] It could hardly

[36] Unconstrained by contact with the real issues, conceptual elaboration may proceed apace: S Smith, *Rights, Wrongs and Injustices* (OUP 2019) 173–74, 181–99 (hereafter Smith, *Rights*).

[37] A Kramer, 'An Agreement-Centred Approach to Remoteness and Damages' in N Cohen and E McKendrick (eds), *Comparative Remedies for Breach of Contract* (Hart 2005) 249, 284.

[38] The discussion here is focused on commercial parties' arguments about inadequacy of damages and the legitimate interest needed to avoid the results of the compensatory default in situations of uncertainty. The possibility of litigation which tries to delve sufficiently deeply into the facts to resolve the uncertainty in these circumstances is not considered. But a quite extraordinary example of what may well be involved was provided by *Douglas Shelf Seven Ltd v Co-operative Wholesale Society Ltd and Kwik Save Group plc (Third Party)* [2007] CSOH 53 (OH), one of a number of Scottish cases on keep open covenants (see the text accompanying n 56). This case, entirely confined to quantum, occupied a preposterous amount of court time, but the resulting 625 paragraph judgment is nevertheless manifestly unsatisfactory. It is quite indefensible that commercial parties which have allowed their affairs to fall into such a state that they try to repair

be more appropriate that the leading Commonwealth case on the issue, *Co-operative Insurance Society Ltd* v *Argyll Stores (Holdings) Ltd*,[39] is so widely misunderstood that the dissenting judgment of Millett LJ in the Court of Appeal which, it is submitted, is the principal source of wisdom on the law of commercial specific performance, has had little effect, our thinking being dominated by a judgment of Lord Hoffmann, with which all his brethren agreed, which barely adds to the consideration of the issues.

In *Co-op v Argyll*, the defendant had taken a 35-year lease on part of the claimant's shopping centre development in order to operate a supermarket. The viability of other businesses in the shopping centre and of the shopping centre itself was, as the parties knew at the outset, heavily dependent on the 'anchoring' operation of the defendant's supermarket. The parties therefore agreed an express 'keep open covenant' of a type common in such leases. When the defendant nevertheless decided to breach its lease because its business, ultimately as a result of a generally depressed outlook, had made a very substantial trading loss with no prospect of change, the claimant itself faced an extensive loss,[40] much of which would, particularly because of certainty problems, have remained uncompensated by an award of damages.[41] On the reasoning we have traced to Treitel, the case for specific performance was very strong.[42] Nevertheless, the House of Lords restored the decision at trial not to award specific performance, and did so for two reasons. One of these, the difficulty of supervising specific performance in these circumstances,[43] has drawn most attention, but it is, with respect, by no means so important as the other reason, which was the existence of a 'settled practice' not to award specific performance in cases of this nature.[44] Lord Hoffmann's judgment merely points to the existence of the settled practice, briefly if firmly criticising the majority in the Court of Appeal for reversing the trial judge's application of it when the case disclosed no reason to do so.[45] To understand the settled practice, it is necessary to refer back to the Court of Appeal.

The refusal of specific performance drew vehement criticism from leading commentators on contract and equity as a failure to apply equitable principles, and the 'sense of fair dealing'[46] behind

them in this way should, regardless of the wisdom of their own legal expenditures, be able to utilise public funds in this way: D Campbell and R Halson, 'The Irrelevance of the Performance Interest: A Comparative Analysis of "Keep-open Covenants" in Scotland and England' in L DiMatteo, Qi Zhou, S Santier, and K Rowley (eds), *Commercial Contract Law: Transatlantic Perspectives* (CUP 2013) 478, 480–81 (hereafter Campbell and Halson. 'The Irrelevance of the Performance Interest').

[39] [1996] Ch 286 (CA) (hereafter *Co-op v Argyll* (CA)); rvsd [1998] AC 1 (HL) (hereafter *Co-op v Argyll* (HL)).

[40] *Co-op v Argyll* (CA) (n 39) 301C–D.

[41] ibid 295A.

[42] Other 'equitable' considerations also spoke against the defendant. Of relevance to the argument here, other third party, smaller commercial tenants also faced uncompensated losses of a type which, in the third edition of his textbook published in 1970, Treitel had hoped *Beswick v Beswick* [1968] AC 58 (HL) might lead the law to address: GH Treitel, *The Law of Contract* (3rd edn, Stevens & Sons 1970) 836–88.

[43] *Co-op v Argyll* (HL) (n 39) 12C–15B. Millett LJ gave this consideration 'little weight', thinking that a claimant which sought an order of specific performance rather than claim damages in the knowledge that the order created possibilities of its own 'evasion' should be regarded as 'the best judge of its own interests': *Co-op v Argyll* (CA) (n 39) 303G.

[44] *Co-op v Argyll* (HL) (n 39) 11D–16A

[45] ibid 19B.

[46] *Co-op v Argyll* (CA) (n 39) 295B (Leggatt LJ).

them.[47] Other commentators did not take this stance, and were able to point to the fact that it was, not the refusal of specific performance, but the Court of Appeal's award of it 'that had caused consternation in the commercial property market'.[48] For Lord Hoffmann was right to say there was a settled practice not to award specific performance, and it had been Leggatt and Roch LJJ who had taken a startlingly novel step. It is submitted they did this because they were, with respect, so enthused with performance interest thinking that they could ascribe no good reason not to provide a remedy in line with it; but there certainly was such a reason.

To enter into a 35-year lease such as was the basis of this case entails, of course, a substantial risk.[49] The most highly competent parties can make only very boundedly rational forecasts about their businesses' prospects over such a time. The parties' contract made some provision to deal with this, particularly in the form of rent review clauses. Such provision could not eliminate the risk that the business would fare so badly as to make breach a sensible course for the tenant (we will ignore the landlord) to adopt (ironically turning the rent review clauses into a source of uncertainty for the landlord). Unlike in the standard case of breach discussed in Chapter 8, such a breach will cause an idiosyncratic loss which must lay either with the claimant landlord if damages are awarded, for quantification on the rules of causation will lead to an uncompensated loss; or with the defendant tenant if specific performance is awarded.

How should this risk be allocated? The only answer which the law of contract should give is that it should be allocated by the agreement of the parties themselves. If they contract on default terms, the risk is allocated to the claimant because the Holmesian choice allows the defendant to breach and pay compensatory damages quantified on the basis of the rules of causation. Though his dissent in the Court of Appeal certainly considers other approaches, Millett LJ described, it is submitted, the basis of good law:

> Over the years countless tenants with the benefit of legal advice have entered into commercial leases ... similar to ... the present ... If they had asked their legal advisers whether this meant that they could be compelled to keep the premises open for business regardless of the financial consequences, I have no doubt that they would have been told that it did not; they would have been advised that such a covenant sounds in damages only. If the courts were willing to compel performance, I do not see how any tenant *properly advised* could safely enter into such an obligation. Yet the covenant is of great commercial value to developers, even if it does sound only in damages. If [such a covenant was specifically enforceable in these circumstances] developers may find it difficult to find anchor tenants willing to submit to such a covenant ... The

[47] Dr Spry felt it so necessary to criticise this refusal that, at a late stage of the preparation of the fifth edition of his book, he included an appendix on *Co-operative Insurance* in order to do so: ICF Spry, *Principles of Equitable Remedies* (5th edn, Sweet & Maxwell 1997) app C.

[48] P Luxton, 'Are You Being Served? Enforcing Keep-open Covenants in Leases' [1998] Conveyancer and Property Lawyer 396, 398.

[49] The background economics of the matter is that the costs of the initial construction or acquisition of premises are so high that terms of great length are needed to amortise the initial investment and leave a profit-making period which justifies that investment. It may possibly be the case that the risk is so high it prevents the parties agreeing, or alternatively leads them to some degree of integration of their formerly separate businesses. What course is taken is, of course, a matter for the parties' entrepreneurial acumen. Integration of this kind is discussed at length in ch 10.

> equitable jurisdiction should not be exercised in a manner which would defeat the commercial expectations of the parties at the time they entered into their contractual obligations.[50]

If the claimant wished to oust the default, it was open to it to do so by negotiation. This is a completely different matter than the court changing the nature of the parties' agreement *ex post* by awarding specific performance. As was mentioned in Chapter 6, it is both undesirable and impossible that the court's jurisdiction should not encompass a residual discretion to deal with exceptional cases which sound on 'equitable' grounds, and that because of the important role it played in *White and Carter (Councils) Ltd v McGregor*,[51] to which we shall shortly turn, the most significant statement of this discretion arguably is that of Lord Watson in *Grahame v Swan and others (Magistrates of Kirkaldy)*:

> It appears to me that a superior court, having equitable jurisdiction, must also have a discretion, in certain exceptional cases, to withhold from parties applying for it a remedy to which, in ordinary circumstances, they would be entitled as a matter of course ... There are, so far as I know, only three decided cases in which the Court of Session, there being no facts sufficient to raise a plea [ie in common law or equity] in bar of the action, have nevertheless denied the pursuer the remedy to which, in strict law, he was entitled. These authorities seem to establish, if that were necessary, the proposition that the court has the power of declining, upon equitable grounds, to enforce an admittedly legal right; but they also show the power has been very rarely exercised.[52]

Leaving its application in *White and Carter* aside and speaking in general terms, acknowledgement of this exceptional discretion must be seen to be a very long way indeed from expanding that discretion to rewrite the parties' contract to privilege some idea of 'fair dealing' over the business efficacy manifested in the parties' intentions, though this was precisely what the majority of the Court of Appeal in *Co-op v Argyll* did. To repeat the wise words of Millett LJ: 'The equitable jurisdiction should not be

[50] *Co-op v Argyll* (CA) (n 39) 305E–G.

[51] [1962] AC 413 (HL Sc) (hereafter *White and Carter* (HL)).

[52] (1882) 7 App Cas 547 (HL Sc) 557 (hereafter *Grahame v Magistrates of Kirkaldy*), quoted by Lord Reid from (1882) 9 R(HL) 91 (HL Sc) 92 in *White and Carter* (HL) (n 51) 430.

I do not pretend to fully understand the relevant law, but I think I can convey what Lord Watson had in mind by 'exceptional' by describing the first of his cases: *Macnair v Cathcart* (1802) Mor 13832, the facts of which, it is vital to realise, arose in the second half of the eighteenth century. By a chance of succession, in 1747 the pursuer's father inherited a substantial parcel of land at the edge of the town of Greenock as it then stood. In circumstances not explained, the pursuer was at the time abroad, evidently out of contact with his family, and knew nothing of this. His sister took possession and took steps to obtain title. In 1777, via her, the land was sold to the defender, a *bona fide* purchaser, who developed it in such a way that it added considerably to the town, 'many valuable houses [having been] built on it'. In 1795(!) the pursuer, it would seem having inherited title from his father, sought to claim the land. His title was, apparently, perfect, but the 'long silence', and the 'great injury and devastation' which would be caused by his retaking possession were the grounds of a bar to his strict legal right (though the defender had to pay him the 'fair value' of the land). I think this would be allowed to be exceptional.

exercised in a manner which would defeat the commercial expectations of the parties at the time when they entered into their contractual obligations'.[53]

Millett LJ clearly was of the opinion that the settled practice stated the best default rule. This is, as it happens, my own opinion,[54] formed after study of *Co-op v Argyll*, but consolidated by research, conducted with Roger Halson,[55] into what might even appear to have been a social scientific experiment on the matter thrown up by the law, for the opposite default was adopted in Scotland just as *Co-op v Argyll* wound its way through the English appeal courts.[56] Interested readers may wish to look at this research to contrast the positions.[57] But the most important thing is not the contrast. The default rule expressed in the common law or consolidated in statute should be what interpretation giving business efficacy to the intentions of commercial parties shows it to be. If interpretation on this basis shows that in a certain setting the default reflecting commercial practice is literal enforcement, then remedies should be awarded on that basis.

This is indeed the case in at least one area of the law. As stated in the leading case of *East Ham Corp v Bernard Sunley and Sons Ltd*,[58] the default rule in cases of defective construction of buildings is that quantification is based, not on the diminution in value between the building as contracted and the building as built, but on the cost to complete the works (or cost of cure, or reinstatement, etc). Cost to complete is, of course, specific performance, but by the claimant or a third party engaged by the claimant when completion by the defendant, in which the claimant will have lost confidence, is impracticable. The claimant's preference for cost to complete can be traced either to the cases involving a true consumer surplus, as was alleged in the leading case of *Ruxley Electronics and Construction Ltd v Forsyth*,[59] which broaches all the issues and shall be discussed below, or to the diminution measure not capturing the commercial claimant's actual loss.[60] The only justification, however, that can be given of adopting a default rule that must go against normal business efficacy as, in other than minor cases,[61] mitigation will be ousted, is that this is what the parties to such

[53] *Co-op v Argyll* (CA) (n 39) 305G.

[54] It is not my opinion that this is the best outcome, for I believe more sophisticated profit and loss sharing arrangements could be superior. The point is, however, that the situation discussed in this chapter is one in which the parties have failed to even attempt the necessary contract planning.

[55] Campbell and Halson, 'Irrelevance of the Performance Interest' (n 38).

[56] *Retail Parks Investments Ltd v The Royal Bank of Scotland plc (No 2)* [1996] SC 227 (IH Ex Div) (hereafter *Retail Parks Investments*) and *Highland and Universal Properties Ltd v Safeway Properties Ltd* [2000] SC 297 (IH).

[57] Whilst 'performance' is an irrelevance in both cases, the starting point of negotiations in anticipation of or after breach is, of course, importantly different. See n 94.

[58] [1966] AC 406, 434G (hereafter *East Ham v Sunley*). The statement of the *East Ham v Sunley* rule in *Linden Gardens Trust Ltd v Lenesta Sludge Disposals Ltd* [1994] AC 85 (HL) 110G (Lord Browne-Wilkinson) is, with respect, completely obscure.

[59] [1996] AC 344 (HL) (hereafter *Ruxley* (HL)).

[60] In *East Ham v Sunley* (n 58), in which the very substantial sum of £21,301 (now *circa* £415,550) was awarded, no attempt was made, or would have been appropriate, to calculate the alternative diminution in value caused by stone facing panels being fixed to a school building in so insecure a manner that the panels fell off or were in a dangerous state.

[61] The policy behind the all but inevitable award of cost to complete in such cases, which must be understood alongside the use of the entire obligation rule, cannot be fully discussed here (though see n 74). It is discussed in Harris and others, *Remedies* (n 1) 45–48, 212. It is this law that would handle the problem for 'the average householder' which was of such concern to Lord Mustill in *Ruxley* (HL) (n 59) 359H–360D.

contracts have agreed, and the statement of the default in *East Ham v Sunley* is persuasively based on this claim.

Whilst, to repeat, we should defer to the default rule which interpretation on the basis of business efficacy shows to have been the intention of the parties, the replacement of the diminution measure by cost to complete is nevertheless bound to lead to difficulty. The disparity between the two measures can mean that after the award the claimant is tempted not to complete the works, especially as in disputed cases the award will exceed the market value of the work to be done, and in some cases may even exceed the value of the entire property when the works are completed![62] This has led to the retention of a discretion to refuse cost to complete damages when the disparity is 'unreasonably' large. A real problem certainly is being addressed here, one which is readily open to exploitation by an unscrupulous claimant.

Ruxley brings a curious symmetry to the discussion of the issues because, as with *Falcke v Grey*, though our understanding of the case has turned on some idea of a true consumer surplus,[63] it is highly likely that this was not the interest motivating the claim for literal enforcement. The claimant in *Ruxley* had built a swimming pool at the defendant's home. It was specified that at its deepest, in the diving area, the pool was to be 7 feet 6 inches deep, but as constructed it was only 6 feet deep there. The defendant refused to make outstanding payments, and brought a counter-claim for cost to complete damages based on the pool being demolished and entirely rebuilt. It having been found that the pool was perfectly fit for the diving which would take place in a domestic setting, and therefore that the diminution in value of the defendant's property caused by the breach was zero, the disparity between the two measures of damages was marked as cost to complete £21,560 (now *circa* £43,000).[64]

The case was decided on the basis that such was this disparity that the discretion to prefer the diminution measure had to be exercised.[65] The case gave rise to such discussion because, to be frank, this outcome was satisfactory to no-one who heard the case,[66] least of all to the majority in the Court of Appeal, which awarded cost to complete on a number of grounds, the most important of which was that 'the bargain was for a personal preference'.[67] To this must be contrasted the specific finding of the Lords that personal preference was not enough: 'it may well be a factor in reasonableness and

[62] In the famous US case of *Peevyhouse v Garland Coal and Mining Company Co* 382 P 2d 109 (Supreme Court of Oklahoma 1962), cost to complete which would have far exceeded the cost of the reinstated mined farm property was not awarded, though it very strongly appears that it should have been had a proper consumer surplus argument been properly made by the claimants: JL Maute, '*Peeveyhouse v Garland Coal and Mining Co Revisited: The Ballad of Willie and Lucille*' (1995) 89 Northwestern University Law School 1341 and JL Maute, 'The Unearthed Facts of *Peevyhouse v Garland*' in DG Baird (ed), *Contract Stories* (Foundation Press 2007).

[63] *Ruxley* (HL) (n 59) 353H.

[64] ibid 354G–H.

[65] ibid 356C–359B.

[66] The Lords, of course, restored an award of £2,500 for loss of amenity made by the trial judge, principally, it seems, because the prospect of awarding nominal damages was intolerable: ibid 365D, 373F–375A. This prospect was one reason *Ruxley* played such a part in the arguments around the performance interest which turn on the perceived unacceptability of nominal remedies that would carry no power of enforcement: ibid 358D, 361A, 370H–371A.

[67] *Ruxley Electronics and Construction Ltd v Forsyth* [1994] 1 WLR 650 (CA) 660H (hereafter *Ruxley* (CA)).

hence in determining what loss has been suffered, but it cannot *per se* be determinative of what that loss is'.[68]

Though it is submitted that the result yielded by the claimant's appeal being ultimately successful is correct, this particular part of the reasoning of the majority of the Court of Appeal is also correct. Though, to repeat, it is inconceivable that some discretion not to make strictly legal awards which are outrageous in the circumstances will not be retained by the courts, the award in *Ruxley*, even though the case drew attention because of the marked disparity between the diminution in value and the cost to complete measures and the apparent unacceptability of nominal damages, should not have been subject to any such discretion.[69] Leaving aside the great difficulty the court must encounter in deciding what is reasonable, a discretionary denial of cost to complete when it was agreed obviously runs counter to the fundamental values of contract. And in this lies the true significance of *Ruxley*.

The judgments in and commentary on the case are based on accepting that the parties agreed that the pool would be, at the appropriate point, 7 feet 6 inches in depth. This is completely implausible, even if, as was the case, the amended contract did stipulate this depth.[70] A contract of this nature obviously allows for margins, and the real question, never properly addressed once it was, dreadfully mistakenly, accepted without much reported discussion, after it seems it was initially denied at trial, that the claimant was in breach,[71] was whether the departure from 7 feet 6 inches actually was a breach. Absolute precision of measurement cannot possibly have been an issue, but nor can precision in any biting sense, for this would have imposed construction costs for which the defendant surely would not have wanted to pay, and which, on basic *Hadley v Baxendale* principles, it would be quite wrong to impose on the claimant if the contract had been agreed on the business efficacy basis of building for ordinary domestic use.

To be perfectly frank, the difference being of 20% certainly is sufficient to have raised the suspicion that there was a breach in the mind of everyone who was involved in or has read the case, including this writer. But it was (very convincingly)[72] found that this made no difference to the value of the pool when put to the domestic use which was the matrix of fact on which interpretation of the contract rested. If this finding of fact was correct, the denial of cost to complete certainly follows. This has been rather strikingly demonstrated by the number of times an hypothetical contract was unwittingly

[68] *Ruxley* (HL) (n 59) 358H–359A.

[69] The absolutely extraordinary *Tito v Waddell (No 2)* [1977] Ch 106, 345F (hereafter *Tito v Waddell*), in which the cost of reinstating land from which phosphate had been mined was claimed to be 1000 times greater than the diminution in value caused by not reinstating, may be a case in which the discretion was rightly applied. The denial of reinstatement certainly was part of a most admirable contract judgment containing much else of value on core aspects of the law of remedies, handed down by one of the greatest equity judges of recent times. But the, as it were, political acceptability of the judgment, and its significance as authority, is very limited because the facts of the case made it an occasion of national and international disgrace that the issues were treated as contractual at all.

[70] *Ruxley* (CA) (n 67) 653H.

[71] ibid.

[72] *Ruxley* (CA) (n 67) 653C–654E. Against evidence of the general standards set by relevant trade associations, little weight, to be polite, was put on Mr Ruxley's that he personally did not feel safe diving and had been prevented from erecting, as he had intended, a diving board.

made the basis of commentary on *Ruxley* by those who disagreed with the decision. Professor Coote, for example, claimed that:

> If, in a case like *Ruxley*, a pool had not been constructed to the depth specified and to the knowledge of the contractor the purpose of building it had been to enable a diver to prepare for the Olympics, so that the minimum specified depth were crucial, it seems most unlikely that the cost of rebuilding would be refused.[73]

But the Olympic speculation is *not* a case like *Ruxley*, indeed it is its opposite, and that is the whole point.[74]

Professor Rowan has interestingly argued that many of the discretionary bars to literal enforcement should be removed, or certainly not allowed to stand as insuperable obstacles to terms specifying literal enforcement remedies which she advises parties wanting literal enforcement to incorporate. Her in itself justified concern appears to be that that those bars run against the agreement of the parties:

> contracting parties should be permitted to agree upon the remedies that ensue from a breach of their agreement. This would give responsibility for determining the level of protection for the performance interest to those best placed to understand the issues at stake, enabling them to fashion remedies to their idiosyncratic circumstances.[75]

However, as this passage leads one to suspect, Rowan's argument is combined with a normal assumption that what the parties would want to agree is a higher degree of protection of the performance interest than the present law by default provides, and this is most implausible. The above passage is followed with:

> Importing negotiation from the context of primary obligations to the realm of remedies would supplement the default regime, allowing parties to circumvent perceived remedies in the existing panoply of remedies.[76]

But we should not assume that when the parties expressly specify their primary obligations they implicitly specify that those obligations must be tantamount to unconditionally performed. They almost never do this by default, no matter how much

[73] B Coote, 'Contract Damages, *Ruxley*, and the Performance Interest' [1997] Cambridge Law Journal 537, 544.

[74] I do not deny the significance of the claim made by Mr Ruxley's counsel in a subsequent article that the decision would pose difficulties for small building works clients who want those works carried out just as they wished: IE Jacob, 'Is Near Enough Good Enough?' (1995) 139 Solicitors' Journal 676. This article is a companion piece to the well-known dissent of Brian Davenport QC when the Law Commission recommended a rebalancing of the entire obligation rule: Law Commission, *Pecuniary Restitution for Breach of Contract (Report)* [1983] EWLC 121, 36–37. The point argued here is that the extent of the parties' liabilities should be determined by their agreement (framed with an effective presumption in favour of the client by the entire contracts and cost to complete rules), and not by an abstract commitment to the performance interest (or indeed an opposite abstract commitment).

[75] S Rowan, *Remedies for Breach of Contract* (OUP 2012) 207 (hereafter Rowan, *Remedies*).

[76] ibid.

the lexical form of the specification looks otherwise—in England and Wales[77] prior to the Court of Appeal judgment in *Co-op v Argyll* 'keep open!' was universally agreed to mean 'shut if you will pay to do so'—and it is, with respect, quite wrong to claim otherwise.[78]

Rowan's views on *Ruxley* in this connection display the defect in the way she puts her case:

> an express provision that damages should be assessed as the cost of curing breach may have availed the promisee in *Ruxley*... If enforceable, it would have enabled him to demand that the swimming pool which was constructed contrary to specification should be rebuilt to the contractually agreed depth. The reasonableness of the demand would have been irrelevant, allowing a solution eminently more protective of the performance interest.[79]

Whilst one sees Rowan's point, *Ruxley* was a case where an express provision should have been supererogatory because the contract surely was agreed on an *East Ham v Sunley* basis, and in fact when an earlier breach left a crack in the pool's bottom, the claimant, anticipating what would have been the outcome of litigation, remedied this by completely reinstalling the pool 'free of charge'.[80] The crucial difference, which is erased by a general commitment to the performance interest, between this matter and the matter over which litigation was brought, is that the defendant actually had no interest in performance regarding the depth of the pool. It was found at trial that the defendant did not intend to rebuild the pool,[81] and so an award of £21,560 would have been a windfall[82] to set-off against the pool's total cost of £38,564.[83] There seems, one is obliged to say, no doubt that the defendant was prepared to say whatever was necessary to achieve the result he wanted[84] at the end of a contractual relationship which had become very sour.

Cost to complete is something of an anomaly within the overall law of literal enforcement, but the anomaly can be understood, and in this sense accommodated within the overall law, by reference to the intentions of the parties in, first, literal enforcement generally, and then in cost to complete in particular. That their agreement contemplated, even if only implicitly, that the claimant had a true consumer surplus should be sufficient to oust the compensatory damages default, and allow of the appropriate form of literal enforcement. But in all commercial cases the ouster should

[77] And in Scotland prior to the innovation in *Retail Parks Investments* (n 56): Campbell and Halson, 'The Irrelevance of the Performance Interest' (n 38) 471–79.

[78] So Rowan regrets that the parties in *Co-op v Argyll* did not include 'an effective specific performance clause' to reinforce the keep-open clause because the former 'would have been conducive to the protection of the performance interest': Rowan, *Remedies* (n 75) 210. But what Rowan means by 'protection of the performance interest' is, with respect, precisely what, as Millett LJ showed us by reference to the undoubted settled practice, the parties did not, as a matter of fact determined by business efficacy, agree.

[79] Rowan, *Remedies* (n 75) 215. This passage concludes with reference to the award for loss of amenity.

[80] *Ruxley* (CA) (n 67) 652F.

[81] ibid 655A.

[82] *Ruxley* (HL) (n 59) 363E.

[83] The defendant also pursued an even greater windfall by arguing that the contract was entire: ibid 363B.

[84] See n 72.

have to be express. However, the one case where the ouster would not seem to need to be express is cost to complete under *East Ham v Sunley*, for there, it seems reflecting parties' intentions, the default is cost to complete. Confusion undoubtedly has been created because the *East Ham v Sunley* default covers, not only true consumer surplus, but also cases, like *East Ham v Sunley* itself, where, as the claimant is not a consumer, there could not be a consumer surplus but, the crucial point, in order to avoid an idiosyncratic commercial loss, the works were going to be completed. The resulting law is, to be precise, that when works are going to be completed, the default measure is cost to complete. And if this is what is agreed, then Rowan is right that this should not be overturned (granting the reservation for truly exceptional cases) by discretionary references to reasonableness.

There must be a way of distinguishing between cases in which the claimant does or does not genuinely want the works to be completed, or the law of cost to complete under *East Ham v Sunley* is unacceptably open to abuse. There are worse cases than *Ruxley*,[85] but let us continue with this case which, however undeservedly, did become the focus of discussion. Having failed to convince the trial court that he would rebuild the pool, the defendant gave undertakings to both appeal courts that he would do so. At a first look, this would seem to deal with the problem of windfall awards, but the undertaking was dismissed as 'irrelevant' and 'unnecessary' because it would go against the English courts' general insistence that they have no concern with what a successful claimant does with its damages.[86] There are good and bad reasons for this which go beyond the law of contract, but there is a very good reason central to that law.

An undertaking will be (leaving procedural issues aside) irrelevant and unnecessary because, if cost to complete damages are challenged, surely it will be integral to the argument the party seeking those damages must make that the works will be completed. If this party does not intend to complete, where is the loss to be compensated by cost to complete,[87] other than, of course, in some incoherent idea that breach itself is a substantial loss? By making its argument honestly, the party gives the undertaking.

[85] One can hardly conceive of a less meritorious cost to complete claim than that brought in the famous US case *Jacob and Youngs Inc v Kent* 129 NE 889 (Court of Appeals of New York 1921), which was discussed in *Ruxley* (HL) (n 59) 366E–367B. However, a comparable English case, also discussed in *Ruxley*, ibid 371H–372B, is *Sealace Shipping Company Ltd v Oceanvoice Ltd, The Alecos M* [1991] 1 Lloyd's Rep 120 (CA). The claimant bought a merchant vessel which was not, as the contract provided, delivered with a spare propeller. There is no market in propellers of this sort, so the claimants sought cost to complete damages to have a spare specially made at a cost of US$200,000. Of course, in the event of certain breakdowns, the vessel might require a new propeller to be made, but the risk of this happening was slight and the benefit of having a spare to hand correspondingly small (vessels typically were not sold with a spare), and the arbitrator did not believe that the buyer would use the award to have the propeller made: ibid 122 cols 1–2. The arbitrator's award of US$1,100 as the scrap value of the anchor was restored by the Court of Appeal. It is impossible to believe the buyer would have paid for the small benefit it would have received from having a spare, especially when the US$200,000 is set against the total price of the vessel of US$2.45m, and difficult to believe that the vessel would have been delivered without a spare by a seller conscious of having agreed cost to complete.

Cases of a similar character arising from affirmation are discussed below.

[86] *Ruxley* (HL) (n 59) 364H–365A.

[87] *Tito v Waddell* (n 69) 335A–B:

> When the court refuses to order the doing of some expensive but largely futile work, the difference in the value of the property to the plaintiff with the work done and without it may be great or it may be small. He may or may not be able to establish that, although on the market the difference is negligible, there are reasons, whether idiosyncratic or not, why it is a matter of great

Ruxley is a particularly unfortunate case in this regard at one point because it seems the defendant professed to have changed his mind over rebuilding the pool, and so gave his undertaking, just to further his intent to punish the claimant by mulcting it in the cost to complete damages.[88] But in general what is necessary is, not the undertaking, but the intention to complete the works, and recognising this puts a very different light on the reasonableness of completion.

There will be a difficulty, commensurate with the *prima facie* unreasonableness of completing the works when the costs of doing so far exceed the value to be gained, in interpreting the parties' agreement to have intended cost to complete. Though *East Ham v Sunley* places the onus of raising the matter on the party which wishes to confine damages to the diminution measure, arguing for *prima facie* unreasonable cost to complete must always be possible, but it must always be hard. A virtue of the Lords judgment in *Ruxley* is that, in the end, the reasonableness of the discretion to deny cost to complete is, albeit inconsistently, overall merged with reference to the unreasonableness of (ie the implausibility of objectively finding it to have been the pool built in perfect conformity with the specifications) the defendant's intention ever to have secured an agreement to do it. It is submitted that this is the basic sense to be found in passages such as this:

> What constitutes the aggrieved party's loss is in every case a question of fact and degree. Where the contract breaker has entirely failed to achieve the contractual objective, it may not be difficult to conclude that the loss is the necessary cost of achieving that objective. Thus if a building is constructed so defectively that it is of no use for its designed purpose, the owner may have little difficulty in establishing that his loss is the necessary cost of reconstructing. Furthermore, in taking reasonableness into account in determining the extent of loss it is reasonableness in relation to the particular contract and not at large. Accordingly, if I contracted for the erection of a folly in my garden which shortly thereafter suffered a total collapse it would be irrelevant to the determination of my loss to argue that the erection of such a folly which contributed nothing to the value of my house was a crazy thing to do.[89]

This focus, not on *ex post* discretionary judgments of reasonableness by courts, but on *ex ante* considerations of reasonableness as they form the intentions of the parties, is valuable, its valuableness being only little diminished by one being able to find it clearly exhibited a century earlier in *Wigsell v The Corporation for the School for the Indigent Blind*.[90]

> moment to him. In damages one always comes back to the fundamental question, that of the loss or injury that the plaintiff has suffered, and the sum of money that will compensate him for it.

[88] *Ruxley* (HL) (n 59) 373E (Lord Lloyd):

> Does Mr Forsyth's undertaking ... make any difference? Clearly not. He cannot be allowed to create a loss, which does not exist, in order to punish the defendants.

[89] ibid 358D–F. The 'ugly fountain' used in Restatement (First) Contracts § 346(1)(a) illus 4 is omitted from Restatement (Second) Contracts § 348(2).

[90] (1882) 8 QBD 357 (QB). In this case, cost to complete damages were sought in connection with the claimed breach of a covenant to build a very substantial wall. But though the covenant made no express mention of it, that covenant was rightly interpreted as resting on the parties' intentions that the wall was to

Behind the doctrinal issues, it is only if one thinks solipsistic self-interest is legitimate that one can not only find virtue in *Ruxley*, a case in which a party wished to avoid paying its bills and to punish the other party, and conducted itself misleadingly before the court in order to do so, but think it is a case that shows grave defects in the positive law of remedies. All that is important about this eccentric case is the attitude taken towards it that allows one to think a contract can be made—not agreed—which asserts only one party's interest, and then be obliged to invoke a judicial discretion to avoid the consequences of doing so. One then has to seek, and fail, to put decisions about reasonableness on a sound footing, because one has dispensed with the sound footing one had in the intentions of the parties. Once it is accepted that the contract was to build a pool suitable for domestic use, and that the construction firm's interests had to be taken into account (and leaving aside the problems caused by the conduct and argument of the defendant), *Ruxley* should have solved itself. But for this to be possible, it has to be grasped that the mutual recognition of the parties' interests that structures the law of remedies, exemplified by mitigation, is by default the basis of the parties' intentions. It is right that this default should be able to be ousted, but this must be done by agreement clearly expressed in the parties' manifestations of their intentions.

The overwhelming response to Lord Hoffmann's judgment in *Co-op v Argyll* has been to deplore the weight he gave to the difficulty of supervision, and to say awards of specific performance should not do this in future.[91] The credulous assumption behind this is that making specific performance more widely available would lead to a greater amount of performance of primary obligations.[92] In cases where a true consumer surplus is not involved, ie in all commercial cases, this would not be the significance of a more ready award of specific performance. For such parties, whose interest is monetary, the award of specific performance is an award of a chose in action which will be used in bargaining with the defendant in order to achieve a settlement. Once this is appreciated, that a primary obligation is performed or not can be seen as in itself irrelevant.[93] The question is whether a party should have its position in post-breach

be built to enclose a projected asylum. A remedy literally enforcing the covenant, regardless of the difference between the diminution measure and cost to complete, would have been awarded were the project to have gone ahead. But the project's abandonment meant that cost to complete damages, if awarded without regard to the parties' intentions, would have been a windfall: ibid 364:

> it was also open to the plaintiffs to do what they have done, viz, bring this action for damages, in which event they will be under no obligation whatever to expend the amount recovered in erecting the wall, and most probably would never think for a moment of any such expenditure, which to us, at least, would seem a simple waste of the money.

[91] Burrows, *Remedies* (n 2) 418–19.

[92] D Friedmann, 'Economic Aspects of Damages and Specific Performance Compared' in D Saidov and R Cunnington (eds), *Contract Damages* (Hart 2008) 165.

[93] In *Attica Sea Carriers Corp v Ferrostaal Poseidon Bulk Reederei GMBH, The Puerto Buitrago* [1976] 1 Lloyd's Rep 250 (hereafter *The Puerto Buitrago*), the defendant charterers of a merchant vessel acknowledged liability for US$400,000 following breach of its obligation to redeliver the vessel in good repair. This quantum represented the difference between the vessel in good repair and in the state in which it was proposed to redeliver it. The claimant owners insisted that the vessel be redelivered in good repair. The repairs would cost US$2m, but, even in good repair, the vessel, which the charterers had proposed scrapping, would have been worth only US$1m: ibid 251 col 1. The precise dispute was over affirmation, but the effect, of course, would be that of specific performance (ibid 255 col 1), and the Court of Appeal refused affirmation, with the result that the defendant's liability was confirmed to be US$400,000. The point about this case is

negotiations be very substantially improved by the award of specific performance, the 'buying off' of which becomes the starting point of those negotiations.[94]

An unfortunate separation seems to have arisen between the consideration of these issues from the perspective of the general principles of contract and from the perspective of equitable jurisprudence, for, of course, some of the leading cases of the latter give penetrating consideration to the issues, exemplified by AL Smith LJ's judgment in *Shelfer's* case.[95] The aspect of the issue which should be stressed here is that captured in Lord Westbury LC's insistence in *Isenberg v East India House Estate Co* that it was not the proper function of a court of equity 'by granting a mandatory injunction, to deliver over the defendants to the plaintiff bound hand and foot, in order to be made subject to any extortionate demand that he may by possibility make [*sic*]'.[96] Once one recognises that the function of specific performance in commercial cases is improvement of compensation, not compulsion of performance, points like Lord Westbury's should place a very large question mark over responding to the possibility of damages leaving the claimant undercompensated by increasing the availability of specific performance in contract.

In sum, the law of literal enforcement generally is undermined by doctrinal mistakes which follow from a downplaying of the defendant's interests itself traceable to a belief that, in disregard of the necessity of mutual recognition, solipsistic self-interest is a legitimate form of contractual action. When parties negotiate on the default terms of the law of remedies, their allocation of the risks of liability are based on an assumption of compensatory damages. But in the laws so far examined in this chapter, claimants which, after breach, come to believe that what they have negotiated will leave them uncompensated, have mounted arguments that the inadequacy of damages in this sense should allow them to obtain a literal enforcement remedy, and these have sometimes met with a sympathetic reception in cases which have become focal points of attention. In the course of this, the equitable bars on literal enforcement have come under criticism, and it is true that, operating at the level of discretionary withholding of the parties' remedies, they are indefensible. But their substantial recognition of the defendant's interests is wholly defensible. It should, however, be seen to be operative *ex ante* in the parties' agreed intentions, not reserved for *ex post* adjustment of what are generally mistaken to be their agreements.

As a matter of doctrine, the confusion to which I am trying to draw attention has, of course, its basis in the way that, 150 years after fusion, the separation of common

that, though yet another occasion for lamentation about insufficient protection of the performance interest, there was never any possibility whatsoever of the vessel being repaired by anyone no matter what the Court decided! Endorsement of the affirmation would merely (leaving aside an issue about continued payment of charter hire) have enormously improved the claimant's ability to secure a settlement much in excess of US$400,000.

[94] There is, of course, a theoretical argument for making specific performance the default remedy based on its possible effect on post-breach negotiations: A Schwartz, 'The Case for Specific Performance' (1979) 89 Yale Law Journal 271 and TJ Muris, 'The Costs of Freely Granting Specific Performance' [1982] Duke Law Journal 1035.

[95] *Shelfer v City of London Electric Lighting Co (No 1)* [1895] 1 Ch 287.

[96] (1863) 3 De GJ & S 263, 273; 46 ER 667, 641.

law and equity still permeates the law of remedies for breach of contract.[97] I have little doubt this separation should ultimately be abolished. I have even smaller doubt that changes to it should be made in the smallest increments. Any such changes must balance the interests of the parties, not *ex post*, but in an *ex ante* interpretation of what they actually agreed, the pattern being the outstanding dissent of Millett LJ in *Co-op v Argyll*.

Distinct from, but obviously related to, this instance of a need for doctrinal reform lies another such instance. That the various literal enforcement remedies are available under significantly different conditions is a legacy of their having been developed in substantial ignorance of what it was they each and all were trying to achieve. We can conclude this chapter by looking at the main attempt that has been made to give these remedies some unity, which more than adequately shows the difficulty of any such effort whilst solipsistic self-interest is regarded as legitimate: the legitimate interest under *White and Carter*.

The Legitimate Interest

The pall which *White and Carter* casts over the law of remedies is not so much a product of the case itself as of a widespread misunderstanding partially generated by it being impossible to draw a *ratio* from it, to some extent because the deciding judgment of Lord Reid is, as Professor Carter observed and as we shall see, 'uncharacteristically vague',[98] but more because the facts of the case are, even now, very inadequately known.[99] In the case, the defender attempted to repudiate a three year

[97] A Burrows, 'We Do This at Common Law But That at Equity' (2002) 22 Oxford Journal of Legal Studies 1.

[98] JW Carter, '*White and Carter*: How Unreasonable?' (2012) 128 Law Quarterly Review 490, 491 (hereafter Carter, 'How Unreasonable?') 491.

[99] *White and Carter* still cries out for 'legal archaeological' explanation after the fashion which, though I believe R Danzig, '*Hadley and Another v Baxendale* and Others' in R Danzig and GR Watson, *The Capability Problem in Contract Law* (2nd edn, Foundation Press 2004), first published in 1975, was the first example, is inevitably associated with the late Professor Simpson. This is so in a particular way. Studies like Danzig's and, indeed, Simpson's of *Carlill's case* (AWB Simpson, 'Quackery and Contract Law: *Carlill v Carbolic Smokeball Company* (1893)' in *Leading Cases in the Common Law* (repr edn, OUP 2001) valuably deepen our knowledge. But, as was mentioned in ch 1, Simpson's study of *Raffles v Wichelhaus* (AWB Simpson, 'The Beauty of Obscurity' in *Leading Cases*, ibid) made sense of the formerly utterly incomprehensible. Professor Macmillan's study of *Bell v Lever Bros* (C Macmillan, *Mistakes in Contract Law* (Hart 2010) 257–78) falls into this latter category. One looks for *White and Carter's* Simpson or Macmillan.

What I surmise from the reports is as follows. The pursuer was a substantial business operating throughout the UK. The terms on which it sought to do business included a clause (Clause 8 which will be discussed in the text accompanying n 140) which gave it a very advantageous position on breach by the other party. This clause had been brought into doubt by a 1952 Scottish case, *Langford and Co Ltd v Dutch* 1952 SC 15 (CS) (hereafter *Langford v Dutch*), which the pursuer had challenged in an unreported case in which judgment was given in England by the Court of Appeal on 21 May 1958, and at first instance in *White and Carter*, which was heard on 6 February 1959 in the Dumbarton Sherriff's Court. The pursuer's argument on an appeal heard by the Second Division of the Inner House of the Court of Session was intended to lead to the issue being considered by the House of Lords, and the gratifying result for the pursuer was that *Langford v Dutch*, ibid was there overruled.

My own 2002 speculation (Harris, and others, *Remedies* (n 1) 165) about the pursuer's motivations was, in its defence, based on the legitimate interest as it had come to be understood in the case law and commentary. However, not only was it a speculation with no basis in the reported facts, which caused me disquiet at the time, but I now believe it is contradicted by those facts as so far known.

advertising contract, performance of which was to commence four months hence, on the very day its employee had mistakenly agreed it. The pursuer's affirmation, which in theory would have led to the unwanted three year performance being carried out, was, however, endorsed only by a bare majority of the House of Lords, reversing the two Scots courts which had heard the matter. The contract on which the pursuer relied was described as 'extortionate' by Lord Patrick in the Court of Session,[100] and the minority in the Lords described the pursuer's argument as a 'startling' one[101] having 'strange' consequences.[102] To take but one example selected because of the authority of its source, 15 years later Lord Denning MR, quoting the eighth edition of *Cheshire and Fifoot*,[103] called the result 'grotesque'.[104] The eighth edition was the first to which Professor Furmston contributed, and this description reflects the tone of his note on the case,[105] one of a number of such notes deprecating *White and Carter* which appeared as quickly as the process of publication allowed.

To bring the issue into the focus required here, *White and Carter*, as Lord Keith pointed out,[106] defeats the entire purpose of anticipatory repudiation under *Hochster v de la Tour*,[107] which is to allow the claimant an early opportunity to mitigate, both in its own interests of possibly securing an alternative in a timely manner, and in the interests of the defendant, which may have to compensate lost expectation and incidental expenses, but will avoid the 'reliance' expenditures of performance.[108] The result in *White and Carter* seems to endorse a complete disregard for mitigation, and as a matter of policy it is unworthy to say that mitigation is confined to damages, and so does not extend to the power to elect to terminate or affirm because, of course, *White and Carter* matters only because of the impact affirmation has on the quantification of the sum of money, 'damages' or not, that the defendant ultimately has to pay the claimant.[109] The position which is claimed to rest on *White and Carter* is, in sum, an indefensible instance of disregard for the values of contract in the law of remedies for breach,[110] and it is deplorable that contesting this basic point evidently still can give

[100] *White and Carter Councils) Ltd v McGregor* 1960 SC 276 (CS) (hereafter *White and Carter* (CS)).

[101] *White and Carter* (HL) (n 51) 442 (Lord Keith).

[102] ibid 432 (Lord Morton).

[103] GCH Cheshire, CHS Fifoot and MP Furmston, *Law of Contract* (8th edn, Butterworths, 1972) 600.

[104] *The Puerto Buitrago* (n 93) 255 col 1.

[105] MP Furmston, 'The Case of the Insistent Performer' (1962) 25 Modern Law Review 364.

[106] *White and Carter* (HL) (n 51) 439–40.

[107] (1853) 2 El & Bl 678, 690; 118 ER 922, 926 (hereafter *Hochster v de la Tour*).

[108] In *Frost v Knight* (1872) LR 7 Exch 111, 113 (Ex Ch) the criticism about to be discussed below of the rule in *Hochster v de la Tour* was rejected *inter alia* because that rule was 'for the common benefit of both parties' (Cockburn CJ).

[109] Framed with the ultimate effect on quantum of, as we have seen, a different specific rule in mind, the wise views of Mann LJ in *Ruxley* (CA) (n 67) 660D (emphasis added) seem particularly apt to the *White and Carter* situation:

> the damages [awarded] should reflect a reasonable *culmination* of the relationship which has occurred between the parties. Thus damages will not reflect an unreasonable failure to mitigate loss.

[110] JW Carter, A Phang and Sock Yong Phang, 'Performance Following Repudiation: Legal and Economic Interests' (1999) 15 Journal of Contract Law 97. On this disregard in light of the more recent litigation I have nothing to add to J Morgan, 'Smuggling Mitigation into *White and Carter v McGregor*: Time to Come Clean?' [2015] Lloyd's Maritime and Commercial Law Quarterly 575 (hereafter Morgan, 'Time to Come Clean?').

rise to high value litigation over 'wholly unreasonable' claims made in contempt of the defendant's interests.[111]

The main way in which disregard for mitigation influenced *White and Carter* was that Lord Hodson, with whom Lord Tucker agreed, seemed to hold that, as a matter of law, the power to elect was entirely discretionary, so that the pursuer could 'choose', not being confined to act in such a way that 'the court thought ... reasonable'.[112] Lord Hodson acknowledged that, if the issue in the case had been one of specific implement, then the relief sought would have been subject to equitable discretion. But, for him, the precise point was that affirmation was not such a case. Going beyond issues arising from the law of action for the price and of debt which the case raises,[113] holding the power to elect to be discretionary ultimately rests on thinking captured in Asquith LJ's *dictum* about 'an unaccepted repudiation [being] a thing writ in water', which Lord Hodson approved.[114] The defenders may have been 'unfortunate [to] have saddled themselves with an unwanted contract ... but there is no equity which can assist [them]. It is trite that equity will not rewrite an improvident contract when there is no disability on either side'.[115] It will be argued that Lord Hodson came to the right decision in the case, but to the unclear extent that he thought that the treatment of affirmation should be fundamentally different to the treatment of specific performance, he was, with respect, quite wrong.[116] This point is very much rubbed home when a defendant continues to insist that it has repudiated, and so at the due date either will not perform or will not pay anything other than damages quantified on the basis of mitigation, for if the claimant then seeks a final remedy of specific performance, this will require substantial legal argument.[117]

[111] *MSC Mediterranean Shipping Co SA v Cottonex Anstalt* [2015] EWHC 283 (Comm); [2015] 2 All ER Comm 614 [121] (hereafter *MSC Mediterranean Shipping* (QB)). This part of the claimant's argument was an attempt 'in effect, to seek to generate an unending stream of free income': ibid. This decision was in substantial part reversed, but in terms which seem to have left intact the valuable observations on mitigation of Leggatt J, as he then was: *MSC Mediterranean Shipping Co SA v Cottonex Anstalt* [2016] EWCA Civ 789, [2017] 1 All ER (Comm) 483 [47]–[50].

[112] *White and Carter* (HL) (n 51) 445.

[113] ibid 444. Lord Keith's views *contra* are at ibid 435–37.

[114] *Howard v Pickford Tool Co Ltd* [1951] 1 KB 417 (CA) 421 (hereafter *Howard*); quoted in *White and Carter* (HL) (n 51) by Lord Hodson at 444 and Lord Keith at 438. This may be the most significant instance in the law of contract of the confusion caused by being seduced by, as Lord Keith put it, a 'graphic phrase' without relating it to 'the circumstances in which it [was] used'. Lord Keith's argument distinguishing *Howard* does not, with respect, make it sufficiently clear that that case should have had no bearing whatsoever on *White and Carter*. *Howard* was not a case of anticipatory breach at all, but was about a possible breach *simpliciter*, though then called a repudiation, which certainly would have been 'accepted'.

[115] *White and Carter* (HL) (n 51) 445.

[116] The minority sought to make the crucial point: ibid 433 'the appellants are claiming a kind of inverted specific implement' and 437 'the appellants are saying: "We shall do something which the courts will not enforce" '(Lord Keith).

[117] Because of the impossibility of fully understanding the proceedings on the basis of what we now know of them, I relegate to a footnote the ironic point that, leaving what Lord Reid said of the defendant's co-operation aside, it is all but inconceivable that *White and Carter* could ever literally have amounted to a case of claiming payment for a completed primary performance. The contract was agreed (and repudiated) on 26 June 1957. Performance was to begin on 2 November 1957, and to be completed on or about 30 October 1960. The first payment was due on 9 November 1957. Clause 8 was activated on or about 30 November 1957. Proceedings must have been issued in 1958, for, as has been mentioned, the case was first heard on 6 February 1959. All this makes sense only if the issue was accelerated payment without the pursuer performing, for surely an unchallenged endorsement of affirmation at this time would have led to settlement.

I do not believe that Lord Hodson found for the pursuer on the basis that the power to elect was discretionary in the thing writ in water sense, and his judgment was much closer to the judgment of Lord Reid than is generally allowed.[118] Lord Reid did not merely think the defender's position was unfortunate. He clearly implied that its contract was 'improvident or oppressive', a type of contract from which 'Parliament has on many occasions relieved parties'. But providing such relief was something which the 'common law [ie including equity] can do only in very limited circumstances', and, not finding those circumstances to obtain in the instant case, in which the pursuer 'may accept the repudiation … or he may if he chooses disregard … it',[119] he found himself 'unable to avoid the conclusion' that he had to find for the pursuer.[120] Like Lord Hodson, Lord Reid wanted to avoid a wide scrutiny of how a party might 'enforce its full rights under a contract': 'It might be, but it never has been, the law that a person is only entitled to enforce his contractual rights in a reasonable way, and that a court will not support an attempt to enforce them in an unreasonable way.'[121]

Finding himself in this most uncomfortable position, Lord Reid, it is submitted, decided to work against the repetition of such a result by so discussing the possibility of the residual equitable jurisdiction set out, as we have seen above,[122] by Lord Watson in *Grahame v Magistrates of Kirkaldy* in such a way that it was effectively expanded to include the defendant's co-operation and the legitimate interest as conditions which had in future to be taken into account. Let us put the former to one side and quote the famous passage setting out the latter:

> It may well be that, if it can be shown that a person has no legitimate interest, financial or otherwise, in performing the contract rather than claiming damages, he ought not to be allowed to saddle the other party with an additional burden with no benefit to himself. If a party has no interest to enforce a stipulation, he cannot in general enforce it: so it might be said that, if a party has no interest to insist on a particular remedy, he ought not to be allowed to insist on it. And, just as a party is not allowed to enforce a penalty, so he ought not to be allowed to penalise the other party by taking one course when another is equally advantageous to him.[123]

That this passage has done a very great deal to make us conscious of the role mitigation should have in the law of affirmation in particular, and the law of literal enforcement in general, is to Lord Reid's immense credit. There are few passages in the law of contract which have done so much to force upon our understanding the necessity of recognition of the defendant's interests, and therefore the mutual recognition of the parties' interests. But this passage is topped and tailed by two sentences that have undermined its basic thrust, and limited the effect it has had. Let us turn to them.

The sentence immediately preceding the vital passage tells us that what was to be set out as the legitimate interest was 'a general equitable principle or element of public

[118] *Salaried Staff London Loan Co Ltd v Swears and Wells Ltd* 1985 SC 189 (CS) 193–94.
[119] *White and Carter* (HL) (n 51) 427.
[120] ibid 431.
[121] ibid 430.
[122] See the text accompanying n 52.
[123] *White and Carter* (HL) (n 51) 431.

policy which requires this limitation of the contractual rights of the innocent party'.[124] As the legitimate interest now is so central to literal enforcement, it is enormously regrettable that Lord Reid saw it, in the way with which we are after earlier discussion now familiar in other forms of literal enforcement, as *ex post* equitable adjustment of the legal liabilities of the parties. Before returning to what fundamentally is wrong with this, it must be emphasised that it gives the courts the very difficult task of balancing those liabilities, their efforts to do so in an in itself very significantly large number of high value, typically shipping, cases after *White and Carter*[125] remaining 'perennially controversial'.[126] After 20 years of such efforts,[127] the problem was captured in *Clea Shipping Corp v Bulk Oil International Ltd, The Alaskan Trader (No 2)*[128] when, after rather despairingly trying to reconcile two important cases which had come down either side of the line Lord Reid had drawn—*The Puerto Buitrago* refusing affirmation, *Gator Shipping Corporation v Trans-Asiatic Oil Ltd SA and Occidental Shipping Establishment, The Odenfeld*[129] endorsing it—Lloyd J could firmly conclude only that Lord Reid *had* drawn a line, as indeed he had:

> there comes a point at which the court will cease, on general equitable principles, to allow the innocent party to enforce his contract according to its strict legal terms. How one defines that point is obviously a matter of some difficulty, for it involves drawing a line between conduct which is merely unreasonable ... and conduct which is *wholly* unreasonable. But however difficult it may be to define the point, that there is such a point seems to me to have been accepted.[130]

Though I believe I can show how it can be done, it undoubtedly is the case that reconciling the legitimate interest with the result in *White and Carter* is a 'puzzle'.[131] In the first place, if the anachronism be allowed, neither Lord Reid nor anyone else who heard the case showed that the pursuer had a legitimate interest! The Scots courts and the minority in the Lords thought the pursuer's conduct illegitimate, and Lords Hodson and Tucker's thing writ in water thinking made the point otiose. What Lord

[124] ibid 430–31.

[125] D Winterton, 'Reconsidering *White and Carter v McGregor*' [2013] Lloyd's Maritime and Commercial Law Quarterly 5.

[126] Morgan, 'Time to Come Clean?' (n 110) 576.

[127] For the state of the law after 50 years see *Isabella Shipowner SA v Shagang Shipping Co Ltd, The Aquafaith* [2012] EWHC 1077 (Comm); [2012] 2 Lloyd's Rep 61, and *MSC Mediterranean Shipping* (QB) (n 111).

[128] [1984] 1 All ER 129 (QB) (hereafter *The Alaskan Trader*).

[129] [1978] 2 Lloyd's Rep 357 (QB) (hereafter *The Odenfeld*), discussed in the text accompanying n 148.

[130] *The Alaskan Trader* (n 128) 137j–138b.

[131] Carter, 'How Unreasonable?' (n 98) 491.

It does not, with respect, assist Professor Smith's ingenious attempt to find a place for 'the *White and Carter* exception' in his new philosophy of the entire subject that he can do no more than leave a complete speculative blank when it comes to the *locus classicus*: S Smith, *Rights, Wrongs and Injustices* (OUP 2019) 139 n 18:

> Lord Reid did not explain why the claimants had a legitimate interest in performing the contract. Unless they had already done the work (which seems unlikely), the only possible interest would seem to be that by displaying McGregor's advertising on their bins they were advertising the possibility of putting advertising on bins—an interest that would have been difficult to quantify.

Reid precisely said, in the sentences immediately following the famous passage quoted above, was that:

> the respondent did not set out to prove that the appellants had no legitimate interest in completing the contract and claiming the contract price rather than claiming damages; there is nothing in the findings of fact to support such a case, and it seems improbable that any such case could have has been proved. It is, in my judgement, impossible to say that the defendant should be deprived of their right to claim the contract price merely because the benefit to them, as against claiming damages and reletting their advertising space, might be small in comparison with the loss to the respondent: that is the most that can be said in favour of the respondent.[132]

Though this reasoning surely is the epitome of the uncharacteristic vagueness of which Carter complained, it does set up a default position that the pursuer had a right to affirm which the defender would have had to oust if it was to be able to insist on termination, and as the defender had made no attempt to do so, Lord Reid found for the pursuer. Leaving aside the result in *White and Carter* itself for a moment, and looking at the law after the case in general, the problem is not so much vagueness but that, with great respect, Lord Reid chose the wrong default![133] The point is not that mitigation should be central to the election to terminate or affirm, though it should. The point is that, by default, this is the parties' intention. I am only too aware of a need to apologise for repeating, yet again, that when parties contract on default terms, their intentions are that the liability they undertake will be to pay compensatory damages quantified according to the rules of causation, and after *Hochster v de la Tour* it should be unarguable that this applies to affirmation just as much as to other parts of the law of remedies.[134] Lord Reid's position would make anticipatory breach impossible. A party contemplating repudiation would find itself 'bound hand and foot', and able to escape its primary obligations only after negotiations which started from, not the cost of compensatory damages after mitigation, but the cost of primary performance without it. In the absence of a contract containing an express permission to anticipatorily breach, a mere academic can only imagine what tactics would be developed to allow a defendant properly advised about the law, not to be frank about its intentions, but to take the very wise course of breaching without admitting that it had done so.

Lord Reid's not adopting thing writ in water thinking and bringing the legitimate interest into consideration had, however, the success he intended, for he did effectively import mitigation into the election to terminate or affirm. But this has only been

[132] *White and Carter* (HL) (n 51) 431.

[133] MP Gergen, 'The Right to Perform after Repudiation and Recover the Contract Price in Anglo-American Law' in LA DiMatteo and M Hogg (eds), *Comparative Contract Law: British and American Perspectives* (OUP 2016).

[134] Lord Keith, *White and Carter* (HL) (n 51) 439–40, put it this way:

> in *Hochster v de la Tour*, from which the whole law about anticipatory repudiation stems, Lord Campbell plainly indicated that if the courier in that case, instead of accepting as he did the repudiation of his engagement as a cause of action, before it was due to commence, had waited till the lapse of the three months of the engagement he could not have sued as for a debt. The jury, he said, would be entitled to look at all that might 'increase or mitigate the loss of the plaintiff down to the day of the trial' [*Hochster v de la Tour* (n 107) 692; 927].

because in subsequent cases Lord Reid's own incorrect formulation has been reversed and, in a way exemplified by *The Alaskan Trader*, the claimant has had to justify affirmation by showing a legitimate interest in doing so, ie the claimant has had to prove a legitimate interest to oust the default of compensatory damages.[135] It is one of the many ironies generated by *White and Carter* that bringing affirmation into line with specific performance in this way erases the claimed difference between them that so motivated Lord Hodson's thinking.

Of course, all defaults should be able to be ousted by agreement, and the perennial confusion has been caused because it is not realised that, so far as one can say on the basis of the reports, this is what happened in *White and Carter*. The main question posed by the predominant understanding of *White and Carter* is what on earth did the pursuer think it was doing? Its conduct and pleadings are inconsistent with its own self-interest. The pursuer's own pleadings on the Court of Session incidentally show that there was excess demand for its services.[136] Had it terminated and found a substitute, it would have been in Lord Reid's 'equally advantageous' position. Had it not been able to find a substitute within a time which linked doing so to mitigation of the terminated contract, it would have been in a somewhat more advantageous position because it would have received its full expectation years earlier than the contract provided, and have been able to redeploy its resources.[137]

Accepting the predominant interpretation, one comes to think that the pursuer must actually have had what was to be called a legitimate interest in order to act as it did. But if it did, why didn't it in effect say so in order to enormously strengthen its argument? The line it took in legal argument appeared so extremely hazardous a flaunting of good sense that it lost in Dumbarton and Edinburgh, and was lucky to win in London.[138] As that line was met with such little sympathy that the pursuer was not awarded costs in the Lords and no adjustment was made of the costs it suffered below, it will have found its ultimate success a somewhat mixed blessing.[139]

And, in fact, *White and Carter* was not about the default law of affirmation at all. Under the parties' contract, payment was to be made in advance in three annual instalments, the first of which was due one week after the first advertisement had been placed. The case turned on Clause 8, which was in two parts. The first, quoted *verbatim* in the reports of the Scots and English cases,[140] accelerated the payments so that the entire sum became immediately due upon a failure to pay any instalment. The second part, not quoted in either report, *seems* to say that, if the pursuer wished to perform, it could do so even if the defender repudiated; ie it incorporated something like thing writ in water thinking. In the paraphrase of this second part by Lord Justice-Clerk Thomson, the defender would have to 'submit to the counter-performance' and at the

[135] The opposite is maintained in Qiao Liu, *Anticipatory Breach* (Hart 2011) 203–04.

[136] The pursuer's pleadings include a 'lost volume' argument: *White and Carter* (CS) (n 100) 279.

[137] Though he did so with knowledge of the clause in the parties' contract on which the case actually turned, Lord Patrick in the Court of Session recognised a possibility like this: ibid 285.

[138] In addition to the points already made, it would seem that the bare majority finding for the pursuer itself represented a change in position between their Lordships' initial conference about the case and the handing down of the judgment: A Paterson, *Final Judgment* (Hart 2013) 184.

[139] *White and Carter* (HL) (n 51) 446. The pursuer will, I surmise, have looked on all this as the cost of overturning *Langford v Dutch* (n 99).

[140] *White and Carter* (CS) (n 100) 281 and *White and Carter* (HL) (n 51) 427.

end pay the price as a debt which was 'not an action for damages [so] the defender had no right to appeal to any equity, like minimisation of damage'.[141]

It is not possible on the reported facts to fully understand Clause 8 or the way the pursuer framed its claim, but what is certain is that that claim is completely at odds with the predominant interpretation of *White and Carter* as it had nothing to do with the default law of affirmation. Clause 8 was an express assertion of an unfettered power to affirm (or claim accelerated payment to identical or even better ultimate effect), and it seems highly likely that this was to oust a default position in which 'minimisation of damage' would be taken into account. At the cost of a certain imprecision which cannot be corrected at an appropriate length here, one can say that the judgments of the entire Court of Session and the minority of the Lords focused on the question whether Clause 8 was a 'penalty', and found it was. Lord Hodson was, it must be said, scornful of the Court of Session being 'no doubt ... impressed'[142] by the defendant's 'unfortunate' position when reaching this finding, and it was to give effect to Clause 8 that he, as we have seen, insisted that 'It is trite that equity will not rewrite an improvident contract when there is no disability on either side'. It is submitted he was right, not because of anything he said about a thing writ in water as the default law, but because in Clause 8 the parties had expressly agreed to make accelerated payment a form of debt.

This long consideration of *White and Carter* can be drawn to an end with a final comment on Lord Reid. By establishing the wrong default, Lord Reid seems to have done the defender few favours. That the defender failed to seek to prove that the pursuer did not have a legitimate interest is perhaps understandable as it will not have known it should have tried to do so until it left the House of Lords Chamber! But, though not with the enthusiasm of Lord Hodson, Lord Reid saw the significance of Clause 8,[143] which is that under it the pursuer had effectively created a legitimate interest, and that is why it would have been 'improbable' that any case that it had no such interest could have been proved. I believe that Lord Reid both felt obliged to find for the pursuer, but to discourage the pursuer's behaviour in future. With the greatest respect, the vagueness of the argument by which he squared this circle follows from his not seeing the issues in terms of default rules and their ouster. This is far from a criticism in the pejorative sense. How many could have, from the material he had to hand, pushed the law of literal enforcement as Lord Reid did further towards recognition of the necessity of respecting the defendant's interests?

In the course of this discussion of affirmation, some cases have been mentioned in which solipsistic disregard of the defendant's interests is so blatant that the cases are outrageous. It will be clear that one can get carried away with indignation at law of this sort, but the treatment of affirmation does place a question mark against the moral conduct of self-interested commercial actors in receipt of sophisticated legal advice which is all very reminiscent of the consideration loophole cases considered in Chapter 5. It is best to conclude this chapter by reminding ourselves that an undoubted and important problem of allocating idiosyncratic loss lies behind this law. It will be

[141] *White and Carter* (CS) (n 100) 281.
[142] *White and Carter* (HL) (n 51) 445.
[143] ibid 426–27.

recalled that in *The Alaskan Trader* Lloyd J tried to reconcile *The Puerto Buitrago* and *The Odenfeld*, but, as has been argued, *The Puerto Buitrago* is one of the outrageous cases—even Kerr J allowed that there were 'probably' no damages in that case[144]—and the better contrast is between *The Odenfeld* and the *Alaskan Trader* itself.

In *The Alaskan Trader*, claimant shipowners kept a vessel at the charterer's disposal, claiming full hire, for the last seven months of a two year time charter which the charterers had repudiated at the time the vessel was tendered again ready for service after requiring repair during the charter.[145] Having made no attempt to mitigate, the claimant, relying on thing writ in water thinking, seems not have pleaded a legitimate interest.[146] The arbitrator certainly did not find one, thinking the conduct of the claimant a 'commercial absurdity',[147] and Lloyd J found no reason to upset the arbitrator's finding. One can imagine reasons for the claimant's election, but none were put forward, and it is submitted that the law in *The Alaskan Trader* is, as has been claimed throughout this chapter, that the default rule in affirmation cases and all commercial literal enforcement cases save *East Ham v Sunley* cost to complete cases, based on mitigation.

As Lloyd J maintained, Kerr J in *The Odenfeld* also allowed that Lord Reid had drawn a line, but this does not mean that mitigation was at all properly applied. One could see the direction about to be taken when Kerr J held that 'any fetter on the innocent party's right of election whether or not to accept a repudiation will only be applied in extreme cases, viz where damages would be an adequate remedy *and* where an election to keep the contract alive would be wholly unreasonable',[148] for one has to ask what the 'and' adds to the matter. And, as one part of the extremely complicated litigation in *The Odenfeld*, it was accepted that if the charterers had repudiated, the owners and connected parties had a legitimate interest in affirmation because they would suffer a loss from termination which they would not be able to quantify in damages:

> it is said that a claim for damages would have been an adequate remedy and that this had been assigned to the plaintiffs. In practice, however, this is an oversimplification. In practice it is an extremely difficult and lengthy process to assess damages in a situation such as this. How are they to be fairly assessed, when at the time of the repudiation the charter still had about 6½ years to run with many possible variables in the market rate and the performance of the vessel? Of course, the law provides some answer, but having to establish a claim for damages puts a shipowner into a very different position from that of being entitled to hire under a subsisting charter.[149]

144 *The Odenfeld* (n 129) 374 col 2.

145 Though there had been a repudiation before the vessel broke down, the case turned on the charterer's refusal to take the vessel back after repair. As the arbitrator acutely noted, there is therefore a question whether the case concerned repudiation, ie anticipatory breach, at all, and, in this sense, though the arbitrator could not be expected to know or even be concerned about this, this was a case actually close to *Howard* (n 114): *The Alaskan Trader* (n 128) 131h, 138f.

146 ibid 132e.

147 ibid 131j.

148 *The Odenfeld* (n 129) 374 col 1.

149 ibid col 2.

All these questions are in a sense good ones, for they indicate the existence of an uncompensated loss, and we are back to Treitel's seeing uncompensated loss as evidence of inadequacy of damages. But we are now in a position to realise that these questions should have occurred to the *Odenfeld* claimant at the stage of negotiating the charter, and as they didn't, it is the claimant which failed to deal with the possibility of idiosyncratic, uncompensated loss. One can understand why the claimant, now aware of the risk it has run, asks these questions at the stage of providing a remedy. But to give the claimant the answers it wants at this stage, is to overturn the intentions of the parties, their liabilities as determined by their agreement being subsumed to the claimant's solipsistic wish to improve the position it agreed; at, of course, the cost of the interests the defendant had secured by that agreement.

Conclusion: The Illegitimate Interest

The law of specific performance has an unquestionably valuable function in regard of what has here been called the true consumers' interest. The response to legal goods being unique in the sense relevant to bring this interest into play seems so sound as to be more the product of a long settled attitude than of decided law, and that other legal forms of economic goods can display an equivalent to that uniqueness is wholly possible. If we put commercial and consumer land cases to one side, the law of the true consumers' interest is not of much practical significance.[150] What has been of very considerable significance is the adoption of uniqueness to commercial cases in which there cannot possibly be a consumers' interest, which has left a lasting effect on the entire law of literal enforcement, reducing it to fundamental incoherence.

The ideas of compulsion of performance and inadequacy of damages as the ground of this, which are entirely appropriate in cases of true consumers' interest, have been turned on their heads. In contradiction of what is claimed in theories of substitutionary damages, in the actual law compulsion of performance is sought as a substitute for compensatory damages. The most important ground on which damages are now found to be inadequate is that they are *accurately* quantified according to the rules of causation. A claimant which, no doubt typically with reason, believes that damages will not fully compensate the loss which, as a matter of fact, it suffers, obliquely pleads this as inadequacy of damages, thereby enlisting the court's efforts to reverse the allocation of risk of idiosyncratic loss which the parties had agreed. The top hat is placed on the whole spectacle when the claimant successfully claims it has a legitimate interest in, in effect, undermining the basic values of the law of contract, the mutual recognition of the parties' interests being subordinated to the claimant's solipsistic exploitation of the possibilities the law allows to avoid the consequences of what it had agreed.

It is extremely significant that the least nuanced welcome that Lord Reid's expression of the legitimate interest has received in a major case has been the adoption of it to the purpose of evaluating agreed damages clauses by Lords Neuberger and Sumption

[150] See the text accompanying n 18.

in *Cavendish Square Holding BV v Talal el Makdessi; ParkingEye Ltd v Beavis*: 'the law will not generally make a remedy available to a party, the adverse impact of which on the defaulter significantly exceeds any legitimate interest of the innocent party'.[151] But this was because their Lordships were perfectly happy with a law which left the critical decisions in agreed damages, literal enforcement (and many other) cases to be made by courts confident in their capacity to accurately determine 'proportionality'. This chapter may fittingly be concluded with a description of the origins and consequences of this abandonment of the common law of contract.

ParkingEye was, of course, a conjoined appeal, and in *ParkingEye Ltd v Beavis*[152] the defendant parked in a car park managed by ParkingEye Ltd on the behalf of a landowner, which operated a retail park served by the car park, doing so, it was found, under a contractual licence the terms of which were made known to him by signs of a number and nature sufficient to give reasonable notice of those terms.[153] The material term was that a driver could park her or his car for free for two hours, but a driver staying any longer would incur, as the signs said, a 'parking charge' which was subject to variations in ways we need not discuss and will treat as £85 for a longer stay of any period. The defendant overstayed by almost an hour and did not respond to demands for payment of the £85.[154]

On the one hand, it must be said that the claimant could not possibly quantify with certainty any loss that the defendant caused, indeed any conceivable loss so quantified could not be more than miniscule, and not even a loss of this size this was actually claimed. But, on the other hand, it can also be said that the defendant's conduct, if unsanctioned and so freely repeatable by others, including those who wished to use the car park but not the retail park at all, would have made the claimant's management of the car park in the way it did impossible.[155] In a context in which the cognoscenti were aware that the penalty rule was changing, the claimant conceded that the £85 was not a pre-estimate of damages, indeed that it actually lost 'nothing' by the defendant's breach, and that 'the predominant purpose of the parking charge was to deter motorists from overstaying'.[156]

Putting aside so far as possible the intended change to the specific law of agreed damages, the question is whether the claimant had a legitimate interest in conducting its business in this way, and, of course, in a sense it did:

> the predominant purpose of the parking charge was to deter motorists from overstaying ... although ParkingEye was not liable to suffer loss as a result of overstaying motorists, it had a legitimate interest in charging them which extended beyond the recovery of any loss ... deterrence is not penal if there is a legitimate

[151] [2015] UKSC 67; [2016] AC 1172, [29] (hereafter *ParkingEye*).

[152] [2015] EWCA Civ 402; [2015] RTR 27.

[153] *ParkingEye* (n 151) [94].

[154] This was a deliberate act by the defendant, Mr Barry Beavis, organised with the support of the Consumers' Association, which intervened, intended to test car parking policies such as the claimant's. One speculates that Mr Beavis and the Association rather missed a public relations trick by not extending his overstaying beyond a minute. But Lords Neuberger and Sumption would not, it seems, have been influenced by this (ibid [111]), and, on the terms they decided the case, this no doubt would have been right.

[155] ibid [98].

[156] ibid [97].

> interest in influencing the conduct of the contracting party which is not satisfied by the mere right to recover damages for breach of contract.[157]

This was set in the context of the law of literal enforcement generally, typified by specific performance:

> More generally, the attitude of the courts, reflecting that of the Court of Chancery, is that specific performance of contractual obligations should ordinarily be refused where damages would be an adequate remedy. This is because the minimum condition for an order of specific performance is that the innocent party should have a legitimate interest extending beyond pecuniary compensation for the breach. The paradigm case is the purchase of land or certain chattels such as ships, which the law recognises as unique. Because of their uniqueness the purchaser's interest extends beyond the mere award of damages as a substitute for performance.[158]

It would be supererogatory to offer a criticism of this as a statement of the law of any aspect of the law of literal enforcement *qua* remedy at this point; this entire chapter is a criticism of it. Let us just look at what has had to be said to try to justify the law thus stated as a result of an agreement between the claimant and the defendant. It was a major part of Mr Beavis' argument concerning The Unfair Terms in Consumer Contracts Regulations 1999[159] that ParkingEye Ltd's business model, in which the company's revenue was completely derived, not from a charge for parking as such, but from charging overstayers, ie from charging, not for ParkingEye Ltd's own performance but for inevitable breaches of contract by overstayers, with obvious implications for the level of such charges, was indefensible.[160] We submit that, in terms of the default law of literal enforcement, it was indefensible.

As a consumer, the defendant had a right, which it should be possible but practically speaking very hard to trump, to have the compensatory default rule applied, for, of course, the default expressed the defendant's, and all consumers', normal intention on entering into an agreement of this nature. But ParkingEye Ltd's model was not based on charging for parking, or for compensation of loss of that payment, at all. This is to say, it is but remotely connected with agreeing payment for a service, and not connected at all with the principle of compensation for loss, though these are the very stuff of the common, but it transpires naïve, understanding of private contractual rights on the basis of which consumers would have entered into a contract with ParkingEye Ltd. It is not just that £85 is a substantial sum for most of the citizens of the UK. It is that the disparity between zero, the amount ParkingEye Ltd conceded it would lose as a result of Mr Beavis's breach, and £85 is (if a certain mathematical inexactitude may be allowed) infinity, and if that disparity is not extravagant or exorbitant, then what possibly could be?

157 ibid [97], [99].
158 ibid [30].
159 SI 1999/2083 (UK). Subsequent and prospective changes to these Regulations in light of unceasing public concern about these charging practices need not concern us here.
160 *ParkingEye* (n 151) [107]–[113].

In a subsidiary but essential part of their judgment, Lords Neuberger and Sumption rightly asked what the 'reasonable motorist' can be regarded as having agreed:

> The charge is prominently displayed in large letters at the entrance to the car park and at frequent intervals within it ... Could ParkingEye, 'dealing fairly and equitably with the consumer reasonably assume that the consumer would have agreed to such a term in individual contract negotiations?' The concept of a negotiated agreement to enter a car park is somewhat artificial, but it is perfectly workable provided that one bears in mind that the test ... is objective. The question is not whether Mr Beavis himself would in fact have agreed to the term imposing the £85 charge in a negotiation, but whether a reasonable motorist in his position would have done so. In our view a reasonable motorist would have agreed. In the first place, motorists generally and Mr Beavis in particular did accept it. In the case of non-negotiated standard terms that would not ordinarily be entitled to much weight. But although the terms, like all standard contracts, were presented to motorists on a take it or leave it basis, they could not have been briefer, simpler or more prominently proclaimed. If you park here and stay more than two hours, you will pay £85. Motorists could hardly avoid reading the notice and were under no pressure to accept its terms.[161]

Lords Neuberger and Sumption's conclusion therefore that the incurring of charges was entirely the responsibility of the driver[162] turns on, with respect, missing the essential point about the legitimate interest, which is that it is an ouster of a default agreement based on compensatory expectations. A reasonable driver would expect to pay for overstaying. A reasonable driver would not expect to pay, indeed would bitterly resent paying, when the 'overstaying' was some trivial infraction wholly unrelated to causing any loss which the driver could reasonably have in mind. ParkingEye Ltd's business model was based entirely on the expectation that very substantial revenues will accrue from, precisely, trivial infractions.

For essentially the reason given by Denning LJ in *J Spurling Ltd v Bradshaw*,[163] it must be said that to think agreement to ParkingEye Ltd's business model could be reasonably secured through the notices given by the company is, with respect, a flat abnegation of the proper consideration, 'broadly and from both sides', of the issues.[164] It is an of abandonment of the proper regulatory function of the law of contract. As with the exemption clauses discussed in Chapter 7, the penalties in *ParkingEye* can be thought to have been agreed in a way which meets the ethical standards of contractual agreement only at the cost of absurdity. It is all highly reminiscent of those post-war notice cases involving clauses so prejudicial to the consumer that they stimulated the passage of The Unfair Contract Terms Act 1977.[165]

ParkingEye Ltd may have 'had an interest in inducing [the defendant] to observe the two-hour limit in order to enable customers of the retail outlets and other members

[161] ibid [100].
[162] ibid [111].
[163] [1956] 1 WLR 461 (CA) 466.
[164] *ParkingEye* (n 151) [106].
[165] c 50 (UK). See Law Commission and Scots Law Commission, *Exemption Clauses: Second Report by the Two Law Commissions* (Report) [1975] EWLC 69, para 11.

of the public to use the available parking space'.[166] It also had a far greater interest in there being a great many breaches, or it would have had no revenue, something Lords Neuberger and Sumption of course see,[167] but to which they, with respect, do not give remotely sufficient weight. Business efficacy is not a matter of what ParkingEye Ltd needed to do to get its business to work.[168] It is a matter of what it could get motorists to objectively agree.

Now, what was done in *ParkingEye* should, in a doctrinally and theoretically important sense, be possible. It is one of the principal arguments of this chapter that the compensatory damages default should, subject to Lord Watson's equitable jurisdiction, be able to be ousted by agreement. But there *must* be agreement. And though this writer finds it impossible to conceive of ParkingEye Ltd's business model, based as it is on substantial charges for inevitable and trivial breaches which *prima facie* should be ignored as *de minimis*, surviving an adequate test of contractual agreement, there certainly was such agreement in the other matter which reached the Supreme Court.[169] Cavendish Square Holding BV and Mr Talal el Makdessi were competent contracting parties if any parties ever have been, and this matter should have been left alone, as it would have been under the previous law. The joinder of the two cases in *ParkingEye* is evidence of a fundamentally mistaken approach.

It would be quite wrong to discuss the exploitation of parking charges without mentioning the role of the government, for, leaving aside the public bodies which levy charges, the current parking system should not be traced to some (illusory) contractual agreement but to recent primary legislation, and it can operate only with the active support of government agencies, notably the Driving and Vehicle Licensing Agency, which plays an essential role providing (selling it at a loss to the parking companies) the information that makes the automated, very high volume tracing of car 'keepers' possible.[170]

But the Supreme Court judgment in *ParkingEye* is playing a most unusual, if not unique, and unedifying part.[171] Though I am unaware of any precise data, many

[166] *ParkingEye* (n 151) [107].

[167] ibid [97].

[168] Although the term was not used in the judgment, *ParkingEye* gave, as was quickly pointed out in a number of comments, culminating in the warm approval of the case in S Rowan, 'The "Legitimate Interest in Performance" in the Law on Penalties' [2019] Cambridge Law Journal 148, 153–54, substantial support to the performance interest argument:

> where [compensation] fails to protect the wider contractual objectives of the parties, there is now acceptance that more robust protection of performance is appropriate. The distinguishing characteristic of damages clauses is that it is the parties themselves rather than the courts that identify this need. Since [*ParkingEye*], the courts will help them meet this need and achieve better performance by enforcing damages clauses more extensively and flexibly.

After earlier discussion of the Rowan's views, I do not think it is necessary to say more than that this specific analysis repeats the basic mistake made by the Supreme Court. So engulfing is the fundamental concern with supporting ParkingEye Ltd's performance interest in its business model that the regulatory function of the legitimate interest, and behind this of the compensatory principle in damages for breach of contract, just vanishes.

[169] *Makdessi v Cavendish Square Holdings BV* [2013] EWCA Civ 1539; [2014] 2 All ER (Comm) 125.

[170] L Butcher, *Parking Policy in England*, House of Commons Briefing Paper SN02235 (29 January 2018) and R Sykes, *The Parking Charges (Code of Practice) Bill*, House of Lords Library Briefing (20 December 2018).

[171] D Campbell and R Halson, 'By Their Fruits Shall Ye Know Them' [2020] Cambridge Law Journal 405.

thousands of small claims proceedings have to be brought to enforce charges like that levelled on Mr Beavis, and whilst the majority will be perfectly routinised, there are thousands of challenges to these charges made in proceedings described as of 'high temperature' in a remarkable County Court judgment by DDJ Harvey which reviewed the general situation.[172] These proceedings are characterised by the claimants all but ritually citing *ParkingEye* to justify themselves, and this is done in a way 'calculated', in DDJ Harvey's view, 'to be *in terrorem* of defendants'! This squalid state of affairs is in large part the result of thinking about the legitimate interest that has so abandoned the moral guidance of mutual recognition that it will endorse anything the claimant wishes to do in its solipsistic self-interest. The incomprehension and outrage of motorists, who cannot reconcile these charging practices with their default belief that contractual damages should be based on compensation of loss, is an important and highly significant lay response to the doctrinal mistakes about the legitimate interest and literal enforcement which have been discussed in this chapter.

[172] *One Parking Solutions Ltd v Ms W* (unreported, Lewes County Court 5 February 2020).

10

The Spectrum of Contracts

Presentiation and Adjustment

Introduction: The Concept of Contract Planning

In Chapters 1 and 3, I endorsed the welfare claim essential to the legitimacy of the market economy that the production of economic goods by business organisations is a system of consumer sovereignty. Facilitating choice by consumers themselves poses specific issues, but as was pointed out in Chapter 3, and as the commercial nature of most of the case law discussed in that chapter evidences, choice by consumers is only a particular aspect of the universal problem of rational choice by any economic actor. It unarguably is the case that business organisations, despite their information gathering and computational capacities typically being greater, and perhaps immensely greater, than those of consumers, face the same problem that under positive transaction they cannot possibly satisfy the informational demands of general competition, and must act with bounded rationality. This applies to the basic decisions about the products a firm should make or acquire, how it should attempt to make or acquire them, and about the scale and scope at which the firm should attempt to operate; the decisions which give a firm its nature (and upon which its existence depends).[1] Our focus in this chapter is on how, and how well, the law of contract sets the legal framework for a firm's decisions to buy its inputs, sell its outputs, and organise its processes.

The issue which is of particular importance to a criticism of the classical law of contract and the welfarist response to the classical law's shortcomings is that which was shown in Chapter 9 to be central to the law of literal enforcement: idiosyncratic loss.

[1] In E Penrose, *The Theory of the Growth of the Firm* (4th edn, OUP 2009) 50–51 entrepreneurial competence successfully to identify 'productive opportunities' is a response to:

> The fact that the future can never be known with accuracy means that the planning of business firms is based on expectations about the future which are held with varying degrees of confidence.

Contractual Relations. David Campbell, Oxford University Press. © David Campbell 2022.
DOI: 10.1093/oso/9780198855156.003.0010

Given positive transaction costs and bounded rationality, undertaking a primary obligation to perform inevitably generates a risk of non-performance, and the latent secondary obligation to provide a remedy for non-performance provides security against this risk; indeed, as was set out in Chapter 1, this security is the essential reason for the existence of the law of contract. In Chapter 9, *ex post* attempts to claim literal enforcement were explained as claimants' responses to their *ex ante* failure to agree a remedy which would satisfactorily compensate them. The bounded rationality of such parties evidently extends to unawareness of the nature of the security actually obtained by entering into a contract on the default basis of the remedy being compensatory damages quantified according to the rules of causation. That their solipsistic attempts to undo their agreements has sometimes met with success is a serious criticism of the persistence of classical elements (albeit often expressed in neologisms) in the law of remedies.

In Chapter 2, it was noted that Wolfgang Friedmann identified the provision of 'insurance against calculated economic risks' as one of the functions of contract. Though I will continue to speak of risk, it is now essential to recognise that this, in its intended sense entirely correct, use of 'calculated … risks' requires refinement. The principal way contract provides this 'insurance' is through compensatory damages in standard cases of the transfer of generic economic goods. It was claimed in Chapter 8 that the remedies for breach of contract handle these cases so well that they appear to be cases of Macaulay's non-use. Sophisticated commercial parties are well aware, however, that, even in these cases, actually obtaining compensation may be problematic. A loss and a liability may be perfectly well quantified, but this will be of little comfort to the claimant if the defendant is insolvent or otherwise unlikely to satisfy a judgment. The enormous range of devices which may be used to provide the security of a 'self-help' or 'real' remedy beyond recourse to the 'judicial' remedies predominantly addressed in this book is a substantial part of commercial law proper,[2] and that range of devices extends beyond contract to property and company law.[3]

The problem addressed in this chapter is the law's regulation of the attempts of parties who are aware that the contracts they wish to make would create a risk of idiosyncratic loss, and so (in addition to other steps) seek to agree terms which will avoid, minimise, or acceptably apportion the 'inadequacy' of compensation of such loss. Such parties are to various degrees aware that the default remedy, based on standard cases, cannot acceptably deal with the risk generated by their projects because the probability and magnitude of loss cannot be quantified to the requirements of the rules of causation, particularly certainty. Though I have called, and will continue to call, this problem one of risk, it is not entirely right to do so.

The great economist FH Knight famously distinguished two senses of 'risk': one when it is a 'quantity susceptible of measurement', and the other when it is 'something distinctly not of this character', and referred to this second form of risk as 'uncertainty'.[4] Any firm will, over the course of its activities, face uncertainty of this sort,

[2] Professor Goode manages to convey the gist of the issues in a single note to his seminal book: E McKendrick, *Goode on Commercial Law* (6th edn, Penguin Books 2020) para 3.108 n 410.

[3] The intertwining of contract, property, insolvency, and the reality of the remedy in the creation of the *Romalpa* clause is explored in an exemplary manner in S Wheeler, *Reservation of Title Clauses* (Clarendon Press 1991).

[4] FH Knight, *Risk, Uncertainty and Profit* (Dover Publications 2006) 19–20.

and, of course, *ceteris paribus*, the greater the scale and scope of the firm, the larger the uncertainty will be, and Knight saw responding to this uncertainty as the key entrepreneurial function. A most important response is to avoid projects which generate uncertainty, or to bring about (up to a point) effective avoidance by creating a 'negotiated environment' in which the uncertainty is broken down into more controllable elements.[5]

The contractual projects discussed in this chapter involve the possibility of idiosyncratic loss which is so uncertain that it cannot be dealt with in this way. These are the 'specie' of contracts which, as was discussed in Chapter 2, in the earlier work which brought his thinking to such attention, Macneil called 'relational contracts', this sense of relational depending on the contrast with the 'discrete contracts' which compose the other pole of the 'spectrum' of contracts. It was argued in Chapter 2 that the most valuable contribution of the relational theory, principally attributable not only to Macneil but to Macaulay and his colleagues, has been to show that all contracts are in a more fundamental sense relational, for they are all based on a moral relationship of mutual recognition, and subsequent chapters have sought to demonstrate this by an examination of agreement, consideration, and remedy in all contracts.

But in this chapter, in light of this understanding of the ubiquity of the relational foundation of contract, we shall turn to the contribution that can be made by employing the relational contract as a specific legal concept.[6] In Chapter 2, it was noted that in later work Macneil came to use a different terminology to denote the relational, in the sense of as opposed to the discrete, contract, and I myself have previously used the term 'complex' for this purpose.[7] Such efforts seeming to be completely unavailing, in this chapter I shall use the term relational to convey the sense of a specie of contract, trusting to the context to make the sense clear. To begin the discussion, for convenience, though it has already been quoted in Chapter 2, a crucial passage setting out the spectrum of contracts shall again be given here:

> contractual ordering of economic activity takes place along a spectrum of discrete and relational behaviour. At one end are relatively discrete transactions. Discrete transactions are contracts of short duration, involving limited personal interactions, and containing precise party measurements of easily acquired objects of exchange, for example money and grain. They require a minimum of future co-operative behaviour between the parties and no sharing of benefits or burdens. They bind the parties tightly and precisely. The parties view such transactions as free of entangling strings, and they

[5] RM Cyert and JG March, *A Behavioural Theory of the Firm* (2nd edn, Blackwells 1992) 167:

> Organisations avoid uncertainty ... They avoid the requirement that they anticipate future reactions of other parts of their environment by arranging a negotiated environment. They impose plans, standard operating procedures, industry tradition, and uncertainty absorbing contracts on that environment. In short, they achieve reasonably manageable decision situations by avoiding planning where plans depend on predictions of uncertain future events and by emphasising planning where plans can be made self-confirming through some control device.

[6] H Collins, 'Is a Relational Contract a Legal Concept' in S Degeling, J Edelman, and J Goundkamp (eds), *Contract in Commercial Law* (Lawbook Co 2016).

[7] D Campbell, 'What Do We Mean By the Non-use of Contract?' in J Braucher, J Kidwell, and WC Whitford (eds), *Revisiting the Contracts Scholarship of Stewart Macaulay: On the Empirical and the Lyrical* (Hart 2013) 168–77.

> expect no altruism. The parties see everything connected with such transactions as clearly defined ... If trouble is anticipated at all, it is anticipated only if someone or something turns out unexpectedly badly ... At the other end of the contract spectrum are ongoing relations ... The relations are of significant duration ... Close whole person relations form an integral part of the relation ... The object of exchange typically includes both easily measured quantities ... and quantities not easily measured ... Future co-operative behaviour is expected ... benefits and burdens of the relation are to be shared rather than entirely divided and allocated ... The entangling strings of friendship, reputation, interdependence, morality, and altruistic desires are integral ... Trouble is expected as a matter of course ... Finally, the participants view the relation as an ongoing integration of behaviour to grow and vary with events.[8]

The sociological concerns behind the normative schemas that became the most familiar feature of Macneil's work were never intended to overwhelm his legal contractual concerns, but they largely did, and the consequences have been unfortunate. With particular regard to our concerns in this chapter, it is to be regretted that an analysis of the legal techniques of 'contract planning' which Macneil published in 1975 as 'A Primer of Contract Planning' has remained quite obscure,[9] though I am unaware of any other treatment of those techniques which so valuably assists the theoretical discussion of the extent to which the positive law does and does not support such planning.

As has been mentioned, in Chapter 9 we discussed the *ex post* attempts, at the stage of remedy rather than agreement, of claimants who had come to realise that they faced an idiosyncratic loss to, generally wholly illegitimately, seek literal enforcement which would avoid the default rules of causation. Unwelcome proposals to alter the default remedy rules to accommodate the failures of such claimants contrast sharply with the law's response to parties which have foreseen this possibility—'Trouble is expected as a matter of course'—and *ex ante* seek to provide for its management. For when pursuing this commendable course of action, these parties encounter serious obstacles posed by the classical law. To understand Macneil's contribution to dealing with this major problem, we must step back to the fundamental concept of his analysis of the law of contract: 'presentiation'.

Presentiation in the Discrete Contract

Macneil argued that the forms of contract running along the spectrum of discrete to relational contracts were distributed by degrees of what he called 'presentiation'.[10] It would seem to be unfortunate that Macneil chose to use this ugly term, which never

[8] IR Macneil and PJ Gudel, *Contracts: Exchange Transactions and Relations* (3rd edn, Foundation Press 2001) 14–15 (hereafter Macneil and Gudel, *Contracts*).

[9] IR Macneil, 'A Primer of Contract Planning' (1975) 48 Southern California Law Review 627. The material in this paper formed the framework of the second part of all editions of Macneil and Gudel, *Contracts* (n 8).

[10] IR Macneil, 'Restatement (Second) of Contracts and Presentiation' (1974) 60 Virginia Law Review 586 (hereafter Macneil, 'Presentiation').

really caught on,[11] to express the valuable—this word is not strong enough—idea that contractual agreement serves to make 'present' in the contract the obligations, and consequent risks of non-performance, that the parties undertake:

> Presentiation is ... a recognition that the course of the future is bound by present events, *and* that by those events the future has ... been brought into the present ... traditional contract law systems are among the greatest intellectual expressions of presentiation ... When we conclude that a manifestation of mutual assent to a future exchange and to a method for effectuating that exchange is a promise, when each party binds himself not to change his mind and fail to carry out the exchange, then the future has been bound and presentiation has been accomplished ... The ability to act now on the basis of something which we know will not come into being until the future is one of the most productive human tools. Mutual assent in contracting is one of the ways we exercise this ability ... traditional contract law created a legal structure which in theory attempted to presentiate not just part of the relation between contracting parties, but virtually all of it ... The aim was to establish, insofar as the law could. the entire relation at the time of the expressions of mutual assent. Total presentiation through 100% predictability was sought as of the time of something called the offer.[12]

Presentiation gives effect to the essential function of the legal contract to provide security of performance by identifying the risks of non-performance and allocating them to the parties at the time of the agreement, so that non-performance gives rise to an adequate remedy. It is vital to recognise that, though errors about this are of course inevitable, these risks are risks in Knight's sense of the term, in that they give rise to liabilities quantified according to the rules of causation in a way that makes them certain and proximate (and unavoidable), ie calculable.

It will be recalled that in the previously given quotation setting out the spectrum of contracts, Macneil claimed that: 'If trouble is anticipated at all [in discrete contracts], it is anticipated only if someone or something turns out unexpectedly badly', and this captures the common expectation of contracting parties that primary obligations, not only ought to be, but normally will be performed. But this cannot be enough. The contract is made only because risks of non-performance are anticipated—why else make a contract?—though with, as we have seen in Chapters 8 and 9, varying degrees of clarity about this, and the point of presentiation is to allocate those risks. The presentiation may be to various degrees precise, depending on the sophistication of the contract, but these degrees embrace widely expressed risks such as 'non-delivery'. In a discrete

[11] That this word remains part of the language at all would seem to be due to Macneil. The source for this word in IR Macneil, 'The Many Futures of Contract' (1974) 47 Southern California Law Review 691 800 n 310, was the first edition of the OED, which was completed in 1933. In this edition and in the second edition of 1989, the word was described as rare, often a lexicographical prelude to subsequent omission, but in the third edition of 2007 this description was omitted. The reprieve was caused by Macneil. The only example given in the first edition of the use of the word or its derivatives since 1860 was 'The Many Futures'. The further examples given in the second and third editions are all quotations derived from Macneil.

[12] Macneil, 'Presentiation' (n 10) 592–93.

contract, risks may be regarded as, as it were, objectively present in the minds of the parties during their negotiations, and liability for those risks may therefore plausibly be believed to have been allocated according to the intentions of the parties expressed in the agreed terms of the contract. Highly sophisticated secondary markets in these liabilities have grown up in institutional support of the basic security provided by contractual compensation of loss.

The discrete contract works only if liability under it is strict in a sense which will be fully explained below but which we may initially approach by considering the dictum of Lord Edmund-Davies in *Raineri v Miles*: 'In relation to a claim for damages for breach of contract, it is immaterial why the defendant failed to fulfil his obligations and certainly no defence to plead that he had done his best'.[13] Without such strict liability, leaving aside all other arguments turning on the parties' responsibility institutionalised in the doctrine of sanctity, the expectations the parties can form based on the contract become incalculable, and making the risk of future events calculable is the entire point of presentiation. The standard of liability I am driving at is often described as the rule in *Paradine v Jane*,[14] a description adopted here, not because I have any authority to claim what the detailed law of this ancient case actually was,[15] but because the *dicta* of Rolle J expressing the rule captures a definite, and it will be argued welcome, position in the modern law:

> when the party by his own contract creates a duty or charge upon himself, he is bound to make it good, if he may, notwithstanding any accident by inevitable necessity, because he might have provided against it by his contract. And therefore if the lessee covenant to repair a house, though it be burnt by lightning, or thrown down by enemies, yet he ought to repair it.[16]

The modern doctrine of frustration of contract established in *Taylor v Caldwell*[17] is, though *Paradine v Jane* was mentioned only in the pleadings,[18] of course based on a rejection of this rule, so that the defendant's liability for the unavailability of music hall premises engaged by the claimant was discharged because those premises had been destroyed by fire 'without the fault of either party',[19] and performance had thereby become 'impossible'.[20] Though they were as a matter of legal history developed entirely independently, common mistake and frustration have come to be recognised to address the same problem of risk allocation,[21] and they have been combined as the

[13] [1981] AC 1050 (HL) 1086G.
[14] (1647) Aleyn 26; 82 ER 897 (hereafter *Paradine v Jane*).
[15] I particularly set aside issues arising from use of the term 'absolute' rather than 'strict': D Ibbetson, 'Absolute Liability in Contract: The Antecedents of *Paradine v Jane*' in FD Rose (ed), *Consensus ad Idem* (Sweet and Maxwell 1996) 30–37 and D Ibbetson, 'Fault and Absolute Liability in Pre-modern Contract Law' (1997) 18 Journal of Legal History 1.
[16] *Paradine v Jane* (n 14) 27.
[17] (1863) B & S 826; 122 ER 309 (hereafter *Taylor v Caldwell*).
[18] ibid 831; 311.
[19] ibid 832; 312.
[20] ibid 833; 312.
[21] J Swan, 'The Allocation of Risk in the Analysis of Mistake and Frustration' in BJ Reiter and J Swan (eds), *Studies in Contract Law* (Butterworths 1980). The first work Swan cites, Patterson's pathbreaking analysis of risk allocation, had some anticipation of the, as it were, joint treatment of common mistake

'initial' and 'subsequent' aspects of a law of 'impossibility'.[22] This combination surely required that the laws of the two doctrines should converge, as it is unacceptable that the grounds and consequences of discharge for the same reason should, as they did, vary widely.[23] This has not happened,[24] indeed it might fairly be said that as a matter of doctrine the opposite has happened,[25] but, it will be argued, this is largely because such convergence never became a substantial issue for commercial parties. In order to understand this, it is necessary to describe two aspects of the law of impossibility.

It is in the nature of these excuses that impossibility taken literally was bound to be expanded. 'Physical' impossibility of performance, such as is occasioned by complete destruction of the subject matter, is not the issue. Though he came to focus on impossibility, in his first statement of the law and reasoning behind his decision in *Taylor v Caldwell*, Blackburn J said non-performance could be excused because 'the performance of [the] contract has become unexpectedly burthensome or even impossible',[26] obviously envisaging what later came to be seen as the significantly different (it isn't) excuse of frustration of purpose. The history of the modern laws of common mistake and frustration for 50 years after *Bell v Lever Bros Ltd*[27] and a century after *Taylor v Caldwell* was one of overall expansion of the grounds of excuse in order to deal with a suitably unexpected burden, however occasioned. Pursuit of a defensible sense of 'suitably' has involved some of the most truly absurd distinctions that have ever been drawn in the common law, even going so far as to include that between substance and quality (or attribute) proper only to the metaphysics of Spinoza.[28]

But what was the rationale of excusing an unexpected burden at all? Two possibilities can be identified in *Taylor v Caldwell*. The defendants argued that 'there was a general custom of the trade and business of the plaintiffs and the defendants, with respect to which the agreement was made ... and which was part of the agreement'[29] that

and frustration: EW Patterson, 'The Apportionment of Business Risks Through Legal Devices' (1924) 24 Columbia Law Review 335, 347–53, 355–57 (hereafter Patterson, 'Apportionment').

[22] JC Smith, *Law of Contract* (1st edn, Sweet & Maxwell 1989) 162–63 (now 352–53); now PS Davies, *JC Smith's Law of Contract* (3rd edn, OUP 2021) 352–53 and R Brownsword, *Smith and Thomas' Casebook on Contract* (14th edn, Sweet & Maxwell 2021) para 23-001.

[23] The flat unacceptability of the problem was strikingly illustrated at an early stage by (leaving aside the contrasts within the frustration cases themselves) the contrast between the results in *Chandler v Webster* [1904] 1 KB 493 (CA) and *Griffith v Brymer* (1903) 19 TLR 434 (KB).

[24] A creditable attempt to do so was made in *Amalgamated Investment and Property Co Ltd v John Walker and Sons Ltd* [1977] 1 WLR (CA) (hereafter *Amalgamated Investment v Walker*).

[25] The acknowledgement by Lord Phillips MR in *Great Peace Shipping Ltd v Tsavliris Salvage (International) Ltd* [2002] EWCA Civ 1407; [2003] QB 679 (hereafter *The Great Peace*) [61] that 'consideration of the development of the law of frustration assists with the analysis of the law of common mistake' can hardly be said to have been supported by the outcome of that case for common mistake, save in the sense argued in the main text.

[26] *Taylor v Caldwell* (n 17) 833; 312.

[27] [1932] AC 161 (HL) (hereafter *Bell v Lever Bros*).

[28] ibid 218. As reported, *Bell v Lever Bros* is literally incomprehensible, and it has been made comprehensible to us (though absolutely not as a coherent law of common mistake) by the researches, entirely comparable to those of the late Professor Simpson, of Professor Macmillan: C Macmillan, 'How Temptation Led to Mistake: An Explanation of *Bell v Lever Bros Ltd*' (2003) 119 Law Quarterly Review 625; C Macmillan, 'The Trial: How Procedure Shapes Substance' (2008) 19 King's Law Journal 465 and C Macmillan, *Mistakes in Contract Law* (OUP 2010) 259–79 (hereafter Macmillan, *Mistakes*).

[29] *Taylor v Caldwell* (n 17) 839; 31.

no liability could arise for impossibility of performance due to accidental fire. Had the parties agreed their liabilities on this basis, the result of the case would have been correct,[30] and I will return to this, but it was found that there was no such custom. Blackburn J nevertheless maintained that in contracts which, as he believed:

> the performance depends on the continued existence of a given person or thing, a condition is implied that the impossibility of performance arising from the perishing of the person or thing shall excuse the performance [this] excuse is by law implied because from the nature of contract it is apparent that the parties contracted on the basis of the continued existence of the particular person or chattel.[31]

Amongst the arguments Blackburn J gave for recognising this 'excuse . . . by law implied' is that it had its parallel in what we now recognise as the law of common mistake prior to *Bell v Lever Bros*,[32] for The Sale of Goods Act 1893, s 6 rendered a contract for the sale of specific goods void when 'without the knowledge of the seller [the goods had] perished at the time of sale'.[33] The account Chalmers himself gave of the drafting of this section[34] cannot, with respect, be correct,[35] for s 6 had no clear basis in the prior case law, and therefore would seem, marring Chalmers' general achievement in The Sale of Goods Act 1893, to be a term implied by law as this was meant in the discussion of implied terms in Chapter 3.

Though it would be wrong to say this was Chalmers' intention with s 6, terms implied by law are not derived from the common law, but are implied by the courts for welfarist reasons. To call them implied may be thought to reconcile them with respecting the intentions of the parties,[36] but the fiction

[30] To stress what I trust is obvious, I am driving not at the 'implied term' theory criticised by Lord Radcliffe but at an implied term which states the agreement of the parties. Though saying this does not entirely commit one to the interpretation of the contracts in the cases, the way the same Court of Appeal effectively distinguished *Krell v Henry* [1903] 2 KB 740 (CA) and *Herne Bay Steamboat v Hutton* [1903] 2 KB 683 (CA) was right in principle. In saying this, and in the argument about common mistake and frustration made generally in this chapter, I seek to build on, albeit by somewhat restating, JC Smith, 'Contracts: Mistake, Frustration and Implied Terms' (1994) 110 Law Quarterly Review 400 (hereafter Smith, 'Contracts').

[31] ibid 839; 314.

[32] ibid 837; 313–14. Blackburn J was the author of a treatise on sale in which he dealt with the common law prior to s 6 in a way similar to the way Chalmers came to do: C Blackburn, *A Treatise on the Effect of the Contract of Sale* (William Benning and Co 1845) 151–61.

[33] The Sale of Goods Act 1979, s 6. Section 7 (now the 1979 Act, s 7) is a 'frustration' provision concerning perishing after an agreement to sell but before risk has passed. 'There are no reported cases bearing directly upon the section': MG Bridge, *The Sale of Goods* (4th edn, OUP 2019) para 4.42.

[34] MD Chalmers, *The Sale of Goods Act 1893* (2nd edn, William Clowes & Sons 1893) 17.

[35] The first and principal authority Chalmers cites in support of s 6 is *Couturier v Hastie* (1853) 9 Ex 103; 155 ER 1250; affd (1856) 5 HLC 673; 156 ER 43. Chalmers was misled by this very difficult case, and his synopsis of it is equivocal and, in the end, at fault. The case as reported was not decided on the basis of (allowing the anachronism) common mistake, 'mistake' nowhere being mentioned in the judgment: PS Atiyah, '*Couturier v Hastie* and the Sale of Non-existent Goods' (1957) 73 Law Quarterly Review 340 and Macmillan, *Mistakes* (n 28) 181–86. In 1908, Sir Frederick Pollock said that *Couturier v Hastie* 'shows how a large proportion of the cases which swell the rubric of relief against mistake in the textbooks (with or without protest from the text writer) are really cases of construction': F Pollock (ed), *The Revised Reports*, vol 101 (Sweet & Maxwell 1908) vi. This is the reason perceptively given for cases of common mistake proper being said to be 'few and far between' in *The Great Peace* (n 25) [85].

[36] D Ibbetson, *A Historical Introduction to the Law of Obligations* (OUP 1999) 224: 'a façade of party intention'.

involved[37] cannot be better exposed than it was by Lord Radcliffe when giving the foundational account of why frustration is allowed to be an excuse:

> there is something of a logical difficulty in seeing how the parties could even impliedly have provided for something which *ex hypothesi* they neither expected nor foresaw ... perhaps it would be simpler to say at the outset that frustration occurs whenever the law recognises that without default of either party a contractual obligation has become incapable of being performed because the circumstances in which performance is called for would render it a thing radically different from that which was undertaken by the contract. *Non haec in foedera veni*. It was not this that I promised to do.[38]

It was in this spirit that Denning LJ had taken advantage of what he described as 'the great case of *Cooper v Phibbs*',[39] in which 'Terms were *imposed* so as to do what was practically just', to breathe new life into common mistake in *Solle v Butcher*.[40]

In a way which will not be described, but can be compared to the history of the law of negligence between *Home Office v Dorset Yacht Co*[41] and *Murphy v Brentwood DC*,[42] than which there can be no greater criticism of a policy effected through the common law, all this had to be put into overall reverse[43] as it increasingly dawned that, in effect, there really was no way of distinguishing these excuses from the reason for breach by all good faith parties: bounded rationality.[44] No other than a fraudulent party would enter into a contract knowing or foreseeing it was going to breach it, but, on the other hand, what would be left of the law of contract if the defendant knew an easy way to be excused whenever it failed to perform?[45] The basic senses

[37] *Hirji Mulji v Cheong Yue SS Co Ltd* [1926] AC 497 (PC (HK)) 504: 'the law is only doing what the parties really (*though subconsciously*) meant to do for themselves' (emphasis added).

[38] *Davis Contractors v Fareham UDC* [1956] AC 969 (HL) 728–29.

[39] (1867) LR 2 HL 149 (HL).

[40] *Solle v Butcher* [1950] 1 KB 671 (CA) 693, 696 (hereafter *Solle v Butcher*).

[41] [1970] AC 1004 (HL).

[42] [1991] 1 AC 398 (HL).

[43] J Cartwright, 'The Rise and Fall of Mistake in the English Law of Contract' in R Sefton-Green (ed) *Mistake, Fraud and Duties to Inform in European Contract Law* (CUP 2005) 65:

> The growth in mistake which was promoted by Lord Denning is being cut back. Mistake is not dead, but its place in the law of contract is being reassessed.

With great respect, though this is not Cartwright's intention, his strongest defences of mistake relate it to being 'rooted firmly in the parties' own agreement' (ibid 81), ie they are not defences of welfarist common mistake at all.

[44] To put the point more generally, the parties being in a contractual relationship is all that distinguishes breach and excuse for impossibility from all the other responses to 'unforeseen' changes in relevant conditions of production which are, in a sense, what economic activity is: FA Hayek, 'Competition as a Discovery Procedure' in *The Market and Other Orders* in *Collected Works*, vol 15 (Routledge 2014) 311:

> *all* economic adjustment is made necessary by unforeseen changes; and the whole reason for employing the price mechanism is to tell individuals that what they are doing, or can do, has for some reason for which they are not responsible become less or more demanded.

[45] For convenience, though it was discussed in ch 1, I quote again the *dictum* of Baggallay J in *Tamplin v James* (1880) LR 15 Ch D 215 (CA) 217–18:

> The defendant cannot be allowed to evade ... performance by the simple statement that he has made a mistake. Were such to be the law the performance of a contract could rarely be enforced upon an unwilling party who was also unscrupulous.

of 'mistake' and 'foreseeability' which distinguish them from the senses of mistake or foreseeability that apply whenever a contract made in good faith is breached have never emerged, because they could never emerge, from a completely incoherent case law. Nothing, really, could drive home the point more fully than that *Bell v Lever Bros* itself contains an impeccable statement by Lord Atkin of what the law should be,[46] which the case as interpreted obviously undermined, but then a haunting awareness of the contradiction between what correctly had been said and what seemed to have been wrongly done in that case essentially confined the law of *Bell v Lever Bros* to the textbooks.[47]

The devising of novel solutions by desperate recourse to equity or unconscionability which was a hallmark of Lord Denning's contract adjudication, though it typically had no basis in precedent (this was its point), unarguably had positive as well as negative results across the law, as was acknowledged in Chapter 5, and we turn to the measure of success he had with estoppel later in this chapter. But *Solle v Butcher* was never defensible unless one's commitment to welfarism is so firm that it sanctioned all but random adjudication,[48] and the position left by *The Great Peace* is wholly welcome, for, it is submitted, it signals the end of common mistake both in equity and in law.[49] The Court of Appeal arguably was obliged to affirm what *Bell v Lever Bros* and *Solle v Butcher* has come to stand for,[50] but this would be to affirm nonsense that parties have all but ignored, although now even more than previously one thinks we may wait some considerable time before any party is foolish enough to fund the overruling of *Bell v Lever Bros* by trying to take a claimed excuse of common mistake so far as the Supreme Court. One looks at the instances when frustration still is used in argument before the senior courts with amazement.

The laws of common mistake and frustration fundamentally contradict the basic function of contract to allocate the risks of non-performance by the contracting parties. These laws cannot be traced to the (implicit) intentions of the parties, but are exogenous limits placed by the operation of a mandatory rule of law upon the extent to which the parties to a contract can assume risk and therefore cut across the allocation of risk by the parties themselves. It has not been possible to 'provide . . . any theoretical basis at all'[51] for the belief that giving the courts the power 'to achieve a result which is just and reasonable'[52] in this way was either a wise thing to do in itself, or that courts would be competent to do it.

46 *Bell v Lever Bros* (n 27) 224 (HL):

> it is of paramount importance that contracts should be observed, and that if parties honestly comply with the essentials of the formation of contracts—ie agree in the same terms on the same subject-matter—they are bound, and must rely on the stipulations of the contract for protection from the effect of facts unknown to them.

47 J Beatson, A Burrows, and J Cartwright, *Anson's Law of Contract* (30th edn, OUP 2016) 311: 'It is not surprising that the strictness of the test for common mistake has resulted in a dearth of cases on the subject.'

48 After expressing puzzlement over want of argument drawing on 'such an important principle of equity—if it exists', Professor Sir John Smith concluded that '*Solle v Butcher* is difficult, if not impossible, to reconcile with established principles of the common law': Smith, 'Contracts' (n 30) 418.

49 J Morgan, 'Common Mistake in Contract: Rare Success and Common Misapprehensions' [2018] Cambridge Law Journal 559 (hereafter Morgan, 'Common Mistake').

50 SB Midwinter, '*The Great Peace* and Precedent' (2003) 119 Law Quarterly Review 180.

51 *National Carriers Ltd v Panalpina (Northern) Ltd* [1981] AC 675 (HL) 687H (Lord Hailsham).

52 *(Joseph) Constantine SS Line v Imperial Smelting Corp Ltd* [1942] AC 154, 186 (Lord Wright).

The source of the unwisdom of Blackburn J's 'extraordinary decision'[53] in *Taylor v Caldwell*, absurd and unfair in itself after the implied term in fact had not been found to exist, and which has caused 'an enormous number of problems',[54] was his (one has no doubt unconscious) focus on 'impossibility' (in the case and in his treatment of what was to become The Sale of Goods Act 1893). The performances could not take place. So what? The claimant wasn't asking for a miraculous restoration of the premises. It was asking for damages, to which impossibility is irrelevant:

> where a man will for a valuable consideration undertake to do an impossible thing, though it cannot be performed, yet he shall answer in damages.[55]

Impossibility is the purest diversion. The parties provide for the possibility of non-performance by the remedial terms they agree, which are default compensatory damages, with some possibility of literal enforcement. These terms are not, until this is imposed, that the defendant should be excused and some apportionment other than that the parties themselves decided upon be applied, for it is 'immaterial why the defendant failed to fulfil his obligations'.

The post-war extent of the (in various ways long held) influence of the beliefs that parties should be released from the obligations they had agreed to deal with economic risk, and that courts are better able to allocate that risk which they come to repent, is part of the history of welfarism which we discussed in connection with consideration in Chapter 5. These beliefs defeat the entire purpose of the law of contract in facilitating the market economy,[56] and with this, of particular relevance to us here, the effort Macneil analysed as presentiation,[57] and so should have no place in the law of contract.[58] There is a huge repertoire of legal devices which can be used to allocate

[53] C Macmillan, '*Taylor v Caldwell* (1863)' in C Mitchell and P Mitchell (eds), *Landmark Cases in the Law of Contract* (Hart 2008) 199.

[54] ibid 203.

[55] *Thornborrow v Whitacre* (1705) 2 Lord Raym 1164, 1165; 92 ER 270, 271.

[56] *Companhia de Navigaceo Lloyd Brasiliero v CC Blake* 34 F 2d 616, 619 (US 2d Cir 1929) (Learned Hand J):

> No doubt we have gone a long way since *Paradine v Jane* ... but a promise still involves risks that the promisor may find it burdensome or even impossible to meet ... Its very purpose is to give assurance to the promisee against hazards of the future.

[57] It must be made clear, however, that the relational theory which it is sought to develop here has had a marked sympathy towards, not only making adjustment more coherent by criticism of the aspects of the classical law that work against this, but allowing what would here be called welfarist intervention on the broad grounds of impossibility and purposelessness. Macaulay and to a lesser degree Macneil certainly did so, but the clearest expression of this, though itself very conscious of the difficulties and expressed in cautiously sensible terms, was RE Speidel, 'Court-imposed Price Adjustments Under Long-term Supply Contracts' (1981) 76 Northwestern University Law Review 369 and RE Speidel, 'The New Spirit of Contract' (1982) 2 Journal of Law and Commerce 193, 206–08. See, however, the reference to another aspect of the late Professor Speidel's views in n 58.

[58] The exception, which in one sense I fully accept but which I propose only briefly to mention, is when the legal regulatory framework under which the agreement was made is fundamentally altered by act of state. By this is not meant that unanticipated changes under existing laws are made, as in *Amalgamated Investment v Walker* (n 24), but that frameworks are fundamentally changed, as in *Reilly v The King* [1934] AC 176 (PC). In normal, peacetime conditions the problem really is one of the state making (or failing to make) adequate transitional provisions, but of course changes outside of such conditions may call many other issues into question. *Fibrosa Spolka Akcinya v Fairbairn Lawson Combe Barbour Ltd* [1943] AC 32 (HL) (P Mitchell, '*Fibrosa Spolka Akcinya v Fairbairn Lawson Combe Barbour Ltd*' in C Mitchell and P

risk once it is presentiated[59]—in a sense commercial law beyond the general principles of contract is the law of these devices—but the basic device in the case of legal goods, which we may use as a pattern for other economic goods, is to strictly allocate all the risks of providing the good to the seller and all the risks of payment to the buyer. This device is adopted because the parties are of the opinion that the risk of an unforeseen event can be managed in line with the default rules of remedies, and the negotiation of a more refined, and therefore, given positive transaction costs, more expensive device is not justified.[60] Whilst one might claim (though I categorically do not agree with the claim) that, with the benefit of hindsight of the course of events in connection with a specific contract, the courts can adjust the parties' liabilities to advantage, this is an entirely different thing to the real issue, which is providing a general framework within which the parties can make their own choices, which analytically involves bearing responsibility for those choices. This framework is provided by the default rules of formation and remedy so far discussed in this book. The attempt to interfere with it on specific occasions in order to make specific adjustments is wrong in principle, and so it is unsurprising that it has been impossible to provide the attempt with 'any theoretical basis at all'. Let us say no more about doctrine but turn to the way all this has become manifest by the laws of common mistake and frustration having fallen into desuetude.[61]

In a paper which has stimulated considerable academic discussion, Ayres and Gertner devised the concept of 'penalty defaults'.[62] These are default rules of contract which yield a result so unattractive that they give an incentive to at least one of the parties to the contract to oust them. The concept may be applied very widely. Ayres and Gertner analysed *Hadley v Baxendale*[63] in these terms, with the penalty for the claimant which fails to give notice of an unusual liability being that that liability is found to be remote. I think the laws of common mistake and frustration are penalty defaults in a narrower and, though I will not argue this, more useful sense. They are laws which are so bad that it is in no party's interest to frame their exchanges with reference to those laws, and if long, continued use—not long formal survival!—is a mark of a good law, then desuetude is the mark of a bad one. It is, of course, implausible to

Mitchell (eds), *Leading Cases in Restitution* (Hart 2006) 276–81) and, in a strong way, *Solle v Butcher* (n 40) (C Macmillan, *Solle v Butcher* in Mitchell and Mitchell, ibid 337–39) were both the products of such changes. Responsibility for impossibility and purposelessness is completely transformed by its being the result of such an act of state, and the principles for dealing with it are authoritatively discussed in RE Speidel, *Contracts in Crisis* (Carolina Academic Press 2007).

[59] Patterson, 'Apportionment' (n 21).

[60] Whilst it is an early expression in contract of the equivocation between giving effect to the choices of individuals and devising objective welfare maximising rules to be imposed on them that came to dominate Posner's thinking, the contribution to the discussion of these issues in RA Posner and AM Rosenfeld, 'Impossibility and Related Doctrines in Contract Law' (1977) 6 Journal of Legal Studies 83 is very considerable.

[61] E McKendrick, 'Force Majeure Clauses: The Gap Between Doctrine and Practice' in A Burrows and E Peel (eds), *Contract Terms* (OUP 2007).

[62] I Ayres and R Gertner, 'Filling Gaps in Incomplete Contracts: An Economic Theory of Default Rules' (1989) 99 Yale Law Journal 87.

[63] (1854) 9 Ex Ch 341; 156 ER 145.

suggest that law-makers actually intentionally set penalty defaults,[64] but this is not to say that they do not exist, brought into existence inadvertently. The laws of common mistake and frustration are patently penalty defaults in this narrower sense. They are so unsatisfactory, in terms of understanding both when they will apply and, if they do apply, what the consequences of that application will be, that parties who are aware that their contract will place them at risk of unforeseeable events should oust that law. It is for this reason that what are often discussed as matters of common mistake and frustration are in reality the quite different matters of *force majeure* clauses and other agreed devices. The complete formal abolition of both common mistake and frustration, removing a continuing inducement to welfare reducing litigation[65] by improving our awareness of the proper role of contract, would be welcome.[66]

Planning in the Relational Contract

The great majority of debate over whether liability in contract is or should be strict or does or does not involve a larger element of what we might call fault is quite beside the point.[67] The law of contract should not make such issues a matter of mandatory liability. The point of the contractual conception of strict liability is that it should not be strict (or absolute) in any sense imposed by law, but the strictness of the obligation should be the result of the agreement, ie the degree of strictness should be the one the defendant has agreed to accept. Two things follow from this. First, if the parties choose a standard of liability based on fault, then it should be enforced. Let us allow that 'fault' may be usefully employed in distinguishing the standard of liability codified under The Supply of Goods and Services Act 1982, s 13 from that codified under, say, s 14(2) of The Sale of Goods Act 1979. But both are in their different way strict, and in relation to both 'it is immaterial why the defendant failed to fulfil his obligations and certainly no defence to plead that he had done his best'.

Secondly, though the language of fault is becoming very strained, the parties may, of course, contract away from the standard allocation of risks by presentiation discussed above. If a seller agrees to deliver a legal good, it is liable for the risks of non-delivery because by default it has agreed to bear those risks. But if a *force majeure* clause is incorporated, the seller will not be liable in this way, not because it has been excused its default liability, but because it never agreed to accept such liability. I have mentioned that there is a huge repertoire of devices which has been developed to manage presentiated risk in this way. These shade into the form of contract planning which Macneil argued

[64] EA Posner, 'There Are No Penalty Default Rules in Contract Law' (2006) 33 Florida State University Law Review 563.

[65] Morgan, 'Common Mistake' (n 49). Until common mistake receives its 'quietus', Morgan believes the law should be that stated by Leggatt J, as he then was, in *Dana Gas PJSC v Dana Gas Suhuk Ltd* [2017] EWHC 2928 (Comm); [2018] 1 Lloyd's Rep 177.

[66] The continued formal existence of these laws can have a disruptive bearing on the interpretation of parties' attempts to agree their own arrangements: E McKendrick, 'Frustration and Force Majeure: Their Relationship and a Comparative Assessment' in E McKendrick (ed), *Force Majeure and Frustration of Contract* (2nd edn, Lloyds of London Press 1995).

[67] GM Cohen, 'How Fault Shapes Contract Law' in O Ben-Shahar and A Portas (eds), *Fault in American Contract Law* (CUP 2010).

involves the progressive abandonment of presentiation,[68] and it is to clarify this argument, which addresses perhaps the most important doctrinal controversy in the classical law of contract, that I now turn.

Positive transaction costs obviously impose the limits of bounded rationality upon presentiation; why else are there ever good faith breaches? Presentiation in standard cases deals with breach by referring to the default remedies, and deals with those cases where it is anticipated that the default will not suit by ousting it with a bespoke provision for handling the presentiated risk. But there are some important, mutually advantageous exchange opportunities which cannot be taken on this basis as the parties realise *ex ante* that those opportunities involve, not possibilities which the parties can manage as risks, but Knightian uncertainties which would only be compounded were they to be treated as quantifiable risks. These are what Macneil originally called relational contracts, and they are fundamentally based, not on presentiation, but on contract planning.

Let us consider, first, the economic and then, secondly, in the next section of this chapter, the legal aspects of Macneil's fullest hypothetical example of a relational contract: of how 'a smelting operation—Smelter—might secure the coal needed for its operations'. Smelter might, of course, make a '[s]pot purchase from a stranger of 500 tons in a market of many sellers, Seller's agents delivering the coal by truck dumped at Smelter's yard, cash paid on delivery of each load'.[69] The particular spot contract may itself be presentiated, but, of course, Smelter can obtain no security of future price or even supply under this arrangement, and if such security is valued, as it will be when the production processes involve very considerable fixed costs and asset specific investments which can be profitable only above a certain throughput,[70] other devices may be considered, and Macneil describes a range of alternatives culminating in the substantial vertical integration of Coal Mine into Smelter:

> (1) Smelter contracts with Coal Mine to buy all the coal it requires during one year; the specified price is subject to a quarterly escalator clause based on a designated market. (2) Same ... except that in addition to the escalator clause there is a provision: 'Should a party become dissatisfied with the price, the parties agree to negotiate about a new price and, in the absence of agreement, to refer the matter to X as arbitrator to determine a fair and equitable price.' (3) Same ... except that the latest

[68] At the cost of anticipating the argument in order initially to stress a point which should no longer require stressing, despite the undeniable differing or contradictory statements about it which may be found in Macneil's huge corpus, this 'abandonment' is a feature of increasingly relational contracts and not an abandonment of presentiation *tout court*, which remains appropriate as the dominant mode of agreeing discrete contracts, as well as having some role in all contracts.

[69] IR Macneil, 'Economic Analysis of Contractual Relations: Its Shortfalls and the Need for a "Rich Classificatory Apparatus"' (1981) 75 Northwestern University Law Review 1018, 1025 (hereafter Macneil, 'Economic Analysis').

[70] In regard to economies of scale, A Chandler, *Scale and Scope* (Belknap Press 1990) 24 tells us:

> These potential cost advantages ... could not be fully realised unless a constant flow of materials through the plant was maintained to assure effective capacity utilisation ... In the capital intensive industries the throughput needed to maintain minimum efficient scale requires careful co-ordination not only of the flow through the processes of production but also of the flow of inputs from suppliers.

contract, entered into this year, is for 20 years rather than one; requires Coal Mine periodically: to provide Smelter with extensive cost information; to allow Smelter's experts to monitor mining operations; and to receive from Smelter recommendations respecting new equipment, improved methods of management and the like.

Smelter and Coal Mine also agree to build and operate a conveyer belt system from minehead to smelting plant, sharing the capital costs equally and operating the conveyer system jointly. As part of the deal Smelter gives Coal Mine a five-year loan to cover part of Coal Mine's costs of the conveyer system and, in order to satisfy other lenders, guarantees Coal Mine's half of a 20-year mortgage loan on the conveyer system. (4) Same ... except that the payment by Smelter to Coal Mine is in return for 20% of Coal Mine's shares rather than a loan; Smelter is guaranteed two seats on Coal Mine's Board of Directors.[71]

Let us accept that the spot commodities contract is a paradigm of a presentiated, discrete contract. Moving along the spectrum of contracts to the open requirements contract works against presentiation because, to mention only a few issues, the parties are accepting a residual price uncertainty despite the incorporation of the escalator clause fixed by a standard of reference, and the contract itself generates the possibility of solipsistically self-interested, or opportunistic, action precisely because the advantage the contract is intended to create will reduce ease of access to alternative buyers and sellers—an example of the situation often described as bilateral monopoly.[72] The shortcomings of using the standard of reference can be avoided by taking the step of referring the matter to an independent third party expert,[73] but for this referral to work the parties would have to comply with the adjudication process in good faith, including by the adequate provision of information which, in their respective positions, only one of them initially would possess. Macneil's example continues through to forms of organisational integration of the buying and selling function, and I return to this in the conclusion of this chapter. Let us now focus on the contracts made as an alternative to spot contracting.

In these increasingly relational contracts, presentiation is replaced by provision for the 'adjustment' (I shall defend the use of this term in the next section of this chapter) of initially specified obligations.[74] 'Somewhere along the line of increasing duration and complexity, trying to force changes into a pattern of original consent becomes both too difficult and too unrewarding to justify the effort',[75] and the basic aim of the negotiation of contracts is no longer to fix obligations (and therefore liabilities) at the

[71] Macneil, 'Economic Analysis' (n 69) 1025–26.

[72] OE Williamson, *The Economic Institutions of Capitalism* (Free Press 1985) 61 (hereafter Williamson, *Economic Institutions*) describes the 'fundamental transformation' by which 'what was a large numbers bidding condition at the outset is effectively transformed into one of bilateral supply [and demand] thereafter'.

[73] Without at all meaning to imply a criticism of Macneil's knowledge of arbitration, which was encyclopaedic, he did not express himself perfectly well here. He will have meant a third party adjudicator from whose decisions, if the adjudication system broke down, there would be recourse to arbitration (or litigation).

[74] IR Macneil, 'Contracts: Adjustment of Long-term Economic Relations Under Classical, Neo-classical and Relational Contract Law' (1978) 72 Northwestern University Law Review 854 (hereafter Macneil, 'Adjustment').

[75] ibid 901.

time of agreement but to provide for their adjustment during the course of performance. To speak more precisely, all welfare enhancing relational contracts[76] must have some presentiated elements or, to the extent that they could make sense as exchanges at all, they would be unanchored, and so provide insufficient guidance to the parties and invite opportunism.[77] So, although tight presentiation is eschewed, some initial identification, perhaps within wide parameters, of obligations, and some identification of the appropriate methods of making adjustment, including resolving disputes, is undertaken through planning. (It is only when contract has been entirely replaced by planning, ie when then production process is entirely subsumed within what it is proper to regard as one economic firm, that the element of separateness of the interests of the parties, even when those interests require active co-operation under contractual planning, disappears, replaced by general commitment to the success of the firm.) Though Macneil modified some of its basic concepts as we shall see, 'A Primer of Contract Planning' remains the most theoretically coherent examination of the legal devices used for facilitating the orderly adjustment of their obligations by contracting parties.

Though planning plays a vital role in devising a welfare enhancing relational contract, such a contract cannot work unless the parties adopt an attitude of conscious co-operation in the realisation of what in a most important respect is seen as a joint project when deciding upon the performance and adjustment of their obligations. Though a discrete contract is mutually beneficial, it is not co-operative in the sense we now need to develop in order to understand the relational contract, because each party is, perfectly legitimately,[78] indifferent to the realisation of the other's benefit in a

[76] It is, however, notoriously the case that some forms of, in particular, military procurement do, in fact, allow adjustment in a way that impairs or destroys rational budgeting. There are a number of variants of the 'cost plus' contract, some of which are valuable, indeed indispensable, if certain complex projects are to be undertaken by private firms. However, in a 1951 address to the American Bar Association (KC Royall, 'Forms of Military Contracting: Incentives v Non-excessive Profits' (1951) 37 American Bar Association Journal 97), Mr Kenneth C Royall, a former US Secretary of War, said that under the 'cost plus percentage of cost' contract widely used during World War I:

> there was no incentive for the contractor to perform efficiently or to keep the costs down. On the contrary, it was to his financial advantage on a specific contract to run the costs up, because this meant a larger fee or profit to the contractor. Consequently, this form of contracting fell into disrepute and has now been outlawed by statute.

[77] Macneil, 'Adjustment' (n 74) 887–88:

> However important flexibility for change becomes in economic relations, great need will nevertheless always remain for fixed and reliable planning. Or in the terms emphasised here, presentiation will always occur in economic relations since it tends to follow planning as a matter of course.

[78] Macneil's earlier criticisms of the values of discrete contracting undermined all the attempts he made to give them a definite place in his general normative schemes. He did sometimes seem to conceive of discrete contracting as a very inferior form of relational contracting, which had the paradoxical effect that he often failed to distinguish the 'co-operation' brought out by the mutual advantage of exchange between actors indifferent to each other's goals and the conscious co-operation over the realisation of goals in the relational contract: eg IR Macneil, 'Whither Contracts?' (1969) 21 *Journal of Legal Education* 403, 405:

> We ... think of economic exchange as being extremely individualistic and selfish, rather than co-operative [but in fact] exchange represents a species of human co-operation ... exchange involves a *mutual* goal of the parties, namely the reciprocal transfer of values. And this is true however strongly the 'economic man'—the 'as-much-as-possible-for-as-little-as-possible-in-return-man'—may dominate the motivations of both parties to an exchange.

way that the parties to a relational contract cannot be. This is the property of economic action which, as we saw in Chapter 5, PH Wicksteed, responding to criticism of 'the economic motive', called 'non-tuism'. The discrete contract is legitimately based on the *fixity* of the obligations set out in its terms.[79] It is essential to recall that, as we saw in Chapters 3, 4, and 5, good faith is an essential condition of avoiding opportunism in the interpretation and therefore performance of even these contracts.

But in a relational contract the parties have, precisely, not fixed important obligations in this way, and so must perform, and in particular adjust their performance, by reference to a joint goal. Of their nature, open-ended provisions create a particular possibility of being interpreted and performed in an opportunistic fashion, and, though the document and the quality of its drafting is itself vital, no document can ultimately prevent this. The plausibility of writing contracts in an open-ended fashion turns on assuming a co-operative attitude to the resolution at the appropriate time of the problems initially left open-ended. Without a shift in attitude, formal provision for flexibility is fruitless, for one cannot create a co-operative attitude by writing it down that such an attitude will be taken to contingencies as they arise. One needs the attitude to make the writing have any meaning:

> there can be present a 'sense of productive increase from the relationship which can dwarf variations in expectation, or of long-term anticipations of mutual benefit that dwarf variations in shares received by parties'. This anticipatory, commonly held 'sense' of the parties may virtually obliterate any present separation as maximisers, thereby making them effectively a single maximiser.[80]

Against this background, we should now expand on the quotation from Macneil used to illustrate the criticism of the economic motive in Chapters 4 and 6, which motive he often placed at the heart of the discrete contract:

> An individual utility maximiser may be perfectly well aware of the fact that the deal he makes creates exchange-surplus, but his *sole* concern about that utility is to grab as much of it for himself as he can. He will feel nothing but regret at whatever amount is snared by the other party and nothing but happiness that the other failed to secure more of it. That is not, however, the case in relational exchange ... Relational exchange ... creates circumstances where the long-run *individual* economic (material)

It was wrong to describe mutual commitment to a process as mutual commitment to a goal, and the consequences of this mistake for Macneil's thinking about both senses of the relationality of contracts were substantial.

[79] RA Hillman, *The Richness of Contract Law* (Kluwer 1997) 244, 252:

> [Though] business parties often believe that flexibility and compromise, not resort to the 'letter of the law', will ensure success in a business relation ... Of course, not every contract raises a duty to adjust when circumstances change. For example, a party may not reasonably expect her counterpart to renegotiate terms if the agreement is a one-time deal involving a standardised commodity.

[80] Macneil, 'Economic Analysis' (n 69) 1023–4. Macneil quotes from a letter sent to him by ST Lowry: ibid 1020 n 3.

> interests of each party conflict with any short run desires to maximise individual utility respecting the goods in any particular exchange; the more relational the exchange, the more artificial becomes the idea of maximisation. The capacity of an exchange to produce exchange-surplus … constitutes a pool of wealth which can be shared as well as grabbed, shared not to make a gift but out of deep economic self-interest … Over time, exchanges made with … long-run motivations produce norms to which the participants expect to adhere and to which they expect adherence from other parties.[81]

Macneil evidently was trying to do at least two things with the spectrum of contracts, which set out not only a range of techniques of economic organisation in the play between presentiation and planning, but also a shift in the ethical attitudes of parties to discrete and relational contracts. It is not remotely to detract from Macneil's achievement to say that trying to do both of these things in the way he did undermined each of them. Though, as has been said, all relational contracts must have presentiated elements or they would be unanchored, this does not sit naturally with the ethical distinction between discrete and relational contracts, and Macneil's repeated attempts to restate his point were overwhelmed by the widespread perception that his position was that in a relational contract the law did not really matter. Empirical case studies do show that when the parties to a relational contract encounter difficulties that put a strain on their planned provision for adjustment, they often innovate solutions that cannot plausibly be directly related to those provisions, and may even defy them, but are in line with, indeed are a product of, the consciously co-operative attitude that identifies the relational contract.

This inevitably led to relational contracting being closely identified with Macaulay's non-use of contract and use of non-contractual relations, and in particular with the distinction which Macaulay came to describe as that between the 'real' and the 'paper deals'. In all this, the 'sociological' concept of relational trust discussed in Chapters 2 and 4 emerges which is distinct from, indeed in an important sense opposed to, the 'economic' concept of trust, and in this sociological concept there is little left of the discipline of contract planning, of which (neither Macaulay nor) Macneil ever wanted to lose sight, though this is the tendency of the sociological concept. For a focus on how parties deal with the situation where the written contract can even be a hindrance, though it has been enormously stimulating, is a distraction from the fundamental question of why the legal contract can take such an unproductive form.

What I believe should emerge from Macneil's spectrum, but what he himself, despite his great labour over statements trying to say this, could not clearly draw out is a distinction between two approaches to contracting which are both perfectly ethically legitimate in their appropriate situations, those situations including being mixed in varying proportions along the spectrum of contracts. The discrete contract previously taken as standard in this book is based on obligations fixed by presentation to which 'relational' adjustment—typified by giving an excuse for non-performance—would be quite wrong. In contrast, the relational contract is based on adjustable obligations the

[81] IR Macneil, 'Exchange Revisited: Individual Utility and Social Solidarity' (1986) 96 Ethics 567, 578–79.

fixing of which would be quite wrong. It is at this point that Macneil should have had his greatest impact on contract doctrine, for the classical law, and in particular the doctrine of consideration, has not been able to provide coherent answers to the questions which the use of adjustment must pose, and the resulting accumulation of *ad hoc* doctrinal developments, creating what Macneil regarded as the prevailing body of 'neo-classical' law,[82] still leaves the law of contract in an 'abrasive' relationship with the practice of relational contracting:

> No comprehensive doctrinal structure has developed in American neo-classical contract law to answer systematically the questions [posed by relational contracting]. The closest it comes to providing such a structure is the doctrine of consideration, which pervades much thinking on the subject. Consideration doctrine, however, by no means deals comprehensively with all the questions. For one thing the doctrine normally impedes change if it operates at all, thus implementing discreteness and presentiation as of the 'original formulation' ... Such [a law] will, however, continue to rub in an unnecessarily abrasive manner against the realities of coexistence with relational needs for flexibility and change. Only when the parts of the contract law system implementing discreteness and presentiation are perceived, intellectually and otherwise, not as an independent system, but only as integral parts of much larger systems, will unnecessary abrasion disappear. By no means will all abrasion disappear, of course, because real conflict exists between the need for reliability of planning and the need for flexibility in economic relations. What will disappear is the abrasion resulting from application of contract law founded on the assumption that all of a contractual relation is encompassed in some original assent to it, where that assumption is manifestly false. The elimination of that assumption ... would eliminate the unnecessary abrasion.[83]

It is to the remedy of these shortcomings of the doctrine of consideration that I now turn.

The Adjustment of 'Existing Obligations'

The incoherent necessity of practical benefit

The rule that existing obligations are insufficient consideration, or its functional equivalent, is, it is submitted, analytically necessary to the executory contract. In the interval between agreement and completion of performance, a shift in the circumstances attendant upon that performance may give one party an incentive and the power to force a renegotiation of the contract by threatening not to perform.[84] Of course, such a threat is a breach, but one can easily conceive of situations arising which make the legal remedy of limited practical value, and in such situations parties threatened with

[82] Macneil, 'Adjustment' (n 74) 865–86.
[83] ibid 874–75, 888.
[84] See the text accompanying n 123.

non-performance may agree to provide greater consideration for the same performance.[85] The law of contract's basic response has been to find that the promisee, the obligations of which do not change from those already existing, has not changed its legal position, and so has furnished insufficient consideration for the renegotiation.

The leading authority is, of course, *Stilk v Myrick*.[86] In the course of a round voyage from London to the Baltic, two members of a crew, the full complement of which was 11 (plus the captain), deserted whilst the ship was in port at Cronstadt. The captain of the ship was unable to recruit new hands and, whilst in Cronstadt, agreed with the nine remaining crew that, if necessary, they would themselves complete the remainder of the voyage, sharing the wages which would have been paid to the deserters. A further attempt to recruit was unavailing, and the ship returned to London shorthanded, at which point the owners of the vessel refused to make the extra payment, for which one of the seamen brought an action. *Stilk v Myrick* obviously involved the very important policy question of what could be required of seamen in response to hazards at sea,[87] but Lord Ellenborough's contract reasoning saw that behind this lay the general issue of opportunistic renegotiation, which was addressed as a matter of the insufficiency of existing obligations.

It is essential to first determine what the seamen's existing obligations were, and the case presents some difficulties over this which have a bearing on the law of existing obligations' ability to give expression to the relational contract. I have in previous work said that the property of a relational contract at which Macneil was trying to drive was 'flexibility'.[88] This certainly had sanction in what Macneil had written, but I now think this is the wrong term, and that, as I have said above, what is at issue is 'adjustment'.[89] It is wrong to place too much weight on niceties of definition, but I think it is helpful to say that *Stilk v Myrick*, the paradigm discrete contract, required flexibility of the seamen in the performance of their primary obligations, but denied them the capacity to require the adjustment of the terms establishing those obligations. As Gilmore acutely pointed out, *Stilk v Myrick* 'can hardly be described as a case in which a dissatisfied party insists on more pay for the *same* work',[90] and it is stretching things to claim that 'a doctrine of maritime law under which the members of the crew are required to exert extraordinary efforts, indeed to venture their lives, to rescue [a] ship from an emergency' can easily cover a renegotiation which took place whilst 'the ship was safe

[85] This is the 'situational monopoly' analysed in MJ Trebilcock, 'An Economic Approach to the Doctrine of Unconscionability' in BJ Reiter and J Swan (eds), *Studies in Contract Law* (Butterworths 1980) 392–96.

[86] (1809) 2 Camp 317; 170 ER 851 (hereafter *Stilk v Myrick*). This is Campbell's report of the case. As is well known, Espinasse's report, (1809) 6 Esp 126; 170 ER 851, does not convey the consideration argument at all. An unusually sympathetic explanation of this which gives food for thought is P Luther, 'Campbell, Espinasse and the Sailors: Text and Context in the Common Law' (1999) 19 Legal Studies 526, 526–540.

[87] ibid 540–49.

[88] D Campbell and D Harris, 'Flexibility in Long-term Contractual Relationships: The Role of Co-operation' (1993) 20 Journal of Law and Society 166.

[89] 'Modification' or 'variation' may, of course, also convey the necessary distinction from flexibility, but both have now acquired a certain legal status and definition by their use in decided law, and it is upon this use that I propose to improve. I am, in particular, anxious to distinguish the outright dropping of the requirement of consideration for what are termed 'modifications' under Uniform Commercial Code § 2-209(1). This has, in my opinion, created specific difficulties in addition to the general difficulty of substituting reliance for consideration in the US law briefly mentioned in ch 5.

[90] G Gilmore, *The Death of Contract* (2nd edn, Ohio State University Press 1995) 27.

in port in Cronstadt [and] not in imminent peril from the sea'.[91] But, crucially, it was held that both flexibility and a commitment to the entire voyage had been fixed by agreement at the outset:

> Before they sailed from London they had undertaken to do all that they could under all the emergencies of the voyage. They had sold all their services till the voyage should be completed. If they had been at liberty to quit the vessel at Cronstadt, the case would have been quite different ... the desertion of a part of the crew is to be considered an emergency of the voyage as much as their death; and those who remain are bound by the terms of their original contract to exert themselves to the utmost to bring the ship in safety to her destined port.[92]

In sum, the seamen's contract required flexibility from them in the performance of their obligations, but prevented the adjustment of the terms of the contract.[93] Though *Stilk v Myrick* involved what would now be regarded as an employment contract which has a certain flexibility at its heart, this will be a common situation in many simple contracts,[94] though not as common as the delivery of perfectly standard legal goods which does not require such a degree of flexibility (despite, as was argued particularly in Chapters 3 and 4, the successful performance of even this obligation turning on good faith in interpreting what the obligation requires). The point of relevance here is that the existing obligations doctrine plays a crucial role in facilitating discrete contracting.

It has been quite otherwise in regard of what now should be seen as the specie of relational contracts. As with the other grounds of insufficiency discussed in Chapter 5, the existing obligations doctrine is formulated in an abstract manner which posits the underlying issue in far too wide a manner, and as a result its scope is indiscriminate. It not only rightly renders unenforceable changes to what should be fixed obligations in discrete contracts, but it also wrongly renders unenforceable the adjustments that are the basis of relational contracts. The difficulties were most interestingly demonstrated even in one of the cases by which the current English law tries to parry them: *Williams v Roffey Bros and Nicholls (Contractors) Ltd*.[95] The defendant, which held the main

[91] ibid 26.

[92] *Stilk v Myrick* (n 86) 319–20; 1169.

[93] The claimant's suggestion that *Stilk v Myrick* was binding in *Hartley v Ponsonby* (1857) E & B 872; 119 ER 1471 received no discussion, but the ground on which it was effectively distinguished is, it is submitted, clear and cogent. The claimant seaman and his colleagues had engaged on a round voyage from Liverpool to Port Philip, Australia, returning via ports to be specified to final port in the UK. In Port Philip, 17 of the crew deserted, and the captain agreed to make an additional payment (to, it appears, nine) of the 19 remaining seamen, only four or five of which were able seamen, if the ship could set sail for Bombay, where extra hands might be, and were, obtained. The enforceability of the extra payment was due to the reduction in complement amounting to the ship being unseaworthy, exceeding the flexibility that could be required of the seamen: ibid 877; 1473:

> for the ship to go to sea with so few hands was dangerous to life. If so, it was not incumbent on the plaintiff to perform the work. He was a free man. There was therefore a consideration for the contract. It would, of course, have been entirely different if the ship were not safe in port but in peril.

[94] H Collins, 'The Employment Relationship as a Relational Contract' (2021) 137 Law Quarterly Review 426, 427–28.

[95] [1991] 1 QB 1 (CA) (hereafter *Williams v Roffey*).

contract for refurbishment of a local authority block of flats, subcontracted the claimant to do carpentry work. The work proceeded badly, and the claimant entered into financial difficulty over completing it. The prospect clearly arose of the work not being completed unless the claimant was given a substantial additional payment.

Conscious of both the practical difficulty of finding a substitute and that its contract with the local authority contained a time penalty clause, the defendant agreed to revise upwards the staged payments so that a total of £10,300 would be paid in addition to an originally agreed £20,000. The claimant resumed work, but the dispute continued, and after the defendant made only one of the staged payments, the claimant quit the still unfinished works, which the defendant had to engage others to complete, with the resultant delay exposing it to one week's penalty. The claimant brought an action for a wrongly quantified sum, but was awarded damages which were based on the agreement to pay the additional £10,300 being in principle enforceable,[96] and these damages were confirmed by the Court of Appeal.

Leaving aside other issues, on the face of it holding this agreement to be enforceable flies directly in the face of *Stilk v Myrick*, which, though general questions about its current significance were raised,[97] was stated to be the law,[98] and distinguished (or its application to the instant case 'refine[d] and limit[ed]',[99] or made less 'rigid',[100] or made more 'modern')[101] on the basis that, by agreeing to return to the works, the claimant conveyed what has come to be known as a 'practical benefit'.[102] Though I can identify nothing spelling this out, this must have been seen as additional to the consideration the claimant furnished for the £20,000, and so could support the payment of the £10,300. This judgment was a good one in a most important sense in that it came to the right conclusion, and did so in a way which avoided[103] the disaster of overruling *Stilk v Myrick* without being aware of a superior alternative.[104] But, with respect—and one does wonder whether the Lords Justice would have challenged the point if it was discussed truly *ex cathedra*—the judgment is at root logical nonsense, and I will set aside both the equivocation about *Stilk v Myrick* and the more general ratiocination

[96] ibid 6G, 7E–G. It is not possible to relate the agreement or the damages awarded to the sum by which, as will be discussed, the pricing of the works was vitally found to be too low.

[97] ibid 16C, 18G–H, 21A.

[98] ibid 16C, 19D, 20D–H, 21B.

[99] ibid 16B (Glidewell LJ).

[100] ibid 18G (Lord Russell LJ).

[101] ibid 23C (Purchas LJ).

[102] The term was used but twice (ibid 11B, 13B) in the judgment, both times in an incidental manner by Glidewell LJ, but it has been so used in subsequent discussion that that use now is settled: *Re Selectmove Ltd* [1995] 1 WLR 474 (CA). An alternative term of much longer provenance, 'factual benefit', has been used, eg H Beale (ed), *Chitty on Contracts* (34th edn, Sweet & Maxwell 2021) paras 6.069–6.072, though it is not to be found in the judgment at all.

[103] Russell LJ did, however, regret that no argument had been made that might have led to a general law of estoppel: *Williams v Roffey* (n 95) 17G–18F. This would have been just a different route to an exaggeration of the doctrinal incoherence left by the case.

[104] As has been noted in ch 5, a long history of contemplating judicial legislation about some or all of the absolute fundamentals of consideration, which in relationship to the present discussion would require going beyond *Central London Property Trust Ltd v High Trees House Ltd* [1947] KB 130 (KB) (hereafter *High Trees*) and *Williams v Roffey* (n 95), has so far thankfully come to nothing: see most recently: *MWB Business Exchange Centres Ltd v Rock Advertising Ltd* [2018] UKSC 34; [2018] 2 WLR 1606 [18], [20].

about the benefit and/or detriment of one or both parties, which depressingly calls to mind more than a century of scholasticism,[105] in order to focus on the basic issue.

Surely the seamen's performance conveyed as much 'practical benefit' to the captain as did the subcontractor's to the contractor. Surely the same thing can be said of cases in which liabilities are adjusted down, certainly including *Foakes v Beer*[106] itself. Why on earth would promisors ever agree an extra obligation of this kind unless they thought there was a practical benefit to be had? But regarding some practical benefits as insufficient, ie not as legal benefits,[107] is the entire point of the doctrine of existing obligations! And if practical benefit is logical nonsense, then so equally is the promissory estoppel drawn from *High Trees*, which, when considered outside of the court, cannot sensibly be justified as reasoning from precedent.[108] This is so regardless whether promissory estoppel is confined, as it has been by barely plausible arguments desperate to prevent it completely undermining consideration,[109] or whether it is an alternative general form of liability.[110] The current law of swords and shields[111] and decreasing and increasing pacts[112] may represent doing the best one can, but it nevertheless is a Heath Robinson contraption because the best one can do has been limited by an inability coherently to distinguish between discrete contracts based on

[105] A striking spectacle is presented by Lord Purchas LJ's purported disregard of 'detriment' (*Williams v Roffey* (n 95) 23D) and the then Denning LJ's commentary on *High Trees* (n 104) from which detriment also disappeared: AT Denning, 'Recent Developments in the Law of Consideration' (1952) 15 Modern Law Review 1, 6. I will not here amplify the general arguments made in ch 5 to show just how much this was *déjà vu* all over again.

[106] (1883–84) LR 9 App Cas 605 (HL) 622–23 (Lord Blackburn):

> all men of business, whether merchants or tradesmen, do every day recognise and act on the ground that prompt payment of a part of their demand may be more beneficial to them than it would be to insist on their rights and enforce payment of the whole. Even where the debtor is perfectly solvent, and sure to pay at last, this often is so. Where the credit of the debtor is doubtful it must be more so.

Lord Blackburn originally had intended to dissent on this point.

[107] As it was pertinently put by the defendants in *Williams v Roffey* (n 95) 11B.

[108] FAR Bennion, 'Want of Consideration' (1953) 16 Modern Law Review 441. As Professor Bennion was perfectly well aware, forms of response to the undoubted problems Denning J addressed had, of course, been registered in the case law. AT Denning KC was able to rely on some forerunner of his own later judgment in *Marquess of Salisbury v Gilmore* [1942] 2 KB 38 (KB) 51–52.

[109] KCT Sutton, *Consideration Reconsidered* (University of Queensland Press 1974) 89:

> the subsequent judicial history of the doctrine has become one of containment, of constriction, and of confinement within narrow limits, lest the orthodox theory of consideration be undone.

Sutton, ibid 142, himself regretted that what I agree with him in believing was Lord Denning's original intention of introducing a general reliance based law of liability had 'foundered on the rock of judicial conservatism'.

[110] See the discussion of *Waltons Stores (Interstate) Ltd v Maher* (1988) 164 CLR 387 (HCA) in ch 5 and in the text accompanying n 210.

[111] *Combe v Combe* [1951] 2 KB 215 (CA) 224 (Birkett LJ). *Baird Textiles Holdings Ltd v Marks and Spencer plc* [2001] EWCA Civ 274; [2002] 1 All ER (Comm) 737 [32]–[40], [49]–[55], [78]–[98] (*hereafter Baird Textiles* CA) confirmed the shield not a sword aspect of the English doctrine of estoppel, though Judge LJ disapproved of this 'misleading aphorism' (ibid [52]) and, as will be argued below, the Court was open to a general plea of estoppel.

[112] GH Treitel, *Some Landmarks in the Law of Contract* (Clarendon Press 2002) ch 1. Professor Treitel is hardly responsible for this law, but it does partake of the quality of the idea of 'invented' consideration he was long prepared to countenance; indeed the passage in which he in 1966 introduced the idea could have been written with *Williams v Roffey* in mind: GH Treitel, *The Law of Contract* (2nd edn, Stevens & Sons 1966) 47.

obligations which are fixed, and relational contracts based on obligations which can be adjusted.

Reconciling *Stilk v Myrick* and *Williams v Roffey*

The commendable motivation behind the judgment in *Williams v Roffey* was that, for a reason to be discussed, the Court of Appeal correctly concluded that it had been the 'true intention of the parties when they arrived at the agreement' to make the £10,300 payable, and the Court's 'finding about consideration' was tailored to 'reflect' that intention.[113] That it was an agreement rested on there being 'no finding, and no suggestion, that in this case the promise was given as a result of . . . duress'.[114] Though it would seem that the underlying point may be traced (under, of course, differently stated law) to the time of *Stilk v Myrick* itself,[115] since 1975[116] an explicit concept of 'economic duress' had been used to focus on forced renegotiation as a way of narrowing down the excessive scope of the existing obligations doctrine.[117] Its use in this specific manner was considered in *Williams v Roffey*,[118] but it was categorically denied that the promise to pay the £10,300 was vitiated by such duress.[119]

Though such recourse to economic duress is a step in the right direction, *Williams v Roffey* presents many of the difficulties, inherent in the use of a doctrine which must connote the 'physical' overbearing of a will to explore what is really an issue of the

[113] *Williams v Roffey* (n 95) 19A, 18H.

[114] ibid 16B.

[115] A remarkable paper, BF Brody, 'Performance of a Pre-existing Contractual Duty As Consideration: The Actual Criteria for the Efficacy of an Agreement Altering Contractual Obligation' (1975) 52 Denver Law Journal 433, sought to use what would now be called economic duress to resolve a conflict between US cases markedly similar to *Stilk v Myrick* and *Williams v Roffey*; but these were both cases decided by the Supreme Court of New York in the same month of 1817!

[116] *North Ocean Shipping Co Ltd v Hyundai Contraction Co Ltd, The Atlantic Baron* [1979] QB 705 (Com Ct).

[117] *Vantage Navigation Corp v Suhail and Saud Bahwan Building Materials, The Alev* [1989] 1 Lloyd's Rep 138 (Com Ct) 147 col 1:

> Now that there is a properly developed doctrine of the avoidance of contracts on the grounds of economic duress, there is no warrant for the Court to fail to recognize the existence of some consideration even though it may be insignificant and even though there may have been no mutual bargain in any realistic use of that phrase.

Subsequent to *Williams v Roffey* see eg *Adam Opel GmbH v Mitras Automotive (UK) Ltd* [2007] EWHC 3481 (QB) [42] (David Donaldson QC) (hereafter *Mitras Automotive*):

> The law of consideration is no longer to be used to protect a participant in such a variation. That role has passed to the law of economic duress, which provides a more refined control mechanism, and renders the contract voidable rather than void.

Though *Pakistan International Airlines Corp v Times Travel (UK) Ltd* [2021] UKSC 40 seems to have settled the possibility, which had remained far too long a matter of uncertainty, of 'lawful act' duress, the emerging clarity over illegitimate renegotiation has, it is respectfully and regrettably submitted, suffered a reverse by, *inter alia*, an inappropriate subjective requirement of the defendant's 'bad faith' (ibid [112] (Lord Burrows)) being introduced into the evaluation of the situation when a claimant is given 'no alternative but to waive its pre-existing rights . . . by illegitimate pressure' (ibid [17]), This requirement was not, however, supported by the majority (ibid 45–57] (Lord Hodge; Lord Reed PSC, Lord Lloyd-Jones, and Lord Kitchin JSCC concurring)).

[118] *Williams v Roffey* (n 95) 13H–16A.

[119] ibid 16B, 17E, 21D.

procedural fairness of a contract between parties which are not even natural legal persons,[120] of using economic duress to prevent opportunism in the adjustment of obligations.[121] Explicitly recognising the specie of the relational contract allows us to markedly more clearly state the issue at which economic duress is driving in adjustment of obligations cases. In essence, this shows how we may coherently distinguish *Williams v Roffey* from *Stilk v Myrick* so as to leave both intact.[122]

A law derived from duress will tend to inquire whether the claimant made a threat; in *Williams v Roffey* a 'threat' to quit the works.[123] A claimant aware of the law (and respecting ordinary courtesy) may do well to couch his intentions in a tactful manner, but the question of the explicitness of a threat in *Williams v Roffey* is a distraction as the crux of the matter was perfectly clear to both parties. In light of the realities of the situation, even an explicit statement of an intention to quit the works for a legitimate reason cannot be a threat (just as a 'veiled threat' backed by no legitimate reason is a threat).[124]

The claimant was not, in truth, in the best of positions to establish the legitimacy of its actions, and therefore to its entitlement to an extra payment which would have reversed its fortunes under the contract.[125] It should not be forgotten that, unlike in *Stilk v Myrick*, in which the seamen did actually perform extra work, the claimant in *Williams v Roffey* did only what he originally had promised to do.[126] Moreover, one reason the works encountered financial difficulties was that the claimant had failed to supervise his workforce adequately.[127] It should not be possible for a claimant to make an enforceable demand for extra payment to cover for its own shortcomings. But the significance of these shortcomings was overridden by the other reason for the financial difficulties,[128] which is that the original price of £20,000 was too low to enable the work to be done satisfactorily and profitably, though this, of course, would initially seem to add to the claimant's difficulties as it *had* agreed the pricing. However, one Mr Cotterell, a surveyor employed by the defendants, estimated the correct price as £23,783, ie the original price was over 15% too low.[129]

Now, of course, it is of the essence of the discrete contract that the price paid for a legal good or service might be too high or low in the judgment of objective third

[120] PS Atiyah, 'Economic Duress and the Overborne Will' (1982) 98 Law Quarterly Review 197.

[121] R Halson, 'Opportunism, Economic Duress and Contractual Modifications' (1991) 107 Law Quarterly Review 649. The substance of this article revised to take proper account of *Williams v Roffey* is to be found in R Halson, *Contract Law* (2nd edn, Pearson 2013) ch 12.

[122] *Mitras Automotive* (n 117) [41], though I wish to insist that David Donaldson QC's observations are correct on the law as it is currently understood.

[123] The facts, eg *Williams v Roffey* (n 95) 10F, led Purchas LJ to claim (ibid 21D) that the extra payment was actually at the initiative of the defendants, but, as his Lordship's perceptive account of the 'particular circumstances' that led to a 'pragmatic point of view' (ibid 22H) being taken by both parties towards the extra payment shows, the question of which party took the 'initiative' is by no means, as his Lordship implies, determinative. The image of a threat is just too crude for the actual situation.

[124] *B & S Contracts and Designs Ltd v Victor Green Publications Ltd* [1984] ICR 419 (CA) 424B.

[125] R Halson, 'Sailors, Sub-contractors and Consideration' (1990) 106 Law Quarterly Review 183, 185.

[126] *Williams v Roffey* (n 95) 19C.

[127] ibid 10D.

[128] ibid. On the reported facts of the case, including the quantification of damages, it is not possible to reach a completely satisfactory understanding of the decision, but the broad reason for that decision may clearly be grasped.

[129] ibid.

parties, or even of the payer in retrospect, but the price remains fixed. But though we have seen there are presentiational limits to adjustment, literally fixing an initial price is tantamount to unknown in all but the simplest construction contracts, and was specifically found not to be appropriate in *Williams v Roffey*.[130] Estimating the price of construction works is a relational contractual undertaking which normally cannot be, and as a matter of fact is not, based on presentiation, ie by allocating risks at the time of the original agreement, but on estimates which are designed to be adjusted under a monitored process.[131] This is why the standard forms of construction contract are predominantly concerned with providing for adjustment; why the parties to construction contracts typically make extensive provision for adjustment; and why (within limits) opposition to adjustment is normally considered both legally unsupportable and practically most unwise.

The trial judge, Mr Rupert Jackson QC, as he then was, perceived all this very acutely:

> The judge quoted and accepted the evidence of Mr Cottrell to the effect that a main contractor who agrees too low a price with a sub-contractor is acting contrary to his own interests. He will never get the job finished without paying more money. The judge therefore concluded: 'In my view where the original sub-contract price is too low, and the parties subsequently agree that the additional monies shall be paid to the sub-contractor, this agreement is in the interests of both parties. This is what happened in the present case, and in my opinion the agreement [to make the extra payment] does not fail for lack of consideration'.[132]

It was because the Court of Appeal followed the judge in recognising that construction contracts are meant to be adjusted that, as has been mentioned, it concluded that it had been the 'true intention of the parties when they arrived at the agreement' to make the £10,300 payable, and now, we can add, it was the parties' intention that the payment was enforceable because it was legitimate in that type of contract (just as it would be illegitimate in a discrete contract such as *Stilk v Myrick*).[133] Economic duress turns on the legitimacy of the 'threat', but this is fundamentally determined by the nature of the original obligation. Not being able to distinguish between discrete and

[130] ibid 13H.

[131] Construction examples are very important in that part of Macneil's casebook on contract planning: Macneil and Gudel, *Contracts* (n 8) pt 2.

[132] *Williams v Roffey* (n 95) 10F–H.

[133] The point was soundly addressed in a modern case decided on ground of economic duress: *Atlas Express v Kafco (Importers and Distributors) Ltd* [1989] QB 833 (Com Ct). The claimant carrier effectively miscalculated the payment it required to deliver the defendant's goods to Woolworths, a very important customer. The defendant agreed the payment in good faith. When it became aware of the miscalculation, the claimant refused to make the delivery without an extra payment, and the defendant, conscious of the practical difficulty of finding a substitute and of the harm it would suffer if it failed to supply Woolworths, paid part of the extra demanded, but then argued that the extra payment had been made under economic duress. The responsibility for the calculation, and therefore the miscalculation, being found to lie with the claimant, its demand was illegitimate and the payment therefore secured by duress. But, though the judgment was an important one in the development of economic duress, Tucker J, perhaps, with respect, not entirely comprehending, raised a question about the proper role of the doctrine for he also concluded that, 'In any event', the agreement to pay the extra was unsupported by consideration: ibid 841D.

relational contracts, the Court of Appeal perforce came up with practical benefit in order to tailor its 'finding about consideration' to 'reflect' the parties' intention. We can get rid of the entire Heath Robinson effort (including estoppel) by developing what has so far been a theoretical distinction as a doctrine of the English law recognising the relational, in the sense of as opposed to discrete, contract. The most blatant obstacle in our way is, of course, *Baird Textiles*, but before turning to this I wish to conclude this section of this chapter by making clear the implications of viewing *Williams v Roffey* as a relational (and *Stilk v Myrick* as a discrete) contract for the doctrine of consideration.

Ultimately our difficulties stem from the way that *High Trees* and *Williams v Roffey* have been understood to stand *in opposition* to the doctrine of consideration's attempt to make the existence of a bargain a requisite of contractual enforceability.[134] The recognition of the relational contract allows us to see this is wholly misdirected. For what consideration do the parties to a relational contract furnish? It cannot be strict liability to perform obligations as originally specified, for those obligations are, precisely, capable of adjustment. The consideration is a reciprocal commitment to operate the adjustment process in good faith. The issues can be seen in the first three of the relational devices Macneil sets out in his smelter example, which are increasingly refined versions of a requirements contract.

Though they have received very substantial doctrinal[135] and empirically informed theoretical[136] debate in the US,[137] and explicit provision is made for them under UCC § 2-306, requirements and output contracts feature but little in Commonwealth discussions of the general principles of contract or of the sale of goods,[138] though in their various specialist forms they are, of course, subject to close analysis in legal commentary on specific industries. Leaving quantity and perhaps price open obviously poses fundamental problems for classically understood agreement. The use of requirements and output contracts would seem to be one of the confirmations of Macaulay's 'non-use' understood in the sense of non-contractual relations replacing unhelpful formal law because these contracts have generated little litigation.[139] Such contracts obviously

134 M Lobban, '*Foakes v Beer* (1884)' in C Mitchell and P Mitchell (eds), *Landmark Cases in the Law of Contract* (Hart 2008) 266–67.

135 Eg on the law prior to the Uniform Commercial Code, HC Havighurst and SM Berman, 'Requirement and Output Contracts' (1932) 27 Illinois Law Review 1, and on the Uniform Commercial Code as a response to this law: Note, 'Requirements Contracts Under the Uniform Commercial Code' (1954) 102 University of Pennsylvania Law Review 654.

136 eg VP Goldberg and JR Erickson, 'Quantity and Price Adjustment in Long-term Contracts: A Case Study of Petroleum Coke' (1987) 30 Journal of Law and Economics 369.

137 The claim that these contract may be anticompetitive has also generated considerable discussion. The claim is dismissed in RH Bork, *The Antitrust Paradox* (rev edn, Free Press 1993) ch 15.

138 The Sale of Goods Act 1893 made provision for the related issue of leaving the price unstated. Section 8(1) of the 1979 Act allows that the price 'may be left to be fixed in a manner determined by the contract, or may be determined in the course of dealing between the parties', and s 8(2) provides that the buyer must pay a reasonable price when 'the price is not determined as mentioned in' s 8(1). Section 9 provides for third part valuation. Once *Walford v Miles* [1992] 2 AC 128 (HL), discussed in ch 2, is taken out of the equation as these contracts are not at all agreements to agree of the sort that should not, indeed cannot, be enforced, then the law seems free of major problems. But, of course, taking *Walford v Miles* thinking out is the difficult part. The leading case, *May and Butcher v R* [1934] 2 KB 17 (HL), posed particular problems because it did have agreement to agree aspects: C Twigg-Flesner and R Canavan, *Atiyah and Adams' Sale of Goods* (14th edn, Pearson 2021) 30.

139 PS Atiyah, 'Contract and Fair Exchange' in *Essays on Contract* (rev edn, Clarendon Press 1990) 337:

could possibly be challenged for want of certainty of agreement,[140] or, the point to be made here, for want of consideration,[141] for it is implicit in the concept of requirements and output contracts that the quantity actually bought or sold may be zero.[142]

Even if those circumstances in which there is no actual exchange of the subject matter of the contract, and therefore it might be said there is no actual benefit or detriment, are rightly put to one side, a claim that there is no legal benefit or detriment will always arise if the focus remains on that subject matter. No change of legal position regarding the actual exchange of subject matter might ever take place. But the focus should be on the legal benefit and detriment of accepting a binding obligation to act in good faith towards the other party regarding the set of possible exchanges of the subject matter, even if that set includes the possibility of zero. Uniform Commercial Code § 2-306(1) defines the quantity provided for in requirements and output contracts as 'such actual output or requirements as may occur in good faith', and this core of § 2-306 is sound even if, as must be acknowledged, the overly elaborate wording of the section in full has given rise to avoidable problems (in addition to unavoidable ones) in determining the application of good faith to specific circumstances.[143]

At issue is the same fundamental obligation of good faith established by the rules of agreement, consideration, and remedy as they apply to the standard, discrete contract. In Chapter 9 we saw how these rules have been misapplied in connection with

> the basic problem with these arrangements is that they seem one-sided and for that reason unfair; however, the fact is that most such arrangements are to be found in commercial context where they do in fact make perfectly good sense and where there is no serious element of unfairness, so that in the result such contracts are normally upheld without too much difficulty.

[140] The fundamental issues discussed in ch 4 in relationship with *Arcos Ltd v EA Ronaasen and Son* [1933] AC 470 (HL) lay behind the attempt to exploit the requirements of certainty of agreement in *Hillas and Co v Arcos Ltd* (1932) 127 LT 503 (HL). Those issues were dealt with by the recently dramatically elevated Lord Wright applying the wisdom of the maxim 'words are to be interpreted so as to give effect to the subject matter rather than defeat it' to an option on its face devoid of essential detail: ibid 514 col 2:

> in contracts for future performance over a period, the parties may neither be able nor desire to specify many matters of detail, but leave them to be adjusted in the working out of the contract. Save for the legal implication [of the detail], such contracts might well be incomplete or uncertain; with that implication in reserve they are neither incomplete nor uncertain ... even if the construction of the words used may be difficult, that is not a reason for holding them too ambiguous or uncertain to be enforced if the fair meaning of the parties can be extracted.

[141] And so the occasions when doctrinal difficulties have actually caused problems, a situation which will be discussed below in connection with *Baird Textiles*, seem particularly unjustifiable: JN Adams, ' Consideration for Requirements Contracts' (1978) 73 Law Quarterly Review 73, 84:

> in spite of the prevalence of requirements contracts, the question of their legal enforceability may be of less importance than might be thought ... Whilst however the law of contract may in a sense be irrelevant to much of what goes on in real life, surely courts should not refuse recovery in the name of doctrinal tidiness when occasionally they are resorted to?

[142] CR Gutenberg, 'And Then There Were None: The Requirements Contract and the Buyer Who Does Not Buy' (1989) 64 Washington and Lee Law Review 871.

[143] A range of these is interestingly canvassed in the majority opinion handed down by Posner J in a case which Macneil and Gudel, *Contracts* (n 8) 302–12 excerpt to facilitate discussion of requirements contracts: *Empire Gas Corp v American Bakeries Co* 840 F 2d 1333 (US 7th Cir 1988). Kanne J's dissent, ibid 1342–43, turned, not on whether requirements could be reduced to zero, but on whether the operation of good faith required the buyer to explain itself.

seeking remedies for the breach of contracts which the parties fail to recognise are radically non-standard. In this chapter we have examined the attempts to plan for this when parties recognise their contracts are not standard, or discrete, but relational. This higher degree of self-consciousness of the nature of their obligations is what has emerged from the relational contract as it has so far been predominantly understood as a specie of contract.

But this higher degree of self-consciousness will be very difficult to fully grasp if, accepting that solipsistic self-interest is the basis of exchange and contract, one is unable to acknowledge that the standard, discrete contract itself rests on good faith. It is not good faith that distinguishes the discrete from the relational contract. Both rest on good faith. But in the former it is the good faith of accepting strict liability to perform a fixed obligation; in the latter it is the good faith of accepting (in itself a strict liability) to consciously co-operate in a process of adjustment. In Chapter 5, we saw that there is no logically or normatively compelling reason to accept consideration as the reason for the bindingness of contracts absent recognition of bargaining in good faith. The doctrinal hollowness produced by adherence to the classical conception of self-interest has led to the truly over-elaborate response to legitimate cases of adjustment in the, to repeat, Heath Robinson contraption of increasing and decreasing pacts. But it would seem that, on our current understanding, obligations to adjust in relational contracts also present 'one of the secret paradoxes of the Common Law'[144] just as much as strict responsibility in executory discrete contracts.

Prior to the vertical integration of Coal Mine, Macneil's smelter example is based on the agreement of various relational devices, including expert monitoring during a 20-year requirements contract. As Terence Daintith recognised some 30 years ago in connection with long-term retail distribution contracts, 'a more explicit judicial recognition of [the] relational components of [such] contracts [has] the attractions of [a] consequently increased harmony of judicial language and action'.[145] The hope that this could be realised generally has proven forlorn, and so we are left with the literal illogic of *High Trees* and *Williams v Roffey*. Let us now conclude this discussion by turning to the major obstacle to the progress which Daintith desired: the disregard of the relational contract in *Baird Textiles*, which must be put in the context of our understanding of industrial organisation.

Conclusion: The Place of the Relational Contract in Industrial Organisation

Though it received attention only after the appearance of the 'The Problem of Social Cost' in 1960,[146] it is significant that Coase's article on 'The Theory of the Firm'[147] was

[144] Anon (Sir Frederick Pollock), 'Review of JG Pease and AM Latter, *The Student's Summary of the Law of Contract*' (1914) 30 Law Quarterly Review 128, 129, discussed in ch 5.

[145] T Daintith, 'Vital Fluids: Beer and Petrol Distribution in English Law' in C Joerges (ed), *Franchising and the Law* (Nomos Verlag 1991) 177.

[146] RH Coase, 'The Problem of Social Cost' in *The Firm, the Market and the Law* (University of Chicago Press 1986).

[147] RH Coase, 'The Nature of the Firm' in *The Firm, the Market and the Law* (n 146) (hereafter Coase, 'The Nature of the Firm').

published, to little or no recognition, in 1937, and that Coase conceived its argument in 1932.[148] Coase began 'The Nature of the Firm' by addressing a then influential statement of what we can anachronistically recognise as general competition and asked whether this was an accurate description of empirical market economies. Answering that it was in fact 'a very incomplete' picture',[149] Coase pointed to the existence of firms in the market economy, for within firms allocation is by command under the hierarchical authority of management, ie is by planning which is private but nevertheless is 'akin to what is normally called economic planning',[150] and therefore 'the distinguishing mark of the firm is the suppression of the price mechanism,'[151] for which 'is substituted the entrepreneur-co-ordinator, who directs production'.[152] But if general competition automatically yielded a Pareto optimum, why should the market ever be voluntarily suppressed? Coase's answer was that the presence of the transaction costs of exchange sets a limit to the exchanges necessary for Pareto optimality, and this being the case, methods of allocation other than the market might be better than the market.

Coase was at this time a socialist enthusiastic about the possibilities of public ownership, and the question that drove the research that led to 'The Nature of the Firm' was whether a generally planned economy could be superior to a market economy.[153] Thinking, not merely communist or socialist thinking, on the firm was dominated by the concept of returns to scale, which seemed to convey an overwhelming advantage to increasing the size of economic organisations, and initially it was not obvious to Coase why it would not be wise to run an economy, as Lenin had put it, 'like a single factory' under 'complete planning'.[154] Coase's socialism was initially somewhat modified (and subsequently completely 'fell away' as he himself later put it)[155] because over the course of writing 'The Nature of the Firm' he arrived at the view that in a competitive market economy the relationship of private planning within firms and market allocation outside them was in principle hugely superior to general planning.

The market not being costless, the firm will emerge as an alternative. However, the firm has its own transaction costs, the costs of private hierarchy, and there will come a point where the firm reaches its optimum size because its further growth would

[148] RH Coase, 'The Institutional Structure of Production' in *Essays on Economics and Economists* (University of Chicago Press 1994) 8. These articles were the two works specifically cited when Coase was awarded the Nobel Prize in 1991, and as Coase, born 1910, said 'it is a strange experience to be praised in my eighties for work I did in my twenties' (ibid).

[149] Coase, 'The Nature of the Firm' (n 147) 35.

[150] ibid.

[151] ibid 36.

[152] ibid 35–36. Though Coase had taken some law classes in the course of his BCom degree, he was careful to limit his claim to competence in the handling of legal materials and doctrine, but in 'The Nature of the Firm' he showed great understanding of the nature of a contract of service as it makes possible the planned direction of labour.

Coase has not, in my opinion, received sufficient credit for being an economist of his generation prepared to, within his powers, properly engage with legal doctrine; not even, incredible to say, in respect of the law of nuisance, our understanding of which he has transformed: D Campbell and M Klaes. 'What Did Ronald Coase Know About the Law of Tort?' (2016) 39 Melbourne University Law Review 793.

[153] D Campbell and M Klaes, 'The Principle of Institutional Direction: Coase's Regulatory Critique of Intervention' (2005) 29 Cambridge Journal of Economics 263.

[154] VI Lenin, 'The State and Revolution' in *Collected Works*, vol 25 (Progress Publishers 1964) 474, 433.

[155] RH Coase, 'The Nature of the Firm: Origin' in OE Williamson and SG Winter (eds), *The Nature of the Firm* (OUP 1991) 39.

involve bringing within the firm allocations which it would be cheaper to leave to the market outside the firm. Within a competitive market economy, the size of firms, and hence the overall optimum size of the firm sector (and therefore the market sector) will be determined by 'competition' between market allocation and planned allocation, and this is an enormous advantage over the generally planned economy from which such competition is theoretically eliminated: 'In a competitive system, there is an "optimum" amount of planning!'[156]

This claim, or Coase's particular formulation of it, has become a cornerstone of the welfare argument for the general market economy, not only in contrast to the generally planned economy, but, as it were, internal to the market economy itself. It is at least part of a reconciliation of the existence within the market economy of organisational elements of 'monopoly' as it was defined in Chapter 6, with the belief, central to the later Coase's views but clearly traceable to the process of writing 'The Nature of the Firm', that, 'broadly speaking',[157] 'our economic system is in the main competitive'.[158] 'The Nature of the Firm' was written against a background of dissatisfaction with 'black box' conceptions of the firm, in which planning within the firm was given no effective role as outputs were regarded entirely as a function of the prices of the factors of production and anticipated demand. Coase himself referred to an influential formulation of this dissatisfaction, DH Robertson finding in the market economy 'islands of conscious co-operation like lumps of butter coagulating in a pail of buttermilk'.[159] The merit of Coase's formulation is that it not merely notes the existence of extensive private planning, but coherently relates the growth and size of firms, and therefore the sizes of the sectors of private planning and unplanned market allocation, to the competitive environment of the general market economy, and so provides a general framework for the economic, but at its heart institutionally informed, analysis of what is generally called industrial organisation.[160]

Of the important criticisms that have been made of Coase's argument, the one that is directly relevant to our concerns here, is not entirely a fair one. Even in 'The Nature of the Firm', Coase did not draw a 'simplistic' contrast between 'firm' and 'market' allocation.[161] He instead allowed that 'the degree to which the price mechanism is superseded varies greatly [and so] the amount of "vertical" integration ... varies greatly from industry to industry and from firm to firm',[162] with the implication that in general 'it is not possible to draw a hard and fast line which determines whether there is a firm or not'.[163] Coase used what are now recognised as requirements contracts to

[156] Coase, 'The Nature of the Firm' (n 147) 37 n 14. See further Coase, '"The Nature of the Firm": Origin', ibid 38–39.

[157] RH Coase, 'George J Stigler' in *Essays on Economics and Economists* (n 148) 203.

[158] RH Coase, 'The Nature of the Firm: Meaning' in Williamson and Winter (eds), *The Nature of the Firm* (n 155) 54 (hereafter Coase, 'Meaning').

[159] Coase, 'The Nature of the Firm' (n 147) 35; quoting DH Robertson, *Control of Industry* (rev edn, CUP 1928) 85 (now DH Robertson and S Dennison, *Control of Industry* (new edn, CUP 1960) 73).

[160] RH Coase, 'Industrial Organisation: A Proposal for Research' in *The Firm, the Market and the Law* (n 146) 61–62.

[161] Coase, 'Meaning' (n 158) 55; responding to B Klein, RG Crawford, and AA Alchian, 'Vertical Integration, Appropriable Rents and the Competitive Contracting Process' (1976) 21 Journal of Law and Economics 297, 326.

[162] Coase, 'The Nature of the Firm' (n 147) 36.

[163] ibid 40 n 21.

illustrate a stage between 'a very short-term contract' and the emergence of a firm.[164] In later work, Coase himself produced notable case studies of the behaviour of firms which occupied such stages in the organisation of their industry,[165] and, through his editorship of the *Journal of Law and Economics* and other uses of the stature he enjoyed sought to encourage detailed work on the contractual arrangements entered into by firms.

It nevertheless is the case that Coase himself did not attempt to provide any general theoretical account of the range of institutional organisational forms of statement. This type of work was not, in fact, his métier. It has principally been Oliver Williamson who has integrated Coase's comparison of the transaction costs of market and firm with other seminal contributions to the analysis of *inter alia* bounded rationality, opportunism, authority, and trust to produce a new institutional, or transaction cost, economics of the industrial organisation of the general market economy.[166] In this account, Macneil's relational contract (and the distinction between the discrete and the relational contract) plays a vital role,[167] for Williamson adopts the spectrum of contracts, and then expands the forms of contract it includes to include hierarchical organisation,[168] in which acceptance of what Barnard seminally called the 'authority' of the executive[169] displaces contractual non-tuism.[170] Macneil's relational contract has in this way been made an important component of the analysis of certain central questions of economics.[171]

The full significance of this for our concerns can emerge only when it is appreciated that the intermingled fluidity of the forms that contracts and firms may take along Williamson's expanded spectrum speaks of a crucial, welfare-enhancing feature of the market economy. Competition is by no means restricted to price (or quality, sales effort, etc) set within 'within a rigid pattern of invariant conditions, methods of

[164] ibid 40. The treatment of the law of sales in 'The Nature of the Firm' is perfunctory.

[165] RH Coase, 'The Acquisition of Fisher Body by General Motors' (2000) 43 Journal of Law and Economics 15. This paper's criticism of an earlier analysis of the episode by Benjamin Klein and others generated a highly charged debate: R Coase, 'The Conduct of Economics: The Example of Fisher Body and General Motors' (2006) 15 Journal of Economics and Management Strategy 255.

[166] Coase was always very generous about Williamson's role in the formulation of an approach which, as he was obliged to acknowledge RH Coase, 'The New Institutional Economics' (1998) 88(2) American Economic Review (Papers and Proceedings) 72), was commonly traced to him: RH Coase, 'Coase on Posner on Coase' (1993) 149 Journal of Institutional and Theoretical Economics 96, 98:

> Williamson's influence has been immense. In a real sense, transaction cost economics, through his writing and teaching, is his creation.

[167] Williamson was at pains to stress Macneil's part: OE Williamson, *The Mechanisms of Organisation* (OUP 1996) 355–56.

[168] Williamson, *Economic Institutions* (n 72) ch 3.

[169] CI Barnard, *The Function of the Executive* (Harvard University Press 1938) ch 12. To what extent, if any, those in the role of employee do or should recognise this authority is, of course, amongst the most controversial of social issues. But, in contrast to the agency theory of the firm, the institutional economics of the firm grounded in empirical analysis stands on the claim that employees largely do and should recognise this authority.

[170] In the way it also displaces non-tuism, the fiduciary obligation proper is, on our current understanding, a difficult boundary case between contract and hierarchy. An attempt to, if this is the right word, unify the economic and sociological categories which interestingly runs up against that difficulty is DG Smith, 'The Critical Resource Theory of Fiduciary Duty' (2002) 55 Vanderbilt Law Review 1399.

[171] J McLaughlin and R Eladi, 'Ian Macneil and the Relational Contract Theory: Evidence of Impact' (2014) 20 Journal of Management History 44.

production and forms of industrial organisation'.[172] Rather, 'in capitalist reality [the] kind of competition that counts'[173] is competition for:

> the new consumers' goods, the new methods of production or transportation, the new markets, the new forms of industrial organisation that capitalist enterprise creates ... organisational development from the craft shop and factory to such concerns as US steel illustrate ... the ... process of Creative Destruction that is the essential fact about capitalism.[174]

The law of contract has to set a framework for economic action, and we have seen that it has to be a framework which facilitates freedom of choice. But this must apply to business organisations' choice of contract terms, and, we now see, forms of contractual and non-contractual organisation.

It took, as has been said, the 1960 publication of 'The Problem of Social Cost' for the 'The Nature of the Firm' to be brought into proper perspective. It was at this time that, essentially independently of the US-dominated new institutionalism,[175] a fruitful, though largely marginal to the core concerns of professional economics,[176] 'neo-Marshallian'[177] tradition in post-war British economics made what can now be seen as a parallel contribution to the theory of industrial organisation.[178] 'The

[172] JA Schumpeter, *Capitalism, Socialism and Democracy* (5th edn, George Allen & Unwin, 1976) 84.

[173] ibid.

[174] ibid 83.

[175] FH Stephen, 'Economics and Work Organisation' in FH Stephen (ed), *Firms, Organisation and Labour* (Macmillan 1984). This brief review of the field is an introduction to a set of economics papers presented at a 1982 UK conference which included contributions by Williamson (and Professors Goldberg and Marglin).

The first UK work on industrial organisation of which I am aware which made an attempt to develop a position based in detail on Williamson (and therefore on Coase and Macneil) was made by a legal academic: T Daintith, 'The Design and Performance of Long-term Contracts' in T Daintith and G Teuber (eds), *Contract and Organisation* (De Gruyter 1986). This outstanding paper has not received the recognition it deserves, especially for its acute analysis of 'Macaulay's non-use' even in so important an activity as the worldwide trade in iron ore.

[176] The figure I am about to discuss, GB Richardson, became so discouraged by a lack of attention paid to his views that is reminiscent of the early fate of 'The Nature of the Firm' that in 1974, two years after his now recognised as seminal paper on 'The Organisation of Industry' on which I will focus was published, he withdrew from academic research at the age of 50 and became the Chief Executive of Oxford University Press. (He had much other experience of business and public regulation of business; GB Richardson 'Introduction' in *The Economics of Imperfect Competition* (Edward Elgar 1998)). His significance began to be properly appreciated only in the 1990s: PE Earl, 'George Richardson's Career and the Literature of Economics' in NJ Foss and BJ Loasby (eds), *Economic Organisation, Capabilities and Co-ordination* (Routledge 1998).

[177] Alfred Marshall, Professor Political Economy at Cambridge between 1885 to 1908, can be regarded as, if not a founder, then the first to give a general statement of neo-classical economics in his *Principles of Economics* (variorum edn, Macmillan 1961), which first appeared in 1890. Though undoubtedly the most important figure in the founding of professional economics in the UK, Marshall was highly sceptical of what he saw as a threatening tendency of economics to over-emphasise mathematical and abstract approaches at the cost of empirical relevance. He himself produced a number of important empirical studies, notably *Industry and Trade* (Macmillan 1919). The British neo-Marshallian tradition both attempts to develop theoretical concepts specific to Marshall and more generally to confine theoretical analysis to a role conducive to the production of work of empirical relevance. In this last sense, Coase saw his own approach as fundamentally Marshallian: RH Coase, 'Marshall on Method' in *Essays on Economics and Economists* (University of Chicago Press 1994).

[178] PWS Andrews, 'Industrial Analysis in Economics: With Especial Reference to Marshallian Doctrine' in *The Economics of Competitive Enterprise* (Edward Elgar 1993).

Organisation of Industry', the principal paper on this topic of one of the central figures, GB Richardson, was published in 1972.[179] It was, unbeknown to Richardson,[180] effectively a critique of 'The Theory of the Firm', and an anticipation of the broad direction in which Williamson took the discussion,[181] and indeed is of greater interest on the specific form of co-ordination on which Richardson focused, inter-firm co-operation. Richardson wrote:

> I was once in the habit of telling pupils that firms might be envisaged as islands of planned co-ordination in a sea of market relations. This now seems to me a highly misleading account of the way in which industry is in fact organised. The underlying idea, of course, was of the existence of two ways in which economic activity could be co-ordinated, the one, conscious planning, holding sway within firms, the other, the price mechanism, operating spontaneously on the relations between firms and between firms and their customers ... I imagine that this account of things might be acceptable, as a harmless first approximation, to a large number of economists. And yet ... it ignores the existence of a whole species of industrial activity which, on the face of it, is relevant to the manner in which co-ordination is achieved ... What I have in mind is the dense network of affiliation by which firms are inter-related ... if the student closes his textbook and takes up a business history, or the financial pages of a newspaper, or a report of the Monopolies Commission ...he may find [that Firm A] is a joint subsidiary of firms B and C, has technical agreements with D and E, sub-contracts work to F, is in marketing association with G and so on. So complex and ramified are these arrangements, indeed, that the skills of a genealogist rather than an economist might often seem appropriate for their disentanglement ... Firms are not islands but are linked together in patterns of co-operation and affiliation. Planned co-ordination does not stop at the frontiers of the individual firm but can be effected through co-operation between firms. The dichotomy between firm and market, between directed and spontaneous co-operation, is misleading; it ignores the institutional fact of inter-firm co-operation and the assumes away the distinct method of co-ordination that this can provide.[182]

The detail of Richardson's explanation of this form—its 'distinct method'—need not concern us here, but in essence he argues it arises because certain activities must be co-ordinated to a degree that cannot as a practical matter possibly be achieved through repeated discrete exchanges,[183] but those activities remain so dissimilar that completely

[179] GB Richardson, 'The Organisation of Industry' in *The Economics of Imperfect Competition* (Edward Elgar 1998) (hereafter Richardson, 'Organisation'). See further GB Richardson, 'Some Principles of Economic Organisation' in NJ Foss and BJ Loasby (eds), *Economic Organisation, Capabilities and Co-ordination* (Routledge 1998).

[180] The paper ends with a footnote reference to Coase which appears to be a mere addition, an impression confirmed by a passage in the 'Introduction' written for *The Economics of Imperfect Competition* (n 176) xvii.

[181] Though it is not the point on which I shall focus, Richardson's overall conception of industrial organisation was of a 'continuum' comparable to Williamson's expansion of Macneil's spectrum, though stopping at inter-firm co-operation, so not extending to full integration: Richardson, 'Organisation' (n 179) 147.

[182] ibid 143–44, 155. Richardson did not make explicit his reference to Robertson, but would have been right to assume that his audience in the *Economic Journal* will have appreciated it.

[183] ibid 150.

integrating them under a single corporate authority would place an avoidable and excessive burden on that authority (which, I might add, then would have to try to replicate, inevitably in an inferior way, the inter-firm co-operation through a form of intra-firm delegation).[184] Though its precise nature and significance is a matter of legitimate dispute,[185] that Richardson did describe an important dimension of organisation within the market economy is not.[186] This is in itself sufficiently shown by the fact that one of the examples Richardson gave of the 'fullest manifestation' of this form was Marks and Spencer, rightly regarded as Richardson wrote as an immense national success.[187] Marks and Spencer could, Richardson tells us, 'Nominally' be classified as a retail chain:

> but in reality they are the engineers or architects of complex and extended patterns of co-ordinated activity. Not only do Marks and Spencer tell their suppliers how much they wish to buy from them, and thus promote a quantitative adjustment of supply to demand, they concern themselves equally with the specification and development of both process and products. They decide, for example, the design of a garment, specify the cloth to be used and control the process even to laying down the types of needles to be used in knitting and sewing ... Marks and Spencer have laboratories in which, for example, there is development work on the use of nylon, polyester and acrylic fibres. Yet all this orchestration of development, manufacture and marketing takes place without any shareholding by Marks and Spencer in its suppliers and without even long-term contracts ... The co-operation of Marks and Spencer and its suppliers is based most obviously on a division of labour between production and marketing; but ... Marks and Spencer performs a variety of services in the field of product development and process control ...beyond the capability of the supplying firms.[188]

In February 2001, the Court of Appeal was required to address an agreement the form of which was a significant element of the organisation of Marks and Spencer's business, and refused to give it any legal weight whatsoever. Baird Textile Holdings Ltd had for over 30 years been one of the main suppliers of clothing to Marks and Spencer, until in 1999, by which time it was one of only four such suppliers, Marks and Spencer, without prior notice, declared its intention to end that relationship at the expiry of the

[184] ibid 152.

[185] Perhaps the principal use to which Richardson's and other neo-Marshallian's views have been put is in the analysis of the 'clustering' of industries in what are now called 'Marshallian industrial districts', the discussion being traced to Marshall, *Principles* (n 177) ch 10. Of value in itself, this treatment associates Richardson's views with a 'local' rather than a general form or organisation, and so does not in my opinion represent the fullest exploitation of those views. Rather it to some extent represents the dominance of the views identified with Williamson over the way those concerned to capture real institutional structures now approach the general market economy.

[186] R Arena and C Charbit, 'Marshall, Andrews and Richardson on Markets: An Interpretation' in NJ Foss and BJ Loasby (eds), *Economic Organisation, Capabilities and Co-ordination* (Routledge 1998).

[187] In 1960 Andrews (PWS Andrews and FA Friday, *Fair Trade* (Macmillan 1960) 56) observed that:

> in one lifetime Marks and Spencer have changed from everything-at-a-penny barrows in a small North of England area to nation-wide 'penny bazaars', and thence to the great multiple chain store with a specialisation in clothing, whose contribution to the standard of living in Britain no-one of working-class origins can overlook.

[188] Richardson, 'Organisation' (n 179) 145–46, 152.

then current production season.[189] In line with Marks and Spencer's long established practice, its relationship with Baird had been conducted though complex links over Baird's management, its planning in all areas and its conduct of production that very fulsomely fleshes out the inter-firm co-operation that Richardson described, indeed extending it as Marks and Spencer exercised very extensive influence over Baird's corporate strategy in dealing with and even acquiring other businesses, and in making investment in its business generally.[190]

Richardson emphasised that though he sought to draw attention to inter-firm co-operation, he:

> by no means [took] the view that where there is co-operation, competition is no more. Marks and Spencer can drop a supplier ... Firms form partners for a dance but, when the music stops, they can change them. In these circumstances competition is still at work even if it has changed its mode of operation.[191]

This possibility no doubt is an attraction of inter-firm co-operation as it reduces the organisational, commercial, and legal difficulties which would attend ever having to reduce the scope or size of a fully integrated operation. Nevertheless, Richardson maintained that:

> The essence of co-operative arrangements ... would seem to be the fact that the parties accept them with some degree of obligation—and therefore some degree of assurance—with respect to their future conduct. But there is certainly room for an infinite variation in the scope of such assurances and in the degree of formality with which they are expressed. The blanket manufacturer who takes a large order from |Marks and Spencer commits himself by taking the appropriate investment and organisational decisions; and he does so in the expectation that this company will continue to put business his way. In this instance, the purchasing company gives no formal assurance but its past behaviour provides suppliers with reason to expect that they can normally rely on getting further orders on acceptable terms. The qualification 'normally' is, of course, important, and the supplier is aware that the condition of orders is conditional on sustained demand for blankets, satisfaction with the quality of his manufacture and so on. In a case such as this any formal specification of the

[189] *Baird Textiles* CA (n 111) [1], [5]. The background to the case was an extremely profound shift in Marks and Spencer's former policy of typically obtaining very long-term supply from a small number of British sources to seeking supply from a range of overseas sources with much lower unit labour costs: N Tait, 'Marks and Spencer Dramatically Shifts Supplier Base' (2000) 41(6) Bobbin 20. This followed a remarkable turndown in Marks and Spencer's trading performance at the end of the 1990s which in its turn led to the acrimonious removal of the company's long served and formerly extremely successful Chairman and Chief Executive Sir Richard Greenbury: G Beaver, 'Competitive Advantage and Corporate Governance: Shop Soiled and Needing Attention! The Case of Marks and Spencer plc' (1999) 8 Strategic Change 325. Sir Richard gave evidence for Baird about the nature of its relationship with Marks and Spencer under the former strategy, the facts of which were not challenged.

[190] The most convenient summary of the situation is in Baird's statement of claim which Morison J quoted at length when ruling on Marks and Spencer's application for summary judgment before trial: *Baird Textile Holdings Ltd v Marks and Spencer plc* [2000] All ER (D) 865 (Com Ct) [8].

[191] Richardson, 'Organisation' (n 179) 155–56.

> terms and conditions of the assurance given ... would scarcely be practicable and the function of good will and reputation is to render it unnecessary.[192]

In one of the most blatant ever examples of the law of contract's classical doctrines preventing it from coming to terms with the realities of a commercial situation, it was held in *Baird Textiles* that no contract could be implied for want of certainty.[193] It is hardly specific to *Baird Textiles*, though the case certainly is a strong example, that there could be no question of enforcing a contract in the sense of ensuring that future detailed commitments, whatever they were, were performed. How could the courts even know what those commitments were when the whole point is that the parties didn't? But this was not the nature of the relief sought. Before the breakdown in their relationship, that relationship accounted for between 30% and 40% of Baird's annual turnover, and something approaching 20% of Marks and Spencer's clothing purchases, with a value of circa £200 million.[194] What was sought was damages of £53.6 million representing lost expectation and reliance estimated over the three years which would in the circumstances have been the period of reasonable notice of termination.[195]

But the very nature of the contract Baird claimed to exist was turned even against this, for it was held that co-operation over repeatedly fixing and adjusting the terms of supply meant that there was no:

> objective criteria by which to assess what was a reasonable quantity or price [Marks and Spencer did not allocate] business from year to year in accordance with some formula ... The annual allocation was separately determined in each year in the light of the circumstances then prevailing.[196]

From this it was concluded that the claim for damages had no prospect of success when, with respect, the *petitio principii* involved in this conclusion is stark. If Marks and Spencer could just end the relationship, the damages were uncertain, or indeed non-existent. But if it couldn't, then those damages were quantifiable to a perfectly acceptably certain standard based on evidence of previous trading.

Baird Textiles has been criticised by Mulcahy and Andrews from a relational perspective drawing on Macneil, the basic thrust of which is that the 'contractual umbrella' which Baird argued had existed,[197] and which, in the sense of there being some such economic arrangement, unarguably did exist, should be recognised to be

[192] ibid 146.

[193] I set aside the subsidiary argument that 'the lack of certainty confirms the absence of any clear evidence of an intention to create legal relations' (*Baird Textiles* CA (n 111)) as a rhetorical innovation supporting the unarguably uncomfortable conclusion about uncertainty. It would be wrong to deny there are varying uses of the doctrine, but, as was discussed in ch 5, if it is used at all precisely, the intention to create legal relations argument is applied to deny enforceability to identifiable agreements, not to deny that they were agreements.

[194] ibid [5].

[195] ibid [11]. When obliged to argue the estoppel in the alternative, it seems Baird tried to state all its losses in terms of reliance in order to avoid the obvious doctrinal problems, but found itself dragged down into the morass of those problems by a Court of Appeal utterly unable to look through the doctrine to the actual issues: ibid [78]–[98].

[196] ibid [29].

[197] ibid [7], [22].

an enforceable contract, which is what the Court of Appeal denied.[198] Mulcahy and Andrew's exposure of the Court of Appeal's incapacity to even recognise the commercial necessity of the law of contract facilitating what in this chapter has been called adjustment is very telling,[199] and the points of relational theory about which I would disagree with them are, with an exception shortly to be discussed, so relatively minor that their discussion here would be unjustified. But what does recognising an umbrella *contract* involve?

In their discussion of umbrella contracts, Mouzas and Furmston emphasise the economic value of umbrella 'agreements' using *Baird Textiles* as an example, and conclude that 'contracting parties need to draft their umbrella agreements in such a way that their expectations are manifested with certainty and predictability [in a way which will be recognised by the courts ignorant of or averse to the relational theory], and they need to include mechanisms for continuous negotiation'.[200] Now, of course, after *Baird Textiles*, this may well be good advice. Were the law in the state left by *Baird Textiles*, a party in a situation like Baird's would be very wise to do as Mouzas and Furmston say, ie try to give their agreements sufficient 'certainty' that an English court would recognise them. But this would be to require Baird and Marks and Spencer to do exactly what they did not want to do, obliging them to give up at least some of the economic advantages of the form of organisation they chose in order to obtain its legal recognition.[201] This is not what the law of contract is meant to do; in fact frustrating the parties' choice of form of organisation because that form is not congruent with uncomprehending doctrine is the very opposite of what the law of contract is meant to do.[202]

Highly conscious of the extreme undesirability, in fact impossibility, of the courts 'gap-filling' the details of Baird's and Marks and Spencer's performance, Morgan has generalised this into an argument about the undesirability and impossibility of enforcing complex relational norms, concluding that it is 'certainly' right that default rules should envisage discrete contracting, with the parties entirely free, of course, to elaborate on top of this relational norms the legal enforcement of which

[198] L Mulcahy and C Andrews, '*Baird v Marks and Spencer*' in R Hunter, C McGlynn, and E Rackley (eds), *Feminist Judgments* (OUP 2010) 201–2.

[199] ibid 199–201. Right at its time—the issue is how far it continues to be so—L Mulcahy, 'Telling Tales About Relational Contracts' in D Campbell, L Mulcahy and S Wheeler (eds), *Changing Concepts of Contract* (Palgrave Macmillan 2013) 213 observed that:

> the judiciary has been unwilling to engage with the challenges posed by the work of scholars such as Macneil in any meaningful way.

[200] S Mouzas and MP Furmston, 'From Contract to Umbrella Agreement' [2008] Cambridge Law Journal 37, 49.

[201] In their paper, the overall argument of which I confess I find unclear, Mouzas and Furmston seem to recognise this: ibid 48:

> If Marks and Spencer had [originally chosen] to incorporate their deal with Baird in a legally enforceable agreement, it seems very unlikely that it would have survived without amendment or renegotiation for thirty years.

But this was not very unlikely; it was impossible. Baird and Marks and Spencer wanted greater possibility of adjustment than they thought compatible with a basic 'contract' which needed continuous 'amendment or renegotiation' in the way Mouzas and Furmston mean.

[202] Lord Mance expressed the correct principle in *Baird Textiles* CA (n 111) [78]; but unfortunately misinterpreted the parties' intentions.

is 'unnecessary'.[203] Writing at a different level of awareness of the theoretical issues than the Court of Appeal, Morgan is critical of an 'enigmatic and vague reference'[204] in the judgment of Morritt VC (not addressed by Mulcahy and Andrews or Mouzas and Furmston) on which, in my opinion, the case turns. My view of the matter is, however, the opposite of Morgan's.

Baird's argument of 'the wide proposition' that 'necessity' is not the test for the implication of a contract' was, with respect, very unwise, and this became clear when and Morris VC flatly dismissed that argument:

> In connection with the wide proposition counsel referred to academic discussion with regard to 'relational contracts' and the legal implications to which they may give rise. But the articles which he produced did not suggest that the normal rules as to the implication and formation of contracts or the usual requirements of certainty did not apply to 'relational contracts'. Accordingly it is to those rules that I turn.[205]

As we have seen, Baird made enormous investments in its reliance on a continuing relationship with Marks and Spencer. These could not possibly have been wise, in fact they would have been lunatic, had not that reliance been justified. One does not ask for implication of elaborately certain or definite details; one asks, despite the Court of Appeal's constant refrain, only for what is obvious and necessary for business efficacy when one asks that it be implied into Baird's and Marks and Spencer's relationship that it could not be summarily brought to an end. It is clear that Baird and Marks and Spencer's intention was not to have a court ever supply details of their relationship; but it was even more clear that it was their intention that simple abandonment of that relationship should be out of the question, and the relief sought of compensation for loss caused by a failure to provide notice was perfectly possible and wholly apposite.[206]

[203] J Morgan, 'In Defence of *Baird Textiles*' in Campbell and others (n 199) 187–91 (hereafter Morgan, *Baird Textiles*).

[204] ibid 169.

[205] *Baird Textiles* CA (n 111) [16].

[206] A rightly very influential paper, RE Scott, 'A Theory of Self-enforcing Indefinite Agreements' (2003) 103 Columbia Law Review 41, distinguished between requirements contracts and the like which are enforceable under US law, and 'deliberately incomplete' (ibid 1642) agreements such as that in *Baird Textiles* which, as much case law showed, are not enforceable. Professor Scott solved the 'puzzle' (ibid 1645) of the choice of parties to 'write deliberately incomplete agreements in the shadow of a robust indefiniteness doctrine' (ibid 1644) by reference to the parties' belief that the agreements were so mutually advantageous as to be self-enforcing. A strong commitment to the moral value of 'reciprocal fairness' (ibid 1661–75) played a large part in grounding this belief.

It does not seem consistent with acknowledgement of the legal history of the effort needed to get relatively simple requirements contracts recognised to strongly contrast their enforceability now to the unenforceability of deliberately incomplete contracts. But Scott generally does not pursue the idea of developing the tension within the current law so that *the law* better facilitates relational contracting because he largely discounts the possibility of such development. The point becomes acute when 'reciprocity fails' (ibid 1693). Even then Scott thinks that the law has no role because 'legal sanctions and voluntary co-operation may be incompatible' (*ibid*). If the remedy is literal enforcement of detailed obligations, then this is right. But a law of contract based on actualising the awareness of relational contracting as a form of the good faith basis of all contracts need not be confined to this remedy. Nor need such a law retain other classical doctrines the paradoxical acceptance of which has led Scott to long maintain a 'break' between the law of contract and relational contracting. It is the basic claim of this book that the development of the modern law of contract has been a process of the positive law itself relinquishing this acceptance.

When, after 30 years, the occasion arose that conduct wholly in contravention of the parties' intentions required the court to act, it was the parties' intention that it should act, and establishing this required merely the application of the 'normal rules as to the implication and formation of contracts'.[207] Had it been allowed to proceed to trial, the real issue of 'certainty' that would have had to be settled was, not what the parties would do in a continuing future relationship, but the quantification of Baird's loss. It is submitted that, even given the undoubted recent deterioration in Marks and Spencer's business prospects which is the background of the case, this would pose no difficulties not encountered in, if it may be put this way, ordinary complex litigation.

To take Morgan's point the other way round, it is, of course, important that parties should (let us leave issues of fraud and actual physical duress aside) be free to enter into arrangements entirely on an 'honour' basis, a widely used practice of commercial value discussed in Chapter 5. But, as was argued in that chapter, the honour basis is a pronounced moving away from the default position of liability integral to the very idea of contract, and so that basis simply cannot be accepted to be the result of a normal interpretation of business efficacy, *a fortiori* in a situation of a *Baird Textiles* complexity. (It is tangential to the point I am trying to make that I cannot possibly conceive of such a situation ever arising from negotiations on what was really an honour basis.) It seems, in fact, that there may be a flaw in Richardson's account of Marks and Spencer when he insisted that the company could 'drop a supplier'.[208] This would appear to be an occasion on which the verisimilitude Richardson characteristically obtained by use of the business vernacular let him down; but in fact Marks and Spencer could *never* 'drop' a supplier. It might bring its relationship with a supplier to an end because of the supplier's incompetence,[209] or, the situation Richardson envisaged, because there was projected to be no demand for the goods the supplier could possibly furnish. But this is not the same as dropping; it is the opposite of dropping.

I have said, and will say, very little about Baird's alternative pleading of an estoppel, not so much because the estoppel as sword is not the English law as because, as was argued in Chapter 5 and earlier in this chapter, it is completely unsatisfactory that promissory estoppel ever should yield a different outcome, of either sword or shield type, to contract. Baird surely highlights the shortcomings of our understanding of exchange and contract that have made recourse to estoppel seem necessary. Though *Baird Textiles* confirmed the sword not a shield aspect of the English law of promissory estoppel, all three judgments handed down in the Court of Appeal clearly held open the possibility of the English law adopting something like the Australian position under *Waltons Stores*, strongly hinting that if this had been the law, then liability could have been found in *Baird Textiles*.[210] It should be mentioned that this completely undermines the certainty point in *Baird Textiles*, for how could what was certain enough

[207] J Wightman, 'Commentary on *Baird Textile Holdings v Marks and Spencer Plc*' in R Hunter, C McGlynn, and E Rackley (eds), *Feminist Judgments* (OUP 2010) 188.

[208] See the text accompanying n 191.

[209] Sir Richard Greenbury's evidence was that even this never happened to a major supplier; rather high level meetings would be arranged to discuss the situation with the aim of revising the processes at fault: *Baird Textiles* CA (n 111) [3]. One nevertheless assumes totally fruitless meetings could have led to the relationship eventually being ended.

[210] ibid [39], [52]–[53], [96]–[98].

for an estoppel not be certain enough to be a contract?[211] But this is by no means the main point.

For how could it have been possible to fixate on a possible solution which could arise from a doctrine which had been known from its inception to be a forced and unsatisfactory innovation, instead of giving business efficacy to a commercial relationship, the existence and importance of which was never in doubt, by simple reference to the core values of the law of contract? The true significance of the reference to estoppel in *Baird Textiles* is what it tells us of the way that contract was viewed. It would have been possible, in the 'equitable' world of 'promise' and 'reliance' (and, by an extension the Court of Appeal itself was unequipped to make, of 'relational contracts') to enforce Baird's and Marks and Spencer's relationship. But the *Baird Textiles* Court of Appeal's world of classical contract is a world of solipsistic self-interest and, unless parties are bound according to definite rules, they can do as they wish. Even our best commentators make the mistake of portraying contract as an amoral system. Morgan explicitly hortatively says on the basis of his analysis of *Baird Textiles*: 'Long let the amorality of English commercial law continue'.[212] Dr Morgan means to criticise the view of relational contract as a 'warm, human co-operative relation' discussed in Chapter 2, and in this he is right. But the way he goes too far is significant. For amorality does not, as Morgan's other work overwhelmingly shows,[213] describe the character of the law of contract. I hope throughout this book to have plausibly argued that the mutual recognition of the parties, so flatly denied in *Baird Textiles*, is the immanent morality of the law of contract, which that law has striven to express through the concept of good faith. Why has consciousness of this immanent morality not emerged in an adequate form; and indeed has emerged in the markedly inadequate form of welfarism? It is to the underlying social dimensions of this question that we now turn in the conclusion of this book.

[211] Ibid [98].
[212] Morgan, *Baird Textiles* (n 203) 189.
[213] Eg his views on mitigation discussed in ch 8.

PART 3

CONCLUSION: THE NATURE OF ECONOMIC ACTION AND THE NATURE OF THE LAW OF CONTRACT

11
Absolute Knowledge of the Law of Contract

Absolute Knowledge

All of the major works of GWF Hegel are difficult to read, and the difficulty is extreme in the case of the *Phenomenology of Spirit*, even though Hegel conceived of this book as an introduction to the philosophical system he later set out in other works.[1] It would be entirely understandable if readers, looking for a less painful way to grasp the secret,[2] were lured by a final chapter entitled 'Absolute Knowing' to prematurely turn to the end. But should they do so, they would be terribly disappointed, for all they would find there is the material discussed earlier in the book, but now adequately restated in light of what has been learned from that discussion.[3]

In 'Mastery and Servitude', the section of the *Phenomenology* which develops the concept of mutual recognition central to our analysis of the law of contract,[4] the struggle between those enjoying positions of dominance attributable to social power and the dominated is shown to be fruitless even for the former. Domination seems to entail the satisfaction of respect from the dominated. But the dominant cannot obtain true self-consciousness of worth in this way, as they can never be assured of the authenticity of a respect which is based on explicit or implicit coercion. To obtain self-consciousness of worth, the dominant must recognise the hollowness of coerced

[1] GWF Hegel, *Phenomenology of Spirit* (CUP 2018) preface (hereafter Hegel, *Phenomenology*).

[2] Marx had a poor opinion of JH Stirling, *The Secret of Hegel* (2nd edn, Thoemmes 1990), a once influential but now completely obsolete commentary on Hegel first published in 1865. 'Hegel himself', in Marx's view, 'would not understand it': Letter from Karl Marx to Frederick Engels (23 May 1868) in K Marx and F Engels, *Collected Works*, vol 43 (Lawrence and Wishart 1988) 39. In his early studies, Marx had himself called the *Phenomenology* 'the secret of the Hegelian philosophy' (K Marx, 'Economic and Philosophical Manuscripts of 1844' in K Marx and F Engels, *Collected Works*, vol 3 (Lawrence and Wishart 1975) 329 (hereafter Marx, '1844 Manuscripts')), but by this he was referring to its function as an introduction as Hegel conceived it.

[3] TS Eliot, 'Little Gidding', *Four Quartets* in *The Poems of TS Eliot*, vol 1 (Faber & Faber 2015) 208:

And the end of all our exploring
Will be to arrive where we started
And know the place for the first time.

[4] Hegel, *Phenomenology* (n 1) 108–16.

Contractual Relations. David Campbell, Oxford University Press. © David Campbell 2022.
DOI: 10.1093/oso/9780198855156.003.0011

respect, and that genuine worth requires the replacement of the relationship of domination with a relationship of basic social equality, in which differences of natural power may be a source of genuine respect. Absolute knowledge of the adequate form of ethical life is universal mutual recognition. This argument does not require, indeed it must eschew, the application of a superior, exogenous moral principle to the relationship of the dominant and the dominated. It is an endogenous, immanent critique of the alienated satisfaction derived from coerced respect.

The argument of this book may be stated in this way: the satisfaction a party may obtain from solipsistically self-interested contractual action which renders agreement a mere show is illegitimate and inadequate. Contractual action which is legitimate because it actually constitutes an agreed bargain, and therefore constitutes a mutually advantageous exchange, must reproduce a relationship of mutual recognition of each party's autonomous power to choose. The law of contract must objectively state this requirement in laws which are facilitative conditions of the agreed bargain, and it has attempted to do through the development of a general concept of good faith. The ontological basis of exchange and contract is, not the individual economic actors or contracting parties, but their social relationship. Adequate consciousness of this ontology replaces solipsistic self-interest with self-interest formed in recognition of the social relationship of mutual recognition. This consciousness is absolute knowledge of the law of contract.[5] In light of the history of modern western political ideas and the influence of that history on our current theoretical and political understanding of the economic freedom of the individual, the achievement of this consciousness, which actualises individualism, should best be regarded as a form of socialism: liberal socialism.

Liberal socialism must be emphatically distinguished from an 'ethical' socialism which conceives of imposing an exogenous, higher moral principle upon economic action.[6] Having discussed RH Tawney's criticisms of the acquisitive society, surely the principal contribution to British ethical socialism,[7] in Chapter 1, I now merely repeat that Tawney fundamentally misunderstood the nature of self-interested economic

[5] I have benefitted from reading J von Platz, 'Absolute Freedom of Contract: Grotian Lessons for Libertarians' (2013) 25 Critical Review 107, but I must say I did so at least a decade after I first conceived of this chapter heading.

[6] Nothing could more clearly demonstrate the futility of seeking to draw hard and fast boundaries between unarguably overlapping varieties of political belief than the inclusion of Orwell, who in ch 1 was quoted when setting out the liberal socialism advocated here, as a major contributor to British ethical socialism in the principal work on the subject: N Dennis and AH Halsey, *English Ethical Socialism* (Clarendon Press 1988) ch 5. It is not in search of theoretical profundity (as distinguished from literary learning) that one turns to Orwell but for an atmosphere, rather than a philosophy, of live and let live, including the celebration of 'lowness' as a legitimate aspect of cultural life mentioned in ch 3. An account of ethical socialism that states that it 'requires of all its adherents an unusual integrity of private and public life' (ibid 97) was, with respect, bound to have trouble with Orwell, and in particular Dennis and Halsey have to endorse the Left Book Club's criticism of Orwell's contemptuous ridicule of displays of superior-mindedness by socialist and communist political activists when it, without consultation with the author, omitted that ridicule from the first edition of *The Road to Wigan Pier*, though they mention only the criticism and not the omission (ibid 104).

Putting the point the other way, Dennis and Halsey do not include TH Green, though, despite his truly liberal impulse acknowledged in ch 6, I believe his 'positive' views were akin to Tawney's: M Carter, *TH Green and the Development of Ethical Socialism* (Imprint Academic 2003).

[7] In a remarkable convergence of views, Hugh Gaitskell's opinion that Tawney was 'the Democratic socialist *par excellence*' (H Gaitskell, 'Postscript: An Appreciation' in RH Tawney, *The Radical Tradition* (Penguin 1964) 211 was echoed by Tony Benn's belief that there were 'none greater' than Tawney in the

action. The point that should be added here is that Tawney's criticisms were so fundamental as to amount to a denial that economic action even had a morality. 'Modern society', he believed, 'is sick through the *absence* of a moral ideal'.[8] But economic action does have a moral ideal, autonomy, and that ideal is the legitimate basis of the market economy. The entire point of liberal socialism is, not to pass a superior judgement on the substance of the exercise of economic freedom by an individual, but to actualise voluntary choice by that individual. The general economy of actualised choice is the social market, 'the only sort of free economy likely to survive in the years to come, and the only sort that deserves to survive'.[9]

The argument here will have completely failed if it is read as a yet further hortation to adopt a 'third way' between capitalism and socialism. The argument that liberal socialism is the actualisation of liberal individualism must, to put the point in a fulsome manner, retain and expand the celebration of the outcomes of exchange and contract as the product of freedom, even on occasions when those outcomes are believed to be substantively wrong. This is in sharp contrast to the tone of resigned acceptance with which advocates of the third way have sought to ally the profane 'efficiency' of 'the market' to the higher ethics of planned organisation, those ethics supposedly gaining effectiveness (indeed being saved from fatuity) by the appropriation 'of whatever elements [are thought] good from the [market] adversary [whilst] keeping up all the severity of ... former censures upon that adversary'.[10] The third way is merely a rhetorical trope excusing this *ad hocery*: the maximalist welfare state's equally tedious parallel to dialectical materialism's reduction of the dialectic to what Hegel had long previously called a 'monotonous formalism'.[11]

The self-congratulation about their daring novelty displayed by many of the leading contemporary exponents of the third way[12] reflects an ignorance or disregard of the fact that social democracy always has had,[13] because it has always had to have, the third way at its heart. Even its greatest contributors have failed adequately to draw a social morality from self-interest. In the first half of the 1930s one finds Beveridge looking for a 'halfway house between Cobden and Lenin',[14] and Keynes for a 'third alternative'

British 'tradition of socialist writing': T Benn, 'Foreword to the 1981 Edition' in RH Tawney, *The Attack and Other Papers* (Spokesman 1981).

[8] RH Tawney, *RH Tawney's Commonplace Book* (CUP 1972) 9 (6 May 1912) (emphasis added). *The Acquisitive Society*, first published in 1921, develops, and somewhat changes, the views expressed in RH Tawney, 'The Sickness of Acquisitive Society' (1919) 17 (no 67) Hibbert Journal 353, which were essentially reprinted in RH Tawney, *The Sickness of an Acquisitive Society* (Fabian Society 1920).

[9] J Gray, 'The Moral Foundations of Market Individualism' in *Beyond the New Right* (Routledge 1993) 123.

[10] E Caird, 'Individualism and Socialism' in D Boucher (ed), *The British Idealists* (CUP 1997) 179. *Apropos* of the point about to be made about the long history of the third way, it should be noted that Caird wrote this in 1897 with particular reference to the views of Sidney Ball, an important member of the early Fabian Society.

[11] Hegel, *Phenomenology* (n 1) 32.

[12] A Giddens, *The Third Way* (Polity Press 1998); P Mandelson and R Liddle, *The Blair Revolution* (Faber 1996) and P Mandelson, *The Blair Revolution Revisited* (Politico's 2002). Mr Blair himself conceived of this revolution as a restoration of 'ethical socialism' over a 'quasi-scientific ... economic determinism' derived from Marx: T Blair, *Socialism*, Fabian Pamphlet 565 (Fabian Society 1994) 2.

[13] P Diamond (ed), *New Labour's Old Roots* (Imprint Academic 2014). As a matter of UK party politics, Conservatism has, of course, also long had its third way: H Macmillan, *The Middle Way* (William Pickering 1994).

[14] WH Beveridge, 'Prices and Planning' in *Planning Under Socialism* (Longmans and Co 1936) 107.

to Asquith and Stalin.[15] But liberal socialism is not a third term. No clash between 'asocial', 'market', and 'social' intervention arises when self-interest is conceived of as social action which cannot exist without regulation and therefore must have an ultimately public justification; though that justification is that economic action has no social purpose. Cases for intervention should be claims that in exceptional, if perhaps extremely important, cases, an alternative governance structure imposing a purpose will improve welfare judged by the same social criterion.[16]

If the argument of this book is allowed to have plausibility, then a serious difficulty arises. Liberal socialism *should* emerge from the immanent critique of liberal individualism. But the end of *laissez faire* has yielded the maximalist welfare state, and with respect to our specific concerns, the death of the classical law of contract has yielded welfarism. The relational morality of exchange and contract in the form of a highly contested concept of good faith remains merely what Gunther Teubner memorably called an 'irritant' in the law of contract.[17] Why has this happened? The answer to this question requires us again to turn to the views of Karl Marx.

Marx's Critique of Alienation

The labour theory of value

As we saw in Chapter 2, Marx's criticism of capitalism is not fundamentally directed at inequality (or exploitation and immiseration) but at alienation. In the first instance, this is a criticism of the experience of work[18] reduced to 'abstract labour'[19]

[15] JM Keynes, 'Mr Keynes Replies to Shaw' in *Collected Writings*, vol 28 (CUP 2013) 32.

[16] RH Coase, 'The Problem of Social Cost' in *The Firm, the Market and the Law* (University of Chicago Press 1988) 154 (hereafter Coase, 'Social Cost'):

> it is, of course, desirable that the choice among different social arrangements for the solution of economic problems should be carried out in broader terms than [the value of production, as measured by the market] and that the total effect of these arrangements in all spheres of life should be taken into account.

I have discussed the role of what has been called here the social criterion in Coase's approach in D Campbell, 'Ronald Coase's "The Problem of Social Cost"' (2016) 35 University of Queensland Law Review 75, 82–86 (hereafter Campbell, 'Coase').

[17] G Teubner, 'Legal Irritants: Good Faith in British Law or How Unifying Law Ends Up in New Divergences' (1998) 61 Modern Law Review 11. My use of Teubner's felicitous term decouples it from the issues of legal transplantation on which he focused in this paper.

[18] K Marx, *Capital*, vol 1 in K Marx and F Engels, *Collected Works*, vol 35 (International Publishers 1996) 639 (hereafter Marx, *Capital*, vol 1):

> within the capitalist system, all methods for raising the social productiveness of labour are brought about at the cost of the individual labourer; all means for the development of production transform themselves into means of domination over, and exploitation of, the producers; they mutilate the labourer into a fragment of a man, degrade him to the appendage of a machine, destroy every remnant of charm in his work and turn it into hated toil; they estrange him from the intellectual potentialities of the labour process ... distort the conditions under which he works, subject him during the labour process to a despotism the more hateful for its meanness; they transform his lifetime into working time, and drag his wife and child under the wheels of the juggernaut of capital.

[19] ibid 51–56, 196–209.

when economic activity is directed towards the accumulation of profit, which is itself oriented towards the exchange-values of goods.[20] As economic activity is a matter of economic actors' mutual allocation of their labour; to direct it by profit and exchange-value constitutes, Marx argued, the profound alienation of labour's social ontology in 'a state of society in which the process of production has mastery over man instead of being controlled by him'.[21] Consciousness that economic activity is a social relationship is lost to economic actors as that relationship 'assumes, in their eyes, the fantastic form of a relation between [goods as] things' which Marx called the 'fetishism of commodities'.[22]

Marx's views on the alienation of labour were not principally derived from his studies of what he generally called 'classical political economy' but from his attempt to restate Hegel's own critique of alienated beliefs in the 'materialist' terms of a philosophical anthropology of 'labour' widely understood as humanity's active engagement with the natural world of which it is part.[23] But Marx, heavily influenced by a criticism of 'Modern economics . . . based on Adam Smith's *Wealth of Nations*' which Friedrich Engels published in 1844 in a journal Marx edited,[24] recognised at a very early stage in the development of his views that 'the anatomy of . . . civil society . . . has to be sought in political economy'.[25] He accordingly engaged in two periods of economic studies, the second of which, begun in 1858 when he became resident in London after expulsion from the Continent, led to the publication of volume one of *Capital* in 1867. So often dismissed as dogmatic or even in a derogatory sense theological, Marx's communism was based on *inter alia* an intellectually productive, because enormously scholarly, immanent critique of classical political economy.[26] It is only after acknowledging this that one can with decency argue that Marx's economics err in a most fundamental way, as I do in support of the criticism of welfarism in the final chapter of this book. But first, let us further explore the light that I have argued Marx's views shed on the inadequacy of the classical law.

[20] Ibid. I have whenever possible replaced Marx's term 'commodities' with 'goods'.

[21] ibid 92.

[22] ibid 83.

[23] These views of Marx as developed through a focus on the *Phenomenology* are set out in Marx, '1844 Manuscripts' (n 2) 330–46.

[24] F Engels, 'Outlines of a Critique of Political Economy' in K Marx and F Engels, *Collected Works*, vol 3 (Lawrence and Wishart 1975) 420. Marx fulsomely acknowledged his indebtedness to this work when, some 15 years later, he began the publication of his mature economic views: K Marx, *A Contribution to the Critique of Political Economy* in K Marx and F Engels, *Collected Works*, vol 29 (Lawrence and Wishart 1987) 262 (hereafter Marx, *Contribution*). This 'Preface' to *A Contribution to the Critique of Political Economy* became the principal statement of the 'materialist conception of history'.

[25] Marx, ibid 264.

[26] Eventually intended to be worked up into a fourth volume of *Capital* on 'the history of the theory' (Marx, *Capital*, vol 1 (n 18) 11), Marx's views on political economy were made available (in a somewhat abridged form) as *Theories of Surplus Value*, edited by Karl Kautsky, between 1905 and 1910, Kautsky taking this material from the enormous body of notes Marx wrote between 1861-63 which is now entirely available in English: K Marx, 'Economic Manuscript of 1861-63' in K Marx and F Engels, *Collected Works*, vols 30-34 (Lawrence and Wishart 1988-94) (hereafter Marx, '1861–63 Manuscript'). The overall interest of the *Theories* is perhaps most clearly demonstrated by II Rubin, *A History of Economic Thought* (2nd edn, Ink Links 1979), a textbook Rubin prepared for a course on the history of economic thought based on the *Theories* which was given in the USSR in the twenties, Rubin being purged in 1930, subsequently horribly treated, and killed probably in 1937.

The core concept of Marx's economics is, of course, the labour theory of value. We saw in Chapter 2 that Marx very strongly distinguished between the use-value and the exchange-value of a good, and he regarded this, or more precisely the analysis of the particular form it takes in the labour-process under capitalism,[27] as 'fundamental' to his contribution to economics.[28] A general exchange economy requires that goods are exchanged in regular proportions of each other, and this implies a common denominator between the goods determining that proportion. A good's use-value cannot form this denominator.[29] Use-values are use-values precisely because they are different, and to say the use-value of a pair of shoes can be measured in terms of a number of coats is senseless. The denominator must lie in exchange-value, or rather the value of each good which exchange-value expresses in a ratio, and:

> If ... we leave out of consideration the use-value of goods, they have only one common property left, that of being products of labour ... All that [goods] now tell us is that human labour has been expended in their production, that human labour is embodied in them. When looked at as crystals of this social substance, common to them all, [goods] are values.[30]

The determination of the value of a good is, then, exclusively a matter of labour inputs into exchange-values, with use-values playing no part:

> on a given basis of labour productivity the production of a certain quantity of articles in every particular sphere of production requires a definite quantity of social labour time ... this proportion ... has no inner relation to the usefulness of these articles or the special nature of their use values.[31]

Examined, as it were, qualitatively,[32] as a sociological claim[33] that it is the social relationships between economic actors which determine the production and consumption of goods, the labour theory of value is a profound truth.[34] By the fetishism of

[27] Marx, *Capital*, vol 1 (n 18) 51–56, 187–209.

[28] Letter from Karl Marx to Friedrich Engels (24 August 1867) in K Marx and F Engels, *Collected Works*, vol 42 (Lawrence and Wishart 1987) 407.

[29] In the developed capitalist economy the denominator is, of course, in the first instance money. But this can be put to one side as Marx's derivation of the function of money as the general medium of exchange from the theoretically and historically prior exchange of goods for one another, money as the universal good avoiding the limitations of barter, is at its core uncontroversial: Marx, *Capital*, vol 1 (n 18) 103–56.

[30] ibid 48.

[31] K Marx, *Capital*, vol 3 in K Marx and F Engels, *Collected Works*, vol 37 (Lawrence and Wishart 1998) pt 2 (hereafter Marx, *Capital*, vol 3).

[32] PM Sweezy, *The Theory of Capitalist Development* (Monthly Review Press 1942) ch 2.

[33] NI Bukharin, *Economic Theory of the Leisure Class* (Monthly Review Press 1972) 35–36:

> any economic theory depends on certain presuppositions having a sociological character and serving as the basis of an investigation of the economic phase of social life. Such presuppositions may be clearly expressed or may remain unformulated . . .but they cannot be absent. The political economy of Karl Marx possesses such a basis in the sociological theory of historical materialism.

[34] There is an element almost of tragedy about the way that the immense efforts Marx took over the presentation of the argument of *Capital* have not prevented it being the case that that argument is often more clearly presented in other of his writings, including correspondence and works unpublished at his death or not intended for publication. One of the leading works of British Marxist economics, MH Dobb, *The*

commodities, Marx was in the first instance criticising what he argued was an alienated belief, part of the structure of capitalism, that economic activity is determined by the values goods had as intrinsic, naturally given properties. In an example made famous by Smith as 'the paradox of value', diamonds are believed just to have greater value than water.[35] Beliefs of some such sort unarguably are ubiquitous features of life in the market economies, but this should be explained as a particular instance of a necessary abbreviation in our everyday understanding of complex social processes.[36] An every-day, and in that context perfectly defensible, belief that diamonds *are* more valuable than water held by all but the most obtuse would be open to a challenge[37] that would lead towards the social truth that the labour theory seeks to express.[38] But the intrinsic value of goods in this sense simply is not a feature of neo-classical economics, which are predicated on the recognition that prices are social constructs.[39]

It would be quite different if theoretical arguments that goods have an intrinsic value were persisted in, and, pointing to what unarguably were such arguments in economics prior to the marginal revolution,[40] Marx went on to claim that these arguments

Political Economy of Capitalism (2nd edn, Routledge & Kegan Paul 1940) 39 had recourse to quotation from 1847 *The Poverty of Philosophy* to describe the fundamental point at which the labour theory is trying to drive, and this was repeated in another work of such status, RL Meek, *Studies in the Labour Theory of Value* (2nd edn, Lawrence and Wishart 1973) 145. K Marx, *The Poverty of Philosophy* in K Marx and F Engels, *Collected Works*, vol 6 (Lawrence and Wishart 1976) 143 (hereafter Marx, *Poverty of Philosophy*) reads:

> In principle, there is no exchange of products—but there is the exchange of the labour which co-operates in production.

35 A Smith, *The Wealth of Nations* in *The Glasgow Edition of the Works and Correspondence* (Clarendon Press 1976) 44–45 (hereafter Smith, *Wealth of Nations*).

36 G Simmel, *The Philosophy of Money* (Routledge Classics edn, Routledge 2011) 186–88.

An attempt to draw on both this account of the 'reification' of social relationships with Marx's fetishism of commodities was made in G Lukács, *History and Class Consciousness* (Merlin Books 1973) 83–222. This attempt is, in my view, basically misdirected, but it certainly has had great influence on the history of social theory. György Lukács' whose early intellectual development was heavily influenced by Simmel, is arguably the greatest of interpreters of Marx, with *History and Class Consciousness* being, given the limited number of Marx's writings available when it was written, a miracle of understanding.

37 The challenge may, of course, not be purely theoretical, as in the 'story' Smith related in his lectures of a wealthy merchant who paid a huge price for water 'in the deserts of Arabia': A Smith, *Lectures on Jurisprudence* in *The Glasgow Edition of the Works and Correspondence*, vol 5 (Clarendon Press) 496 (hereafter Smith, *Lectures*).

38 Smith, *Wealth of Nations* (n 35) 49:

> The greater part of people . . . understand better what is meant by a quantity of a particular commodity than by a quantity of labour. The one is a plain palpable object; the other an abstract notion which, though it can be made sufficiently intelligible, is not altogether so natural and obvious. When . . . money has become the common instrument of commerce . . . it comes to pass that the exchangeable value of every commodity is more frequently estimated by the quantity of money than by the quantity of labour or of any other commodity which can be had in exchange for it.

39 C Menger, *Principles of Economics* (Libertarian Press 1994) 52 n 4, 120–21 (translation amended):

> it is evident that goods-character is nothing inherent in goods and is not a property of goods, but is merely a relationship between certain things and men, the things obviously ceasing to be goods with the disappearance of the relationship . . . Value is nothing inherent in goods, no property of them, nor an independent thing existing by itself. It is a judgement economising men make about the importance of the goods at their disposal for the maintenance of their lives and well-being.

40 Marx, *Capital*, vol 1 (n 18) 94.

reflected the generally alienated, capitalist understanding of economic activity. Squarely facing these arguments during his studies involved Marx in complexities now of interest only for the history of economics,[41] and his summary comments in *Capital* are sufficient here: 'So far no chemist has ever discovered exchange-value either in a pearl or a diamond'. Only 'economic discoverers' had done so.[42]

The labour theory also had, as it was of course required to have if it were to be corroborated by theoretical economics, a quantitative dimension in providing an account of the formation of prices, which after all are the determinants of economic activity as perceived by economic actors. The publications of *A Contribution to the Critique of Political Economy* in 1859 and volume one of *Capital* in 1867 received all but no notice,[43] and the theoretical discussion of Marx's economics which effectively began only after Engels published volume three in 1894 focused on the transformation of the values of goods into their prices which that volume set out.[44] The reader will no doubt be relieved that, as will be argued in the next and final chapter, Marx's concept of value is so profoundly mistaken a basis for his entire economics that it is unnecessary here to say anything about this 'transformation problem'. The point that must be noted here is that in moving from value to prices Marx was trying to explain the economic phenomena, if we understand the term strictly, of prices in terms to which the specific effects of the social relations constitutive of economic activity were, at each and every one of the explanation's many stages, absolutely intrinsic.

It was in this that Marx thought he moved beyond even those economists committed to the market for whom he had a profound respect because they themselves were grasping the truth of the labour theory, of which Smith and David Ricardo were markedly the most important.[45] In his earliest economic researches, Marx had in fact himself rejected the labour theory,[46] and was brought to belief in it by the study of particularly Ricardo.[47] With Smith and Ricardo in mind, in *Capital* Marx acknowledged that:

> Political economy has indeed analysed, however incompletely, value and its magnitude, and has discovered what lies beneath these forms. But it has never once asked the question why labour is represented by the value of its product and ... by the magnitude of that value.[48]

[41] Marx, '1861–63 Manuscript' (n 26) 298–305, 312–53.

[42] Marx, *Capital*, vol 1 (n 18) 94.

[43] Marx's wife's disappointment at the 'silence' which met the publication of her husband's books, the product of labours which dominated, and were frequently a grave burden on, her life and the lives of her children, is very moving: Letter from Jenny Marx to Friedrich Engels (23 or 24 December 1859) in K Marx and F Engels, *Collected Works*, vol 40 (Lawrence and Wishart 1983) 574 and Letter from Jenny Marx to Ludwig Kugelmann (24 December 1867) in K Marx and F Engels, *Collected Works*, vol 42 (Lawrence and Wishart 1987) 578.

[44] Marx, *Capital*, vol 3 (n 31) 185.

[45] Marx, '1861–63 Manuscript' (n 26) vol 31, 7–200, 387–578; vol 32, 7–208.

[46] K Marx, 'Comments on James Mill' in K Marx and F Engels, *Collected Works*, vol 3 (Lawrence and Wishart 1975) 211.

[47] Marx, *Poverty of Philosophy* (n 34) 120–25.

[48] Marx, *Capital*, vol 1 (n 18) 91.

But it is one thing to show that behind the exchange values of goods lies the truth that economic activity is a matter of social relationships. It is another thing again to ask why economic activity should have such a form that it is conducted on the basis of the general exchange of values. Even Smith and Ricardo, Marx argued, believed that capitalist exchange was the form of economic activity 'eternally fixed by Nature for every state of society',[49] and on this basis the social relationships that constitute 'the form of value' were simply accepted.[50]

Intended as a joke at the expense of socialist utopianism, Ricardo once contrasted the economics which will hold 'as long as society is constituted as it now is' to those which might apply to 'Mr Owen's parallelograms', by which, of course, he meant Robert Owen's new towns, which were organised on a grid pattern.[51] But in *A Contribution to the Critique of Political Economy*, Marx successfully turned the joke back on Ricardo.[52] Smith's presentation of the labour theory involved a description of the hunting of beavers and deer in an 'early and rude state of society', so that:

> If among a nation of hunters ... it usually costs twice the labour to kill a beaver which it does to kill a deer, one beaver should naturally exchange for or be worth two deer.[53]

When Ricardo sought to build upon Smith's views in *The Principles of Political Economy and Taxation*, one finds, as Marx observed, that these primitive hunters calculated the value of their tools and labours as if 'in accordance with the annuity tables in use on the London Stock Exchange in 1817'.[54] Ricardo, who prior to retiring to theoretical work had had great success on the financial markets, had the hunters, not merely proportionally valuing the different weapons necessary to kill a beaver and a deer, but taking into account, for example, nice considerations of amortisation:

> suppose the same quantity of labour was necessary to make both weapons, but that they were of very unequal durability; of the durable implement only a small portion of its value would be transferred to the commodity, a much greater portion of the value of the less durable implement would be realized in the commodity which it contributed to produce.[55]

49 ibid 91 n 2. Once again, there are fuller statements of the point elsewhere in Marx's writings, eg Marx, *Poverty of Philosophy* (n 34) 174:

> When the economists say that present-day relations—the relations of bourgeois production—are natural, they imply that these are ... in conformity with the laws of nature. These relations therefore are themselves natural laws independent of the influence of time. They are eternal laws which must always govern society.

50 Marx, *Capital*, vol 1 (n 18) 57–58.

51 D Ricardo, *On Protection to Agriculture* in *Works and Correspondence*, vol 4 (CUP 1962) 222.

52 Marx, *Contribution* (n 24) 300. The joke is repeated in condensed form in Marx, *Capital*, vol 1 (n 18) 87 n 1.

53 Smith, *Wealth of Nations* (n 35) 65.

54 Marx, *Contribution* (n 24) 300.

55 D Ricardo, *The Principles of Political Economy and Taxation* in *Works and Correspondence*, vol 1 (CUP 1951) 23.

Though Ricardo did indeed in this way make what remains an important point in economic theory (with which we are not concerned) in this passage, that this passage was not merely historically implausible[56] but in an important respect comically absurd did not strike Ricardo, nor a great number of subsequent commentators, and this affirms, I think, Marx's point about the conception of capitalist economic relations as eternal and natural: 'The parallelograms of Mr Owen appear to be the only form of society, besides the bourgeois form, with which [Ricardo] was acquainted'.[57] And Smith, it is essential to recall, advocated *laissez faire* because 'Little else is required to carry a state to the highest degree of affluence ... brought about by the natural course of things'[58] as 'the obvious and simple system of natural liberty establishes itself of its own accord'.[59] From its inception, Marx's entire economic thought can be seen as a rejection of this claim. But what are we to understand Smith to have meant by 'natural'?

The natural and the social in the Age of Commerce

Smith fundamentally ascribed the historically unprecedented wealth of what he called the 'Age of Commerce'[60] to the development of the economy-wide division of labour:

> It is the great multiplication of the division of labour which occasions, in a well-governed society, that universal opulence which extends itself to the lowest ranks of people ... without the assistance and co-operation of many thousands, the very meanest person in a civilized country could not be provided, even according to, what we very falsely imagine, the easy and simple manner in which he is commonly accommodated. Compared, indeed, with the more extravagant luxury of the great, his accommodation must appear extremely simple and easy; and yet it may be true, perhaps, that the accommodation of a European prince does not always so much exceed that of an industrious and frugal peasant as the accommodation of the latter exceeds that of many an African king, the absolute master of the lives and liberties of ten thousand naked savages.[61]

[56] MI Finley, *The Ancient Economy* (Chatto & Windus 1973) 21:

> [Alfred] Marshall's title [*The Principles of Economics*] cannot be translated into Greek or Latin. Neither can the basic terms such as labour, production, capital, investment, income, circulation, demand, liability, utility, at least not in the abstract form required for economic analysis. In stressing this, I am suggesting, not that the ancients were like Molière's M Jourdain who spoke prose without knowing it, but that they in fact lacked the concepts of an 'economy' and, *a fortiori*, that they lacked the conceptual elements which together constitute what we call 'the economy'. Of course, they farmed, traded, manufactured, mined, taxed, coined, deposited and loaned money, made profits or failed in their enterprises. What they did not do, however, was to combine these particular activities conceptually into a unit. Hence Aristotle, whose programme was to codify the branches of knowledge, wrote no *Economics*.

Marx's acute views on Aristotle on exchange may be found at Marx, *Capital*, vol 1 (n 18) 69–70.

[57] Marx, *Contribution* (n 24) 300.

[58] D Stewart, 'Account of the Life and Writings of Adam Smith LLD" in A Smith, *Essays on Philosophical Subjects* in *The Glasgow Edition of the Works and Correspondence*, vol 3 (Clarendon Press 1980) 322.

[59] Smith, *Wealth of Nations* (n 35) 687.

[60] Smith, *Lectures* (n 37) 14.

[61] Smith, *Wealth of Nations* (n 35) 22–24.

Though *The Wealth of Nations* is in large part a set of prescriptions for the governmental economic policies which will allow the division of labour to flourish, it would be misleading to say that Smith saw the division of labour as the *result* of such policies:

> This division of labour, from which so many advantages are derived, is not originally the effect of any human wisdom which foresees and intends that general opulence to which it gives occasion. It is the necessary, though very slow and gradual consequence of a certain propensity in human nature which has in view no such extensive utility: the propensity to truck, barter, and exchange one thing for another.[62]

Two strands to Smith's argument must be distinguished.

First, the entire point of Smith's view is that the Age of Commerce is not universal but must be distinguished from the earlier and ruder states of society from which it emerged. The Age of Commerce was the highest of 'four stages' in the development of human society, the preceding stages being the Age of Hunters, the Age of Shepherds, and the Age of Agriculture.[63] Marx's own periodisation of human progress[64] was influenced by the four stages theory,[65] and, though it markedly emphasised a theme of conflict which played only a subordinate role in that theory, is essentially comparable to it,[66] with one exception of immense significance to which we turn in the concluding chapter. But in one respect Marx's critique of the acceptance of the naturalness of capitalist economic activity implies a truly fundamental criticism of Smith's understanding of the Age of Commerce.

Of the source of the propensity to truck, barter, and exchange, Smith says:

> Whether this propensity be one of the original principles in human nature, of which no further account can be given; or whether, as seems more probable, it be the necessary consequence of the faculties of reason and speech, it belongs not to our present subject to inquire. It is common to all men, and to be found in no other race of animals ... Nobody ever saw a dog make a fair and deliberate exchange of one bone with another dog. Nobody ever saw one animal by its gestures and natural cries signify to another this is mine, that yours.[67]

It can be seen that Smith conceived of the propensity to truck, barter, and exchange in the form of a propensity to *exchange* in the 'fair and deliberate', ie proportionate

[62] ibid 24.

[63] Smith, *Lectures* (n 37) 14.

[64] Marx, *Contribution* (n 24) 263.

[65] Eg K Marx, 'Economic Manuscripts of 1857-8 [*Grundrisse*]' in K Marx and F Engels, *Collected Works*, vols 28-29 (Lawrence and Wishart 1986-87) vol 28, 24 (hereafter Marx, *Grundrisse*). These references in Smith, clearly central to the views Marx developed on wages and the working class, profits and the capitalist, and the limits to capitalist production, are to Smith, *Wealth of Nations* (n 35) 82–105, 111, 264–67.

[66] Letter from Karl Marx to Joseph Wedemeyer (5 March 1852) in K Marx and F Engels, *Collected Works*, vol 39 (Lawrence and Wishart 1983) 62.

I do not claim to have discovered either the existence of classes in modern society or the struggle between them. Long before me, bourgeois historians had described the historical development of this struggle between the classes, as had bourgeois economists their economic anatomy.

[67] Smith, *Wealth of Nations* (n 35) 25–26.

and consensual, manner in which exchange takes place in developed market economies, and this is read back into the calculations primitive hunters make about killing beavers and deer. This is to locate in an innate feature of human nature as such the social relationships which constitute market exchange, and this cannot be reconciled with the account of the forms of progress in the four stages theory and its culmination in the Age of Commerce. No-one ever saw a dog make an exchange; but no-one ever saw a primitive hunter make an exchange, if by exchange one means exchange displaying the relational properties of rational economic action this book has tried to describe which make a general market economy—the Age of Commerce—possible. The point is not only to *situate* one's economics in economic history and economic sociology, for, of course, Smith did this in a remarkable way in *The Wealth of Nations*,[68] which for this reason takes its place amongst those Scottish Enlightenment historical and social writings[69] which are some of the most important contributions of this sort ever made.[70] The point is to have an understanding of economic action which is not founded on what seem to be naturalistic assumptions about such action, but in which any assumptions made are in principle themselves to be understood in terms of the history, politics, and sociology which constitute the social ontology of the action.[71]

It does not, of course, remotely diminish Smith's achievement to say that the difficulties which the views criticised by Marx have created for our understanding of exchange, contract, economic action, and human progress have been very considerable, one of these being the persistence of an alienated view of economic action as solipsistic self-interest when such economic action integrally involves, as Smith certainly sought to say,[72] the external[73] and internal[74] facilitation of self-interest as mutual recognition.[75] With particular reference to our concerns here, in Chapter 1 emphasis was

[68] Eg ibid 689–95.

[69] The two works which have received most contemporary attention are A Ferguson, *An Essay on the History of Civil Society* (CUP 2012) and J Millar, *The Origin of the Distinction of Ranks* (Liberty Fund 2006).

[70] Marx therefore related his criticism of Smith and Ricardo to these works: Marx, *Grundrisse* (n 65) 17–18.

[71] JR Hicks, *Value and Capital* (2nd edn, Clarendon Press 1946) 23:

Pure economics has a remarkable way of producing rabbits out of a hat—apparently *a priori* propositions which apparently refer to reality. It is fascinating to try to discover how the rabbits got in; for those of us who do not believe in magic must be convinced that they got in somehow.

[72] D Campbell, 'Adam Smith and the Social Foundation of Agreement' (2017) 21 Edinburgh Law Review 376, 376–94.

[73] Smith, *Wealth of Nations* (n 35) 687 (emphasis added):

> Every man, *as long as he does not violate the laws of justice*, is left perfectly free to pursue his own interest in his own way.

[74] A Smith, *The Theory of Moral Sentiments* in *The Glasgow Edition of the Works and Correspondence* (Clarendon Press 1976) 83:

> [An individual who dares] look mankind in the face . . . must . . . humble the arrogance of his self-love, and bring it down to something which other men can go along with. They will indulge it so far as to allow him to be more anxious about, and to pursue with more earnest assiduity, his own happiness rather than that of any other person . . . In the race for wealth and honours and preferments, he may run as hard as he can, and strain every nerve and muscle, in order to outstrip all his competitors. But if he should justle, or throw down any of them, the indulgence of the spectators is entirely at an end. It is a violation of fair play, which they cannot admit of . . . they do not enter into that self-love by which he prefers himself so much to this other.

[75] In Smith scholarship following J Viner, 'Adam Smith and *Laissez faire*' in *The Long View and the Short* (Free Press 1958), first published in 1927, that Smith's view of *laissez faire* was by no means minimalist but

placed on the way that Smith saw persuasion as central to exchange. In his *Lectures on Jurisprudence*, Smith depicted persuasion as antecedent to the propensity to truck, barter, and exchange, explaining it in a similar way:

> If we should inquire into the principle of the human mind on which this disposition of trucking is founded, it is clearly the natural inclination everyone has to persuade.[76]

There must, of course, be a natural capacity of this sort for exchange to be possible at all, but the law of contract exists because there is also a natural capacity for quite the other thing, and an explanation of the existence of a general economy in which the economic actor formulates its economic action on the basis of persuasion cannot have recourse just to nature. Smith's account of exchange based on persuasion, and of the system of natural liberty which rests on that account, is therefore both indispensable, and yet seriously inadequate, to the understanding of the social relations that natural liberty addresses.

Conclusion: Self-interest at General Competitive Equilibrium

In the course of this book's general advocacy of Pareto optimisation, it has been argued that influential criticisms of the market economy that have led to the maximalist welfare state and to very important welfarist changes to the core doctrines of the law of contract carry far less weight than they are widely accorded. Fashioned in the background political atmosphere generated by the rejection of the acquisitive society, these criticisms have failed to make a focused attack on the solipsistic self-interest of neoclassical economics and the classical law of contract. In a paradoxical sense accepting this self-interest as integral to the market economy, these criticisms have become criticisms of the market economy *tout court*. As I discuss in the final chapter, it has not been, because it is not, possible to sustain a criticism of the market economy *tout court*, with the result that welfarism has taken what I have hoped to show, mainly by pointing to its consequences for the welfarist law of contract, is an intractably incoherent position. But the point is that the welfarist criticism of the classical law has very badly

involved a sophisticated conception of regulation (including intervention) is beyond dispute. But the reconciliation of what have been claimed to be his contradictory views on human action as variously motivated by sympathy (expressed in *The Theory of Moral Sentiments*) and self-interest (expressed in *The Wealth of Nations*), generally known as 'the Adam Smith problem' traceable to HT Buckle, *History of Civilisation in England*, vol 2 (Parker, Son and Bourn 1861) 449, continues to be attended with basic difficulties. I believe Buckle's overall account, ibid 432–57, to be much more subtle than it is generally taken to be, despite A Oncken, 'The Consistency of Adam Smith' (1897) 7 Economic Journal 443, 444, which argued that Buckle 'emphatically upheld the homogeneity of Smith's two works'. This turns on the refinement of Smith's view of 'economic' self-interest such as is attempted here. Nevertheless, the predominant theme of current commentary on Smith would seem to be an unwarranted stress on the 'social' side of Smith's views on sympathy which follows from a fundamentally misconceived condemnation of the 'economics' of self-interest: E Rothschild, *Economic Sentiments* (Harvard University Press 2001).

[76] Smith, *Lectures* (n 37) 352. At ibid 493–94 Smith says that we should 'cultivate the power of persuasion', and of course this is right. But the cultivation is of a given power.

missed what should have been its target: the economic and legal production of solipsistic self-interest.

The core of an alternative, adequate approach may be set out by drawing into a general position the comments that have been made on the work of late Ronald Coase throughout this book. Coase acknowledged that pure analytic results of great value could be derived from the model of general competitive equilibrium, and in what has come to be known as 'the Coase theorem',[77] he himself provided a partial restatement of the model which has, in my opinion, yielded one of the pure analytic results—at general equilibrium social costs are zero—of greatest value since Arrow-Debreu.[78] But the essential point for us here is that Coase has been one of the most successful *critics* of the extent to which neo-classical economics has sanctioned the direct use of general competition assumptions in the formulation of policy, including the use of the Coase Theorem in this way,[79] which use he has called 'thoroughly bad' or 'pernicious':

> Contemplation of an optimal system may suggest ways of improving the system, it may provide techniques of analysis that would otherwise have been missed, and, in certain special cases, it may go far to providing a solution. But in general its influence has been pernicious. It has directed economists' attention away from the main question, which is how alternative arrangements will actually work in practice. It has led economists to derive conclusions for economic policy from a study of an abstract model of a market situation.[80]

Though he subsequently formed an accurately pessimistic view of how far his call had been heeded,[81] in 'The Problem of Social Cost' Coase called for a basic 'change of approach',[82] and in his Nobel Lecture he argued that that this change would 'ultimately transform the structure of microeconomics'.[83] Any analysis of or policy proposal for an empirical situation has, at its heart, to deal with the institutional shaping of the basic motivations of, and capacities for, economic action, without which whatever was said would be so devoid of concrete content as to be of extremely limited positive or normative value:

[77] Coase, 'Social Cost' (n 16) 97–104.

[78] Campbell, 'Coase' (n 16) 77–82, 90–92.

[79] RH Coase, 'Notes on the Problem of Social Cost' in *The Firm, the Market and the Law* (University of Chicago Press 1988) 174:

> The world of zero transaction costs has often been described as a Coasean world. Nothing could be further from the truth. It is the world of modern economic theory, one which I was hoping to persuade economists to leave.

[80] RH Coase in EW Williams and RH Coase, 'The Regulated Industries: Discussion' (1964) 54 The American Economic Review (Papers and Proceedings) 192, 194–95.

[81] RH Coase, 'The Firm, the Market and the Law' in *The Firm, the Market and the Law* (University of Chicago Press 1988) 1 (hereafter Coase, 'Firm, Market, Law'):

> My point of view has not in general commanded assent, nor has my argument, for the most part, been understood.

[82] Coase, 'Social Cost' (n 16) 153.

[83] RH Coase, 'The Institutional Structure of Production' in *Essays on Economics and Economists* (University of Chicago Press 1994) 10 (hereafter Coase, 'Institutional Structure').

> It makes little sense for economists to discuss the process of exchange without specifying the institutional setting within which the trading takes place since this affects the incentives to produce and costs of transacting ... The time has surely gone in which economists could analyse in great detail two individuals exchanging nuts for berries on the edge of the forest and then feel that their analysis of the process of exchange was complete.[84]

The absence of concrete content has led, as Coase strikingly observed, to the curious disappearance of markets from the standard economics of exchange:

> Markets are institutions that exist to facilitate exchange, that is, they exist in order to reduce the cost of carrying out exchange transactions. In an economic theory which assumes that transaction costs are non-existent, markets have no function to perform, and it seems perfectly reasonable to develop the theory of exchange by an elaborate analysis of individuals exchanging nuts for apples on the edge of the forest or some similar fanciful example. This analysis certainly shows why there is a gain from trade, but it fails to deal with the factors which determine how much trade there is or what goods are traded ... the influence of the social institutions which facilitate exchange being completely ignored.[85]

Once the point is acknowledged, the remedy is as obvious as its execution has proven to be extremely demanding:[86] 'The process of contracting needs to be studied in a real world setting [through] the explicit introduction of transaction costs into economic analysis ... Let us study the world of positive transaction costs'.[87]

A belief that in any empirical situation an optimal allocation will result from economic action exhibiting the unbounded rationality which is a logical corollary of the existence of zero transaction costs is a grave mistake in policy formulation. And now, especially after Coase's injunction to study the world of positive transaction costs, it is almost never *expressly* denied that the assumption of zero transaction costs is 'very unrealistic'[88] because there is always 'a cost of using the price mechanism'.[89] However, for reasons on which our earlier criticism of Smith and Ricardo was intended to shed

[84] ibid 12.

[85] Coase, 'Firm, Market, Law' (n 81) 7–8.

[86] In large part the problem is the reluctance within economics and related disciplines to actually do the sort of work needed to satisfy the demand for detailed institutional knowledge which is really the thrust of 'The Problem of Social Cost': D Campbell, 'The Sense in Coase's Criticism of Pigou' (2017) 13 Journal of Law, Economics and Policy 39, 44–49. Coase's own numerous studies of various economic activities provide the methodological example, and in perhaps his most perfectly realised paper, his detailed knowledge about one such activity, lighthouse provision, reveals that what had been regarded as an axiomatic proposition about welfare economics rests on little such knowledge indeed: RH Coase, 'The Lighthouse in Economics' in *The Firm, the Market and the Law* (University of Chicago Press 1988). The comparison to Macaulay's argument, not only for the study of 'law in action', but for the study of law in action to be knowledgeably conducted, is very close: S Macaulay, 'Law and the Behavioural Sciences: Is There Any There There?' (1984) 6 Law and Policy 149.

[87] Coase, 'Institutional Structure' (n 83) 9, 11.

[88] Coase, 'Social Cost' (n 16) 114.

[89] RH Coase, 'The Nature of the Firm' in *The Firm, the Market and the Law* (University of Chicago Press 1988) 38.

light, we should grasp that the fundamental issue is, not that establishing zero transaction costs is impossible, though it is; it is that doing so would involve us in flat logical contradiction.[90] Realising the assumptions of general competitive equilibrium would not perfect the model; it would destroy it.[91]

Let us consider one of Coase's descriptions of transaction costs:

> In order to carry out a market transaction, it is necessary to discover who it is that one wishes to deal with, to inform people that one wishes to deal and on what terms, to conduct negotiations leading up to a bargain, to draw up a contract, to undertake the inspection needed to make sure that the terms of the contract are being observed, and so on.[92]

Obtaining information, deciding what to do, and negotiating an agreement are, in one important respect, costs, and if one focuses on this, then one should drive those costs down. But these things are not *only* costs. What contract could be made without gathering information, deliberating a decision, and negotiating? If one really eliminated all the transaction costs of exchange, the exchange would not take place cost-free; it would not take place. What are in a first sense costs are in another, and more theoretically profound, sense essential facilitative conditions of economic action. Failing to grasp this prevents us adequately understanding how economic action ever takes place at all.

We get into an area where our language becomes absurd because the theory of general competition makes a fundamentally impermissible assumption, not that transaction costs are zero, which is a permissible and valuable assumption when kept within its theoretical bounds, but of the existence of the economic actor making an exchange. At zero transaction costs, the economic actor is perfected, but only because the existence of rational choice and peaceful exchange somehow survive in a situation where information gathering, deliberation, and negotiation are costless, ie do not exist. But at the bliss of zero transaction costs, exchange *itself* is unnecessary. Goods would simply just be allocated by a process which it is impossible to conceive in any concrete manner. Perhaps the best way to put this is that if one looks at the issues only in terms of costs, then exchange itself is a cost, and at a general competitive equilibrium, not just the transaction costs of exchange, but exchange itself, is reduced to zero.

As with Smith and Ricardo, but in a way which the extreme abstraction of the model markedly exaggerates, general competition assumes that economic action just *has* the

[90] The argument I am about to make is an argument about the human being in the specific form of the economic actor in a market economy. It is a different argument from arguments that general competitive equilibrium is incompatible with necessary claims about the nature of human agency as such, of which Schackle's claim that the model requires 'dismissing *time* from [the] concerns' of the 'theoretician [who] was perhaps unaware of the degree to which he was carrying abstraction' is an outstanding example: GLS Schackle, *Epistemics and Economics* (Transaction Publishers 1992) 151.

[91] There are undoubtedly indications that Coase had some sense both of the issues raised by Schackle and the issues it is sought to raise here, eg Coase, 'Firm, Market, Law' (n 81) 14–15, where Coase quotes SNS Cheung, *Will China Go Capitalist?* Hobart Paper 94 (Institute of Economic Affairs 1986) 3:

> the assumption of private property rights can be dropped without the least negating the Coase Theorem [ie the claim that general competition will yield an optimum].

[92] Coase, 'Social Cost' (n 16) 114.

form of exchange as it has been developed in the market economies. Coase's approach obliges us to question whether in any particular situation welfare-optimising exchange is possible, and this is of the first importance in its proper domain, but it itself does not fundamentally investigate the very *form* of economic action. But, to point out what it is hoped has now become clear, such action is the product of a specific economy and society, and what are for one purpose transaction costs are also social relations facilitative of exchange. The formulation of policy intended to promote Pareto optimisation therefore always requires active, thoroughgoing investigation into whether these relations exist or can possibly be established.[93] Their existence should never be assumed in policy formulation.

One essential part of this investigation has to be into the existence or possible establishment of the legal institutions which culminate in a law of contract that will foster the morality of mutual recognition necessary for general, welfare-enhancing exchange. When engaging in this, one has to be conscious that adequate self-interest cannot be solipsistic, and that we have been set the task of actualising the immanent morality of neo-classical economics and of the classical law of contract. An adequate law of contract has to be fundamentally restated so as to clearly articulate the relationship of mutual recognition on which it is based.

It is surely significant that the late Harold Demsetz, unarguably one of the leading contributors to the development of our understanding of property rights after Coase, has said that:

> we must be careful in economics when ethical beliefs are brought into the analysis. Economic analysis neither makes nor needs an ethical presumption regarding motivation. Analysis depends only on the assumption of rational maximisation.[94]

This is not an identification of a lack of ethics in economic action. It is an assertion of, to put it this way, an ethic of self-interest which is possible only because of a lack of awareness of the contradiction involved in making such an assertion about economic action. This axiomatic equation of legitimate economic self-interest with solipsistic self-interest makes the views even of such as Demsetz inadequate to the understanding of their subject; the stability of the market economy composed of general exchange.[95]

[93] In his Nobel Lecture, given in 1991, Coase, 'Institutional Structure' (n 83) 12, drew the following lesson from 'recent events in Eastern Europe':

> ex-communist countries are advised to move to a market economy ... but without the appropriate institutions no market economy of any significance is possible. If we knew more about our own economy, we would be in a better position to advise them.

I attempted to apply this lesson to a very admirable analysis of the use of the law of contract remedies in the former USSR in D Campbell, 'Breach and Penalty as Contractual Norm and Contractual Anomie' [2001] Wisconsin Law Review 681.

[94] H Demsetz, *The Economics of the Business Firm* (CUP 1995) 28.

[95] Driven by anxiety to describe the fundamentally non-market aspects of the public company in 'market' terms, the agency theory of the corporation to which Demsetz was a principal contributor gave both an account of managerial authority which suppressed the empirical fact that it has an ethical basis and an account of the 'contracts' on which the company is based which are at complete variance to the empirical contracts which a company enters into with its employees. The extraordinary result is that the company in the agency theory is a pure empirical fiction: D Campbell, 'The Role of Monitoring and Morality in Company Law: A Criticism of the Direction of Present Regulation' (1997) 7 Australian Journal of Corporate Law 343.

This understanding, both of the law of contract and of exchange in general, is possible only on the basis of consciousness of the moral relations that constitute both:

> a relational approach to contracts and their remedies in which efficiency analysis is reached only by working to it through relations, rather than assuming them away *ab initio* [should] seem more attractive than it now does as a tool of economic analysis. Such an approach ... will lead to more realistic and effective analysis of the material and necessarily social aspects of contracts and contract remedies. This [is] also ... the true role of economics.[96]

But, as shall now be discussed in the final chapter, acknowledgement of this moral relation does not, however, justify the rejection of self-interest either in the maximalist form of the welfare state, or in welfarism in the law of contract. Welfarism has replaced one fundamentally inadequate understanding with another.

[96] IR Macneil, Contract Remedies: The Needs for Better Efficiency Analysis' (1988) 144 Journal of Institutional and Theoretical Economics 6, 29.

12
The Maximalist Welfare State, Inchoate Communism, and Betterment

The Natural and the Social in Socialism

Though I have argued that Marx's claim that Smith's and Ricardo's understanding of exchange involved an alienated view of economic action is correct, the position that Marx thought was sanctioned by that argument itself even more seriously misunderstands such action. Having shown that economic action is not a matter of just the 'natural', he treats it as a matter of just the 'social',[1] and this approach led Marx to grossly overstate the possibilities of change in humankind's relationship to nature.[2] The consequences have been, trying to choose one's language carefully, enormously theoretically and politically negative. We can focus our discussion on these consequences as they have influenced the regulation of the market economy by the law of contract if we return to the labour theory of value, and specifically to its fundamental

[1] K Marx and F Engels, *The German Ideology* in K Marx and F Engels, *Collected Works*, vol 5 (Lawrence and Wishart 1976) (81) (emphasis added) (hereafter, Marx and Engels, *German Ideology*):

> The reality which communism creates is precisely the true basis for rendering it impossible that anything should exist independently of individuals, insofar as reality is nevertheless only a product of the preceding intercourse of individuals.

[2] E Meiksins Wood, 'The Separation of the Economic and the Political in Capitalism' (1981) I/127 New Left Review 66, 72.

> Marx's purpose ... is to stress not the dualism of the 'material' and the 'social' but the definition of the material by the social.

On the implications of this position for the explanation of the nature of economic action, see E Meiksins Wood, *The Origins of Capitalism* (Verso 2017) 34:

> [In the] old models of capitalist development ... the capitalist market was both an immutable natural law and the perfection of human choice and freedom. The antithesis of such models would be a conception of the capitalist market that fully acknowledge its imperatives and compulsions, whilst recognising that these imperatives are rooted not in some transhistorical law but in historically specific social relations, constituted by human agency and subject to change.

Contractual Relations. David Campbell, Oxford University Press. © David Campbell 2022.
DOI: 10.1093/oso/9780198855156.003.0012

inability to come to terms with the place of consumption in the economics of the market.

The British criticism of the labour theory of value

British writings on Marx's concept of value from the decades around the formation of the Labour Party were of marginal theoretical importance at the time,[3] and are now of only historical interest.[4] Their significance is their failure to grasp Marx's basic intentions, for that has been the fundamental reason that they were unable to offer any substantial resistance to the rejection of the labour theory which has dominated British social democracy, to which George Bernard Shaw, in his self-appointed role as the economic theorist of the early Fabian Society,[5] was central. Shaw was a member of a group of Fabians, all of whom were to become influential figures, convened in 1885–86 for the study, in French, of volume one of *Capital*,[6] and he influentially reviewed the English translation which appeared in 1887.[7] Shaw never seems to have altered his very positive view of an account of capitalist exploitation and its inevitable collapse which he associated with the bulk of volume one of *Capital*, ie minus the theory of value, seeing it as a sort of communist firming up of the 'sentimental' message of *Hard Times*.[8] But at the time of his participation in the important study group and of his review, he could not have held a lower opinion of the labour theory. He called it a 'blunder',[9] one of a number of 'clumsy' 'muddlements',[10] and he even included Marx, with Henry George and John Ruskin, in a demeaning trio of 'great propagandist amateurs of political economy'.[11]

Shaw's opinion of Marx is preposterous, one consequence of this being that Shaw's economics have never themselves repaid theoretical scrutiny.[12] But this by no means

[3] S Macintyre, *A Proletarian Science* (corrected edn, Lawrence and Wishart 1986) ch 7. Though they are tangential to his account, the early works of Maurice Dobb overlap with Macintyre's period, and he is at pains to point out that those works are of a qualitative difference in lasting interest.

[4] The apparent glaring exception to this is the theory of capitalist imperialism in JA Hobson, *Imperialism* (3rd edn, Unwin Hyman 1988), which has played, particularly through its influence on Lenin, an important part in the development of Marxist economic and political theory after Marx. But, though this need not be argued here, Hobson's views are not and cannot be derived from Marx's analysis of value.

[5] GB Shaw, 'Postscript [to the 1948 'Jubilee' edition]: Sixty Years of Fabianism' in GB Shaw (ed), *Fabian Essays* (5th edn, Pickering & Chatto 1996) 213 (hereafter Shaw, 'Sixty Years').

[6] ER Pease, *The History of the Fabian Society* (Bibliobazaar 2006) 58 (hereafter Pease, *History*) and Letter from George Bernard Shaw to John Maynard Keynes (30 November 1934) in JM Keynes, *Collected Writings*, vol 28 (CUP 2013) 37 (hereafter Shaw to Keynes (30 November 1934)).

[7] GB Shaw, '[Three Notices of] Karl Marx and *Das Kapital*' in RW Ellis (ed), *Bernard Shaw and Karl Marx* (Random House 1930).

[8] Letter from George Bernard Shaw to John Maynard Keynes (11 December 1934) in JM Keynes, *Collected Writings*, vol 28 (CUP 2013) 40. See further n 38.

[9] Shaw, 'Sixty Years' (n 5) 228.

[10] GB Shaw, 'On the History of Fabian Economics' in Pease, *History* (n 6) 217 (hereafter Shaw, 'History').

[11] Shaw, 'Sixty Years' (n 5) 219.

[12] In an admirable display of tact, when contributing to a commemoration of Shaw's 90th birthday, Maurice Dobb managed to write a piece on Shaw's economics which celebrated their polemical success, which he (Dobb) attributed to Marx's continuing influence, without saying anything whatsoever about the substance of those economics: M Dobb, 'Bernard Shaw and Economics' in S Winsten (ed), *GBS 90* (Hutchinson 1946).

detracts from their very considerable significance for the way that any positive reference to Marx in the history of British social democracy has been all but totally confined to rhetoric; indeed it is an important aspect of that significance. After the remarkable success of the 1889 *Fabian Essays in Socialism*, in which Shaw's chapter on economics took the line described above,[13] Engels felt that Shaw's views were sufficiently important to spend an, admittedly dismissive, line or two on them when he brought out volume three of *Capital* in 1894.[14] Engels comments were, however, directed at the one aspect of Shaw's economics which are sound, because entirely derivative. Shaw seems to have had a sort of apotheosis about the labour theory[15] after eventually grasping the brilliant criticism of volume one made in 1884 by PH Wicksteed.[16] Wicksteed's important contribution to the winning of acceptance for marginalist economics, which has been taken up at points throughout this book, was allied with an abiding concern for social reform that made him sympathetic to socialism, and indeed led him to acknowledge the 'extreme importance' of the 'latter portion' of volume one, though he could not see that it stood 'in any logical connection with the abstract reasoning [about value] of the early chapters'.[17] I shall not refer in detail to Wicksteed's criticism, but shall apply it, as it were, directly to Marx.

There are certain immediate objections to the labour theory of value, which Marx saw and with which he sought to deal early in the development of that theory, which arise from the way he separated use-value and exchange-value.[18] If the value of a good was a matter only of the labour needed to produce it, then any good produced should have an exchange-value. But in all modes of production goods are produced in order to be consumed, and so under capitalism they must have a use-value in order to enter into exchange, ie to have an exchange-value: 'nothing can have a value without being an object of utility. If the thing is useless, so is the labour contained in it; the labour does not count as labour, and therefore creates no value'[19].

Marx was able to maintain his very strong separation between use-value and exchange-value in respect of goods which were produced for sale which do not find a buyer because no buyer finds them useful. Being unsold, these goods do not have a value because they have, to put it this way, failed to become goods. Marx's distinction between use-value and exchange-value can, let us allow, deal with this case. A good which cannot be sold has no value, regardless of how much labour is embedded in it. But, certainly with the hindsight provided by the success of the marginal revolution, it is clear that, though the class of unsaleable goods which cannot have a price, or have a

[13] GB Shaw, 'Economic' in GB Shaw (ed), *Fabian Essays in Socialism* (Jubilee edn, Pickering & Chatto 1996) (hereafter Shaw, 'Economic').

[14] F Engels, 'Preface' in K Marx, *Capital*, vol 3 (in K Marx and F Engels, *Collected Works*, vol 37 (Lawrence and Wishart 1998) pt 2 (hereafter Marx, *Capital*, vol 3) 13.

[15] Shaw, 'History' (n 10) 217. Shaw had previously tried to defend the labour theory against Wicksteed, only to be most politely but even more emphatically shown to be completely confused: GB Shaw, 'The Jevonian Criticism of Marx' and PH Wicksteed, 'The Jevonian Criticism of Marx: A Rejoinder' in RW Ellis (ed), *Bernard Shaw and Karl Marx* (Random House 1930).

[16] PH Wicksteed, '*Das Kapital*: A Criticism' in *The Commonsense of Political Economy* (rev edn, Routledge & Kegan Paul 1933) (hereafter Wicksteed, *Das Kapital*).

[17] ibid 724.

[18] Marx, *Capital*, vol 1 in K Marx and F Engels, *Collected Works*, vol 35 (International Publishers 1996) 639 (hereafter Marx, *Capital*, vol 1) 50–51.

[19] ibid 51.

zero price, is important, this is a highly restricted view of the influence of use-value on price, and is quite wrong. It turns on distinguishing a class of 'failed' goods, on which use-value has a determining effect, from the class of 'successful' goods which are exchanged, the value, and therefore ultimately the price, of which was to be determined, Marx claimed, by labour inputs alone.

But it is not possible to draw this line between the products of labour which do find a buyer and those which do not, for the value of a good which is able to be sold is also a function of both supply and demand. The same factors of supply and demand which Marx acknowledged will, in an, as it were, on/off manner, prevent some goods from having a value at all, also enter into the determination of the value of goods which are exchanged, those factors' respective roles having to be analysed, as it was Wicksteed's main aim to argue, at the margin. Price from the outset reflects both the production cost of the good's supply and the effective demand for it, the prediction of both of which is a crucial function of the entrepreneur. The level of investment in production, which is a very significant influence on the cost of production, is a function of predicted demand. At a further level of analysis, prediction of demand also enters into the amount of investment in capacity building, ultimately in research and development, which itself enters into the determination of the technological conditions of production, ie the amount of labour needed for production. Marx's, in itself correct, acceptance that demand determines the zero value of goods that do not sell is simply not consistent with treating the value of goods that do sell as determined only by labour inputs.

Wicksteed was therefore right to say that it emerges from Marx, not that abstract labour is the only property common to goods, but rather that, if I may modify Wicksteed's term, *abstractly useful* labour is that property.[20] In the general market economy, production and consumption, or supply and demand, always from the outset determine the price of a good.[21] In Chapter 11, we saw Marx scathingly observe that 'So far no chemist has ever discovered exchange-value either in a pearl or a diamond'.[22] But equally no chemist has ever discovered use-value in any good, for use-value, like exchange-value, albeit in a distinct manner, is a form of human action determining price.

It therefore must be acknowledged that Marx's distinction between use-value and exchange-value invited the disdain with which Shaw regarded it. The point, however, is that Shaw purported to retain the criticism of capitalist production for profit as a doomed system which at some vague and general level he derived from Marx,[23] and it is essential to recognise that this cutting-off of the criticism of capitalist profit from

[20] Wicksteed, *Das Kapital* (n 16) 712.

[21] Save in the exceptional case of goods which cannot be provided in competitive supply, the 'uniqueness' of which was discussed in regard of remedies in chs 8–9.

[22] Marx, *Capital*, vol 1 (n 18) 94.

[23] Shaw to Keynes (30 November 1934) (n 6) 215:

> that ... lines of disruptive strain [are] there and can be got rid of only by the abolition of 'real' property is beyond all sane question. At present, Marx's demonstration of the blind ruthlessness of capital in the pursuit of 'surplus value' (practically of cheap labour) is producing a dangerous conflict.

its theoretical root has become a defining feature of British social democracy.[24] The detail of what Marx actually argued may be all but forgotten, but the rejection of profit and the market severed from that detail live on. In one sense it could be said that this has reduced the criticism of profit to mere rhetoric, but the way in which this has happened has had great importance for the theoretical underpinning of the maximalist welfare state.

The annihilation of demand and the demand for the unconditioned life

How could Marx have come to place such weight on a distinction so fragile as that which he drew between use-value and exchange-value? I believe he did so because this distinction seemed to locate the superiority of economic governance by planning, which was essential to the overcoming of the alienation of labour, in the scientific analysis of capitalism. Though the most famous formulation of the point was due to Engels,[25] the belief that Marx's critique of capitalism was a 'scientific socialism' quite distinct from purely moralistic or utopian socialism was central to Marx's own thought.[26] But that critique is imposed on, ie it cannot be drawn from, the analysis of economic action, nor, more generally, from a plausible philosophic anthropology of humankind's relationship with nature.

We have seen that Marx's claim that the direction of economic activity by the capitalist pursuit of profit follows from conceiving of value as a matter of labour inputs alone. In Chapter 3, we saw that essentially this way of seeing the issues, in which the imperatives of business organisations are the real drivers of consumer demand, lies behind the many claims that the market economy is not an economy of consumer sovereignty. Consumer sovereignty cannot have weight because in the determination of the value of goods, use-value, to repeat, plays no role in determining production. As consumers of course choose to buy goods because of their use-values, this approach eliminates the influence of consumer demand from the determination of the prices of goods.

But, as we have seen Marx stress, even the capitalist must produce saleable goods. In the 1857–58 notebooks now universally known as the *Grundrisse*, Marx very interestingly tells us that capital 'creates a particular surplus value ... because it cannot create

[24] Even the views of CAR Crosland, discussed later in this chapter, ultimately display this character. In A Crosland, *The Future of Socialism* (William Pickering 1994), first published in 1956, 'the aims of socialism' were said to include, for reasons explicitly distinguished from 'the Ricardo-Marx labour theory' (ibid 88), 'The objective of substituting for unrestricted competition and the motive of personal profit some more social organisation and set of motives' (ibid 89). These reasons were principally ethical, but also included an 'economic' objection to 'the actual material results of classical capitalism' (ibid 91), 'The inner contradiction of capitalism, according to Marx, [being] its tendency to huge accumulations of profit' (ibid 415). This is right, but only up to the point where one is obliged to acknowledge that the historical lesson that 'The *real barrier* of capitalist production is *capital itself*' (Marx, *Capital*, vol 3 (n 14) 248) in which Marx's economics culminate is manifested in 'the law of the tendency of the rate of profit *to fall*': ibid (emphasis added).

[25] F Engels, *Socialism: Utopian or Scientific?* in K Marx and F Engels, *Collected Works*, vol 24 (Lawrence and Wishart 1989).

[26] K Marx and F Engels, *Manifesto of the Communist Party* in *Collected Works*, vol 6 (Lawrence and Wishart 1976) 514–17 (hereafter Marx and Engels, *Communist Manifesto*).

an infinite one at once'.[27] Concerned only with accumulation, capital would prefer an infinite, instant surplus, but it cannot create one because capitalism is but one mode of humankind's relationship with nature, and the 'fact that the production of use values, or goods, is carried on under the control of a capitalist and on its behalf does not alter the general character of that production'.[28] The structural principle of capitalism may be surplus value, but the production of saleable commodities is essential, for 'commodities are not paid for twice over, once on account of their use-value and again on account of their value'.[29] The capitalist actually must have:

> two objects in view: in the first place, he wants to produce a use-value that has a value in exchange, that is to say, an article destined to be sold, a commodity; and, secondly, he desires to produce a commodity whose value shall be greater than the sum of the values used in its production . . . His aim is to produce not only a use-value but a commodity also; not only use-value, but value [and] surplus value.[30]

It is at this point, in my opinion, that the fracture occurred in Marx's economics which made communism bound to, thankfully, fail in the liberal democracies.[31] We saw in Chapter 1 that Engels and Marx celebrated the historically revolutionary role that capitalism has played by vastly expanding the possibilities of human aspiration. It is essential at this stage of our argument to stress that this revolutionary role is experienced as an expansion of possibly achievable needs or wants:

> [under capitalism there takes place] the discovery, creation and satisfaction of new needs arising from society itself, cultivating all the qualities of a social man and producing him in a form as rich as possible in needs . . . producing man as the most total and universal social product possible . . . with a corresponding system of ever more extended and ever more varied needs . . . Hence the great civilising influence of capital.[32]

[27] Marx, 'Economic Manuscripts of 1857–8 [*Grundrisse*]' in K Marx and F Engels, *Collected Works*, vols 28–29 (Lawrence and Wishart 1986–87) vol 28, 260 (hereafter Marx, *Grundrisse*).

[28] Marx, *Capital*, vol 1 (n 18) 187.

[29] ibid 170.

[30] ibid 196. It is truly jarring that the following passage, a concession of the entrepreneurial function in a developed market economy, is to be found in the part of volume one on fetishism:

> The division of a product into a useful thing and a value becomes practically important only when exchange has acquired such an extension that useful articles are produced for the purpose of being exchanged, and their character as values has therefore to be taken into account, *beforehand*, during production (ibid 84 (emphasis added)).

[31] I Kristol, 'On Corporate Capitalism in America' in N Glazer and I Kristol (eds), *The American Commonwealth 1976* (Basic Books 1976) 136:

> there is no case, in any country that can reasonably be called 'capitalist', of . . . class conflict leading to a proletarian revolution. Capitalism, precisely because its aim is the satisfaction of 'common' appetites and aspirations, can adequately cope with its own class conflicts, through economic growth primarily and some version of the welfare state secondarily.

[32] Marx, *Grundrisse* (n 27) vol 29, 336.

But though this is central to Marx's overall conception of progress, his developed economics of capitalism simply contradict it because they give no weight to the consumer demand in which this expansion is principally manifested, wholly subjecting it to the criticism of capitalism as the pursuit of profit.[33] In this way, Marx surrendered any hope of purchase on the political aspiration of the common citizens of the liberal democracies, as he set at nought the value of the material wealth and the freedom to choose which those citizens enjoy, and have politically struggled to ensure they enjoy,[34] in the market economy.[35] Of course, great achievements must be attributed to socialisation, including the New Liberal and the Beveridgean welfare state, in considerable part in response to working class political pressure for the creation of social citizenship;[36] but this was reform or extension of the potential of the market economy. For when Smith told us, as we saw in Chapter 11, that in the Age of Commerce 'the division of labour ... occasions ... that universal opulence which extends itself to the lowest ranks of people',[37] he captured the essential, positive feature of capitalism in a way with which Marx, and Marxism, have never been able remotely to come to terms. In the capitalist societies which were to be communism's natural home, common citizens have had far, far more to lose than their chains. This was emphatically the case, not merely at the time of the death of Engels, but even when[38] he and Marx made the

[33] E Wilson, *To the Finland Station* (Doubleday 1940) 295:

> On the one hand, Marx is telling you in *Das Kapital* that a certain 'historic' development, indispensable for the progress of the race, could only have been carried out by capitalism; and, on the other hand, he is filling you with fury against the wickedness of the people who have performed it.

[34] Struggle over employment and employment conditions or over levels of consumption by organised labour was, Marx believed, a limitation on proper working class consciousness. In ch 2 I quoted the question set in K Marx, *Value, Price and Profit* in K Marx and F Engels, *Collected Works*, vol 20 (Lawrence and Wishart 1985) 148 (hereafter Marx, *Value, Price and Profit*):

> [Ought] the working class ... renounce their resistance against the encroachments of capital and abandon their attempts at making the best of occasional chances for their temporary improvement. If they did, they would be degraded to one level mass of broken wretches past salvation [Nevertheless, instead] of the *conservative* motto '*A fair days wage for a fair day's work!*' they ought to inscribe on their banner the *revolutionary* watchword '*Abolition of the wages system!*'.

The value of such resistance was to 'school' the working class into the eventual abandonment, or transcendence, of economic choice about such matters under socialism and communism: K Marx, 'Instructions for the Delegates etc' in Marx and Engels, *Collected Works*, vol 20, ibid 191–92.

[35] There are other ways in which this point could be put relating to other dimensions of Marx's thought, all of which boil down to an idea of distinguishing 'revolution' from 'reform' (R Luxemburg, 'Reform or Revolution?' in *Rosa Luxemburg Speaks* (Pathfinder Press 1970)). The liberal socialism which informs this book turns on the belief that, as an issue of any substance for the assessment of the relevance of Marx's thought to the liberal democracies, this distinction was shown to have less than no value by late nineteenth-century revisionism after Edouard Bernstein, for the reform *is* the revolution. Such vitality as the distinction enjoyed in the liberal democracies in the twentieth century has largely been a reflection of the political success of Bolshevism.

[36] R Aron, *The Century of Total War* (Derek Verschoyle 1954) 355: 'Socialism has ceased in the West to be a myth because it has become a part of reality'.

[37] A Smith, *The Wealth of Nations* in *The Glasgow Edition of the Works and Correspondence* (Clarendon Press 1976) 22 (hereafter Smith, *Wealth of Nations*).

[38] Engels' and Marx's early indictments of poverty, of which F Engels, *The Condition of the Working Class in England in 1844* in K Marx and F Engels, *Collected Works*, vol 4 (Lawrence and Wishart 1975) and K Marx, *Wage-labour and Capital* in K Marx and F Engels, *Collected Works*, vol 9 (Lawrence and Wishart 1977) are the centrepieces, were directed at the consequences of the process of capital formation that gave rise to industrialisation which Marx called primitive accumulation. They do not have a part in the theory

claim that chains were all the working class had to lose,[39] a claim which has resounded ever since, despite the unmanageable contradiction of it appearing in the course of one of the most fulsome encomiums to capitalist achievement ever written.

As we have seen particularly in Chapter 3, giving weight to consumer choice is a difficult regulatory task. But, as part and parcel of the approach which underpinned Marx's ultimate disinterest in problems of equality, consumer choice is excluded from his economics by theoretical fiat, so that I am unaware of any significant consideration of the role of such choice anywhere in his work. What on the face of it is overwhelming counter-evidence to this claim, the lengthy treatment of the circulation of capital in volume two of *Capital*, is extraordinary. It is foolish to deny the importance of volume two in the history of social theory,[40] but nevertheless this is an awkward thing to say as the book is barely readable, largely because it hardly addresses its real subject matter. Circulation is entirely described at a structural-functionalist level (though the system involves contradictions which will bring about its collapse), and the actual empirical basis of circulation—sale of consumer goods and services—plays no significant part! In what is the most outright implausible part of *Capital*, Marx treats the facilitation of buying and selling,[41] and indeed commerce as such,[42] as a mere expenditure on unproductive labour, one of the '*faux frais*' or incidental expenses of production which must be completely distinguished from the creation of value.[43] There are isolated passages in Marx's economics which pass moral judgements on consumer choices,[44] but these are irrelevant to his core argument, the logical end-point of the criticism of abundance discussed in Chapter 3, that consumer demand in any way at all represents choices to be valued, and, given this, business organisations' entrepreneurial attempts to identify

of developed capitalism. *Capital*, vol 1 and its extremely abridged statement for directly political purposes in *Value, Price and Profit* (n 34) are directed at capitalism after what Marx called the real subsumption of labour to capital had taken place. Despite the view which we have seen Shaw express (see the text accompanying n 8), it is, in my view, impossible to deny that there is a sense of improvement in the empirical picture of factory labour painted in vol 1, such as the limit on the working day and the regulation of labour conditions, and some note of balance emerges from the substance, if by no means from the rhetoric, of both vol 1 and *Value, Price and Profit* (n 34). In sum, the picture painted in *Capital*, vol 1 cannot entirely be read as Shaw so influentially read it.

39 Marx and Engels, *Communist Manifesto* (n 26) 519.

40 The reproduction schemas in K Marx, *Capital*, vol 2 in K Marx and F Engels, *Collected Works*, vol 36 (Lawrence and Wishart 1997) chs 17–22 (hereafter Marx, *Capital*, vol 2) are essential to the structure of *Capital* as a whole. There is also essential material on the reproduction of constant capital elsewhere in volume two, but all this, in my opinion, would have been better merged with material now in volume three.

41 K Marx, 'Economic Manuscript of 1861–63' in K Marx and F Engels, *Collected Works*, vols 30–34 (Lawrence and Wishart 1988–94) 447 (hereafter Marx, '1861–63 Manuscript'):

> legal proceedings, contracts, etc … relate only to the conditions made between the owners of commodities as buyers and sellers of commodities; they have nothing to do with the relation of capital and labour. Those who perform these functions may thereby become the wage labourers of capital; this does not make them productive workers.

42 Marx, *Capital*, vol 1 (n 18) 170.

43 Marx, *Capital*, vol 2 (n 40) 135.

44 Eg in comments directed at consumption by capitalists, Marx, '1861–63 Manuscript' (n 41) 449 tells us that:

> A large part of the annual product … consists of extremely paltry products (use-values) serving to satisfy the most miserable appetites, fancies, etc.

consumer wants simply vanish because it is the organisations that completely determine the wants.[45]

To the extent it is right to say it exists at all, consumer choice features in *Capital* in the analysis of the value of labour power. The value of labour power is the cost of its reproduction, ie the continuation of the supply of labour,[46] and Shaw was fundamentally attracted to volume one by what he saw as its depiction of the capitalist seeking to drive this cost down to its minimum. Leaving aside the ways in which this is just wrong, such a point would have been for Marx very much a subsidiary point to the reproduction of labour-power being, if it may be put this way, a demand of the capitalist, not the labourer:

> We must never forget that the demand for productive consumption is … *a demand of the capitalist*, whose essential purpose is the production of surplus value, so that he produces a particular commodity [labour] to this sole end.[47]

It is very jarring to realise that what is being described here is the working class's choice of consumption of goods *in toto*. Specific criticisms of the power of choice are, however, redundant in Marx because his approach annihilates choice *in toto*:

> The individual consumption of the labourer [is] a factor of the production and reproduction of capital [but the] fact that the labourer consumes his means of subsistence for his own purposes, and not to please the capitalist, has no bearing on the matter. The consumption of food by a beast of burden is none the less a necessary factor in the process of production because the beast enjoys what it eats.[48]

One of the principal contributions to Marxist value theory after Marx was Nikolai Bukharin's 1927 response[49] to the founding Austrian economist Eugen von Böhm-Bawerk's famous criticism of Marx.[50] Though written after the appearance of volume three of *Capital* and focusing on the transformation problem, Böhm-Bawerk's criticism essentially turned on the point made by Wicksteed. As economics, Bukharin's

[45] It is, in my opinion, irremediably unclear why Marx thought any expenditure was made on the *faux frais* of production. An explanation of the enormous 'sales effort' made by large corporations is integral to later Marxist economics, notably PA Baran and PM Sweezy, *Monopoly Capital* (Monthly Review Press 1966) ch 5. But this can be related to Marx only in the sense that it retains the overwhelming sense of the irrelevance of consumer choice to production determined by capitalist structural imperatives, and so gives no possible role whatsoever to the entrepreneurial function.

[46] Marx, *Capital*, vol 1 (n 18) 177–86. Marx acknowledged that the reproduction of labour-power was not an, as it were, purely physical matter, and that there was an 'historical and moral element' in labour-power's value: ibid 181. But though this acknowledgement played a significant part in his criticisms of an 'iron law of wages' which he claimed had such a physical basis (K Marx, *Critique of the Gotha Programme* in K Marx and F Engels, *Collected Works*, vol 24 (Lawrence and Wishart 1989) 91–92), Marx could not connect the historical and moral element to the positive account he gave of the increase of needs as the increase of civilisation which was discussed in ch 1 because this would have undermined his entire economics.

[47] Marx, *Capital*, vol 3 (n 14) 187 (emphasis added).

[48] Marx, *Capital*, vol 1 (n 18) 572.

[49] NI Bukharin, *Economic Theory of the Leisure Class* (Monthly Review Press 1972).

[50] E von Böhm-Bawerk, 'Karl Marx and the Close of His System' in PM Sweezy (ed), *Karl Marx and the Close of His System by Eugen von Böhm Bawerk and Böhm-Bawerk's Criticism of Marx by Rudolf Hilferding* (Merlin Press 1975).

response is based on acceptance of the labour theory, and so ultimately is a failure for the reasons we have seen, but it was a failure of great significance as it was at the heart of the belief that bourgeois economic categories, including money, need be of no relevance, indeed would be an hindrance, to economic calculation by Bolshevism in power. With Evgeny Preobrazhensky, in 1919 Bukharin published *The ABC of Communism*, an intendedly popular treatment of the issues which arguably was Bolshevism's principal general statement until it was suppressed and its authors executed during the purges of the late 1930s. This historically important book claims that, as with Engels' famous remarks about the state,[51] the monetary system would wither away and 'Communist society will know nothing of money'.[52] This view played a major part in the catastrophe of War Communism,[53] the Bolshevik attempt upon taking power to revolutionarily reconstruct the economy which is the episode of outright communist chaos and horror which can most clearly and justly be linked to Marx's own thought.[54] It is of direct relevance here that Bukharin's thinking instructively turns on the attitude to consumer choice which underpins the Marxist concept of value.

Writing of the exploitation of labour power, Bukharin and Preobrazhensky commented upon the following 'very interesting characteristic of capitalist society', that it:

> Does not itself produce the things which are necessary and useful to it; instead of this, the capitalist class compels the workers to produce those things for which more will be paid, those things from which the capitalists derive the largest profit. Whisky, for example, is a very harmful substance, and alcoholic liquors in general ought to be produced only for technical purposes and for their use in medicine. But throughout the world capitalists produce alcohol with all their might. Why? Because to ply the people with drink is extremely profitable.[55]

Does one really believe that alcohol is produced for recreational purposes *only* because it is extremely profitable? One should go on to ask why *this* good is extremely profitable, but surely the point that demand representing voluntary choice plays an essential economic role even in this case, where manipulation of the consumer can be a particularly serious issue, is not worth debate. It really does show the singular distortion of the understanding of market economics to which the labour theory gives rise that such a belief could ever be entertained.

[51] F Engels, *Anti-Dühring* in K Marx and F Engels, *Collected Works*, vol 25 (Lawrence and Wishart 1987) 268 (translation amended): 'the government of persons is replaced by the administration of things ... The state ... withers away' (hereafter Engels, *Anti-Dühring*).

[52] NI Bukharin and EV Preobrazhensky, *The ABC of Communism* (University of Michigan Press 1966) (hereafter Bukharin and Preobrazhensky, *ABC*). See further N Bukharin, 'The Economics of the Transition Period' in *The Politics and Economics of the Transition Period* (Routledge and Kegan Paul 1979) 155: 'a process of "self-negation" of money'.

[53] A Nove, *An Economic History of the USSR* (rev edn, Penguin Books 1982) ch 3 (hereafter Nove, *Economic History*).

[54] S Malle, *The Economic Organisation of War Communism 1918–21* (CUP 1985) ch 4.

[55] Bukharin and Preobrazhensky, *ABC* (n 52) 32.

Though he was hardly able to maintain it with the force of Bolshevism, as an instance of the criticism of profit-seeking he retained after rejecting the labour theory, Shaw identified 'the drink traffic' as 'the most popular branch of commercial enterprise' because 'it yields high profits'.[56] To concede this degree of prominence to the drink traffic might reflect that fact that Shaw was, it seems as a reaction to his father's drunkenness, himself teetotal, but, of course, the significance of Shaw's views is that they were in a strong way representative. Shaw's concern would, of course, be perfectly legitimate if it were balanced; but it was not. Shaw gave no weight to the choice to recreationally consume alcohol, which is viewed merely as an obstacle to be overcome, so far as possible.

Shaw threw his great powers behind the Fabian Society's campaign to establish 'a municipalised drink traffic which should check drinking at the point of excess'.[57] It followed from the defining gradualism of Fabianism that this aspiration, which allows of some recreational consumption,[58] is not an instance of authoritarian foolishness entirely comparable to Bukharin and Preobrazhensky's envisaging the end of drinking in Russia, but it is important to see why this allowance was made. The Fabian policy was designed to be distinct from prohibition, but only because the main proponent of that policy, the Society's Secretary, ER Pease, had reluctantly concluded, after a review of the principally American experience, that 'prohibition cannot be enforced when enacted'.[59] But even this degree of compromise was to no avail. Reviewing the campaign in the history of the Society which he published in 1916, after more than 20 years of great Fabian influence, Pease was sorrowfully obliged to conclude that this was 'one of the few causes taken up by the Society which have made but little progress in popular favour'.[60] The goal was dropped, not for reasons of respect for the consumer choice which opposed it, but, as with a great many such consumer policies intended to deny and defeat consumer choice, only for reasons of political accommodation.

The belief that production is solely governed by the pursuit of profit, and with it a corollary tendency 'to deprecate' the value of 'free consumers' choice', though this is 'really to show a lack of common human observation' because the satisfaction of choice '*is* freedom and it *is* happiness',[61] has become central to left-wing thought in the liberal democracies. As it was put in 1960 by CAR Crosland, with RHS Crossman the last major Labour politician to display other than a caricature understanding of Marx and a potential to productively relate the concerns of classical social theory to social democratic politics:

[56] GB Shaw, *The Common Sense of Municipal Trading* in *Essays in Fabian Socialism* (rev edn, Constable 1932) 183 (hereafter Shaw, *Common Sense*).

[57] ibid.

[58] In an early instance of a now common interventionist practice, Shaw, ibid 184 even believed that the municipalisation policy might so diminish brewers' and publicans' profits that, hilariously, drinking would have to be subsidised from the rates!

[59] [ER Pease], *Municipal Drink Traffic*, Fabian Tract 86 (Fabian Society 1898) 4. Tracts adopted as policy documents by the Society were not published under their author's name, but Pease identified himself as the author of this Tract in Pease, *History* (n 6) 234. The American evidence was provided by numerous local and State prohibitions. The Volstead Act lay 20 years into the future.

[60] ibid 134.

[61] D Jay, *The Socialist Case* (2nd edn, Pickering & Chatto 1996) 255, 257 (hereafter Jay, *Socialist Case*).

> a section of the Left displays a profound aversion to (other people's) high consumption. Condemning the affluent society as 'degenerate' and 'irresponsible', they bid us not to 'come to terms' with it ... But while a puritan government of one's own life is admirable, a pharisaical attitude to the lives of others is revolting.[62] It seems particularly nauseating today when, for the first time in history, entire populations, and not just privileged minorities, have escaped from 'the normal condition of mankind'—squalor, hunger, deprivation and despair. For myself, I rejoice in this as the most beneficial social development in world history; and I detest the grudging reaction of those who have never themselves known poverty, or what it means to scrabble and scrimp and starve and scheme simply to get the basic decencies of life, never mind the luxuries. An excessive love of money is odious' but money, *some* discretionary money, is the essential condition—which the mass of people have utterly lacked until recent times—of privacy, a dignified family life, and reasonable hope for the future. Of course there are innumerable things wrong with the affluent society. But why, the moment that the workers acquire the cars, the holidays, and the gadgets which the critics have been enjoying all their lives, should they be condemned as 'fatty' and 'degenerate'?[63]

As the limit on such measures is grudging acceptance rather than actual respect for consumer choice,[64] measures for coercively intervening in the choice of goods have become normalised in the maximalist welfare state. Shaw expressed his views on alcohol in terms which anticipated what would now be called the identification of a negative externality calling for corrective taxation.[65] These views were given some prominence in the argument by which AC Pigou made the externality (though he did not use that term) a pillar of modern welfare economics.[66] Let us leave aside the other shortcomings of the externality as a guide to policy which led Coase to claim, as we saw in Chapter 5, that its 'central role in welfare economics [has had] results which

[62] The distinguished political theorist Colin Crouch has tried to explain the sale of iPads as the result of 'a firm [finding] that it could make them, and [setting] about generating a demand by clever marketing ... the role of consumers in all this was passive': C Crouch, *The Strange Non-death of Neo-liberalism* (Polity Press 2011) 26–27. I have personal experience of ready academic critics of bingo, horoscopes, cars, meat, etc finding this a troubling argument. And what if Crouch had picked, not on the I understand now rather old hat iPad, but on the iPhone?

[63] CAR Crosland, 'Radical Reform and the Left' in *The Conservative Enemy* (Jonathan Cape 1962) 128–29. Crosland's corollary view of advertising is set out in CAR Crosland, 'The Mass Media' in *The Conservative Enemy*, ibid.

[64] In a passage unchanged from the first edn of 1937, in 1947 Jay, *Socialist Case* (n 61) 256 observed that 'No sane man would presumably advocate the entire abolition ... of customer's choice', but he did so in response to 'Those who wish to "plan" everybody's consumption': ibid 257.

[65] Shaw, *Common Sense* (n 56) 183:

> Suppose the drink trade were debited with what it costs in disablement, inefficiency, illness and crime, with all their depressing effects on industrial productivity, and with their direct cost in doctors, policemen and prisons, etc, etc, etc! ... It would at once appear that ... the pleasures of drunkenness are costly beyond all reason.

[66] AC Pigou, *The Economics of Welfare* (5th edn, Transaction Books 2002) 186, 192. This reference is to the main text of the *Economics of Welfare*, established in the 4th edn of 1932. *The Common Sense of Municipal Trading* first appeared 1904 and Pigou had referred to it in this way in both the 1920 1st edn of *The Economics of Welfare* and the book of which it was in effect a much expanded revision, *Wealth and Welfare* of 1914.

have been wholly unfortunate'.[67] The externality's fundamental shortcoming is that because, as is so often insisted in criticism of neo-classical economics, general equilibrium can never exist, then market failure is universal and externalities are 'ubiquitous'.[68] The mere identification of an externality therefore cannot itself be *any* guide to the occasions of intervention, but in an instance of a writer losing control of his ideas which is noteworthy even against the background of a discussion of Karl Marx,[69] in 'Pigouvian' welfare economics after Pigou the identification of *any* externality may, depending on the political situation, become the occasion of intervention. The belief 'that when "externalities" are found, steps should be taken by the government to eliminate them'[70] has become an essential feature distinguishing the maximalist from the Beveridgean welfare state, and in this way 'methodologically sound' cases for 'piecemeal' intervention have become swamped by a 'utopian' social engineering that knows no principled bounds.[71]

Perhaps not unexpectedly to those familiar with Shaw's character, Shaw described in strong terms indeed what he regarded as the emphatic confirmation by the political history of the twentieth century of the gradualist political tactics definitive of Fabianism, tactics which certainly had been under vehement anarchist and communist attack right from the inception of the Society.[72] Looking back in 1948 he said:

> though socialist may be substituted for capitalist governments in twenty four hours it by no means follows that industry and agriculture, religion and art and their professions, land and capital, can be transferred from private to public ownership and management in twenty four hours or completed even within twenty four years. Crushing proof of this has come from Russia, where the disciples of Karl Marx, the Arch Anti-capitalist, in 1917 established what Marx called 'The Dictatorship of the Proletariat'. After a few years of anti-Fabian catastrophic policy which brought their country to the verge of ruin and a bit over, they were forced to announce a New Economic Policy which was in fact Fabian, and which has had a prodigious civilising success, besides carrying its union of Society republics through a frightfully destructive war against all the military might of Germany and her allies.[73]

[67] RH Coase, 'The Firm, the Market and the Law' in *The Firm the Market and the Law* (University of Chicago Press 1988) 26, hereafter Coase, 'Firm, Market, Law'.

[68] ibid.

[69] Pigou was sympathetic to socialism, but whilst he seems on occasion to have acknowledged the possibility of an ultimately completely planned economy, his views in this respect were so gradualist, and in such conflict with his belief that 'the working of self-interest is generally beneficent' (discussed in ch 1), that those views have no real definition, and he was, for all practical purposes, committed to some form of mixed economy: AC Pigou, *Socialism Versus Capitalism* (William Pickering 1994) 137–38.

[70] Coase, 'Firm, Market, Law' (n 67) 26.

[71] KR Popper, *The Open Society and Its Enemies* (5th edn, Routledge and Kegan Paul 1966) vol 1, 158.

[72] The very name of the Society was chosen as a response to that attack, with the cover of very first Fabian Tract carrying an epigraph in praise of the wisdom of the Roman general and dictator Quintus Fabius Maximus Verrucosus, whose agnomen 'Cunctator', 'delayer', connotes the broad nature of his military tactics: [WL Phillips], *Why are the Many Poor?* Fabian Tract 1 (Fabian Society 1884) (Phillips' authorship is identified in Pease, *History* (n 6) 230).

[73] Shaw, 'Sixty Years' (n 5) 215.

War Communism was indeed 'Anti-Fabian' in the sense that it was a now scarcely believable utopian indulgence by the Bolshevik Party made possible only by terror, and the New Economic Policy did mark a return to some sort of accommodation with reality.[74] But Shaw's fulsome praise of the New Economic Policy and subsequent USSR policies up to the Second World War includes praise of—it is sufficient to mention just this—the collectivisation of agriculture, and what he said in 1948 merely is a continuation of views he had expressed during the 1930s which could be seen to be foolish at the time.[75] One always has to guard against being overly sympathetic towards attempts to do what one oneself believes should be done, but these views represent far more than a failure of this sort, and the crucial point is that Shaw became critical only of the Bolshevik *means*. He was not critical of, say, public ownership and management of the means of production for aiming towards, as he saw it, the abolition of private property, and his economics remained directed at the utopia which lay beyond the end of capitalism. His essay on economics in the *Fabian Essays* concluded thus:

> The science of the production and distribution of wealth is political economy. Socialism appeals to that science and … routs it in incurable disaster. Henceforth the bitter cynic who still finds the world an eternal and unimprovable doghole [who] repeats the familiar misquotation 'the poor ye shall always have with you'[76] lose their usurped place among the cultured and pass over to the ranks of the ignorant, the shallow, and the superstitious … It is to economic science—once the dismal, now the hopeful—that we are indebted for the discovery that though the evil [of capitalism] is enormously worse than we knew, yet it is not eternal—not even very long-lived, if we only bestir ourselves to make an end of it.[77]

The bounds of what should be done to achieve that end that Shaw acknowledged are only the bounds of what at a particular time it is politically possible to do; a limit ultimately set by the refractory wills of those whose lot one is certain one is trying to improve.

[74] Nove, *Economic History of the USSR* (n 53) chs 4–6.

[75] Eg in GB Shaw, *The Rationalisation of Russia* (Indiana University Press 1964) 91, an unfinished summary of the impressions he formed of the USSR during a visit in 1931, echoes of which sound in other of his works, including the prefaces to some of his plays, Shaw tells us that:

> the cardinal difference between an English and a Russian prison is that in England a delinquent enters as an ordinary man and comes out as a 'criminal type', whereas in Russia he enters … as a criminal type and would come out an ordinary man but for the difficulty of inducing him to come out [from prison!] at all.

The point is that such views were not extreme in their milieu, and S Webb and B Webb, *Soviet Communism: A New Civilisation* (reissued 2nd edn, Longmans, Green and Co 1941), from which the question mark at the end of the title of the first edition had been removed, may take pride of place amongst many works to similar effect.

[76] Though the misquotation may indeed be familiar, I do not think Shaw expressed himself perfectly well. He meant the very common drawing of the opposite conclusion from that which is drawn in Scripture. Deuteronomy 15:11 tells us that:

> the poor shall never cease out of the land: therefore I command thee, saying, thou shalt open thine hand wide unto thy brother, to thy poor, and to thy needy, in thy land.

[77] Shaw, 'Economic' (n 13) 27.

Shaw's significance hardly now lies in any of the detail of his views but in the general attitude in British public life that he did a great deal to create. When Shaw died in 1950, the abolition of private property in the form of widespread nationalisation of industry and services had become practical politics, but if this enthusiasm has since waxed and waned, the more important attitude, definitive of the maximalist welfare state, has enjoyed secular growth. This is the attitude, compared to which the mere abolition of private property seems an almost concrete proposal, of presuming intervention to be good, and so in principle of unlimited scale and scope, because the economics of self-interest should not be applied to the altruistic bestowing of benefits by public bodies which are above such considerations.[78] In an irony as striking as it is important, and as was inevitable if Beveridgean limits were regarded only as unfortunate restrictions on the maximalist welfare state, the criticism of the acquisitive society has given rise to a 'taste for the unconditioned life'.[79] Though it has emerged from the struggle for civil citizenship:

> the unconditioned life [is] something different from enjoying rights and decent treatment from one's fellows. It was to act as if nothing stood in the way of every wish.[80]

The unconditioned life is subject to a strikingly similar criticism to that made of the acquisitive society. The difference between them is that the latter is based on (an inaccurate identification of) an absence of morality in the in-principle constrained private demand for goods in the market economy, whilst the former is based on (an accurate identification of) an in-principle unbounded public expenditure when sanctioned by the purposive morality of the maximalist welfare state.[81]

The taste for the unconditioned life meets with such gratification as it does only because it is pandered to by an 'unconstrained vision' of the possibilities of intervention.[82] I wish to focus on two aspects of this political culture relating to the practice of regulation as it is understood here,[83] or perhaps two ways of looking at the same point from opposite directions.[84] First, whilst it is not, as was pointed out in Chapter 6,

[78] A Downs, *An Economic Theory of Democracy* (Addison Wesley 1957) ch 15.

[79] J Barzun, *From Dawn to Decadence* (HarperCollins 2000) 781.

[80] ibid.

[81] D Bell, *The Cultural Contradictions of Capitalism* (2nd edn, Heinemann 1979) 220–26 contrasted 'the public household' as originally conceived as 'the management of state revenues and expenditures ... for the satisfaction of public needs ... as against private wants [provided by] the market, which seeks to serve diverse private wants', and was critical of the 'hedonism' of 'the prodigal idea of private wants and unlimited ends'. But the establishment of 'normative economic policy in the 1960s [and] normative social policy in the 1960s [created] new and deep dilemmas for the society':

> the public household now becomes the arena for the expression not only of public needs *but also of private wants* ... And this raises a fundamental question of restraints. The economic constraint on private wants is the amount of money that a man has ... But what are the constraints on political demands?

[82] T Sowell, *A Conflict of Visions* (Basic Books 2007) 15–17.

[83] Of the conditions for successful democracy set out in the consideration of the relationship of socialism and democracy in JA Schumpeter, *Capitalism, Socialism and Democracy* (5th edn, George Allen & Unwin 1976) 289–96, three at least do not, on balance, now apply: 'the effective range of political decision should not be extended too far'; 'electorates and parliaments' must exercise 'Democratic Self-control'; and there should be 'a large measure of tolerance for difference of opinion'.

[84] Even within the confines of a study of forms of regulation, however (D Campbell, 'The Market in the Theory of Regulation' (2018) 27 Social and Legal Studies 545, 551–52), our focus on the collapse of

disputed that good cases for extensive, important interventions can be made, so that those interventions should indeed be welcomed, the normal standards for assessing whether an intervention will enhance welfare have become normally slovenly, with the consequence that the marginal returns to intervention are very oftenly negative. Though Ronald Coase is widely thought to have had a bias against intervention, I am convinced that, first, his judgements about cases for this, though as we shall see they were overwhelmingly unfavourable, were objectively made, though I disagree with a number of them;[85] that, secondly, the, as it were, method he proposed for making such judgements is intrinsically objective;[86] and, thirdly, that he was justified in tracing the slovenliness of welfare economics to defects in Pigou's basic approach.[87]

In an episode with a particular resonance in the history of welfare economics, but the main significance of which is that it is an otherwise perfectly commonplace example of policy formulation, Shaw's and Pigou's punitive taxes on alcohol consumption have been levied in response to the widespread 'binge-drinking' which now disfigures British city centres, even though this was caused, not by spontaneous changes to personal action, but by a governmental change to the regulatory regime intended, as indeed it has, to increase the 'night-time economy' of those cities. The slovenliness of the formulation of this policy, and the reckless disregard of unintended but very likely side effects would be striking were they not normal.[88] It is in this light that we should understand why Coase's very wide experience of case studies for intervention led him to conclude that cases of successful intervention were rare, and acknowledge a strength in his claim that:

> the most probable reason we obtain these results is that the government is attempting to do too much—that it operates on such a gigantic scale that it has reached the stage at which, for many of its activities, the marginal product is negative. We would expect to reach this stage if the size of an organisation were allowed to expand indefinitely. I suspect this is exactly what has happened—the continued expansion of the government's role will inevitably lead us to a situation in which most government activities result in more harm than good.[89]

discipline over piecemeal regulation should be complemented by a discussion of the way that Keynesian macro-economic management has shifted from being a counter-cyclical policy, as it was devised, to an intendedly permanent state of stimulation of economic activity: JM Buchanan and RE Wagner, *Democracy in Deficit* in JM Buchanan, *Collected Works*, vol 8 (Liberty Fund 2000).

[85] D Campbell and M Klaes, 'What Did Ronald Coase Know About the Law of Tort?' (2016) 39 The Melbourne University Law Review 793 (hereafter Campbell and Klaes). This paper is in large part a response to perhaps the most substantial claim that Coase was biased in this way by a Commonwealth legal scholar: AWB Simpson, 'Coase v Pigou Re-examined' (1996) 25 Journal of Legal Studies 53; revised as AWB Simpson, 'The Story of *Sturges v Bridgman*: The Resolution of Land Use Disputes Between Neighbours' in G Korngold and AP Morriss (eds), *Property Stories* (2nd edn, Foundation Press 2009).

[86] Campbell and Klaes (n 85) and D Campbell, 'Ronald Coase's "The Problem of Social Cost"' (2016) 35 University of Queensland Law Review 75, 83–88.

[87] D Campbell, 'The Sense in Coase's Critique of Pigou' (2017) 13 The Journal of Law, Economics and Policy 39.

[88] D Campbell, 'Alcohol-related Disorder and the Nature of the Problem of Social Cost' [2005] Public Law 749.

[89] RH Coase, 'Economists and Public Policy' in *Essays on Economics and Economists* (University of Chicago Press 1994) 62. Expressing these views in 1974, Coase's concluding sentence of this passage was: 'My surmise is that we have reached this stage'.

The welfarist attitude towards the law of contract emphasises a second, in a sense opposite, aspect of intervention in the maximalist welfare state. Not only is there a general ungrounded confidence that intervention will work, but this stage of the typical non-argument about the wisdom of intervention follows in the wake of a general disrespect of the voluntary choices which are to be improved. The most obviously unwelcome specific aspect of this is the growth of the law of negligence and the compensation culture it has founded discussed in Chapter 5. However, this is but part of a disregard for freedom and sanctity of contract, the more important because it is more generally corrosive of respect for the responsibility evidenced in voluntary choice. Bentham set up a sort of presumption against intervention by claiming that (imperative) law is in itself a mischief because it analytically must coercively alter action.[90] To yet again repeat, such a consideration does not preclude intervention, but it does show that the mischief of imperative law has to be found to be outweighed by the mischief avoided. Bentham's first substantial discussion of a situation in which this was not shown was when the mischief to be avoided:

> was such as might, on some occasions, be mischievous or disagreeable, but the person who gave his *consent* to the performance of it. This consent, provided it be free and fairly obtained, is the best proof that can be produced that, to the person who gives it, no mischief, at least no immediate mischief, upon the whole, is done. For no man can be so good a judge of the man himself what it is that gives him pleasure or displeasure.[91]

What is left of this, as a principle, in the welfarist attitude to the law of contract?

In Chapters 3 and 4, we saw that the doctrine of agreement which, by bracketing the range of alternatives which should be actively considered, makes voluntary choice possible in circumstances of radically imperfect information and radically limited computational competence, is viewed as manipulation; which it is when set against some absurd standard of an absence of 'coercion'.[92] In Chapters 5, 6, and 7, we saw that the doctrine of consideration which, by stipulating that payment is the only way to acquire scarce goods through voluntary transfer, makes rational choice between mutually exclusive alternatives possible, is viewed a 'fallacy'; which it is when set against some never coherently specified standard of superior allocation reeking of sanctimoniousness. In Chapters 8, 9, and 10, we saw that the doctrine of remedy which, by bringing about appropriate forms of co-operative response to the error which is inevitable in the face of risk and uncertainty, minimises the costs of such error, is criticised as 'seriously defective'; which it is when this crucial aspect of the unrivalled performance of the general market economy is absurdly viewed as a failure to 'attach a value' to the performance of fundamental obligations. This fundamental disrespect for exchange and contract is

[90] J Bentham, *An Introduction to the Principles of Morals and Legislation* in *Collected Works* (Clarendon Press 1996) 158.

[91] ibid 159.

[92] EW Patterson, 'Compulsory Contracts in the Crystal Ball' (1943) 43 Columbia Law Review 731, 741:

> if a man is deemed not to 'consent' because he was induced by pressure outside himself, then consent becomes a useless concept in the administration of justice.

a major constituent of the atmosphere in which it seems sensible to make all sorts of improvements to the law of contract, and improvements to welfare by intervening to restrict the Pareto region of that law's operation, though when they have gone beyond the bounds of the Beveridgean welfare state, those improvements have been fundamentally a mistake.

Planning, scarcity, and inchoate communism

The attempt I have made to in substantial part derive the argument of this book from detailed knowledge of the views of Karl Marx runs wholly counter to the intellectual spirit of the age. The time when the defence of liberal democracy and the market economy was thought to require such knowledge is long past, and the atmosphere in which Marx's views on exchange and contract are now intellectually regarded is, I think, most graphically captured in Richard Rorty's—the point is he was far from an ignoramus about the issues—having made a boast about not finishing *Capital*.[93] The argument here is that we must conceive of the law of contract as the legal institutionalisation of market socialism because this is necessary for a *desirable*, *general*, *practical* reform of the way that contracts serve, as we saw Macaulay put it in Chapter 2, as 'devices for conducting exchanges'. This obliges the book to confront the paradox, initially approached in Chapter 1, involved in believing that Marx could ever offer anything of value for reform of exchange and contract, for he undoubtedly thought that exchange was of its nature so bad that further human progress posited its ultimate abolition in communism. Those whose views demand serious attention who are in express, reasoned agreement with this view are now a vanishingly small group, perhaps an empty set. But it is essential to give serious attention to those whose views are an implicit, intellectually confused assertion of what I will call inchoate communism, for these views underpin the maximalist welfare state and welfarism in contract.

That knowledge of the detail of Marx's economics, and really of his thought *in toto*, is now very restricted has been unfortunate in two ways of relevance to our concerns. The first is that a restated critique of the alienation of economic action, in which Marx must be an essential point of reference, is, it was argued in Chapter 11, the necessary basis of the adequate understanding of exchange and contract as based, not on solipsistic self-interest, but on self-interest conscious of the moral relationship of mutual recognition. This consciousness, it has been suggested, is best seen as a liberal form of socialism, and an economy constituted of exchange of this nature is the social market, not as some *ad hoc* combination of the 'individual' and the 'social', but which is a market in which consciousness of the social ontology of economic action is known to be the condition of the reproduction of autonomy in a general system for allocating economic goods.

The second way in which disregard of Marx has been unfortunate is that it has prevented the drawing of the lesson which has had to be drawn from the utter implausibility of the way Marx himself ultimately saw the issues. In the section on the

[93] R Rorty, 'A Spectre is Haunting the Intellectuals: Derrida on Marx' in *Philosophy and Social Hope* (Penguin Books 1999) 210–11.

fetishism of commodities in *Capital*, volume one, Marx described the alternative to the alienated society he had described:

> Let us now picture to ourselves, by way of change, a community of free individuals, carrying on their work with the means of production in common, in which the labour power of all the different individuals is consciously applied as the combined labour power of the community ... The total product of our community is a social product. One portion serves as a fresh means of production and remains social. But another portion is consumed by the members as means of subsistence. A distribution of this portion amongst them is consequently necessary ... apportionment in accordance with a definite social plan maintains the proper proportion between the different kinds of work to be done and the various wants of the community ... The social relations of the individual producers, with regard both to their labour and to its products, are in this case perfectly simple and intelligible ... The life-process of society ... based on material production, does not strip off its mystical veil until it is treated as production by freely associated men, and is consciously regulated by them in accordance with a settled plan.[94]

Sustained criticism of Marx's concept of communism as a form of association,[95] and *a fortiori*, of the actually existing communist experience of 'utopia in power',[96] is supererogatory. For our purposes, it is necessary to make only two points about the former: first, it rests on the abolition of scarcity; and secondly, it cannot be derived from an immanent critique of capitalism.

There is almost nothing of any definiteness in all of Engels' and Marx's vast published and unpublished corpus about, if this word be allowed, the organisation of communism.[97] To the extent this follows from their rejection of the exogenous ideals of socialist utopias, this is correct. Marx's most famous statement of this rejection was his refusal in the Afterword to the second German edition of volume one of *Capital* to write 'recipes (Comtist ones?) for the cookshops of the future',[98] but a more substantial statement may be found in *The Civil War in France*:

[94] Marx, *Capital*, vol 1 (n 18) 89–90. A particular aspect of what Marx is driving at is that competition '*is* ... externalised ... as an outward necessity' only because 'social conditions ... assume the form of objective powers', and therefore competition's 'chaotic collisions' will be eliminated in a form association which moves beyond the 'limited basis of the domination of capital': Marx, *Grundrisse* (n 27) vol 29, 39, 40, 47.

[95] A Walicki, *Marxism and the Leap to the Kingdom of Freedom* (Stanford University Press 1995).

[96] M Geller and A Nekrich, *Utopia in Power* (Hutchinson 1986).

[97] The passages on industrial organisation of which I am aware which have some definiteness amount to the continuation of capitalist technique: eg Marx, *Capital*, vol 1 (n 18) 361–62. The most substantial discussion of actual technique is the all but unknown F Engels, 'On Authority' in K Marx and F Engels, *Collected Works*, vol 23 (Lawrence and Wishart 1988) 423–24. I have said that discussion of actually existing communism is supererogatory, but it is necessary to note the portentousness of this theme, leading as it did to the paean to capitalist technique, which amounted to a complete unawareness of the transaction costs of hierarchical order, in Lenin's views which were actually to be put into practice: VI Lenin, *The State and Revolution* in *Collected Works*, vol 25 (Lawrence and Wishart 1964) 443, 474:

> [Under] complete planning ... it is quite possible, after the overthrow of the capitalists ... to proceed immediately, overnight [to create] a single, country-wide 'syndicate' [so that] The whole of society will have become a single office and a single factory.

[98] Marx, *Capital*, vol 1 (n 18) 17 (translation amended).

> The working class … have no ready-made utopias to introduce *par décret du peuple*. They know that in order to work out their own emancipation, and along with it that higher form to which present society is irresistibly tending by its own economical agencies, they will have to pass through long struggles, through a series of historical processes, transforming circumstances and men. They have no ideals to realise but to set free elements of the new society with which the old collapsing bourgeois society itself is pregnant.[99]

If, however, this is to work as a rejection of utopian socialism in favour of a new society which develops tendencies in existing society, then providing *some* detail about those tendencies, and how they would be realised in communism, was essential. Having rejected exogenous ideals, one must be able to derive endogenous 'ideals'. A successful critique analytically implies an alternative. But that Engels and Marx provided effectively nothing about communist organisation has been, as Miliband rightly put it, Marxism's Achilles' heel.[100]

The early works of Engels and Marx contain a number of blissfully attractive descriptions of communist life, which there can be no doubt drove all their subsequent work. In the 'Preface' to *A Contribution to the Critique of Political Economy*,[101] Marx referred to *The German Ideology*, a philosophical work he and Engels wrote in 1845–46 which could not then be published for political reasons, and was not available at all until after Engels' death, but the first part of which has had an important, and in the post-war period very important, influence on the interpretation of *Capital*. The following now famous passage gives a communist account of the division of labour:

> as soon as the division of labour comes into being, each man has a particular, exclusive sphere of activity which is forced upon him and from which he cannot escape. He is a hunter, a fisherman, a shepherd or a critical critic, and must remain so if he does not want to lose his means of livelihood; whereas in communist society, where nobody has one exclusive sphere of activity but each can become accomplished in any branch he wishes, society regulates the general production and thus makes it possible for me to do one thing today and another tomorrow, to hunt in the morning, fish in the afternoon, rear cattle in the evening, criticise after dinner, *just as I have a mind*, without ever becoming a hunter, fisherman, shepherd or critic.[102]

How work could be socially co-ordinated on this completely unconstrained basis is impossible to say, beyond that, as we have seen Marx claim in volume one, it will be co-ordinated by 'freely associated men, and … consciously regulated by them in accordance with a settled plan'.[103] The attractiveness of this lyric passage in *The German*

[99] K Marx, *The Civil War in France* in K Marx and F Engels, *Collected Works*, vol 22 (Lawrence & Wishart 1986) 335.
[100] R Miliband, 'Lenin's *The State and Revolution*' [1970] The Socialist Register 309.
[101] K Marx, *A Contribution to the Critique of Political Economy* in K Marx and F Engels, *Collected Works*, vol 29 (Lawrence & Wishart 1987) 264.
[102] Marx and Engels, *German Ideology* (n 1) 47 (emphasis added)
[103] Obviously, saying even this much involves a contradiction between 'just as I have a mind' and 'settled plan'. But the point is that it has proven fruitless to make even this much inquiry into these statements.

Ideology, though Engels and Marx would have bitterly resented the comparison, is reminiscent of nothing so much as Fourier's belief that when humankind has managed to achieve a rational, combined order in its eighth social period, it will find it is able to cultivate more or less all the Earth, eliminate extremes of temperature, turn the seas into an inexhaustible source of refreshment ('the kind of lemonade known as *aigresel*'), domesticate useful fish, etc, etc.[104] That Marx 'never considered the organisational implications of his ideas',[105] and was 'oblivious of the inescapable opacity and indirectness of communication and decision in [all] large bodies of men ... let alone those organised around a large and complex productive system',[106] has meant that his conception of communism is so devoid of practical meaning as to be, in my opinion, senseless, and certainly irrelevant to the consideration of the very issues that constitute economics,[107] politics,[108] and, indeed, human aspiration.[109] The truly fundamental question is how it could be that Marx, the interest of whose 'materialist' views on human agency in the context of humanity's relationship to its natural environment remains very great, could suffer from this lacuna?

We must return to the famous passage of *The Critique of the Gotha Programme* discussed in Chapter 2, in which the socialist stage of post-capitalist society which bears 'defects [which] are inevitable in the first phase of communist society, as it is when it has just emerged after prolonged birth-pangs from capitalist society'; is contrasted to the:

> higher phase of communist society, after the enslaving subjugation of the individual to the division of labour, and thereby the antithesis between mental and physical labour, has vanished; after labour has become not only a means to life but life's prime want; after the productive forces have also increased with the all-round development of the individual, and all the springs of common wealth flow more abundantly—only then can the narrow horizon of bourgeois right be crossed in its entirety and society inscribe on its banners: From each according to his abilities, to each according to his needs![110]

In Chapter 2 it was noted that 'From each according to his abilities, to each according to his needs' is not an egalitarian principle. It is a principle which makes equality irrelevant. We should now note that neither is it an altruistic principle. Such absolutely

[104] C Fourier, *The Theory of the Four Movements* (CUP 1996) 47–56.

[105] A Nove, *The Economics of Feasible Socialism* (George Allen & Unwin 1983) 59 (hereafter Nove, *Feasible Socialism*).

[106] C Taylor, *Hegel and Modern Society* (CUP 1979) 153.

[107] Nove, *Feasible Socialism* (n 105) 10.

[108] A MacIntyre, *After Virtue* (2nd edn, Duckworth 1985) 260–62.

[109] A Gorz, *Critique of Economic Reason* (Verso 1989) 95–96:

> the question why [human beings] aspire to achieve free, autonomous self-realisation will not be answered as long as it is seen from the perspective adopted by Marx. For him, this question simply did not arise because ... he saw history as the process by which meaning took possession of the real, this meaning being ... the fully developed individual becoming master of nature and of the process by which nature was mastered.

[110] K Marx, *Critique of the Gotha Programme* in K Marx and F Engels, *Collected Works*, vol 24 (Lawrence and Wishart 1989) 87.

unconstrained action makes even altruism irrelevant; one just does as one wants. As we saw in Chapter 1, Engels and Marx believed capitalism constituted the closure of the 'pre-history of society' by furnishing the conditions that made communism scientifically possible rather than a mere utopia. They believed that the wealth capitalism had generated made it possible, by a movement to a different, communist, form of social organisation, to end the scarcity of economic goods by which humankind had experienced the refractoriness of nature. The limits on human possibility were limits imposed by capitalism after it had played its 'historically most revolutionary part'. This purely social view of the conditions of human existence seemed to allow communist association to eliminate the refractory sense in which humankind, even after the achievements of capitalism, must experience nature.[111] In such bliss, all competition over resources is meaningless, and so the movement towards communism can be conceived as a process of the state withering away,[112] for without scarcity, let us allow, there is no occasion for (class) conflict, and so no need for a state.[113]

It is only if one is possessed of the 'peculiar idea that a fundamental change in the whole universe will go hand in hand with the proper organisation of human relations'[114] that Marx's views make even the most rudimentary sense, and no-one should be so possessed. If all that is causing the economic problem is adherence to capitalist relations of production that have done their historical work, then clearing them away leads to wholly unconstrained freedom. The relationship between humankind and nature captured in use-value can be grasped directly, without the historically frustrating mediation of exchange-value. But if scarcity is an existential condition, then the issue facing capitalism will face any concretely conceivable mode of production, of which set communism, a mode of production in which this condition is not to apply, is therefore not a member.[115]

The crucial point has, to my knowledge, been best captured by Hume in his explanation of the origin of justice in the *Enquiry* into morals which he himself considered his best work, though it has been eclipsed by his explanation of property in other works:

[111] K Kosik, *Dialectics of the Concrete* (Reidel 1976) 152:

> Though nature for man is humanised, in industry, in technology, science and culture, this does not imply that nature is in general a 'social category'. Cognition of nature and its mastery is socially conditioned, and nature is a social category, changing through history, in *this* sense; but the absolute existence of nature depends on nothing and on no-one.

[112] Engels, *Anti-Dühring* (n 51) 268.

[113] JP Sartre, *Critique of Dialectical Reason* (New Left Books 1976) 145–46:

> What is striking in Engels' interpretations, and often in Marx's too, is that the references to scarcity are almost incomprehensible . . . taken literally [they] would have us believe that . . . it is the mode of production which, through the institutions that it conditions, produces the social scarcity of its product, that is to say, class inequality.

[114] A Schmidt, *The Concept of Nature in Marx* (New Left Books 1971) 163.

[115] A Gorz, *Farewell to the Working Class* (Pluto Books 1982) 119:

> Politics is not morality, just as morality is not politics. Politics is the site at which moral exigencies confront external necessities. This confrontation will last so long as, in Hegel's phrase, consciousness does not encounter the world 'as a garden laid out for its benefit'. The quotation is from GWF Hegel,

The Phenomenology of Spirit (CUP 2018) 326 (hereafter Hegel, Phenomenology).

> Let us suppose that nature has bestowed on the human race such profuse *abundance* of all *external* conveniences that ... without any care or industry on our part, every individual finds himself fully provided with whatever his most voracious appetites can want, or luxurious imagination wish or desire ... No laborious occupation required: No tillage: No navigation. Music, poetry, and contemplation form his sole business. Conversation, mirth, and friendship his sole amusement. It seems evident that, in such a happy state, every other social virtue would flourish and receive tenfold increase; but the cautious, jealous virtue of justice would never one be dreamed of. For what purpose make a partition of goods where everyone has already more than enough? ... Why call this object mine when, upon seizing of it by another, I need but stretch out my hand to possess myself of what is equally valuable? Justice in that case being totally *useless*, would be an idle ceremonial and could never have place in the catalogue of virtues.[116]

Though Marx's engagement with Hume was very limited, he would have agreed with this way of seeing the issues, with the difference that, as he believed that capitalism *had* potentially 'bestowed on the human race such profuse *abundance* of all *external* conveniences', he would have maintained that, once communism was established, every individual *would* find 'himself fully provided with whatever his most voracious appetites can want, or luxurious imagination wish or desire'.

We have seen that Marx conceived of capitalism as a specific mode of production, the most recent of an historical succession of such modes, which had raised human progress to unprecedented heights. As was claimed in the previous chapter, Marx had in this way reached the same point as had the Scottish Enlightenment view of history represented by Smith;[117] the Age of Commerce is the capitalist mode of production. The difference is, of course, that whereas Smith saw no further possibility of a further stage of *fundamental* social change and improvement,[118] Marx posited communism

[116] D Hume, *An Enquiry Concerning the Principals of Morals* in *The Clarendon Edition of the Works*, vol 4 (Clarendon Press 1998) 13. One is not obliged to agree with all aspects of Hume's explanation of property to recognise that he regarded justice as social ontologically prior to property in the sense that (D Hume, *A Treatise of Human Nature* in *The Clarendon Edition of the Works*, vol 1 (Clarendon Press 2007) 315):

> Our property is nothing but those goods whose constant possession is established by the laws of society; that is by the laws of justice ... A man's property is some object related to him. This relation is not natural but moral, founded on justice ... showing its origin in the artifice and contrivance of man.

[117] There are intricacies in relating Hume to the four stages theory that cannot be discussed here. But Hume did, of course, recognise a general contrast between present 'times of industry and refinement' in 'which there is more exchange and commerce of all kinds', and 'the rude, uncultivated ages' which were 'the first ... ages of any state': D Hume, 'Of Money' in *Essays Political, Moral and Literary* in *The Clarendon Edition of the Works* (Clarendon Press 2021) 224–25.

[118] This statement must be put in the context of Smith being acutely aware of what would now be called the social costs of capitalism, including what could well be called the alienation of work caused by the division of labour: Smith, *Wealth of Nations* (n 37) 781–82. This theme, undoubtedly in part drawn from Scottish Enlightenment thought, is also prominent in Hegel's account of 'civil society': GWF Hegel, *Elements of the Philosophy of Right* (CUP 1991) s 243. The gross misinterpretation of Smith as an uncritical advocate of capitalism has been paralleled by a similar misinterpretation of Hegel's concept of the modern state, and in particular what he meant by what has been called 'the end of history': GWF Hegel, *Lectures on the History of Philosophy*, vol 3 (Kegan Paul, Trench, Trübner 1896) 551:

precisely as such a stage, or, vitally importantly, of socialism and then communism as succeeding stages.[119]

One could in principle derive from capitalism a form of socialism understood in this broad sense, as the derivation would have to, but could, be argued from the basis of capitalist possibility. But there is no other than a utopian ground for deriving communism from capitalism,[120] for the end of scarcity has to amount, disastrously, to 'an absolute separation between two historical eras'.[121] The end of scarcity cannot satisfy Marx's own criterion of successful critique,[122] as opposed to utopian criticism, because it cannot be derived from the immanent critique of the classical political economy of his time, nor, we should now add, from the neo-classical economics of ours, both of which absolutely turn on the ineluctability of scarcity. Even if one accepts the possibility of socialism, it is wholly illegitimate to extend this to a claim that doing so further shows the possibility of communist society, for it does nothing of the sort. Though it is essential to the Marx's overall conception, socialism cannot lead from capitalism to communism, for even if one allows, for the sake of argument, that a socialist general plan could in some sense be more 'efficient' than market order, no growth in wealth under socialism can remotely approximate to the abolition of scarcity.[123] Communism is a higher phase defined by the absence of 'defects [which] are

> A new epoch has arisen in the world. It would appear as if Spirit had at least succeeded in stripping off from itself all alien ... existence and apprehending itself at last as absolute Spirit ... This is the whole history of the world ... the up to the present time, and the history of philosophy in particular ... Now, indeed, [philosophy] seems to have reached its goal, when this absolute self-consciousness, which it had the work of representing, has ceased to be alien, and when Spirit accordingly is realised as Spirit ... This, then, is the standpoint of the present day, and the series of spiritual forms is with it for the present concluded.

119 It will be recalled that in Chapter 11 a passage was quoted from Letter from Karl Marx to Joseph Wedemeyer (5 March 1852) in K Marx and F Engels, *Collected Works*, vol 39 (Lawrence and Wishart 1983) 62:

> I do not claim to have discovered either the existence of classes in modern society or the struggle between them. Long before me, bourgeois historians had described the historical development of this struggle between the classes, as had bourgeois economists their economic anatomy

The letter continues at 62–63:

> My own contribution was (1) to show that the *existence of classes* is merely bound up with *certain historical phases in the development of production*; (2) that the class struggle necessarily leads to the *dictatorship of the proletariat*; (3) that this dictatorship itself constitutes no more than a transition to the *abolition of all classes* and to a *classless society*.

120 S Moore, *Marx on the Choice Between Socialism and Communism* (Harvard University Press 1980).

121 G Sorel, *Reflections on Violence* (CUP 1999) 129.

122 Marx and Engels, *German Ideology* (n 1) 49:

> Communism is for us not a state of affairs which is to be established, an ideal to which reality will have to adjust itself. We call communism the real movement which abolishes the present state of things. The conditions of this movement result from the now existing premise.

123 O Lange, 'On the Economic Theory of Socialism' in O Lange and FM Taylor, *On the Economic Theory of Socialism* (University of Minnesota Press 1939) 141:

> It is quite conceivable that ... wealth increases ... and an increasing number of commodities are distributed by free sharing ... until, finally, all the prime necessaries of life are provided for in this way ... Thus Marx's second phase of communism may be gradually approached.

As a general position, this would be possible only if the goods which constituted prime necessaries were identified by central authority, a purely formal achievement in complete contradiction of Marx's aspiration.

inevitable in the first phase of communist society', but nothing could more thoroughly demonstrate the abandonment of Marx's own criterion of successful critique than that one can make no more of this than that communism therefore is a process of the elimination of the capitalist 'survivals' in socialism.[124] This is an entirely negative contradiction of immanent critique *which itself has no determinate content.*

The failure of Marx's communism has the significance it has because it was the failure of a leading, indeed over 'economic' issues the leading, modern European representative of rationalism in social thought which now, even more than when Berlin so strongly criticised the 'positive doctrine of liberation by reason',[125] is such an influence in the liberal democracies, though the main thing about it is that, in the confidence of its knowledge of what is right, it is opposed to liberalism as liberty and to democracy as majority rule. The attractions of seeing no limitation to the possibilities of a rationally ordered humanity, vividly exemplified in the young Engels' and Marx's visions of communism, are undeniable;[126] which is why insisting on framing policy in consciousness of such limitation, though so necessary,[127] is so difficult. Leszek Kolakowski chose his language very wisely when he drew his magisterial intellectual history of Marxism to an end by saying, as few have had more authority than he to say, that 'Marxism has been the greatest fantasy of [the twentieth] century',[128] for fantasies are not without attraction.

However, writing in 1978 Kolakowski was, with respect, wrong to claim that, in the liberal democracies, 'At the present time it is obvious to all except a handful of New Left adolescents that socialism cannot literally "satisfy all need" but can aim only at a just distribution of insufficient resources.'[129] It is now glaringly obvious that views which cannot recognise scarcity save as a political obstacle still demand huge political attention. The reason the indispensable critique of merely legal freedom has led to the maximalist welfare state, and the indispensable critique of the classical law of contract has led to welfarism, is that the advocates of both generally do unconsciously affirm Marx's view of scarcity. By far the most profound argument ever made for the abolition

[124] L Althusser, 'Contradiction and Overdetermination' in *For Marx* (New Left Books 1977) 114. In his autobiography, Arthur Koestler described his personal experience of holding this position whilst living in the USSR in the 1930s: 'I learnt to classify automatically everything that shocked me as "the heritage of the past" and everything I liked as "seeds of the future"': A Koestler, *The Invisible Writing* (Collins 1954) 53.

[125] I Berlin, 'Two Concepts of Liberty' in *Four Essays on Liberty* (OUP 1969) 144.

[126] In 1944, it was remarked in G Orwell, 'Arthur Koestler' in *Complete Works*, vol 16 (Secker and Warburg 1998) 400 that:

> The Russian Revolution ... started out with high hopes. We forget these things now, but a quarter of a century ago it was confidently expected that the Russian Revolution would lead to utopia. Obviously this has not happened.

But although in the next five years Orwell was about to produce perhaps the most effective anti-communist books ever written in English, his basic views about a, were it able to be implemented, desirable British economic policy remained unchanged.

[127] FA Hayek, *The Constitution of Liberty* in *Collected Works*, vol 17 (University of Chicago Press 2011) 80–81:

> the case for individual freedom rests chiefly on the recognition of the inevitable ignorance of all of us concerning a great many of the factors on which the achievement of our ends and welfare depends. If there were omniscient men ... there would be little case for liberty.

[128] L Kolakowski, *Main Currents of Marxism* (Clarendon Press 1978) vol 3, 523.

[129] ibid 528.

of capitalism lives on, in necessary ignorance of the detail of that argument and the reasons for that argument's failure, in an inchoate aversion to profit and market.

The implications of the contrast between Marx's intellectual achievement and the complete failure of the political action based on that achievement have been simply ignored, leaving only the unconstrained appetite for intervention that characterises the unconditioned life of the maximalist welfare state.[130] That state knows no principled bounds to interventionist expenditure; and welfarism in contract rightly sees freedom of contract as wholly unsuited to pursuit of 'the ideals of social justice [and] the communitarian values which gave birth to the welfare state'.[131] Though continual compromises have to be reached with mundane 'economic', 'political', and 'social' 'realities', the 'principle' of the maximalist welfare state and welfarist contract is an inchoate communism in which the naturally given conditions of economic action are seen as difficulties which can be overcome with sufficient political will. Such recognition as there is that in the development of the general market economy institutionalised in the law of contract humankind has responded to these natural conditions in a way which, because it was not and could not have been 'planned',[132] has created an historically unprecedented increase in welfare, is not taken as a counsel to deepen our inadequate understanding of how this could possibly have been done, and, rather after the fashion of the common law, to cautiously build on it, if, on occasion, even more cautiously intervening in it.[133] Rather, in themselves completely uninteresting identifications of externality are occasions of remorseless complaint that in what has been done one can always identify market failure.

In a crucial sense, the foundation of this is disrespect for the core doctrines of the law of contract in which economic exchange is institutionalised as a practice. In our current understanding, the law's basic doctrinal shape is interminably criticised because of its virtues: agreements are made possible without complete negotiation; bargains which are not paid for are not enforced; and performance which conveys no

[130] I formulated these views some considerable time prior to the incredible success of T Piketty, *Capital in the Twenty First Century* (Belknap Press 2014), and I am relegating to a footnote a discussion of this extremely important cultural phenomenon because, to be frank, it is a somewhat embarrassingly emphatic a confirmation of those views. It is very significant that Piketty felt it advantageous to give his book the resonance which its title was bound to convey, but the opportunism of his doing so when he had a low opinion of Marx based on an ignorance of Marx's work which really does link Piketty to Shaw is deplorable. The argument about structural tendencies of capitalism which Piketty tries to build on what I understand are important achievements in the analysis of the distribution of wealth is—and one should understand this literally—vacuous. The attractiveness of Piketty's book is entirely attributable to its seeming to legitimate a further rise in the tax take in the maximalist welfare state: D Campbell, 'The Fetishism of Divergence: A Critique of Piketty' (2015) 15 The Journal of Corporate Law Studies 183.

[131] H Collins, *The Law of Contract* (1st edn, Weidenfeld & Nicolson 1986) 1.

[132] A Ferguson, *A History of Civil Society* (CUP 1995) 119:

> Every step and every movement of the multitude, even in what are termed enlightened ages, are made with equal blindness to the future, nations stumble upon establishments, which are indeed the result of human action, but not of human design.

[133] Hayek cited some form of the passage from Ferguson ibid on numerous occasions throughout his work, and he concluded one such of these, FA Hayek, 'Individualism: True and False' in *Studies in the Abuse and Decline of Reason* in *Collected Works*, vol 13 (Liberty Fund 2018) 74, by claiming that:

> the fundamental attitude of true individualism is one of humility towards the processes by which mankind has achieved things which have not been designed or understood by any individual and are indeed greater than individual minds.

benefit is not compelled. It is not understood that this is the doctrinal shape necessary to facilitate the economic action of autonomous, self-interested, socially interdependent, boundedly rational economic actors in a natural world that, in one aspect, is refractory. But individual and social self-consciousness of the necessity of this shape is absolute knowledge of the law of contract.

The justification offered for this uncomprehending criticism of the market is the claimed unacceptability of the fundamental cultural feature of Tawney's acquisitive society, solipsistic self-interest. But the self-interest which motivates economic action in the market economies, legally institutionalised in the shape of the doctrines of the law of contract, is nothing of the sort; it is the inherently relational, ie other-regarding and moral, self-interest of mutual recognition. Let us conclude this argument by analysing the current prospects for the law of contract in light of this understanding of its nature.

Conclusion: Self-interest and Betterment in the Relational Law of Contract

The argument of this book is that solipsistic self-interest is an alienated form of economic action, and that the non-alienated economic actors must be self-consciousness of the social relationship of mutual recognition that makes possible exchange, Pareto optimisation, a stable market economy, and therefore the reproduction of autonomy as the principle for the allocation of economic goods. I have drawn on the critique of alienation in a tradition of which the principal figures are Immanuel Kant, GWF Hegel, and Karl Marx, focusing on Marx's critique of the naturalness of solipsistic self-interest as of crucial importance. Immanent critique of the classical law of contract reveals an always denied but always ineliminable concept of good faith has been necessary for the coherence of the law, and that absolute knowledge of this necessity should now be actualised in consciousness of the fundamental contractual relation of mutual recognition.

In the welfarist law of contract that has replaced the classical law, this immanent critique has not been carried out. That the law of contract *should* take its shape in order to facilitate the voluntary exchanges constitutive of the market economy is denied because perceived moral and economic market failure, generally tainting the choices of consumers and therefore the significance of demand, is taken to be endemic. The content of welfarism is given by *ad hoc*, exogenously driven interventions, including both outright reductions of the Pareto domain and innovations in the law which have seriously diminished and will further diminish the coherence of the law of contract. The justification of this ultimately is the perceived superiority of 'consumer-welfarism' over 'market-individualism',[134] but not only would I personally find this superiority wholly questionable were one to have to choose between the values which set up this opposition, the far more important point is that one does not have to choose between these alternatives; indeed one has to choose to discard the positing of the opposition.

[134] JN Adams and R Brownsword, 'The Ideologies of Contract' (1987) 7 Legal Studies 207.

Though the immanent critique of the law of contract must be endogenous to that law, refusing to bring in exogenous principles, acquiring absolute knowledge of the law of contract does not leave the positive law as it was. Knowledge of 'the *true* in the *shape* of the *true*'[135] is radically different from former inadequate knowledge,[136] and should be the basis of a radical restatement of the law which makes it adequate to that knowledge. The positive law of contract is in part constituted by its own inadequate, solipsistic understanding of self-interest, which forms part of the interpretative background to the following of, and adjudication upon, its rules. The classical law of contract therefore continuously threw up fundamental doctrinal and practical problems focused around the concept of good faith, eventually producing a state of affairs that famously came to be described as the death of contract. The predominant response to these problems has, however, been misguidedly welfarist in the sense that that response *did* import exogenous principles into the criticism of the classical law, itself producing a state of affairs that I have called inchoate communism. This seemed necessary because the classical law's conception of self-interest is paradoxically first accepted by welfarism in order to then totally reject it, this rejection being an important constituent of the political culture of the maximalist welfare state. But exchange, the market economy, and contract have always required that self-interest be constituted of a relationship of mutual recognition, and consciousness of this allows us to restate, in profound criticism of the maximalist welfare state, the fundamental achievement of economics as conceived by Smith: the 'rehabilitation of desire'.[137]

As Marx saw it, the criticism of Smith's and Ricardo's natural conception of the economic actor opened the way to the ending of scarcity. Communism therefore analytically implies a radical criticism of the philosophic anthropology of the economic actor on which this book is based.[138] If the scarcity of economic goods through which

135 Hegel, *Phenomenology* (n 115) 23.

136 ibid 467.

137 C Lasch, *The True and Only Heaven* (WW Norton 1991) 52.

138 Communist attempts to describe post-capitalist humankind have been so risible that it would be unhelpful to engage with them here. What is now striking about them is the contrast between what was promised and what was believed to be justified by having made that promise. It is both dreadful and laughable that in 1924, whilst still a principal member of the Bolshevik government, Leon Trotsky described the vision which was the ultimate justification of his part in devising policies of extreme ruthlessness in the following terms: L Trotsky, *Literature and Revolution* (University of Michigan Press 1960) 256:

> Man will become immeasurably stronger, wiser and subtler; his body will become more harmonised, his movements more rhythmic, his voice more musical. The forms of life will become dynamically dramatic. The average human type will rise to the heights of an Aristotle, a Goethe, or a Marx. And above this ridge new peaks will arise.

The characteristic forms of Western Marxism are not couched in this tone. A sophisticated rejection of the liberal philosophic anthropology of economic action is, for example, the basis of the influential criticism of 'possessive individualism' in CB Macpherson, *The Political Theory of Possessive Individualism* (Clarendon Press 1962), which gained a particular prominence as it formed the basis of Macpherson's long introduction to the Pelican edition of *Leviathan*. Macpherson's views have an undeniable appeal derived by relying on Marx to go far beyond the criticism of the acquisitive society. But the initial plausibility of these views rests on an essential negativity, for the statement of what is wrong with possessive individualism is not burdened with a statement of an alternative, and when the necessity of a concrete alternative is appreciated, the statement of what is wrong takes on a different complexion. This becomes acutely clear when Macpherson criticises Rawls' views as 'severely limited' because they are based on acceptance of the need to manage inequality, for this is necessary 'only within a class-divided society': CB Macpherson, 'Revisionist Liberalism' in *Democratic Theory* (Clarendon Press 1973) 89.

the human being experiences the refractoriness of the natural world does not obtain, there is no basis for this anthropology, nor for the law of contract which legally institutionalises the market economy as humankind's most productive response to scarcity. There is, in particular, no basis for legitimate self-interest, even if this is not solipsistic self-interest but the self-interest of mutual recognition. Just as immanent critique of market order must yield the plan if communism is possibly to be justified, and Marx's argument for communism is a complete failure because it does not do so, so the immanent critique of self-interest must yield a conception of the communist human being which can associate on the basis of 'from each according to his abilities, to each according to his needs!'. That no credible or even comprehensible explicit defence of this position is possible has not prevented the maximalist welfare state and welfarism from effectively maintaining it, even though the force of the negative criticism of the acquisitive society has been turned into the incoherence of the unconditioned life by the lack of a principled 'social' alternative. What is needed is a conception of actual self-interest conscious of its social constitution. This is potentially available in Smith.

Though we have seen Smith ascribe the propensity to truck, barter, and exchange to human nature, this ascription must be, to put it this way, derivative. One does not truck, barter, or exchange—ie make a contract—as an end in itself. One does this in order to obtain economic goods, and when doing this one is in turn driven by self-interest. Self-interest exercised through the propensity to truck, barter, and exchange is motivated by 'the desire of bettering our condition':

> a desire which, though generally calm and dispassionate, comes with us from the womb, and never leaves us until we go into the grave. In the whole interval which separates those two moments, there is scarce perhaps a single instant in which any man is so perfectly satisfied with his situation as to be without any wish of alteration or improvement of any kind.[139]

The justification of the institutionalisation of market order in the law of contract is that it does facilitate what it is ultimately right to call a system of natural liberty, for economic action is spontaneously motivated by the natural desire of betterment:

> The ... constant ... effort of every man to better his condition, the principle from which public and national, as well as private, opulence is originally derived, is frequently powerful enough to maintain the natural progress of things towards improvement.[140]

Macpherson cannot really be said to propose a way of dealing with the Hobbesian problem of order, for in the absence of the social form of possessive individualism, the problem is dissolved, or withers away. Oakeshott was simply dismissive of Macpherson. If one could believe that individual character in the modern European state was given by the entirely negative formation of possessive individualism, then 'one is capable of believing anything': M Oakeshott, *On Human Conduct* (Clarendon Press 1975) 242 n 1.

[139] Smith, *Wealth of Nations* (n 37) 341.
[140] ibid 343.

The desire for betterment analytically is an aspect of the philosophic anthropology of the economic actor on which this book is based, and we can now adequately understand why this is so. As was argued in Chapter 1, the finite but free human being must experience its given situation as a limit which it wishes to surpass. In respect of its natural environment, this impulse takes the form of the desire for betterment. Betterment is, it is submitted, an ahistorical constituent of human character, which Marx should have recognised as a 'general' factor common to all modes of production,[141] just as much as he recognised labour as directed at the production of use-values as such a factor. It was capitalism's achievement to so develop the social relations which facilitate betterment that the division of labour's extension of opulence to the lowest ranks could take place. This is the lesson of the four stages theory *and* of Marx's account of progress, up to the point where Marx purported to go beyond the Age of Commerce. This was a mistake of such enormous consequences because betterment *is* a general human motivation which reaches its productive culmination in the Age of Commerce. In a society in which the supreme principle of morality is autonomy, economic action *must* be motivated by betterment, and the social purpose of purposeless endorsement of betterment *must* be regarded as the legitimate foundation of the economy.

In the classical law of contract, the affirmation of the freedom of purposeless betterment was identified with solipsism in the pursuit of self-interest. But exchange, Pareto optimisation, and market order cannot rest on this basis. The development of the law of contract since it may be said to have taken its definite shape in the mid-nineteenth century has therefore been driven by a contradiction between solipsistic self-interest and self-interest based on the relationship of mutual recognition. In legal doctrine, this contradiction has been generally expressed in the denied necessity of a concept of good faith. The predominant form of the criticism of the classical law has, however, been a welfarism which is at profound variance with the essential purposelessness of Pareto optimisation institutionalised in voluntariness of agreement. The valuable contributions that welfarism has made towards the establishment of social citizenship have increasingly been supplanted by an authoritarian imposition of socially desired outcomes which is fundamentally opposed to freedom of contract, and is ultimately traceable to the inchoately communist political culture of the maximalist welfare state.

Immanent critique of the classical law shows, however, that voluntary agreement many be actualised on the basis of adequate self-consciousness of the relationship of mutual recognition. Whilst there is a very valuable distinction to be drawn between what in his earlier work Ian Macneil called discrete and relational contracts, the more important point, one of the points essential to our understanding of the nature of exchange, is that *all contracts are relational*. Self-consciousness of this social constitution of the individual economic actor may best be regarded as a liberal form of socialism, and the general economy based on exchange of this nature is the social market.

[141] GA Cohen, *Karl Marx's Theory of History* (Clarendon Press 1978) 151–52.

Index

For the benefit of digital users, indexed terms that span two pages (e.g., 52–53) may, on occasion, appear on only one of those pages.